1981

MODERN
WORLD
THEATER

# MODERN WORLD THEATER

*A Guide to Productions
in Europe and the United States
since 1945*

Siegfried Kienzle

*Translated by Alexander and Elizabeth Henderson*

Frederick Ungar Publishing Co.    *New York*

Translated from the German

*Modernes Welttheater*

by arrangement with the original publishers,
Alfred Kröner Verlag, Stuttgart

# *Translators' Foreword*

This book is a survey of the postwar theater throughout the world, as seen through the eyes of a young European critic and aided, in the choice of works analyzed, by the program statistics of German-language theaters. Of the 755 plays discussed in the original German work, *Modernes Welt-theater,* this English version includes 563, and another 15 have been added by the author for this English edition.

In his Foreword to the original edition the author explained that the purpose of the work is not to trace lines of development, but to give a cross-section of the theater within a certain period. For practical convenience 1945 was chosen as the starting date of the period covered. No attempt has therefore been made to set in perspective the work of such writers as Brecht, Camus, or Tennessee Williams, who are here represented only by their later, post-1945 work. As the author stated, the aim of this survey of contemporary drama is not so much to pronounce definitive judgments as to examine potentialities, to understand each work from the viewpoint of its own aims, and to evaluate its success in achieving them.

The present English edition follows the German original in arranging the works discussed in alphabetical order of authors and, under each author, in alphabetical order of titles. In all cases where a play was originally written in English, or an English-language version of the play is known to exist, the English title is given as the main entry heading. This is followed by the original title in parentheses in the case of plays written in languages other than English. Wherever possible the translator's name is given, together with details of publication or at least stage production. While every effort has been made to trace existing English translations of plays and the relevant details, the fact that in some cases no such translation is indicated is not to be taken as proof that no translation exists. Where no evidence of the existence of an English version of a play could be found, the entry heading consists of the title of the play in its original language, followed by an English rendering in [square] brackets.

## ABRAMOW, Jaroslaw
(Poland, born 1933)

LICYTACJA *[The Auction]*. One-act play. Prose. First performance March 18, 1962, Warsaw, Teatr Ateneum. Time: the present. Place: Poland.

Arthur Stronski puts up for sale the car, once driven by Goering, that was captured in battle—a 1942 Maybach with special armor plating. Two prospective buyers recognize each other; they are the *Reichsmarschall*'s former driver, who has come over from West Germany for the auction, and the Polish partisan who had captured the car. The two former enemies enthusiastically exchange reminiscences of the battle and become so engrossed in their grotesque military game and heroic posturing that they forget all about the auction. In the meantime a businesslike young man examines the car for its practical features such as maximum speed and fuel consumption. He advises Arthur that the unprofitable "old toboggan" is good for nothing but the scrap heap. The trader indignantly retreats into the transfigured past: "That's the young generation! That's the price they pay for our blood, our heroism, and all our sacrifices. For them it's not profitable." An exposure of the military romanticism of war veterans, who imagine their inflated war reminiscences constitute a privilege.

## ACHARD, Marcel
(France, born 1899)

SAVEZ-VOUS PLANTER LES CHOUX? *[Do You Know How to Plant Cabbages?]*. Farce in three acts. Prose. First edition Paris 1951. First performance November 4, 1946, Lyons, Théâtre des Célestins. Time: the present. Place: stationmaster's office at a small railway station.

The worthy stationmaster, Sylvain Caporal, is blessed by two presences likely to introduce upsetting surprises into his placid middle-class life: a pretty seventeen-year-old stepdaughter, Violette, and a sharp-tongued mother-in-law, Madame Landrol. But what grieves this Frenchman's patriotic heart much more is the absence of a male heir. Then Fragnol, a classic simpleton as old factotum, gives him the secret recipe: lots of spinach and even more sport. It proves a good tip. Year after year a new offspring appears, until the proud father begins to have suspicions of his own performance. Just when Caporal crowns his achievements with the birth of quintuplets and is duly decorated as a unique paragon of a progenitor, a coded letter arrives that seems to confirm the existence of a lover. But in the end it turns out to be a letter addressed to Violette, and the little railway employee can go on basking in his glory.

A masterpiece of stagecraft that, with its definite types, explosive farcical situations, and superbly comic language, will always be sure of a public.

A SHOT IN THE DARK (L'Idiote). Comedy in three acts. Prose. First edition in L'Amour est difficile, Paris 1960. First performance September 23, 1960, Paris, Théâtre Antoine. Adapted by H. Kurnitz, New York, Random House, 1962. Time: the present. Place: examining magistrate Sévigné's office in Paris.

Camille Sévigné, a newly appointed examining magistrate in Paris, has to deal with a tricky case. Miguel Ostos, chauffeur of banker Beaurevers, has been shot dead. Lying beside the corpse was the chambermaid Josefa, unconscious but clutching a gun in her delicate hand. She seemed straight out of Eden with her lack of clothing but somewhat less than Eden-sent in regard to her innocence. Word comes from above that the case is to be solved quickly and discreetly; but what Josefa blurts out in her naive unconcern implicates wider and wider circles of increasingly important people.

A fast-moving actor's play that is all of a piece; Achard handles even a criminal theme in the high-spirited vaudeville manner.

### ADAMOV, Arthur
(France, born 1908)

L'INVASION [The Invasion]. Play in four acts. Prose. Written 1949. First edition Paris 1950. First performance November 14, 1950, Paris, Studio des Champs-Elysées. Time: the present. Place: a room at Pierre's.

Pierre and his young wife Agnes devote their entire life to the manuscript which his deceased brother-in-law Jean left behind in a huge trunk. The whole room is cluttered with piles of confused and often illegible notes. With painstaking, time-consuming labor several versions must be produced in order to reconstruct the original. Pierre watches jealously over his life's work, to which he devotes every minute of his time; he excludes first his assistant Tradel, and eventually even Agnes, from collaboration because they do not work with sufficient care. The neglected woman finally accepts the purposeful advances of the "first comer" and leaves her husband, who works so hard he does not even notice. His mother rejoices at Agnes's de-parture, and when she is betrayed by her first comer, the mother spitefully bars her return home. In the meantime Pierre has at last found selfhood, resolutely tearing up the manuscript and wanting to get back to a normal life. When he realizes what has happened he commits suicide. The mother takes up the stylish pose of a Niobe martyred by destiny.

Men experience themselves only as functions, as defenseless victims of an automatic, anonymous sequence of events. Adamov gives the following in-terpretation: "By 'invasion' I mean the creeping encumbrance of the indi-vidual by his own pressing occupations, by the presence of other individuals who in their turn are encumbered by their own worries, and finally by the thrust of external events hard to reconcile with the inner life." He presents the situation of modern man devoured by the Moloch of an illusionary task—the life of free self-realization and spontaneity having long been displaced by standardized reactions—with the utmost economy, making do with a minimum of characters and action.


PAOLO-PAOLI, THE YEARS OF THE BUTTERFLY (Paolo-Paoli). Play in twelve scenes. Prose. Written 1957. First edition Paris 1957. First per-formance May 24, 1957, Lyons, Théâtre de la Comédie. Translated by Geoffrey Brereton, London, Calder & Boyars, 1964. Time: 1900–1914. Place: Paris.

Early twentieth-century power politics is transposed into the cosy chintz setting of the lower-middle class in strict proportion, for the selfish motiva-tions and aims of world politics and of politics among knickknacks and sofas are the same. The victor in the merciless power struggle among the politically interested priest, the liberal-minded industrialist, and the defi-ant proletarian is ultimately Paolo-Paoli, a petit bourgeois who dabbles in bohemianism and displays a propensity for anarchistic speechmaking. The ambitious Paolo exploits every opportunity for his butterfly trade. He is getting lucrative supplies not only from the convicts in remote Cayenne, among them the innocently condemned workman Marpeaux, but also from the native children in Abbé Saulnier's mission. Skillfully, Paolo prevents Marpeaux's rehabilitation and takes advantage of his wife Rose, not only as cheap labor but also as his mistress. The feather dealer Hulot-Vasseur has fallen completely under Paolo's sway through his collector's passion. Business prospects are further enhanced when Paolo's wife Stella becomes Hulot-Vasseur's mistress. At the margin of Paolo's purposeful game is Cécile de Saint-Sauveur, an officer's wife ashamed of her poverty and who is ruth-lessly exploited by the butterfly trader. Between scenes there are interpolations of documentary material—photographs, newspaper headlines, quotations from historic speeches—which magnify this array of human villains to the world scale.

PING-PONG (Le Ping-Pong). Play in two parts. Prose. Written 1955. First edition in Théâtre II, Paris 1955. First performance March 2, 1955, Paris, Théâtre des Noctambules. Translated by Richard Howard, New York, Grove Press, 1959, and by Derek Prouse, London, Calder & Boyars, 1962. Time: the present. Place: Paris.

It is not certain what most attracts the students Victor and Arthur to the Café L'Espérance—the pretty waitress Annette or the pinball machine, whose "system" they vainly try to discover. Arthur has worked out a new way to organize the gambling business and is now trying, unsuccessfully, to get an interview with the mysterious Monsieur Constantin, the grand old man of the slot-machine concern. Both Sutter, the boastful cashier of the gambling pool, and the dandy Roger, Constantin's secretary, distract the two students with excuses and try to put them off. At last Arthur gets through to Monsieur, who accepts his idea. This wins him Annette, who covets a more promising job in the slot-machine business. But soon things turn sour. Madame Duranty, the manager of the café, first takes over a bathing establishment and then a dancing school. Sutter, too, turns against the gambling business, which has led to a brawl in which Annette is killed. Victor has become a doctor but remains addicted to gambling. As old men, the two friends play ping-pong together, get into a heated discussion about the rules of the game, in the end disregard the rules, and play as though possessed. Victor finally collapses, dead.
The pinball machines run by an anonymous company are a symbol of life: people are irretrievably at the mercy of the slender chance of gain; they passively put up with the fact that the machines often break down, always cheat the players of their stakes, and usually disappoint their expectations. The magic of the rolling ball keeps the whole world spellbound.

TOUS CONTRE TOUS [All Against All]. Play in two parts. Prose. Written 1952. First edition in Théâtre I, Paris 1953. First performance April 14, 1953, Paris, Théâtre de L'OEuvre. Time: the present. Place: an imaginary country.

A fanatical fight of "natives" against hated "refugees" has plunged the country into political chaos. The native workman Jean Rist has lost his girl friend Marie to the refugee Zenno. This disappointment, together with failure in his trade, turns him into a rabid refugee hater; he becomes a demagogic rabble-rouser, sets up extermination camps, and organizes a comprehensive liquidation campaign. For the sake of Marie he gives his personal enemy Zenno a chance to escape with the help of a false passport. The project goes wrong; Marie is killed and Zenno becomes an ally of Darbon, who ousts Jean from rulership of the masses. This political reversal makes privileged citizens of the refugees. Jean goes underground as a "refugee," lives in another town, and becomes engaged to the refugee girl Noémi. Yet another political upheaval revives the persecution of refugees, and when native partisans arrest Jean as an enemy of the people, he disdains rehabilitation (because of his bloodstained past) and chooses to be shot with Noémi and his mother. Zenno has taken the precaution of a timely change of opinion and once more comes to no harm.

In this didactic play about ceaseless discrimination, Adamov demonstrates with merciless objectivity that the miracle of survival has to be paid for with the loss of self-respect and human dignity. Images of the most recent past suggest to the playwright a madly careering witch hunt, in which men, blinded by a mania of destruction, are driven along by some catchword or other. He deliberately situates the political conflict in an unrealistic no man's land and represents his characters as mathematical functions with opposing signs.


## AHLSEN, Leopold
(Germany, born 1927)


DER ARME MANN LUTHER [The Poor Man Luther]. Television play. Prose. Written 1964. Acting edition Munich, Drei Masken, 1964. First performance January 21, 1965, Westdeutscher Rundfunk. Time: February 18, 1546. Place: Eisleben and unspecified dream setting.

In the hour of his death Martin Luther is alone with his struggle for clarity. Flashbacks repeat the scenes of his life. There is the defiant resistance to his father, the early religious doubts, the tormenting conflict over his mission, the growing despondency of not being able to fulfill the inscrutable will of God. His path is marked by historical figures: there is the prior, who is fond of his rebellious pupil but cannot share the latter's reforming zeal; there is Cardinal Cajetan, who on the pope's behalf demands a recantation; there are ordinary politicians, such as Sickingen, Florian Geyer, Hutten, who exploit the reformer's work in the interests of their own ambitions; there is the cold rationalist Erasmus of Rotterdam who would rather be master in the realm of reason than a humble servant in the realm of faith;

there are fanatics on both sides, such as Thomas Müntzer and the vituper-
ous monk; there are opportunists seeking personal advantage in the religious conflict, such as the cobbler who wants Protestantism to provide a
justification for polygamy or Staupitz who in return for his faith gets a
comfortable sinecure from the Roman clergy. In the end Luther is aware
of closer ties with his bitterest opponent, the Emperor Charles V, than with
the swarm of his sly supporters, for he and the emperor both feel that they
have failed. The emperor is faced with the invalidation of his life's work,
of the world order, of law, even of God's providence. "Before you it was
unthinkable that anyone should be outside the Church and yet religious.
Oh, I loved it all, the settled forms, the strict hierarchy, the truth established once and forever. The institution and God were one, form and
content were one. . . ." Now a piercing unrest has come into the world and
will not be silenced by any certainty. The reformer's testing time throws a
light on history. The individual's rebelliousness against an inherited world
order, as expressed in his skepticism and revolt, tears away the cloak of
certainty for centuries to come. "Never again will an institution be the sole
source of blessedness, unalterable, infallible. For me it's as though God had
vanished altogether out of our hearts, our world. There is no certainty
any more."
The sequence of associations in thought, with their spasmodic movement,
determines the structure of this dream play, which even in its stage version
is influenced by the techniques of television drama.


SIE WERDEN STERBEN, SIRE *[You Will Die, Sire]*. Comedy in nineteen
scenes. Prose. Written 1963. Acting edition Munich, Drei Masken, 1963.
First broadcast as the radio play *Tod eines Königs [Death of a King]*
March 13, 1964, Bayerischer Rundfunk, Munich. First stage performance
June 12, 1964, Berlin, Schloßparktheater. Time: 1483. Place: Plessis
Castle near Tours.

The subject of this study of death, a study carried out with clinical precision, is King Louis XI of France (reigned 1461–1483), a cynical, cruel,
unpredictable, malicious cripple. Following a stroke he realizes that his
days are numbered and feverishly seeks for assurances about the hereafter.
The inevitability of death becomes the touchstone for the various attitudes
expressed by the personages surrounding Louis. The fear-ridden despot
seeks consolation and help from all of them. They include St. Francis of
Paola, who feels secure in his Christian faith; the bloated, decrepit harlot
Perette, who finds eternal bliss in every zestful moment of life. She has
no fear of death because in her animal carnality she feels at one with all
of nature's creatures. Even the monarch's personal physician Cottier has

no understanding of the king's unease, since for him the world is merely a collection of neatly dissected organs, mere soulless matter susceptible of physical measurement. So Louis seeks salvation from those who are themselves threatened by death. For Bishop Balue, the former chancellor who has been in prison for decades, death will be a release. Derisively the king condemns him to live on. Olivier Necker, the hated present chancellor whose fate will be sealed by the king's death, is a political gambler and as such looks forward calmly even to his own end. Louis' frantic searchings are not satisfied even by an encounter with death in all its crude reality—a poisoning and the examination of a dying man. Caught in the whirlpool of transience, he wants to take with him the assurance that he has left behind something enduring. His son Charles, as misshapen and full of hatred as he himself is, will carry on into history the same evil obsession. Louis' testament is falsified by the triumphant courtiers and turned into its opposite. Nothing remains but a stinking corpse which is hurriedly buried. Louis becomes a symbol of man and his eternal predicament, which none can escape. In his dread he, as an individual, has no foothold. Those about him are safe and secure, each for himself, made so by his philosophy, prejudices, or, at worst, indifference. Louis cannot believe either in himself or in others.

The fear of death develops into the crucial situation in which a man first becomes comprehensible to himself. Ahlsen explains: "The basic pattern of this essentially philosophic and reflective play is that of exploring, of circling around a single problem that from beginning to end remains the same tormenting fear. There is no action. Paralysis, fixation, and being spellbound are the keynotes of the events portrayed and must be made immediately evident in the dramatic pattern." That pattern has "only a single theme . . . carried to the point of monomania, namely, death. The death of a man. Death as a phenomenon of our existence." The outcry of a creature who sees the verification of life and the endurance of the spirit betrayed and surrendered in the horror of putrefaction was expressed at the beginning of this century in Hans Henny Jahnn's *Pastor Ephraim Magnus, Die Krönung Richard III,* and *Der Arzt, sein Weib, sein Sohn.* But what in Jahnn was the tragedy of an anguished predicament becomes in Ahlsen's hands witty, even sardonic comedy.

## AIKEN, Conrad Potter
(United States, born 1889)

MR. ARCULARIS. Play in two acts. Prose. After Aiken's short story. First edition Cambridge, Mass., 1957. First performance 1949, New York, Provincetown Playhouse. Time: the present. Place: operating theater and ship.

A psychological study in depth leads Aiken to meditation about man and the universe in lyrical language and sequences of images in reminiscences and dreams. The individual escapes into hallucination, which is to disclose to him the sense and justification of a chaotic reality: We're all of us fixed little parts in a vast logical dream." All men are "parts of myself, symbols of something in the brief little microcosm of my soul. As I, in turn, am perhaps a symbol of something in each of yours."
In front of the students in the operating theater, a complicated heart operation is performed on Mr. Arcularis. Under the anesthetic, the patient imagines that he is cured, leaves the hospital, and starts out on a voyage by ship. The passengers Arcularis meets are the doctors and nurses of his hospital reality. Miss Snell, his dreamy, warm-hearted nurse, looks after him on the ship as well in the person of Diana Dean. In a milieu of high society proceeding by conversation through a life without problems, Arcularis wastes away. Clairvoyantly he feels the icy emptiness of infinity closing in on him. In his sleep he repeatedly walks to a mysterious coffin in the cold-storage vault and is firmly convinced that it is his own resting place. Snatches of memories and failures from his childhood, of his mother's death and of adultery flit through his mind and are clarified in the lucidity of this strange no-man's ship "anchored between walls of ice and rime." In the operating theater the surgical intervention is successful, but the patient is dead.

## ALBEE, Edward
(United States, born 1928)

THE AMERICAN DREAM. One-act play. Prose. Written 1960. First edition New York 1961. First performance January 24, 1961, New York, York Playhouse. Time: the present. Place: a living room.

*The American Dream* is a social satire on the standardized American way of life, exemplified in the puppets Daddy, Mommy, Grandma, and the athletic young man with his stereotyped film-star smile. Distorted clichés and the vestiges of a deformed reality are the ingredients of Albee's collage of banalities. Mommy tyrannizes the family with strident bad temper and an exasperating flow of talk. Daddy is seriously ill; she married him only for the sake of his money. Now she wants to dispatch Grandma, her mother, who has built herself an imaginary better world of carboard boxes, into an old people's home. Daddy and Mommy sit waiting with a bad conscience for Grandma to be taken away. But instead the strangely confused Mrs. Barker appears. She once helped the family to adopt a child, who grew up a headless, gutless monster with feet of clay, and eventually died —Albee's sarcastic version of the end product of American supercivilization. The dazzling obverse to this is "the American dream," a jobless boy who bewitches Grandma with his empty white-toothed smile. He is a soulless husk: "I have no longer the capacity to feel anything. I have no emotions. I have been drained, torn asunder . . . disemboweled. I have, now, only my person . . . my body, my face. I use what I have . . . I let people love me . . . that is all it comes to. . . . And it will always be this." Grandma introduces him into the family as a new son. Mommy is delighted and displays her faded charms. Grandma is happy that she has given her family a new chance for self-delusion and secretly slips out of the house. She resolutely dismisses the audience: "I don't think we'd better go any further. . . . Let's leave things as they are right now . . . while everybody's happy . . ."

THE BALLAD OF THE SAD CAFÉ. Play in nine scenes. Prose. After the novella by Carson McCullers. First edition New York 1963. First performance October 14, 1963, New York, Martin Beck Theatre. Time: the past and the present. Place: Miss Amelia's café.

Love binds together three entirely different people. This love does not bring happiness, security, and salvation but a dark, elemental catastrophe that overtakes its victims, a visitation that burns up the lovers and drives them into blind self-destruction. A dwarf, an amazon, and a reformed scoundrel persecute each other out of unrequited love. The complete lack of response to which each is condemned becomes the precondition of feeling. These outcasts do indeed spend themselves in hopeless love, but any affection proffered only calls forth hatred. They are so permeated with pride, self-torment, egotism, and masochistic self-debasement that their love, too, degenerates into a new, even more devastating form of loneliness. They are really clinical cases, about which—outside psychiatry—nothing more need be said. But McCullers and Albee succeed in breaking through to an existential dimension. For Albee, eroticism is the one field in which contemporary man still is a problem to himself, however much he may

otherwise entrench himself in his civilized environment that is increasingly
free of problems. Notwithstanding all his predetermined and calculable
reactions, he is shaken by the spontaneity of the unconscious. What the
ancients expressed by the "doom of destiny," what in later literature was
meant by the encounter with chaos, that, for Albee, is man's blind bondage
to desire.

The narrator tells of the glory and decline of the café, now deserted and
boarded up. It was here that Miss Amelia, a quarrelsome giantess who
could hold her own with any man in a brawl, used to carry on her liquor
trade. She was a hard-hearted, cold, and rapacious woman, after nothing
but money until her cousin Lymon, a deformed dwarf of whose family
relationship and indeed of whose existence she had never known, came to
live with her. Amelia readily allows herself to be tyrannized by the cripple's
tantrums. She is consumed by an exclusive love for him and, because he
likes to be merry and mix with people, she turns the liquor shop into a
café for his sake. At this stage Marvin Macy comes back unexpectedly from
prison. In his reckless youth he had fallen in love with Amelia, married
her, and made over to her all he owned; but, held at bay by her herculean
strength, he was never allowed to make love to her. This tragically ridiculous marriage had lasted only ten days. After that Macy took off, full of
hate for the world, and became a criminal. Now he returns to settle his
accounts. Cousin Lymon is as though spellbound by this aura of crime.
Just as Amelia lavishes the pent-up emotions of her unlived life on the
ugly dwarf and is rewarded by nothing but ingratitude, so Lymon in turn
pines for the brutal contempt that Macy metes out to him. He leaves his
inconsolable protectress and follows his idol with doglike devotion. When
the neurotic tension finally finds an outlet in a wild struggle between
Amelia and Macy and the powerful woman seems to be winning, the little
hunchback gives the decisive turn to the fight. The ill-assorted friends
smash up the café, pilfer the cash, and leave Amelia, beaten for life. Since
then the unhappy woman has been hiding in her crumbling house. The
epic doom of these flashbacks and reflections is captured in a loose sequence
of scenes: events that are suffused with a strange, diagnostic coolness.


THE DEATH OF BESSIE SMITH. Play in eight scenes. Prose. Written 1959.
First edition New York 1960. First performance November 21, 1960,
Berlin, Schloßpark-Theater. Time: September 26, 1937. Place: Memphis,
Tennessee, and environs.

The play is based on the actual circumstances of the death of Bessie Smith,
Empress of the Blues. This famous Negro singer was hurt in a bus accident
in 1937 and left to bleed to death while the slight injuries of the white

passengers were being looked after. Albee wants to make use of these facts in a challenging accusation; for theatrical effectiveness, he shifts the emphasis in important respects. The jobless Negro Jack has fastened onto the aging Bessie, who has tired of the ceaseless rush of show business and is drowning memories of her fading career in drink. Jack wants more golden eggs from his goose and tries unscrupulously to whip her up to new successes; drunk himself, he causes the fatal accident. With the severely injured Bessie he erupts into the bored, crumbling world of a provincial hospital. He is turned away. For the nurse, racial fanaticism is merely an outlet for her erotic frustration. The liberal-minded intern is prepared to render medical assistance, but the nurse, who is his mistress, thwarts him in order to gratify her love-hate. She destroys the doctor's career. She also despises the Negro male nurse who outwardly shares her racial hatred; but he bleaches his skin and slavishly imitates the habits of the whites he secretly admires.

This dramatization lessens the collective guilt of the whites and turns the spell of a mad witch hunt into a clinical study akin to Tennessee Williams' Southern hothouse world of sexual pathology.

TINY ALICE. Play in three acts. Prose. Written 1964. First edition New York 1965. First performance December 29, 1964, New York, Billy Rose Theatre. Time: the present. Place: the cardinal's garden and the library in the castle.

Since Pirandello the disintegration of reality has become a recurrent theme of literature. The progress of the natural sciences has increasingly brought home even to the general public the disturbing, crucial, and irrevocable discrepancy between the object's physical properties, significance, and effects and its appearance. The world accessible to sensory perception has become a schematic pattern of atoms, electromagnetic fields, and kinetic forces. This reality can be expressed only in mathematical formulas and the physicists' models. It is the abstraction, the inaccessible actuality of being, the thing-in-itself, that Albee tries to reproduce in the intertwining relationships of his characters. The experimental nature of our existence, simulation, analogy, and functional dependence—all these Albee takes in a literal sense and makes his characters perform in front of a model that is a miniature mirror image of their world. The problem of identity becomes a challenge to reality. People are functions of their given potentialities, and the riddle of their existence turns into a question of semantic interpretation.

The quest for God, the individual's response to the challenge of sexual experience, and his response to the immense capital that may dominate choices are also treated as abstractions, as intangible sources of energy, as a means for modifying reality, and as condensed formulas for potential events.

Julian, a lay brother in the cardinal's service, all his life has striven for the pure, unadulterated concept of God, stripped of any Sunday-school prettiness and teleological interpretation. He voluntarily exiled himself in a lunatic asylum for six years to try to rediscover faith in a nonpersonal, purely transcendental God, that is, faith in a higher moral necessity in Kant's sense: "My faith and my sanity . . . they are one and the same." Suddenly the philosophic dreamer is confronted with life and its temptations. An errand on behalf of the cardinal leads him to Miss Alice, whose enormous donations support revolutions and cultural establishments alike, at once buttressing and undermining existing régimes, never allowing events to stand still. Julian is sent into this mirror world by the cardinal to secure the lion's share of Miss Alice's fortune for the Church. The fanaticism of the abstract idea is shown in the tension between feigned reality and its magical counterpart in the scale-model castle. Julian yields to Alice's courtship as a sacrifice of himself. After the wedding he is overjoyed in the belief that the woman he loves is now his forever and that the permanence and reality of his happiness are ensured. With gentle cynicism he is reminded of the "tiny Alice" of the doll's house. Only this abstraction can meet Julian's claim for exclusivity. What in his years of solitude tormented him as the problem of identity has now, in the field of human interrelations, become the touchstone of communication. Julian refuses to allow symbols to restrict reality and vitiate it by turning it into clichés. His experience of love is to be as unique as his experience of God. But the possibility of reaching another person depends not on one's own powers of expression but on the other's capacity to understand. Alice despairs of the self-deception that is imposed upon her, the self-deception of complete communion with her partner: "I have tried to be . . . *her*. No; I have tried to be . . . what I thought she might, what might make you happy, what you might use as a . . . what? We must . . . represent, draw pictures, reduce or enlarge to . . . what we can understand." In utter bewilderment Julian has to stand by as the butler covers up the furniture, and Alice's lawyer, who is her rejected lover and serves as her devil's advocate, prepares everything for her departure. Julian's desperate protest ends when the lawyer shoots him. Left alone in the empty house, the dying man accepts his senseless destiny and stands by the "tiny Alice" of his imagination.

Albee employs not only symbols and leitmotivs—the repeated description of the dark attic as an image of being locked into oneself, the figure of Butler in whom name and profession coincide—but also visual symbolism and significant tableaus.

WHO'S AFRAID OF VIRGINIA WOOLF? Play in three acts. Prose. Written 1962. First edition New York 1962. First performance October 13, 1962, New York, Billy Rose Theatre. Time: the present. Place: living room at George's.

George is a college professor who is ruining himself with drink. He and his wife Martha have invited his younger colleague Nick and his wife Honey for a late drink. The older couple keep up the illusion of companionship only in a merciless struggle between the sexes. They humiliate and torment each other and each gets satisfaction out of the other's helplessness and suppressed hate. The guests are nothing but prompters who introduce new variants into this relentless sadism. George married Martha for opportunist reasons; she was the daughter of the influential college president. She, in her turn, has a neurotic father fixation and tries to refashion George to fit this model. George vainly resists this depersonalization; having failed as a writer, he has taken to drink. They play macabre "party games" to fan the excitements of their stale existence; childless, they pretend they have a son and the invented behavior of this invisible offspring is used by each to mortify the other. The other couple, the biology teacher Nick and his hysterical wife, Honey, are held together by crude egotism. Honey had forced the marriage by pretending to be pregnant; she is pathologically afraid of having a baby and vomits for hours on end. George cynically drives his wife into adultery with Nick and revels in his own self-abasement. He spitefully tells her of the death of their fictitious son and gloats over her nervous collapse. Martha thinks up new torments, and yet she knows that all this is only an expression of their buried love for each other. "George who is good to me and whom I revile; who understands me and whom I push off . . . ; who keeps learning the games we play as quickly as I can change the rules; who can make me happy and I do not wish to be happy . . . whom I will not forgive for having come to rest; for having seen me and said, 'Yes, this will do'; who has made the hideous, the hurting, the insulting mistake of loving me and who must be punished for it." Half nightmare, half clowning, this is vivisection of the soul carried *ad absurdum*. Playful nursery rhymes reflect the banality of the action and are so distorted as to assume a menacing air; hence also the title of the play echoes the cadence of "Who's afraid of the big, bad wolf?"

THE ZOO STORY. Play in one scene. Prose. Written 1959. First printed
in *Evergreen Review,* No. 12, March/April 1960. First edition New York
1960. First performance September 28, 1959, Berlin, Werkstatt des Schillertheaters. Time: the present. Place: Central Park, New York.

Peter, a successful executive in a publishing firm and the contented father
of a family, has his Sunday calm abruptly disturbed. As he sits on a park
bench, Jerry accosts him and tries every means of provoking the respectable citizen in his attempt to find some *vis-à-vis* in the inescapable emptiness—whether it be friend or adversary—and thus to become comprehensible to himself. In this ocean of indifference his last support had been his
landlady's repulsive and vicious dog: "I loved the dog, and I wanted him
to love me . . . if you can't deal with people, you have to make a start
somewhere . . . where better to make a beginning . . . to understand and
just possibly to be understood . . . a beginning of an understanding, . . .
than with a DOG." But he failed in that attempt to come close to some
creature, even if it was only the meanest, most disgusting, most maltreated
mongrel, on which to lavish his love. Convinced of the superfluousness of
his existence, Jerry remains alone. He comes to blows with the shocked
Peter, whose life has no problems and is neatly ordered in every respect,
down to the care of his parakeets. Jerry presses his knife into Peter's hand
and throws himself upon it. Only as a victim bleeding senselessly to death
does Jerry find his place in Peter's cozy middle-class world.
The hopeless isolation of modern man and his unrelatedness are captured
in the image of the zoo, that railed-off world where the individual seeks
an answer that does not exist, "what with everybody separated by bars
from everyone else, the animals for the most part from each other, and
always the people from the animals. But, if it's a zoo, that's the way it is."


## ALBERTI, Rafael
(Spain, born 1903)


EL TRÉBOL FLORIDO *[Flowering Clover].* Tragicomedy in three acts.
Prose. Written 1940. First edition in *Teatro,* Buenos Aires, 1950. First performance March 3, 1955, Göteborg, Municipal Theatre. Time: the present. Place: "an island in the sun, amid a blue sea, under a blazing sky."

A sort of ballad full of nature magic and fantastic folklore: Loving and
dying, in obscene revelry and archaic lamentation, the characters disport
themselves amid a setting where all creation breathes the spirit of Pan.
In animal and forest disguises, they celebrate the nocturnal clover festival;

for each, his individual life is a reenactment of ancient, primitive myths. The people bear the mark of the irreconcilable conflict between the land and the sea, between the blind miller Silenos in the mountains and the fishwife Umbrosa on the shore. Silenos' daughter Aitana is betrothed to Martin who is Umbrosa's son; but Aitana secretly loves Martin's brother Alcyon. Jealously the parents lurk in wait for the union of the hostile elements; however, the blind miller wants to preserve his daughter for the earth so he strangles her. The action, colorful and fantastic, makes play with obscure oracles, vineyard choruses, Dionysian rites, and grotesque faunlike figures.

## ANDERSON, Maxwell
(United States, 1888–1959)

ANNE OF THE THOUSAND DAYS. Play in three acts. Prose and verse. First edition New York 1948. First performance December 8, 1948. New York, Shubert Theatre. Time: 1526 to 1536. Place: England.

Before her execution, Anne Boleyn, the second wife of Henry VIII, king of England, thinks back upon the strange story of her marriage, which is seen in a succession of rapid fade-outs. The king has rejected Mary Boleyn, his mistress for many years, and desires her younger sister Anne. The girl breaks off her engagement and, under duress, submits to the impetuous ruler. But even as Henry's mistress she maintains a reserve, an inner resistance, which binds the otherwise so fickle lover to her side. Anne furthers her plans with cold determination. Henry is made to divorce his legitimate spouse Katharine and to defy the pope in order to marry Anne. To satisfy her, he endangers his realm and brings many of his best friends to the block, including Sir Thomas More. As soon as she is queen, Anne's ambitions leave her; she wants to be nothing but a loving wife. But Henry's passion was fanned only by her resistance. When the longed-for male heir to the throne fails to appear, he turns to Lady-in-Waiting Jane Seymour. False witnesses accuse Anne of adultery and she is to be exiled. She insists, however, on the legality of her marriage to give her daughter Elizabeth a claim to the succession, and chooses the death sentence.

The historical events are presented in interspersed verse passages and stylized flashbacks. The love-hate of two forceful personalities is magnified to the scale of the fateful conflicts of a whole epoch. Like Duncan, Eliot, and Fry, Anderson sets out to present an anti-illusionist historical tragedy in metrical language, without foregoing the established means of theatrical entertainment.

BAREFOOT IN ATHENS. Play in two acts and six scenes. Prose. Written 1951. First edition New York 1951. First performance October 31, 1951, New York, Martin Beck Theatre. Time: near the end of the fifth century B.C. Place: Athens.

A lecture course in civic responsibility is presented in historical garb. American didacticism becomes humanly natural and timeless through the example of one individual proving himself in the face of censhorship and wars, a sham trial, and the temptations of power. Socrates inwardly welcomes the false accusations by which he is brought to trial, for at last he can propound his humanitarian views before a large audience. He passionately defends the aims of democracy. But the Spartan king Pausanias saves the sage from the citizens' fury by dictatorially destroying the freedom of Athens. The uncompromising urge for truth, which makes Socrates doubt the existing order and probe its legitimacy, earns the disturbing mentor the death sentence. Again Pausanias offers the philosopher his help. But Socrates chooses the deadly cup of hemlock, because the regimentation of opinion in a dictatorship would be spiritual death to him. "May I reckon the wise to be the wealthy and those who need least to be the most like the gods."

JOAN OF LORRAINE. Play in two acts. Prose. First edition New York 1946. First performance October 29, 1946, Washington, D.C., Lisner Auditorium. Time: the present. Place: a stage with medieval scenery.

Anderson dramatizes history not by actualization but by simultaneous stratification of past and present. Within the overall frame of a stage rehearsal, he realistically motivates the dissolution of identity—a theme borrowed from Pirandello. Jimmy Masters, the director, is rehearsing the play *Joan of Lorraine*. He disagrees with the way the part is conceived by his leading lady, Mary Grey, who wants to represent Joan as an ecstatic saint. In the course of many mishaps in the company and of discussions with her fellow actors, Mary gradually, from scene to scene, develops a more complex conception of the part. The financial sponsor of the production is arrested for fraud and Masters, against his better judgment, puts up a large amount for bail to get him released so that the performance can take place. In defiance of the opposition and incomprehension of her family, of the corrupt court of the dauphin, and of the ill will of the clergy, Joan tries with cunning and persuasion to fulfill her mission, and ultimately goes to the stake with composure. Mary realizes that she, too, can fulfill her artistic mission only by continuous compromise, yet keeping intact her inner certainty of vocation. She drops her reservations about the miracle girl of Domrémy and gives herself up trustfully to the part, in which it is granted her to discover her true self.


## ANOUILH, Jean
(France, born 1910)


ANIMAL GRAB (also: *Catch as Catch Can*) *(Foire d'empoigne)*. One-act play. Prose. Written 1959. First edition in *Pièces Costumées*, Paris 1960. First performance May 14, 1960, The Hague, Kgl. Schouwburg. Translated by Lucienne Hill. Time: 1815. Place: Palais des Tuileries, Paris.

With a surprise action, Napoleon has driven out Louis XVIII and begun his hundred days' reign. The kowtowing politicians quickly adapt themselves to the new situation by changing their opinions. Napoleon is a cynical and self-satisfied poseur. He much prefers the unprincipled knavery of his police minister Fouché to the ecstatic enthusiasm of the young Lieutenant d'Anouville, whose romantic self-sacrifice is nothing but a nuisance to him. After Napoleon's final fall, Fouché serves the restored Bourbon king with equal compliance, while d'Anouville, deprived of a rewarding purpose for his ardent dream of a heroic death, is plunged into tragicomical disillusionment by Napoleon's advice: "Don't talk too much about ideals to your kids. That's no luggage for life." This is Anouilh's entertaining contribution to the theme of heroes and hero worship. He skeptically exposes the dubiety of great ideals and sets the small things of life against the narcotic effect of high-sounding phrases, which are so dangerous and uncontrollable precisely because they are vague.


ARDÈLE (also): *The Cry of the Peacock*) *(Ardèle ou la marguerite)*. One-act play. Prose. First edition Paris 1949. First performance November 4, 1948, Paris, Comédie des Champs-Elysées. Translated by Kitty Black, London, John Lane, 1951, and by Lucienne Hill in *Five Plays,* Vol. 2, New York, Hill & Wang, 1958–1959, and in *Ardèle and Colombe,* London, Methuen, 1959. Time: before the First World War. Place: the hall of a castle.

This farce on matrimonial morals and taboos is, as it were, the negative of a tragic love story, for the unhappy lovers themselves, who choose a common death, are neither heard nor seen. Their truth, their striving for the absolute, can be comprehended only in negation, in the distorted grimace, in the perversion of their feelings. Ardele, a plain and elderly hunchback, loves the tutor, another hunchback. The family might put up with a love affair, but to their horror Ardele is so depraved as to insist on marriage. The general, who is the head of the family and Ardele's brother, locks up the disgraceful offender in her room and in all haste calls a family council. His younger sister, the countess, forms a mutually distrustful trio with her husband and her lover. The general himself has been pursued by his ailing wife's peacock cry of "Leon! Leon!" and consoles himself with a chambermaid. Only Nicolas, the general's youngest son, who has lost his adored Natalie to his eldest brother, stands up for the lovers, who are, nevertheless, driven to suicide by the family's ill will. The children in this family have long ago discovered their favorite game—they play mummy and daddy, talking grandiloquently of love while beating each other with mounting fury.

Anouilh admits that he owes this grotesquely clear-sighted ending to Roger Vitrac's *Victor, ou les enfants au pouvoir*, but Anouilh turns the surrealist's monstrosity into a cynical stage bravura of laissez-faire: "Thank God we are ridiculous, otherwise the whole story would really be too sad."

BECKET, OR THE HONOR OF GOD (Becket ou l'honneur de Dieu). Play in four acts. Prose. First edition Paris 1959. First performance October 1, 1959, Paris, Théâtre Montparnasse. Translated by Lucienne Hill, New York, Coward McCann, 1960, and London, Methuen, 1961. Time: twelfth century. Place: England and France.

Like Fry and Eliot, Anouilh sees the tragic conflict between King Henry and his chancellor Becket as one of two contrasting existential positions and irreconcilable worlds of experience. The cleric Thomas Becket stems from the oppressed Saxons; spiritually homeless, he looks for security and self-forgetfulness among the noisy vitality of the Norman ruling class. This sociological background explains the ardent friendship which has united him since his youth with the carefree, worldly, sensuous king. His inner solitude gives Becket the equanimity which makes him a successful dilettante in everything, as worldling and boon companion, as statesman and chancellor, as priest and courtier. He remains a dilettante because that is what he wants to be, without committing himself. He can keep his distance and need not get involved.

For reasons of state Henry makes his friend Archbishop of Canterbury, the highest dignitary of the church in England. For the first time Becket is faced with a real task, for the first time he feels the fascination of the challenge of a situation where he is needed: "I used to be a man without honor. Suddenly I had an honor that I never dreamed would be mine. The honor of God. An honor as hard to grasp and as tender as a perse-

cuted royal child." Without reservations he serves his new office, resigns
the chancellorship, and glows with ascetic fervor. He becomes the unbending advocate of the rights of the church against the absolute rule of the
king. Embittered, the king persecutes his former friend. He hates in him
not so much the new opponent as the faithless friend whom he cannot
understand. Becket's transformation has devalued the companionship of
the past, has turned it into a lie; he has betrayed the king and made him
an outcast. This is why Becket must fall, a victim of the murderous attack
by the four barons. Years later Henry goes through the farce of having himself lashed by monks as a penance, and by this unworthy trick not only
regains his good conscience but also the acclaim of his people as well. Between the two antagonists the petty hucksters scurry to and fro, the eternal
survivors of politics. The pope, King Louis of France, Folliot the power-
hungry bishop of London, and Henry's perfidious royal brood all nimbly
pursue their own interests in the shadow of the great conflict. Again a
young monk is Anouilh's torchbearer in a shameful world. Two opposing
experiences of the world are locked in a fatal struggle, fired again and
again by mutual contradiction. But the ruthless dialectic is tempered by
immense charm.

THE CAVERN (La Grotte). Play in two acts. Prose. First edition Paris 1961.
First performance October 4, 1961, Paris, Théâtre Montparnasse. Trans-
lated by Lucienne Hill, New York, Hill & Wang, 1966. Time: the present.
Place: kitchen and drawing room at the count's.

Anouilh diverts himself by making the playwright appear in the part of
a commentator, who vainly tries to bring together in a well-constructed,
significant play the characters who are thrown into disarray by life. Conflicting intentions, inertia, inflexibility of theatrical machinery, temporal
and spatial resistances, and, not least, the intractability of the characters
who refuse to accept the tasks assigned to them by the author produce a
vibrant and multiple web of interrelationships. The play does not have
Pirandello's dialectical brilliance; it is heavier, less clear-cut, displaying
not mental acrobatics but profound bewilderment in the face of life.
Marie-Jeanne, the cook, has been stabbed. A police inspector is investigating the case and tries to make a perfect detective-play out of his scenes.
The playwright-commentator is more ambitious than that. He presents
the antecedent events in flashbacks, but must admit that the events defy
interpretation. All he can find is separate and hopelessly isolated individuals, divided by life into two hostile camps: the carefree and light-
hearted in the aristocratic rooms, and the oppressed servants cowering in
the cavernous basement kitchen where they work off their hatred and lust

on each other. The cook Marie-Jeanne has been hardened by life and made cynical. Once she was the count's mistress, now she rules the servants with vicious tenderness. The seminarian is her illegitimate son, whose future she means to assure by the clerical gown; all it has done for him is to make him an outcast. For a brief moment he believes himself safe in the kitchenmaid Adele's love, but soon his mother disrupts the affair and ruthlessly enforces her own plans for the future. Plunged back into her former hopelessness, Adele agrees to be sent off to an oriental brothel. The seminarian, with his ardent innocence, turns to the men of good will—or rather, to a woman, the countess: "If you could think of something which just once would make God's pitiless justice smile. . . ." The impotence of his idealistic heart appeals to the countess, who in her life of luxury has vainly hoped to do good some time. For the first time she faces life's dark side and proposes to ask Adele, the despised, downtrodden girl, to be godmother to her own new baby. Glowing with the pure spirit of sacrifice, the countess learns that her spontaneous move will never be more than a theatrical gesture to the others, a self-indulgent whim. Adele, whom poverty has driven to get rid of her own unborn child, flings all the hatred and enmity her miserable existence has inspired in her in the face of the countess and her guileless benevolence. In a jealous dispute with Leon, Marie-Jeanne is fatally wounded and dies. The playwright-commentator despairs of the tragic banality of these destinies: "Senseless cruelty! . . . The whole story should never have happened. . . . I cannot believe that life is as ugly as that."

CECILE, OR THE SCHOOL FOR FATHERS (Cécile ou l'école des pères). Comedy in one act. First edition in Pièces brillantes, Paris 1952. First performance October 28, 1954, Paris, Comédie des Champs-Elysées. Translated by Luce and Arthur Klein, in From the Modern Repertoire, Ser. 3, Eric Bentley, ed., Bloomington, Ind., Indiana University Press, 1956. Time: eighteenth century. Place: garden with Chinese pavilion.

The aging Don Juan, Monsieur Orlas, has taken the young and capricious Araminthe into his house, ostensibly as governess for his daughter Cecile but really in the surreptitious hope of a gay interlude to relieve the boredom of his life's autumn. Cecile loves and is loved by an impoverished aristocrat, who, since Orlas rejects his suit, plans to elope with her. By changing clothes with Cecile, who takes Araminthe's place at a nocturnal rendezvous with Orlas, Araminthe lures Orlas into making the most daring propositions to his own daughter. Thus exposed as a hypocritical lecher, Orlas is in no position to withhold Cecile's hand from her lover, and, for the sake of his own reputation, must willy-nilly propose marriage to Araminthe.

To celebrate the double engagement, the cunning governess has baked a fine cake in advance.

This charming little play was Anouilh's wedding gift to his own daughter Catherine, herself an actress; it is also a gracious tribute to Molière and Marivaux, Anouilh's masters in the eternal art of "playing the game."

COLOMBE (also: *Mademoiselle Colombe*) *(Colombe)*. Comedy in three acts with an epilogue. Prose. First edition in *Pièces brillantes,* Paris 1952. First performance February 1952, Paris, Théâtre de l'Atelier. Adapted by Louis Kronenberger, New York, Coward McCann, 1954; translated by Denis Cannan in *Five Plays,* Vol. 2, New York, Hill & Wang, 1958–1959, and in *Ardèle and Colombe,* London, Methuen, 1959. Time: 1900. Place: stage and dressing rooms of a theater in Paris.

The old theme of the cuckold serves for an analytical and merciless exposure of the illusionary world of the theater—an exposure, however, which at the same time exalts this intoxicating and seductive medium of transforming and being transformed. The musician Julien, an ultrahonest and uncomplicated bourgeois, while on military service leaves his young wife Colombe in the care of his mother Alexandra, the famous tragic actress. The little flower-girl Colombe, his white dove, was becoming a good, faithful, and unassuming housewife, but she finds herself propelled into a novel world of poisonous magic, glorious malice, and sweet deception—and to her astonishment becomes increasingly aware of her talent for playing a part, indeed a heroine's part, in this world. She begins to experiment with herself, flits with virtuosity from one lover to the next, discovering in each experience a new facet of her own capricious, glittering self, and is enchanted by the maze of lies. The moment when Julien in utter bewilderment grasps what has been going on and sees his whole world collapsing is for Colombe merely another opportunity for a brilliant scene. She is just an unprincipled, childishly cruel little animal, who lives with complete naturalness according to her own inner law, that is, yields unreservedly to every temptation, which gives her enjoyment a certain kind of innocence. Her antics are shown against the background of tawdry glitter and ravishing makeup: there is the high-strung, aging diva and her vain poetaster; there is Surette, the poor, downtrodden secretary; Desfournettes, the smutty lecher and theater director; and Madame Georges, Alexandra's stolid dresser—they all glow in the most venomous and seductive colors through the jungle of mendacity.

THE FIGHTING COCK (L'Hurluberlu ou le réactionnaire amoureux). Comedy in four acts. Prose. Written 1958. First edition Paris 1959. First performance February 5, 1959, Paris, Comédie des Champs-Elysées. Translated by Lucienne Hill, New York, Coward McCann, 1960, and London, Methuen, 1967. Time: the present. Place: the general's country house in France.

The general, a political crackpot (hurluberlu means "scatterbrain") with a passion for causing trouble, is not taken seriously by the authorities, but simply retired. He marries young Aglae, conscientiously waters his cucumbers and cabbages, and produces children. He also wins the collaboration of the village dignitaries in his conspiratorial hobby, including the doctor, the down-at-the-heels Baron Belazor, the local Don Juan, and a trigger-happy scrap merchant. The general's eldest (illegitimate) daughter Sophie makes friends with Tarquin Edward Mendigales, an exasperating modern smart aleck, who at once stages one of today's fashionable "antiplays"—a malicious skit on the Theater of the Absurd. When the general calls the young worldling to account for seducing Sophie, Tarquin fails to understand her father's hopelessly outmoded indignation. The uppercut which floors the general is a symbol for this latter-day Don Quixote's tragicomic defeat at the end of a life squandered on dreams, which eventually cost him his neglected wife as well. He is at last overtaken by events. And yet it is this ridiculous, old-fashioned blunderer who alone keeps faith with himself in a world of unprincipled opportunists. "What one needs in life is courage . . . and enough good humor to act the comedian."

THE LARK (L'Alouette). Play in two parts. First edition Paris 1953. First performance October 16, 1953, Paris, Théâtre Montparnasse. Translated by Christopher Fry, London, Methuen, 1955, adapted by Lillian Hellman in Five Plays, Vol. 2, New York, Hill & Wang, 1958–1959, and Random House, 1966. Time: fifteenth century. Place: France.

The French public did not take too kindly to the idea that, of all people, the skeptic Anouilh, with his bent for frivolity, should venture upon the subject of their national saint. It seemed all too obvious that neither a solemnly sacred play nor any glorification of martyrs was to be expected from him. But after the first performance, the astonished critics had to note yet a new facet of the playwright. No longer, as in his early pièces noires, does he treat the historical material as a medium for bitter, maliciously sarcastic accusations, but instead looks at history in a playful, bittersweet mood of serene comprehension. The result is a legend of beautiful spontaneity verging upon the fairy tale. A significant example of this new style of glittering irony is the final tableau, a quick improvisation of the coronation at Rheims: "Bells, a salute of cannon, a flight of doves, a play of light perhaps, which throws the reflection of the cathedral's stained glass across the scene, transforming it. The curtain falls slowly on this beautiful scene." This baroque enrichment in expression, this delight in color and ornament look forward to Anouilh's *Becket*.

The events in the life of Jeanne, the shepherd girl from Domrémy, are set within the framework of a trial; all the decisive scenes in the Maid's life are reenacted for purposes of evidence before Bishop Cauchon's court and the Spanish inquisitor. All the participants wait in the background for their cue, link the separate scenes, and often step outside the action with their explanations. Jeanne is not so much a saint in unearthly glory as a simple human being with sound common-sense, humor, and tenacity, who, once she has accepted a task as just, energetically carries it to its successful conclusion. She has a practical sense for what is immediately needed, and this helps her to hold her own in relation to her harsh parents as well as to the conceited squire Robert de Vaucouleurs, the intimidated Dauphin, and the malevolent courtiers. For the Earl of Warwick, the English general, this imperturbable girl becomes the symbol of free France and for this very reason she must be destroyed—the "imponderable" which, without question, was "Joan: singing like a lark in the sky over the heads of your French armies on the march. . . . This lark singing in the sky, while we all take aim to shoot her down: that seems very like France to me." The most diverse motives and accusations appear behind the arguments of the court, which has but one aim: to bring Jeanne to the stake. This end is the symbolic end of all Anouilh's numerous unreasonable little girls who so stubbornly and uncompromisingly defend justice; who keep putting the bigoted, hypocritical world to the inconvenience of having to do away with its tiresome monitors; who by their persevering failures in this world perform deeds far transcending it. It is more, therefore, than a striking stage direction if Anouilh brings the play to a close with an improvisation of Jeanne's triumph, the coronation at Rheims.

MEDEA *(Médée)*. One-act play. Prose. Written 1946. First edition in *Nouvelles pièces noires*, Paris 1946. First performance 1948, Brussels. Opera by Andras Kovach, first performance January 23, 1967, Saarbrücken, Stadttheater. Translated by Lothian Small in *Plays of the Year*, Vol. 15, New York, Ungar, and London, Elek, 1957, and by Luce and Arthur Klein in *The Modern Theatre*, Vol. 5, and *Collected Plays*, Vol. 2, London, Methuen, 1967. Time and place: not specified.

Because Jason is getting older, he wants to settle down to a quiet life, while Medea's passions are still untamed and her adventurous spirit is ill at ease among the sedentary Greeks. Jason has left behind him the world of daring and decision, and now even wants to blot out the memory of it; he dissociates himself from Medea, to whom he no longer has ties. Medea is segregated with the nurse in a wagon while Jason marries Creusa, the king's daughter, and thereby acquires the right of domicile in Corinth. This treason reawakens Medea's primitive nature; blood and crime once led her to Jason, blood and crime shall end their union. She wants Jason to kill her, but he has become a respectable citizen and will not pay such a price for his new happiness. Thus Medea takes it upon herself to purify the world by a blood-bath; she poisons Creusa, stabs her own children, and kills herself. Jason bows to the disaster and rises above himself. For him the only redemption is death, but in the meantime he will make good use of the time left to him, do his duty in life, and govern Corinth to the best of his ability.

The ancient myth is psychologically illuminated in terms of a supreme test for men who have to make their way in this world without the guidance of a higher authority; Jason's conflict develops from the destiny rooted in his own nature.

L'ORCHESTRE *[The Orchestra]*. Concert piece in one act. Prose. First published in *L'Avant-Scène* No. 276, November 1962. First performance February 10, 1962, Paris, Comédie des Champs-Elysées. Time: the present. Place: café at a spa.

A compact study of the Pagliacci tragedy is turned into farce to avoid sentimentality. A ladies' palm-court orchestra is playing its soulful tunes, but behind the dreamy fiddling lies a junk-heap of broken lives. Patricia, the first violin, is a frustrated spinster who vents the hatred of her unfulfilled life on her aged mother. Pamela, the second violin, is driven by primitive instinct to yield to every temptation and wallows in her supposed affection for her little daughter. Both women glory in the feeling of doing their duty while they ruin the human beings in their care. Ermeline, the viola, and the hunchback flautist Leona busily exchange gossip, and Monsieur Leon, the hack pianist, tries to forget his ailing wife in the arms of the cellist Suzanne Delicias. For Suzanne, this love is a surrogate for the great artistic career which she has failed to achieve, and she kills herself when Madame Hortense, the double bass and leader of the orchestra, purposefully takes possession of Leon. The others have to pull themselves together and hide their grief behind a mask of gaiety: "Smile . . . charm! An impeccable bearing, whatever happens!"

ORNIFLE OU LE COURANT D'AIR [*Ornifle or The Draft*]. Comedy in five acts. Written 1955. First edition Paris 1955. First performance November 3, 1955, Paris, Comédie des Champs-Elysées. Time: the present. Place: Ornifle's room, Paris.

Anouilh sees Don Juan as a child of our own time, sensual, calculating, cynical, and licentious. Life has become a game of cheating and bluffing, taking chances and ruthless destruction, and the partner is God: "But I know that he wins the game. He plays with marked cards. He has all the aces. But when will he play them?"

Count Ornifle de Saint-Oignon began as an unsuccessful lyric poet seriously concerned with art, but then sold his talent for worldly gain and now writes lyrics for popular songs and whatever else is well paid. He produces spicy song hits for the former scrap dealer Machetu, who is now in show business, just as readily as he supplies Father Dubaton with a few moving verses about Jesus. In addition he skillfully keeps the wheels of publicity moving, adds another link to the unbroken chain of his lady loves in the person of a young budding actress to whose "artistic" education he wants to contribute, and soothes the hysterical secretary Mademoiselle Supo, who, to her despair, is the only woman anywhere near Ornifle whom he has left alone. The young physician Fabrice, an illegitimate son of Ornifle's, turns up with the intention of calling his mother's unscrupulous seducer to account at the point of a loaded gun. Before he can do so, Ornifle collapses with a heart attack, and while Fabrice tends him with all his medical skill, the irrepressible papa plots to seduce Marguerite, his son's fiancée. He dies of heart failure just when he sets out for a rendezvous with her.

Ornifle adds a fascinating new variant to the French character comedy's gallery of types; this play on a vain, playful sensualist forever running away from himself and drugging himself so as not to have to stand up to his conscience is that rarity where tragedy dissolves in airy froth and the casual commonplace of comedy takes on an undertone of destiny.

LA PETITE MOLIÈRE [*Madame Molière*]. Play in two parts. Written 1959. First published in *L'Avant-Scène* No. 210, December 1959. First performance June 1, 1959, Bordeaux Festival (Compagnie Madeleine Renaud). Time: seventeenth century. Place: France.

The life of the upholsterer's son Jean Baptiste Poquelin, who under the name of Molière has taken his place in world literature, provides the material for a historical piece painted on a broad canvas; planned originally as a film scenario for Jean-Louis Barrault, the play is broken up into a multiplicity of static shots. What made Molière the inspired mocker that he was, was acceptance of his failure as a tragic dramatist. His mistress, the actress Madeleine Béjart, opens up the way of success for him with her connections. With growing fame the poet slips away from the aging actress and marries her young sister Armande. The game is reversed only too soon; Molière is betrayed by his flirtatious wife. His last consolation is young Baron, growing up to be the greatest actor of his time; but he, too, succumbs to Armande's seductions. At Madeleine's deathbed the poet, himself fatally ill, speculates on the meaning of his confused life: "With one hand you give, with the other you take. We warm each other, hurt each other. But at least one is not alone."

This play is Anouilh's idiosyncratic contribution to the tradition of the "artist's drama" from Goethe and Oehlenschläger through Laube and Gutzkow to Hauptmann, Penzoldt, and Jahnn. Its attraction lies not so much in poetic expression as in refined stage techniques and their playful application in parody.

POOR BITOS. (Pauvre Bitos ou le dîner de têtes). Play in three acts. Prose. Written 1956. First edition in Pièces grinçantes, Paris 1956. First performance October 10, 1956, Paris, Théâtre Montparnasse. Translated by Lucienne Hill, New York, Coward McCann, and London, Methuen, 1964. Time: the present. Place: an old priory in France.

A savagely bitter attack on the mediocrities who, under the cloak of office and duty, indulge their own base instincts. French public opinion was outraged that Anouilh should have chosen to denounce some of the nation's political sacred cows, and as a result, for some years the author refused to have this play performed abroad.

Before selling his inherited priory to an oil company, the country squire Maxime invites his friends to a so-called dîner de têtes, where every guest, otherwise in modern dress, has to wear a mask representing a character of the time of the Revolution. This historical assembly is to give the host his opportunity to humiliate a man he detests, his former fellow-student Bitos, who thanks to dogged ambition has risen to the position of deputy public prosecutor; this evening, when he appears as Robespierre, his bigoted self-righteousness is to be shattered. Tense with ambiguity, the dialogue makes Bitos completely identify with the bloodthirsty, self-righteous executioner of the Revolution. The destruction which Robespierre, a zealous puritan out of weakness and lack of imagination, wreaks on his more sybaritic contemporaries has its counterpart in the cruelty with which Bitos, the despised son of a washerwoman, prosecutes those whom life has favored with success and a happy disposition. Bitos vainly tries to justify the bloodstained record of his office. In Franz Delanoue he is confronted with an especially brutal example of his own malevolence: at his instance, the maximum penalty was imposed on the perpetrator of a harmless piece of boyish mischief, thus ruining the rest of a young man's life. In a night-mare Bitos relives the humiliations and privations of his despised life. Then the aristocracy begin to flatter him, only to humble him more than ever by tripping him up on the unfamiliar, slippery parquet floor of society. In his vanity, Bitos falls into the trap; he gladly avails himself of the right of asylum offered him in precisely those circles which he attacks so violently because they are inaccessible to him. His eyes are eventually opened by Victoire, whom he has—unsuccessfully—courted. Embittered, he once more hardens into the vindictive figure of self-righteousness.

Anouilh shows us the tragedy of our century: justice as an instrument of mediocrity, politics as a tool of the petite bourgeoise. The machinery of the law is set in motion only in order to satisfy the hatred and envy of those who have had little from life.

THE REHEARSAL *(La Répétition ou l'amour puni)*. Play in five acts. Prose. First edition Paris 1951. First performance October 26, 1950, Paris, Théâtre Marigny. Translated by Lucienne Hill in *Five Plays*, Vol. 1, New York, Hill & Wang, 1958–1959, and by Pamela Hansford Johnson and Kitty Black, New York, Coward McCann, 1962, and London, Methuen, 1961. Time: the present. Place: the château of Ferbroques.

Anouilh has come to see life as so close to make-believe and masquerade that he uses the device of a play within the play to confront people with the reality of their feelings and aspirations. A party of aristocrats, frivolous, light-hearted, mischievous, dissipated, and amiable, disregard the modern age just as the modern age disregards them. Assembled at a château, they perform Marivaux in rococo dress. The amorous combinations of Mari-vaux's *Double Inconstancy* reflect the reality of those concerned: the count between his mistress Hortensia and the countess, who in her turn has at her side her jealous lover Villebosse. On the margin of this burnt-out crater of the soul, the action is commented upon by Hero, an alcoholic. Young, innocent Lucile, who has been employed to look after a group of orphans housed on the château grounds, finds herself in this spectral world propped up by nothing except the daily pursuit of pleasure. The count at once assigns her the leading part in the play and—in his role he is nicknamed "The Tiger"—begins to stalk his appetizing prey. Unexpectedly, a deep passion grips the two entirely different individuals. The countess, usually ready to overlook her husband's affairs, senses the danger of this encounter and tries to get rid of Lucile by a feigned theft of jewelry. Under the pres-sure of this plot Lucile runs away. The count is faced with deciding whether to go on with his rake's progress, an aging man going through the gestures and witty words of noncommitment, or whether, for the first time in his life, to give himself up to a hard, challenging happiness. The graceful rehearsal has turned into a real test of character.


RING ROUND THE MOON (L'Invitation au château). A charade with music in four scenes. Prose. Written 1947. First edition Paris 1948. First performance November 5, 1947, Paris, Théâtre de l'Atelier. Translated by Christopher Fry, New York, Oxford University Press, and London, Methuen, 1950. Time: the present. Place: conservatory at a château.

The mistaken identities of identical twins, a theme popular with play-wrights from Plautus to Shakespeare and Goldoni, serve the purpose of merciless social criticism. Hugo, the "young man about town," is anxious to cure his melancholy twin brother Frederic of his unrequited love for the flirtatious Diana Messerschmann, and to this end arranges for the ballet dancer Isabelle to be decked out as a seductive beauty for a ball, in the course of which she is to attract Frederic's affections; thereafter, she is to disappear once more into the obscurity of her shabby existence. Isabelle resists the indignity of this game with more and more determination, but in so doing succumbs to the charms of the icy cynic Hugo; eventually, how-ever, she sees through this vain dazzler and hesitantly grows fond of the unimpressive Frederic. All this passes across the stage at a riotous pace. For once it is not anonymous fate, but a blasé charmer who arranges the play and distributes the parts, yet the hopelessness of Anouilh's characters, who are governed by their cues and functions, is the same as ever: "One is alone. That much is certain. One can do nothing for one another except play the game." And again, as always in Anouilh, it is a young person, Isabelle, who stakes her longings and her unfulfilled life against a perverted world. She is surrounded by the caricatures of bitter, angry social satire: the paralyzed Madame Desmermortes, owner of the château and the twins' aunt, who vents her clever, crafty malevolence on her mousy, acidulated companion Mademoiselle Capulat; Isabelle's mother, a piano teacher, who makes up for her life's disappointed hopes in exasperating volubility; the rich financier Messerchmann, who lives on noodles and plain water and dreams of the happy past when he was still a small tailor in Cracow; and the butler Joshua with his inimitable dignity.
The play is a milestone in the development of Anouilh, that master of the art of saying angry things in pretty words.

ROMEO AND JEANETTE (also *Fading Mansions; Jeanette) (Roméo et Jeanette)*. Play in four acts. Prose. Written 1945. First edition in *Nouvelles pièces noires,* Paris 1946. First performance 1946, Paris, Théâtre de l'Atelier. Translated by Donald MacDonagh *(Fading Mansions)* for London production, 1949, and by Miriam John in *Five Plays,* Vol. 1, New York, Hill & Wang, 1958–1959, and in *Collected Plays,* Vol. 2, London, Methuen, 1967. Time: a summer between the two world wars. Place: Jeanette's house in a village in France and a summerhouse in the woods.

Like Shakespeare's *Romeo and Juliet,* this play has two lovers who seem made for each other and for a happy marriage. And again life plays one of its incomprehensible cruel tricks and disrupts the idyll by a sudden, inexplicable, senseless passion which causes the couple's ruin. The beauty of life can be understood only when it is seen to be precarious and imperiled.

The young, capable teacher Julia is embarrassed by having to disclose her family's sordid circumstances to her fiancé Frederic and his mother. Julia's father is a drunkard who forever puts on an act of sentimental self-pity; her brother Lucien, "a sorry cuckold," wallows in mordant, self-tormenting cynicism, and her sister Jeanette is an embittered, precocious girl who becomes the mistress of Azarias, the owner of the local castle, in order to maintain her family. In a fit of hatred Jeanette explodes at the philistine, cheap respectability of the visitor, because Frederic's mother kills the pet cockerel for lunch. Frederic intervenes, and with alarming suddenness the two young people from entirely different backgrounds are seized by a mutual passion. But the past is stronger: Frederic feels tied to Julia, who is driven to a suicide attempt by this incomprehensible betrayal. In her bewilderment, Jeanette marries Azarias. But the lovers lack the strength for a lifelong lie; they let themselves drift out to sea together in search of a common death.

The play is a *pièce noire* overshadowed by ruin and hopelessness; it does, however, preserve a touch of humanity in the saving grace of suffering, in the poetic aura of self-sacrifice.

THE WALTZ OF THE TOREADORS *(La Valse des toréadors)*. Play in five acts. Prose. Written 1951. First edition Paris 1952. First performance January 8, 1952, Paris, Comédie des Champs-Elysées. Translated by Lucienne Hill, New York, Coward McCann, 1957, and London, Elek, 1956. Time: the present. Place: the general's room.

Seventeen years ago, at a ball, General St. Pé, then a dashing cavalry captain, found—as the "Waltz of the Toreadors" played—the great passion of his life, Ghislaine de Sainte-Euverte. But his hysterical wife managed with the help of a sham paralysis to chain him to herself; for her the waltz was the prelude to enjoying her life with successive lovers. The nagging guilty conscience for a planned but never performed betrayal turns the general into a poseur who dictates his memoirs and gladdens the heart of the chambermaid who happens to be at hand. Suddenly Ghislaine appears, not as young as she was but gaily chirping with a teen-ager's undiminished zest; she brings two letters which prove the wife's adultery with Doctor Bonfant, the physician. The "girl's" impetuous eagerness to set him free for a joint future somewhat embarrasses the now indolent general and sets off a chain reaction of suicide attempts by his wife and his sweetheart, neither of whom wants to be outdone by her rival. Finally Ghislaine finds consolation with Gaston, the secretary and illegitimate son of the general; the general himself with the new maid; and his wife in the gleeful pleasure of having won.

On the face of it, this is hilarious, brilliantly staged theater, relying for its electrifying effects on drawing-room comedy, farce, and even slapstick effects; but behind it all one senses bitter resignation and a merciless objectivity which sees men degraded into puppets of chance trying to forget their irreparable loneliness in hectic grimaces: "There is no point in trying to understand either one's adversary or one's wife. In fact, it is best to understand no one at all, otherwise one goes to the dogs."

## ARDEN, John
(England, born 1930)

ARMSTRONG'S LAST GOODNIGHT. An exercise in diplomacy. Three acts. Verse and prose. First performance May 7, 1964, Glasgow, Citizens' Theatre. Time: about 1530. Place: Scotland.

Arden's ironically detached chronicle play, which deals pretty freely with its historical material, is to be understood, according to the author, as an analogy to many a double-tongued sharp practice in the Congo crisis. Law and morals have become things to be manipulated, the dependent variables of politics.

In meditative cynicism the statesman Lindsay compares his office with the business of a pimp who panders to "the base lusts and deficiencies of humanity. The material of my craft, in fact. Accept them, make use of them, for God's sake enjoy them. . . ." As the setting for his exposure, Arden chooses that turning point at the end of the Middle Ages when the ancestral natural law was being superseded by expediency's variable reasons of state.

After decades of strife, James V, the adolescent king of Scotland, seeks peace with England for his exhausted realm. The robber barons of the Border, who had waxed rich through raids transfigured into patriotic and heroic exploits, refuse to abandon this "chivalrous" life. They sack English monasteries and farms and thus provoke reprisals, and the conclusion of peace is put off again and again. The royal ban pronounced upon the most powerful of the brigands, Johnny Armstrong of Gilnockie, remains ineffective in the inaccessible forests. At this juncture Sir David Lindsay, educator, court poet, and king-of-arms, steps in with his flexible "divide and rule" policy. The Laird of Wamphray is supposed to kill Armstrong, but is himself lured into an ambush by his forewarned adversary and delivered up to the vengeance of his arch enemy Stobs. Lindsay adapts himself to the new situation, offers Armstrong the king's pardon and a governor's post—intended originally as Wamphray's reward—and thus wins the robber laird over to James. At court, meanwhile, Lord Johnstone, Wamphray's liege, though guiltless, is thrown into prison in order to gain the good graces of Lord Maxwell, Armstrong's protector, reputed to be in England's pay. Church and nobility form an alliance to resist Lindsay's plan of strengthening the Border barons, and foil Armstrong's appointment. Armstrong thereupon angrily takes again to raiding, and discovers in Luther's doctrine an excuse for his insurrection. Lindsay sets a trap for him with the king's word of honor; unarmed and—like Wamphray before him—betrayed, Armstrong meets his death. The stuttering giant falls a victim to his own naiveté, which all his life had made him waver between the ruthless indulgence of his own power and the desire for recognition at court. The dead man's possessions are rapidly put to good use as bribes in the power game.

The different settings are seen side by side on the stage, like toys, and the successive incidents of the epic chronicle are linked by songs. Arden, who was familiar with the alfresco style of medieval subjects from his adaptation of Goethe's *Götz von Berlichingen,* uses a gnarled, antiquated language, but replaces Berlichingen's straightforward rebelliousness with bitter satire, which turns ideals into points of view.

LIVE LIKE PIGS. Seventeen scenes. Prose and songs. First edition Harmondsworth, England, 1961. First performance September 30, 1958, London, Royal Court Theatre. Time: the present. Place: a post-war council estate in a north-country industrial town.

In this play Arden shows the fracture in the modern social structure by which initiative is traded for safety, instinct for social convention with its shelter of inconspicuousness. The outsider is either domesticated or destroyed within the system. Arden sets before us one of those antisystems that disturb and trouble the cosy peace of the settled. Exuberant nomads come into spontaneous and violent conflict with the decency standards of the lower-middle class. Arden explains: "When I wrote this play I intended it to be not so much a social document as a study in differing ways of life brought sharply into conflict and both ways losing their particular virtues under the stress of intolerance and misunderstanding." Arden's concern is with the incompatibility of these different worlds, but he does not take sides or present one of them as ideal. The middle class, too, indulge their brutality and amorality, but they preserve the appearances.

The municipal authorities have expelled the Sawney family from their caravan and established them on a housing estate—but it is not to their liking. The half-gypsies, free as the birds, have hitherto had a lot of fun, and they do not intend to exchange that existence for a daily round of duties. They pilfer and drink as they always did, and the house becomes a pigsty. The mediocre ordinariness of their neighbors, the Jacksons, acts as a provocation to rudeness. Jackson, the respectable family man, has a bit of fun with Rachel, Sawney's termagant wife. Rachel's son Col naively takes it for granted that he can do the same with Jackson's daughter Doreen. But this is too much for the neighborhood and, in a wave of fury, the outsiders are almost lynched. The Sawneys are saved thanks only to the police, whom they have always so despised, and with much relief the family sets off on its untamed ways once more. The social experiment has failed.

Arden presents a series of colorful episodes and figures (the half-gypsy Blackmouth, the Old Croaker, the indestructible Sailor) and makes effective use of folk words and of ballads which provide a foil and bind the scenes together.

SERGEANT MUSGRAVE'S DANCE. An unhistorical parable. Prose and songs. Written 1959. First edition London 1960. First performance October 22, 1959, London, Royal Court Theatre. Time: eighty years ago. Place: a mining town in the north of England.

Alternating between slapstick and folk song, Arden shows how man's bewilderment in the face of other men and their power is reflected in hero worship and agitation for peace. Pacifism in the absolute, pursuing its aim with fanaticism and violence, is a traitor to and negates itself. Arden makes his intentions plain: "I have endeavoured to write about the violence that is so evident in the world, and to do so through a story that is partly one of wish-fulfillment. I think that many of us must at some time have felt an overpowering urge to match some particularly outrageous piece of violence with an even greater and more outrageous retaliation. Musgrave tries to do this."

Sergeant Musgrave and three privates take up quarters in one of the desolate mining towns of northern England, and as a recruiting party they are made welcome by the authorities. The mayor, who is also a mine owner, sees the queen's men as natural allies in his endeavor to avert a strike of the exhausted, restive workers and hopes thereby to press the ringleaders into military service. But Musgrave and his companions are deserters from the colonies. The treacherous raids of the natives and the even more cruel reprisals of the English on innocent hostages made Sergeant Musgrave aware of a divine mission: he wants to mobilize mankind against war and, if need be, turn the Gatling gun on the lukewarm and the indifferent, so as to win the masses for his aims. Young Sparky, the gayest of Musgrave's party, wants to escape with Annie, the barmaid, into a quiet, uncomplicated happiness but pays with his life for this betrayal of the idea. Musgrave organizes a big peace demonstration in the marketplace and instead of the Union Jack runs up the skeleton of Billy Hicks, a son of the town who met his hero's death overseas. The crowd is carried away by the brawling dance around the beer barrel. Musgrave is arrested and learns with consternation from the publican's wife that his reforming zeal has done nothing but increase misery in the town.

A new and rather unlikely style for a somewhat antididactic play is tried out, using numerous songs, touches of folklore, and vigorous popular speech, and having the courage to be ridiculous.


THE WORKHOUSE DONKEY. A vulgar melodrama in two acts. Prose and songs. First edition London 1964. First performance July 8, 1963, Chichester Festival Theatre. Time: the present. Place: a Yorkshire industrial town, somewhere between Sheffield and Leeds.

A small-town satire on threadbare party ethics and petit-bourgeois corruption serves to unleash all the tricks of modern stagecraft; prose and rhymed verse, songs, pantomime, melodrama, audience participation, and repeated breaks in theatrical illusion are used in order to give a tragicomic demonstration of a sociological law. The unprincipled majority casts out two incorrigible outsiders who indulge in the old-fashioned luxury of convictions of their own and live according to them.

Charlie Butterthwaite, the workhouse boy, has all his life done the donkey work that others did not want to soil their hands with. As a strike organizer and labor leader he used his native intelligence and toughness to bring the Labour Party to power in the town. With some misgivings but without protest, party friends and foes alike put up with the gruff and boisterous tyrant, who can always get the crowd, and hence success, on his side. Then Colonel Feng is appointed chief constable. He has an incorruptible sense of duty and is determined to take drastic action against the general nepotism and abuse of office. He proceeds sternly against Labour's Butterthwaite, who couldn't care less about the rules, and in his own interests organizes a fictitious robbery of the borough treasury. Feng also wishes to expose the brewer Sweetman, the local leader of the respectable and bigoted Conservatives who strengthen their party funds from the returns of a less-than-respectable nightclub. A tricky hunt now sets in; the aldermen play off Butterthwaite and Feng against each other, to divert attention from their own shady activities, and Feng's subordinates are so corrupt that all the surprise raids by his police are leaked out beforehand. The town follows this chain of failures with derisive interest. Dr. Blomax, a physician come down in the world and a cunning schemer, is the scandalmonger who, though despised by all, eventually gets the better of everyone. Feng is deprived of his office for incompetence, and Butterthwaite, who has long been a thorn in the flesh of his own party, is dropped by them in a sudden bout of moral indignation. The worthy alderman Sweetman redeems the image of his party by turning the brothel into a picture gallery. With admirable social cohesion across all party barriers and political differences, the townspeople have given yet one more splendid demonstration of how to erect an honest façade behind which to hide the same old unsavory deals.

## ARDEN, John, and D'ARCY, Margaretta
(England)

ARS LONGA, VITA BREVIS. One-act play in seven scenes. Prose. First edition London 1965. First performance January 12, 1964, London, LAMDA Theatre. Time: the present. Place: somewhere in England.

A farce on a doctrinaire who reduces himself to absurdity. An honorably dusty college appoints an art master, Antiochus Miltiades, who distrusts any kind of freedom in art and drills his class with such commands as "constructivism the only permissible abstraction, but realism the keynote." His students draw only geometrical shapes on graph paper, with mechanical precision. The intoxication of commanding power precipitates the would-be foot-soldier into a grotesque battle: "We must preserve rigidity, we must remember that unless we can subordinate ourselves wholeheartedly to the enthusiasm of total control we shall disintegrate." With burning enthusiasm Antiochus enrolls in the Territorials, and during

maneuvers is accidentally shot by the headmaster. The art master happily
dies his hero's death, and equally happily his widow pockets the subscrip-
tion raised by the school. The money at long last assures her of a comfortable existence. The caricatured figures and situations are matched by
the telegraphic style of the language, which is reduced to a series of
proposals.

## ARDREY, Robert
(United States, born 1908)

SHADOW OF HEROES (also: *Stone and Star*). Play in five acts. Prose.
Written 1958. First edition New York 1958. First performance October
7, 1958, London, Picadilly Theatre. Time: 1944–1956. Place: Hungary.

In a somewhat offhand manner the political facts of postwar Hungary and
the private destiny of its statesmen are pressed into a causal nexus. Putting
aside the question of the extent to which these facts really add to our
knowledge, as the author intends, or how much had to be simplified and
sacrificed for the sake of dramatization, the play remains a stylistically
interesting attempt to put documentary reporting on the stage by means
of a series of action shots linked by the author as commentator.
After the collapse of the German front, the leaders of the left gather in
1944 under Soviet auspices in order to set up communism in Hungary.
They include the chief of the resistance movement, Laszlo Rajk, and his
wife, Julia; the party ideologists Ernö Gerö and Matyas Rakosi, who have
returned from a stint in Moscow as *Apparatschiks* and blind executors of
Stalin's commands; and the plumber Janos Kadar, the only proletarian
among the party strategists and as such supposed to win over the broad
masses to the system. Rajk takes over the Ministry of the Interior, later
becomes foreign minister, and tries to loosen the bonds which tie Hungary
to Moscow as a satellite state. He is accused of Titoism and executed;
Kadar, his former friend, acts as a willing hangman's assistant to the powers
that be. The Khrushchev "thaw" sweeps away the Stalinists and Julia
succeeds in obtaining her husband's official rehabilitation. But then the
revolution of October 1956 breaks out, inspired by Rajk's ideas of ideal
communism. The protagonists of force—Kadar and Mikoyan—gain the
upper hand with the help of Russian tanks. Julia and Imre Nagy are lured
out of their asylum in the Yugoslav Embassy and arrested.

## ARRABAL, Fernando
(Spain/France, born 1932)

GUERNICA *(Guernica)*. Play in one scene. Prose. Written 1959. First edition in *Théâtre II,* Paris 1961. First performance May 7, 1960, Celle, Schloßtheater. Translated by Barbara Wright, in *Plays,* Vol. 2, London, Calder & Boyars, 1967. Time: 1937. Place: a ruined house in Guernica.

The old Basque Fanchou and his wife Lira have been buried under rubble during a bomb attack. Like frightened children they flee from the incomprehensible horror of death and take refuge in everyday commonplaces. While sinking more and more deeply into the rubble, they quarrel about trifles, cantankerously defend their opinions, and torment each other with persistent malice. Their concern is not how to save each other but the tree in front of the window, which, as a symbol of freedom, must be safeguarded. Fanchou finds an excuse even for the inhuman destruction of the town—after all, the bombs have to be tried out somewhere. Eventually the couple are killed by a direct hit. Two colored balloons rise upward. A spiteful officer, who had kept threatening to handcuff Fanchou, vainly tries to shoot down the toys that irresistibly float into the sky. A writer who had long prowled around the couple like a hyena and is enraptured by their "heroic death" drafts the outline of a novel about it.
Several associations from Picasso's picture have been worked into this admonitory play on abused humanity. With bitter mockery in this requiem for the town destroyed in the Spanish Civil War Arrabal depicts people who lack even the narcotic of highflown phrases by which to give themselves the illusion of being victims and heroes. Thus they are nothing but helpless cattle slaughtered in the ordinary course of events.

ORISON *(Oraison)*. One-act play. Prose. First edition in *Théâtre,* Paris 1958. First performance April 13, 1958, Paris, Théâtre de Poche. Translated by Barbara Wright in *Plays,* Vol. 1, London, Calder & Boyars, 1962. Time and place: not specified.

A blasphemous jest of terrifying consistency: People have become so wicked that they are wicked without motive or purpose. Thoughtlessly, with primitive unconcern, just as children break their dolls, men kill and indulge in aberrations, are bored and eventually play at being religious. But all good intentions are condemned to failure, for faith in goodness is long extinct.
A married couple sit in front of the coffin of their child, whom they have killed, and out of boredom start reading in the Bible. They are fascinated

by the novel world it opens up to them, and they decide "to become good" —that will be less boring and perhaps very nice. It may even turn out to be useful. The couple decide not to kill anyone again, and to give up adultery, theft, and lying. Still, they have some slight misgivings in beginning their new life: "It will become boring. Boring just like everything else. We shall grow tired of it."

PICNIC ON THE BATTLEFIELD (Pique-nique en campagne). One-act play. Prose. First published in Les Lettres Nouvelles, No. 58, March 1958. First edition in Théâtre II, Paris 1961. First performance April 23, 1959, Paris, Théâtre de Lutèce. Translated by Barbara Wright in Plays, Vol. 2, London, Calder & Boyars, 1967. Time: the present. Place: bare earth.

The senseless murder of war is reduced to absurdity in a picnic. The soldier Zapo has trouble coping with a roll of barbed wire, some shells, and a complicated military order. All the greater is Zapo's relief when suddenly his parents turn up and surprise him with an excellent picnic: as petits bourgeois they cannot understand the complexities of war. They are all enjoying their meal when suddenly the enemy soldier Zepo bursts upon them. Willy-nilly Zapo has to take him prisoner. He poses for a martial snapshot, and with this surely his military duty is amply fulfilled. Two zealous ambulance men are busy looking for wounded warriors, but all they find is Mother's finger, which she injured when slicing onions. Zapo and Zepo, to their surprise, keep discovering more and more things they have in common. Both groan under the burden of military service, and they have similar hobbies to amuse themselves during the long periods of waiting in the trenches: Zapo knits, Zepo makes flowers out of cloth. Both get the same propaganda slogans. An unexpected nuisance drops from the sky—bombs, but an umbrella provides ready protection. A burst of machine-gun fire eventually mows down the incorrigible peace-lovers. With happy zeal the ambulance men do their duty.

THE TWO EXECUTIONERS (Les Deux Bourreaux). A melodrama in one act. Written 1957. First edition in Théâtre, Paris 1958. First performance April 13, 1958, Paris, Théâtre de Poche. Translated by Richard Howard, New York, Grove Press, 1960, and by Barbara Wright in Plays, Vol. 1, London, Calder & Boyars, 1962. Time: none specified. Place: a very dark room.

A cosy family scene is distorted to the point of horror in order to expose the vicious lies of our time, and has equipped itself with an ideological toolbox for its deeds of violence. Homicide is replaced by denunciation,

deliberate treason by the pious self-deception of a "surmounted past."
Françoise denounces her husband Jean to two executioners and causes him
to be taken to the torture chamber. Greedily Françoise listens for the
screams of the tortured man. In front of her two sons Benoît and Maurice
she lets herself go in heartrending self-pity. Benoît accepts her as the
angelic mother who was tormented by her husband. Maurice loves his
father, but is helpless in the face of his mother's and brother's hypocrisy.
With the suffering mien of the Good Samaritan she opens Jean's wounds
with her nails and "disinfects" them by rubbing in salt and vinegar. He
dies of his injuries. Maurice wants to stop, in silent accusation. But the lie
with its pulsating vitality is even stronger than the noble idea that his dead
father has become for him. He makes his peace with his inhuman family,
for right is where the survivors are.

## ASMODI, Herbert
(Germany, born 1923)

DIE MENSCHENFRESSER *[The Man Eaters]*. Comedy in eleven scenes.
Prose. Acting edition Zurich, Stauffacher, 1962. First performance De-
cember 31, 1961, Bochum, Schauspielhaus. Time: the present. Place:
England and Morocco.

This comic crime play wavers between the pleasant humor of such boulevard theater successes as *Risky Marriage* and *Arsenic and Old Lace,* and
the horrible murder used as a vehicle of contemporary satire. England has
been disturbed by a series of perfect crimes. Rich members of high society
have repeatedly been found dead, each one a suicide by potassium cyanide.
The playboy Peter Body solves the riddle by having his fiancée marry the
murderer, making sure that his future mother-in-law is murdered in time.
The expert murderer is Sir Bogumil Octopus, an enthusiastic lover of
Homer and collector of antique statues, who has to drive the owners of
antiquities to suicide so that he can appropriate their treasures. This
worthy art lover has in his service a fakir whose methods of torture can be
held out as a threat to the occasional unwilling candidate for suicide,
should the amiably proffered dose of potassium cyanide not be tasty
enough. Bogumil is executed, not for the series of murders—proof against
him cannot be found—but for the death of the fakir, for whose heart attack
he is not responsible. Peter takes back his fiancée, almost undamaged, the
poorer by the loss of a mother-in-law, but the richer by a double inheritance and the grace of the queen.

PARDON WIRD NICHT GEGEBEN *[Pardon Will Not Be Granted]* (also: *Schuwaloff und der Weltfrieden [Zhuvalov and World Peace])*. Comedy in four acts. Prose. Written 1958. Acting edition Munich, Drei Masken, n.d. First performance July 30, 1958, Munich, Kammerspiele. Time: the present. Place: drawing room, hotel, castle.

Some shady aspects of art and politics are studied; apart from yielding a highly explosive piece of grotesquerie, the outcome is a melancholy aphorism: "I'm rather afraid one has to be a bit of a fool to dream of world peace, but then it's better for a fool to dream of it than no one at all."
The talented young painter Schuwaloff has been caught up in the art boom. His work has been promoted by the dealer Ambrosius Krell, who now with the consortium Aschenboom and Rumschedel want to kill the painter in order not to spoil the market by glutting it with good pictures. With the help of drugs and regular shooting practice, the painter's wife Nina is trained to murder her husband and thus safeguard business interests. The American, James Pappel, is an equally dubious patron, interested in the young Russian only because he wants to use him as grounds for divorce from his wife Dorothy. The only one to help Schuwaloff without an ulterior motive is Princess Stefanie. Her brother Bonifaz is obsessed with dreams of world peace; at his castle he conducts daring experiments in coexistence with wolves and sheep and ruins his family with his expensive ideas. To cure him of his delusions, Krell and his consortium organize a four-power summit conference for him. On this occasion the money strategists try to liquidate each other and finally are devoured by the wolves, who have suffered a regrettable reversion to type. As a result of this bloodbath Bonifaz is cured of all his unrealistic dreams of peace. Then a stranger is announced, by trade an art dealer, and once more a web begins to spin around Schuwaloff.
Asmodi seems to have taken refuge from his own bitter insights in farce and the absurd.

## AUDEN, Wystan Hugh
(England, born 1907)

THE AGE OF ANXIETY. A baroque eclogue in six parts. Free verse. First edition New York 1947. Time: Second World War. Place: New York and imaginary dream landscape.

On the basis of Pound's and Eliot's attempts at a heightened poetic language, Auden strives in the varying verse forms of *The Age of Anxiety* for a metaphysical view of the universe. He attempts a comprehensive, two-dimensional world view and deliberately makes the poem a vehicle for the message of Christian living and redemption. He shows man's experience of himself between the hubris of ever new technological achievements making yet more dangerous threats and the chaos of a meaningless, inorganic mass society.

In a bar in New York four customers listen to a radio news bulletin from the battlefields of the Second World War. Stirred by the destructive mania that has gripped the whole world, the four individuals break out of their own indifference and put their trust in conversation. All of them are failures and are drowning in drink the emptiness and loneliness of the daily round in a big city. They brood about themselves and, going beyond their personal failure, grasp the deeper causes of humanity's degeneration and fanaticism in this "age of anxiety." The fourfold self-examination is conditioned by the contrasts of this chance encounter. The widower Quant is a simple clerk; Malin, a medical intelligence officer in the Canadian Air Force, is an intellectual congealed in icy cynicism; Rosetta is a department-store buyer with a zest for life; and Emble is a lighthearted dandy in naval uniform. Into these four people's visions, reminiscences, and dreams, Auden blends the varying aspects of psychoanalytical diagnosis appropriate to each case, aspects of easy sensuousness or religious fervor. In their visions they traverse the settings of human life: nature in her inexhaustible self-renewal impassively obeying her own laws; civilization idolized as an end in itself; the museums enclosing in their coffins the cultural heritage of whole epochs whose art no longer touches men's hearts. The seven circles of purgation in Dante's *Purgatorio* have here turned into a review of the "seven selfish ages" and a journey through the "seven stages." Feelings of guilt and yearnings for salvation allow the four people no respite in their quest. The apocalyptic nightmare of a disintegrating world presses in on them more and more closely, until they come to their senses in the alcoholic vapors of the bar. Rosetta invites them all for a nightcap in her apartment and tries, in the "masque" of sensations, to win the elegant Emble for the escape from self by a brief night of love. Sobered, she eventually realizes that the only thing that can bring true security into the exile of earthly existence is the Christian message of redemption.

## AUDIBERTI, Jacques
(France, 1899–1965)

LA BÊTE NOIRE *[The Black Beast]*. Play in three acts. Prose. First edition Paris 1945. Included under the title *La Fête noire [The Black Feast]* in *Théâtre II,* Paris 1952. First performance December 3, 1948, Paris, Théâtre de la Huchette. Time: uncertain. Place: somewhere in the mountains.

"The beast" is the symbol of unrestrained instincts. The crowd wants to hunt the beast and destroy it, without noticing that in the heat of the chase and in their bloodlust they become more and more bestial themselves. The beast is in the crowd and among them. Once more the archaic symbol is combined with the most modern knowledge of mass psychosis.

The physician Dr. Felicien has been driven to the mountains by his unsatisfied desire for the warmth of a woman's body. The peasant girls Alice and Mathilde recoil from the agonizingly tense demands of this involuntary ascetic. Soon afterward Mathilde is found dead, dreadfully mutilated by a sexual murderer: "the beast" has claimed its first victim. Under the leadership of Felicien and the sharpshooter Lou Desterrat, the population gathers for a far-ranging chase. An odd collection of grotesque figures flits across the scene: Mme. Palustre, the resolute ice-cream vendor; Monsignor Morvellon, with an odor of sanctity and sweetness as provocative as a whore's perfume, "who dispenses grace with intolerable kindness and pours it upon all the world, including God"; and the ludicrous manservant Bellenature. Eventually a skinny goat is triumphantly shot as "the beast." This deed earns Felicien world renown as a scientist as well as a lucrative trade in the "beast's" alleged hair and teeth. Alice knows that she herself is the ferocious beast—she is a woman endowed with Circe's magical power to transform everyone around her into beasts. When she gives herself to Felicien, both of them shudder, for they feel the presence of the black beast. Lost to the world in a rapturous ritual dance, the pair is discovered by Lou and the curtain falls as he stands with his knife pointed at them.

Man's being possessed by demonic powers is expressed in the style of the writing and the dramatic structure. The language of the play is like lush Mediterranean vegetation, the characters are glittering dream images under a southern sky, "all softness and flowering ashes," with perpetually changing outlines in changing associations, present and yet out of reach, like the beast.

LA FOURMI DANS LE CORPS *[Ant in the Flesh]*. Play in two parts. Prose. Written 1961. First edition in *Théâtre IV*, Paris 1961. First performance October 14, 1961, Darmstadt, Landestheater. Time: 1875. Place: the ladies' home of Remiremont.

With a skeptical and ironic delight in theatrical fun that is occasionally close to the absurd, the author describes an obstinate virgin's conversion to love. Young Jeanne-Marie Barthelemy de Pic-Saint-Pop turns her back on the world and enters the ladies' home of Remiremont, where the residents are divided between the zestful "bees" and the praying and law-abiding "ants." The first thing the inspired spinster does with her zeal for renunciation is to sabotage a ballet entertainment by which the "bees" are trying to bring a little fun into the greyness of life at the home. Marshal Turenne, who nearly lost his life as a result of two excited ladies' playing with a cannon, threatens to march against the home with the royal army. A four-year-old boy, who in the panic has taken refuge in her otherwise so well-guarded bed, suddenly awakens in Jeanne-Marie the motherly feelings of a loving woman. By luck it turns out that Turenne's adjutant is her persistent and platonic admirer Roger du Marquet, a young officer with a philosophical addiction to cocoa. In these circumstances she has no trouble saving the ladies' home, but now she wants to find out the secret of love that was so long withheld from her. Embattled as usual, she forces Marquet at the point of a gun to give her a "lesson." Although the little boy has in the meantime been replaced by an ugly changeling, she is determined to adopt the misshapen creature and to start a new, fulfilled life together with Marquet.
A profusion of witty diversive effects, ranging from precious language through the cool development of the action to ludicrously caricatured characters, turns this play into a triumph of the stage.

LA LOGEUSE *[The Landlady]*. Play in three acts. Prose. Written 1954. First edition in *Théâtre III*, Paris 1956. First performance July 7, 1960, Cologne, Kammerspiele der Städtischen Bühnen. Time: the present. Place: Mme. Cirqué's apartment.

Audiberti chooses a mythical symbol—the sorceress Circe who transforms men into beasts in the *Odyssey*—for the struggle between the sexes and projects it into modern life.

The beautiful and zestful landlady Mme. Cirqué has waited all her life for the one man who is her superior in vitality and willpower. In her frustration, the passionate woman has enslaved all the weaklings that surround her and transformed them as she pleased. Her husband, formerly a minister, now earns a miserable living as a milliner; her daughter Crista is nervous and on the point of suicide; their neighbor Pierre, who used to be a competent mechanic, now despairs of ever becoming as great a musician as she has made him want to be. Monsieur Tienne, allegedly a teacher, arrives, rents a room, and begins to contradict the self-confident lady. This is so unusual a circumstance for Mme. Cirqué that she is quite fascinated and lets Tienne take her away. All the others sigh with relief and return to their former and appropriate occupations. But Mme. Cirqué soon returns. Tienne, it turns out, is really a police inspector detailed to carry out a secret investigation of her boardinghouse; the numerous cases of suicide, murder, and madness in Mme. Cirqué's circle have at last begun to worry the authorities. Once more Madame's victims are pressed into their abhorred parts. Ultimately even Tienne becomes a victim. Under the spell of Mme. Cirqué's hypnotic powers, he has left the police force and really becomes a teacher, but in the end he is made to occupy the place of her milliner husband, whom she has sent away.

POMME, POMME, POMME *[Pomme, Pomme, Pomme]*. Comedy in two acts. Prose. First edition in *Théâtre V,* Paris 1962. First performance September 7, 1962, Paris, Théâtre de la Bruyère. Time: the present. Place: Paris.

Dream and imagination clash with reality; help in facing up to life comes not from a psychiatrist but from a clown, whose circus tricks are the expression of a redeeming power of destiny that is released by a demonic game.
Dadou and Vévette, newly married, spend their life in idle dreams and tender dalliance on the park benches of Paris—much to the annoyance of Dadou's strict papa, a comfortably placed tax official who has to pay for this rosy bliss. He engages the services of Zozo, a magician, entomologist, and jack-of-all-trades, and his radiant and naive assistant Miss Pomme, to make his young good-for-nothing son change his idle ways. Zozo and his foolery go to work. He dazzles Dadou with the prospect of an effortless way of accumulating great riches: pebbles sprinkled with water make cheap motor fuel. Other stratospheric projects of this kind, suitably explained in bombastic foreign words, ultimately so enrapture Dadou that he is roused into action. Pomme, with her rustic cunning, is supposed to possess the formula for the crucial invention. Much to Vévette's exasperation, Dadou

thereupon brings all his charms and seductions into play to gain the heart of the apple-cheeked girl, and takes her into the household. Zozo's plan is to make work palatable to Dadou not because of its moral value, but as a pretext for play. Eventually Dadou is led to accept reality without having to give up his dreams. As a precaution, a fat, menacing bluebottle from Zozo's kit of magic props is left behind, to guard against any relapse into sweet idleness.

Songs, pantomime, and all the stylistic means of the grotesque are used in this lighthearted and colorful theatrical entertainment.

QUOAT-QUOAT [Quoat-Quoat]. Play in two scenes. Prose. Written 1945. First edition in Théâtre I, Paris 1948. First performance January 28, 1946, Paris, Théâtre de la Gaîté Montparnasse. Time: the reign of Napoleon III. Place: cabin of a mail boat.

The young archaeologist Amédée is traveling on the secret assignment of recovering the Emperor Maximilian's treasure in Mexico, and plans to take this opportunity to investigate the legend of the primitive god Quoat-Quoat. The ship's captain subjects him to elaborate regulations, supposed to safeguard the secrecy of the mission. Nevertheless the captain's pretty daughter Clarisse, by kittenish flirtation, worms the truth out of Amédée, whereupon the captain triumphantly condemns him to be shot. A Mexican adventuress is a new temptation for Amédée; she gives him a stone of Quoat-Quoat endowed with the power of destruction. Amédée, condemned to death as he is, hands the Mexican woman over to the captain in the hope of thus obtaining his pardon by legal means. Nothing, it would seem, can save a man so fanatically law-abiding. At the last minute, Mme. Batrilant, a commercial traveler in Bordeaux wine, reveals herself to be the true envoy in charge of the treasure-hunting mission. Amédée's assignment was fictitious and meant to cover the real agent. The captain indifferently pardons him, but when Amédée realizes that he owes his life merely to his own unimportance, he chooses to be executed. By this time the captain is tired of driving people to their ruin. With the help of the Mexican god's stone he sinks the boat and all its passengers and crew.

Quoat-Quoat is a parable on the rootlessness of modern man—drifting along in a ship, cheated of satisfaction by an unreal task, and teased by temptations. A cynical and malevolent captain constructs compulsive situations in which the human guinea-pig is bound to be defeated. A profound pessimism underlies all the theatrical levity: Man in his predicament can look to no superior moral authority or standard of value; even the captain is no longer the guide and master of his ship, only the instrument of a nameless system. The only free decision man can take is to destroy himself.

# AYMÉ, Marcel
(France, 1902–1967)

CLERAMBARD (also: *The Count of Clerambard) (Clérambard)*. Comedy in four acts. Prose. Written 1949. First edition Paris 1950. First performance March 13, 1950, Paris, Comédie des Champs-Elysées. Translated by Norman Denny, London, Lane, 1952, and an adaptation from it by Alvin Sapinsley and Leo Kerz, New York, French, 1958. Time: the present. Place: Clerambard Mansion.

In tragicomic intransigence a Don Quixote of faith runs full tilt against life's established ways, that is, egotism and carelessness. The Count of Clerambard has set each member of his aristocratic family to work on knitting machines, so that they should earn by piecework the money needed to pay off the mortgages. His son Octave would much prefer to marry the rich and ugly daughter of the lawyer. The count himself provides for the table by busily shooting unpedigreed but well-nourished dogs and cats. One day St. Francis of Assisi appears to him and transforms him into a zealous practicing Christian. To the horror of the ladies, every spider has henceforth to be welcomed as a brother and fellow-creature of God. And as for Octave, he is to marry the village hussy after whom he has lusted, and thereby set an example of humility and charity. A psychiatrist is called in to deal with this shocking case of disturbance to society, whereupon the saint converts the rest of the family as well. Together they will now roam the country in a trailer and preach the Gospel.
This is a play with paradoxes in the borderland between fairy tale and frivolous farce, and it exploits the comic situation without much concern for the serious theme.

MOONBIRDS *(Les Oiseaux de lune)*. Comedy in four acts. Prose. Written 1955. First edition Paris 1956. First performance December 15, 1955, Paris, Théâtre de l'Atelier. Adapted by John Pauker for New York production, October 9, 1959, Cort Theatre (typescript New York 1959, Hart Stenographic Bureau). Time: the present. Place: a boarding school near Paris.

Alexandre Chabert is headmaster of a boarding school for hopelessly obtuse pupils. The assistant master Valentin, who has married Chabert's daughter Elisa out of "pure absent-mindedness," is lost in his daydreams; he tries to make up for the missed opportunities of his childhood in his love for Sylvie, one of the pupils, and discovers that he has the power to transform humans into birds. Soon he foists feathers upon everybody who gets in the way of his love: the lecherous Professor Bobignot, his own exasperating mother-in-law, and all potential rivals among the students. School supervisors and inspectors trying to investigate the mysterious disappearance of these people are also banished to the cloud cuckooland. The world gradually becomes an aviary full of Valentin's shrieking, chirping, whistling, and cheeping victims. But with the new moon Valentin's magic powers wane. He can at best only manage hybrids, and eventually everybody regains human shape. Valentin loses Sylvie to the student Martinon; all she wanted to achieve with her flirtation was to get by more easily in the examinations.

Was all this boisterous clowning really meaningless? Certainly not. This is a farce with ingredients of slapstick, the Theater of the Absurd, and the fairy tale, and there is more to it than meets the eye. The yearning for a bird's free existence, for the bliss of dwelling in the sky, which has inspired literature since Aristophanes, will live on in rowdy students, stuffed-shirt schoolmasters, and silly provincial ladies. The moonbirds' spell of metamorphosis will not be lost; it will live on in human longing.

LES QUATRE VÉRITÉS *[The Four Truths]*. Play in four acts. Prose. First edition Paris 1954. First performance January 23, 1954, Paris, Théâtre de l'Atelier. Time: the present. Place: Trévière's study and laboratory.

Aymé chooses a paradoxical action as a setting for his satirical attacks on philistine deception. Olivier, a chemist working in his father-in-law's laboratories, has proof that his wife Nicole did not go to Montauban, as she said, to visit an old aunt, but on a far less harmless visit to Cannes. His jealousy is met by protests of injured innocence. Olivier has just developed a truth serum and wants to make Nicole take it, but she agrees only on condition that he himself as well as her parents also take it. After the injection the whole family is gripped by a mania of confession, and the chance witnesses of the incident—some friends, a plumber, and the postman—hurriedly take flight. Papa Trévière, a henpecked husband with a passion for butterflies, turns out to be a crafty ladykiller, and his so respectable wife a vicious sadist. Olivier himself has married only for opportunist reasons and betrays his wife with the laboratory assistant. The one thing drowned by the general hubbub is Nicole's confession, for the sake of which the whole brainwashing has been organized. Olivier vainly tries later to establish the truth. He must resign himself to the fact that what makes women charming is that they are not always transparent. Absolute truth kills the illusions and secrets which alone make life tolerable: ". . . even the most limpid life hides many small lies. . . . There are detours in a man's soul which have meaning only for himself. . . . Lying is a normal activity of the mind, and as healthy as any other. The mere fact that it can be abused is no reason to condemn it."

## BAGNOLD, Enid
(England, born 1896)


THE CHALK GARDEN. Comedy in three acts. Prose. First edition New York 1956. First performance April 11, 1956, London, Theatre Royal. Time: the present. Place: Mrs. St. Maugham's living room.

The play is characteristic of the psychoanalytical approach of Anglo-Saxon playwrights and their therapeutic orientation. Extreme cases of human instability, criminals and psychopaths, are made to test each other.

The chalk garden, condemned to infertility by its lime and chalk rocks, becomes the symbol of the topsy-turvy environment. All her life, old Mrs. St. Maugham has tried to make the rocks flower, and for this reason has patiently put up with the tyrannical gardener-butler Pinkbell. She neglects her sixteen-year-old granddaughter Laurel, who tellingly characterizes herself as a case that can be found in Freud. The child hates her mother Olivia, who has married for the second time, and as a result she has become neurotic and a pyromaniac, who keeps inventing monstrous accusations, such as rape, and likes nothing better than to act out famous criminal cases with an appropriate cast. In this macabre game she finds a willing partner in the servant Maitland, who has served a prison sentence for refusing to do his military service. At this stage Miss Madrigal is engaged as a new governess for Laurel and soon her matter-of-fact humanity straightens out all these clinical cases. Laurel is reconciled with her mother and returns to an orderly family life; Madrigal remains as a comfort to the old lady and even manages to make the withered chalk garden flower. In the end it turns out that Madrigal, the redeeming angel, had years ago been convicted of the murder of her stepsister, but was finally acquitted for lack of conclusive evidence. Only an outcast can succeed in giving new content to the unsettled relationships of human society.


## BALDWIN, James
(United States, born 1924)


BLUES FOR MISTER CHARLIE. Play in three acts. Prose. First edition New York 1964. First performance April 23, 1964, New York, ANTA Theatre. Time: the present. Place: Plaguetown, U.S.A.

The play is based on an actual event: the murder of a Negro youth in Mississippi, in 1955, and the acquittal of his murderer. But Baldwin makes it more than a mere factual record by the stylized multiple set of his Plague-

town, and by the voices of the people personified as Whitetown and Black-
town. Charlie of the title is the nickname for all white people. Motives are
given almost mythical significance: for instance, the whites being fascinated
to the point of obsession by the sexual potency of the blacks and the whites'
ability to affirm themselves only by the use of the revolver.

The various patterns of behavior are shown by means of contrasted types.
One of them is the young Negro Richard, a dope addict who returns from
New York to his home town. Provocative and rebellious, he insists on
equal rights. He humiliates the Negro-hater Lyle Britten, who shoots and
kills him because he has to recover his "dignity." Under pressure of public
opinion led by the newspaper editor Parnell James, Britten is brought to
trial. His wife gives false testimony, accuses the dead Richard, and Britten
is acquitted. Britten is a white man whose racial arrogance has no economic independence behind it, and who, as a result, sinks ever deeper into
his hatred. The blacks boycott his shop and thereby threaten his livelihood. The Negro clergyman Meridian Henry, Richard's father, wishes to
secure his people's rights by nonviolence, but finally and despairingly wonders whether his Christian humility does not ultimately leave the Negroes
more hopeless than ever, thus increasing the tyranny of the whites. The
Negro girl student Juanita, through whose love Richard had hoped to
make a new beginning, represents the younger generation, whose efforts
toward emancipation are beaten down by the whites. Baldwin sees white
society as a waxworks of self-righteous and bigoted puritanical types with
the white clergyman Phelps as their unctuous spokesman. Among them
Parnell James is a white outsider and the only person to speak up for the
blacks, but he nevertheless sticks by his friend Britten. Baldwin shows the
murderer not as a villain but as an average petit bourgeois who insists
all the more uncompromisingly on the alleged privileges of his race and
community, and is obviously a failure as an individual.

For Baldwin the problem is not to condemn a single individual, but to
make the criminal understand his crime, which over generations has been
condoned through prejudice and indifference and excused as a mere cava-
lier offense. Baldwin disrupts the sequence of time and space by means of
flashbacks, unusual perspectives which create a loosely connected series
of scenes.

# BAUM, Vicki
(Austria, born 1888)

GIGI *[Gigi]*. Comedy in six scenes. Prose. After the novel of the same title by Colette (1945). Written 1953. Acting edition Berlin, Bloch Erben, n.d. First performance February 24, 1954, Paris, Théâtre des Arts. Time: around 1900. Place: Paris.

The society theater tends to produce star parts, and Gigi has all the ingredients of a sure-fire hit—a package of humor, sentimentality, and frivolity wrapped up with a thoughtful moral. The heroine is the flapper Gigi, a lively, carefree, lighthearted girl growing up under the care of her grandmother Alvarez, her great-aunt Alicia, and her mother, Andrée. Madame Alvarez was once a famous beauty, the toast of the demimonde. Her daughter is a wretched singer in the chorus at the opera and vainly longs for the glitter of a similar demimonde career. For the three women, Gigi becomes an essential prop to their memories and longings. The girl is not to waste away in the insignificant respectability of a bourgeois existence, "perhaps become a milliner or a postman's wife." She is brought up for a life of luxury, of travel, balls, gambling, *chambres séparées,* champagne, and to be a precious jewel at the side of an elegant, wealthy gentleman who may—their imagination runs riot—be replaced at will. So Gigi is trained to be a brilliant coquette, indolently ornamental. But all the time the unruly, childishly naive, spontaneous, high-spirited nature of the girl keeps breaking out. Even if Gigi has no talent for being a great courtesan she at least has the family tradition for it, and she finally realizes that she is honor bound not to evade this duty. To the great relief of the women concerned with her education, the sugar king Lachalle, a man of the world with a touch of scandal to his name, is already enchanted by Gigi. The practiced charmer is to introduce Gigi to the smart world with a little affair. But Gigi has always known Lachalle merely as her faithful playmate Tonton, and she is outraged by his proposal. With all the impetuosity of her simple heart she reproaches him with his affairs. This outburst of her injured feelings is applauded and relished by the family as a "splendidly managed, exciting scene." Only Lachalle is hurt; he proceeds to make an old-fashioned, honorable proposal which leads Gigi to a happy marriage.

## BECHER, Johannes R. (Robert)
(Germany, 1891–1958)

WINTERSCHLACHT *[Winter Battle]* (also: *Schlacht um Moskau [Battle for Moscow])*. A German tragedy in five acts and a prologue. Prose and blank verse. Written end of 1941, altered versions 1953 and 1956. First printed in *Internationale Literatur,* No. 3–6, Moscow, 1942. First edition Berlin 1953. First performance November 9, 1952, Prague, Army Theater. Time: October 1941 to January 1, 1942. Place: the eastern front and a town in Germany.

Proclaiming his ideal of world communism in *Winterschlacht,* Becher takes into account the altered circumstances of the popular propaganda drama, but does not alter its means, which range from the glorification of freedom and posterlike, black-and-white set designs to patriotic quotations from Hölderlin and Arndt. Whereas Brecht delivers his message by proceeding from one argument to the next and seeking to sharpen the critical insight of his public, Becher aims at the spectator's spontaneous emotions, at passionate identification with his view of the world. Ecstatic language alternates with descriptive realism, lyrical passages recur as keynotes, and the monologues are given emphasis with blank verse.

Corporal Johannes Hörder and his friend Sergeant Major Gerhard Nohl reach the top of a hill. Hopefully, they set up a signpost: "To Moscow—100 kilometers." Hörder is honored as an "unknown soldier," receives the Iron Cross, and has to look on helplessly while he is made an instrument of propaganda. Nohl sees through the Nazi party functionaries' thirst for power and their practice of denunciation, the weaknesses of the officers, no less than through the egotism of the aristocrats of Tsarist days who return from exile behind German tanks. He deserts and with leaflets urges his former comrades to make peace. Despite some doubts, Hörder is still full of patriotic idealism. During his Christmas leave he breaks with his father, who, as an associate judge in a "People's Court," causes Nohl's family to be executed, and, while at the front, had shot his own son, Johannes' older brother, from behind, for his socialist opinions. Now, after a dramatic discussion, the father is killed under the Christmas tree by his own wife. Johannes refuses to liquidate Russian partisans and is executed by party fanatics. The one character who survives snowstorms and hunger alike is the sly cook Oberkofler, a sort of Good Soldier Schweik, who, subservient but scornful, serves the general staff officers and at the same time opens the soldiers' eyes to the reality of war behind all the pompous words. The final moral is spoken by the commander of the Red Army: "Take note that for our foes no road leads to Moscow! But our hearts stand open to our friends."

## BECHER, Ulrich
(Germany, born 1910)

FEUERWASSER *[Firewater]*. A German-American tragedy in three acts and an epilogue. Prose. First edition in *Spiele der Zeit,* 1957. First performance November 29, 1952, Göttingen, Deutsches Theater. Time: 1946. Place: Yorkville, the German quarter in New York.

This is sociological documentary and clinical study rather than tragedy. Charlie Brown's bar is the gathering place for a motley crew of postwar failures. There is a popular alcoholic preacher, a pickpocket, a bum who comes from a good family, and similar jetsam. The young schoolteacher Nelly dreams timidly of a better future. Charlie, who knows that he will die shortly of lung cancer, sacrifices himself for her. He lets himself be stabbed to death by a gangster, and his savings give a chance of happiness to the girl whom he has secretly loved. The pulp fiction story is given some depth by the hopelessness of a generation that, brought up for war, cannot make terms with peace.

## BECKETT, Samuel
(Ireland, born 1906)

ENDGAME *(Fin de partie)*. One-act play. Prose. First edition Paris 1957. First performance April 3, 1957, London, Royal Court Theatre. Translated by the author, London, Faber, 1958 and New York, Grove Press, 1958. Time: not specified. Place: bare interior.

Until Beckett the end of a tragedy coincided with the catastrophe, which gave the drama its justification and meaning. Beckett turns this consequence of the game's end into the sequence of the end game. People are reduced to objectified ciphers and participate in events without any will of their own—aimless, unrelated, outside history. Devoid of intentions and perspective, they are, after the final loss of all potentialities and freedom, identified with nothing but themselves and their momentary reactions. Beckett's first play expresses the paralysis of awaiting an arrival; *Endgame* has to do with a repeatedly delayed departure, that of Clov. The characters are throughout hemmed in by uncertainty, menaced by latent failure, for it is never clear whether their task is to wait inactively or to break out of this hypnotically paralyzing state by some decision.
Four people exhaust their strength in a struggle against the burden of self-consciousness. They invent meaningless actions in order to give them-

selves the illusion of having a purpose. They cling to props in order to feel assured of some causal connection. Feverishly they think up stories and tell them to each other with tantalizing monotony, feigning sympathy and companionship. But the actions spend themselves, the props drop from their hands, the stories dry up. The individual has lost the capacity for experiencing the world as a whole and breaks up into partial functions. Hamm is blind and unable to move. His world is the wheelchair. His son Clov cannot sit. Hamm's parents, Negg and Nell, have lost both their legs in a tandem accident and are wasting away in two refuse bins. These maimed human beings seem to be the only survivors on an earth withered and burnt out by some catastrophe. The parents die, the son Clov wanders off aimlessly. Hamm is left alone in a world deprived of meaning. Once again the blind man goes through the everyday motions of a day that no longer exists: taking off his cap and putting it on, wiping his glasses. Disgruntled, he throws away the props. As at the beginning of the play, he finally dozes, his face covered with a handkerchief—extinguished, congealed into a chance object.


HAPPY DAYS. Play in two acts. Prose. First edition New York 1961. First performance September 17, 1961, New York, Cherry Lane Theatre. Time: not specified. Place: the desert.

*Happy Days* is a play of senseless but ceaseless euphoria. The transports of bliss and hope, however, are not felt as affirmative, but as an expression of mechanical, almost vegetative, automatic activity devoid of conviction. Beneath the burning sun, Winnie is embedded waist deep in a mound of sand and is unable to move. Behind her back and out of her reach, her husband Willie crawls about near his hole in the sand. With endlessly renewed fascination Winnie goes through the motions of everyday life: morning prayer and a song, brushes her teeth, uses makeup. Reason enough to be happy, for "No better, no worse, no change." Invisible, Willie reads out disconnected headlines from his newspaper, which, by association, encourage Winnie's persistent monologues. Self-centered, these two people have long become everyday objects to each other. An ant crawling in the dust creates for one brief moment the shared experience of a sudden laugh. But immediately they are afflicted by doubt; did each of them perhaps laugh at something different, irrevocably locked in his own world and his own sensations? Eventually Winnie has sunk up to her neck into the sand, but undeterred she praises the many "mercies . . . of the happy days." In morning coat and top hat, her husband wears himself out in a futile attempt to reach her. The couple are hopelessly at the mercy of the piercing ring of a bell that marks the progression of the "happy days." All means of expression are now completely dismantled and the loose parts are employed for purposes other than originally intended: language turns into babbling noise, gestures congeal in automatism, the face is blurred in disintegrating grimaces. Everything is done blindly, without any impulse from the soul. What happens, happens of its own accord. Problems are skeletonized and deformed even as they are taken up: the indecision in the idle byplay with the little parasol, or the painful discord between concept and reality that gapes in absurdities: "I speak of temperate times and torrid times, they are empty words. . . . I take up this little glass, I shatter it on a stone—I throw it away—it will be in the bag again tomorrow, without a scratch, to help me through the day. No, one can do nothing." Scraps from lyric poems, "wonderful . . . unforgettable" lines, useless and mendacious beauty interrupted by helpless hemming and hawing to bridge sudden gaps in memory, stand out like exotic ornaments in the trite small talk.

We are shown in voluptuous detail how the humdrum trifles—from teeth-brushing to the vacant humming of some musical hit—are much more enduring and more truthful than all emotions and idealism.

KRAPP'S LAST TAPE. One-act play. Prose. First edition London 1959. First performance October 28, 1958, London, Royal Court Theatre. Set to music in an opera by Marcel Mihalovici, 1961. Time: a late evening in the future. Place: Krapp's den.

A paradoxical situation—the monologue of a lonely old man conversing in self-delusion with the lifeless equipment of a tape recorder—is sensitively exploited to convey elementary existential experiences: the awareness of transitoriness, the power of the past to shape the present. The free play of associations, which elsewhere in modern literature serves as a medium for self-expression, is here replaced by a technical device: The mechanical act of winding the tape backward and forward creates at will the vision of the past which determines Krapp's experience of the present.
Krapp, an unsuccessful writer, has recorded his life on a massive archive of tapes. He plays back the recording he made on his thirty-ninth birthday. On that day, too, he had listened to a recorded tape—the birthday impressions of himself at twenty. Reminiscences, lost opportunities, experiences and disappointments, the whole shadowy reality comes through only in cynical retrospect, rendered by the sound montage of two interlocking periods of life. All that remains of Krapp's life now is surly comment on the past, and finally he falls silent: "Nothing to say, not a squeak. What's a year now? The sour cud and the iron stool . . . Crawled out once or twice, before the summer was cold. Sat shivering in the park, drowned in dreams

and burning to be gone. Not a soul. Last fancies. Keep 'em under!" Empty
and silent the "last tape" runs on.


PLAY. One-act play. Prose. First published in *Evergreen Review,* Vol. 8,
No. 34, December 1964. First edition London 1964. First performance
in German, June 14, 1963, Ulm (Germany), Stadttheater. Time and place:
not specified.

The three voices in this fuguelike composition represent three contrasting
existential experiences which strike sparks from each other and are petrified in the cyphers $W_1$, $W_2$, and M. A man, his wife, and his mistress were
chained to each other for a lifetime by jealousy, hatred, and helpless entanglement. Each of them eventually committed suicide, in order to find
a way out of the agonizing and endless sequence of disputes, reconcilia-
tions, escapes, renewed reunions, and renewed explosions of hate. Now they
are confined up to their heads in tall gray urns. "Faces so lost to age and
aspect as to seem almost part of urns. . . . Their speech is provoked by a
spotlight projected on faces alone. . . . Faces impassive throughout. Voices
toneless . . ." They are not aware of each other. Each of them believes the
other two to be still alive and happily united. Their halting and mono-
syllabic words merge in a litany of frustration. The rhythm of these scurrying, disconnected words alternates with prose passages in which the past
is conjured up. Three modes of experiencing the same events intermesh
flexibly and on different levels of meaning: "Is it that I do not tell the
truth, is that it, that some day somehow I may tell the truth at last and
then no more light at last, for the truth?" Eventually the whole play is repeated, word for word. Here again the hopeless awareness of being cast
out, of being irredeemably alone, is the only thing people can grasp: "Are
you listening to me? Is anyone listening to me? Is anyone looking at me?
Is anyone bothering about me at all? . . . And that all is falling, all fallen,
from the beginning, on empty air. Nothing being asked at all. No one
asking me for anything at all."


WAITING FOR GODOT *(En Attendant Godot).* Tragicomedy in two acts.
Prose. Written 1952. First edition Paris 1952. First performance March 7,
1953, Paris, Théâtre de Babylone. Translated by the author, New York,
Grove Press, 1954. Time: not specified. Place: a country road.

Vladimir and Estragon, two tramps, are out on a gloomy, desolate plateau.
They are waiting for "Godot"; but no one knows whether he exists or not,
and if he does, where. At the end of each of the two acts a small boy holds

out the promise that Mr. Godot will certainly come tomorrow. The end always rolls back to the beginning, in a circular course of absolute standstill. Camus' Sisyphus myth is here condensed into a stage nightmare. This hopeless world sustained by ceaseless self-delusion is abruptly disturbed by the appearance of Pozzo, the symbol of brutal force at its worst, leading his victim Lucky on a rope, a picture of utter human degradation. On Pozzo's command this wreck of a man is made to "think," and proceeds to utter a stream of incoherent conceptualizations, the refuse of language, the crumbled sweepings of the symbols of our cultural tradition, a spectral chaos of nonsense and aberrational associations, the last particles left over from the demolition of the spiritual world. The tramps do not join this pair who have found Godot within themselves in tormenting reciprocity. Vladimir and Estragon go on waiting, and they retain the innocence of inactivity by projecting responsibility and justification both for themselves and the world onto the intangible, that is, onto Godot.

The title of the play sums up a host of antecedents and possibilities: action and solution, sense and senselessness, aim and unattainability. The play allows scope for the most contradictory interpretations: Godot is meant to stand for God, or nothingness; for guilt, or redemption. There is no point in trying too hard to translate this parable into concrete terms; it should be taken literally for what it is: a dismal clowning, that is to say, an attempt at a timid laugh by which to give oneself courage in the face of the incomprehensible.

## BEHAN, Brendan
(Ireland, 1923–1964)

THE BIG HOUSE. One-act play. Originally written for radio. Prose. Written 1958. First published in *Evergreen Review,* Vol. 5, No. 20, September–October 1961. First performance 1960, Ireland. Time: 1923. Place: country manor in Ireland.

A period piece from the days of the Irish struggle for home rule after the First World War is presented in a sequence of symbolic vignettes. For centuries an old English family, the Baldcocks, have been living on their Tonesollock estate in Ireland. Their comfortable feudal arrangement is disrupted by the terror of the liberation movement when the Irish Republican Army blows up a barracks. The activities of the British police make the situation even more tense. In consternation, the Baldcocks emigrate to good old England, leaving behind their agent Chuckles to manage the estate. Chuckles is a rascal from the Dublin slums and, under the cloak of good Irish patriotism, plunders the estate with his pal Angel. The crops, cattle, furniture, even the lead roof are sold and the proceeds turned into hard liquor for thirsty Irish throats. More than that, his knavish trick appears as a deed of national heroism, for four hundred years ago Cromwell's soldiers had taken the land with an equal disregard for justice and had given it to the Baldcocks. Chuckles glories in his role of a belated avenger of the violated national honor as he squanders the wealth entrusted to him in ostentation and drink. When the Baldcocks' naive love of nature eventually draws them back to Ireland, the unfaithful steward cynically pretends not to know them, but leaves.

A documentary of restless times is turned into a pithy study of Irish vitality and joy of life.


THE HOSTAGE. Play in three acts. Prose. First edition London 1958. First performance October 14, 1958, London, Theatre Workshop. Time: the present. Place: a lodging house in Dublin.

With the help of songs, folklore, and realistic snapshots, the epic of the Irish struggle for independence is soberly portrayed from the point of view of the victims' everyday life and of the minor hangers-on. Grandiose words about a national mission are debased: they are used as a drug to help the unsuccessful middle class hide its own failure behind a heroic pose; they are buried under the persistent daily cares and worries; they pale before the miracle of true sentiment. So, too, self-tormenting cynicism and the social challenge evident in the description of the slums are turned into the timeless struggle against human failure and for achievement.

Pat, once a militant member of the illegal Irish Republican Army, has in his old age become the caretaker of a miserable rooming house whose boarders include male and female streetwalkers, a former police inspector, Mulleady, who has been dismissed for fraud, and "Monsewer," a strange fanatic and passionate bagpiper. Irish partisans take the young British soldier Leslie as a hostage and hide him in the house; he is to forfeit his life unless the British authorities revoke the planned execution of an Irish assassin. The arrival of a stranger creates a sensation in the usual round of boasts, brutality, drink, and vulgarity, and everyone is startled into taking an unequivocal position. The soldier himself is too innocent to grasp the fanatical reasons for the reprisal. A tender love blossoms between him and the country girl Teresa. The British attempt a raid to liberate the hostage, but in the course of it the boy is shot. This accident also seals the fate of the young Irishman who was to be saved by Leslie's abduction. Indifference takes over once more. Teresa alone will henceforth nurse in her heart a memory of her unfulfilled yearnings.

THE QUARE FELLOW. A comedy drama in three acts. Prose. Written 1955. First edition London 1956. First performance May 24, 1956, Stratford, Theatre Royal. Time: the present. Place: a prison in Ireland.

Behan's "prison ballad" moves along without any dramatic action, using only a sequence of snapshots to render the atmosphere of prison life. The main figure, the "quare fellow" who is due to be hanged at dawn, does not appear at all, but in the oppressive hours of the night preceding his execution he dominates the thoughts and feelings of the prisoners and warders alike. The man in the death cell is a reproach that weighs on all of them. The powerlessness of men who cannot help any more finds an outlet in trivialities, seeming indifference, hunger for sensation, and mindless fulfillment of duty. Bets are taken on the odds for a sudden reprieve; the convicts boast of their terms spent in allegedly famous prisons; incorrigible bums quarrel about cigarettes and a secret swig; the warders pursue their little plots for promotion, patronize the toughest among their wards, and do their best to be wholly functional, to remain inaccessible to all human stirrings: "We're in it for the three P's, boy, pay, promotion, and pension, that's all that should bother civil servants like us." A government official gives forth unctuous phrases and "Himself," the hangman, expertly calculates the necessary height of the drop for a clean break of the neck. The one ray of light that penetrates this gloom comes, as always, from the oppressed and humble of this world: the Gaelic song of a young Irishman whose love of his country has landed him in jail, and the unreasonable sympathy of a warder who drowns his own helplessness in drink.
Behan raises no protest against capital punishment, concealing his purpose behind the spell of these scenes. But this sober record of a life ending in legal murder is all the more disturbing: "Himself [the hangman] has no more to do with it than you or I or the people that pay us, and that's every man or woman that pays taxes or votes in elections. If they don't like it, they needn't have it."

## BEHRMAN, Samuel Nathaniel
(United States, born 1893)

JANE. Comedy in three acts. After a story by Somerset Maugham. Prose. First edition New York 1952. First performance February 1, 1952, New York, Coronet Theatre. Time: the present. Place: Mrs. Tower's house in London.

Jane Fowler, an elderly widow, a shockingly grumpy fanatic for truth, busy knitter, gossip, decides to marry the architect Gilbert Dalney, who is twenty years her junior. She transforms herself into a capricious drawing-room heroine, who with smiling diplomacy patches up the marriage of her sister-in-law Milly Tower, arranges the future for a young couple, and eventually finds a more appropriate husband for herself in an aged newspaper baron.

*Jane* is a masterly piece of society theater, entirely constructed with an eye to the star's virtuoso part. As straight entertainment it is not concerned with originality, but does successfully present the familiar with good taste and sophistication.

## BELLOW, Saul
(United States, born 1915)

THE WRECKERS. One-act play. Prose. First published in *New World Writing*, Vol. 6, New York 1954. Time: the present. Place: living room in a shabby apartment.

One of the salient literary manifestations of the American "beat generation." A city official wants to build a school on a site occupied by a house and has offered the couple living there a large sum if they will leave. But the husband insists on his rights until the last minute and with delirious vandalism eventually demolishes the scene of his fifteen years of marriage. The past with all its memories and circumspections is ruthlessly done away with. Neither the mother-in-law's outcry nor the city official's protests can keep the man from settling his accounts. Outraged, the wife looks for something that in their common life was valuable enough to be preserved. But when she, also, tries to find relief in destruction, feeling that "maybe the best way to preserve the marriage is to destroy the home," the man will have none of it. The mere fact that someone shares his anarchism at once puts it in doubt and turns it into a pose and a lie.

# BERNANOS, Georges
(France, 1888–1948)

THE FEARLESS HEART (also: *The Carmelites) (Dialogues des Carmélites)*. Play in five scenes. Prose. After the story "Die Letzte am Schafott" by Gertrud von Le Fort (1911). Written winter 1947–1948, originally as a film script. First published posthumously Paris 1949. First performance, in German under the title *Begnadete Angst,* June 14, 1951, Zurich, Schauspielhaus. Adapted, in French, for the stage by Marcelle Tassencourt and Alfred Béguin. Opera by Francis Poulenc, 1957. Translated by Michael Legat, London, John Lane, and Westminster, Md., Newman Press, 1952, and by Gerard Hopkins *(The Carmelites),* London, Collins, 1961. Time: April 1789 to July 1794. Place: town house in Paris and Carmelite convent at Compiègne.

Bernanos' drama of religious faith is concerned more with symbolism than with dramatic action. The historical fact behind it is the death by guillotine of sixteen Carmelite nuns on July 17, 1794. Fear of life and anxiety have driven the young aristocrat Blanche de la Force—"Born out of fear, into an age of fear"—into the convent. What she finds there while still a novice is not peace but the challenge of having to take a stand in the upheavals of the Revolution. Blanche is present when the aged prioress dies her difficult death. The convent is not a place of security but of lifelong, terrible trials. Mother Marie, in whose care young Blanche is placed, is a woman of unbending faith. She warns the young girl of the heavy cross of the vow, which is forbidden by the new atheistic popular government. Mounting fear drives Blanche back to her home in Paris. Her family has perished in the Revolution; she herself might save her life by posing as the misled victim of the clergy. But fearlessly she takes her stand as a member of the Carmelite order and follows her sisters to the guillotine. She takes the place of the absent Mother Marie, who has fanatically struggled all her life for the grace of martyrdom. The true martyr was not the Christian zealot, it was frail little Blanche, astray all her life on the dark byways of her fear.

### BETTI, Ugo
(Italy, 1892–1953)

CORRUPTION IN THE PALACE OF JUSTICE *(Corruzione al Palazzo di Giustizia)*. Play in three acts. Prose. Written 1944. First published in *Sipario,* Vol. 4, No. 35, March 1949. First performance January 7, 1949, Rome, Teatro delle Arti. Translated by Henry Reed in *The New Theatre of Europe,* Corrigan, R. W., ed., New York, Dell, 1962. Time: the present. the Palace of Justice in "a foreign city."

Betti, who was himself a judge, uses a case of abuse of justice to probe the problem of guilt and punishment, involvement and redemption. A career-hunter unscrupulously makes his way over innocent victims. He achieves what he set out to do, but suddenly grace proves stronger than success, which he forgoes in order to win back his inner freedom by a confession.

Judge Erzi has to clear up a case of corruption in the Palace of Justice, and conducts an investigation of senior officials. Confidential records and judicial opinions have been disclosed. In an effort to exculpate themselves, the officials direct suspicion on Vanan, the president of the Supreme Court, a defenseless old man. Judge Cust, the real culprit, manages by double-dealing to deprive Vanan of his office, honor, and reason and to drive his daughter Elena to suicide. He coldly provokes his rival Croz until the latter succumbs to a heart attack. Cust's way to the presidential office is open. But with the appointment in his hands, he confesses his guilt and sacrifices his ambition to justice.

CRIME ON GOAT ISLAND (also: *Island of Goats) (Delitto all'Isola delle Capre)*. Play in three acts. Prose. Written 1948. First published in *Teatro,* Vol. II, No. 2, November 1950. First performance October 20, 1950, Rome, Teatro delle Arti. Translated by Henry Reed, London, French, 1960 and San Francisco, Chandler, 1961. Time: the present. Place: a lonely house on a heath.

"Goat Island," a crumbling house parched by the sun and standing in a lonely southern landscape, shelters three women: Agatha, who has been abandoned by her husband, her daughter Silvia, and her sister-in-law Pia. Suddenly young Angelo turns up, brings news of Agatha's husband, and with unquestioning naturalness takes the latter's place. He removes the burdensome frustration of this loveless life and with a Pan-like innocence and unconcern seduces all three women: "If we are true to our nature

everything is easy. Then we feel as though we are sleepy and stop thinking . . . only then we know some calm. The calm of grass, of animals, of
stones." But there is no durable salvation in this escape into elementary
existence. Doubts and shame, jealousy and self-contempt create discord
among the women. When Angelo climbs down into the well, Agatha pulls
the rope ladder away and leaves her lover to die. The irrevocability of this
deed, she hopes, will give her peace.

Metaphysical symbolism is expressed through a realistic love tragedy. Eros
is temptation and destruction, but at the same time is the only possibility
of self-realization, a bait of destiny: "Our salvation lies in sin. Only damned
pride wants the opposite. . . . But that has nothing to do with the senses.
. . . It belongs to the realm of the soul, the restless, raging, self-destructive
soul that wants to break free of human nature."

THE FUGITIVE (La Fuggitiva). Play in three acts. Prose. Written 1952–
53. First edition in Teatro postumo, Bologna 1955. First performance
September 30, 1953, Venice, Teatro Da Fenice. Translated by G. H.
McWilliam, San Francisco, Chandler, 1964. Time: the present. Place:
Italy.

A criminal story provides the situation in which people are forced to pause
in the flight from self and to give an account to themselves. The courts,
which come into action in the case of murder, are the symbol of the world's
salvation: "There is peace when all questions are placed in the hands of
the judges. To hand oneself over to them means handing over not merely
a person, but above all a psychological plight. . . . To be convicted means
to be understood." Every detail in the action points symbolically beyond
itself.

The deputy official Daniele Manniscoli gets more and more deeply into
debt, and his wife Nina, in her turn, loses enormous sums at cards to his
superior, Giulio. This double indebtedness stands for undischarged obli-
gations to life, for being at the mercy of a superior creditor's demands
and powers. Daniele secretly absconds to a mountain village and tries to
escape across the frontier. Dr. Ferzi, a mephistophelian tempter, reinforces
him in this plan and offers his support: Is the individual to be held responsible for his physical and psychological makeup, which he has to accept without contradiction? Although Daniele's marriage with Nina has
long broken up, he is driven to call on her once more. She, in the meantime, has evaded Giulio's financial claims by surrendering to his advances
and then poisons him. Daniele helps her in her distress, disposes of the
corpse, and thereupon is himself accused of the murder by Nina. Both flee
to the frontier. Nina is shot by a policeman. In a dream scene the two fugi-

tives are confronted and called to account by all the counteracting forces in their lives. There is the commissioner—"the law"; a chance passer-by, "the world"; Giulio's mother, "conscience"; the murdered Giulio, "the victim"; Dr. Ferzi, "the tempter." The couple willingly accept their destiny and with their humility rout Ferzi.

The plot is of the penny-dreadful kind, but with the help of simultaneous scenes, dream images, film montage, and alienation-effect commentaries (a passer-by reads out the crime from a newspaper, and the scenes of the case are faded in), it is magnified into a symbol of world judgment.

THE QUEEN AND THE REBELS *(La Regina e gli insorti)*. Play in four acts. Prose. Written 1949. First published in *Sipario,* Vol. VI, No. 51, May 1951. First performance January 5, 1951, Rome, Teatro Eliseo. Translated by Henry Reed, Harmondsworth, Penguin, 1958 and Ulanov, Barry, ed., in *Makers of the Modern Theatre,* New York, McGraw Hill, 1961; London, French (acting edition), 1957; and in *Three European Plays*. Time: the present. Place: hall in an imaginary country.

Rebels in an imaginary country frantically try to find the widow of the deposed dictator, who, styling herself "Queen," leads the counterrevolution. The prostitute Argia discovers her in the disguise of a peasant girl. Argia and her lover Raimondo, who serves the rebels as an interpreter, thereupon plan to blackmail the Queen. When the Queen tells them that she is fleeing and trying to rejoin her child, Argia is moved and lets her go. Soon afterward the Queen is shot. In order to save the dead woman's child, the prostitute poses as the Queen and faces the firing squad—happy to have found for the first time in her life a worthwhile task: "I have acquired a son . . . and memories. If memory survives at all, the radiance of this night will always be with me."

Man is at the mercy of the political events which keep him going. He can liberate himself only by accepting sacrifice and suffering and thereby unlocking the meaning of life. The play is set in our time but aims at timelessness and the glorification of man's Christian rebirth.

## BILLETDOUX, François
(France, born 1927)

CHEZ TÖRPE *(Va donc chez Törpe)*. Comedy in four acts. Prose. First edition in *Théâtre,* Paris 1961. First performance September 26, 1961, Liège Festival. Translated by Mark Rudkin, in *Two Plays,* London, Secker & Warburg, 1963, and New York, Hill & Wang, 1964. Time: the present. Place: parlor in an old inn in central Europe.

Again and again, from Cocteau to Casona, the writers in Romance languages have equated the magic of death and femininity. Billetdoux shows us a handful of failures, their longing for salvation, and their terror of life. Their last consolation lies not in religion, ideologies, the narcotic of illusions, or any real drug but in Miss Ursula-Maria Törpe's inn, somewhere at the edge of the world. One human being again becomes another's refuge from life. Fading, awkward Miss Törpe gives them all courage by listening to them, helpless but full of good will; she calms them and gives them the courage to let go of themselves at last, the courage for suicide: "They're all . . . like shadows that have fetched up here, that lose themselves in the general, groundless despair which crowds around me. And I am like an ocean, all I can do is to accept their despair with good grace. I cannot dam up anything any more. I am like them." Inspector Töpfer is charged with investigating the background of this series of suicides. He interrogates people and doggedly looks for a culprit. The explanation must lie in Miss Törpe's destructive influence upon her guests: "Your guests . . . seem to be dependent upon you, as upon a mother, a mistress, a trade-union secretary or a father confessor." The inspector decides to try to win these would-be suicides back to life; his sense of order and his robust competence in life are outraged by this anarchy of the spirit. Since words prove unavailing, he assembles the guests, at the point of a tommy-gun, to explain his charitable purpose. But in proving Ursula to be a criminal, all he does is to cause another suicide, for Hans Meyer, who has hopelessly loved her for years, desperately takes all the responsibility upon himself and shoots himself. The inspector closes the inn. Ursula wants to break out of her predestined fate and entrusts herself and her fortune to the uncomplicated, resolute policeman. She dreams of her future life's work—they will build nursery schools, dwellings, factories. The realistic inspector meanwhile makes arrangements for the first night they are to spend together.

CHIN-CHIN (Tchin-tchin). Comedy in four acts. Prose. Written 1958. First edition in Théâtre, Paris 1961. First performance January 26, 1959, Paris, Théâtre de Poche Montparnasse. Translated by Mark Rudkin, in Two Plays, London, Secker & Warburg, 1963, and New York, Hill & Wang, 1964. Time: the present. Place: Paris.

Two people of conflicting temperament are brought together by a ridiculously tragic destiny and try with the inadequate means left in the rubble of their existence to build another meaningful whole but ultimately identify themselves with their own failure. The author explains: "The problem of the play is the furious certainty that there is no sense in a joint effort to find the center of one's own existence, that one partner—in this case Grimaldi—can give away everything and approach life naked and as though new-born, while the other, Pamela, stays the course, hypnotized by her ideas and emotions, the sterility of which she seems long to have known."

The meeting of the respectable, ultrasober Englishwoman Mrs. Pamela Puffy-Picq and the exuberantly temperamental Italian Cesareo Grimaldi is occasioned by the open deception of their French spouses, the physician Dr. Picq and pretty Marguerite, who have been dallying with true Parisian frovolity and without regard to diplomatic conventions. In anger and humiliation the two victims meet in a café and laboriously try to overcome their spontaneous antipathy and blatant differences of temperament. Pamela manifestly is stronger on virtue than on charm, habitually serves as president of charity clubs, is "solemn, well equipped with principles, judgments, rules and the banner of justice. . . . Absolute, immoderate, military!" Now she is all injured vanity. She despises Cesareo, the tipsy dreamer, whose quick, childish temper is followed at once by readiness to forgive. He feels the fault in his marriage may lie in his own deficiencies and wants to set Marguerite free to be sure she will be happy. While Pamela cuts herself off from life in hard self-assurance, he gives himself over wholeheartedly to the fleeting moment: "I am nothing but an endless quest for something or other." More and more frequently the ill-assorted couple turn up in cafés and small restaurants, drink heavily, and in shabby hotels vainly pursue the illusion of a love not meant for them. Both their lives have gone to pieces. In an endless alcoholic twilight they torment each other in hate and self-pity. Each turns the other into his own nightmare. The only thing they have in common is a punching-bag, a symbol of their spiritual state, on which they let off all their unsubdued tensions and frustrations. Only when both have sunk to the state of down-and-out tramps and Pamela steals her own son's wallet for the sake of the daily ration of drink, do the would-be lovers unite in gentle, carefree, happy-go-lucky vagabondage. Their spiritual and physical dissolution becomes their liberation.

COMMENT VA LE MONDE, MÔSSIEU? IL TOURNE, MÔSSIEU! *[How's the World, Môssieu? It's Turning, Môssieu]*. Comedy in four acts and some songs. Prose. First edition in *Théâtre II*, Paris 1964. First performance March 11, 1964, Paris, Théâtre de l'Ambigu. Music by Joseph Kosma. Time: winter 1944 to autumn 1945. Place: Germany, France, United States.

The leader myth is satirized in divergent settings. The relationship between Don Quixote and Sancho Panza is reversed; the unworldly dreamer and idealist has become the servant, the compliant tool, and the primitive egotist has taken the dominating part. In addition to this perversion of Cervantes' baroque scale of values, there is no longer any faith in an overriding order: "There is no freedom on earth as yet, and men's souls are tormented in the confusion of things." The duel between two contrasting temperaments also illustrates Brecht's thesis of the right which is always with the survivor.

The American prisoner of war Job and the Frenchman Hubert Schluz meet in a German concentration camp. Job, known as "Woopy the Boss," is the egotist driven by his elementary urge to live; he coolly weighs his chances and acts according to strict utilitarian principles. Life proves Job's tough inconsiderateness to be the only right method and confirms it by success. Hubert believes in humanity; he wallows in noble sentiments, and however often he is disillusioned and abused, he at once constructs a new utopia from the ruins of his hopes. He sacrifices himself in order to help others. But his ideals of self-sacrifice and his humanitarian romanticism are merely means of voluble self-assertion. As drawn by Billetdoux, this idealist is not a noble youth in the romantic Schiller manner but a sort of zestful Schweik—cunning and quick at repartee, the born underling who always follows his leader.

Job is hungry in the concentration camp and thinks nothing of satisfying his hunger with the meat of his dead fellow-sufferers. Hubert procures him some extra food and lets him into the secret of a common plan to escape. The American, in a stolen *Schutzstaffel* uniform, gives the signal for revolt only in order to shoot at the other inmates and by this double treason to make sure of his own escape. He takes Hubert along solely for his knowledge of German. After the war, the two meet again, Job now an American officer and Hubert an inmate of a camp of deportees. Again, the Frenchman is the subservient partner who helps Job—by this time tired of war—to desert. Hubert shelters him in his own family. Job's primitive nature soon revolts against the limitations of his underground existence. He takes possession of Hubert's wife and denounces Hubert to the French. Hubert leaves his home and country in order to follow Job to America. Constantly abused, tormented, and humiliated, the Frenchman at last reaches the land of his desires, the boundless open spaces of the pioneers. Job is killed in a family vendetta, and Hubert, cheated of his ideology, remains alone and helpless in the unknown.

All the action is concentrated in the dialogue between the two protagonists. The environment—the concentration camp, idyllic French middle-class family life, the coarseness of the lower class, and the world of the Texas cowboy—is indicated only by pantomime and sometimes by a clue in the dialogue. Songs are added as a counterpoint, to break up and generalize the action and to show the stereotyped attitudes and motivations of the victims who do not appear as persons in the play. The songs of the Russian soldiers and of the Negro military policeman lament the conflicts of all those condemned to kill. In song, the young SS soldier doggedly marches toward the promised final victory, in song the peasant woman grieves for the happiness that could have been hers but was prematurely destroyed by the war, and in song the rabbi covers up his powerlessness with a "litany to help people to die."

IL FAUT PASSER PAR LES NUAGES [*Passing through the Clouds*]. A middle-class epic in five movements. Prose. Written 1963. First edition in *Théâtre II,* Paris 1964. First performance October 22, 1964, Paris, Odéon Théâtre de France. Time: 1963. Place: a small town near Bordeaux (stylized contemporary setting).

The individual with a longing for the absolute, who violently defies convention in order to leap into something "entirely different," achieves nothing but a satirically caricatured family catastrophe. The author says ironically: "I have written here the poem of an alley cat which, at a time when the tomcats inconsiderately disported themselves right and left, pulled itself up into the middle classes. . . . Out of instinct, concerned both for her kittens and herself, the cat begins to scratch and bite, so that each kitten should go forth into the world and be exposed to its drafts and learn it is not so easy to get along as one might think. But perhaps it is also about something else altogether."

Claire Verduret-Balade, once despised and pushed around with her illegitimate son Jeannot, has acquired respectability and wealth by her marriage. To her dismay, her power grows. She dominates the family and the factory. Everyone around her takes refuge in her motherly protection; everybody looks for security by foregoing freedom. Jeannot has become a bank manager but is incapable of coping with his sexual life. Claire's second son, Pierre, is her puppet as manager of the family concern. Another son, Lucas, dreams of social reforms and gets into debt. Claire recognizes that her solicitude has turned the people in her care into spineless weaklings. Clos-Martin, the dead sweetheart of her youth, appears to her and

makes her realize that she is merely a function of her environment's
lethargy: "But to be a lady is no occupation for a genuine woman . . . I
haven't done what I should have done, either for myself or for anyone
else . . . I should like to be absent, that's precisely what I should like."
Gripped by a desire for self-effacement, Claire proceeds to pull down the
façade of her respectability. She sells the factory for next to nothing, also
the vineyard, the bank, and the country property. Having suddenly to fend
for themselves, all the members of the family fail. Jeannot loves his secretary Adeline, but marries her mother just to be under someone's tutelage
again. Pierre is driven by his anxiety into suicide. Claire and her little son
Pitou are left alone and penniless to face the outraged middle-class world.
But she does not give up her hope of "passing through the clouds" toward
the light.

The play is conceived as an orchestral work in five movements: Overture,
Andantino, Allegro Pathétique, Molto Vivace, and Aubade. In the author's
own words, the play is to be taken as "a concerto or, if preferred, as the
gradual beginning of an impromptu 'jam session.' I am, therefore, not
interested in changing the scene quickly nor in ubiquity but in the connections, in the unknown or so-far unanalyzed vibrations between two or
more human beings at any one time: while they are not together, are engaged in different occupations, and subject to different moods." It is in this
sense that the author uses monologues in polyphonic overlay, choreographic
sequences, pantomime, and clowning.


## BLAŽEK, Vratislav
(Czechoslovakia, born 1925)


PŘÍLIŠ ŠTĚDRY VEČER [And All That on Christmas Eve]. Comedy in two
parts. Prose. First published in Divadlo, XI, No. 7, Prague 1960. First
edition Prague 1960. First performance June 9, 1960, Prague, Comedy
Theatre. Time: the present. Place: Prague.

The conflict of the generations is shown, apparently in the private sphere
but in fact as a symptom of social grievances and misdirected political
education. Without foregoing the "positive hero" who follows the orthodox
line, the author courageously enters a plea for the idealist outside the party,
who fights against the injustice of the party organization. Individualism is
no longer a crime against the state but a stage in the development of
personality.

Antonin Novák is entirely dedicated to his work for the state and society.
He runs his nationalized establishment "exactly as well and correctly . . .

as a piece of work is turned on the lathe." Suddenly—and on Christmas Eve, at that—he is confronted with his own family troubles. His daughter Hanka wants to marry Thomas, by whom she is pregnant. Outraged by the injustice of the party apparatus, Thomas wants to have nothing to do with the state, adopts an "ironical attitude," and prefers working as a furniture mover to pretending socialist allegiance and thereby purchasing admission to the university. During the night Antonin reaches a decision concerning Thomas. He not only welcomes Thomas into the family but shows him the way to a more objective approach: it is possible to have faith in the world's capacity to improve.

The moralizing tale is leavened by formal devices: the actors address their comments directly to the audience and parody their own roles as "positive heroes."

## BÖLL, Heinrich
(Germany, born 1917)

EIN SCHLUCK ERDE [A Mouthful of Earth]. Play in three acts. Prose. First edition 1962. First performance December 22, 1961, Düsseldorf, Schauspielhaus. Time: imaginary future. Place: an artificial island.

The "end-game" of mankind, which has destroyed itself by its mania for progress and organization, becomes a didactic work about lost earth. Earth —"it was bread and blossom; it was tree and bed for the willing; it was the peace of the dead, and water swallowed it up"—stands for everything that was true to nature and life and has now abdicated and been replaced by standardized functional formulas. Whereas Beckett evokes a state of absolute atrophy, a motionless nightmare pressure, Böll starts up a many sided argument, sharp and lively as a ferret. Associations become illuminating symbols. A role which is nothing but a rigid thesis is contrasted with another which has recovered the innate originality of play.

A catastrophe has made the earth sink into the sea. On artificial islands the descendants of the few survivors establish a rigid, impersonal world of robots. Overalls of different colors indicate who belongs to what caste in this anthill state, and man, a function of varying value, is moved up and down on the line of caste, promoted and demoted. The lowest level is the colorless "Crestians," outlaws branded because of their recurring human feelings. Blue is the color of the innumerable laborers, whose hopes of rising in the hierarchy make them perpetually willing slaves. But the fact that with this attitude they are so universally employable excludes them from any chance of promotion. Green, red, and white are the further grades in the hierarchy of those who give and receive orders; these "specialists," are headed by a despotic, ambiguous being, the "expert" in gold. Divers are continuously and frantically at work raising from the sea objects belonging to the epoch of the "drinkerers." Billboards and a plaster apple provide the self-satisfied descendants with material for the most contradictory hypotheses about their ancestors. In the hustle and bustle of the castes can be seen ambition and servility, as well as the courage to contradict and the emergence of spontaneous human feeling. The two "uncoloreds" Hack and Dräs win the love of the girls Berlet and Simone, who selflessly accept loss of caste for the sake of love. Outlawed and menaced as they are, they form an islet of free humanity. They rediscover for themselves the pleasure of play and the blessing of fire, the joy of giving and the miracle of love. On the swaying floor of modern pontoons they have gained "a whole mouthful of earth"—the security of community. The sterile system of functions is punctured by the children which they have and the "hearth" which thus comes into the world. The language of the play, with its abstract substantives, its strange alienation, and its ironic style, is stiff and made to serve the author's aim of extreme nonrealism.

## BOLT, Robert
(England, born 1924)

FLOWERING CHERRY. Play in two acts. Prose. First edition London 1958. First performance November 4, 1957, Edinburgh, King's Theatre. Time: the present. Place: the Cherrys' kitchen and garden in a London suburb.

The destiny of a small soul on the border between humdrum reality and illusion is described. The trenchant dialectic with which Ibsen exposed self-deception is softened in poetic gentleness.

All his life the insurance-company employee Cherry has dreamed of giving notice with a flourish and of moving to the country to a flowering orchard. When he loses his job, he hides the failure from his family and takes to drink, stealing from his wife Isobel's household money. The woman realizes that even now he is not prepared to make reality of his dream of flowering cherries, but is content with the miserable pose of the misunderstood nature-lover. Isobel has loved in him the man he might have been; she leaves him just as he himself has abandoned his dream. Dying, Cherry sees his yearning fulfilled—a sea of flowering trees. The small disappointments of his children Judy and Tom in their love and in their professions are complementary colors in this world that founders weakly in self-pity and delusion.

A MAN FOR ALL SEASONS. Play in two acts. Prose. First edition London 1960. First performance July 1, 1960, London, Globe Theatre. Time: 1530–1535. Place: London.

Sir Thomas More, statesman and scholar, who was canonized in 1935, is interpreted not as the hero of a martyr's drama but as personifying the individual freedom that cannot be defeated even though it may be destroyed. He puts the decision of his own conscience above the law and the power of ruling authority, and for this goes to his death: "But since we . . . have to choose, to be human at all . . . why then perhaps we *must* stand fast a little—even at the risk of being heroes . . . finally . . . it isn't a matter of reason; finally it's a matter of love."
King Henry VIII wants to dissolve his childless marriage with Catherine of Aragon for reasons of state and personal inclination. Sir Thomas More, the lord chancellor, obstinately refuses to accept the legal sophistries by which this wrong is to be glossed over. He is banned and his family suffers need. More obliging politicians, such as Thomas Cromwell and Richard Rich, are promoted and set up as judges over the "innocent man." The king breaks with the pope, establishes the Church of England, and demands that the Oath of Supremacy be tendered by all upon his divorce. More refuses the oath and is convicted of high treason. His relatives do not understand him, but reproach him with cruelty and vain obstinacy; his friendship with the Duke of Norfolk is disrupted when More scornfully rejects his well-meant suggestion for a compromise; his opposition is exploited by the political maneuvers of the Spanish ambassador, Chapuys. The chronicle is commented on and explained by the "Common Man," who appears on the scene in various parts, including More's treacherous household steward, his jailer, the foreman of the jury, and eventually the headsman who executes More. It is he, the turncoat, who always promotes his own interests by serving whoever happens to be in power, who is the idealist's real counterpart. The "Common Man" acts as a kind of compère for the individual scenes, which dissolve into each other.


THE TIGER AND THE HORSE. Play in three acts. Prose. First edition London 1961. First performance August 24, 1960, London, Queen's Theatre. Time: the present. Place: Jack Dean's study in an English university town.

Man's loneliness in a thoroughly socialized, materially secure environment amid its institutions, and his fear of reality, from which he shies away in panic like a horse from a tiger, are demonstrated with reference to the acute problem of the nuclear bomb and a confusing multiplicity of other problems, not always with optimum returns.

The Deans' façade of bourgeois family happiness is decked out with special glitter when the head of the family, Jack Dean, the master of the college and future vice-chancellor of the university, celebrates his birthday. But when the student Louis presents a petition for the banning of nuclear weapons, the fragility of this cultivated worthiness becomes abruptly obvious. Gwendoline, whose marriage with Jack has gone cold with empty formality, and who wastes her motherly impulses on growing flowers, would subscribe with enthusiasm to the call for total disarmament except that she must remain silent for the sake of her husband's career. Her repressed self-reproach leads to mental breakdown. She destroys a painting by Holbein, a loan from the city. Thereupon Jack throws to the wind the tolerant detachment he has displayed all his life, gives up his career, and takes his stand by the side of his wife and her deed. As a result, his inhibited daughter Stella in her turn reaches a true companionship with Louis.

## BOND, Edward
(England, born 1935)

SAVED. Thirteen scenes. Prose. First edition London 1966. First performance November 3, 1965, London, Royal Court Theatre. Time: the present. Place: South London.

The situation and the setting have already been seen in Shelagh Delaney's *A Taste of Honey*. In it juveniles are abandoned to their own devices; the egotistic adults with their lack of understanding and the outsider who introduces some humanity hope for security in return. Bond carries the conflict further. The social disruption is vented on the baby that Pam, herself in many ways still a child, has brought into the world but refuses to care for. As a result of their early biological precosity, of the absence of authority, and the general lack of standards, all these juveniles are exposed to a situation that is mentally and spiritually too much for them.
Pam takes Len back home with her. The youngster, diffident and sensitive, is at first abashed by the girl's aggressiveness. But then he tries to make this chance encounter give significance to his whole life, dreams of a future together, but without protest loses Pam to Fred, the leader of a street gang. A cycle of degradation and self-torment sets in. Pam clings to Fred, who mistreats and humiliates her. Len feels that he is needed and selflessly takes care of the girl, who turns against him in outbursts of hysterical hatred. Pam cannot bear having to be grateful. There is a troublesome accident—she has a child. Len is the only one to take any trouble about the

baby, but he looks on silently while the gang, with an infantile destruction mania, stone the baby to death. Fred goes to jail. On his release he finally breaks with Pam. The parents are outsiders in this world—Mary, middle-aged, who tries to tempt Len with crude lust, and Harry, who hides his helplessness under brutality. Hysterical scenes and pointless violence bring Len to the point of leaving the house. Then Harry, who only a little while before had been attacking him, persuades him to stay. For the first time one of these people brings himself to admit a relationship and to accept it.


## BORCHERT, Wolfgang
(Germany, 1921–1947)


THE MAN OUTSIDE (Draussen vor der Tür). A play that no theatre will put on and no public will want to see. Prose. First edition Hamburg 1946. First performance November 21, 1947, Hamburg, Kammerspiele. Translated by David Porter, Norfolk, Conn., New Directions, and London, Hutchison, 1952. Time: 1945. Place: Hamburg.

This, the only directly personal drama on the unknown soldier of the Second World War, is the work of a man who died of a lung disease the day after the first performance. The work is a summing up, not only of a life but also of a style and of a particular experience. For these lemures who haunt a world that has collapsed into trouble there can be no reconstruction. And the expressionistic style that strives to make plain the inexpressible through visions of dread, scraps of dreams, and cosmic symbols is too earnestly concerned with its own ecstasy and its own emotions of compassion to learn, afterward, to laugh at itself in the irony of mere play.

Beckmann, a noncommissioned officer and one of the many "homecomers" for whom there is no longer a place at home, seeks death in the river Elbe. Death is a stout undertaker and war profiteer who looks on with "dear God," that frail old man "in whom no one believes any more," while the Elbe, that termagant, returns the would-be suicide to the bank. Beckmann, who again and again finds himself "the man outside," vainly tries to make a new start. To find with a girl the security he hopes for, he would have to swindle the "one-legged man" outside the door. The colonel, to whom he wants to hand back responsibility for an especially bloody suicide-squad raid, has long since comfortably settled down in his bourgeois world and considers the admonishing voice that of a madman. The manager of a variety show thinks that Beckmann's story is not spicy enough to ensure success. But against suicide there is always "the other . . . the inciter, the undercover man, the disturber . . . the optimist." Beckmann's parents, petty collaborators, have been driven to their death in the denazification wave. Their right to live has been transferred to a Frau Kramer and her aggressive commonness. Everything that Beckmann has known and experienced is turned into whirling associations of fear. And "men look past each other, speechless and brimful of sorrow," until a helpless silence covers everything.


## BOST, Pierre
See PUGET, Claude André


## BRANCATI, Vitaliano
(Italy, 1907–1954)


RAFFAELLE [Raphael]. Comedy in three acts and a prologue. Prose. First published in Botteghe Oscure, No. 2, 1948. First edition in Teatro, Milan 1957. First performance February 7, 1961, Padua, Teatro Verdi. Time: 1944–1945. Place: Italy.

One of the marginal yes-men who have to pay for the heroic pose of their superiors is described in tragicomical farce. In the days of Fascism Raphael, with a prudent eye on the main chance, joined the party and volunteered for the Home Guard—to scant effect, for no one paid any attention to the insignificant fellow from a small mountain village and his vociferous patriotism. Just when the Allies arrive, he is suddenly notified of his appointment as Fascist federal secretary for the province. This untimely honor brings him before a mock court-martial by the high-spirited victors who mete out a mock death sentence. His brother Giovanni, a loud-mouthed grouser and dogged opponent of the eternal yes-man Raphael, intervenes and saves Raphael, who at once launches into effusive thanks. He is incorrigible and cannot help taking this splendid opportunity to attract notice and make sure of his reward for a life of uncritical submission.

## BRANDSTAETTER, Roman
(Poland, born 1906)

LUDZIE Z MARTIREJ WINNICY *[The People of the Dead Vineyard]*. Play in four acts. Prose. First performance December 19, 1957, Warsaw, Teatr Polski. Time: 1813. Place: an Andalusian village during the Spanish War of Liberation.

The author takes up a historical vantage-point for the representation of the cardinal problem of his Polish homeland, the human conflicts in an occupied country. The young peasant woman Inez despises her husband Pedro Manarez, who in loyal submission puts up with the excesses of the French occupation. She is captivated by the heroic pose of Fernando Oviedo, who has become a passionate resistance fighter since the enemy devastated his vineyard. The French discover his secret store of weapons. While Fernando flees to the mountains, Pedro takes the blame upon himself in order to prevent the murder of hostages. Overwhelmed by her husband's quiet greatness, Inez betrays Fernando in order to save Pedro. But her self-conquest seems as futile as the suicide of the Polish officer Borowski, who capitulates to inhumanity. Napoleon's defeat at Leipzig sweeps away the alien rule in Spain and Pedro Manarez regains his freedom. Ferando wants to have Inez executed for treason, but is overcome by Pedro's matter-of-fact humanity. Pedro at once sets to work in order to make the dead vineyard thrive again and to help the man for whose sake he lost not only his wife, but very nearly his life as well.

MILCZENIE *[The Silence]*. Play in three acts. Prose. Written 1951–1954. First performance April 4, 1957, Warsaw, Teatr Wybrzeże. Time: 1951. Place: Warsaw, living room at Ponilowski's.

A contemporary period piece born of the misery of oppression disguises the elemental rebellion as a clinical study in order to pass the domestic censorship. Even the family, the closest human tie, crumbles under the pressure of the totalitarian regime. Suspicions and estrangement, fear and self-contempt make men into desperate loners, who fail to fight for a better future only because they identify with dictatorship as an expression of their hatred of themselves: "Can one love or hate the air? I breathe the air. When I am without air, I suffocate. That's why my bitterness does not kill my faith, nor my faith my bitterness."
In a world of regimented opinions, the writer Xavier Ponilowski has been driven to drink. He cannot come to terms with the fact that the communist

ideals, for which he fought in his youth, now in practice turn against people. He brought up his daughter Wanda in strict adherence to these ideals; now a teenager and fanatic champion of world revolution, she cannot understand his misgivings. These, she is sure, must be the fault of her stepmother Irene, who preserved her religious faith against all obstacles. Unexpectedly Xavier's friend Peter Niedzicki turns up and wants to hide with Xavier for a few days before fleeing abroad. Although Xavier is afraid, he cannot very well refuse, since he himself was saved years ago by Peter when the Communists were being persecuted. The Ponilowskis' neighbor, the public prosecutor Felix Witowicz, has cynically resigned himself to being the instrument of a murder machine and as such condemned to silence and violation of the law. He cannot forget the humiliations of his poverty-stricken youth and importunes Irene with his advances. She is for him the incarnation of all the luxury and beauty he has always had to deny himself. His obscure remarks about the visitor intensify the family's fear. Wanda eventually denounces the enemy of the people to the security police. She pretends to have done so at Xavier's insistence and is triumphant when Irene, who now despises her husband, leaves him. At this point the presecutor's better nature wins the upper hand and he tells the truth to the woman he loves. Irene is prepared to make a new beginning with her hopeless marriage. But in the meantime Xavier has poisoned himself. He has irrevocably chosen silence.


## BRANNER, Hans Christian
(Denmark, 1903–1966)


THE JUDGE *(Søskende)*. Play in three acts. Prose. First edition Copenhagen 1952. First performance December 13, 1951, Stockholm, Kungliga Dramatiska Teatern. Translated by A. Roughton in *Contemporary Danish Plays,* London, Thames & Hudson, 1955. Time: the present. Place: Judge Olden's study.

Like Ibsen, Banner studies the conflict between the generations and on self-deception. But while Ibsen always gives his plays a didactic conclusion of faith in the world's capacity to improve, Banner rests content with analysis. The dream of a better self remains a dream, mere playing with possibilities.
Two brothers and a sister meet again, after many years, at their father's deathbed. The pedantic careerist Arthur, the zestful and worldly Irene, and the cynical playboy Michael have always been divided by distrust and prejudice. For one moment they dream of a common life in rural isolation.

Then their ambitions and pursuit of pleasure drive them asunder once more. The psychologically differentiated conclusions meet the requirements of unity of time, space, and action.


# BRECHT, Bertolt
(Germany, 1898–1956)


THE CAUCASIAN CHALK CIRCLE *(Der kaukasische Kreidekreis)*. Play in five acts and a prologue. Prose and verse. Written 1943–1945. Music by P. Dessau. First published in *Sinn und Form,* first special issue on Bertholt Brecht, Berlin 1949. First edition in *Versuche 13,* Berlin 1954. First performance (in English) May 4, 1948 by students at Northfield, Minnesota, Norse Little Theatre, Carleton College; in German, Berlin 1954. Translated by Eric and Maja Bentley, Minnesota, University of Minnesota Press, and London, Oxford University Press, 1948; republished in *Two Plays,* New York, Grove Press, and London, Calder & Boyars, 1957. Time: after the end of the Second World War. Place: a Caucasian village .

Klabund, in his version of the old Chinese theme, makes the test of tearing the child in the chalk circle the glorification of motherhood. Brecht, with his dialectical doubts, turns the idea of the fable inside out. He distrusts the hackneyed emotional values just as much as the privileges of birth and the myth of the language of blood. The child is awarded not to the mother with her socially approved rights, but to the maid who in loving and daily devotion to duty has proved that the child should "belong to where it is, to those who are good for it." It seems unhelpful provocation and paradox that Brecht shows us no issue to the conflicts of this world. Kindness and justice, truth and reality cease to be identical. Only Azdak, the inspired rogue, can do good as an incompetent judge delivering a deliberately wrong judgment.

The servant girl Grusha saves the governor's child in her care from the upheavals of the revolution. She escapes with the child to the mountains and for its sake endures poverty and persecution by the army. In order to give the child a home, she renounces her love for the soldier Simon and enters into a loveless marriage. The governor's wife claims the child, which ensures her of a rich inheritance. The heartbroken Grusha in her turn pretends to be the child's mother. Judge Azdak is a former village clerk and no legal expert, though rich in practical wisdom. He has Solomon's test of motherhood performed in the chalk circle. Imperiously the governor's wife pulls the child to herself, while Grusha lets go of it in pity: "I've raised it. Shall I now tear it in two? I can't do it." She is allowed to keep the child and to contract a second marriage, with Simon.

In order to point the lesson, Brecht places the play within a framework. The goatherders of a Caucasian village turn a fertile valley over to the orchard *kolchoze* which, to the community's benefit, is to get better returns from the land: "The children to the motherly women, so that they should prosper . . . and the valley to the irrigators, so that it should bear fruit." To mark their gratitude and obligation, the fruitgrowers act the didactic play, whose epic structure is underscored by the commentary of the folk singer Arkadi as well as by songs and dances.

HERR PUNTILA AND HIS SERVANT MATTI (also: *Mr. Puntila and His Man Matti,* and *Puntila*) *(Herr Puntila und sein Knecht Matti).* A folk play in twelve scenes. Prose and verse. Written 1940–1941 after Finnish folk tales and a draft of a play by H. Wuolijoki. Adapted for opera, libretto by Palitzsch and Wekwerth. Opera by Paul Dessau, 1966. First edition in *Versuche 10,* Berlin 1950. First performance June 5, 1948, Zurich, Schauspielhaus. Translated by Gerhard Nellhaus, New York, Columbia University, 1959. Time: the present. Place: southern Finland.

Brecht's doubts of method and dialectical skepticism repeatedly bring him back to the ambivalence of all existence. In *The Caucasian Chalk Circle,* motherhood breaks down into two contradictory behavior patterns. The "good woman" of Szechwan must turn to self-negation for the sake of survival. Puntila, finally, is forced into a perilously grotesque double nature in which to live out the conflict between his own warm-heartedness and the social class to which he belongs and which has formed him. Brecht, for all that he presents capitalism as destructive of all human values, is at pains to avoid any black-and-white characterization in depicting the class struggle. *"Puntila* is anything but a play with a political message," he remarks in his notes. "The part of Puntila, therefore, must never for a moment nor in any of its particulars be divested of its natural charm; it will be no mean challenge for the actor's art to make the drunken scenes poetic and tender, with as much differentiation as possible, and the sober scenes as little grotesque and as little brutal as possible."

In a prologue, the milkmaid introduces the main character, Puntila the estate owner, that "sort of prehistoric animal *estatium possessor* . . . notoriously voracious and quite useless." When drunk, the landlord of Kurgela is affable and extravagant. Magnanimously he gets engaged in one drunken morning to the smuggler's daughter Emma, the telephone operator, the milkmaid, and the chemist's assistant, and he urges his own daughter Eva to set a humanitarian example by marrying the simple chauffeur Matti. But the proletarian wants a practical-minded, hard-working wife and refuses the young lady of the manor. Puntila's alcohol-induced euphoria soon wears off. When sober, he is selfish and brutal, a bully who turns his four fiancées away from the estate and forces Eva to marry the stupid diplomatic attaché Eino Silakka. Matti wants to help the girl rid herself of her unloved admirer and arranges a common sauna bath. But even this scandal has no effect on Puntila's social ambitions and on the diplomat dowry-hunter. Another bout of drinking transforms Puntila once more into an enthusiast. He suddenly thinks up a supreme pleasure. Matti has to break up all the valuable drawing-room furniture and pile it up on the billiard table to represent the Hatelma mountain. Sitting on top of his pile of broken furniture, Puntila launches into rapturous tirades. Matti leaves this waning upper-class household and joins the workers: "it is time that your servants turn their backs on you. They'll soon find a good master once they are their own masters."

DER PROZESS DER JEANNE D'ARC ZU ROUEN 1431 *[The Trial of Jeanne d'Arc at Rouen in 1431].* Adapted for the stage (in collaboration with B. Besson) from the radio play by A. Seghers. Sixteen scenes. Prose and verse. First edition in *Stücke XII,* Berlin 1959. First performance November 23, 1952, Berlin, Theater am Schiffbauerdamm. Time: 1430–1946. Place: a village in Touraine and Rouen.

The theme is not the spiritual life of the martyr, but Jeanne d'Arc's political and social function in the people's struggle for freedom. Brief episodes in court alternate with popular scenes, with the revolutionary murmur from below.

In obeying her voices Jeanne is not God's instrument, but acts on the basis of her understanding of historical necessity. Everything supernatural in the character of Jeanne is rationalized in the dialectical distinctions with which she defends herself before the tribunal. Every touch of the other-worldly is secularized into the practical wisdom of the daughter of the people, as when Jeanne justifies her attempted flight by saying: "But there's the proverb that God helps those who help themselves." Jeanne calls her inner voice "divine" because it proves to be useful and helpful: "It always guarded me well. It taught me to be good and to go regularly to church." In accordance with the Marxist interpretation of history Jeanne's supernatural ties are to be understood as merely a stage in historical development and conditioned by its terminology.

The ecclesiastical court under Bishop Cauchon embodies the forces of reaction that serve the English occupying army. Jeanne is dangerous to the Church not because of her warlike deeds, but because of her reason and her courage in accepting new standards and questioning the universal authority of the Church: "Jeanne, we have shown you how serious it is and how dangerous to pry inquisitively into things which pass man's understanding and to believe new things, and even to devise new and unusual things, for the devil knows very well how to take advantage of curiosity." Jeanne is in despair because she feels abandoned by the people. She signs the recantation because she feels that any further resistance is meaningless. Martyrdom and a heroic death seem to her justified only if they bring about political results. On the market place and in the taverns her suffering becomes political gunpowder. People sing derisive songs about Cauchon and gather together against the English oppressor. From all this Jeanne plucks up courage once more to accept her destiny and to die at the stake. Her death is a beacon signal for the popular rising by which France is liberated.

Epigraphic superscriptions to the separate scenes, folk songs sung as commentary at the beginning and end, and the counterpoint of the popular scenes give the story the objective quality of a report.

THE RISE OF ARTURO UI (also: *The Resistible Rise of Arturo Ui,* and *Arturo Ui) (Der aufhaltsame Aufstieg des Arturo Ui).* Prologue, 17 scenes and an epilogue. Iambic verse and prose. Written March/April 1941 in collaboration with M. Steffin. Music by H.-D. Hosalla. First published in *Sinn und Form,* second special issue on Bertolt Brecht, Berlin 1957. First edition in *Stücke IX,* Berlin 1957. First performance November 10, 1958, Stuttgart, Staatstheater. Translated by H. R. Hayes, New York, 1957, and by George Tabori for New York production November 11, 1963, Lunt-Fontanne Theatre. Time: 1938–1939. Place: Chicago.

With a posterlike simplification of types Brecht retraces in the Chicago gangster world the Nazi assumption of power. In order to show the American public the genesis of the Third Reich, Brecht bases his plot on the story of a Chicago gang and their takeover of a cauliflower trust. In so doing Brecht has helped to influence and strengthen the communists' opposition to and distrust of capitalism and their equating of fascism with the capitalist economy. Brecht himself interprets *Ui* as a parable intended to destroy the dangerous respect for the great killers fostered by custom. "The circle is drawn deliberately narrow to take in only the state, industrialists, aristocrats, and the lower middle class. . . . The great political criminals must absolutely be exposed, and preferably to ridicule. Because they are not really great political criminals, but the perpetrators of great political crimes, which is something altogether different."

The gangster Arturo Ui (Hitler) and his pistol-carrying henchmen face bankruptcy. In its turn the cauliflower trust has its worries as a result of the economic crisis. The only thing that can set the finances right is a government loan for a fictitious port development. The aged party boss

Dogsborough (Hindenburg), the national idol and incorruptible upholder of the law, knows the scheme is a swindle and resists at first, until he is presented with the shipyard, which has been extorted from its owner Sheet (General Kurt von Schleicher). As a secret beneficiary, Dogsborough is now quite willing to misappropriate government funds and distribute them among his accomplices. But when an investigation committee gets wind of the matter and comes to interrogate him at his new country house, he stands before them helplessly. Ui's great chance has come: reluctantly and fearfully Dogsborough makes him his personal adviser and thus confers political respectability on the gangster. Ui's pals, the lame Givola (Goebbels), who conducts his murderous business in a flowershop and with the help of flowery oratory, and the stout killer Giri (Goering) clear up the situation. Obviously the only one who could have embezzled money is Sheet, the official owner of the shipyard. Unfortunately, he is killed before the judicial inquiry, also another man who is inconveniently in on the secret. In order to intimidate the population and to justify terror as a "protective measure," Ui organizes a conflagration; after the farce of a trial for the "grocer's warehouse fire" he has a drunken tramp convicted of the crime and executed.

"With menaces and pleas, with flattery and abuse, with gentle pressure and steely embrace," Ui gets the whole of Chicago into his power. All the traders pay him substantial protection money in order to be safe from the raiding parties of his lieutenant, Ernesto Roma (Röhm). Ui then wants also to take under his wing the neighboring small town of Cicero (Austria), where he has an opponent in the militant newspaperman Dullfeet (Dollfuss), who adheres to such old-fashioned ideas as freedom and humanity. As a moral alibi, Ui liquidates his loyal comrade Roma and concludes an alliance with Dullfeet. The newspaperman reacts with silence rather than with loud praise. He is removed, and Ui assumes power in Cicero as well.

In this drama Brecht uses the noise and brutality of the baroque horror play: "In order to give the events the significance which unfortunately attaches to them, the play must be staged in the grand style, preferably with obvious resemblances to the Elizabethan history plays, that is, with curtains and platforms." He also makes satirical use of quotations, such as Antonius's speech from Shakespeare's *Julius Caesar,* with which Ui practices public speaking. The appearance of Roma's ghost to foretell calamity is borrowed from *Macbeth,* and the negotiations with Dullfeet, a dialogue modeled on the garden scene in the first part of *Faust,* turns on the Gretchen complex and moral issues. Between scenes, historical parallels are flashed on a screen.

SCHWEIK IN THE SECOND WORLD WAR (also: *Schweik in World War II*) *(Schweyk in zweiten Weltkrieg)*. Eight scenes with a prologue, an epilogue, and two interludes. Prose and verse. Eight lyrics, music by Hanns Eisler. Written 1942–1944. First edition in *Stücke X*, Berlin 1957. First performance January 17, 1957, Warsaw, Polish Army Theatre. Translated by William Rowlinson, London, 1966, and by Max Knight and Joseph Fabry, New York, Random House (?1967). Time: Second World War. Place: Prague and outside Stalingrad.

The character of Schweik as presented by Brecht is representative of the author's own rule-of-thumb morality in which "right is only on the side of the survivor." As long ago as 1928 Brecht was working on a dramatization of Jaroslav Hašek's famous novel, and this play is a sequel to Hašek's political satire. Schweik, the cunning dolt, gets on well enough even under the regime of terror, by giving way, obsequiously making himself indispensable and for the rest, sabotaging what he can by mischievously imitating and thus exposing his superiors' devotion to regulations: "If you want to survive in wartime, just do exactly as the others and what is the usual thing to do, nothing ever out of the ordinary, just down with you until the time when you can bite."

The dog-seller Schweik, a regular customer at one of the Prague inns, manages with his deliberately stupid garrulous talk to play off the Gestapo agent Brettschneider and the *Schutzstaffeln* group-leader Bullinger against each other. The photographer Baloun, who is apt to lose all his sense in his eagerness to guzzle, is kept going by honest and respectable means thanks to Schweik's turning into goulash the pure-bred dog he has "organized" for Bullinger.

Schweik creates confusion as a forced laborer, and as a soldier at Stalingrad he marches with zeal. The "interludes in higher regions" are monstrous puppet shows showing Hitler and his staff involving the "little man" in their strategy. In the epilogue Hitler meets Schweik on the snow-covered Russian plain—a helpless puppet running away from the truth coming face to face with the "little man": "The times change, the grand design changes. The men of power must stop in the end. The stones roll on at the bottom of the river Moldaua. The great does not remain great, nor the small, small."

DIE TAGE DER COMMUNE *[The Days of the Commune]*. Play in 14 scenes, with three lyrics. Prose and verse. Written 1948–1949 in collaboration with Ruth Berlau. Music by Hanns Eisler. First edition in *Versuche 15*, Berlin 1957. The song "Keine oder Alle" appeared in *Svendborger Gedichte*, 1939. First performance November 17, 1956, Karl Marx-Stadt (Chemnitz), Städtische Bühnen. Time: January to May 1871. Place: Paris, Bordeaux, Frankfurt/Main.

In his revolutionary drama *Die Niederlage* [*The Defeat*], Nordahl Grieg depicts the collapse of the Paris popular rising of 1871 as due to disunity, abuse of power, thirst for revenge, and personal egotism. Brecht makes use of Grieg's material and some of his characters in the attempt to find in the pessimistic renunciation of revolution an honorable justification of popular sovereignty. The defeat is seen by Brecht as a moral victory because it is based on the Communards' rejection of terrorism: "in this struggle there are none but bloodstained or severed hands."

The Prussian army and Bismarck's political maneuvers have brought France to the brink of collapse. The French statesmen Favre and Thiers cede Alsace-Lorraine to the victor, agree to reparations, and hand over arms and fortifications for a commission. The workers rise against the surrender of Paris and seize the guns which were intended for delivery to the Germans. The National Guard disassociates itself from the government, which has fled to Bordeaux, and sets up the new system of communes. The central committee wishes to assume power legally and prepares for a general election. The revolutionaries renounce any seizure of the state treasure or attack on Versailles, the headquarters of the enemy. High politics are mirrored in the destinies of a handful of the Parisian petite bourgeoisie. The seamstress Cabet and her son Jean, a member of the "Papa" (the revolutionary National Guard), the free-thinking schoolmistress Geneviève, the former seminarian François Faure, and Philippe the baker are all full of enthusiasm for the utopia of freedom, despite the shortage of food and no pay. They are harassed by their unwonted responsibility as delegates and department heads. On the barricades they defend their freedom and finally lose their lives in the street fighting. From a safe distance the aristocrats and the magnates of industry enjoy the bloodbath and resume their privileged positions.

Verbatim records of committee meetings are read and alternate with realistic popular scenes and with songs, among them "Keiner oder alle" ("All or None").

THE VISIONS OF SIMONE MACHARD *(Die Gesichte der Simone Machard).* Four scenes. Prose and verse. Written 1941–1943 in collaboration with Lion Feuchtwanger. Music by Hanns Eisler. First published in *Sinn und Form,* Berlin 1956. First edition in *Stücke IV,* Berlin 1957. First performance March 8, 1957, Frankfurt/Main, Städtische Bühnen. Translated by Arnold Hinchuffe, London, 1961, and by Carl R. Mueller, New York, Grove Press, 1965. Time: June 1940. Place: yard of the inn "Au Relais" in the small French town of St. Martin.

This is Brecht's second variation on the Jeanne d'Arc theme. Here the Maid is not a political agitator, as in *St. Joan of the Stockyards,* but a trustful girl of childish innocence. In the midst of war and egotism she alone feels the seduction of goodness, and is foolish enough to be honest. Brecht sees a carefully calculated connection between profit and destruction: "In the vanguard are the military vehicles, the vehicles carrying the booty bring up the rear. Men are mowed down, but the corn is reaped. Therefore, wherever they go, the cities collapse, and wherever they leave, there is a bare desert."

Simone Machard, a young girl, still almost a child, has to perform in the inn the heavy work of her brother André, who has been reported missing at the front that is crumbling under the German tank attack. Her enthusiasm is fired by reading about the fearless Joan of Arc, and she rebels against her employer Soupeau, who refuses to serve any food to the soldiers but always has some delicacies for deserting high officers and extorts exorbitant prices from the refugees. The mayor gives up trying to do anything against so much unscrupulousness, which goes so far as to divert requisitioned trucks to profiteering deals in china and silver. Simone dreams of herself as St. Joan, her brother André appears to her as an angel with a stirring message, and the mayor is the weak Dauphin. The girl opens the hidden stores of food to the refugees and destroys the reserve of motor fuel which Soupeau has refused the army and is now about to cede obsequiously to the German occupation troops. Simone, threatened by collaborators, cursed by her parents, and disowned by the people whom she helped, is taken to a lunatic asylum for reeducation. The refugees, roused by her deed, set fire to their quarters which they are now supposed to hand over to the enemy.

The conflict is not with the external enemy, but in the French themselves— the opportunist adherents of Pétain, the collaborators with their patriotic slogans, and the eternally oppressed people who are always ready to be subservient and come to terms with the powers that be. The resistance drama is thereby turned into a pessimistic exposure transcending any political message. The dream interludes serve as a didactic explanation of reality.

## BREFFORT, Alexandre
(France, born 1901)

IRMA LA DOUCE *(Irma-la-Douce)*. Musical in two acts. Prose and lyrics. Music by Marguerite Monnot. First performance November 11, 1956 Paris, Théâtre Gramont. English book and lyrics by Julian More, David Heneker and Monty Norman. Time: the present. Place: Paris.

This musical owes its worldwide success not, like its Broadway prototypes, to social criticism and psychological characterization, but to sheer stage effects, excitement, choreographic dynamism, the parody of the romantic appeal of "Paris at Night" and the satirical portrayal of its apache world.
Night after night Irma la Douce comes out best in the prostitutes' amorous business at the Pont de Caulaincourt. She falls in love with Nestor, a penniless law student, chooses him as her new protector, and leaves the pimpboss Polyte-le-Mou. Nestor soon becomes jealous of Irma's paying admirers and adopts a double role: disguised as Monsieur Oscar, in frock coat and beard, he hands out a ten-thousand-franc note every day to Irma at their amorous encounters. In return, Irma gladly agrees to give up the rest of her clients. She faithfully hands over her gains to Nestor every day, who reinvests them as Oscar at night; during the day he scrubs floors to earn his living. When he returns from work, tired and disgruntled, he finds Irma gushing about her ever kind and elegant friend Oscar. Nestor is so depressed by this that he takes to brooding about the way of the world and decides in a rage to "get rid" of his rival; he throws his gentleman's clothes into the Seine, is convicted of Oscar's murder, and is deported to Cayenne. In the most roundabout way he escapes to Paris, is rehabilitated, and marries Irma. The couple's modest but henceforth respectable domestic bliss is crowned by the arrival of twins, who naturally have to be named Nestor and Oscar.

## BRIDIE, James (Osborne Henry Mavor)
(England, 1888–1951)

DAPHNE LAUREOLA. Play in four acts. Prose. First edition London 1949. First performance March 23, 1949, London, Wyndham's Theatre. Time: the present. Place: Soho restaurant and a summerhouse in a garden of suburban London.

In a nondescript Soho restaurant the Polish student Ernest notices an elderly, tipsy lady who rapturously recalls her somewhat disreputable past. Ernest is fascinated by the idea of "saving" this unknown creature. To the eyes of this generous visionary, she turns into Dante's Beatrice and into Daphne Laureola, who evaded Apollo's advances by changing into a laurel tree. He confesses his love to the stranger, and learns that this "glorious lady of his mind" is wasting away in the golden cage of marriage to a multimillionaire and procures herself the illusion of licentious freedom with the help of a string of escapades. When her husband dies, Lady Pitts shrinks from a happiness which rests not upon herself, but solely upon Ernest's extravagant dreams. She marries her manservant, whom she despises, and curtly dismisses the young enthusiast: "They make up something out of their heads and borrow our faces and our bodies to clothe it, like washing off a line."
This brilliant tour de force, a tender play modulating between the nostalgic and the grotesque, makes its effects with the help of mythology and dialogue, and through the "great scene" of the final reckoning and touching resignation.

## BROD, Max
(Germany, born 1884)

AMERIKA [America]. Comedy in two acts. Based on the unfinished novel by Franz Kafka. Acting edition Frankfurt/Main, Fischer, 1957. First performance February 28, 1957, Zürich, Schauspielhaus. Time: 1890. Place: America.

Guileless and vulnerable, Karl Rossmann, aged sixteen, expelled from school and home for a flirtation, arrives in America. His blind trustfulness is a challenge to the meanness and trickery of the people he comes in contact with. "The filth here is not really a tangible filth. But it is as though everything had been badly used and as though no cleanliness could

ever put it right again." On the passage across the Atlantic the boy, a
steerage passenger, takes up the cause of a dissatisfied stoker with the stubbornness of a fanatic for justice. His uncle Jacob, a self-made millionaire,
takes the newcomer at his market value and finds a place for him in a
profitable system that combines training and duty. Karl's timid attempt
at greater freedom ends in his being ruthlessly thrown out. Karl takes up
with a couple of hoodlums, who rook him while he is romantically convinced that he has realized his ideal of comradeship. Some charitable people
get him a job as an elevator operator, but in the end have to give him up
because his shady companions always manage to exploit his childlike simplicity. After a suicide attempt, Karl finds himself staring with amazement
at an advertisement which promises work "to everyone in his place." Karl
is overwhelmed with the feeling of being needed and appreciated, of getting security and a livelihood from the community, not as an exceptional
case but as one among many, without distinction or exception. Could this
be a dream, or perhaps already the other world? The hotel maid Therese,
for whom he has a tender regard, appears to him as an angel blowing a
trumpet and tells about the worldwide "Theater of Oklahoma" that includes all men in its summons and will make them happy. On this stage
of many lands everyone can play the part for which he is destined. The
management, kind and just, takes care of the welfare of all. Overjoyed Karl
trusts his future to this new opportunity. But the nature of this opportunity is not specified.

This dramatization can give only the broadest outline of an innocent simpleton's way of purification *per aspera ad astra*. Is redemption to be found
in the illusion of the theater, in the wish-fulfilling dreams of one who is
tired of life, or in the Christian promise of paradise? The question remains
open, a smiling enigma signifying either hope or resignation.


DAS SCHLOSS *[The Castle]*. Play in two acts. Based on Franz Kafka's
novel. Written 1953. First edition Frankfurt/Main 1964. First performance May 12, 1953, Berlin, Schloßpark-Theater. Time: not specified.
Place: village in the neighborhood of the castle.

Josef K., having lost his way, arrives cold and exhausted at a village and
asks for shelter. But the parish, ruled by an invisible hierarchy of officials
in the castle, rejects any stranger. "Unfortunately you are somebody after
all, you are a stranger, the sort of person who is superfluous and always in
the way, the sort of person who causes us no end of trouble." K. claims to
be the newly appointed surveyor, and this white lie acts as a challenge
to the incalculable bureaucratic system. To his astonishment his appointment is confirmed by the castle. He is given two assistants, Jeremiah and

Arthur, two grotesque and malicious trolls who spy on him. In vain K. tries to obtain from the anonymous authorities some job to do, some confirmation of his existence. The messenger Barnabas refers him to the chairman of the parish council and the latter makes him a school porter subordinate to the teacher. It is not only his desire for activity, but also his brief happiness with the barmaid Frieda, that embroil K. in the vicious circle of authorities. When he finally bursts in on the official Bürgel, the latter turns out not to be the appropriate authority. More and more sunk in lethargy, K. lives out the parable of the doorkeeper who bars his access to the sanctuary. K. spends his life in waiting, in doing nothing, locked out from his goal, and only when he dies learns that this particular entrance door was reserved for him alone and will now be closed forever. Unctuously, all those who had driven K. to his death pronounce an obituary at his grave. Breathlessly Barnabas announces that the authorities have taken a decision on the "K. case": "He has of course no right of domicile among us. That is indubitably clear from the files. However, in view of the fact that his application was so persistent and pressing, and was so completely in order, the right of domicile is herewith accorded to him *ex gratia* and officially conceded."

In *The Castle,* a disturbing parable of the collapse of the individual beneath the power of a ruling system that defies understanding, Kafka's quizzical humor, with its grotesque and macabre touches, plays on images of the human situation, of man exposed to increasing loneliness and menace.


## BROSZKIEWICZ, Jerzy
(Poland, born 1922)


GŁUPIEC I INNI *[The Fool and the Others]*. Tragifarce in two scenes. Prose. First performance September 25, 1960, Katowice, Teatr Wyspiański. Time: the present. Place: a room at Lullek's and the judge's office.

In sudden alarm Lullek interrupts the writing of his memoirs, runs away from his customary surroundings, and goes to a judge, from whom he demands severe punishment for all his sins of omission in a life hitherto free of care and responsibility. Has not Lullek bribed his friend, the tax inspector, by being too flattering and obliging? Did he not act as a procurer when he advised a girl who could not decide between two admirers to take the more lovable of the two? And when an overhasty conclusion of his drove someone to his death, was that not sheer murder? Lullek seems to find security solely in awareness of his guilt, by deceiving himself with hallucinatory self-accusations. The judge is angry and feels he is being attacked. But if he were to acquit Lullek, the fool would appeal to the supreme court. And so he is tried for the murder of a man who never lived, who acquired a mere theoretical existence as the result of an error in a document. In despair Lullek realizes that he is caught in the trap of circumstantial evidence. He is convicted, but jumps out of the window. The judge and Lullek's family break into a wild dance of joy at the inconvenient pursuer of the truth who has at last been got rid of. But with a shy snicker, the immortal Lullek appears among the audience and turns up the lights.

Clowning of the virtuosity of a Chaplin is displayed in the problems of guilt and responsibility, individual and community, human being and institution. Sins of omission and of thought, and all the doubts of society and its conventions are worked into a grotesque, disturbing image.

KONIEC KSIEGI VI [The End of Book VI]. Play in two acts. Prose. First performance February 29, 1964, Warsaw, Polskie Teatr. Time: around 1540. Place: Frauenburg.

The scientist whose knowledge leads him into conflict with the powers that be, into mortal danger and spiritual loneliness, is a key figure of modern drama from Brecht to Dürrenmatt. In most dramatizations, the decision has been between black-and-white alternatives, opportunist self-betrayal or martyrdom. Broszkiewicz—a voice from a close-to-liberal people's democracy—suggests a "policy of gradualness" by eliminating the rigid either/or solution and presenting instead the stubbornness of contradictory human nature.

Many years have passed since Nicholas Copernicus completed his great work *De revolutionibus orbium coelestium,* in which he proved that the earth revolves around the sun—in sharp contradiction to the Catholic dogma that the earth is the center of the universe: "We were wretched and mortal indeed, verminous and lepers and blind on the day of our birth and death—pity of pities! And yet bravely at the center of the heavens' vault. In such a place one can afford to be the most piteous of the piteous." Copernicus is afraid of the consequences of his discovery and tries to keep out of trouble. He retires to remote Frauenburg, on the frontier of civilization, attends to his duties and leaves his manuscripts unpublished. By small compromises he hurts those near him, but purchases from his bishop the fool's freedom of research. At the insistence of the Church, Copernicus sends away Anna Schilling, his mistress for many years, and refuses a poor sinner his promised support. Rheticus, a Wittenberg disciple of Copernicus' and a man alternating between ambition and indecision, eventually persuades the master to publish his great work and to reinstate himself by cheap concessions. This purpose is to be achieved by an effusive dedication to the pope and a hint at the convenient new calendar system. Disinterested search for truth has capitulated to opportunism for the sake of survival and ultimate triumph.

The décor, representing a Gothic church, permits all the characters and settings to be seen simultaneously and simplifies the transitions among the various levels, with their intercrossing back and forth of comment. Everyone has an assigned place in this world stage, from the spiteful pamphleteer Gnaphaeus, who writes polemics in the pay of the clergy, to the fanatically pious Sister Beate and the malevolent informer Plotowski. It is "functional theater" and contributes to the action.

## BRUCKNER, Ferdinand
(Austria, 1891–1958)

HEROISCHE KOMÖDIE *[Heroic Comedy]*. Play in three acts. Prose. Written 1938–1939. First edition in *Historische Dramen,* Berlin, 1948. First performance September 12, 1946, Vienna, Volkstheater. Time: 1810–1815. Place: Paris, Coppet, Stockholm.

Bruckner gives an ironic and at the same time sympathetic picture of Madame de Staël, the eccentric and courageous idealist who always comes to grief on the political consequences of her acts: "A born victor knows that victory means nothing else than being the stronger, even if that involves the renunciation of what one has fought for. . . . You could have often been victorious. But you always preferred defeat in order to avoid renunciation."

Germaine de Staël returns to Paris, only to be exiled once more to her Swiss residence at Coppet by Napoleon's police minister, Fouché. Some of her malicious and brilliant bon mots about the emperor, published with mischievous relish by the *Moniteur,* spur the emperor to fury against her, the "plague of Paris." Germaine's friend of many years, Benjamin Constant, her companion-in-arms in political struggles, is weary of the senseless attacks on the unconquerable Corsican. He separates from Madame de Staël and marries a worthy housewife from Braunschweig. Marshal Bernadotte, who has been awarded the Swedish throne, has every sympathy for Germaine but refuses to follow her cry to arms against Napoleon and thus to endanger the peace of his new fatherland. In the romantic Lieutenant Rocca she finds an ally who accompanies her on a propaganda trip to Russia. Germaine fires the Tsar's resistance and lives to see Napoleon defeated on his Russian campaign. She dreams of a free republican

France, but instead witnesses the return to power of the Bourbons with their fawning partisans, and the restoration of their corrupt system. Germaine is on the point of giving up and retiring into blissful private life with Constant, who has returned to her. But then she becomes excited by the fate of Norway, which at the Congress of Vienna is to be traded to Sweden, and she issues a new call to freedom. She wants to realize freedom in the absolute, without compromise, and as a result her intention becomes a futile utopia.

DER TOD EINER PUPPE [A Doll's Death]. Tragedy in two acts. Verse. First edition in Zwei Tragödien, Cologne, 1956. First performance October 11, 1956, Bochum, Schauspielhaus. Time: the present. Place: hall in a country house.

The increasing perfectionism of modern life which levels out everything personal and makes it into a mechanical function is distilled into a parable of deliberate artificiality.
At a mannequin parade—the citadel of standardized exclusivity in the fashion cult—a young widow named Adrienne watches a display of wedding dresses. Brought up as a doll-like beauty without a soul, her immaculate appearance has never been spoiled by any show of feelings; as a child, she was beaten for crying. Her first husband, whose face was always hidden behind a cloud of cigar smoke, never touched Adrienne's mouth and hair in order not to damage their beautiful shape. And even her present fiancé Paul, a painter, tries to make art so perfect in her that it reverts to nature. Marthe, one of the mannequins, who falls in love with Paul, pretends to faint and her spontaneous emotions awaken his masculinity. He ravages his fiancée's refined façade and releases the first tears she has shed in her life. However, for Paul the attempt at self-realization was only a fleeting compulsion. Disillusioned, Adrienne takes her life and, dying, becomes the centerpiece of a show.
The play is an attempt to give intensity to contemporary problems in their present-day settings and to give them the validity of a parable by the use of the methods of antique tragedy—the chorus of four mannequins introduces pauses in the action and the verse and unrealistic scenes provide detachment.

**BUDJUHN, Horst**
See ROSE, Reginald

# BULATOVIĆ, Miodrag
(Yugoslavia, born 1930)

GODOT JG DOSAO *[Godot Has Come]*. Variations on a very old theme in three acts. Prose. First performance May 28, 1966, Düsseldorf, Schauspielhaus. Time: not specified. Place: a swamp.

Bulatović takes the characters of Beckett's *Waiting for Godot* and confronts them with Godot—for Beckett the symbol of unconscious longings, justification, menace, or destiny, but for Bulatović a very live and realistic figure, a man like any other. Beckett's multivalent existential symbols are made concrete. Beckett's imminent action, his spontaneous, eternally renewed game has become a parable with a counterplot, sudden changes, and an often all-too-obvious practical application. And thus we get a tragedy about an unknown Messiah and mankind not measuring up to the promise. Bulatović provides more specificity of environment, uses symbols by way of commentary, uses educational associations and historical allusions and even manages to produce a type of theater out of the spontaneous interplay of paradoxes, and to derive the model for his play from the interpretations that theoreticians have so far lavished on Beckett.

The two tramp-clowns Vladimir (Didi) and Estragon (Gogo)—the master Pozzo and his obedient companion Lucky, that barking and whining human wreck on a dog's leash—are in the middle of a swamp, in constant peril of sinking into the teeming multitude of frogs and reptiles. Only the hope of Godot, the great unknown, gives their existence meaning. For the two clowns, Godot is an uncertain promise; for the exploiter Pozzo with his Nordic pride of race, Godot is the butt of furious rejection and negation. Panic and lethargy, despair and hectic euphoria unite and divide the characters. Bulatović works out more sharply the difference in the temperaments of the two clowns. Didi is an intellectual, forever tormented by scruples, inhibited, lost in abstractions; Gogo is the partner who plays up to him, almost feminine in his pliancy, wholly yielding to spontaneous and primitive sensations of fear, gaiety, and comfort. Pozzo is a health fanatic and poses as a patron. Suddenly, announced by the boy, Godot turns up—an amiable, simple baker, a Chaplin-like figure dusty with flour, who proceeds not to the apotheosis that all are waiting for, but to the most obvious deeds of matter-of-fact humanity. He brings to the wretches love, bread, and freedom. With no false modesty he fulfills the expectations of the sex-starved postmistress and is ready to give the others his nourishing flour. But the swamp dwellers have lived too long on excrement; they refuse the unfamiliar food with disgust. Godot's freedom is suspected to be a particularly insidious form of tyranny. In a grotesque battle Godot liberates Lucky, who at once uses his liberty to oppress Pozzo in turn, and to give himself airs as "a poet with a predilection for symbols that no one understands." At an imaginary press conference, Lucky sets up his system of oppression, in which people are lulled by being glorified as heroes. Everyone turns on Godot, the inconvenient outsider, in an orgy of accusation; he is brought to mock trial. All defend the community against the national enemy and traitor. An imaginary execution ends Godot—his existence is passed over in silence, his good intentions are ignored. The postmistress betrays him and the memory of his love to a new lover, and even the boy gives him up, since Godot has come without message or privilege— a simple man, who lives, works, and naively enjoys his life. The boy cannot understand this stranger and wants to kill him. Godot continues on his way, disappointed but not discouraged. He preserves intact within him his conviction that his gentle mission will one day win through.

Bulatović displays his predilection for posterlike symbolism and thereby diminishes his theme. The clowns have a heart in common—the frequently wounded, humiliated, abused heart of mankind. Their hats are the seat of their mental faculties and at the same time a food store. Symbols enriched with sociological significance are conjured up: a train thunders past on bleeding tracks, carrying a load of hogs as first-class sleeping-car passengers. A military parade and a mass demonstration produce as crude and superficial an effect as the tree standing ready with the rope for a potential suicide. Sound effects, too, are used as commentary: the screaming brakes of the locomotive, detonations of explosives, the ecstatic shouting of a crowd at a football game, the screech of a jet plane, the creaking of a mattress. The one fixed element is the atmosphere of the circus, evidenced in the music, the clowning, the numbered placards announcing the scenes, and the direct addressing of the audience.


## BURROWS, Abe
(United States, born 1910)


CAN-CAN. Musical comedy. Prose and verse. First performance May 7, 1953, New York, Shubert Theatre. Time: 1893. Place: Paris.

The Paris demimonde at the turn of the century provides the subject and the main character of this play, which skillfully drives home its effects in a mixture of frivolous revue, Montmartre romanticism, and petty bourgeois satire.

La Mome Pistache, proprietress of a Paris nightclub, is in serious trouble The city fathers of Paris have forbidden the provocative can-can dance and thereby taken away from Paris nightlife the lucrative sensation dear to all tourists' hearts. Judge Aristide Forestier, who is at the same time a friend and ardent admirer of the leg-throwing arts, successfully lodges an appeal in the courts against this embarrassingly respectable ruling, and when the gentlemen of the bench come to carry out an agitated inspection on the spot, he has them all conquered by the grisettes. A play within the play offers splendid opportunities for spectacular effects and breath-taking dances—not only the can-can of the title but also an apache ballet and a skit on striptease. A comic subplot, involving the soubrette Claudine and her rival admirers, the Bulgarian sculptor Boris and the art critic Hilaire, contributes the satirical undertone.


## BUZZATI, Dino
(Italy, born 1906)


UN CASO CLINICO *[A Clinical Case]*. Comedy in two parts. After the author's short story of the same title. First edition Milan 1953. First performance May 15, 1953, Milan, Piccolo Teatro. Time: the present. Place: Italy.

Kafka's nightmare of the omnipotence of anonymous authorities is reduced to a theatrical satire on the overelaborateness of welfare institutions. Modern medicine with its multiplicity of clinical applications, its boundless diagnostic and prophylactic possibilities, needs a victim on which to exercise itself in order to justify its own existence. And thus an individual gets caught in the machinery of the health service. As he moves from one set of specialists to the next he is gradually taken apart. He is deprived of everything that constitutes his personality, his unique human existence: his work, his environment, his interests. What remains is a spineless wreck, material for the dissecting knife.

The businessman Giovanni Corte pays a courtesy call at a clinic and for fun allows the modern apparatus to be tried out on him. He is persuaded to undergo a minor operation, stays on for postoperative treatment, and remains indefinitely. The seven stories of the clinic mark the stages of his decline. He starts out on the seventh floor, which houses the patients in almost complete health; then he is implacably moved down, first under some pretext or as a result of alleged mistakes, then under impersonal rules and eventually by force, until he reaches the bottom floor, the waiting room for the dying. Corte's mother tries in vain to get him away from this process of clinical dissolution. As the curtain falls he is at the point of death.


IL MANTELLO *[The Overcoat]*. One-act play. After a short story written in 1940. Prose. First performance March 14, 1960, Milan, Teatro del

Convegno. Opera by Luciano Chailly: first performance May 11, 1960, Milan, Teatro della Pergola. Time: the present. Place: a house in the mountains of Italy.

Realistic folklore and symbolic apparitions of the dead are combined, not always smoothly, in this scenic *memento mori*. Signora Anna cannot resign herself to her son's having been reported missing in the war and steadfastly believes that he will return. Suddenly her Giovanni does in fact turn up unexpectedly and talks of a mysterious officer who is waiting for him outside and who will take him along once more into the unknown. He obstinately refuses to take off his overcoat. The family's long-deceased ancestors recognize him as belonging to the realm of the dead. When eventually a corner of the coat is lifted, everybody can see the mortal wound. The dead soldier is taken back into the silence by his mysterious captain.

L'UOMO CHE ANDRÀ IN AMERICA *[The Man Who Will Go to America]*. Comedy in two acts. Prose. First published in *Il Dramma,* No. 309, June 1962. First performance April 23, 1962, Naples, Teatro Mercadante. Time: the present. Place: Italy.

There is a striking contrast in this play between the ambiguous theme, whose dark symbolism is reminiscent of Kafka, and a realistically drawn satire of contemporary conditions.

The "America Prize," the highest distinction in the field of painting, is awarded only rarely and at irregular intervals. All painters long for this incontestable confirmation of their creative achievement and in a businesslike manner strive for it in the confusion of the various isms of the day. Only Antonio Remittenza keeps himself apart as an unnoticed outsider. All his life he has been obsessed with trying to express in color the world as he sees it, and in the end is devoid of all hope. Suddenly he receives a visit from a representative of the unknown group that awards the America Prize. The mysterious messenger, who appears in different shapes according to the situation and his mission, informs the aged Remittenza that he has been awarded the prize. With a shock the painter, who thus sees his life's aim fulfilled, realizes that this favor must be at once the climax and the end of his work, salvation and death at the same time. The ceremony of the award is to be held in America, and he sets out for this legendary distant country, where all troubles and doubts come to an end: no one has ever returned after the award.

A colorful and humorous satire on the dubious practices of the modern art business is presented in the loose manner of a sketch, without losing the mysterious undertone of destiny implied in a prize that means death.

## CAMOLETTI, Marc
(France, born 1925)


BOEING-BOEING *(Boeing-Boeing)*. Comedy in two acts. Prose. First published in *L'Avant-scène,* No. 240, April 1961. First performance December 10, 1960, Paris, Théâtre de la Comédie-Caumartin. Translated by Beverley Cross, London production 1962, New York production 1965; London, Evans Drama Library 1967. Time: the present. Place: Bernard's apartment in Paris.

The interior decorator Bernard, a young and carefree bon vivant, has given his whole heart to airline stewardesses—no less than three of them. The women are of different nationalities and their work is a guarantee of charm, wit, and timely departure. When Judith's plane from Stockholm touches down at Paris in the evening, Jacqueline has already left at noon for Cairo, and Janet is not due from New York until the next morning. This perpetual motion of love provides Bernard with a cozy life with three fiancées, each of whom believes herself to be the only one. He thus gets variety at little cost. But suddenly bad weather upsets the international timetable and, by bringing the three women together, creates even worse atmospheric disturbances in Bernard's dovecote, until with some relief the harassed lover takes refuge in wedlock.
A hilarious and frothy entertainment in the best boulevard tradition, this comedy relies on well-tried situations, such as mistaken identities, abrupt reversals of fortune, and verbal acrobatics.


## CAMUS, Albert
(France, 1913–1960)


THE JUST ASSASSINS *(Les Justes)*. Play in five acts. Prose. First edition Paris 1950. First performance December 15, 1949, Paris, Théâtre Hébertot. Translated by Stuart Gilbert, in *Caligula and Three Other Plays,* New York, Knopf, 1958. Time: 1905. Place: a large town in Russia.

Camus transfers the inner conflicts of his own resistance activity to an episode in Russian history: the murder of Grand Duke Sergei by anarchists in 1905.
Stepan, a revolutionary toughened by hatred and a will to destroy, is not deflected from his struggle either by inner doubts or by human sympathy: "Nothing is ruled out that can serve our cause." He has nothing but con-

tempt for the young idealist Ivan Kaliayev, who does indeed want to over-throw the tyrants, but without getting personally involved in doing wrong. Kaliayev has thwarted a bomb attempt on the Grand Duke in order to save some children. He has his own answer to Stepan's unbending purposeful-ness: "I have agreed to kill in order to overthrow the tyranny. But behind your words I see emerging another tyranny, which, if it should seize power tomorrow, will make of me a murderer whereas I mean to be an agent of justice." In a second attempt on the Grand Duke's life, Kaliayev succeeds in killing him, and subsequently refuses to appeal for certain pardon and goes to his death for his convictions. The girl Dora, who loves him, will continue his struggle in token of their bond.

The problem of "dirty hands," which can free the world from evil only by doing further evil in the name of justice, can be solved for Camus only by the voluntary death of atonement: "I do not want for the sake of dead justice to contribute to existing injustice."

THE POSSESSED (Les Possédés). Play in three parts after the novel by Dostoevsky. Prose. First edition Paris 1959. First performance January 30, 1959, Paris, Théâtre Antoine. Translated by Justin O'Brien, New York, Knopf, and London, Hamish Hamilton, 1960. Time: 1860. Place: a small town in Russia.

One of numerous Dostoevsky dramatizations and, like most of them, less than fully successful. Doubts of the existence of God, yearning for redemp-tion, voluptuous sinning and remorse, man's irremediable entanglement in the world that finds expression in a vast and confused array of seductions, duals, brawls, suicides, murders, carousing, and conspiracies—all this de-mands the epic breadth and the larger-than-life characters of the great Russian novelist. Transition to the medium of the stage is bound to diminish and destroy the proportions of these wide-ranging novels. In this novel, the characters are personified instincts and spiritual passions; on the stage, they become pathologically distorted romantics and nihilists in an overdone thriller.

Professor Stepan Trofimovich Verkhovensky has found a cosy niche as tutor and parasite in the home of the rich widow Barbara Petrovna Stavrogina, a bigoted matchmaker. His son Peter Stepanovich is a political fanatic, for whom revolutionary aims are an outlet for his murderous instincts. Nich-olas, Barbara's son, wastes his life in debauchery and unscrupulous seduction, and ends by committing suicide.

The excesses of this corrupt society are exemplified by a parable from the Gospel of Luke which is the motto of the complex action: "Then went the devils out of the man, and entered into the swine: and the herd ran

violently down a steep place into the lake, and were choked. . . . Then they went out to see what was done; and came to Jesus, and found the man, out of whom the devils were departed, sitting at the feet of Jesus, clothed, and in his right mind: and they were afraid." (Luke 8: 33–35.) Like Dostoevsky, Camus seems to take refuge in a vague yearning for redemption. Clearly, Camus includes in the "devils and possessed" the Communist reality of present-day Russia, and hopes that a miracle will lift the political menace from our age: "The devils that go out of the man . . . they are, of course, our sores, our impurities, and the sick man is Russia. . . . But as the impurities go out of him, they go into the swine, and that means us, my son, the others, and we rush off as though possessed, and we will die. But the sick man will be cured and will sit at the feet of Jesus and all will be cured. . . . Yes, Russia will be cured some day!"
Camus sets the action in an epic frame and places the narrator Grigoreiev in front of the drop curtain as an ironically detached commentator.


STATE OF SIEGE (L'État de siège). Play in three parts. Prose. Written 1946. First edition Paris 1948. First performance October 27, 1948, Paris, Théâtre Marigny. Translated by Stuart Gilbert, in Caligula and Three Other Plays, New York, Knopf, 1958. Time: an indeterminate present. Place: a fortified town in Spain.

For Camus's brand of ethically oriented existentialism, man's absurd, mechanized, and fundamentally unfree existence acquires meaning and redemption only when an individual resists the deadly menace and by his voluntary sacrifice generates a positive counterforce. Of the formal aspects of this play, Camus explains: "This is not a play of traditional structure, but a spectacle in which it is my avowed intention to mix all the forms of dramatic expression, from the lyrical monologue through pantomime, simple dialogue, farce and chorus to the 'collective theatre.' "
"The Plague" takes hold of a town in the form of a brutal man in uniform who, through his secretary—no longer a woman, but the personification of bureaucratic function—sets up a deadly apparatus of power, complete with watchtowers, barbed wire, trumpets, propaganda slogans, manipulated voting, mass executions, and death patrols: "One plague, one people! . . . Concentrate, do as you are told, keep busy—Deport, torture." The rulers (the Governor) betray the people in the hope of saving their own skins; the underlings (the Alcalde) at once come to terms with the new powers. Only the young physician Diego has the courage to resist. He forgoes the private happiness he might find with Victoria, the girl he loves, and sacrifices himself for the community. By choosing his own destruction, he forces the regime of the Plague into retreat. But it remains as

a menace—a menace to be resisted over and over again by selfless individuals fighting for life and freedom—man's task and test in time and eternity.


## CANETTI, Elias
(Bulgaria/Austria/England, born 1905)

HOCHZEIT *[Wedding]*. Play in one act with a prologue. Prose. Written 1931–1932. First edition Berlin 1932. First performance November 3, 1965, Braunschweig, Staatstheater. Time: the present. Place: old Mrs. Gilz's house.

Behind his cynical mask, Canetti is a moralist. His fun is envenomed, his satirical temperament aims to shock and provoke. Sometimes obscene, sometimes macabre, *Wedding* did create quite a storm among the well-mannered, passive theater public of West Germany. The play is a witches' sabbath of lust for life, sex, and possession. Vileness has become so commonplace and blatant that all taboos are swept aside. There is neither story nor characterization, but only a spontaneous, carnal reaction to interchangeable, disposable objects of sexuality.

Death and marriage are very close together in the house in Kindly Street, which is the goal of every sort of covetousness. Despite the helpful urging of her granddaughter, old Mrs. Gilz, the owner of the house, is in no hurry to pass on to a better world. Down below, the caretaker's wife lies dying. Her husband won't fetch the doctor, because "praying is cheaper!" Upstairs at the home of Segenreich the architect, an uproarious wedding party is being held for his daughter Christa. Making good use of the last opportunity, she quickly gives herself to the loquacious idealist Horch and lines up three expert boy friends for the forthcoming boredom of marriage. Her mother, "with her youthful heart and exuberant figure," leaves her lover of many years for her daughter's bridegroom, who is simultaneously pursued by Marie, the fourteen-year-old nestling of the family, who goes to work alternating sex appeal and tears. The respectable wedding guests join in the general woman-swapping. As doctor, pharmacist, and undertaker, they are professional associates, since they are all concerned with taking potential corpses through to the final stage. Along with the taboos, all conventions, indeed all natural limits, are suspended. Dr. Bock, the family physician, crawling under the table and lecherously fumbling for his prey, is renowned for being the ladies' man who never lets them down, despite his eighty years. Then Horch proposes a party game. They are to imagine the end of the world has come. What would each of them do for his nearest

and dearest? Round the ring go question and answer in this psychological probe. Each one thinks only of the satisfaction of his desires. Then an earthquake suddenly turns the game into reality. Panic-stricken, each thinks only of his own life. When Segenreich blocks the door, he is knocked down by his own children. The pharmacist forestalls his wife's murder plan and throttles her. Whimpering, foaming at the mouth, tearing each other to pieces, these beasts in human form crowd to the exit behind which is nothing but the void. The last word is with the speculators who, over a world in ruins, are already discussing their projects and haggling about whether they can get six times the price for land. Out of the wreckage is heard the voice of the old woman, Mrs. Gilz, whose death was a general subject of speculation, saying: "I'm still alive. Still ali . . ."
Canetti's characters are only contrived figures to demonstrate the collective symptoms of degeneracy, of unbridled self-destruction, of bestiality. There is no development in the action; no character stands out. A loosely knit, frequently overlapping sequence of dialogues continually reveals new facets. The language is that typically Austrian mixture of the rude dialect of Vienna's lower class and stilted officialese.


KOMÖDIE DER EITELKEIT [A Comedy of Vanity]. Drama in three parts. Prose. Written 1933–1934. First edition Frankfurt/Main, 1950. First performance February 6, 1965, Braunschweig, Staatstheater. Time: none specified. Place: an imaginary state.

What begins as a bad habit becomes a prejudice, the prejudice hardens into a taboo, the taboo leads to lynch law, and finally lynch law turns into a totalitarian, strait-jacket regime that stifles all life. There is no resisting the current of discrimination. Canetti makes his parable begin at the terminus of this development.
The scriptural ban on images is given the force of a dogma. All pictures and photographs, all mirrors and glasses are to be destroyed under penalty of death. In an orgy of destructive fury the people make a bonfire of the playthings of vanity. Thus everyone becomes anonymous to himself, ceases to have access to his own appearance and, for lack of any resemblance, also loses contact with his fellow men. But the desire for self-affirmation finds substitutes. Franzl Nada, the emaciated odd-job man, makes a rewarding business out of becoming a streetcorner flatterer. Peddlers rent at exorbitant charges a little fragment of mirror in which people can see their image for a brief, coveted moment. Blackmailers and informers flourish. The supporters of the system organize themselves in cadres of officials. They become Fourthship leaders and moderators of Sextodecimoships, and as such propose to put out the eyes of all suspects and thus to eliminate the last glimmer

of reflections from the world. In order to break out of isolation, to snatch a word or a glance of sympathy, people hit upon the most extraordinary expedient: "People literally lie in wait for someone to say something about them. They know nothing about themselves. They don't see themselves. No one who can speak, speaks to them. Through a lifetime no one has paid attention to them. So at night they lie down in the street, so that people will stumble over them. They thus compel attention to themselves. It's really blackmail. They are famished, these people, it's unbelievable!" Emilie Fant is a good businesswoman; she sets up a mirror cabinet where for a large fee anyone can admire himself. Enraptured with himself, her regular customer Heinrich Föhn delivers a speech about himself in which he champions "everything genuine and unadulterated, everything immaculate and pure, everything unfalsified and true," in short, the rebirth of the ego, of the sole ego, the supreme ego. The masses are captivated. Inspired by the drug of these phrases, they overthrow the antimirror dictatorship and replace it with the self-mirror dictatorship. Föhn gets a monument and a new myth arises.

In this play, as elsewhere, Canetti makes no attempt at development in the action and the leading characters. He interprets a sociological hypothesis by means of a social utopia that consists only of facets. But these will-o'-the-wisp snippets are so intense that they constitute an autonomous creative principle and can dispense with dramatic construction.


THE NUMBERED (Die Befristeten). Play in two parts with a prologue on old times. Written 1952. First edition in Dramen, Munich, 1964. First performance (in English) November 5, 1956, Oxford, Playhouse. Time: not specified. Place: an imaginary state.

Canetti imagines a world which has lost its fear of death but with it also its spontaneity. Men are machines whose market value and working life are known precisely. Once again Canetti takes an abstract model for an object lesson on a theme, which in this case is "fatalism as a mass phenomenon." The characters are embodiments of a thesis, the action is dialectical argument made visible. Canetti releases men from their fear of death and removes the last factor of uncertainty in a mechanized world. Life has become a manageable calculation. The years of a man's life are capital which can be computed and allocated: "We come into the world with a certain capital of life. It does not diminish and it does not increase. You cannot be robbed of any of it, it is registered in your name and is not negotiable. You cannot get rid of it because it is paid out to you only in annual installments. You alone know how much you have; so no one can interfere . . . If you know how to manage it, you have something of your life. You only have to know what you buy with your time."

Everyone knows the day he is to die, and uses as his name the number of years apportioned to him, but keeps his true age secret, under strict taboo. This is the basis of a scale of privileges. Men are high, middle, and low according to their expectation of life: Mr. Eighty-eight is envied, the boy Eight is hardly worthy troubling about. People carry about with them a sealed capsule containing the dates of their birth and death. Death is no longer an event; it is called the "moment," and when it arrives, only the "Capsulan," the all-powerful administrator of the system, may look into the capsule. The only one who does not know his age is Fifty. Thus he also does not know how long he has yet to live. This doubt makes him rebel against the self-assurance of the others. He contests the inevitability of the "moment" and is forced to make a public recantation. He examines the mysterious capsules and finds them empty. Triumphantly he exposes the capsule cult as a world-wide self-deception. To his horror Fifty discovers that the steady order is disrupted forever. Fear and insecurity, passions and crimes drive men along—into the freedom and anarchy of their impulses.


## CAPOTE, Truman
(United States, born 1925)


THE GRASS HARP. Play in two acts after Capote's novel of the same name. Prose. Written 1952. First edition New York 1952. First performance March 27, 1952, New York, Martin Beck Theatre. Time: the present, late September. Place: the Talbo family's house, the town, and a wood.

A gentle and poetic play, *The Grass Harp* is concerned less with everyday realities than with human dreams and longings. The nature pantheism which Walt Whitman's *Leaves of Grass* introduced into American literature with a solemn missionary purpose has subsided into an unpretentious, tender idyll—lyrical musings more compellingly suggestive of the unspoken than of any valid claim to a so-called message.

Verena Talbo, an elderly, extremely energetic and self-assertive woman, dominates her family circle, including her dreamy sister Dolly, her teen-age nephew Collin, and the good-natured, garrulous and lazy Negro maid Catherine. Dolly lives in a world of wishes remote from reality. She possesses the recipe for a famous popular nostrum for dropsy, the legacy of a gipsy. Verena wants to develop it into a profitable industry and has already interested the wily physician Morris Ritz in her project. Faced with these menacingly real claims, Dolly escapes into the woods and, with Collin and Catherine, finds shelter in a hidden, windswept farm house. There she blissfully communes with nature and in these hours of peace encounters Charlie Cool, a judge and lover of fairy tales, who has run away from the dignity and duties of his office and pursues the dreams of his youth. Dolly lacks the courage to give herself to this starry-eyed happiness. The uproar among the bigoted philistines and her own sense of duty drive her back to Verena, whose once high-handed and tyrannical spirits disappeared when the admired Dr. Morris Ritz was exposed as a quack. Charlie will henceforth be part of Dolly's small, dreamy world—but the happiness between the two shy people is sensitively left in the realm of yearning.

## CAPPELLI, Salvato
(Italy, born 1911)

DUECENTOMILA E UNO [Two Hundred Thousand and One]. A report in two acts. First published in Il Dramma, No. 358, July 1966. First performance May 4, 1966, Milan, Piccolo Teatro. Time: November 20, 1965. Place: courtroom in the United States.

Like Kipphardt and Weiss, Cappelli chooses a semidocumentary play about a trial in an attempt to illustrate our century's conflict of conscience. The individual experiences himself as the agent of political crimes, the implications of which he cannot see at the moment of action. The crisis of responsibility is brought on only in retrospect. Cappelli gives the theme a new dimension by centering his play on the attitudes and behavior of persons who themselves have nothing to do with the crime in question, but who consciously accept the collective guilt for it and irrevocably identify themselves with it by a punishable offense of their own. The play is the final one of Cappelli's trilogy on the crisis of conscience. Of the two earlier plays, Il Diavolo Peter [The Devil Peter] dealt with man's responsibility before God, and Incontro a Babele [Encounter at Babel] with the responsibility of the individual to the community. In Duecentomila e Uno the author freely adapts facts from the life of Major Eatherly, the Hiroshima pilot, to raise the question of the possibility and extent of personal responsibility in an age of prefabricated ideologies.

The nurse Gloria Wilton has to account to a military commission of inquiry. She was the only eyewitness when Major Nicola Fafour shot his superior officer General Greene. Twenty years ago, in 1945, Greene was in command of the bomber from which Dafour, the gunner, released the atom bomb over Hiroshima. Gloria took part in the psychiatric test by which an attempt was made to determine the effects of mass destruction upon the soldiers ordered to carry it out. The conflict of conscience is simplified into an organic malfunction, a psychopathic defect, that can be cured by treatment. With Dafour, the sense of guilt takes the shape of a dragon seen in hallucination. His two comrades Burket and Diamond are shaken by convulsions of remorse, while the third, Brickt, takes refuge with his unease in a Dominican monastery. Only Greene is hard-hearted enough to allow himself the excuse of political justification. A few years later all of them have superficially settled down in life. They hide their scruples under the pride of being national heroes, or feel themselves to have been the chosen instrument of God in castigating His creatures with the bomb. Only Dafour has remained a schizophrenic outsider, who flings his aggressive challenge at the rest of the world and feverishly imagines a deed of violence which is to stop mass murder forever. As time goes on, the atom bomb, mass murder on call, becomes an ordinary ingredient of current thought, a familiar bogey of politicians and editorial writers. Dafour decides to kill Greene as a sign of protest. Brickt tries vainly to convert him to private remorse and introspection, which would not only be riskless and avoid imperiling one's own person, but would also not disturb the existing order. But Dafour's sense of his mission is too strong for the monk to break, and Brickt takes his own life in despair. Gloria has so far tried in vain to restore to Dafour his psychological balance and the hardened conscience that is the standard equipment of our society. Now she fights for the murder that is to liberate Dafour, and accompanies him to see the general. Dafour breaks down in the face of Greene's cold self-assurance, and it is Gloria who shoots Greene. Only a truth drug wrests from her the confession, which the military hush up. The 200,000 victims of Hiroshima are joined, twenty years later, by one more. The conflict of conscience remains unsolved.

Cappelli interrupts the external frame of the investigation with fade-ins which are often compressed into purely pantomimic quotations of the past and are accompanied by acoustical leitmotivs, such as the roar of the aircraft. The dialectic of the theme is externalized in pure theatrical effects (for instance, the thriller device of the double shot).

## CARLINO, Lewis John
(United States, born 1932)

CAGES. Two one-act plays for one evening. Prose. First edition New York 1963. First performance June 13, 1963, New York, York Theatre. Time: the present. Place: hotel room/studio-bedroom.

Illusions are acted out on the theme of being "locked in." Two one-act plays are coupled under the common title *Cages,* the symbol of irremediable isolation. Both variants of imprisonment are the result of the sex war. In both cases the woman, with her willingness for self-surrender wins.

In *Snowangel* John tries to find the illusion of a lost happiness with Connie, the tippling old prostitute. He forces her into words and gestures alien to her in order to recall a long-past amorous encounter with a "nice girl." But the prostitute is angered by this debasement into an object and a toy. Even in her depravity she demands to be taken seriously as a human being, and tells of the only love of her life. With touching clumsiness John takes on the part of this imaginary partner and for a few hours gives Connie the gift of the illusion that she is beautiful and loved.

*Epiphany* throws a spotlight on the sex struggle distorted to the point of absurdity. The husband is an impassioned but unpaid ornithologist who also does the housework; his wife is a successful advertising manager and supports the household. Both have become specialists, slaves of their professions, who see in each other only an uninitiate who gets in the way. The droll children's games by which they try to create an illusion of companionship are merely an outlet for mutual torments. The husband feels cheated of his hereditary claim to domination and thinks up a grotesque revenge: by means of "epiphany" he will transform himself into a rooster and return to the evolutionary stage of winged creatures. He equips himself with a steel beak sharp as a knife, with claws and a coxcomb; he cuts off the telephone connection and locks the doors. Two bags of chickenfeed henceforth are the limits of their world. Desperate and helpless, the woman is at the mercy of this madness, by which she is to be condemned to the existence of a submissive clucking hen. Suddenly the man begins to cackle excitedly and lays an egg. His feigned virility has failed and his triumphant crowing is nothing but a pitiful clucking. Sympathetically the woman resumes command. The play is a sly farce on the American social order, equally skillful in the use of psychoanalysis and the absurd.


TELEMACHUS CLAY. A collage for voices in two acts. Prose. First edition New York 1964. First performance January 7, 1964, New York, Writers' Stage Theatre. Time: the present. Place: empty stage.

The figure of Odysseus' son Telemachus, a homeless wanderer in search of his father and who repeats his father's Odyssey, finds its counterpart in the destiny of an uprooted intellectual. The latter bequeathes his as yet unborn son nothing but the message that he is to go out into the world to seek his father, because in that search he will find himself. Telemachus Clay lives in the small provincial city of Downsville Town and dreams of becoming a poet. He has never known his father. One summer his mother Agatha gave herself to four migrant workers in nearby fields. At twenty, Telemachus abandons the girl Barbara, who is expecting a baby by him. The uncertainty of his origin and the unfulfillment of his vocation attract him to Hollywood. He makes a living by washing dishes. The curvaceous starlet Ginger takes him to the parties of influential personalities. Nadine, the wife of the writer Collin Adler, repays an amorous debt by getting him work with a film crew as a board snapper, where he has to carry out the producer's commands automatically. At last he is able to give a reading of his script, but his public is merely a group of drunken mockers. The homosexual producer Warren poses as his patron to tie Telemachus to himself. A brawl lands Telemachus in jail. Collin finds his cynical philosophy confirmed by universal prostitution. Telemachus, who wants to proclaim ideals rather than manufacture love stories, will never make his way in Hollywood. At Downsville Town the body of an unknown tramp, one of his four fathers, is found. Odysseus has returned; but meanwhile Telemachus roams the highways of America.

Eleven actors sit on the stage in a half-circle and recite and act out the individual scenes, which are announced, explained, and linked by the "Prophet." The action is connected and counterpointed on a purely aural level in a simultaneity reminiscent of Dylan Thomas' *Under Milk Wood*.

## CARROLL, Paul Vincent
(Ireland, born 1900)

THE WAYWARD SAINT. Comedy-fantasy in three acts. Prose. First edition New York 1955. First performance February 17, 1955, New York, Cort Theatre. Adapted as opera libretto by Mark Lothar, 1967. Time: the present. Place: sitting-dining room of Canon McCooey's presbytery near the Northern Irish border.

The naive fantasy and folklore of Carroll's Irish gift of gab are put at the service of a clerical comedy that is at once rollicking and innocently pious, transcendental, earthy, and funny.

Old Canon Daniel McCooey with his resolute charity and St. Francis-like simplicity is a nuisance not only to his bishop but to hell itself. The cunning old man preaches to domestic animals, does good without reference to any dogma, and is worshiped as a saint by the people. The church takes the canon's animals away and as a punishment subjects him to the merciless, bigoted domination of the housekeeper Miss Killicat. Hell proceeds with more diplomacy and sends a tempter along in the person of the worldly Baron Nicholas de Balbus. By devilish tricks he makes the canon believe that he has the miraculous power of bewitching the bishop. Prayer leads the canon back to humility. He is prepared to submit to the bishop and never to be wayward again. The bishop, however, has seen the light and

calls the canon to Rome in order to present him to the pope as a new
saint. What can the old man do in these circumstances except be as wayward as ever and oppose his bishop once more?

## CAU, Jean
(France, born 1925)

LES PARACHUTISTES *[The Paratroopers]*. Play in seven scenes. Prose.
First edition Paris 1963. First performance March 24, 1963, Paris, Studio
des Champs-Elysées. Time: during the Algerian war. Place: Algeria.

As in Genet, the political background of the Algerian war is reflected in a
bizarre and extravagant inferno, which created a theatrical scandal in
France. The whole play is one drunken orgy, made up indiscriminately of
murder prompted by a gambling instinct, lust for power, gloating over filth,
bloodlust, and sexual perversion. No one has any choice, everything is
predetermined. Some are born to assume the part of corpses in this filthy
war, others become murder machines: "When you kill one, you must kill
more and more to be able to sleep. . . . The only way is to kill without
thinking." Cau has explained that the paratroopers were neither good nor
bad, neither just nor unjust, but simply personified the war and were its
instruments and innocents. "They are children. They play the terrible
and entertaining game that is called war. They personify the force of war,
the Arabs personify suffering and hope. But I wanted the voices of the
executioners and the victims to combine and mingle sometimes, for there
is no fight—however cruel it may be—which does not have its fascination
and its celebration of secret unions between victims and executioners in
the dead of the war's night."
Under their corporal, Gros Bébé, a group of paratroopers are torturing
the two Arab prisoners Hocine and Ahmed to get them to talk. A third
Arab, Saïd, managed to escape, and the soldiers' whore Mora offers him
safe shelter. But doggedly Saïd sticks to the national cause, is captured and
killed in a senseless fight. His comrades casually note: "We have one more
hero!" The paratroopers and the Arabs—the torturers and their victims—
spend themselves in macabre games of love-hate, whether they take a
morbid delight in imagining their comrade's heroic death, enjoy the ecstasy
of sudden penitential raptures, or yield to the fascination of exploring the
possibilities of treason and a change of allegiance.
In scornful mockery the author sneers at the futile efforts of committees on
human rights far away in Europe that distribute their manifestos and show
lack of power to do anything against the army as an institution. But the

balance between friend and foe has long been struck; men are united only in the bestiality of subconscious instincts finding an outlet in crime and perversion.

## CÉSAIRE, Aimé
(Martinique, born 1913)

UNE SAISON AU CONGO [A Season in the Congo]. A play about Patrice Lumumba in three acts. Prose and verse. First edition Paris 1966. First performance autumn 1967, Venice. Time: January 1960 to January 17, 1961. Place: the Congo.

Césaire attempts a theatrical epitaph for Patrice Lumumba, but it is more a pious duty than political drama. The history of the Congolese independence struggle is presented in a chronological series of stills. Lumumba, but recently mistreated in jail, becomes prime minister of the new state. He fights against the indolence and corruption of his colleagues. Soon party strife bursts out and extends even to the brands of beer. At the urging of Belgian bankers, the rich mining province of Katanga secedes from the state. Belgian troops intervene as a result of native excesses. Lumumba uses the police to terrorize the church. The United Nations intervene. Hammarskjöld takes a strictly neutral line and drives Lumumba into the arms of Moscow. President Kala, a good Christian, dismisses the premier. Lumumba manages to escape from prison and proclaims a counter-government. He rejects cooperation with Kala and is handed over to his enemies in Katanga, where he is butchered. Hammarskjöld admits that he was misinformed by his colleagues and laments his guilt.
The play is spoiled by wavering uncertainty between documentary and lyrical apotheosis of a martyr. Metaphors drawn from folklore and lyrical lamentations are interspersed with radio proclamations and speeches. Bankers talk in nursery rhymes. A zanza player with his songs links the scenes. The characters are equally uncertain. Alongside historical figures such as Hammarskjöld and Lumumba and various national types, there appear other real persons under fictitious names; for example, Baudouin appears as Basilio, Tshombe as Tzumbi, Mobutu as Mokutu, and Kasavubu as Kala.

## CHAYEFSKY, Paddy
(United States, born 1923)

GIDEON. Play in two acts. Prose. First edition New York 1962. First performance November 9, 1961, New York, Plymouth Theatre. Time: June 1100 B.C. Place: Manasseh, the mountainous country west of the Jordan in Biblical Palestine.

A play woven of many strands: religious fervor and playful irony, symbolism and reality, deliberately simple legend and the discussion of eschatology in all its immanent contradictions. On these many different levels the author takes up the cardinal theme of Western man's tragedy, that is, the Promethean confrontation between the individual trying to prove his own value and the meaning of his existence in the face of superior divine or fateful powers, and those extrahuman powers. Yet Chayefsky's gentle skepticism enables him to avoid pathos and tragic inevitability in this inherently pathetic theme. He stands the Promethean problem on its head, as it were: man's inherent claim to freedom and his needs are not fulfilled by any sort of long-invalidated heroism and the cathartic rigor of the ancient tragedy, but man experiences himself as human precisely in his own inconstancy, his mistakes and his shortcomings, and realizes himself and his claim to being in the perpetual interplay of mastery and entanglement, delusions of grandeur and the exposure of frailty, semblance and reality.

The people of Israel have forsaken Yahweh, God of their fathers, and offer sacrifices to the heathen Baal, beseeching him to save them from the depredations of the warlike Midianites. God comes to earth as an angel to reveal his divinity to Israel by a miracle and to lead the erring people back to their true faith. He selects Gideon, the simplest of the simple, to go out with the most cowardly of his people to destroy the powerful enemy. Gideon, who has been pushed around and despised all his life, resists being stirred out of his comfortable insignificance. But when a surprise attack by the Midianites causes a panic, he takes the lead in defensive action. Seasoned warriors including Shillem and Hezekiah are appalled at his strategic ignorance, while the fanatic dreamer Malchiel becomes a vociferous disciple of the new prophet. Gideon, the new military leader, wavers between self-satisfied pomposity and peevishness, for he keeps making a fool of himself and does not measure up to his responsibilities. After the miraculous victory he takes refuge in bumptious arrogance, because he cannot bear merely receiving everything as an unmerited grace from God, and owing nothing in life to his own merit. Even when he eventually capitulates to God's glory, the angel resigns himself to the knowledge that man's megalomania and hubris will always divide the creator from his creatures.

The angel commands the Midianite elders to be slain. But Gideon is so enraptured by the seductive charm of Orpah, the daughter of the Elder Onzi, that he takes her as his concubine and pardons the condemned. Complacently he lends his ear to a rationalistic theory which explains the victory as having come about without God's help, solely by his own strategic genius, as an inevitable consequence of historical, economic, sociological, psychological, and cultural factors. The angel indignantly reproaches Gideon with his repeated betrayals. The man despairs of his own shortcomings and revokes his pact with God: "It is too much for me, this loving God. I cannot manage it. I am a plain man and subject to imperfect feelings. I shall betray you many times, and you shall rise in wrath against me and shall punish me with mighty penalties, and I cannot continue in this way, my Lord . . . I tried to love you, but it is too much for me. You are too vast a concept for me. To love you, God, one must be a god himself." Mortal fear seems to be the only thing that can tie the creature to its creator. Gideon entreats God to retire once more into his former inaccessibility and thus to grant men the unique grace of being able to deny and ignore God. Only then would the world of men find meaning and justification in its quests and aspirations. God and man face each other, perplexed. God despairingly sees himself abandoned by his creation and dissolves into invisibility. He implores Gideon to turn back, but the latter is already deaf to God's word. The angel proclaims God's judgment in words of thunder, but his love for mankind prevails: he leaves the children of this earth their delusions and conceit, for these alone seem to be the foundation of their happiness.


THE TENTH MAN. A legend in three acts. Prose. Written 1959. First edition New York 1960. First performance November 5, 1959, New York, Booth Theatre. Time: the present, a winter's morning. Place: small synagogue near New York.

Like Ansky in *The Dybbuk,* Chayevsky in *The Tenth Man* revives elements of Hasidic demonology in the songs, dances, and colorful folklore of Judaism. Their contrast with New York's big-city life provides an opportunity for social satire and psychological subtlety without encroaching upon the play's real subject, which is the miracle of inner rebirth, a modern catharsis of compelling simplicity. This compound of mysticism, psychoanalysis, the grotesque, legend, conjuration of spirits, and dialectic glows with the entrancing colors of Chagall. The contrasting elements are held in suspense by skeptically detached irony. A small Jewish community has made a bare synagogue for itself out of a shabby store. The members are always having trouble gathering the *minyan,* the ten needed for the service, as the law commands. Foreman brings his eighteen-year-old granddaughter, Evelyn, to the synagogue, to save her from the lunatic asylum. Evelyn is possessed by a dybbuk: in Jewish folklore a wandering soul that can find no rest because of an injustice suffered in life, enters a living body and, through the madness of that body, demands expiation and justice. Foreman is appalled when he recognizes in Evelyn's confused talk the soul of a Polish girl whom he had once seduced and abandoned. While the former rabbi, Hirschman, prepares for a solemn exorcism of the demon, the rationalist Schlissel sees the case simply as schizophrenia. To allow the ceremony to go forward, a tenth man is brought in from the street. He happens to be the lawyer Arthur Brooks, a man so worn down by an unhappy marriage that he is on the verge of suicide and is kept going solely by regular sessions with his psychiatrist. Long estranged from and indifferent to the religion of his people, Brooks is disconcerted at the ghostly doings around him. He is struck by the warm-hearted unaffected-ness of the girl Evelyn, who between fits seems to be perfectly normal. He is reluctant to admit the growing attachment he feels for her. He has been disappointed so often, has experienced love so far only as lust and nausea —he is a man possessed by the modern dybbuk of joylessness and bitter-ness. When the evil spirit is to be exorcised by cabalistic magic, the ancient conjuration has its effect not on Evelyn, but on Arthur, who breaks down and is set free from the demon of hard-heartedness and lack of faith. He acknowledges his love for Evelyn and henceforth will devotedly care for her peace of mind.


## CHRISTIE, Agatha (A. Mary Clarissa Miller)
(England, born 1891)


THE MOUSETRAP. Thriller in two acts. Prose. First edition London 1956. First performance November 25, 1952, London, Ambassador Theatre. Time: the present. Place: lounge in an English guesthouse.

The family guesthouse run by Giles and Mollie Ralston in the isolated, snow-bound country house Monkswell Manor is suddenly startled by a visit from the police. Maureen Lyon has been murdered in London by her former foster son George Corrigan, who has thus taken his revenge for the ill-treatment he and his brothers and sisters had to endure. Corrigan, an escaped lunatic, leaves the song "Three Blind Mice" on the scene of the crime and announces in a note that he will seek out two other culprits at Monkswell Manor. Detective Sergeant Trotter is assigned to the protection of the guests, all of whom obstinately deny any connection with the Corrigan case. Which of these strange people will be the next victim—the psychopathic Chris Wren, or Major Metcalf, or shady Mr. Paravicini, or rebellious Mrs. Boyle? Behind what honest mask is the murderer hidden? The classical elements of a crime play—the isolated setting and a small cast of grotesquely contrasting types—are in this case enlivened by creepy effects and an analytical chain of motivations.

TEN LITTLE INDIANS. Brit. Play in three acts after the author's 1939 novel. Prose. First performance November 17, 1943, London, St. James's Theatre. Time: the present. Place: living room in a country house on an island off the English coast.

As in *The Mousetrap,* the ingredients of this play are a hermetically sealed, isolated setting; a small cast of characters who are not acquainted with each other and never know more about each other than the audience does; and, not least, reliance on the moral alibi of unpunished crimes. The calculation behind this construction is ironically manifested in the nursery rhyme "Ten Little Indians," which anticipates and serves as a connecting link to the series of murders.
Judge Wargrave, General Mackenzie, the sour old maid Miss Brent, the psychiatrist Dr. Armstrong, the globe-trotter Lombard, the secretary Miss Claythorne, and the playboy Marston find themselves invited to a country house on an island. There, each of them is confronted by a tape recording discussing a crime dating back a year, and each is brought to trial. One by one the guests, who accuse each other and, panic-stricken, set upon each other, are murdered. Finally when only three remain, a subtly prepared coup brings the solution. This dramatization of the novel cuts down to essentials the background stories and relies entirely on the thriller effect of the situation.

## CHRISTOFF, Daniel
(Germany, born 1926)

NOAH IST TOT [*Noah Is Dead*]. Tragic farce in two acts with prologue and epilogue. Prose. Acting edition Frankfurt/Main, Fischer, 1963. First performance October 21, 1961, Göttingen, Deutsches Theater. Time: the present. Place: hotel lobby.

A disturbing parable which casts light on the fears and distresses as well as on the courage and decisions of our time, in an enigmatic puzzle. Humanity, trapped between banality and hysteria, is struck blind and with oblivious hubris accelerates its own downfall.

A handful of failures, with all their longings and memories, have taken refuge in the run-down, once elegant Hotel Bellevue, which is crumbling away as a result of the blasting required to build a nearby dam. Nobody will admit that his place of refuge may be swept away by the next detonation. The hotel-keeper Leopold is busy planning an extension of the hotel that becomes more of a ruin at every explosion. The soft-drink millionaire de Hogge, whose shareholding gave him the decisive voice in initiating the dam, nonetheless persists in including in his future business projects the hotel which he himself has destroyed. He marries off his son Jülchen, a chatterbox of a mother's boy, to Leopold's daughter Ellen, the only one who wants to escape from this depressing scene. All the rest are captives of their own past—King Jonny, a defeated boxer; Loulou, the unsuccessful cabaret dancer; the old prostitute Rheseda, who has outlived her fame and drowns her disillusionment in alcohol; a frogman excited by purposeless risk; and Mrs. de Hogge, who can communicate her love only to an undemanding fabric dog. Suddenly there appears a vagabond, full of life and confidence, who is looking for lost animals to rescue before the great detonation releases the masses of water. He is amazed to find people living in the utmost danger and urges them to flee. But the lost are infuriated at being disturbed in their opiumlike dream. The boxer kills the intruder, "for no one may with impunity behave in a human way." The stranger's unselfish sacrifice stirs Ellen and Jülchen and brings them together in real companionship. Bravely they set out in life with the determination "not to get involved." The others, however, progress-happy and fascinated by technology, await the great explosion without suspecting that it will mean their end.

The lesson that Christoff wants to teach his contemporaries is overlaid with the symbolism of men's wantonness in accumulating nuclear bombs, their confinement in a circumscribed space, and their individual self-deception. The play's dramatic impact is lost under its calculated effects.


RÜCKKEHR VON ELBA [Return from Elba]. Play in one act. Prose. Acting edition Frankfurt/Main, Fischer, 1963. First performance November 3, 1963, Nuremberg, Städtische Bühnen. Time: the present. Place: an antique shop.

The undigested past that catches up with a man is distilled into a grotesque farce that combines infectious clowning with topical relevance at many levels. The horror play with the shade of Napoleon offers an outlet for the power instincts of the petty bourgeois. The ready pleasure in hurting and being hurt, in insult and humiliation is the motive force of the action. "We remember only things we don't want to talk about." Man's helpless exposure to the moods and inspirations of the moment prevents him from being his true self in any situation. Guilt feelings and disgust drive him to meaningless aggression and make him forever a caricature of his excesses.

Sophie and Eduard, an aging sister and brother, run a poor little antique shop. Max, their shop assistant for many years, has been taken to a lunatic asylum. His growing schizophrenia led him to identify himself with Napoleon and despotically tyrannize the two old people. Sophie and Eduard excitedly took part in this game of unexplored possibilities. They enjoyed the fevered reactions of their mutual hatred for which the dictator now assumed responsibility, and greedily savored the humiliation of slavish adulation. When Max commanded that Eduard shoot his sister as the supposed traitor Palm, the old man, obsessed with his duty, was on the point of carrying out the order. But Sophie, in terror, telephoned the police and the macabre farce came to a sudden end. Such is the background of the two old people who now agitatedly wander about the deserted shop and cannot rid themselves of their exciting past. They abuse Max who destroyed valuable English engravings because they were English. Then again, still trembling from the recent nightmare, they idealize him and act out once more fragments of their former parts, warming to all the excitements and intoxication of power.

The seductions of power are manifest in three refractions: the basic image of Napoleon and his historical associations, his latter-day epigone Max, and the two victims of this madness. Each one projects his repressed wishes and ideals, as well as his destructive impulse and sadism into the dominating image whose attitude he either grimly defends or follows with suspicion. Then Max, released by the asylum as cured, unexpectedly returns. Often enough the old couple have pictured to themselves how they would scornfully show him the door. But now Eduard is once more fascinated by the world of forbidden dreams of power which will be revived by the reappearance of their originator. Disappointed, he realizes that Max has lost all his delusions and has no recollection of anything. Then Eduard, obsessed by the game, takes Max's visit as a pretext for carrying out the command he once received, and he shoots Sophie with all the gusto of a naughty child. This act brings back Max's madness, and oblivious of all else, they are lost in their world of delusions.

## COCTEAU, Jean
(France, 1889–1963)

BACCHUS *(Bacchus)*. Play in three acts. Prose. First edition Paris 1952. First performance December 20, 1951, Paris, Théâtre Marigny. Translated by Mary Hoeck in *The Infernal Machine and Other Plays,* Norfolk, Conn., New Directions, 1962. Time: 1523. Place: audience room in the duke's castle, in a small German town near the Swiss border.

*Bacchus* is concerned with the ambivalence of existence. In a hierarchic world in which good and evil have long been unalterably defined by their utility and expediency for the hierarchy, the demand for goodness and justice is bound to generate dangerous unrest: "His tragedy consists in belonging to no one. . . . Hence he must be mad. The crowd will get rid of him."

According to tradition, the vintage festival in a small town is crowned by the election of Bacchus, who for one week is absolute ruler over land and people. This custom offers an unpredictable outlet for exuberance, and the authorities, led by the duke and his guest, Cardinal Zampi, are anxious to render it harmless. To this end they arrange for the part of Bacchus to be taken this year by Hans, the village idiot, who lost his reason years ago as a result of an inhuman "jest" by the local gentry. As Bacchus, however, Hans surprisingly drops the mask of simplicity, which was merely for self-protection. Vicariously endowed with the power of the inspiring god, he wants to use this power to force goodness and charity on the people, who have long become indifferent. He causes the prisons to be opened, drives the stallkeepers from the church, and proclaims an uncompromising Christianity. The authorities are powerless, the rich see their privileges threatened, and the poor are cheated of their fun. All want to get rid of the inconvenient do-gooder, for goodness is an alarming element of revolt in our selfish world. The cardinal tries to urge a compromise on the ardent idealist; radical goodness, with its claim to be exclusive, total, and absolute, can be realized only by force, and thereby it betrays itself and turns into its own opposite. Hans's ideals not only bring the enmity of the whole town on him, but also lose him Christine, the duke's daughter, who loved the simpleton but recoils from the fanatic. Her brother Lothar admires Hans with romantic enthusiasm. When Hans loses courage in the face of the stake which the destructive crowd has prepared for him, Lothar kills him with an arrow. Bacchus is not to survive his redeeming action in an everyday compromise. Cardinal Zampi immediately realizes the dangers of this martyrdom and invents a pious lie to invalidate it. He announces that Hans had retracted his errors and submitted to the Church. The rebel is now sure of his burial place in consecrated earth, for his aim is destroyed. Hans succumbs as a necessary victim of order. The cardinal, who inwardly feels at one with the pure reformer, cannot look on people as human beings but merely as either members of the Church or godless. That is why he must demolish the messianic challenge of Bacchus, whose aim it had been to bring the redemption of goodness indiscriminately to a united community of all who had been separated from each other for centuries, to the nobility, the burghers, and the peasants, the pious and the heretics alike. The cardinal's way is, for Cocteau, the way of "hard goodness," which comes to terms with reality in order to be efficacious in it. In these terms he wants to "restore to God the intelligence which otherwise serves the devil."

THE EAGLE WITH TWO HEADS (also: *The Eagle Has Two Heads*) (*L'Aigle à deux têtes*). Romantic melodrama in three acts. Prose. First edition Paris 1946. First performance October 25, 1946, Lyons, Théâtre des Célestins. Translated by Ronald Duncan, London, Vision Press, 1948; by Carl Wildman for New York production, December 10, 1964, Royal Playhouse; included in *Five Plays*, New York, Hill & Wang, 1961. Time: the past. Place: the queen's bedroom and library at Krantz Castle in a mythical kingdom.

The story of the Empress Elizabeth of Austria is set in the picturesque environment of Bavarian King Ludwig's mountain castle and turned into a grand spectacle of virtuoso parts, pomp, melodramatic effects, political intrigue, and heightened passions. Cocteau develops the action from the tension between the historical facts and psychological motivation in the experience of the characters. His self-declared intention was to put two ideas on the stage, and out of their conflict to develop a situation in which these ideas should again become human. "A queen with anarchist views and an anarchist with monarchist leanings. . . . They evade their problems and become a problem themselves. They are seen as a constellation, or rather as a meteor which glows for a second and is extinguished at once."

Soon after her wedding, the queen has lost her husband through an assassination. Under the suspicious eyes of her mother-in-law, the archduchess, and under the tutelage of the court, headed by the all-powerful police minister Count von Foehn, she indulges her eccentric whims, travels about aimlessly, and shocks the etiquette-ridden court with the liberties she takes. During a stormy night the poet Stanislas, in full flight, breaks into the queen's bedroom. His rebellious pamphlets have long fascinated her, and in a sudden whim she hides him. His aim of saving the world by an assassination is as unrealistic and eccentric as the queen's desire to accept this death voluntarily for the sake of the ecstasy of a fateful crime. But these

two people who have so far stood merely for institutions are led back to
life through love. Stanislas persuades the queen to take the reins of government into her own hands. Foehn threatens the idealist with a trial
which would compromise the queen. Stanislas is so exasperated by the
feigned mockery of the queen, who thus sees herself cheated of her happiness, that he now carries out the planned assassination for reasons of personal jealousy and then swallows poison.

The play is a late offshoot of historical drama of the sensuous, high-flown,
illusionist kind.


## COWARD, Noel
(England, born 1899)


NUDE WITH VIOLIN. Farce in three acts. Prose. First edition London
1957. First performance November 7, 1956, London, Globe Theatre.
Time: the present. Place: Sorodin's studio.

Dislike of modern art is too popular a subject for the boulevard theater
to miss, and Noel Coward has concocted a farcical mixture out of its char-
latanism and some amorous frivolity. "Nude with Violin" is the last work
left by Paul Sorodin, the deceased abstract painter of world renown. The
family's joyous expectation of their inheritance is damped by the servant
Sebastian's information to the effect that the painter has bequeathed them
nothing but debts. Sorodin, it turns out, could not paint at all, and arranged for his pictures to be produced by whatever lady happened to rule
his heart at the moment. Princess Anya Pavlikov contributed the early
"Farouche" period and the dancer Cherry-May Waterton the "Circular"
period; the world of art has the Negro Obadiah Lewellyn to thank for the
"Jamaican" period. "Nude with Violin," the masterpiece of the "Neo-
Infantilism" period, is the result of the manservant's little son getting to
work with his paintbox. In order not to upset the well-oiled machinery
which keeps painters, critics, exhibitions, the bewildered public, and the
whole lucrative art world going, the art dealer Jacob Friedland doggedly
pays out enormous sums to keep the scandal quiet. And thus the world
may in all innocence go on enjoying modern art and its most famous
master, Sorodin.


QUADRILLE. Romantic comedy in three acts. Prose. First edition London 1952. First performance September 12, 1952, London, Phoenix
Theatre. Time: 1873–1874. Place: South of France and London.

This amorous game of musical chairs makes its points by playing off national and class differences against each other. The Marquess of Heronden elopes to the Riviera with his latest conquest, Charlotte. But this queen of his fickle heart, lured from her arch-bourgeois marriage with the American railroad potentate Diensen by aristocratic grandeur, insists with puritan lack of humor that the marquess is to lead her to the altar. Suddenly the idyll is disturbed; two persons arrive to make up the quadrille. The Marchioness of Heronden, armed with the cool ironic smile of a wife long used to forgiving escapades, and Diensen, a robust self-made man, fetch back their respective spouses. In the process they get to like each other so well that a year later they elope.

Less, perhaps, in the manner of a romance than of a novel, Coward this time tries to vary the boulevard situation by introducing a dose of sentimentality.


## CREIGHTON, Anthony
See OSBORNE, John


## CSOKOR, Franz Theodor
(Austria, born 1885)


CAESARS WITWE [Caesar's Widow]. Play in three acts and a prologue. Prose. Written 1952. Center play in the trilogy Olymp und Golgotha. First edition Vienna 1956. First performance May 3, 1955, Vienna, Akademietheater. Time: 43 B.C. to A.D. 9. Place: Rome.

Calpurnia, "Caesar's ashes," the widow of the murdered ruler, coldly disdains to take any notice of the worldwide struggle for Caesar's inheritance, of the efforts of Augustus to exploit the assassination as a welcome means of political pressure, or of the contorted pose of the victor as a second Caesar. Calpurnia and Augustus clash as opposites in a dialectical contest. Augustus ensures the continuance of his life's work by forcing personality into the forms of the system, even turning Caesar, the great individualist, into the institution of Caesarism. Calpurnia defends the value of the free individual and in her restless searching begins to incline toward Christianity, "toward something that would bind our fleeting being to the eternity in which we pass away, from which we come and which at the same time remains always about us. . . . And perhaps then even suffering would find a meaning, and death, and our blinded heaven with its moldering gods, and we would not then at the end have to gaze into the naked void with horror and disgust as I do now."

The raw material of the historical event is made clear by man's eternal challenge: he must have the courage of decision and prove his worth. This is a drama of ideas that, in Hebbel's sense, sets men and their actions in the twilight of a time of transition, so that even their errors and entanglements acquire meaning and justification as the expression of a fateful play of forces.

## CUMMINGS, Edward Estlin
(United States, 1894–1962)

ANTHROPOS, OR THE FUTURE OF ART. One-act play. Prose. First edition New York 1944. First performance 1960, New York. Time: imaginary future. Place: a cave.

Misgivings at the bombastic phrases of certain politicians and art critics and protest against mass suggestibility by catchwords lead Cummings to an explosive farce with prehistoric allusions.

Three "subhuman creatures," more animal than human, squat around the fire in their cave and try to think up an effective slogan by which to inspire the masses and "kid them along." At last they hit upon the conveniently ambiguous word "evolution" and solemnly announce it to the "muttering snarling grunting squeaking jabbering mob of hide-smothered subhuman dwarfs." The crowd accepts this new ideological drug with quick and simultaneous praise. In the meantime a naked man in the background, unnoticed by all, has painted a mammoth on the wall of the cave. When the theoreticians notice this manifestation of artistic independence, they are indignant, and their anger mounts when the artist dares to confront them with reality. He shows them a noisy steamshovel excavating in front of the cave, and approaches this novel "mammoth" with timid awe. Out of their depth, the subhumans return to their fire and their inexhaustible discussions.

SANTA CLAUS. A morality play in five scenes. Verse. First edition New York 1946. First performance 1960, New York. Time: not specified. Place: not specified.

An allegorical mystery play in lyrical verse confronts the excesses of hyper-civilization with the yearning for simple human values: "O, we are all so very full of knowing/ that we are empty: empty of understanding;/ . . . knowledge has taken love out of the world." Following Klages, the mind is seen as the soul's adversary and salvation lies in a sensuously vital existence close to nature.

Santa Claus, the jovial Father Christmas, sorrowfully tells Death his troubles: he wants to bring the gift of comprehension, but the contemporary world is interested only in science, in realistic knowledge that can be turned into hard cash. Santa Claus follows Death's advice: having exchanged clothes with Death, he goes off to sell the crowd shares in a fictitious "wheel-mine." Mass hunger for sensations makes the fraud so real to the crowd that Santa Claus is held responsible for a mine disaster. Genuine Death is lynched by the angry mob. Santa Claus and a woman are brought together by a child, and the woman thanks him "for making love remember me."

## D'ARCY, Margaretta
See ARDEN, John


## DELANEY, Shelagh
(England, born 1939)

A TASTE OF HONEY. Play in two acts. Prose. First edition London 1959. First performance May 27, 1958, Stratford, Royal Theatre. Time: the present. Place: a sordidly furnished flat in Salford, England.

This study of life in the slums is the extraordinarily mature first work of a self-taught young writer. Without any literary ambitions but with much human warmth, the nineteen-year-old playwright, once a cinema usher, describes her lightless world.
Teen-aged Jo is expecting a baby by a Negro sailor. Her mother Helen is chasing some new adventure and has left the girl alone and penniless in a shabby furnished flat. The homosexual art student Geoffrey befriends the deserted girl, hopefully makes baby clothes, and wants to look after her and marry her. This responsibility transforms his hitherto sterile existence; before he knew her, everything was all the same to him, the whole world seemed senseless—"but now . . ." Helen returns and breaks up the strange idyll. Geoffrey desolately returns to his empty life, and Jo is left to herself with her hate for the child that is to be born.


## DEVAL, Jacques
(J. Boularan, France, born 1894)

LA MANIÈRE FORTE [In the Strong Manner]. Comedy in three acts. Prose. First edition Paris 1953. First performance February 9, 1954, Paris, Théâtre de l'Athénée. Time: the present. Place: casino bar and Simone's bedroom.

In the sparkling fireworks of this play the class conflict is turned into a duel of love. At the roulette table and at parties, the young widow Simone is trying to forget the burdens of her wealth and beauty. She wants to get rid of her lover, the blasé bon vivant Tony; she has had enough of this exquisite "lobster," who makes her suffer but whom she still loves, and feels some "sardine" would be nice for a change. Any sardine will do, but the one she chooses happens to be the commonplace automobile dealer André. For weeks he has been making sheep's eyes at her from afar; in a sudden whim she asks the insignificant, slightly ridiculous little man to act as her latest conquest before the world, to arouse Tony's jealousy. The sardine discharges his task with all the riotous technical means of the theater, including surprise visits in the lady's bathroom, fits of fainting, a sham leap from the window, and an overdose of sleeping pills, not to mention a stuttering friend and an inept maid. With the help of explosively comic situations and bubbling and fluffy dialogue, the lobster is eventually shown up to be nothing but a self-satisfied professional charmer, and the way to a rosy future is open.

TONIGHT IN SAMARKAND (Ce Soir à Samarcande). Symbolic melodrama in three acts. Prose. First edition in Théâtre I, Paris 1951. First performance September 29, 1950, Paris, Théâtre de la Renaissance. Adapted by Lorenzo Semple, Jr., New York, French, 1956. Time: the present. Place: South of France and Le Havre.

Deval takes his tale about kismet and also his title from an oriental legend in which a vizier, afraid for his life, flees to distant Samarkand where he is overtaken by his fate.

The doom-dodger is the lady lion-tamer Nericia. She lives only for her cats, and is courted by the juggler Angelo Farinacci, the millionaire manufacturer Tabourier, and the magician Sourab Kayam. The latter looks into his crystal ball and foretells what will happen on the girl's next birthday. If she chooses Angelo, she will be betrayed; if Tabourier, she will lose her beloved cats. But in either case she will board the steamship "Hollandia," which will sink with all its passengers on her birthday. In an attempt to escape her fate, she marries the magician. Their happy marriage lasts only a few months, for he is arrested for counterfeiting that he had done some years before and takes poison. Nericia calmly books a passage on the "Hollandia" just a few hours before her birthday.

## DONLEAVY, James Patrick
(United States, born 1926)

FAIRY TALES OF NEW YORK. Play in four acts. Prose. Written 1960. First edition New York 1961. First performance December 6, 1960, London (Croydon), Pembroke Theatre-in-the-Round. Time: the present. Place: New York.

Social criticism is accentuated to the point of provocativeness, the provocative turns into paradox, but the paradox becomes conventional and subsides in the established techniques of the Theater of the Absurd. This is the inevitable course awaiting any individual's lifelong effort to hold his own in a standardized environment.
Cornelius Christ, who loafed through his student years, very nearly fails in his profession because of a trifling whim of his chief. He fails in his hobby as an amateur boxer because he allows himself to be knocked out just to be obliging. Society, too, ousts him disapprovingly when he puts into practice a modest individualism. Only extravagant eccentricity wins him the enthusiastic acclaim of New York.
With its fast-moving scenes in the style of cabaret sketches, this play seems to herald a new kind of sardonic mockery in the theater.

## DORST, Tankred
(Germany, born 1925)

FREIHEIT FÜR CLEMENS [Freedom for Clement]. Farce in one act. Prose. First edition Cologne 1962. First performance November 19, 1960, Bielefeld, Städtische Bühnen. Time: the present. Place: a prison cell.

Using a trick borrowed from cabaret, the author turns the theory that the individual is a result of his environment into an oppressive existential diagnosis. Life in prison finds its ultimate consequence in a view which sees the prison as life. Dorst explains: "The play was an attempt to shape an amorphous individual on the stage, in the course of the play, and in so doing gradually to delineate him more precisely: an artistic balancing act, a stage play above all, in which the dialogue was to keep the characters in proper proportion and equilibrium."
The prisoner Clemens, "a young man with a face of which there are thirteen to the dozen," is taken to his cell by the warder and introduced to his new life. This narrow world, which no longer has any outside, must be affirmed and accepted as final and unalterable. Clementine, the warder's

daughter, teaches Clemens a new way of walking calculated to fit his few steps of living space; he learns the only possible way of communication, knocking on the wall; he develops a feeling of being at home, and eventually a perverted ideal of freedom in hermetic isolation. When in the end the doors of the prison open, he stays on, contented and indifferent.

## DROZDOWSKI, Bohdan
(Poland, born 1936)

KLATKA CZYLI ZABAWA RODZINNA *[The Cage or the Family Game]*. Play in one act. Prose. First performance September 13, 1962, Nowa Huta, Teatr Ludowy. Time: the present. Place: room in Cyrillus's apartment in a Polish provincial town.

A "trial" play intended as social criticism is combined with a disturbingly paradoxical parable.
After many years of absence, Cousin Edward Bonk returns to his home town, full of self-assurance and confident of success. He calls on his poor relations. Suddenly the door is bolted. Uncle Cyrillus, the head of a clan of embittered failures, begins a merciless cross-examination: "We have summoned you here in order to cleanse you of the dirt in which you wallow." As a company clerk during the war, Cousin Edward kept out of the fighting, later denounced his friends and mistreated his wife. Edward, however, is a man of the world, and bribes his accusers with clothes, luxury goods, and lucrative jobs. Adam and Lucas compete for appointment as head of the state funeral institute. Anxious to get the better of his rival, Adam threatens Edward with a particularly scandalous revelation. Edward collapses with a heart attack, and Adam has to admit that he was only bluffing. Unctuously the family take leave of their victim: "take unto Yourself the soul of Edward Bonk and forgive him his sins on earth, for he was one of us and in no way different from us who are born in sin and die in sin."

KONDUKT *[The Funeral]*. Play in two acts. Prose. Written 1960–1961. First performance November 21, 1961, Zielona Gora, Teatr Ziemi Lubuskiej. Time: the present, evening and night. Place: a wood.

Life chains people to a senseless, sham task. The façade of human relationship crumbles in the penetrating light of an extreme situation, which is explored from the most divergent points of view.
Two young miners decide that despite every obstacle they will take the

body of their friend Maniek, killed in an accident, safely home to his
native village. In the middle of the wood the truck breaks down. Carrying
the coffin and the flower wreaths, the group stumble through the impenetrable darkness and lose their way. Against the background of this grotesquely macabre situation we are shown the most diverse variants of human shortcomings: vanity, irascibility, malice, petulance. The driver is
after the girl Magda, who has thumbed a lift with the funeral convoy;
she is trying to hide her pregnancy, but one of the party sneeringly reveals
it. An arrogant academic resents the colliers' rough ways. The party delegate is a weakling who can pursue his career, but is physically not up to
the exertions of this nocturnal march. Even the ideal image of the dead
man is shattered in the rebellion of his bearers, who find that their task is
more than they had bargained for. Eventually the local mayor reports that
Maniek had run away from home and if he returned, even dead, his wrathful father would at best bury him in the dungheap.
Although the details are realistic, in the livid atmosphere of unreality
they are distorted to the point of grotesque ambiguity.


## DUNCAN, Ronald Frederick Henry
(England, born 1914)


THE DEATH OF SATAN. Comedy in two acts. Free verse. First edition
London 1955. First performance August 5, 1954, Devon Festival of Arts,
Bideford, Palace Theatre. Time: the present. Place: Hell and Spain.

Shaw, Wilde, and Byron are having a good time in Hell playing cards and
exchanging witticisms. They carry on their earthly life in all its super-
ficiality, for "a man needs no other punishment than memory." Satan is a
spiteful parson; he is the only one who really suffers, because he cannot
mete out greater torments to his guests. Don Juan, accompanied by his
servant Catalion, returns to earth for one year in order to carry out psychological research for Satan on "why people don't suffer . . . in Hell any
more." He is out of his depth in twentieth-century Spain. The luxury
hotel "Don Juan" has been put up next to the statue of the Commandant.
There is nothing left for the seducer to do, for there is no virtue left, no
scruples, and therefore no sin. For the ladies, Don Juan is a pastime like
any other; the husbands treat him with indulgence and comprehension.
Donna Anna is represented in Marcia, the wife of an English novelist; she
has no soul, but gets pleasure flirting with Don Juan. Don Juan runs away,
back to Hell, now a place of relaxation for him. Having lost his last victim,
Satan dies.

A satire on society that juggles with literary allusions to make the point that there is no need for the devil once men make their own hell with loneliness, indifference, and material ambitions. The conversational tone and the poetic flights sometimes obtrude on each other, and the elements of literary caricature and morality play do not always mix.


STRATTON. Play in four acts and a prologue. Free verse. Music by Benjamin Britten. First edition London 1950. First performance October 31, 1949, Brighton, England, Theatre Royal. Time: the present. Place: the hall in Kirnstone Manor and Central Criminal Court, London.

Incest and murder, the ingredients of this family melodrama, are built into an archaic tragedy of fate. Man's sinfulness and longing for salvation merge in the hymn of *vanitas vanitatum:* "What a thing is man,/ Blessed with a spirit/ Damned with a nature/ His eyes seeking heaven/ Whilst his hands construct hell . . . He is both crucified/ And crucifier/Oh, Christ, may Thy Mercy/ Rain compassion on this desert that is man."
The barrister Sir Cory Stratton has a dreamlike vision in which he sees himself strangling his wife Maria. Uneasiness and exaggerated self-righteousness drive him into aggressiveness. He accepts an appointment as judge in the Central Criminal Court and finds self-confirmation in a controversial death sentence. This blood guilt is a repetition of a centuries-old event in Stratton history: One Cory Stratton condemned his own king to death and as a reward was given the family estate of Kirnstone Manor by the new ruler, Cromwell. But once a judge, Stratton longs to be back in his old practice which he had turned over to his son Cory. The father thrusts his son aside and eventually shoots him to gain possession of his son's wife Katherine. Experienced lawyer that he is, he manages to construct evidence of suicide. Katherine sets a trap to provoke a confession from him. Maria is blinded by fear of the truth: "What can a woman do/ But stare at the ashes of her life/ Remembering the flames that were." She has forgiven Stratton, but his self-righteousness founders on her comprehensive gentleness and he strangles her in an act of expiation and submission: "What a thing is man,/ Destroying what he loves,/ Desiring what he hates . . . His life is all despair/ For what is man but pride?"
Like Eliot, Duncan seeks out the mystery in ordinary life. Verse, choric elements, and symbolic language create a metaphysical atmosphere.

## DURAS, Marguerite
(France, born 1914)

DAYS IN THE TREES (Des Journées entières dans les arbres). Play in three acts. Prose. First published in L'Avant-Scène, No. 348–349, January 1966. First performance December 1, 1965, Paris, Odéon. Translated by Barbara Bray and Sonia Orwell, in Three Plays, London, Calder & Boyars, 1967. Time: the present. Place: Paris.

The play's theme, the oppressive awareness of futility and frustration— "ultimately it all comes to the same thing, to work, or not to work. That's how one starts, and then one gets used to it . . . one can't do without it anymore."—determines its structure. People live together in a void and escape into illusions, which merely prove to be another dimension of alienation.

Unexpectedly, Mother arrives from overseas for a short visit with her son in Paris. She is an oppressively comic fossil restlessly driven by her appetite for life, grotesquely overladen with gold trinkets and perpetually hungry. The son is a gigolo living in poverty and seeking consolation for his unfulfilled hopes in grandiloquent talk about his "free existence." His life is shared by the barmaid Marcelle, a lachrymose girl of animal-like inertia, whom he keeps driving away and then using again, only to send her away once more. The mother's visit alters nothing. What brings her to her son is not mother love, but the self-tormenting triumph of being the sole origin of his failure and thus bequeathing an irrevocable provocation to the orderly world of philistines. In boundless motherly pride she brought up her son as a weakling. There were to be no exertions or duties for him. He spends his "days in the trees, as though there were nothing but birds in the world." Mother, too, is a prisoner of her illusions. For a few hours she plays the part of a rich, spoiled factory owner. But her property in a former colony has long been expropriated. She herself is under the domination of her unloved daughter Mimi, an aging spinster from whom she secretly steals to supplement her pocket money. Every one of the characters is alone, exhausted, and without consolation.

With dreamlike assurance Duras places the accents somewhere between psychological study and absurd farce. Behind the clichés of conversation and attitudes she makes us aware of the vibrations of an unspoken sadness, a lament for the peaceful life which each withholds from the others.

THE SQUARE (Le Square). Play in three scenes. Prose. First edition Paris 1955. First performance of an abridged version, 1957, Paris, Studio des Champs-Elysées; of the full version January 15, 1965, Toulouse, Théâtre

Daniel-Sorano. Translated by Sonia Pitt-Rivers and Irina Morduch, New York, Grove Press, 1959, and by Barbara Bray and Sonia Orwell, in *Three Plays,* London, Calder & Boyars, 1967. Time: the present, late afternoon in spring. Place: a square in Paris.

Opportunities and memories, expectations and disappointments ("One thinks nothing has begun as yet, and everything has already happened") are suggested by the spring twilight in the square. Formally, the improvisation is presented in two monologues; contrasting strains of consciousness in the major and minor key are superimposed in many layers, vibrate in harmony, question and answer each other. But no saving understanding ever comes. All that reaches from one to the other is a faint resonance, ambiguous and misleading, creating transitory moments of light or darkness—music of the soul in ultimate inwardness.

A young maid in charge of her employers' child in the square, and an elderly peddler, both insignificant and unimportant people, fall into a conversation which "commits no one to anything." The girl is consumed by vague expectations in which time runs by. She loathes having to spend her life in the kitchen, torments herself with the vexations of her daily round, and passively waits for her servant's existence to come to an end. She is convinced that the moment must come when the sense and *raison d'être* of her life will find fulfillment. Her whole life is to be a bitter advance payment for this unswerving hope. For the utter joylessness of her youth and the loathsomeness of the present can be borne only as a surety for that "later" when real life is to begin. The gentleman next to her is perplexed, but tries to follow these emotions. He is a small peddler who has spent his life wandering from place to place. He is not worried by any expectations, for he always feels brimful with the present. In his wandering, the unknown becomes familiar to him and the familiar always again excitingly unknown. "There are people who get so much pleasure out of life itself that they don't need to hope for anything else." The two lonely strangers try to achieve mutual understanding for the length of an evening hour. But all the girl can see in the peddler's existence is depressing poverty, and her zestful partner cannot understand the groundless dejection of her youth. They part disappointed, both hopelessly imprisoned in their own lives. Perhaps they will meet again some time; it remains uncertain whether this "perhaps" is resignation or hope: "here we all are, after all. It's not that one was so anxious to get into this life, but once one's here, one's got to live. There's nothing else to do."

THE VIADUCTS OF SEINE-ET-OISE (*Les Viaducs de la Seine-et-Oise*). Play in two acts. Prose. First edition Paris 1960. First performance May 8, 1960, Marseille, Théâtre Quotidien. Translated by Barbara Bray and

Sonia Orwell, in *Three Plays,* London, Calder & Boyars, 1967. Time: 1954. Place: Epinay-sur-Orge, a small town in the Département of Seine-et-Oise, France.

A criminal case is the catalyst of a diffused variety of sentiments, ideas, dreams, and longings, of man's resignation in the face of life's incomprehensibility and contradictoriness: "One must not ask too much of people. It is impossible simultaneously to have understood, not to understand any more and still to understand what one understands no longer. Otherwise there would be no problem." The play is prefaced by a bit of impersonal information: All over France parts of a female corpse were discovered in goods wagons, all of which had passed under the viaduct of Epinay-sur-Orge. As a result a harmless married couple of railroad pensioners living nearby were found guilty of the crime of killing their deaf-mute niece, who had run the household for twenty-seven years, and bestially cutting up the corpse. All attempts during the trial to discover a motive for the crime failed; the man was condemned to death, the woman to life imprisonment. Marguerite Duras dissects this occurrence with all her means of sensitive language and poetic lucidity.

A week after the crime, Claire and Marcel try to come to terms with their senseless deed. Trapped in memories of missed opportunities and deluded hopes, the aged couple were driven by an urge for reality, for something unalterable: "There it is. We've got ourselves into a fine mess. A foul crime. . . . So now we can rest assured. We know where we are . . . Think that we'll never again have to become something other than we are! What an event! . . . At first, you understand, it was an amazement. And then later, very soon after, it was calm. But calm of a peculiar kind. A tiring rest. Since then I'm tired. That's how it is." In a bar, where others crave sensation and gossip, the couple probe yet more deeply into the buried understrata of consciousness. As in a dream, as under compulsion, they talk of their niece. They were increasingly driven to distraction by the deaf-mute's primitive innocence, the eeriness of her self-sufficient, enclosed, inaccessible world. Her exasperatingly strong passive equanimity fanned the hatred of the old couple, driven by their moods and restlessness, until that hatred found an outlet in the murder. The couple of lovers in the corner of the bar prove to be a police trap; the man is a detective and proceeds with their arrest. The old people are relieved and calm, only just a little sad that the lovers they met during their last hours together were a fraud. "There would be much more to say, things more or less profound, but all of them, after all, have been more or less said already."

# DURAS, Marguerite, and LORD, James

LA BÊTE DANS LA JUNGLE [The Beast in the Jungle]. Play in six scenes. After the short story "The Beast in the Jungle" by Henry James. Prose. First performance September 11, 1962, Paris, Théâtre de l'Athénée. Time: first half of the twentieth century. Place: England.

A wistful play about missed opportunities in love and life dissolves the present in expectations, memories, and hopes; the six scenes are each punctuated by the passage of years.

At a party at Weatherend House, John Marcher meets young Catherine, the owner's niece. They remember having met some years earlier, in Italy. On that occasion John had told her that he had always had a deep sense of being kept for something rare and strange, possibly prodigious and terrible: something was to happen to him and perhaps overwhelm him. Now he is living in feverish apprehension of this event that is to give meaning and justification to his life: "After all these years I am almost certain that what is to come to me really exists, that it lies in wait for me, amid the twists and the turns of the months and the years, like a crouching beast in the jungle. It signifies little whether the crouching beast is destined to slay me or to be slain." This confession makes Catherine his accomplice. With her secret love for John she accompanies him through his life, through the doubts and the enigma of that promised instant which will never happen. For both of them this gentle play with possibilities is a dream to help them over their unfulfilled life. Their fear of facing the reality of their longing drives them into trifling inessentials: "The appearance of things is always deceptive, but I believe that in the long run it comes to replace the real truth." The years go by. Wistful birthday celebrations, the setting of the successive scenes, are the only consolation Catherine gets for her wasted youth and happiness. Resigned, she eventually dies, and John, so many years older now, begins to wonder whether his ceaseless search for the great event, his lifelong uncertainty about himself, was not precisely the saving grace of his existence. Only at her grave does John at last take stock of the "jungle of his life" and realize what he has missed. Grief for happiness never experienced and now irretrievably lost overcomes him; this is the occurrence uniquely destined for him which he has feared all his life.

The one essentially dramatic event in John's life, the transition from reflection to the experience of suffering, is presented in the impersonal words of the epilogue. The artificial means of this dramatized short story correspond to the self-deception of lifelong, narcissistic introspection.

## DURRELL, Lawrence
(Ireland, born 1912)

AN IRISH FAUSTUS. A morality play in nine scenes. Verse. Written 1963. First edition London 1963. First performance December 18, 1963, Hamburg, Deutsches Schauspielhaus. Time: the Middle Ages. Place: Ireland.

Durrell's Irish Faustus combines within himself the modern nuclear physicist's qualms of conscience and the alchemist's entanglement in belief in demonic spirits and pacts with the devil.

Dr. Faustus engages in scientific research not for its own sake and not to gain fame for himself, but in order to satisfy his yearning for a deeper, more immediate understanding of the world. By the process of gaining more and more knowledge, the seeker of knowledge himself is purified. In this interpretation the old alchemist's dream of transmuting base substances into pure gold becomes a profound, metaphysical symbol. Faustus possesses a ring of alchemist's gold, which his teacher Tremethius once had to make at King Eric's command. Like the ring of the Nibelungs, it was created solely to satisfy the lust for power, is indestructible, and is endowed with fabulous powers. Its possession confers dominion over the earth and the underworld. Faustus wants to escape this temptation of atomic destructiveness and hides the ring. But Queen Katherine discovers the secret and gets hold of the ring with the intention of bringing back to life her deceased husband Eric, now a haunted vampire between life and death. The suspension of the law of nature for the sake of a selfish, purely sensual passion would destroy the scale of values and lead to universal chaos. Faustus recovers the ring. He causes the vampire to be killed and banishes him finally into the realm of the dead. But now Faustus himself is faced with a hard decision. Mephisto, his second self, made up of intellect alone, tries to tempt him with power. As in Werfel's "mirror man," the negative stratum of the ego becomes man's dialectical counterpart. Mephisto tries to persuade Faustus to create a paradise of earthly bliss with the help of the ring, and to use his power in a purely materialistic manner. Faustus withstands this temptation, too, and decides to melt down the ring in the fires of hell. Of his own free will he undertakes his journey into hell, "down to the slag heaps of nature's inmost processes." The sight of boundless horror, of utter despair, makes a new and purer man of Faustus. He returns to earth aged by decades, but full of new energy and confidence. He looks for a new meaning to life in the wilderness with the hermit Matthew. But Faustus is not to be granted a life of solitary contemplation nor the peace and guiltlessness of an observer. Mephisto, his eternal adversary in creative unrest born of yearning and imperfection, remains an inseparable part of his nature. Faustus will set forth into the world again in search of new knowledge and new ventures, and he will know that this also means error and guilt. He accepts this striving for knowledge, where every answer poses a new question and existence is no definite possession but an ever-renewed task: "And where faith is not deep enough to comprehend our sciences/ Nor doubt wide enough to guide us back to stillness? What?/ . . . Yet even death is a becoming . . . In dreams only now reside these ever loved realities."

A somber ballad, full of misty ghosts and Celtic rites, vampires, and conjurations of the dead. Delight in historical and romantic props seems deliberately to displace the spiritual problems.


SAPPHO. A play in verse. Written 1947. First edition London 1950. First performance November 21, 1959, Hamburg, Deutsches Schauspielhaus. Time: seventh century B.C. Place: Lesbos and an unnamed island.

Sappho is shown not as an unworldly dreamer, dwelling idyllically in the beauty of sound, but as a struggling and erring woman, caught up in political currents and suffering from her vocation. She has reached her prime as a mature woman, is occasionally given to stuttering, celebrated as a poet, and respected as a wife and mother. Her husband Kreon is a busy and restless man and gives her complete personal freedom. Her friend, General Pittakos, conducts a war in foreign lands. As for her two children, Sappho feels them "always like/ Small, perfectly composed criticisms of me." Hers is a dull life, day in day out without a wish or purpose, and she is weary and apathetic about it: "towards the ending of your element,/ The summer, lovely, famous and discontented." She meets Phaon, twin brother to Pittakos, a man who of his own free will left the carefree life of the privileged to seek happiness and contentment as a poor spongediver. Sappho has so far given herself to the eager energy of the general; she is now spellbound by his brother's renunciation of wealth. Afflicted by leprosy, Phaon had long ago fled to a lonely island, where in many years of silent self-examination he found his true self. Only one brief night of communion is granted the lovers. Then Phaon returns to his solitude, for he sees that the woman he loves is destined to become a tool in the plans of the powerful. Kreon and Pittakos want to gain possession of the island, the merchant by means of titles recovered from the sea, and the general with the help of his victorious army. Sappho shrinks from so much purposefulness: "Never to question? Always to act?" The pragmatist has his answer ready: "Can we change, really change, anything, or alter/ Any part of the world for the better . . . They are both useless/ In the face of this eternal refraction/ Of the thinking mind touching reality." A portentous oracle drives Kreon and Sappho into exile. Pittakos is elected tyrant, keeps Sappho's children as hostages, and becomes the cause of her son's death. The grief-stricken mother now sets out to destroy the man she once loved, in a battle lasting many years and conducted with every means of intrigue and violence. At the end of her life Sappho has won. Pittakos is destroyed. Instead of song and poetry she now spreads terror, a burnt-out Medea who has lost herself in an ecstasy of destruction.

## DÜRRENMATT, Friedrich
(Switzerland, born 1921)

AN ANGEL COMES TO BABYLON (*Ein Engel kommt nach Babylon*). A fragmentary comedy in one act. Prose. Written 1948–1953. First edition Zürich 1954. First performance December 22, 1953, Munich Kammerspiele; second version April 6, 1957, Göttingen, Deutsches Theater. English version in *Four Plays,* translated by Gerhard Nellhaus et al., New York, Grove Press, 1965, and London, Cape, 1964. Time: mythical prehistoric. Place: Babylon.

A fairy tale of the king and the beggar is made the vehicle of a profound interpretation of the world, in which the beggar stands as the opposite of officialdom, administration, and standardization. The beggar alone is still free for the adventure called life. Since for him the whole of life is an act of receiving the unexpected gift of the moment, he never succumbs to the domination of possession. Kurrubi, the young girl made by God's hand in the image of pure loveliness, is destined for the poorest among men and is taken to the earth by an angel. Here she finds herself between two irreconcilable opponents: Nebuchadnezzar, the King, and Akki, the Beggar. Both want, after their own fashion, to make men happy. The king's way is to eliminate the beggars and appoint them to pensionable jobs as tax collectors. Akki's begging relieves the rich of their superfluity, and he then throws his booty into the sea to preserve the world's frugality and contentment. With the crumbs he quickly feeds a few starving poets. Nebuchadnezzar is locked with his predecessor Nimrod in a millennial struggle for power, which is never settled other than provisionally; in continuous alternation, one is always the footstool of the other. Just now, Nebuchadnezzar has reconquered the throne, and he arranges a beggars' contest in an attempt to convince Akki of the senselessness of his outdated profession. The king is the loser in this tricky dispute and—as the poorest of the poor— is awarded Kurrubi. The girl loves him as an unsuccessful beggar, and thereby so wounds the vanity of the ruler that he cedes God's gift to Akki.

The persistent beggar escapes execution only by bribing the bibliophile hangman with a second-hand rarity and taking over the bloody trade himself. The king wants to share his life with Kurrubi, the whole population longs for this heavenly gift, but nobody is prepared to give up power and possessions and to become the poorest of the poor, to whom alone God's grace is granted. And thus, according to the people's will, Kurrubi is once more given over to the poorest, the most miserable of men—the hangman Akki. He is the only person to accept the girl not as an uncontestable property, but as a promise: "I have no right to you. I got you in exchange accidentally, a piece of heaven stuck to me, only a thread of His grace, weightless and gay, and now a gust of wind carries you away." Nebuchadnezzar, who has sacrificed happiness and the peace of his soul for his kingship, in presumptuous revolt commands the building of the tower of Babel. Human self-assertion is to invalidate heaven. Akki flees with Kurrubi from this world of arrogance toward a new land of daring and decision, temptation and self-conquest.

CONVERSATION AT NIGHT WITH A DESPISED MAN *(Nächtliches Gespräch mit einem verachteten Menschen).* A course for contemporaries in one act. Prose. Written 1952 as a radio play. First edition Zürich 1957. Translated by Robert David MacDonald, produced July 19, 1966 by the Watford Civic Trust at the Palace, Watford, England. Time: the present. Place: the writer's room.

Man's fate is reduced to two contrasting positions, those of executioner and victim. At night a respected writer is awaiting the murderer whom the state is employing to get rid of him as a now undesirable citizen. The executioner climbs in through the window. His destined victim is in despair. He had hoped for an opponent with whom a struggle would have been worthwhile, a despot whom his innocent death would have put in the wrong; the person he actually meets is a nondescript odd-job man of an anonymous system who kills because it is part of his duty and because in return he will one day contentedly draw his pension. Once the compelling sequence of criminal guilt and expiatory justice has given place to general arbitrariness, the executioner comes to be a mere function, signifying nothing. "The higher lives on power borrowed from the lower, and vice versa, an obscure system of power and fear, of greed and shame that encompasses all and finally generates an executioner who is more feared than I am, namely, tyranny that continually drives new masses into the endless lines of its slaughter-houses, meaningless because it changes nothing, but only destroys, for one deed of violence begets another, one tyranny another, again and again, for ever and ever, like the plunging spirals of hell!" The conversation, inconclusive and meditative, turns to Dürren-matt's favorite paradox when finally the executioner consoles his victim before the mortal blow: "It's a victory greater than the victory of the mighty when a man in the hour of his unjust death puts aside his pride and fear, and even his rights, in order to die as children die, without cursing the world. The gentle death of the humble, their peace, which en-folded even me like a prayer, the enormity of their death which was against all reason, these things, which are nothing in the eyes of the world but laughter, nay, less, a mere shrug of the shoulders, all these reveal the im-potence of the unjust, the insubstantiality of death and the reality of the truth, about which I can do nothing, which no hangman's assistant can seize and no prison contain, of which I know nothing except that it *is*, for every man of violence is shut up in the dark, windowless dungeon of himself."

FRANK DER FÜNFTE *[Frank the Fifth]*. The opera of a private bank in fifteen numbers. Prose and lyrics. Music by Paul Burkhard. Written 1959. First edition Zürich 1960. First performance March 19, 1959, Zürich, Schauspielhaus. Time: the present. Place: a town, possibly Zürich, in Switzerland.

This play is a merciless, bitter, grotesque satire on the dictatorship of money. All the characters are like stylized puppets and come alive only in their relationship to money. The style of the *Threepenny Opera* and of *The Rise and Fall of the Town of Mahagonny* is here developed further on a more intimate scale. It is a style that does not attempt mass effects, is of posterlike simplicity; displays of headlines and strong lyrics are set apart from the action. Dürrenmatt defines the piece as "not a work of economics (for that it would be too naive and superficial), but a study of an invented model . . . The value of a play lies in the number of problems it poses, not in its singleness of meaning."

Päuli Neukomm, a locksmith, and Heini Zurmühl are planning a bank robbery. Frank V, the ruler of the last private bank, and scion of a dy-nasty of money despots, cannot bear to look on while the boys get them-selves into jail through their reckless procedure, since their talent for illegality could, with a little discipline, be developed much more profit-ably. The director decides to employ them in his own bank: "the stock exchange will train you, cash will toughen you, capital will educate you." The old-established credit institute has taken its obligation to make a profit so seriously that it has naturally had to develop into a gangster organization: "It's he who has who's got to steal,/ It's he who's rich who has to squeal." The business principle strictly followed is that no honest deal must ever be concluded, and money once paid in should never be paid out again. Clients who are so inconsiderate as to insist on their rights come to a sudden end, as do inquisitive business analysts. At the beginning of his banking career Heini has the honor to be entrusted with an important though passive assignment: he is killed. With due ceremony his corpse is buried as that of Frank V at the bank's private cemetery, for the director, a mass murderer and an enthusiast of the poet Mörike prefers to disappear from the public eye and enjoy the fruits of his crimes in peaceful anonymity. Quite incidentally a minor insurance swindle of some three hundred thousand people comes to light. The bank at this period of "the purest and most ruthless honesty" is facing bankruptcy. The most reliable schemes fail and finally the employees have to sacrifice their savings in order to pay off an unknown blackmailer. Suspicion and discord break out among the business partners. The senior clerk Böckmann is so slow in dying of stomach cancer that he has to be assisted with a small injection, in order to get hold of his property. Frieda Fürst, the permanent fiancée of Egli, the chief of personnel, has chalked up outstanding successes in big business as a call girl, but is waning as an asset as the years go by. Egli, who has postponed the delights of marriage and children for thirty-two years in order to earn still more money, has to stand by helplessly while Frieda is liquidated in the blood-splashed cellar. The remaining well-off members of the bank are continually decimated by fatal accidents or vanish mysteriously. Frank and his wife Ottilie justify themselves with their children Herbert and Franziska, who are being brought up to an honorable existence in high-class boarding schools and have no suspicion of their parents' double life. Then Herbert makes himself known as the blackmailer who wants to acquire possession of the bank—"the only law is that there is none"—and Franziska is the newly appointed call girl— "take cash for this amusement,/ for it keeps you supple to be a pro." Herbert has his father strangled in the strong room, and, as Frank VI, purposefully takes over the direction of the bank. For a few years the public, which has become distrustful, must be lulled with honesty; after that he will apply new ideas to the old jobs.

The younger generation does not take the Fortinbras attitude, always so welcome in the theater because it provides a prefabricated guarantee of purity and idealism. Injustice triumphs, but it is an honest injustice, hard toward itself. Frank VI will not dream as his father did of a sunny garden arbor in which he, a respectable man, will bring up his children on quotations from the classics. Frank V foundered not because of what he did, but because of the fissure in himself, his insincerity. Dürrenmatt is forced to the bitter, challenging conclusions that "In stinking mercy we're all frozen hard,/ the penalties neglected, courts ignored,/ for justice never could be made to pay."

HERCULES AND THE AUGEAN STABLES *(Herkules und der Stall des Augias)*. Comedy in fifteen scenes. Prose. Written 1954 as a radio play. First edition Zürich 1963. First stage performance March 20, 1963, Zürich, Schauspielhaus. Translated by Alexander Gross, produced March 19, 1966 Ealing, England, Quester's Theatre. Time: mythical. Place: Greece.

Dürrenmatt uses the methods of the cabaret to bring on the twilight of the heroes. On one side is the nation that has found its home and security in filth, and on the other the hero who is to provide a moral alibi but is not allowed to change the world.
Heroic deeds have become unprofitable. In performing them Hercules is barely able to cover his expenses, creditors pursue him, and his house in Thebes is swallowed up in his bankruptcy. So the hero has to put up with the evil-smelling job of cleaning stables for King Augeas. At first the hero's rage at the suggestion costs his secretary Polybius a few broken ribs. But then his mistress Deianeira quietly but firmly takes him to Elis, the stock-raising paradise, "all muck and manure." The country lies buried under mountains of dung. Augeas is not so much a king as the most influential peasant who presides over the national council from a milking stool in the stables. Hercules sets to work with a will and plans to wash all the dirt into the sea by diverting a couple of rivers. But first he has to get the proper permits—from the water board, the aliens' office, the engineering office, the labor office, and the manure office. The Interim Commission for Cleansing Affairs intervenes and a countercommission, whose task it is to study the repercussions of a thorough-going demanuring on the country's economy, is repeatedly adjourned. Hungry and unemployed, Hercules spends month after month with Deianeira on a bare mountain. Even his attempt to put on an act as an athlete in the national circus of Elis fails. With nothing accomplished, Hercules sets out for his next heroic deed, killing the cannibal birds of Lake Stymphalis. Deianeira, who had been ready to marry Phyleus, the king's son, goes with him. An improvised interlude gives a glimpse of the future: young Phyleus falls in a duel with Hercules. The hero is killed by the poisoned shirt of Nessus with which Deianeira hopes to win back his love.
The play is a satire on bureaucracy run wild, all too lightly veiled in its antique costume.


THE MARRIAGE OF MR. MISSISSIPPI (also: *Fools Are Passing Through*) *(Die Ehe des Herrn Mississippi)*. Comedy in two parts. Prose. Written 1950. So far three versions (1957, 1964). First edition Zürich 1952. First performance March 26, 1952, Munich, Kammerspiele. English version in *Four Plays,* translated by Gerhard Nellhaus et al., New York, Grove Press,

1965, and London, Cape, 1964. Time: the present. Place: "a room in late middle-class ostentation and transience, which should smell to high heaven."

This is a dance of death of the ideologies which, since the beginning of time, have disputed for woman, that object of desire, that unpredictable, fickle, delightful piece of life. It is a clash not between human beings, but between unrestrained doctrines. Liberty, humanity, man's free will are dissolved in a fixed-star universe of theses and antitheses. With his tongue in his cheek, Dürrenmatt places these philosophical question marks in the setting of a thriller that wallows in a surfeit of murder until it boils over into farce. In this world, constructions, catchwords, and principles have taken over from reality. By slight of hand, murder is turned into a heroic deed, criminals into men of principle.

"For therapeutic reasons" Dürrenmatt puts the final scene at the beginning: Saint-Claude, a life-long champion of world revolution, is shot by three men with red armbands. Having been so obliging as to die, he goes on, as a commentator, to introduce the beginning of the story. The public prosecutor Florestan Mississippi, former doorman of a brothel, is a fanatic for justice of the merciless, Old Testament cast: "The course of history, which has lost the law and won a freedom which cannot for a second be morally justified, must be reversed." He and the entrancing Anastasia, a woman of the world, have got rid of their spouses by poison and now marry as a mutual punishment. Mississippi doggedly persists in his self-righteousness: "What you have done out of an appalling instinct, I did out of moral insight. You have slaughtered your husband, I have executed my wife." The new marriage stimulates him to no less than 350 death sentences, embellished by the graceful presence of Anastasia who, as the "Angel of the Prisons," always has to attend the execution. At some stage the minister of justice, Diego, feels that Mississippi's bloodthirsty purge has gone far enough: "As Minister of Justice it is my duty to assess justice according to what is politically tolerable. Justice is a convention." The public prosecutor makes a fatal mistake; he believes in himself and in his principles even when the latter are no longer expedient. Hence he is locked up in a lunatic asylum. Saint-Claude, the reformer who has joined the Communists, is equally true to himself which leads to his downfall. The Moscow rulers find him inconvenient and have him liquidated. Count Bodo von Übellohe is the only person among these men obsessed with ideologies who has kept himself free for the enterprise of being human, who "risked the adventure of love . . . and was made a fool by love." He, too, fails to win Anastasia, but at least he is the only one to survive. He is simply not important enough to be persecuted. The strange married couple poison each other, and Diego emerges triumphant over this twilight of idolatries. He who, "wanting power and nothing but power, embraced the world" has always been able to revise his opinions and adapt himself at the proper time. In this sort of justice, judge and convict, murderer and victim are only masks worn alternately by the same participants. The chorus of the dead laments this subjection to eternal execution: "An eternal comedy to give brilliance to His glory, fed by our impotence."

THE METEOR *(Der Meteor)*. Comedy in two acts. Prose. First edition Zürich 1966. First performance January 20, 1966, Zürich, Schauspielhaus. Translated by James Kirkup, produced July 28, 1966, London, Aldwych Theatre. Time: the present. Place: a painter's studio.

The problems of religious faith are dramatized with the help of the striking effect of paradox. That a man is resurrected after death is a challenging paradox and at the same time a miracle that lays claim to each individual's faith and puts it to the test.

Schwitter rises from the dead but no longer believes in eternal life, and this turns his resurrection into ceaseless dying, into a death forever retracted and never mastered. In this play Kierkegaard's definition of life's predicament as a "sickness unto death" is taken to its ultimate conclusion. The occasion for Dürrenmatt's macabre and yet merry paradoxes is the myth of the immortality of famous writers as exploited for publicity by the wily tribe of publishers, critics, and literary executors.

Applying the notion of a writer's immortality in the literal sense, Dürrenmatt has Schwitter, a Nobel Prize winner in literature, jump up from his bier again and again, in defiance of all medical beliefs, until his irrepressible vitality dispatches all the others into the hereafter. For months the death of the famous writer has been anticipated in news bulletins and headlines. Officially he is already declared dead on the highest medical authority; in these circumstances he escapes from the luxury clinic into the shabby attic where once, as a starving unknown, he dedicated himself to art. In order to thwart the expectations of his heir, his altogether incompetent son Jochen, he stuffs his whole fortune—two suitcases full of bank notes—into the stove and burns it. Determined to die, Schwitter gets hold of the wife of the host, the painter Nyffenschwander, and startles the "great Muheim" out of his bourgeois smugness. While Schwitter dies again, only to come to life once more among the wreaths and obituary notices, the painter is killed by Muheim in a fit of jealousy, Schwitter's call-girl wife takes poison, and her mother, a lavatory attendant and brothel keeper, sinks into the grave; so does Pastor Lutz. The Salvation

Situations are repeated and details grotesquely overexposed, and it all adds up not so much to a spiritual message as to mere stage entertainment.

ONE AUTUMN EVENING *Abendstunde im Spätherbst)* (also: *Herr Korbes empfängt).* [*Mr. Korbes Receives*] Utopian comedy in one act. Prose. Written 1956 as a radio play; adapted for the stage 1959. First edition Zürich 1959. First performance November 17, 1959, Berlin, Theater am Kurfürstendamm. English version produced at the Open Space Theatre Club, London, November 1968. Time: about 1969. Place: a hotel apartment.

In this theatrical aphorism on the modern bestseller racket, Dürrenmatt is enigmatic, macabre, and fiendishly clever. The original conception as a radio play has been maintained almost unchanged.

Lightly sardonic, the author introduces himself and thus provides the framework. He is the famous and notorious writer Maximilian Friedrich Korbes, Nobel Prize winner and idol of his times. In his successful novels he has discovered the greatness and beauty of murder and described them with thrilling suggestiveness to the delight of the whole world. A timid visitor pushes his way in to see the literary hero. He is Fürchtegott Hofer from Ennetwyl, near Horck, formerly a bookkeeper and now a private detective. Hesitantly he begins to prove that Horbes himself has actually committed all the murders he so fascinatingly described in his twenty-two novels. The proof is so conclusive that Korbes confesses his double life as a professional writer who became a professional criminal. When the visitor threatens court action and combines a touch of blackmail with his sense of justice, all Korbes can do is to burst out laughing. Respectable people do not want him to be punished, all they want is that he keep up the glittering perversity of his crimes. Everyone who has hitherto discovered the truth is locked up in a lunatic asylum. "True literature is not concerned with literature, its business is to satisfy people. They don't hanker for new forms, or for linguistic experiments, least of all for knowledge. They hanker for a life that doesn't need hope, because there is no hope any more, for a life rich in fulfillment and tension, such as can be supplied not by reality in the machine world of the masses, but only by art. Literature has become a drug which takes the place of a life that is no longer possible." The writer now playfully and gracefully exchanges his pen for a revolver. The visitor is to provide the material for a radio play by becoming the twenty-third victim. Terrified, Hofer jumps out of the window and the hotel manager comes in to apologize to his distinguished guest for the intrusion of this obvious lunatic.

THE PHYSICISTS *(Die Physiker)*. Comedy in two acts. Prose. Written 1961. First edition Zürich 1962. First performance February 21, 1962, Zürich, Schauspielhaus. Translated by James Kirkup, *Evergreen Review,* 1963, and in *Four Plays,* translated by Gerhard Nellhaus *et al.,* New York, Grove Press 1965 and London, Cape, 1954. Time: the present. Place: reception room in a mental institution.

When the world in its obsession with progress has turned into a madhouse, the only man who really knows must voluntarily take refuge in the security of a lunatic asylum: "Only in the lunatic asylum are we still free. Only in the lunatic asylum are we still allowed to think. In freedom our ideas are dynamite."
The physicist Moebius has worked out a strategically decisive formula of destruction and has buried his responsibility both as man and scientist in a mental institution. He pretends to see visions in which King Solomon implores the world to desist from its self-destruction. Two emissaries of rival world powers also sham madness and, pretending to be Einstein and Newton, have entered the same institution to keep the peerless scientist Moebius under continuous observation. Each of them has already had to strangle a nurse in order to avoid exposure. Moebius follows this sinister precedent more for reasons of analogy than of logical necessity, and kills the nurse Monika who loves him. The girl wanted to fight for their joint future, but Moebius fears a return to life. To leave would only mean for him a worse imprisonment in camps of silence and secret laboratories. The three physicists decide to stay in the institution with their feigned madness: "We have reached the end of our road. . . . Our science has become terrible, our research dangerous, our knowledge lethal. There is nothing left to us physicists except to capitulate to reality. Reality is not up to us. It founders on us. We must take back our knowledge, and I have taken it back." The owner of the institution, the misshapen, old-maidish Dr. von Zahnd, has long seen through the game of her strange patients, has stolen the decisive formula and handed it over to a world-dominating trust. She, the only true lunatic in the play, holds the world's fate in her hands. With this alarming conclusion Dürrenmatt capitulates to the sense of inevitable doom of our age, in which every serious attempt at a solution loses its meaning.

ROMULUS THE GREAT (also: *Romulus*) *(Romulus der Große)*. An unhistorical historical comedy in four acts. Prose. Written 1948. First edition Zürich 1958. First performance January 10, 1958, Basle, Stadttheater. English version in *Four Plays,* translated by Gerhard Nellhaus *et al.,* New York, Grove Press, 1965 and London, Cape, 1964; under the title *Romu-*

*lus,* adapted by Gore Vidal for production at the Music Box, New York, January 10, 1962. Time: March 15 and 16, A.D. 476. Place: the villa of the Emperor Romulus at Tivoli, near Rome.

Only in comedy is Dürrenmatt's Romulus conceivable, for he prefers to cut a small figure in history as an emperor in order to preserve his greatness as a man. As in Wedekind's *König Nicolo,* the fool's mask gives license for the exposure of a world of secular spuriousness: "It is far greater and far harder to keep faith with a man than with a state."
Romulus has come to realize that to rule successfully means incurring guilt. For Rome has become "a world empire, and hence an institution which publicly practiced murder, robbery, oppression and extortion at the cost of other peoples, until I came." So Romulus chooses passive resistance. He becomes a ridiculous poultry-breeder and makes his living by selling cultural objects to a certain Rupf, an upstart manufacturer of ready-made trousers ("Made in Germany," of course). The last objects to be sold are the busts of ancient poets. But when the Goth demands the emperor's daughter Rea as his wife and in exchange promises to save the whole empire from the approaching army of battle-hungry Goths, Romulus gives him a determined "No" in answer. The poverty-stricken ruler thinks nothing of bartering away all the inherited junk of empire, but he will not sacrifice a human being's happiness to an idea. Rea and her fiancé, the Prefect Spurius, have no more ardent wish than to be allowed to sacrifice themselves for the safety of the empire, but the emperor with his matter-of-fact humanity and horror of emotionalism refuses them the halo of national heroism. All those who cannot renounce their patriotic raptures, with Spurius at their head, plot an attempt on the emperor's life —a bitterly comic travesty of Caesar's murder—but the act of violence founders on the emperor's imperturbable irony. He calmly rejects the accusation of treason: "It is not I who has betrayed Rome, Rome has betrayed itself. It knew the truth, but chose violence, it knew humanity but chose tyranny." In calm inactivity Romulus has watched the empire go to its ruin through its own fault; now he wants to turn over the power and responsibility to the Goth's prince, Ottaker, who with his nephew Theodoric has conquered the empire. The two statesmen, whom the course of history would require to be bitter enemies, find to their amusement that they both like raising poultry and get on splendidly. Ottaker has counter-designs on Romulus and presses the world's dominion upon him, for he sees therein the last chance of checking his people's warlike energy "before the Goths have definitely become a people of heroes." Romulus, with his plans foiled and the prospect of a new Leviathan of an empire bestriding the world, desires death. But even this heroic outcome is denied the anti-hero; he is simply retired with a pension.

The rejection of the heroic pose, the courage of simple humanity, is shown as a sadly unusual, individual case, while the paraphernalia of politics rule unchecked.


THE VISIT (also: *Time and Again*) (*Der Besuch der alten Dame*). A tragicomedy in three acts and an epilogue. Prose. First edition Zürich 1956. First performance January 19, 1956, Zürich, Schauspielhaus. Translated by Patrick Bowles, New York, Grove Press, and London, Cape, 1962; adapted by Maurice Valency, New York, French, 1958. Time: the present. Place: the small town of Güllen.

This play's analytical method and its epilogue, a sarcastic parody on the final verses in Sophocles's *Antigone,* are not its only connection with ancient Greek tragedy. There is also classical mercilessness in taking the premises to their extremes, as well as the catharsis, although that comes not from a god's hand but from prosperity.
The small town of Güllen is hopelessly impoverished. Its last hope is the visit by the oil heiress Claire Zachanassian, who grew up in the town. In case neither the children's choir nor the burgomaster's moving welcoming speech should open the old lady's treasure chest, filled by inheritances from successive husbands, surely the storekeeper Anton Schill, her first love, will know by what tender reminiscences to tap the golden spring of her munificence to the benefit of all. Claire appears in a bizarre costume, borne in a sedan chair by two convicts. In her train are also two blind eunuchs, a panther, and a comfortable coffin. She is full of understanding for the town's distress; it was by her own doing that the formerly prosperous economy of Güllen ended. She has come to exact justice. Schill abandoned her after she bore him a child. He married well and defeated her law suit with false witnesses. This treachery reduced Claire to being a prostitute, until her rise to power began with her marriage to the Armenian oil magnate Zachanassian. Since then she has indefatigably been plotting for her day of reckoning with Güllen's hypocritical respectability. The eunuchs in her entourage are the false witnesses once hired by Schill, her butler is the judge whose verdict deprived her of honor. Now she offers one million for rescuing the town, but in exchange demands Schill's life: "The world turned me into a whore, now I turn the world into a brothel. . . . The only decent people are those who pay, and I pay. Güllen for a murder, prosperity for a corpse." Of course, every one of the dignitaries refuses this barbaric bargain, but they all begin to get into debt and to live beyond their means, as though the promised reward could not fail to materialize. The general anticipation that someone or other will surely get rid of Schill gains so much ground that even Schill's family shares in

the new prosperity. Even the church trusts the others' wickedness and orders new bells on credit. Schill is haunted by the fear of death, to the point of being incapable of flight. He obstinately refuses to oblige the town by taking his own life. Claire knows the world well enough and can afford to sit back in icy calm; meanwhile she marries husbands seven, eight, and nine. Claire's "generous offer" provides the occasion for a splendid press and television show, in the course of which, unnoticed by the public, Schill is strangled by the town's athlete. As if by agreement, the doctor records "death by heart attack." And the newspapers carry the jubilant headline: "Death by joy. Life writes the finest stories." Claire hands over her check, packs her once faithless lover, now finally hers, into the coffin she has brought along, and departs.

Dürrenmatt's often excessive delight in paradoxes and in grotesque distortion is tamed and subordinated to the consistent development of an idea: the terrible accumulation of a collective guilt for which there can be neither a prosecutor nor a judge. For the box crammed full of slogans, from "Let justice be done" to "Necessary sacrifice for the good of the community," always contains some serviceable formula of justification.

DIE WIEDERTÄUFER [The Anabaptists]. Comedy in two parts. Prose and verse. First edition Zürich 1967. First performance March 16, 1967. Zürich, Schauspielhaus. First version entitled Es steht geschrieben [It Is Written]. Time: 1534–1936. Place: Münster and Worms.

The scene and the situation rest on firm historical ground. In 1534 the Anabaptist sect established in Münster a "kingdom of God on earth" that soon degenerated into unbridled profligacy. The troops of the expelled bishop sealed the fate of the unruly city. Out of this situation Dürrenmatt develops the tragic farce of faith forever deluded. The people want to hope, they want their enthusiasm to be fired, and so sacrifice themselves for such ideals as are offered with all the most intoxicating, striking dazzle of rhetorical brilliance. Politics is a matter of show business, the formation of public opinion a combination of grimaces, emotionalism, theatrical display as well as gripping, self-confident imagination. Demagogy and the theater continually play into each other's hands. It is theatrical effect that makes ideology dangerously explosive and gives it its infectious power. The brilliant demagogic showman brings immediacy to the political program, fans the fanaticism of all the hitherto inhibited participants, and sweeps them along in the intoxicated enjoyment of action.

The actor Johann Bockelson, currently "resting," comes to Münster, intrigues his way to the leadership of the Anabaptists and arranges a private end of the world to destroy the city. The result is death and despair for the credulous followers who believe in this play-acting, and applause and princely patronage for the theater-mad deceiver: "Art never fed me, and pimping only a bit/ Now I fatten on religion and politics: but I'm trapped/ I became a baptist from professional poverty/ Jobless, I taught rhetoric to muddle-headed bakers, cobblers and tailors/ And watched how they stirred up the world/ With credulous ideas as though it were sludge/ And at last let them unleash war/ Indeed became their king, thanks to a chance idea/ Now let the devil take it, they believe in me. . . ."

There is an obvious analogy with Calderon's *El gran teatro del mundo*. But what to the Christian of the Baroque Period was a symbol of a higher, divinely appointed order, becomes for Dürrenmatt the expression of deception—anything is possible and everything is unpredictable—and it is the image of inescapable relativity that invalidates everything. When the people of Münster deck themselves out with grotesque names and titles— a butcher as Viscount Gê-Hinnom, the cobbler as the Count of Gilboa, the tinker as Prince of Sichem—it is not of security within the Catholic hierarchy that one thinks, as in Calderon, but of the rapturously savored masquerade in Genêt's *The Balcony*. The grotesque impulse to revolution, it becomes clear, is the fascination of being different, the desire for a new life, so far withheld by reality. Thus politics becomes a festival of wild gestures and rhetoric made up of song, dance, choruses, mime, rigmarole and incantation. It is watched, not by Calderon's God the Father, but by a decrepit old man, bewildered by the confusion of the time, dressed up in bishop's vestments.

Dürrenmatt contrasts two opposed ways of life. On the one hand there is the ham actor Bockelson who makes himself king of the new Jerusalem. His counterpart is Knipperdollinck, who seeks certainty in faith, sacrifices himself and finally ends up on the wheel. Satiated by his burgomaster's existence, he tries to take the Gospel literally. He receives into his house a man who is the lowest, the poorest, among the people, none other than Bockelson, hands over to him power and riches—and thereby surrenders everyone to arbitrary power and to ruin. Bockelson abolishes private property, surrounds himself with a harem and rapturously declaims Seneca while the bishop's troops overrun the crumbled walls of the town. The people are butchered, Knipperdollinck is saddled with the main guilt and executed, the charlatan is pardoned because the princes cannot do without their jester. In the play Charles V and the old bishop are weary, resigned spectators who are kept going only by Bockelson. A monk represents sound commonsense and in consequence is continually threatened with the gallows. In form Dürrenmatt uses a loose sequence of scenes, with playful anachronisms and cabaret-style gags.

# DYER, Charles
(England, born 1928)

RATTLE OF A SIMPLE MAN. Play in three acts. Prose. First edition London 1963. First performance October 2, 1961, London, Richmond Theatre. Time: the present. Place: Cyrenne's small basement flat in London.

This textbook example of Anglo-Saxon psychological theater repeated in Germany the successful run it enjoyed in its home country. Trauma and neurosis serve as a commentary for a realistic social study.
Percy, a mother's darling at thirty-five, as the result of a bet finds himself inside the streetwalker Cyrenne's lodgings. Things cannot take their natural course between those two people, and so each takes refuge in self-deception. They would like to help each other, and to this end each psychoanalyzes the other. The girl's story about her noble birth founders on reality just as much as the sham self-satisfaction behind which Percy hides his unlived life. The symbol for the conversation that never gets anywhere is the rattle Percy has brought along from a football match—a toy that just turns, makes a noise, and leads to nothing.

STAIRCASE. Two acts. Prose. First edition Harmondsworth, England, and Baltimore, Maryland, U.S.A., 1966. First performance autumn 1966, London, Aldwych Theatre (Royal Shakespeare Company). Time: the present. Place: a barber's shop.

Dyer presents the "marriage" of two middle-aged homosexuals as a psychological study, in which he maintains unity of time and place. He makes effective theatrical use of his grotesque, bizarre theme and at the same time expresses self-torment, self-pity, escape into self-dramatization, fear of life, and loneliness.
Charlie Dyer, the broken-down actor, has found a refuge and livelihood with the barber Harry Leeds. The burden of having to be grateful impels him to tease Harry more and more maliciously. He despises and makes fun of the little hairdresser who hides his baldness under a bandage and is unhappy over his age and increasing physical degeneration. Charlie is a cynical poseur who boasts of his great days in the theater. Harry is a sentimental, good-humored lower middle-class type, full of self-pity and obsequiousness. Charlie needs Harry, lets himself be pampered and coddled by him, and humiliates him to get revenge on his partner for his own failures. At a club Charlie carried a transvestite gag a bit too far and

was questioned by the police. He expects a summons to appear in court, and trembles at every sound. At the same time he talks big about a visit from his daughter Cassy, the only legacy of his broken marriage. Spitefully, he throws in Harry's face this actually highly dubious proof of his virility in an attempt to bring pressure to bear on him. In the end Charlie has to admit that the whole of his grand past, about which he boasted so much, is nothing but a lie. The two years when he was supposedly a successful actor were, in fact, spent in jail. All the names of impresarios and stars he mentions are anagrams of his own name. They finally decide to separate. When Charlie pretends to commit suicide, Harry has a heart attack. Sobered, the actor accepts his true dependence and for the first time tries to reach a human relationship with his partner.

Dyer does not evade the human problems of his material, yet maintains an ironic detachment by giving the chief character his own name, and referring to the latter's partner Harry Leeds as only an anagram and imaginary embodiment of Charlie Dyer.

## EHRENBURG, Ilya Grigorevich
(U.S.S.R., 1891–1967)

LEV NA PLOSHCHADI [*The Lion in the Square*]. Comedy in five acts. Prose. First edition Moscow 1948. First performance March 26, 1948, Moscow. Time: after the end of the Second World War. Place: small town in southern France.

Satirical social criticism in a small-town setting with a rather too obvious political bias leads to the obligatory apotheosis of world communism.
The dignitaries of a shabby small town in France, arthritic bourgeois and exploiters of the working class, spend their lives playing cards, pay an occasional visit to the local prostitute, and passively wait for American economic aid. An American, James Law from Jackson, turns up. He is a businessman and a blusterer, perpetually chewing gum, who looks at everything in terms of its dollar value and dismisses what cannot be so calculated as "stupid and immoral." He talks the citizens into giving him their famous monument, the Lion in the Square, which he intends to sell at a high price in America as a souvenir. The manufacturer Deleau welcomes the new ally with the identical speech he used in 1943 for the Germans. France gives up its lion and in exchange gets the American lion-tamer. But when Stalingrad Square is renamed Law Square, the hard-pressed working class intervenes and defends its independence. In the final scene, Ehrenburg has also drawn on national themes, with a Communist Joan of Arc and the International forcefully combined.

## ELIOT, Thomas Stearns
(United States/England, 1888–1965)

THE COCKTAIL PARTY. A comedy in three acts. Verse. Written 1949. First edition London 1950. First performance August 22, 1949, Edinburgh, Lyceum Theatre. Time: the present. Place: London.

The motif from the Alcestis legend of voluntary death as a representative sacrifice of atonement is transposed into the prosperous society of the twentieth century as a life-long quest for self-validation and moral self-fulfillment. Edward and Lavinia Chamberlayne, a married couple mired in luxury and indifference, are giving one of their usual cocktail parties. Lavinia, feeling that her young lover Peter Quilpe is slipping away from her, has gone away and is not at the party. Edward, who is having an affair with Celia Coplestone, could now openly choose a life with her, but he mistrusts his feelings. Lavinia returns to the conjugal home built on lies and estrangement. The couple turn to the authority of destiny, who today can be no one but a psychiatrist—Sir Henry Harcourt-Reilly—in order to find out the truth about themselves and what they are doing. For the first time they see each other without the subterfuges and decorative trimmings of society life: "A man who finds himself incapable of loving and a woman who finds that no man can love her." The psychiatrist reunites these two people whom life has separated, and they are determined to prove themselves in a new companionship: they mature together into true humanity.

Celia realizes that her love was no more than a mistake and a substitute for a vague inner yearning for self-sacrifice. This failure gives her a sense of sin and frustration. Upon Sir Henry's advice she goes to the tropical jungle as a nursing sister where she serves her fellow men, quietly, forgotten by the world. She is killed during an insurrection of natives.
The refined drawing-room of the boulevard play with its little scandals, parties, and liaisons suddenly faces us with the compelling mystery of man's often unfathomable destiny in this world.


THE CONFIDENTIAL CLERK. Comedy in three acts. Verse. First edition London 1954. First performance August 25, 1953, Edinburgh Festival. Time: the present. Place: London, Mulhammer's office and drawing room.

The inner conflicts of human nature and the precariousness of all human bonds are treated with theatrical playfulness rather like Nestroy's "precarious circumstances" and placed in the limelight of bourgeois life. The plot is based on the *Ion* of Euripides, but the classical allegory in which the gods create first confusion in men's feeling and then beautiful clarity can provide no more than a framework for this turbulent farce.
Sir Claude Mulhammer is financially highly successful as a banker, but to draw up the balance sheet of his complicated private life is a problem which defies even so skillful a businessman. He has engaged his illegitimate son Colby Simpkins as his secretary, and expects that his hopeful offspring will so impress his wife, Lady Mulhammer, that she will agree to the young man's adoption. In this way Mulhammer discreetly hopes to remove the blot on the family escutcheon. Lady Mulhammer is delighted at the proposed addition to the family, since she believes Colby to be the long-lost issue of her own escapade many years earlier and flatters herself that all his merits are inherited from her. The labyrinthine situation gets alarming when Colby falls in love with Lucasta Angel, another child of the prolific banker. But at this dramatic possibility of incest the young couple, who have an inkling of their origin, pale and finally part. Suddenly it turns

out that Colby's father was an organist. Defiantly he allows himself to be adopted into the big-money aristocracy, but only to retire to a little village, where he takes to playing the organ and thus demonstrates the inheritance from his true father. Lucasta consoles herself with a bank clerk, who turns out to be Lady Mulhammer's lost son.

Behind all these extravagant mix-ups there looms the question of man's true nature. Man's readiness to identify himself too hastily with every hypothesis and to validate it with the seal of fact is carried *ad absurdum* with all the well-tried devices of comedy. But Eliot does not touch on the more profound question involved in this plot, the question, that is, of where the responsibilities lie in a situation where the search for one lost son eventually reveals three children deprived of father and mother by the caprice of adults.

THE ELDER STATESMAN. Play in three acts. Verse. Written 1958. First edition London 1958. First performance August 25, 1958, Edinburgh Festival, Lyceum Theatre. Time: the present. Place: England.

True not only in its plot but in its position in the author's total output to the analogy with *Oedipus at Colonus,* the work of Sophocles's old age, this play was Eliot's last. His "elder statesman," long petrified in his attitudes, in playing a part, finds at the end of his life that his past is catching up with him: "I've spent my life in trying to forget myself,/ In trying to identify myself with the part/ I had chosen to play." A compromise is struck between the social critic's question of the need of the façade, of the image demanded by society, and Ibsen's question about self-deception and inner truth—and this compromise consists in easing the leave-taking, in ironic detachment. This play of memories is kept in suspense not by actions, which have long been concluded, but only by valuations.

Lord Claverton, a retired statesman and a man from whom life now asks no further effort, has gone to live in a sanatorium. He is not so presumptuous as to wish to wear himself out in office to the end of his life and thus to prove that he is indispensable, but he feels lost in the emptiness of his sudden idleness and cannot invest his new freedom with any meaning. Suddenly two people turn up: Senor Gomez, a shady businessman from overseas, and Mrs. Carghill with her exasperating cheerfulness. Many years ago, on a binge, Gomez was in the car when Claverton, then a student, ran over an old man and never even stopped to look, and Mrs. Carghill was seduced by Lord Claverton and subsequently sacrificed to his career after getting a generous indemnity. At first Claverton tries to hush up these embarrassing indiscretions, but then he admits his shortcomings and leaves the world quietly. The autumnal meditations of this verse comedy are punctuated by contrasting farcical minor characters.

## FABBRI, Diego
(Italy, born 1911)

BETWEEN TWO THIEVES (also: *Man on Trial*) *(Processo a Gesù)*. Spectacle in two parts and an interlude. Prose. First edition Florence 1955. First performance March 2, 1955, Milan, Piccolo Teatro. Adapted by Warner LeRoy, New York, French, 1959; translated by Lucienne Hill *(Man on Trial)* for London production, October 12, 1959, Lyric Opera House. Time: the present. Place: a stage.

This play is a rationalistic reexamination, in a supposedly improvised trial, of the judicial murder of Jesus Christ. In the face of the relativity of guilt and atonement, of the bewilderment implied by an insoluble theodicy where every judgment involves a new accusation, there remains only Kierkegaard's leap into the "wholly different," into the hope of grace and redemption in another world.

Elia, a former professor at Tübingen and an eminent scriptural scholar, has joined a traveling theater group and every evening he reopens with the "Trial of Jesus" in another town. The parts of accusers and defenders are distributed by lot every day. And each day the proceedings, which involve the audience as well, take their different, unrepeatable, spontaneous course. Elia wants to discover whether Israel was guilty of deicide and whether the extermination of the Jews in the Third Reich was a punishment for this. He looks for logic in history, but all he finds in the trial is a confusion of conflicting points of view. Did not Caiphas have to remove the rebel Jesus and his teaching of forgiveness in order to safeguard God's vengeance, in accordance with the Old Testament? Did not Pilate act in strict compliance with the rules and with diplomatic wisdom in reestablishing order in the country? The audience intervenes in the discussion with the controversies of modern philosophies. All of them need faith, which alone justifies existence. Elia forgoes judgment in the trial of Jesus, for God's forgiveness has long spoken the last word. The theatrical performance and its audience are at once the background and the material of the drama. Pirandello's device of disillusionment is used by Fabbri for absolute identification and for proclaiming the message of salvation.

PROCESSO DI FAMIGLIA *[Family Trial]*. Play in two parts. Prose. Written 1953. First published in *Il Dramma*, No. 197, 1954. First performance December 11, 1953, Turin, Teatro Carignano. Time: the present. Place: Italy.

Man's religious rebirth appears in Fabbri's work not so much as an existential phenomenon but rather as a blind flight forward, away from a world rotten with selfishness and lies: "What support would we have in our despair if it were not for that inner certainty incomprehensible to our reason—the certainty of eternal peace in which our love, our sorrow, our suffering will come to rest and be redeemed?"

The girl Bice marries the farm bailiff Libero Casadei. The two want Bice's son Abele, adopted five years before by Professor Eugenio Valenti and his wife Isoline. Isolina desperately fights for possession of the child, and admits to repeated adultery in vain hope of proving herself the mother. She does prove that Libero is wrong in believing himself to be the boy's father, and goes to call on the child's real father, the racing driver Rolando Ranieri, now married in his turn. Three marriages break up under the impact of the Isolina's fanatic obsession. In the turmoil of the adults' egocentricity, the child meets with a fatal accident. Deeply stirred the three couples pluck up courage for a new beginning: "What else can we hold on to in the depth of our sorrow today except the hope of love's eternity?"

IL SEDUTTORE *[The Seducer]*. Comedy in three acts. Prose. First published in *Teatro-Scenario* No. 19, 1951. First edition Milan 1952. First performance October 4, 1951, Venice, Teatro La Fenice. Time: the present. Place: a large town.

The triangle is enriched by a fourth party; the resulting amorous quadrangle relies on irony and slapstick and eliminates the happy ending in a fast-moving theatrical entertainment tailored for star parts.

The "seducer," the manager of a travel agency, has his irresistible charms to thank for a complicated and exhausting private life. As Eugenio he is married to the practical Norma; under the name of Filippo he is the idol of his romantic secretary Alina; and under his third hat as Elio, he is allowed to spoil the fashion model Wilma. It is inconvenient always to have to pretend, the eternal lies do not amuse him any more and therefore begin to weigh upon his conscience. He skillfully arranges for the three ladies of his heart to meet and is happy to see that they at once become close friends. This seems to vouchsafe him triple bliss. But when the women discover the deception, they unite against him and send him packing.

## FAULKNER, William, and FORD, Ruth
(United States, 1897–1962)

REQUIEM FOR A NUN. Play in three acts. After Faulkner's novel of the same name (1931). Prose. First edition New York 1951. First performance October 9, 1955, Zürich, Schauspielhaus. Time: the present. Place: Mississippi.

Behind psychoanalytical self-revelation is glimpsed the mystery of a sacrifice of atonement for the sins of another, a grace by which a human being, driven by her instincts and unjustly persecuted, finds the way to herself. Faulkner takes an appalling child murder as a means by which to work a blessing and demonstrate the moral ambivalence of all being.

The traumatic experience of Temple Drake's forced stay in a brothel has become a voluptuous memory for her. She has long been leading a respectable life, is married to Gowan Stevens, and is the mother of two children. As a "sister in sin" she lifted the "nigger whore" Nancy Mannigoe from the gutter and took her in as a nursemaid. When Temple was about to leave her husband and children and follow a blackmailing gangster, Nancy killed the younger child in order to foil the plan. The shock was to bring Temple to herself and thus to keep the mother with the remaining child. Nancy is condemned to death for her crime, which she committed so that "little children, as long as they are little children, shall be intact, unanguished, untorn, unterrified." Temple, in the investigation, is at first self-righteous and obdurate, but eventually confesses her own great guilt to the governor and pleads for Nancy to be pardoned. The Negro girl is executed. The governor does not have the courage to invalidate the voluntary sacrifice of Nancy's miserable, dissolute, yet unique life. Temple's despairing question, whether one must sin, is soothed by Nancy on the threshold of death: "You ain't *got* to. You can't help it. And He knows that. But you can suffer. And He knows that too. He don't tell you not to sin, He just asks you not to. And He don't tell you to suffer. But He gives you the chance. He gives you the best He can think of, that you are capable of doing. And He will save you."

In this dramatic version, which is rather a narrative in dialogue linked by prose transitions, Faulkner probes further the events of his novel. Only the last few hours preceding the execution are acted out, but the real action lies in Temple's confession.

# FEUCHTWANGER, Lion
(Germany, 1884–1958)

THE DEVIL IN BOSTON *(Wahn oder Der Teufel in Boston)*. Play in three acts. Prose. Written 1948. First edition Los Angeles 1948. First perform-ance March 1949, Frankfurt/Main, Kleines Theater im Zoo. Adapted by N. Buckwald for New York production by the Yiddish Theatre at the Barbizon Plaza, 1952. Time: 1692. Place: Cotton Mather's study in Boston.

In this work of his later years, Feuchtwanger proves himself a champion of humanity and democracy. Basing the play on historical events, he ex-poses the pernicious interlocking of mass religious mania and political struggles for power. Public opinion can be manipulated by demagogues and fanatics. The political persecution to which Feuchtwanger himself was subjected remains actual even though seen through the historical de-tachment of the story.

Reverend Cotton Mather considers himself one of God's elect and rules the people with unyielding severity. His brother-in-law, the enlightened, free-thinking, skeptical physician Thomas Colman, observes bitterly how the privileges of the colony of Massachusetts are surrendered by the clergy to the English king in return for personal power and office. The witch-craft mania, in which Hanna, the adolescent daughter of Parrish, the country clergyman, gets mixed up, is zealously exploited by Mather in a clerical-political campaign. Fascinated, the girl assumes the role attributed to her in this game, and makes decisions on the life and death of many in-nocent people. With her fantastic accusations she first gets rid of personal enemies—the nurse Tituba who, she feels, has insulted her, and the Rev-erend Mr. Burroughs, her father's inconvenient colleague. Colman sees through this terrorization of conscience but yields silently to superior power. The whole countryside is gripped by a mania for killing and every-one is engaged in denunciation. When the clergymen's wives see them-selves threatened with the stake, there are recantations. Hanna confesses that she was an insignificant puppet in the affair and hangs herself. Only Mather persists with pharisaic pride in his mission as the only true be-liever who is to cast out the devil.

Arthur Miller in his play *The Crucible* used local color and the speech forms of the period; Feuchtwanger has perferred terse, depersonalized discussion.

### FIELDS, Herbert, and FIELDS, Dorothy
(both United States; Herbert, 1897–1958, Dorothy, born 1905)

ANNIE GET YOUR GUN. Musical comedy, with music by Irving Berlin. First performance May 16, 1946, New York, Imperial Theatre. Time: 1890. Place: a Western show.

Mass society's expectations in love and professional rivalry in a colorful Western milieu. Annie Oakley is the Western variant of the successful, emancipated rich girl who eventually gives up her privileges for love. In spite of humor and trigger-quick excitement, the sentimental pattern remains visible in the interaction of the characters and guarantees the play its mass appeal.

Annie, a girl grown up in the woods with her gun, is a better shot than the marksman Frank Butler and ousts him from Buffalo Bill's Wild West Show. He joins the rival group under Pawnee Bill. But Annie loves him, and in order to win her adored hero, she lets him win in a shooting competition. A show within the show provides an opportunity for spectacular circus feats and Sioux dances.

Irving Berlin, who made his name almost exclusively with song hits, neglected musical construction in the score for the sake of individual songs. These are sometimes sentimental, sometimes melodramatic, and are strung together in the manner of a revue. One of them, the musical self-portrait of all musicals, "There's No Business Like Show Business," has become a triumphal hymn to the genre.

### FILIPPO, Eduardo de
(Italy, born 1900)

FILUMENA MARTURANO (Filumena Marturano). Comedy in three acts. Prose. First published in Il Dramma, No. 35–36, 1947. First edition in Cantata dei giorni dispari, Vol. 1, Turin 1951. First performance November 7, 1946, Naples. English version in Masterpieces of the Modern Italian Theatre, Robert W. Corrigan, ed., New York, Collier, n.d. Time: the present. Place: Soriano's dining room in Naples.

As actor, author, and manager of a theater company, de Filippo invariably turns to the simple folk and their elementary claims on life for the scripts he writes for himself and his ensemble. Psychological development and

social criticism, farce, sentimentality, folklore, and a moralizing undertone are seamlessly welded in his racy comedies.

To his boundless fury, Domenico Soriano, a wealthy and well-born man,
finds that he has been made a fool of. Filumena had served him faithfully
for twenty-five years as mistress, housekeeper, and motherly counsel in all
calamities. He marries her when he believed her to be mortally ill and had
to fulfill her last wish. Making a miraculous recovery and once more as
strong as a horse, the woman firmly seizes the reins of the household. In a
burst of Neapolitan temperament she throws out the latest mistress of her
incorrigibly zestful "Don Dummi" and takes into the house her three
grown-up sons, of whom nobody had ever heard. Don Dummi, abruptly
deprived of his bachelor's freedom, talks of annulment, but Filumena tells
him that one of her three sons is his. She does not tell him which. Vainly
he tries to find out, and eventually he distributes his paternal pride equally
among all three and renews his familial bliss with Filumena.


## FRISCH, Max
(Switzerland, born 1911)


ALS DER KRIEG ZU ENDE WAR [When the War Was Over]. Play in two
acts. Prose. Written 1947–1948; a third act was deleted in 1962. First
edition Basle 1949. First performance January 8, 1949, Zürich, Schauspielhaus. Time: early 1945. Place: Berlin.

This gloomy romance deals with a man who, desiring happiness, love, and
security, impetuously goes awry and then willingly accepts guilt. In an
afterword Frisch admits: "In an age that is hypnotized by clichés, it seemed
to me not superfluous to bear witness on behalf of those individuals who
don't keep to the rules, but all the same are real and vital." The national
hatreds that divide are overcome by the miracle of love between a German
woman and a Russian, amid ruins, thirst for revenge, and atrocities: "if
we understand God as what is vital in every man, as the incomprehensible,
the unutterable which we can only endure as such where we love; otherwise we always make an image unto ourselves; not being either ready or
willing or able to confront an individual face, we stereotype whole nations
and will not allow them anything but the mask of our own prejudice,
which always signifies a wrong."

During the last days of the fighting in Berlin, Agnes Anders, her little son,
and her husband Horst, who has come back from the front with only one
arm, hide in the scullery of her villa. In the smart rooms upstairs the

drunken Russian victors brawl and roister. When the family is discovered by Jehuda Karp, the Jewish orderly, Agnes decides to face the Russians in her prettiest evening dress. Distrust and fear sow discord between husband and wife. Horst is feverishly waiting for civilian clothes so that he can go underground. The little boy has an accident on the rubbish dump. In a short time Agnes shyly comes to love the young Russian colonel, Stepan Ivanov, whose language she does not understand but whose heart speaks spontaneously to her. Self-reproach and feelings of guilt come between the lovers, but the elemental forces of life keep breaking through. Jehuda in his hatred denounces Horst. Stepan is brought down to earth and leaves the house. He does not want to spoil the brief dream with cheap revenge and leaves behind him a marriage that has hardened into disconsolate meaninglessness.

The three-act 1949 version, the first, accentuates the dramatic conflict and lays much more emphasis on the question of guilt. Horst, a self-righteous bourgeois, is implicated in war crimes and pleads higher orders. And he considers Agnes's relationship with the colonel as justified by a similar *force majeure*. At this indignity Agnes throws herself out of the window.


ANDORRA *(Andorra)*. Play in twelve scenes. Prose. Written 1958–1961. A first prose sketch published in *Tagebuch 1946 bis 1949*. First edition Frankfurt/Main 1961. First performance November 2, 1961, Zürich, Schauspielhaus. Translated by Michael Bullock in *Three Plays*, London, Methuen, 1962 and New York, Hill & Wang, 1964. Time: the present. Place: Andorra, an imaginary country.

A didactic fable on racialism is so consistent in following out the relationships of reality that it achieves the merciless authenticity of a model. The destructive pressure of race discrimination is generated not by brutes, but by a guileless little town, by kind and honest people who, in the security of collective behavior and the safety of doing as everyone does, cast out an individual and brand him as the incarnation of all evil as a pretext and justification for every individual failure: "Suddenly you are as they say you are. That is the trouble. They've all got it in them, but none of them wants it, and where is it to go? Into the air? It's in the air, but it doesn't stay there long, it's got to enter a person so that some day they can get hold of it and kill it."

The Teacher has provocatively announced his son Andri to be a Jewish foster-child. The Andorrans pride themselves on their tolerance, yet everyone tries to give vent to his own, usually suppressed aggressive tendencies in the general hostility which is legitimized by collective anonymity. The

Carpenter asks an exorbitant fee for Andri's apprenticeship and humiliates him with thoughtless injustices; the Sergeant brutally takes the girl Barblin whom Andri worships; when the foreign Senora, Andri's long-lost mother, turns up for a short visit and is killed by a stone thrown at her, it stands to reason that—for the sake of the community's peace of mind—the Teacher's son must be the culprit. "The Blacks," the totalitarian regime of the neighboring country, occupy Andorra. In the humiliating "Jew inspection" to which all must submit, Andri is designated as the victim and executed. Between the scenes the participants are arraigned before a courtroom bar and preen themselves with their disingenuous justifications: "I certainly do not deny that somehow we got caught up in some sort of current movement . . . No one likes a bad conscience, but that's just what they're after. They want us to treat them badly. They're only waiting for it . . . quite apart from the fact that, as far as I myself am concerned, I really fail to see why I should have behaved otherwise. What, after all, has any of us done? Nothing at all."
Detachment and immediacy, abstraction and facts are deliberately held in balance.


THE CHINESE WALL (Die chinesische Mauer). Farce in twenty-four scenes. Prose and blank verse. Written 1946, second version 1955. First edition Basle 1947. First performance October 10, 1946, Zürich, Schauspielhaus. Translated by James L. Rosenberg, New York, Hill & Wang, 1961. Time: not specified. Place: not specified.

The eternal conflicts of human failings in the turmoil of power, fanaticism, bellicosity, avarice, and sycophancy are captured in a motley round of characters. "Contemporary man," at first a detached commentator, then the witness to his own truth and its victim, explains and situates the characters who, called up by historical reminiscences and literary quotations, appear as leitmotivs to break through and resolve the play's situations. Between improvisation and alienation we get a clear view of man's eternal vocation and peril from the temptations of power.
The contemporary commentator presents the building of the Great Wall of China under Emperor Hwang-ti as the model case, as "one of the recurring attempts to bring time to a stop." Tyranny afraid for its continued existence always takes flight forward into yet worse cruelty and oppression. A masquerade, "lemures of an unrepeatable history," demonstrates that of all the chances of fulfillment nothing is left except the clichés that have always surrounded despots: star-crossed lovers, like Romeo and Juliet; Napoleon, the type of conqueror who cannot grasp that he has been out-

dated by radioactivity; King Philip of Spain in the delusion of his Inquisi-
tion; Pilate with the hypocrisy of self-righteousness; Cleopatra, forever
spending herself on success; Brutus, the tyrannicide who wants to destroy
violence by violence; the playboy Don Juan, as weary of life as is the Unknown Girl out of the Seine; and Columbus, in his search for truth, deludes himself with the discovery of America. Time and space are abolished
to expose the extremes of dialectical conflict. Like all tyrants and great
conquerors, Hwang-ti fights exclusively for peace, by which term he understands true, unique, and final order, his own limitless domination of the
world: "For the barbarians are always the others. . . . And civilization,
that is always us. And therefore the other peoples must be liberated; for
we (and not the others) are the free world." The building of the wall is
to make his regime irreversible and to eliminate the future. But this national imperative does not prevent the wall simultaneously becoming the
main reason of discord of corrupt business practices. The Contemporary
can pronounce his twentieth-century warnings only in the guise of a court
fool. Mee Lan, the emperor's daughter, gains from his opposition the
courage to reject the suit of Prince Wu Tsiang, one of those athletic fighting robots indispensable to any ruler. The tyrant has long been trying to
find Min Ko, the "voice of the people" and unique witness to truth, who
has yet to be destroyed. A mute is arrested and his execution is to set the
emperor's mind at peace. Only the fool has the courage to defend innocence in the show trial, in which the ruler has pronounced sentence in
advance. The Contemporary overcomes his fear and rouses himself to an
open accusation of the dictator. But he is not granted the grace of a
martyr's death for his convictions. The court applauds his apocalyptic
vision as a poetic horror story. The emperor honors him as Poet Laureate
and at once presses the warning of nuclear death into service as an effective means of pressure against his political opponents. The mute's mother,
too, who has been called as a witness to testify to his innocence, succumbs
to the power of propaganda, declares her son to be the infamous Min Ko,
and thus makes his death certain. The eruption of Wu Tsiang, who, in his
disappointment, has set himself up as leader of a popular revolt, puts an
end to the farce with a few rifle shots. The mute becomes the new ruler's
welcome prop. The puppets of all ages and regions once more get busy
with spectral activities, while the princess and the fool recognize the futility of their opposition and yet do not despair of their love: "That is reality:
you, powerless, and I, dishonored, thus we stand in this age, and the world
passes over us. That is our story."

The episodic improvisation, elusive in the first version, is more firmly
drawn in the second. The original noncommittal play of man's hopeless
entanglement gained cathartic definition with the defeat of the princess
and the fool as dishonored, tormented witnesses of truth.

COUNT OEDERLAND *(Graf Öderland).* A murder story in twelve scenes. Prose. Written as a first sketch 1946 (published in *Tagebuch 1946 bis 1949),* stage versions 1951 and 1956, final versions February 1961. First edition Frankfurt/Main 1951. Final version in *Stücke I,* Frankfurt/Main 1962. First performance February 10, 1951, Zürich, Schauspielhaus; second version February 4, 1956, Frankfurt/Main, Städtische Bühnen; final version September 25, 1961, Berlin, Schiller-Theater. Translated by Michael Bullock in *Three Plays,* London, Methuen, 1962. Time: the present. Place: an imaginary country.

In a literal sense the individual forced to renounce himself in a standardized civilization and degraded into a mere function of bureaucracy runs amok. In the mechanism of authorities and conventions, life is so predetermined and protected from the unforeseen that an individual's free decision as such becomes a resvolt against the established course of events: "Seriously . . . where would we be without an ax! In this world of paper, in this jungle of limits and laws, in this madhouse of order. . . . There are moments when one wonders why we don't all reach for the ax. We all put up with it, though it means nothing. Work as virtue. Virtue as a surrogate for joy. And the other surrogate, since virtue isn't enough, is pleasure: leisure time, the weekend, the adventure on the screen."
A senseless, inexplicable murder has occurred. A bank teller, a most respectable ordinary citizen, has in a sudden fit killed a totally unknown man with an ax. Everybody is puzzled. Only the public prosecutor looks on this deed as liberating, as a challenge of fate. The outburst of violence seems to him the only way of escaping from the environment and the part assigned therein to each individual. In bewilderment he looks on while Hilde, the maid, with naive unconcern, burns the records, "so that there can be a dance, like the charcoal-burners' dance in the woods when Count Oederland came." The prosecutor takes refuge with the charcoal-burners and hears of the legendary Count Oederland, whose bloody ax once became fateful for the forest dwellers. Fascinated, he identifies himself with this myth of rebellion, kills a few customs officials who bar his way across the frontier, and sets up a pocket of resistance on the bare island of Santorin. His underground movement unites all the discontented under the sign of the ax and eventually stages a revolution and takes over the government of the country. But the chastened prosecutor has to recognize that his idea of basic rebellion, of boundless liberty, annuls itself with the disappearance of the opponent, and that he must now, in his turn, promulgate laws for the conquered state, set up rules, and sacrifice the individual's freedom to a bureaucratic machinery. Despairing and impotent, he is again, as at the beginning, a prop of soulless institutions: "Life is a nightmare, slowly I am coming to grasp that—it's repetition, that's what

it is, and when you bang your head against the wall, that's the curse, that's the limit, and no ax is any use against that. Repetition!"

In the first version, the disillusioned freedom fighter jumps out of the window. His frivolous wife Elsa and her lover—standing for imperturbable banality—are left in possession of the field. In the later version, programmatic scene headings serve to generalize the action, as also do symbolic changes of parts—Hilde, the elfish symbol of the seductive faraway, turns into Inge and Coco (in the first version also into Iris).

DON JUAN OR THE LOVE OF GEOMETRY *(Don Juan oder Die Liebe zur Geometrie)*. Comedy in five acts. Prose. Written 1952, revised 1961. First edition Frankfurt/Main 1953. First performance May 5, 1953, Zürich, Schauspielhaus, and Berlin, Schiller-Theater. Translated by Nell Moody, adapted by Peter Philip, produced March 6, 1956, Bristol (England), Old Vic Company. Time: "a period of good costumes." Place: "a theatrical Seville."

Don Juan is no longer the carefree lady-killer, but distrusts himself and his spontaneous, fickle sentiments. He looks for truth and certainty in a crumbling world. Thus he is turned into one of our own contemporaries, forever torn between the truth as he sees it and the reality of his experience: "I long for what is pure, my friend, for what is sober and precise; I have a horror of the morass of our emotions."

The transience of moods which only too quickly evaporate into shadowy memory, the inner conflicts of meditating, brooding man drive Don Juan to seek refuge in the certainty of forms, the finality of geometrical coordinates. Suddenly he is torn from his geometrical studies and is supposed to marry Donna Anna, the daughter of Don Gonzalos. In order to preserve his freedom, he flees into the park and seduces an unknown woman, who subsequently turns out to have been Anna, while the supposed bride in the wedding gown is the prostitute Miranda, who in this guise approaches her idol Don Juan. As a gesture of cynical challenge Don Juan reverts to his seducer's pose in an attempt to bend reality, which has so far fooled him, to his own whims. Anna drowns herself in the pond. Twelve years later, exhausted, Don Juan must resign himself: "Twelve years of an unrepeatable life: wasted in this childish challenge of blue air that we call the heavens!" With the help of the Bishop of Cordova and a technical trick he stages his "descent to hell," leaving behind in the world his legend and the moral of the sinner's end. He himself finds a cosy nook for his old age by the side of Miranda, whose amorous disposition has raised her to the position of the Duke of Ronda's wealthy widow. He becomes a pedantic grumbler preoccupied with paternal joys and family worries.

The heavens dispose of their challenger not by an apocalyptic thunder clap, but by a comfortable descent into the commonplaces of bourgeois life. The character's spiritual depth—man struggling for the freedom of his will and feelings—is canceled by ironic doubt. The claim for absoluteness is raised and at the same time parodied, and the courage of existential independence broken by knowledge of the provisional nature of existence.

THE FIREBUGS (also: *The Fire Raisers) (Biedermann und die Brandstifter)*. A morality play without a moral in six scenes and an epilogue. Prose. Written 1957–1958, originally as a radio play. First edition Frankfurt/Main 1958. First performance March 29, 1958, Zürich, Schauspielhaus. First performance with the epilogue September 28, 1958, Frankfurt/Main, Städtische Bühnen. Translated by Mordecai Gorelik, New York, Hill & Wang, 1963, and by Michael Bullock *(The Fire Raisers)* in *Three Plays,* London, Methuen, 1962. Time: the present. Place: room and loft at Biedermann's.

The ordinary philistine, who complacently and idly lets things take their course, is branded as the real culprit responsible for political world catastrophes. He thinks only of his own bit of prosperity, yet wants to play the hero to shout down his inner fear. He wants to reassure himself by unconditional compliance and to save himself by coming to terms with the powers that be.

Again and again the firebugs—disguised as harmless peddlers—gain access to houses and in sudden assault destroy the smug bourgeois world. Mr. Biedermann rants against the authorities that afford so little protection. When two vagrant hoodlums, the professional wrestler Schmitz and the waiter Eisenring, with ominous friendliness come to stay with him, he dares not object. The guests prepare gasoline containers, unwind fuses, put detonators in place. They frankly discuss the proposed arson with Biedermann beforehand: "The best and safest concealment, I find, is the plain, naked truth. Strangely enough. Nobody believes it." The host frantically tries to persuade himself that it is all a jest, but at the same time—you never know—he tries to make friends of the two odd jesters, asks them to dinner and, as a sign of his trust, presses a box of matches on them. Eventually he is overwhelmed by the catastrophe which overtakes the whole town. The chorus of firemen—an ironic allusion to classical tragedy —provides a commentary of helpless foreknowledge on this road to ruin, and in conclusion is forced to the hopeless admission that nothing can have less sense than this tale, which, "once kindled, killed many, but, alas, not all, and changed nothing." The epilogue, a satyr play in hell, demonstrates the incorrigible self-righteousness of Biedermann and his wife Babette. The two firebugs—now the infernal hosts who welcome Biedermann—return to earth in order to continue their work of destruction with the help of the good folk to be found everywhere.

Frisch here develops the style which he was later to refine: the times are put on trial on the stage, but without the full rigor of Brecht's didacticism.


NUN SINGEN SIE WIEDER [They Sing Again]. An attempt at a requiem in two parts. Prose. Written 1945. First edition Basle 1946. First performance March 29, 1945, Zürich, Schauspielhaus. Time: during the Second World War. Place: not specified.

This attempt to exorcize the victims of war, both the guilty and the less guilty, on both sides of the front, is something between a mystery play and a documentary. A bitter world of hatred opens up: "We reached for power, for the ultimate violence, to make contact with the real spirit . . . and we have the world in our pocket, whether we need it or not, I see no bounds to our power—that's the awful thing."

The German soldier Karl is ordered by his superior Herbert to shoot twenty-one hostages. The abbot of the solitary monastery is also shot because he knows too much. Karl is horrified at the killing of these innocent victims who go singing to their death—he deserts. When he reaches home and witnesses the conflict of conscience of his schoolmaster father, a member of the party, he hangs himself. As in a dream Karl returns to the distant monastery, now become a strange purgatory where the dead bake bread for each other and drink out of the same jug. Now they enjoy that peaceful life of fulfillment which from the beginning had been destined for them and which they themselves had buried under discord and fanaticism: "This is repentance, our perdition, our redemption." Karl's wife Marie is there too; she and her child had died under the incendiary bombs. The schoolmaster, whose humanistic phrases were swept aside by the war, is shot under martial law on Herbert's orders, and joins the ranks of the dead along with a group of American airmen sent to their death. To the accompaniment of the song of the hostages, friend and foe unite in a great silent community. But the survivors stand at the gravesides and exalt the fallen with patriotic phrases about "not forgetting" and vengeance. "They make of our death what they like, what's useful to them. They take the words out of our life and make a testament of them, as they call it, and prevent us from ripening to more than they are. . . . Everything is in vain, death, life, the stars in heaven, they too are in vain. How should it be otherwise." But despondency gives way to a consoling gentleness: "Love is beautiful. . . . Only love knows that it is in vain, and only love does not despair."

PHILLIP HOTZ'S FURY *(Die große Wut des Philipp Hotz)*. Farce in one act. Prose. Written 1957–1958. First published in *Hortulus* 32, 1958. First edition in *Stücke 2*, Frankfurt/Main 1962. First performance March 29, 1958, Zürich, Schauspielhaus. Translated by Michael Bullock in *Gambit*, No. 4. Time: the present. Place: room in a modern apartment.

An existentialist trifle is inspired by the fun of paradox. The fear of not being taken seriously drives a husband to make a fool of himself.
Phillip Hotz, Ph.D., a writer married to a capricious wife, Dorli, has always preached complete freedom and frankness in marriage. All the same he is hurt when she confesses to an escapade with his friend Wilfrid. He sticks to his principles, is grimly not jealous, and counteracts with an invented adultery with Wilfrid's wife Clarissa, in order not to lose in this questionable competition. Every year Hotz threatens to join the Foreign Legion and revels in the triumph of being tearfully brought home by the terrified little woman. But for once Dorli has committed a gross breach of the rules in this farce of masculine independence by going so far as to withdraw her annual petition for divorce. This appeasement convinces Hotz that he is nothing but an amiable ninny of a husband, a peaceable bourgeois. He flies into a furious rage, locks Dorli in a cupboard, and with the help of a couple of handymen reduces the apartment to splinters. Carefully preserving his fury against rapid exhaustion, Hotz leaves for Marseilles and the Legion. Inwardly he is deeply hurt. However, his myopia makes him unfit for the Legion and, toughened by his fury and as earnest as he can be, Hotz returns to married bliss.
Uproarious scenes alternate with Hotz's comments on himself to produce a comic slice of middle-class life.

SANTA CRUZ *[Santa Cruz]*. Romance in five acts and a prologue. Prose. Written 1944. First edition Basle 1947. First performance March 7, 1946, Zürich, Schauspielhaus. Time: the present. Place: an inn, a castle and Santa Cruz in a dream.

Man is so much at the mercy of his longings and unfulfilled desires, of the pull of the unreal within himself, that he neglects his reality in order to pursue an unattainable dream. The inner conflict is appeased only by the realization that dreams can never signify reality but only a promise. "God intended it all to be much finer . . . we may love one another, all of us, I can see it now: life is different, love is greater, loyalty is deeper, it need not be afraid of our dreams, we needn't kill longing, we needn't lie."

Pelegrin, the cosmopolitan idler, already marked by death, meets Elvira, the vanished yet unforgotten love of a brief, passionate night on the sea of Santa Cruz. Now she is the respected wife of a cavalry officer and mother of seventeen-year-old Viola, but still yearning for the unredeemed promise of that night of love. The cavalry officer in his turn is trying to break out of his solid respectability and longs to get away in search of adventure. Pelegrin's sudden death shocks the couple out of their illusions and helps them to mature into a new companionship and acceptance of reality.

The language is lyrical and pictorial, and, together with filmlike fadeouts, subdues all conflicts in a restrained, impressionist landscape of the soul.

## FRY, Christopher
(England, born 1907)

CURTMANTLE. Play in three acts and a prologue. Verse and prose. First edition London 1961. First performance March 1, 1961, Tilburg (Netherlands), Stadsschouwburg. Time: 1158–1189. Place: England.

Fry adopts neither Anouilh's psychological approach nor Eliot's legend of God's warrior in interpreting the fatal conflict between Henry II, the man who is always right and always does wrong, and his archbishop Thomas Becket, "a man/ Who had gone through life saving up all passion/ To spend at last on his own downfall." The polarity between two personalities and institutions is concentrated in one single formulation. Henry is not against God, but against Becket's view of God; Becket is not against the state, but against the king's way of governing the state. The tragedy of two ideas thus becomes a tragedy of interpretation, and the spiritual conflict turns into a pragmatic one. Both state and church need interpretation if they are to be understood at all, but this makes them changeable and open to question; they give rise to political consequences and personal emotions.

Becket has become indispensable to the king as a friend and counselor, as a resourceful diplomat, and as chancellor. For reasons of state the king appoints Becket Archbishop of Canterbury, the head of the church in England. Becket resigns his chancellorship and demands the independence of the clergy. The king realizes that this would break up the unity of his conception of the world and brings the archbishop to trial: "Why should a man make God my enemy/ And the enemy of a maturing nation." Others quickly try to turn the conflict to their own advantage. The king's confessor Bishop Foliot is ready to subordinate the church to the king in order to promote his own career. France supports the archbishop for political reasons. The common people make him a symbol of their own sufferings and worship him as a saint. Words spoken by the king in a fit of rage lead to Becket's murder by overzealous courtiers. The king's abdication creates discord among his sons, the last survivors of whom enter an alliance with France and take up arms against their father. Abandoned and sick, tended only by the bastard Roger born to him by Blae the whore, "King Curtmantle" dies in the open field after a lost battle. Even the mantle to which he owed his nickname is stolen.

This chronicle play combines stylization, realism, and a sense of the theater.

THE DARK IS LIGHT ENOUGH. A winter comedy in three acts. Verse. First edition London 1954. First performance March 23, 1954, Brighton (England), Theatre Royal. Time: the winter of 1848–1849. Place: Countess Ostenburg's country house in Austria near the Hungarian border.

In Fry's cycle of seasonal plays, this one stands for winter—a time of clarity and calm after the restless confusion of beginning and decline in the spring and autumn. Countess Rosmarin Ostenburg goes through no development, she has reached her end and is at one with herself, fond of life but not afraid of death, serene and filled with gladness that makes even the dark both comforting and familiar: "In our plain defects/ We already know the brotherhood of man."

Much to the disapproval of her family, old Countess Rosmarin Ostenburg shelters in her house the writer Richard Gettner, who is being pursued by the rebellious Hungarians under Colonel Janik. Nobody can understand why she should thus endanger herself and the castle. For although Gettner was once married to Rosmarin's daughter Gelda, he made the girl wretched with his insolence and selfishness, and subsequently joined the Hungarian rebellion as a political adventurer. Gelda is now married to Count Peter Zichy. And Rosmarin does not hesitate to leave her highly respected and lovable son-in-law in the Hungarians' hands as a hostage and thus to jeopardize her family's happiness for the sake of saving the cynical, shady writer: "Life has a hope of him/ Or he would never have lived." Gettner is unable to understand so much humanity and suspects that it hides weakness or a bad conscience. In cynical provocation he takes advantage of the absence of Zichy, who has sacrificed himself for him, and tries to regain Gelda. Rosmarin's son Stefan defends his sister's honor by challenging Gettner to a duel, in which Stefan is wounded. The countess breaks down under all these misfortunes, but still pleads for Gettner. On the point of death, Rosmarin grants asylum to Colonel Janik, who is now in his turn hunted by the government troops. Gettner still fails to understand her selfless generosity, tries to discover some explanation, some hidden motive behind it. Cynically he proposes that she should marry him to settle his debt of gratitude, but Rosmarin merely smiles—she never loved him, merely liked him occasionally. His vanity is hurt: "Will you tell me, then, what I meant to you?/ A penance you gave yourself? Was I/ An exercise in charity/ Which is proving unfortunately fatal?/ Isn't it a sort of inso-lence/ To do for me what you care so little about?/ What in God's name was it I meant to you?" And Rosmarin leaves this world gently with this confession: "Simply what any life may mean." For the first time in his life Gettner, who was ready to escape, now stays to face the situation and waits for the government troops.

The parallelism between the facts (Gettner's exchange for Zichy, the re-versal of the flight situation as between Gettner and Janik) never seems a calculated and moralizing device, but acquires a natural immediacy in the fluent poetic language which dissolves reflection in images and melodies.

THE FIRSTBORN. Play in three acts. Free verse. First edition London 1946. First performance September 6, 1958, Edinburgh, Gateway Theatre, and, in a revised version, January 29, 1952, London, Winter Garden Theatre. Time: the summer of 1200 B.C. Place: Egypt, Pharaoh's palace and Miriam's tent.

In the firstborn's death of atonement, Fry anticipates the Christian sacri-fice of redemption at a time of judgment by the wrathful and revenging God of the Old Testament and raises the question of the meaning and justification of human life. In answer to his firstborn's question, "If I'm to live, shall I know how?" Pharaoh can point only to the world's immedi-ate realities: "A great power, a great people, a living Egypt," and it falls to Moses to reconcile the claims of eternity with time by proclaiming "The morning, which still comes/ To Egypt as to Israel, the round of light/ Which will not wheel in vain./ We must each find our separate meaning/ In the persuasion of our days/ Until we meet in the meaning of the world."

Moses was found in the rushes and brought up by Anath Bithiah, sister to Pharaoh Seti II. Moses was held in high esteem as a general, until he was banished to Midian for defending a Jewish slave. Now Seti needs this "general of excellent perception" and wants him back. Moses is conscious of his mission to lead his people out of slavery. Pharaoh justifies the enor-

mous waste of human life and the reign of terror as means to an end—
the construction of the enduring pyramids, the progress of culture and
civilization: "I have put men to a purpose who otherwise/ Would have had
not the least meaning," but Moses counters this totalitarian view with the
dignity of the individual: "It is the individual man/ In his individual freedom who can mature/ With his warm spirit the unripe world." Moses
meets with resistance and distrust not only in the palace, but also on the
part of his own people, his sister Miriam and her son Shendi. Only
Pharaoh's son and heir Rameses in youthful idealism opts for Moses and
plans to obtain from his father a gradual mitigation of the Jews' lot. But
Moses rejects any compromise: "We're not concerned with hope,/ Or with
despair; our need is something different:/ To confront ourselves." Upon
Rameses's intercession Shendi is made an officer and thereupon turns into
one of the worst oppressors and begins to regard Moses as a danger to his
own privileges. Moses is treated as an outcast for living through the natural catastrophes which fall upon Egypt in the seven plagues "as though
he owned them." Eventually the country's general distress forces Seti to
set Israel free, but he keeps revoking his promise and thus calls forth even
worse afflictions. God decides to "obliterate the firstborn of Egypt/ All the
firstborn." Rameses, the boy free of guilt and full of the best intentions,
must die too, and Moses cannot prevent it. Moses suffers from the deeds
he is called upon to do which lead to the death of innocent men: "I do not
know why the necessity of God/ Should feed on grief."

THE LADY'S NOT FOR BURNING. Comedy in three acts. Free verse. First
edition London 1949. First performance March 10, 1948, London, Arts
Theatre Club. Time: "1400 either more or less exactly." Place: a room in
the house of Hebble Tyson, Mayor of the small market-town of Cool
Clary, England.

In his quartet of seasonal plays, Fry has so far paid his tribute to spring
(*The Lady's not for Burning*), autumn (*Venus Observed*), and winter (*The
Dark Is Light Enough*). The seasons are not merely the foil for the characters' inner life, but their heartbeat. Nature is mobilized dramatically as
an antagonist, as a higher instance, the vehicle of events and destiny. Fry
looks for the spontaneous natural ethos of Pan in the merry paradoxes of
existence. The magic of the seasons' progression, of rise and decline, makes
man one with vegetation in his love, his joy, and his grief. This play belongs to the spring, the time of restless new beginnings, of disturbing fears,
the time of March winds and April showers, of the ascending sun and
urgent hope. Fry asks the producer of this play to think in images of light,
of everchanging April weather, of sunsets, twilight, and the full moon; of

human intellects dancing together, sometimes lightly soaring, sometimes grave and weighty, sometimes the mock of need and misery and then mocking in return.

At Mayor Hebble Tyson's house, guests are expected for a peaceful family celebration, as young Alizon Eliot, just out of a convent school, is to be betrothed to Tyson's nephew Humphrey Devize. But suddenly there is a disturbance. The little town is in the grip of a witchhunt and a doomsday mood. Jennet Jourdemayne is being persecuted as a witch and takes refuge with the mayor. She is supposed to have changed the rag-and-bone man Skipps into a dog. In his turn, the discharged soldier Thomas Mendip seeks to exculpate the girl by confessing to having killed Skipps and demands to be hanged. He is fed up with life. Mayor Tyson and Justice Tappercoom are somewhat confused in the exercise of their office: Jennet swears her innocence, and Thomas will not retract his confession. To earn the gallows, he even pretends to be the devil. To cure Thomas of his "suicidal tendencies," he is to attend the evening's festivities with Jennet. Then the unpredictable April mood takes possession of the mayor's household. Humphrey and his brother Nicholas bash each other about in rivalry over Alizon. The girl elopes with Richard, the mayor's young clerk. With grace, gaiety, and reason the "lady not for burning" puts everyone on the right path again. She arouses love in Thomas and with it a new pleasure in life. Old Skipps turns up, very much alive, and so all the accusations fall to the ground. By the light of a full moon, as the cocks announce dawn, the young couple are allowed to set out.


A PHOENIX TOO FREQUENT. One-act comedy. Verse. First edition London 1946. First performance April 25, 1946, London, Mercury Theatre. Time: antiquity. Place: the tomb of Virilius, near Ephesus.

This one-act play gives us the key to Fry's zestful, vitalistic poetry, which always celebrates the victory of the natural over the unnatural, the freedom of impulsive feeling as against categories and taboos, the power of paradoxical, immediate, sensual existence. The anecdote first told by Petronius has also been used by Lessing, Cocteau, and Hömberg.

Dynamene has retired with her servant Doto to the tomb of her dead husband, with the intention of grieving and starving herself to death and thus following the man she loved into the underworld. But life in its contrariness sends along the young soldier Tegeus. He urges a cup of his wine upon Dynamene, and she, just to strengthen herself for death, willingly accepts it. The senses awaken, the two talk. Dynamene calls her unexpected guest Chromis, because the "breadlike sound" seems apt for one who seems as appetizing to her as "a crisp loaf." They conjure up the places of their childhood. The exuberance of life and love asserts its elementary right over these two young people and they plan a common future. To his alarm Tegeus, who was supposed to guard the corpses of six hanged men, discovers that one of them has disappeared. This means a court-martial for him, and in his despair he decides he will hang himself on the tree to replace the missing corpse. Dynamene, however, offers her husband's body instead. There is no blasphemy or irreverence in her justification of this deed, only an innocent, matter-of-fact humanity: "How little you can understand. I loved/ His life not his death. And now we can give his death/ The power of life." Doto cheerfully raises the bottle to "the master. Both the masters."

The language follows the psychological transformation and shifts from the initial parody of a bombastically expressed unnatural and theatrical death-urge to the celebration of life's victory in diction of folk-song simplicity.


A SLEEP OF PRISONERS. One-act play. Free verse. First edition London 1951. First performance April 23, 1951, Oxford, University Church. Time: not specified. Place: the interior of a church.

This play, which was commissioned by the Religious Drama Society, is not only meant to be performed in a church, but uses the church as a setting and living space, a place for men's doubts and purification.

Four prisoners are quartered in the church: Corporal Joe Adams and privates David King, Peter Abel, and Tim Meadows. First they are shown in their ordinary life—the practical David's quarrels with the dreamer Peter, the invalid Meadow's pains—and then in their true selves, asleep. In their dreams they are faced with hard decisions in situations out of the Old Testament. Personal fear and hope, anguish and doubt are subsumed in the eternal symbols of man's bondage to inevitable fate. "I am history's wish and must come true." In all the changing dream-visions David is the man of action—Cain, King David, and Abraham ("Let me . . . be active . . . whatever damned result")—and Peter the one who suffers, like Abel, Absalom, Isaac.

First Meadows dreams, in the perspective of God, of the fratricide: Cain (David), "a muscular strapling/ With all his passions about him," sees his own sound vitality invalidated by Abel's (Peter's) "angel-sickness" and strangles him, while Adam (Adams) has to look on, powerless. Then David sees himself in his dream as King David, led by political necessity and his own obsession with justice to have his rebellious son Absalom (Peter) killed. In Peter's dream, Peter is the happy boy Isaac, about to be sacrificed by his father Abraham (David). Corporal Adams, finally, dreams of himself and his comrades as the three youths in the burning fiery furnace. The fire of guilt and discord burns off the cords that tied them, and the prisoners' faith in the future survives: "But good's unguarded/ As defenceless as a naked man./ Imperishably. Good has no fear;/ Good is itself, whatever comes . . . Affairs are now soul size./ The enterprise/ Is exploration into God."


VENUS OBSERVED. Comedy in three acts. Free verse. First edition London 1950. First performance January 18, 1950, London, St. James's Theatre. Time: the present. Place: observatory and garden at Stellmere Park, the Duke of Altair's mansion.

The autumnal atmosphere of this play reflects man's involvement in cosmic decline. The blood moves more lethargically, longings are darker, in the hours of the falling leaves the human heart knows what it has missed. The twilight of a solar eclipse dims the illusions, those reflexes of daily self-deception: "We have a borrowed brilliance . . . Here we're as dull as unwashed plates; out there/ We shine. That's a consideration. Come/ Close to paradise, and where's the lustre?/ But still, at some remove, we shine, and truth/ We hope is content to keep a distant prospect."
The aging Duke of Altair has invited three former loves to observe an eclipse with him. The astronomer-epicure feels ready to retire into a comfortable marriage for the rest of his life; his grown son Edgar is to decide which of the three it is to be and hand the mother of his choice an apple. After the eclipse the sunlight is doubly bright as it falls upon Perpetua, the young daughter of the duke's agent, Reedbeck, who has come home unexpectedly from overseas. Entranced, the duke wants to press the apple upon her, but on an impulse she neatly shoots it in two with a pistol, because "it appeared to be, in a misty way/ Like a threat to my new-come freedom." Edgar, too, quickly falls in love with the girl and outshoots his father in the amorous archery contest. Perpetua knows that her father has long cheated the duke and taken a generous amount of the latter's income, and for the sake of her father and the family honor she is prepared to pay the price by accepting the duke's proposal. She meets him at night in the observatory, which suddenly goes up in flames. The actress Rosabel Fleming has set fire to it because she is jealous of the duke's preoccupation with something so inhuman as science. The two stargazers are saved. Perpetua decides she would rather have Edgar; the duke picks Rosabel, the flame of whose love has lit up for him the path of serene resignation.
As the plot proceeds through mythological analogies—the judgment of Paris, the shot of the arrow, and the Saturnian revolt of the young against their father—so the stylized verse language uses semantic analogies. Per-

petua, the "perpetual," is the personification of light and love, the motive power of this world: "I move, and the movement goes from life/ To life all round me. And yet I have to be/ Myself. And what is *my* freedom becomes/ Another person's compulsion." The verse carries the mythological quotations, the exotic names of stars, like ornaments, like invocations of a deeper reality imbued with nature's magic.

## GARDNER, Herb
(United States, born 1934)


A THOUSAND CLOWNS. Comedy in three acts. Prose. First edition New York 1962. First performance April 5, 1962, New York, Eugene O'Neill Theatre. Time: the present. Place: Murray Burns's apartment in New York.

The underlying situation of Saroyan's *My Heart's in the Highlands*—the daydreamer who never grows up and lives by his wits, which are those of a roguish, precocious boy—is made more pointed by maliciously intelligent social criticism. The dissolute television writer Murray Burns lives with his twelve-year-old nephew Nick in a picturesquely squalid bohemian atmosphere. Is Murray a man who has conquered for himself a boundless freedom, out of which he can make war against those who are apparently sure of themselves and successful in life? Or is he simply an unusual egotist, an eternally rebellious simpleton who deludes himself by cranky eccentricities into the self-confidence of a misunderstood genius? The outside world of officialdom and administration erupts into this playful Arcadia in the persons of two file-carrying social workers who want to save Nick by removing him from his questionable environment. The façade of these do-gooders is shaken by Murray's carefree and naive grasp of things. Their self-assurance crumbles and, forgetting her fanatic devotion to duty, the child-psychologist Sandra Markowitz turns into a loving, understanding woman who becomes engaged to Murray. For the self-reliant outsider Murray this means a compromise, a return to ordered society, for "That's the most you should expect of life . . . a really good apology for all the things you won't get."


## GATTI, Armand
(France, born 1924)


CHRONIQUES D'UNE PLANÈTE PROVISOIRE [*Reports from a Provisional Planet*]. Thirty-three reports with inserts. Prose and free verse. First performance October 3, 1963, Toulouse, Capitole. Time: the present. Place: stylized variable settings.

Gatti takes issue with the recent German past, but not in a documentary play like Weiss's or Kipphardt's and not in an illusionistic one like Hochhuth's. Instead, he uses stylized historical facts in analogies and free associations whose multiple refractions exemplify the ambivalence of events more clearly than does straightforward representation concerned with facts. All the more disturbingly does he make us aware of the twin aspects of stupidity and baseness, horror and ridicule, nightmare and farce: "We must figure out some sort of story. Nobody accepts the intolerable truth of today. . . . The only truth with which it is possible to live is the lie." The action takes place simultaneously on three levels whose sharply contrasting dimensions mutually illuminate and explain each other.

A satellite with five astronauts is launched into outer space. Their reports from a "provisional planet" are a frame for the events in the fictitious but clearly recognizable military state of Barbarotia. The action gains yet more detachment by the insertions of bulletins from the concentration camp prisoner Shertoc, which are contrasted with the prose scenes by the use of free verse. When it comes to direct accusations against fascist terror, the play withdraws behind documentation—Gatti does not objectify the horror, but conveys it by the projection of a faded photograph as evidence, or by the alienation effect of a lyrical epitaph on memories that can be no more than fragmentary. Barbarotia, under its anti-Semitic, extreme-rightwing military dictatorship, has unleashed a world war against the rest of the universe—the Starry States, the Piccadilly Circusians, and the Tolstoyevskians. The deputy leader Little Rat (a caricatured Goebbels convulsed by stomach cramps) rouses the "nation of steel" with intoxicating propaganda slogans of final victory and racial domination. He works out a new popular religion which exalts the leader as a mythic superman and guardian of the Holy Grail. At the same time he plans to depose that leader as a lunatic. This national idol turns out to be a robot in the form of a dog, a ceaselessly barking, driveling machine. Details from the National Socialist party history of the Third Reich are reproduced, grotesquely distorted. An omnipotent Plenipotentiary for the Science of Spatial and Numerical Magnitudes represents the influence of astrology on the government. Joel Brand's unsuccessful mission, at Eichmann's instance, to barter Jews for Allied trucks, is transposed into Shertoc's attempt to barter prisoners for carnivorous plants. Nature's secret weapon—a caricature of the Third Reich's psychosis about miracle weapons—is to decide the final victory, but in the end merely provides a pretext for liquidating the government's own counterespionage services. Eichmann is represented by Angel Pupil, the leader of the Black Guard. The ambiguous attitude of the neutrals and the various churches is reflected in the benevolently correct disinterest of the Rousseauvetic Republic and in the unctuous regret expressed by the Church of the Fifteen Sorrows. Rebellion against political terror is left to the powerless individual: Lieutenant Quatrain protests vainly against the mass exterminations. Fast moving shots of realistic details are given distance by fade-out techniques. Jewish auxiliary policemen betray their relatives in order to achieve the daily quota of deportees. After the collapse of the front the political turncoats get ready to redesign their own past. But at this point the astronauts from earth intervene. Their silhouettes conduct a trial by the victors and establish a new order.

A cast of more than one hundred is employed; some scenes last only a few seconds.

UN HOMME SEUL *[A Man Alone]*. Play in eight parts. Prose and verse. First performance May 11, 1966, St. Etienne, Comédie. Time: during the Chinese civil war. Place: China and Formosa.

In a complex dramatic construction, Gatti tries to show how man's consciousness is independent of time, space, and reality. He disintegrates the action into associations and imaginary aspects. But unlike the playwrights of the Absurd, Gatti does not present this play of psychological facets as merely a sensitive tracing of nonlogical affective forces, but mirrors experiences, reflections, and attitudes. With this technique Gatti tries to interpret his theme logically, to get down to lower strata of reality, and to explain connections and correlations in simultaneous juxtaposition. Gatti uses a historical turning point in the Chinese revolution to show how relative appearance becomes and how the external world disintegrates under the impact of spontaneous experience. History is defined in ironical and skeptical terms: "History (woe to the defeated!) consists of the opinion of the majority among a number of persons closely or remotely involved in a particular event. And this opinion (by whatever compromises it has gained the majority) is filtered by interpretations. (Barring accidents, it never had anything to do with what really happened.)"

The Communist partisan leader Li Tche-liu has fled into the trackless Long-chen mountains after a crushing defeat by Kuomintang troops under General Chiang Kai-shek. His only companion is the faithful Tsun-yen. The lost battle is for him nothing but a pledge of future victory. For the grief of the defeated is a challenge and hence must lead to a new, embittered revolt. In an "imaginary trial" Li Tche-liu conjures up memories of the past, expectations of the future, hopes and disappointments of his life in a dream procession of figures: "What does it mean, the present? It is an imaginary trial, which brings together a number of persons (who did or did not exist—who may be dead or alive), who want to discuss what happened in the past and in the future." General Pai Tchun-shi, who, as military governor of the province of Kwangsi was Li Tche-liu's bitter enemy, has begun his shadow existence as representative minister in Formosa, while Communism reigns in China. Pai Tchun-shi's reminiscences and the reports of his accomplice Po reveal other facets of discord

and confusion, but also of Li Tche-liu's persistence. The latter has dedicated himself heart and soul to the revolution; he has sacrificed his family
and friends, had to leave his wife repeatedly in order to take flight. Threatened by arrest, she eventually obeyed her mother and married an officer of
the government army, but in the end sacrifices herself in order to cover Li
Tche-liu's retreat. Li's son is taken as a hostage and tortured by Pai
Tchun-shi to lure Li, who is put in irons on party orders and has to resign
himself to the child's destruction. His daughter Erh-hu is sold by his
father to an American convent, which pays more than a Chinese brothel
would. Everything must serve the cause of the revolution. Li Tche-liu and
his friends are always haunted by the secret fear that the new China for
which they fight may later disavow them as bandits and reject them. While
Li Tche-liu dreams of being honored on Red Square in Moscow, struggles
for power spread through his own ranks. An ideological rival expels him
from the party as a "fractionist." By courageous self-criticism he manages
to justify himself before an official committee, but then a further political
change of direction finally displaces him. In an effort at protecting him,
one after another of his adherents pretend that they are he and die under
Pai Tchun-shi's tortures. The last flashback is the initial situation: Li
Tche-liu and his companion Tsun-yen are hiding in a cave. Tsun-yen tries
to gain the friendship of his idol, to whom he has sacrificed everything.
When he realizes that Li Tche-liu knows nothing except cold party
fanaticism, that family and friends are for him mere means to an end,
mere munitions of varying caliber for the final victory, he kills him. And
the long-dead partisans of the "imaginary trial" march on.

The imaginary figures of the past and the future are distinguished by the
colors of their costumes. The separate "versions" show up in filmic cuts
and sudden lighting effects, and overlap and displace each other.


LE POISSON NOIR [The Black Fish]. Play in six complications, reports,
counter-report, mimodrama, prelude, and finale. Prose and verse. First
published Paris 1958. First performance October 29, 1964, Toulouse,
Théâtre Daniel Sorano. Time: 222–221 B.C. Place: China.

The eternal game of rulers, their struggle for creative self-realization confirming itself in the establishment of a world empire, and the growing
temptation to abuse power are shown in multiple permutations on a cosmic
scale. Men see their nature demoniacally mirrored in animal masks—of
fish and monkeys—and they appear as willow trees and horses, have access
to insights and modes of experience that are not granted to man. Apart
from the disintegration of time and space, the author has also done away
with the inevitability of the forms of existence, which in a ceaseless circle

of transformations leads from man, animal, and plant into the circulation of eternal life itself: "All our life, or its counterpart, is exchangeable. The movement became illegible after hundreds of years and yet is the present, no less durable for all that. . . . Our eternity, that is the last image we did not succeeed in abandoning."

Emperor Ts'in has ruthlessly molded the chaos of warring tribes into a powerful empire and is building the Great Wall of China. He banishes his son Fu Su, an unworthy patron of scholarship. Tan, the ruler of the southern state of Yen, is afraid of the conqueror's drive and sends the sage King Ko to Ts'in's court, where King Ko channels the empire's energies for some years into gigantic irrigation projects and thus to peaceful purposes. But a further increase in Ts'in's power spells destruction for the peace-loving Tan. It would seem that only the emperor's death can avert the threat. An attempt on the emperor's life fails. Ts'in abdicates in order to seek out the black fish, his cosmic counterpart. A doll is placed at the head of the government in place of the vanished emperor, and the mechanism of bureaucracy keeps things going. Tan senselessly sacrifices his life for freedom and a second attempt at assassination, which is condemned to futility in this soulless system.

This tale is the mere scaffolding for a profound improvisation, which makes use of films, loudspeakers, choreographed movement, and chorus to represent conflicting purposes in changing manifestations and contrapuntal orchestration.


TATENBERG II (*La Deuxième Existence du camp de Tatenberg*). Prologue, four actualities, four flashbacks, total recall, and anticipation. Prose and verse. First edition Paris 1962. First performance April 13, 1962, Lyons, Théâtre des Célestins. English version entered in 1967 by Liverpool University for the 13th National Student Drama Festival, Bradford, England, December 28, 1967 to January 2, 1968. Time: after the end of the Second World War. Place: fair-ground on the Danube.

People are projections of their own pasts, incomplete objectivizations of the dynamite in their souls which threatens to tear them to pieces. Gatti explains: "This stage experiment is based exclusively on memory. . . . To trace its course is tantamount to drawing a path which, as it were, runs parallel with visible reality, but has no more than chance coincidence with it. Or better: visible reality becomes a film screen on which memory projected shadows—shadows set in motion by memory's inherent connections and associations."

Hildegard Frölick, the owner of a puppet theater, and the Baltic Jew Ilya Moïssevitch, who runs a "music robot," travel from fair to fair. Their hope of a common future is over and over again buried by memories. Having survived implies guilt, they are utterly incapable of digesting the horror they have lived through and thus cannot break free of the past. Moïssevitch is haunted by his dead comrades from the Tatenberg concentration camp. Abel Antokokoletz acted as *Kapo* for the Germans and thereby earned the hatred of his fellow sufferers. He was killed at the liberation. The athletic Ukrainian Kravchenko and the Spaniard Rodriguez bitterly resented being excluded as foreigners from the community of the Jewish inmates. After the war, Solange Valette becomes the first victim of the "imaginary Tatenberg camp." Searching for her missing son, she turns up on the spectral make-believe railway station which the *Schutzstaffeln* had put up to deceive the candidates for death on their arrival. Rodriguez surrounds her with shy tenderness, but she dies of sheer hopelessness. Solange's son Guinguin, an invalid, now accompanies Moïssevitch on his round of fair grounds. While Moïssevitch is thus haunted by his memories, Hildegard Frölick is plagued by recurring hallucinations of her husband's death. Frölick was shot for neglect of duty when on guard at the front with Captain Von Basseville and Johan Steltenkamp. As masked puppets the dead now dominate the show-booth and Hildegard's life. Moïssevitch vainly tries to remove these monitory figures by force, and vainly looks for consolation in the gentle calm of the Danube landscape: "This river, which is as old as the world, has made me grasp that, in spite of Tatenberg, the leaves have always smiled, and that they still smile." He cannot save himself from the dead.

On three levels—in the concentration camp, in the "imaginary" postwar camp, and in the whirling business of the fair—man is surrounded by the visions of his fear and unease. With the help of film montage techniques, resulting in the juxtaposition of sequences from different periods, the action is developed in terms of the dynamism of explosive associations.


LA VIE IMAGINAIRE DE L'ÉBOUEUR AUGUSTE GEAI *[The Imaginary Life of the Road-Sweeper Augustus Gee]*. Play in four parts. Prose. First published in *L'Avant-Scène* No. 272, 1962. First edition in *Théâtre III*, Paris 1962. First performance February 16, 1962, Villeurbanne, Théâtre de la Cité. Time: first half of the twentieth century. Place: Paris.

The marginal destiny of a man who longs for a little security and must pay with his life for his championship of justice makes this ordinary social drama merely a pretext for a stage vision. The multiple refractions of this life show the ceaseless effort at self-realization, which—and the irony is cruel and consistent—can succeed only in an "imaginary life," in dreams, play, and illusions.

The road-sweeper Auguste Geai is mortally wounded by the police during a demonstration. As he lies dying in the infirmary, the hopes and disappointments of his life pass across the stage like shadows and disappear. At nine years of age, he is seen starving in the poverty-stricken Quartier de la Vierge, a shantytown where the immigrants live; as a young recruit in the First World War he loses Pauline, the only true love of his life, to the temptations of the street. These are the first two existential positions shown in contrapuntal interaction. At thirty, he is resigned. He finds his place in the world, dons the uniform of a road-sweeper and leads an indifferent married life. At every point he comes up against an adversary. In his youth, the black Baron is an atheist tempter; later, the white Baron represents the boss who provokes a strike and thus causes Geai's death. At the end, Geai sees himself just before his death as a pensioner, who hands on to his son Christian, a film producer, the legacy of his fight for freedom and social justice. Christian makes a film of it; the revolt of the individual, for which Auguste went to his death, is exploited commercially and, as an aesthetic trading commodity, smoothly enters that organized world which it purports to oppose. A hectic "dance marathon" expresses the dying man's whirling imaginary world. In flashbacks and anticipations every figure is seen partnered by some particular object of the illusion in which his life was spent—a person, an animal, a working tool, or a fantasy. The various humdrum tragedies unroll in the rhythm of this kinetic trance— and in the end are revealed to be mere skillful arrangements by the showman Christian. "Life is a dream, but a dream that hurts (gun-butts are there for beating). Illusions make us great, and when we lose them, we are small, and with the last of them we disappear (only the gun-butts remain)." The two Barons die in the riot, and, with his two adversaries, the road-sweeper, too, dies. But what Auguste deplores is not the inevitability of having to die, but "having to do it in such great weariness and with so many trifles before our eyes." An inner monologue ramifies and is seen as simultaneous scenes of possibilities and reminiscence. Time and space no longer exist. On seven different platforms of as many colors the dying road-sweeper reenacts his life at the various stages of his development. These stages displace each other, overlap, and always preserve the spontaneity of improvisation.

# GELBER, Jack
(United States, born 1932)

THE APPLE. Play in three acts. Prose. First edition New York 1961. First performance December 7, 1961, New York, The Living Theatre. Time: the present. Place: a restaurant or coffee shop.

The text is written to simulate improvisation. Many elements of the "happening"—though still staged and not spontaneous—are anticipated, such as the apparent fusion of actors and audience into the unity of an experiment and spontaneity taken in the absolute, so that man reacts to the challenge of a meaningless situation by nothing but his unleashed passions. The attempt to preserve the semblance of the documentary, for instance by requiring all of the actors to insert their personal names into the script is equally characteristic of this style of apparently spontaneous invention.

A handful of actors have got together, and this time Anna is "in charge" of the evening. She improvises a session at the dentist's. The nihilist Ajax is the Doctor, Iris the Hustler is his assistant, and the whimpering patients are mimed by the confidence trickster Jabez and the Negro Ace. Spontaneous confessions and psychoanalytical phrases again and again interrupt the set situations of the framing action: "You know our configuration is like the structure of a nucleus." Mr. Stark, a spastic, becomes the butt of sadistic outbursts and is degraded to the state of an animal. At this point Tom, a former silent-screen actor, turns up drunk and boisterous in the auditorium. He starts a fight, dies of a heart attack, but soon intervenes again in the play. Eventually they all confront each other in animal masks which express varying aspects of brutality, rapacity, sexual desire, and banality. They murder each other and yet are kept alive by hatred. The end is paralyzing frustrations: "Isn't it confusing and then just boring? Life is such a bore. . . . You don't know what freedom is until you feel the yoke." They tear a window-display mannequin to pieces and worship the dead props of living. Faith in hygiene and vitamins is elevated to a message of redemption, and everybody wallows in an ecstasy alternating between Messianic aggression and animal-like self-abasement. An apple nibbled by all serves as a challenge to reality.

The play is an orgiastic stunt intended to exert a shock effect.

THE CONNECTION. Play in two acts. Prose. First edition New York 1960. First performance July 15, 1959, New York, The Living Theatre. Time: the present: Leach's pad, a hang-out for heroin addicts.

Jazz and heroin, the narcotics of a languishing and frustrated world, are the theme of this brutal improvisation: "Find a horror. Then you try to tell people it isn't a horror."

Jaybird, the author, and Jim Dunn, the producer, prepare the stage for the informal representation of a narcotics séance. Some jazz musicians are engaged for background and a group of drug addicts are to be photographed in various stages of dissolution. They are Solly, a frustrated intellectual; the psychopath Ernie; and the dreamer Sam. All of them long for the next "fix" and feverishly wait for the "gallant white powder," heroin, supplied by the dope-pusher Cowboy. The naive Sister Salvation is to dispel the suspicions of the police by her presence. The syringe passes from hand to hand, confessions dissolve in a confused babble, and the photographers are busy. The theater professionals are going to use this revolting photographic material for a film, for only publicity can help these depravities to a deeper meaning and lucrative application. The play is a farce wavering undecidedly between provocation and speculation.


## GENET, Jean
(France, born 1910)


THE BALCONY (Le Balcon). Play in two acts. Written 1956. First edition Décines 1956, second version 1960. First performance April 22, 1957, London, Arts Theatre Club. Translated by Bernard Frechtman, New York, Grove Press, and London, Faber, 1958. Time: the present. Place: an imaginary monarchy.

Genet's favorite theme, split identity, is in this play lifted from the sphere of the psychopathic individual, as in *The Maids,* and broadened out into a social problem. Lies and deception, the fascination of being different, lead into an intoxicating and enjoyable masquerade and create the true existence which reality withholds.

Irma's luxury brothel is the scene where men indulge their illusions and emotions, act out extreme situations and contrived experiences: "Ornaments, lace, it is through you that I reach myself, through you that I reconquer lost possessions, with your help that I return to an ancient place from which I was exiled. I stand face to face with my death." Ordinary men escape their humdrum lives and in the brothel perform the rituals of wished-for roles as bishops, generals, or judges. The girls readily enough provide the cues for this imaginary personality cult. Sexual desires have long been smothered in this house by lust for power and the individual's sadistic actions. A revolution of young idealists who, under their leader Roger, believe in reality and want to prove themselves in it, sweeps away the specter of perverted dreams: "the main thing is that the revolution breaks out to show our disgust of play-acting and complacency." However, the people demand not freedom, but the old-established idols of power, to be feared and worshiped. The chief of police presents Irma to the masses as their new queen, and the judge, the bishop, and the general are brought out of mothballs and set in motion like marionettes. They now publicly act out their wish-fulfillment dreams and make use of the magical symbols of power. Everything turns into a function of this system of privileges. The Chief of Police, the head of the previous regime, and Roger, the champion of new beginnings, must both give in to the new authorities. Roger escapes into the brothel in order to dream himself into the part of chief of police—to become a spectator in a world of specters. Topical satire and symbolic ritual are juxtaposed without transitions.

THE BLACKS *(Les Nègres)*. Play in two acts. Prose. Written 1957. First edition Décines 1958. First performance October 28, 1958, Paris, Théâtre de Lutèce. Translated by Bernard Frechtman, New York, Grove Press, and London, Faber, 1960. Time: not specified. Place: empty stage with pedestals in front of black curtains.

The world, inescapably divided as it is between executioners and victims, oppressors and oppressed, is represented by an outlawed, hated race. The intoxication to be found in ritual and spontaneous frenzy provides an outlet for all the emotional eruptions conceivable on life's dark side: "The time has not yet come when one can stage plays that treat of noble things. But perhaps some may sense what lies behind this construction of emptiness and words. We are what we are required to be, and, absurdly, we shall remain that until the end."

On the empty stage four Negro couples in evening dress dance a Mozart minuet around a catafalque. In the gallery, the "court" watches in puppetlike attitudes of detachment: Queen, Valet, Governor, Judge and Missionary—all Negroes grotesquely dressed up as dignitaries of the ruling class which they hate and admire and massacre, and with whose victims they identify in play. The group around the catafalque releases hatred and destructive rapture, fears and longings by festive visual and rhetorical excesses made up of songs, dance, chorus, pantomime, litany, and witchcraft. Any beginnings of coherent action, of concrete connection between the situation and the characters, are drowned in unfettered sensuality. As soon as events begin to have logic and motivation, as soon as relationships are established and action seems comprehensible in terms of reality, Genet shifts by association to another plane. In order to escape a standardized, traceable consistency, he plunges into a free play of aspects and possibilities. The result is that events on various levels are taken up, dropped, and then resumed on another level without logical connection. The catafalque contains the corpse of a white woman who has been sacrificed to the hatred of the blacks as a representative victim. She happened, this time, to be a drunken beggar woman. Archibald Wellington, the "producer," gets Deodatus Village to reproduce the murder in a ritual ceremony. In the course of it, the symbolic act is transformed into the sexual murder by Deodatus, intoxicated with blood-lust, of a baker's wife. Abruptly, the events shift—they become a demonstration in front of a court of law consisting of the watching whites. Tyranny and anarchy face each other in derisive enmity. As a reprisal, the whites chase the blacks into the African swamps and are killed by the natives. A shot is heard offstage—a traitor is executed. The changing facets of the play were meant merely to mask reality. This reality itself is perhaps only a token of things to come, or perhaps reminiscence and witchcraft. The minuet around the catafalque begins once more, masks and props for a new episode lie in readiness. Only Village and Miss Virtue, the despised half-breed and the prostitute, manage to conquer a little piece of reality through their love, and escape the hectic hallucination.

DEATHWATCH (Haute surveillance). One-act play. Prose. Written 1946. First edition Paris 1949. First performance February 26, 1949, Paris, Théâtre des Mathurins. Translated by Bernard Frechtman, New York, Grove Press, and London, Faber, 1961. Time: the present. Place: a prison cell.

This is an autobiographical prison play reveling in its psychologically extreme situation. In monomaniac self-fascination, the particular case of prison psychosis is raised to that of an exceptional world—a hierarchy of physical beauty and murderous strength, brutality, and crime. Somewhere in the prison some cell holds a Negro murderer, famed for his crimes of violence, whose rebellious and terrorizing strength makes him the idol of all the other inmates. Like all the others, Greeneyes, Lefranc, and the teen-age Maurice are governed in their attitude by that invisible, remote, godlike authority. Of the three, Greeneyes, the sexual murderer, is the only one to have received the consecration of bloodshed. The burglar Lefranc and the pickpocket Maurice admire and flatter him. In the compulsion of inescapable proximity all human elements—kindness and hatred, jealousy and pride, revulsion at having to feel grateful—dissolve in a frenzy of hysterical provocations and enmities. Everything turns into a weapon of self-affirmation—the urge to conceal something within oneself just as much as the contrary urge to emotional exhibitionism. Lefranc, the intellectual, writes on behalf of the illiterate Greeneyes to the latter's wife. He sows discord between them and tries to incite Maurice against the murderer. The boy coquettishly excites the men's subconscious desires. Lefranc, the petty criminal, longs for the distinction of committing a capital crime. He invents bloody deeds, paints tattooes on his chest, eventually strangles Maurice, but is still not accepted among the lawless. For he has picked on murder just to show off, whereas Greeneyes was overwhelmed by murder as though by a natural catastrophe.

The style is deliberately anti-illusionist and rejects anything resembling an environmental study: "The whole play goes by like a dream. . . . The movements of the actors are, as far as possible, to be either clumsy or else incomprehensibly swift as lightning."

THE MAIDS (Les Bonnes). One-act tragedy. Prose. First edition Décines 1948, second version Sceaux 1954. First performance April 17, 1947, Paris, Théâtre de l'Athénée. Translated by Bernard Frechtman, New York, Grove Press, and London, Faber, 1954. Time: the present. Place: Madame's bedroom.

Outcasts are condemned to be subservient in the drawing-room world of Madame, never allowed to participate in it. Servants have access to their employer's world only in games and dreams, where they can give vent to their love-hate, their yearnings, and their destructive urge. But Genêt flings no accusation at society. He develops an extreme case by making it into a repeatedly renewed game and a magic ceremony: "I tried to gain enough distance to be able to use a declamatory tone and to put the theatrical upon the stage. I hoped thereby to do away with the characters . . . and to replace them by symbols, which should be as remote as possible from what they really represent and yet closely connected with it, so that they can serve as the sole bond between author and audience. In short, I wanted to make the figures on the stage no more than metaphors for what they are supposed to represent."

As soon as Madame leaves her apartment, her maids, the sisters Claire and Solange, play the game of masters and servants, torment and suffering, oppression and docility: "I have to talk. I must empty myself. . . . Can we continue the game at all? Once there is no one any more on whom I can spit when he calls me Claire, I shall choke on my spittle." By an anonymous denunciation the two maids have caused the arrest of Monsieur and now they learn over the telephone that he has been released. They enjoy their malice as much as they itch for punishment. They imagine how they are going to strangle Madame, and at the same time wallow in the humiliation

which they endure with rapture. Eruptions of hate and penitential writhings are kindled by the unattainable sphere of the masters. So deeply are
they in the grip of the dream of what they will never be, that they dissolve in it even their own reality, their own personal existence. The
phantasmagoria of maid and mistress has long destroyed every human
relationship, even the bond between sisters: "I should like to help you. I
should like to comfort you, but I know I disgust you. I am repulsive to
you. I know it, because you disgust me. Love in servitude is no love." When
Madame returns, they both fuss over her obsequiously. They try in vain
to press poisoned tea on her. She rushes to welcome Monsieur, released
from detention. Claire, in the ultimate identification with her part to the
point of self-annihilation, drinks the poison, while Solange "stands, perfectly still, facing the audience, her hands crossed over as though she were
wearing handcuffs."

THE SCREENS (Les Paravents). Play in seventeen scenes. Prose. Written
1959. First edition Décines 1961. First performance May 19, 1961, Berlin,
Schloßparktheater. Translated by Bernard Frechtman, New York, Grove
Press, 1962, and London, Faber, 1963. Time: the present. Place: Algeria.

A sad ballad tells of man hopelessly lost in a compartmentalized world.
The Arab couple Saïd and Leila are the symbol of utter degradation and
loneliness. They are tied to each other in a marriage that is agony, the
most miserable, most despised creatures on earth. They are outcasts by
destiny—Saïd is the country's "poorest son," Leila its "ugliest and cheapest
daughter," they are outlawed by their own people, and they are hated by
all because they live, although poorly, by theft. Saïd rebels against his
destiny by betraying his people and making common cause with the French
colonial masters in the Algerian revolt. By so doing he deprives himself of
the last place on earth that was his by right. He is torn within himself and
a torment to himself: "Even the stones are too soft for me. Everything
should hurt me, everything should disgust me, nauseate me." Thus Saïd
becomes the prototype of a man who can find no support or security either
within himself or around him. All that is left to him is the narcotic of
being evil. He torments Leila, forces her to hide her ugliness behind a
mask, and runs away from her to the brothel, were, under the rule of the
experienced Warda, all feelings stiffen into a ritual of empty gestures. For
Saïd no contact with people is possible any more. The conjuration of the
dead, which Saïd's mother in a witch's frenzy instigates in an attempt to
break through the isolation of the "screens," turns into a farce of selfishness. Even the dead are divided by discord when they indulge their venge-
fulness against Saïd, the apostate. He is shot by his countrymen. But the

world of the dead rejects him and he is left adrift in a no man's land of the soul. Only Leila was devoted to him with faithful love, but the screens of self-contempt and hard-heartedness in his marriage were impenetrable. The characters are driven through the gloom only by addiction to evil, the fascination of blasphemous negation, the urge for self-destruction, the rapture of self-debasement and simmering hate: "Calamity, miracle-working calamity, which remains to us when all else has vanished . . . calamity, pregnant with mystery, you—will help us. I beseech you . . . still upright on my feet, I beseech you: Make my people fertile! Do not let it want!" It is only in the complete extinction of all that exists, in the ultimate degeneration, that the timid glow of a vague yearning for salvation flickers up: "that I shall rot until the end of the world, so that the world rots." A magically opalescent, unreal stage landscape set in front of empty screens opens up with masks, phantoms, screams and dances, with ecstasy and convulsions, obscenities and anthems.

The theme is constantly projected into and swallowed up by a flickering chaos of crazed means of expression. "There are truths that ought never be obeyed. But precisely those are sung and they become truths because they are sung." People are turned into puppets, dead marionettes into participants. The distorted caricatures of the French masters are stuffed puppets strutting about with artificial pride while a shopwindow dummy hung with the tinsel decorations of whole generations becomes the idol. The destructive spirit of the Algerian rising is exemplified visually by meaningless words scribbled hastily on walls. Both content and form manifest a pervading multiple symbolism against a diffuse background.


## GIBSON, William
(United States, born 1914)


TWO FOR THE SEESAW. Play in three acts. Prose. Written 1957. First edition New York 1959. First performance January 16, 1958, New York, Booth Theatre. Time: the present. Place: New York.

A sure-fire hit in psychorealistic Broadway style, the play is a sentimental and realistic romance of everyday life. The techniques of film cutting are occasionally used in the simultaneous stage settings for melodramatic effects. There are only two characters, both failures in life. The unsuccessful lawyer Jerry Ryan and the jobless dancer Gittel Mosca give each other a brief illusion of happiness. Jerry is in the process of being divorced by his wife, to whom he owes his degree and his job, but when she learns that he is living with Gittel she is jealous and returns to him. Out of pity he wants to pretend to the ailing dancer that he still loves her, but Gittel sees through the deception, gives Jerry his freedom, and returns to her loneliness. In almost psychotherapeutic optimism, they both acknowledge that this encounter has made them fitter for their subsequent life.

## GILROY, Frank D.
(United States, born 1926)

THE SUBJECT WAS ROSES. Play in two acts. Prose. First edition New York 1965. First performance May 25, 1964, New York, Royale Theatre. Time: May 1946. Place: John's apartment in the Bronx, New York.

The play is a study in the behavior of people who are unable to communicate and to give or accept love, of their loneliness, and of the traumata of missed and long vanished opportunities. After his discharge from the army, twenty-one-year-old Timmy Cleary returns to his parents' home. John and Nettie long ago drifted apart, and each tries to win the son as an ally in the daily conjugal warfare. Nettie cannot get over her disappointment that John, the hero of her youthful love, has turned into a philistine. John tries to hide his mediocrity behind the façade of a bully. He wants to boast about Timmy's war decorations, of which he is also jealous. Timmy tries to straighten things out and persuades his father to surprise Nettie with a bunch of roses, but the reconciliation founders on their mutual suspicions. Weary of the quarrels, Timmy leaves his home, where love can take no shape other than a desire to dominate and show off.

WHO'LL SAVE THE PLOWBOY? Play in two acts. Prose. First edition New York 1962. First performance January 9, 1962, New York, Phoenix Theatre. Time: the present. Place: the Cobbs's lower-middle-class apartment in New York City.

An ordinary, unsuccessful middle-class marriage serves to demonstrate the meaning and justification of sacrifice. Is self-sacrifice to be valued for itself or only by its results? Does the responsibility for the consequences rest with the person who sacrifices himself, or with the one who accepts the sacrifice?
During the war Larry Doyle saved the life of his friend Albert Cobb, the plowboy, and is now dying of the injury sustained on that occasion. After fifteen years he calls on his friend to find consolation in the latter's domestic happiness, for which he has paid with his own health. The plow-

boy, whose only aspiration in life had been a farm of his own, has failed in all his hopes and has become a drunkard. The child, for Larry the meaning of his sacrifice, is an idiot. Embittered and disappointed, Albert's wife Helen seeks compensation in adultery. She hates the man who has saved her husband's life and has caused all this misery with his courage. Albert vainly tries to counterfeit a happy domestic life with the help of a strange child. For the sake of his friend, Larry wearily and hopelessly takes part in the pretense, and as the ultimate sacrifice renounces his own despair.

The author is thoroughly at home in his chosen social setting, and uses the psychological play as an approach to greatly simplified metaphysical questions.


## GIMÉNEZ-ARNAU, José
(Spain, born 1912)

MURIÓ HACE QUINCE AÑOS *[He Died Fifteen Years Ago]* Play in ten scenes. Prose. First performance March 17, 1953, Madrid, Teatro Español. Time: the present. Place: Madrid and Southern France.

Man is caught in the battle of ideologies: "I began to suffer when I realized that it was my lot to be hero and traitor at the same time."

Diego, the son of General Acuna, was kidnapped by Communist partisans fifteen years ago, when he was still a child, and brought up in Moscow as a convinced Marxist. He was also trained as a terrorist. Now he is told of his true origins and allowed to go back to his father's home in order to spy on Acuna, who is leader of the Christian-Conservative party. The guileless pleasure of his father, who unreservedly trusts his newly found son, the love of his sister Monica, and family resemblances of temperament all estrange Diego from the world revolution and offer him a security he never knew before. When the party leader orders him to kill his father, he sacrifices himself instead. Acuna quietly sums up the case: "He died fifteen years ago." Diego's sacrificial death is the reference point of the action; antecedents are shown in flashbacks.

## GOMBROWICZ, Witold
(Poland, born 1904)

IWONA, KSIĘZNICZKA BURGUNDA [Yvonne, Princess of Burgundy].
Written 1935. First published in Skemandes, Warsaw, 1935. First performance 1957, Cracow. Time: the legendary past. Place: the royal court
of Burgundy.

The theme of the outsider whose difference puts the majority's conventions in question—the same theme that Klima treated in terms of social
criticism in *A Castle*—is transplanted to a legendary royal court in a
permutation cruel as a game and harmless as a toy. Here, too, an individual
dares to break through the consistency of conventions, the circle of predetermined reactions. Society has only one response to this assault of the
unforeseen: destruction. Society can feel secure in its standards and confirmed in its validity only if everything that contradicts it is eliminated.
In a reckless experiment with himself, Prince Philip is engaged to ugly,
insignificant, ridiculous, silly Yvonne. He means this irrevocable decision
to be a challenge to himself and his own reality, a trick by which to call
forth a new result hitherto beyond his potentialities. Yvonne's deficiencies,
her taciturnity and indifference, her repulsive nature which constitutes
the perfect negation of all the expectations placed in her, become a challenge for the whole court. Everybody takes Yvonne's clumsiness as an
allusion to, and soon as an open exposure of, their own carefully concealed
weaknesses and faults. The otherness of the princess is a reproachful cor-
relative for every individual thus caught out in his hidden guilt. The king
is reminded of the seamstress whose life he once wrecked. The queen is
made to feel ashamed of her sentimental versifying, and the prince's complacency is exposed. All of them secretly plan to get rid of Yvonne. With
spiteful cunning a banquet is arranged in her honor, and she is deliberately
made to choke to death on a fishbone. All are relieved to be among themselves again and during the funeral ceremonies indulge their own irresistibility. This mockery of absolute moral standards is presented in the
setting of a viciously playful choreography of discrimination: cascades of
laughter, sarcastic interludes, voluptuously chiseled displays of malice.

SLUB [The Wedding]. Play in three acts. Rhythmic prose. Written 1945.
First edition Paris 1950. First public performance January 8, 1964, Paris,
Théâtre Récamier. Time and place: not specified.

Man is exposed in a surrealist dream in which not only time and space are dissolved, but also the unity of the personality. The world is visited by a thousand plagues, man is torn by wounds, distorted by baseness. With his faith and longing he tries to invalidate reality and to force the intact ideal down to himself. He cannot do so without the insignia of earthly power, which he acquires by autosuggestion, to realize his dream. But these guilt-ridden, hollow forms of power corrupt the idealist's pure aspirations, make them arbitrary and despotic. In form, the drama is an experiment in the magic of language and speech that invades the field of semantics. It is a musical score of sounds, images, and rhythms, and of silences often signifying the ultimate, extreme vibrations of emotional intensity.

Henryk and his friend Vladźo are plodding through a devastated landscape on the North African front. Henryk's thoughts go back to his home in Poland, desires take voice, and by the force of his longing he conjures up Maloszyce, the village of his childhood. But everything that was once so familiar is distorted and defiled as in a nightmare. His parents run a filthy tavern; Maña, the pure girl to whom he was betrothed, has become a slut. Henryk tries to alter this horrible reality by his system of world order. He kneels down in front of his father, a drunkard crippled by gout, pays tribute to him as a king, and feels himself a prince. But this newly enthroned ruler does not have the strength to celebrate the "wedding" and to restore to Maña, by the sacrament, her virginal purity. The Traitor's mockery degrades into a mere masquerade the attempt at existential transformation, which is blasphemously mimicked by the Drunkard. Insidious flattery drives Henryk into thinking of himself as God incarnate. In the person of the Prince he makes ready to perform his own wedding, dethrones his father and has him tortured, and revels in his own grandiose plans; but he founders on his human shortcomings. His throne has to be protected by his henchman, and the Drunkard easily succeeds in arousing Henryk's jealousy of Maña and Vladźo. In the new reality conjured up by Henryk, Vladźo has become a spineless yes-man, but his mere existence adds to the insecurity of the King, weakens him, and jeopardizes his dream of absolute power. He commands that Vladźo must die, and Vladźo complies. At a sumptuous court ball Henryk intends, as a climax, to perform the "wedding," the ritual of world purification and transfiguration, by his own supreme authority. But the Drunkard cynically thrusts him back into reality, shows him the grimacing masks of his environment, the shabbiness of the sham pomp, and eventually the guilt of the King: Vladźo's corpse is among the dancing guests. Henryk despairs of his humanity that is forever condemned to guilt and impotence.

## GOODRICH, Frances, and HACKETT, Albert
(both United States; Goodrich, no date; Hackett, born 1900)

THE DIARY OF ANNE FRANK. Play in three acts. Prose. Based on the book *Anne Frank: The Diary of a Young Girl*. First edition New York 1956. First performance October 5, 1955, New York, Cort Theatre. Time: July 2, 1942 to November 1, 1945. Place: top floor of a warehouse in Amsterdam.

This deeply disturbing contemporary document of racial persecution is at the same time the tragedy of a misunderstood adolescent. Through the troubles of puberty and through the fortitude of thirteen-year-old Anne is revealed the message of human resilience in suffering and faith. "I have often been downcast myself . . . but never in despair. . . . You know what I sometimes think? I think the world may be going through a phase. . . . It'll pass, maybe not for hundreds of years, but some day. . . . I still believe, in spite of everything, that people are really good at heart."

In July 1942 the Jewish families Frank and Van Daan go into hiding from the Gestapo on the top floor of a warehouse. Dutch friends secretly supply them with just enough to live on, and they spend two years packed like sardines into a tiny space. All day long any sudden movement, any noise means risk of death. The adults are estranged from each other by hysterics, egotism, and fear of death. The well-groomed Van Daan is so hungry that he steals bread from the others' scant rations. Anne, an impulsive, zestful, happy child, suffers especially under this forced isolation. She must relentlessly stifle her protests and can never give free rein to her high spirits. Her diary becomes the confidant of her longings and distress. She experiences a first, timid love for Peter, the Van Daans's teen-age son. A thief who has long known of their hideout finally denounces them and they are arrested by the Germans. Only Anne's father survives the concentration camp and when he returns after the war he finds her diary. His moment of recall forms the framework for this play of an underground existence conjured up by flashbacks and a montage of sounds and voices.

# GRASS, Günter
(Germany, born 1927)

BERITTEN HIN UND ZURÜCK *[There and Back on Horseback]*. A prologue on the stage. Prose. First published in *Akzente,* Vol. 5, Munich 1958, pp. 399–409. Acting edition Berlin, Kiepenheuer, 1960. First performance January 17, 1959, Hamburg, Theater 53. Time: the present. Place: an empty stage.

A farce whose form and theme are a deliberate allusion to the *Faust* prologue explores stagecraft as such. It was originally written as a theatrical contribution for a round-table discussion of comedy.

Oblivious of all else, the clown Conelli rides his rocking-horse, when actor, producer, and playwright suddenly all crowd in on him. They tell him to give up his hopelessly obsolete effects and want to remodel him altogether as a modern attraction. To do so, account has to be taken of tragic and comic aspects, surrealism, psychology, and technical progress. To express alienation, the good old rocking-horse must be turned into a skeleton. But Conelli cannot be persuaded to go along with the remodeling. His inspiration is neither stimulated by a promising bed or by paradoxes. Only in his private life has he a problem capable of dramatic development: he refuses to bless the engagement of his daughter Dorothea to a film cutter. But this problem is not modern enough for the theater bigwigs. So the clown has no way out except to pretend he is dead and to wait for his next performance for the children.

The arguments to be met in theoretical stage shoptalk, such as are inevitable in any group of theater people, are playfully transformed into grotesque fragments of scenes for the sheer joy of the show.

FLOOD *(Hochwasser)*. Play in two acts. Written 1956, second version 1962. First edition Frankfurt/Main 1963. First performance January 21, 1957 Frankfurt/Main, Neue Bühne. Translated by Ralph Manheim and A. Leslie Willson in *Four Plays,* London, Secker & Warburg, 1968. Time: the present. Place: cross section of a house.

This juggling with paradoxes obtains its effects not so much through mime, unruly delight in fun, vitality, and clowning grimaces as through its tone of cool detachment. We sense a joy in intellectual experiment, in the ingenious metaphor for its own sake with no conclusions drawn from it, and in the clear premise disconnected from its predication. Symbols give the play its precisely drawn contours, but traditional logical consistency in

symbolic content is sacrificed, and through the loss of sense these fragments of form recover their native sensuous quality. What brings the play
to life is the fluctuating alternation of predetermined significance and a
continuously re-created expression.

A steadily rising flood drives a group of terrified people to flee for shelter
to the attic. Noah, the master of the house, tries with dogged determination to salvage his life's work, a crazy jumble of candlesticks and inkpots
of all kinds that he has laboriously collected. His sister, dear Aunt Betty,
lives only for the memories which she has tidily hoarded in a sheaf of
photo-albums: "A man without a photo-album is like a coffin without a
lid." His daughter Jutta is more attached to the present than to the past,
and her extremely youthful fiancé Henn does his best to enliven it for her.
His long-lost son Leo, an energetic dynamo, returns home with his friend
Kongo, who was once Bruno the boxer. They tell stories and brag a bit
until Kongo makes such a determined pass at Jutta that Henn without
more ado is banished to the farthest corner of the attic. This is already
the quarters of a pair of rats, Strich and Perle, droll creatures whose behavior is no different from that of humans. They too are telling yarns,
have their cravings, and plan for the future. But these more spiritual
quadrupeds have kept certain ideals and have a bent for human wisdom.
In the intimacy of the family circle, so-called ideals and taboos are cynically and provocatively attacked when, in reply to the reproach "You drag
everything into the muck," Henn receives the answer: "You know, you
have to hide treasures. It's so common, the way gold glitters. A bit of mud
over it and it looks like nothing much. You can always polish it up bright
afterward." Finally the flood subsides, the rats leave the rescuing ark,
Henn gets back his fiancée, and the two friends are anxious to go out into
the world again. They are fed up and want to work off their boredom in
some act of opposition. Patricide is too trite for Leo. Enthusiastically the
friends seize the grandfather clock and carry it off with them to the North
Pole. But first an official of the Damages Control Board has to record the
fact. All Jutta is left with is a well-intentioned tract entitled "Man and
Catastrophe" and the hope of a new and final flood.

Seemingly, all that matters is the basic situation, namely, the threat of
death as a result of some natural catastrophe. But the commonplaces of
small-town life smother the moment of terror at facing oneself which the
proximity of death could make significant. Life and death lose their existential value and, for ratlike human beings, are nothing but a state of
aggregation, a blind condition between vegetating and perishing.


ONKEL, ONKEL *(Onkel, Onkel)*. Play in four acts. Prose. Acting edition
Berlin, Kiepenheuer, 1957. First edition Berlin 1965 (second version). First

performance March 3, 1958, Cologne, Bühnen der Stadt. Translated by Ralph Manheim and A. Leslie Willson in *Four Plays,* London, Secker & Warburg, 1968. Time: the present. Place: Germany.

The failure of a mass murderer is presented with macabre "black" humor. The urge to evil is blunted by the banality of the surroundings.

As a murderer, Bollin is a master. But his unusual gifts are sapped by his pedantic bent. His passion for system kills improvisation, that light touch of inspired imagination that is indispensable in artistic pursuits. "But that's the way it always is! I start something, I set about the preparations with enthusiasm and even with great care, but then I go too far. This blasted specialization of mine breaks through every time!" Bollin had his first training as a killer on teen-agers, then progressed to twins, and later to seamstresses. Hidden under the bed he is lying in wait for Sophie. But her naiveté and the simplicity of her bustling mama, who is determined not to let him catch cold, tame the murderer into reading fairy tales aloud, lending a hand with the crossword puzzles, and winding wool. Bollin decides that the cure for his shattered nerves is a stay in the country. He commits a series of murders of foresters and thus recovers. Forschbach, the head forester, is about to be murdered when some passing children inspire the forester to a lecture on botany, and Bollin is so touched by this passion for culture that he makes a sacrifice for it and renounces the lovely murder. Finally he is fascinated by the death scenes customary in opera. No one excels Bollin the specialist in the touch of verisimilitude. The opera stars clamor to be murdered by him to achieve immortality in splashy headlines. Mimi Landella, the diva, arranges with a photographer to ensure that she will get the right publicity as the latest of the murderer's victims. Then she learns that Bollin is to bestow the same favor on her rival. She makes such a hysterical scene that the mass murderer hurriedly takes flight. Finally, in a gravel pit, Bollin is shot with his own revolver by some children at play to the accompaniment of their begging song, "Onkel, Onkel, haste nich'n Ding." This is the cynical and challenging moral of the story. In our world evil, even on the scale of mass murder, is commercialized, corrupted by cause and purpose. Only little children, with their animal cruelty, are still able to murder in pure innocence, just for fun and games.

ONLY TEN MINUTES TO BUFFALO (*Noch zehn Minuten bis Buffalo*). One-act play. Prose. First published in *Akzente,* Vol. 5, Munich 1958. First edition in *Spiele in einem Akt,* Frankfurt/Main 1961. First performance February 19, 1954, Bochum, Schauspielhaus. Translated by Ralph Manheim and A. Leslie Willson in *Four Plays,* London, Secker & Warburg, 1968. Time: the present. Place: a green landscape with cows.

A cat's-cradle of comic and disturbing associations yields no logical co-
herence and uses instead patterns of strident contrasts. The point of con-
vergence of all the contradictory ideas is the "frigate." All action is reduced
to a sea voyage, seen either as goal or as escape. Thus in the imagination of
the painter Kotschenreuther, milk becomes sail juice; through his pal-
ette harmless grazing cows are transformed into a majestic three-masted
schooner. "In the beginning was the ship. Out of that there came the cow
and out of the cow came chess, then the pyramids were built, then came
journalism and with it railways—who knows what will happen tomorrow?
. . . Above all, you must get rid of these silly titles: cow, ship, professor,
buttercup. They're nothing but deceptions, complexes. Do you think your
cow minds if you say ship to her, or steamer even?" The play goes full tilt
in exploiting the everlasting conflict between mutable reality and the concepts petrified in words, two things which never completely coincide. In a
rusty, scrapped, immovable, locomotive Krudewill, the engine driver, and
Pempelfort, the fireman, tear across the green meadow. They never stir
from the spot, but pretend they are progressing, torment each other, and
dream of the idyllic town of Buffalo which they will soon reach. Trembling, they make out the "frigate," an alarming female and magical figurehead in admiral's gold braid, who firmly brings back to the watery element the two deserting seamen who have taken flight in their dream of
railway travel. The worried pair deny their Buffalo, and mime a whale
hunt in the meadow, while the cowman Axel enthusiastically takes possession of the abandoned locomotive. Suddenly this wreck of an engine starts
to move with the man of reality, the only one who, minding his cattle,
never let himself be carried away by dreams; it goes off to legendary Buffalo.
This is a theatrical lark with many meanings, whose ultimate interpretation is to be found in its immediacy and impulsiveness.


THE PLEBEIANS REHEARSE THE UPRISING. *(Die Plebejer proben den
Aufstand)*. A German tragedy in four acts. Prose and verse. First edition
Neuwied 1966. First performance January 15, 1966, Berlin, Schiller-
Theater. Translated by Ralph Manheim, London, Secker & Warburg,
1967. Time: June 17, 1953. Place: stage of the Theater am Schiffbauer-
damm, Berlin.

Brecht's controversial attitude at the time of the East German June rising
suggested to Günter Grass the idea of a play dealing with a rehearsal of
*Coriolanus* by the Berlin Ensemble—but which hardly measures up to its
theme. The Pirandellian conflict of reality intruding upon the stage gets
in the way of the play's claim to documentary truth, and vice versa. The

author fails to make plain the nature of the politically committed poet, his opportunities and inner contradictions. Grass is in fact as helpless as Brecht; Brecht cannot come to a decision in this reality nor take up an irrevocable position, and Grass cannot gain enough distance to generalize the individual predicament he depicts. Thus the whole thing remains staged dialectic, theses and antitheses, which Brecht, "who knows and hesitates," makes subservient to his theatrical apparatus.

The "Chief" and his Berlin Ensemble are rehearsing Shakespeare—the uprising of the plebeians against their autocratic consul Coriolanus. The rehearsal is interrupted by workmen who are on strike and ask the famous theatrical producer for a sign of solidarity with their opposition to the government. The proletarians demand freedom and lower output targets. Brecht wards them off: "Wherever I look: kneaders of dough who want to bake me into a sabre-rattling hero. . . . A moment ago I still hoped it would have the impetus of a manifesto; now that I read it over, it smacks of elegy." Brecht has no confidence in a popular uprising which has an inner rift from the very outset. People clamor for freedom and tidily throw their sandwich wrappers in the refuse bins; a crowd collects—in a well-mannered way on the officially authorized spaces, to make sure they don't step on the grass. The state's mechanism of rules enslaves the citizens even in their revolt. Fear and suspicion divide men. The actors and stagehands suspect the discontented populace of being *agents provocateurs* and spies from the West, and the strikers are afraid of informers among the actors. The "Chief" sidesteps the issue with a cryptic parable and a spontaneous show of solicitude—he gives the rebels something to eat. The dramaturgist Erwin soothes the people with Shakespeare's parable of the limbs' unreasonable revolt against the belly. The other party, the government, in its turn wants to exploit Brecht's name for its own purposes. The poet Kosanke, official speechifier and national prize winner of the Ulbricht system, demands Brecht's help in the name of the state. Brecht is to calm down the workers with a few words and send them home. Brecht thinks of the one thing he understands and can control—his work for the theater, which will outlast him. He infiltrates the rebels among the stage plebeians of his *Coriolanus* rehearsal and records fragments of conversation on a tape-recorder. Reality is for him nothing but raw material to be sorted out and made comprehensible in his theatrical production. The raw material of facts acquires meaning only when it finds application in art. The collapse of the uprising brings Brecht into conflict with his conscience, when tribute has to be paid once more to the victorious regime: "When the builders were babbling about victory, I found them ridiculous. Only their defeat convinced me. . . ." In order not to endanger his work for the theater, Brecht writes an ambiguous letter of loyalty to the regime and takes refuge in his books. Throughout the play there is alternating prose and verse, of

Shakespeare quotations and an aphoristically simplified language inspired by Brecht and sometimes literally borrowed from him.


THE WICKED COOKS *(Die bösen Köche)*. Drama in five acts. Prose. Written 1956. First published in *Modernes deutsches Theater I,* Neuwied 1961. First performance February 16, 1961, Berlin, Werkstatt des Schillertheaters. Translated by Ralph Manheim and A. Leslie Willson, New York, Harcourt Brace, 1957, and in *Four Plays,* London, Secker & Warburg, 1968. Time: not specified. Place: various settings.

This is the Theater of the Absurd in its grotesque form. With its contortions and grimaces it repeatedly becomes a parody of itself. The course of the action is determined by each moment's mimic intensity, by the fascination of paradox, by sheer delight in captivating nonsense. The only firm point of reference seems to be the basic idea of the play, namely, the hunt for a recipe, a clarifying and explanatory formula that can be taken home safely and easily. It may be that Grass is here mischievously equating the stubborn pack of cooks with the public that wants profound thoughts and can understand an event only when it is presented in a neatly concocted message. But even in this happy-go-lucky foolery that does not pretend to be anything more than just that, fragments of crumbling reality come to the surface. Contorted and deliberately devoid of purpose, they constitute bits of blurred relevance, a key to the cryptographic forms of the experience of being vulnerable, threatened, and afraid of persecution and death.

There are five cooks, radiant in white. They are ranged in a precise hierarchy from Petri, the trumpet-blowing chef, to the junior assistant Benny. In a playful inversion, the symbolic world of white is shown as the origin of the blackest negatives, a lethal, sterile, immaculate pallor. The cooks are in the service of a mysterious employer, the innkeeper Schuster, who is the moving spirit of everything but never makes an appearance. Abruptly and disconcertingly, the cooks break out of the white that is seemingly so harmless, out from the cooking, salt, egg, tiled stove, and snow. Of course, there has to be a victim who is pounded, roasted, peppered, and made to boil over. The beastliness of life is reduced to kitchen work, and its victim—the object offered by life's beastliness to itself—is Herbert Schymanski, known as "the Count." He has committed a capital crime: He refused the function assigned to him and did some cooking. What is more, he did some highly successful cooking and discovered a new recipe. The world of cooks is thrown into an ominous commotion. By means of this culinary secret which he stubbornly withholds, the outsider has shown up the imperfection of their art. He has invalidated their vocation and overturned the order of the world. Singly and together, with pleas and threats, the cooks advance against the Count to wrest his secret from him. Among themselves they become suspicious rivals, lying in ambush for each other. Their community breaks up, interrogation and torture are the only bond among them. The attempt of the cook Vasco to bribe the Count by offering him his fiancé Martha, a hospital nurse in the most immaculate white, is as unavailing as the violence of the tall cook Kletterer who has wrested the domination of the kitchen from Petri. That dark little soup—they want to find out about it. Is it the Count's personal secret? "Not here in my breast! In the street, in a wastebasket, sometimes, too, it runs about, the miserable secret. On three legs, quite slowly, a lame dog, so it toils along from tree to tree and leaves behind a scant afterglow of its lusterless existence." Or is it perhaps a revelation that mankind may not be denied? Perhaps it is "not a recipe at all, but an experience, living knowledge, a change," perhaps life itself taking its unrepeatable course and not to be captured in any formula? In vain the Count assures the pack, his persecutors, how impossible message and understanding have become. He resigns, and he and Martha commit suicide. But the fanatical cooks pounce upon Vasco, who has perhaps acquired the recipe and withheld it from them. The pursuit of a victim goes on. In a ceaseless whirl of delicious superabundant invention, the problem is concealed rather than revealed.

The author's sardonic note continually breaks through, stimulated by the purposelessness of what he is doing. "Such confused stories are profoundly repugnant to me. I require the most economic use of means and tidy motivation. . . . I was almost overwhelmed by the feeling, the unpleasant feeling, of being faced by a symbol, or, what is worse, of having to pass the rest of this night under a symbol." Props are deliberately misapplied to produce an effect of total nonsense: the trumpet as a telescope, the shoe on the table as a flower vase, the frying pan as a tennis racket. The language, too, is full of that kind of meaningless joke: "Once they have taken away the glasses from the shortsighted, they will dispossess the possessive pronouns." However, the ultimate background of this piece of theatrical sleight-of-hand is grief and revolt at the absurdity in the world, at the way one message can be changed into another, at the ambiguity of language, at the disintegration of identity and the agonizing uncertainty of all being.

## GREEN, Julien
(France, born 1900)

L'ENNEMI *[The Enemy]*. Play in three acts. Prose. Written 1953. First edition Paris 1954. First performance March 1, 1954, Paris, Théâtre des Bouffes-Parisiennes. Time: the present. Place: a drawing room.

At first sight this appears to be a triangular situation with melodramatic trimmings, a romantic castle, and murder for jealousy. But unaware a man and a woman, prone to temptation in their human weakness, discover themselves to be instruments in the eternal battle between good and evil, pawns on a theological chessboard. For "unfortunately, no one can have to do with the devil without having to do with God."

Jacques has made his home in the castle of his older brother Philippe and is the secret lover of the latter's wife Elisabeth. Then the third brother, Pierre, suddenly turns up, having left his monastery and now ready in cynical defiance to establish Satan's reign on earth. Elisabeth, whose life between her husband and her lover has so far been an empty one—"I live here with Philippe, with Jacques, with my nurse and all our people, but I can hardly imagine that they exist . . . Everything I love is elsewhere . . ."
—senses in Pierre the great, unknown enemy, who menaces and at the same time fascinates her. She becomes his mistress. What for him is a frivolous adventure and a means of self-assertion, becomes for her a way to God. In her fear and love for Pierre she takes refuge in prayer, and in her sin experiences the grace of illumination. Pierre is strangled by a bandit hired by the jealous Jacques. Philippe, desperately anxious not to lose Elisabeth, is prepared to go on tolerating Jacques as her lover. She, in her turn, is gripped by a strange rapture and wishes to find peace in a convent.

Green does not tell us what will really happen, for he is concerned only with the inner shock which destroys his characters' self-assurance and opens their souls to the working of grace.

SOUTH *(Sud)*. Play in three acts. Prose. First edition Paris 1953. First performance March 6, 1953, Paris, Théâtre de l'Athénée. English version in *Plays of the Year*, Vol. 12, London and New York, Elek, 1955. Time: 1861, on the eve of the War of Secession. Place: Broderick's farmhouse in South Carolina.

This is a play about men at the mercy of their passions, and is conceived not as a pathological study but in terms of the confusion of emotions in a world without faith: "All my books, however remote they may be from traditional and generally accepted religiosity, are certainly religious in nature. All the fears and the loneliness of the characters can always ultimately be traced back to the 'horror of existing' in one form of another— as I think I have called it once"—thus Green notes in his diary. On the eve of the outbreak of the American Civil War, all the human relationships in the home of the plantation owner Edward Broderick are, similarly, disrupted by opposition and strife. His son Jimmy maltreats the Negro slaves who are already beginning to revolt. Regina, who comes from the North, feels misunderstood in this alien world and bestows her love on the Pole Jan Wicziewsky, a homosexual who cynically rejects her. He, in his turn, has a passion for young Eric MacClure, who loves Broderick's daughter Angelina. Rather than give up, the Pole is determined to destroy the object of his passion, and to this end provokes a quarrel with MacClure—but, when it comes to a duel, allows himself to be killed without defending himself. Jan has found the courage for self-sacrifice.

## GREENE, Graham
(England, born 1904)

THE COMPLAISANT LOVER. Comedy in two acts. Prose. First edition London 1959. First performance June 18, 1959, London, Globe Theatre. Time: the present. Place: London and Amsterdam.

The hackneyed triangular situation so often laboriously turned to tragedy is here resolved in serene resignation to the smiling "convenience" of all concerned. Mary wavers between her husband, the dentist Victor Rhodes, and her lover, the antiquarian Clive Root. She does not want to give up either the security of marriage or her children, even though her love for her husband is long spent: "It's killed by the children, by the chars who give notice, by the price of meat." Clive wants to force a divorce and to this end writes an anonymous letter to the husband. But Victor is "complaisantly" prepared to put up with the marriage à trois, and thereby makes Clive the outsider who has to be content with occasional snatched hours. This is social criticism with the sting taken out of it by the moving and humorous conversational tone of a boulevard comedy sure of its effects.

THE LIVING ROOM. Play in two acts. Prose. First edition London 1953. First performance October 31, 1952, Stockholm, Kungliga Dramatiska Teatern. Time: the present. Place: the Brownes' living room.

Greene uses the toolbox of psychoanalysis to draw his caricatures of human weakness and guilt, by which he finally demonstrates the workings of divine grace. Orthodox catholics are shown as pharisees unable to measure up to life. Young Rose Pemberton is helplessly at the mercy of her relatives, the self-righteous and ossified old Brownes—the sisters Teresa and Helen, and her brother Father Hames Browne. As Rose's guardians and the trustees of her inheritance, they hermetically isolate her from the world in order to thwart her love for Michael Dennis, a lecturer in psychology, who cannot break loose from his sick wife. Helen, an embittered old maid, tyrannizes the household with her pedantry—that is, her intimidated sister Teresa and James, an ailing superannuated priest. Because of her fear of death she has every room in which someone once died closed for ever, and the family ultimately huddles in the last remaining corner of the house. After Rose has been driven to suicide, the old people come to realize that they have been hiding only their own coldness of heart and intolerance behind the pretext of doing what was best for their ward; the worst of the disaster is that everything is going to be the same as before: "Three old people have lost a living room, that's all; and the psychologist is left with a sick wife." Suddenly Teresa overcomes her fears; freed at last from the spell of the "closed rooms," she decides that in future she will live in the room in which Rose died.

## HACKETT, Albert
See GOODRICH, Francis

## HACKS, Peter
(Germany, born 1928)

ERÖFFNUNG DES INDISCHEN ZEITALTERS *[The Inauguration of the Indian Age]*. Play in ten scenes. Prose. First edition in *Theaterstücke,* Berlin, 1957. First performance March 17, 1955, Munich, Kammerspiele. Time: October 1491 to October 1492. Place: Spain and on board the ship *Santa Maria.*

A didactic play about the necessity and dubiousness of progress and knowledge. Like Brecht's Galilei, Columbus has to sacrifice his discovery to the interests of the authorities. For the sake of progress he must wrong the people. His idea can be realized only at the cost of humanity. Hacks has suggested that a more indicative title of the play would be "The idea of the world by ship," and explained that: "the character of Christopher Columbus gives only a biased and in many respects false representation of the historical figure. All that the historical Columbus could have been made to show is that under favorable circumstances great deeds can be accomplished by a charlatan and a complete fool, which would be an unworthy and useless moral. But of course the Columbus of the play is not a mere arbitrary invention. Historical plays are based on the fiction that individuals make history, and so they have to adapt the character of the individual to the character of the real maker of history, that is, to the individual's social class. The historical play liberates the hero from the anecdotal, the contingent, it generalizes like any other product of the intellect. . . . The playwright's job is not merely to show how the present should be, but also how the past should have been." The story serves only to illustrate this clear ideological concept in theatrical terms.
Columbus vainly tries to persuade the Spanish court to support his scheme to look for the sea route to India. Adolescent dukes, courtiers and pedants stand in his path. His great project succeeds only when he makes allies of the rulers' greed and pride of race, and of the clergy's thirst for power. In a dream Columbus sees the misery which he brings to the peaceful aborigines of America by exposing them to the civilization and murderous violence of Europe. But the explorer accepts this sacrifice as necessary in order to replace the age of faith by the "scientific age" of knowledge and to take mankind another step forward. This "sub specie doctrinae" of the Marxist view of history is easy to interpret with such a subject matter.

Despite the ideological purpose, there remains the aesthetic charm of a historical reality often mixed with alienation. It is a stylized picture book inspired by dialectical materialism and Hegel's evolutionary theory.


MORITZ TASSOW *[Moritz Tassow]*. Comedy in eleven scenes. Verse. Written 1962. First published in *Theater heute*, No. 2, February 1963. First performance October 5, 1965, Berlin, Volksbühne. Time: September 1945. Place: Gargentin village and estate, East Germany.

Hacks's dream of ideal communism takes refuge in a rough, tender backwoods tale. Putting a literal interpretation on the advent of the classless era, an individual tries to live according to his inborn nature. He is bound to come to grief on the system of political guidance in a bureaucratic state based on rules and regulations: "From now on then you have in mind to lie/ And cheat away into eternal truths/ The cries of moments drowning in the stream/ Of time, eternal truths that daily change." On the orders of the Russian occupying power, Mattukat, the party secretary, is implementing the land reform.

In deepest Macklenburg, the people of the Gargentin estate, led by the swineherd Moritz Tassow, have solved the problem after their own fashion. Captain von Sack, the landlord, and his canting mistress are driven out. For years Moritz has pretended to be a deaf-mute booby; now he creates a vital, sensuous paradise in which even duties consist of inclinations: "The man who really should be reckoned one,/ That's him who does just what he has a mind to,/ And scratches where it itches, not elsewhere/ In sheer embarrassment. . . ." The estate is to provide a place for everyone to express his ego. But Tassow is defeated by the selfishness of the laborers who won't give up their little scraps of capitalism, by the ambitions of the middle-sized farmers who want power and who keep their Nazi underground as a useful instrument of terror, and by the absolutism of the state functionaries. The land is divided up under government supervision. The party doctrine wins and Tassow is deposed. He decides that in future he will take shelter under the fool's cap of the writer in order to indulge his dreams of man's rebirth, and to leave reality to a state which is not his.

The verse is cumbersome and rebarbative, transmutes every expression into remote refractions, and wears its phrases like obligatory masks: "The time's impatient edge has mutilated/ My well-considered choice and made of it/ A wooden yes or no." It all adds charm to this display of dialectics in backwoods clothes.


DER MÜLLER VON SANSSOUCI *[The Miller of Sanssouci]*. A bourgeois comedy. Prose. First published in *Fünf Stücke*, Frankfurt/Main 1965.

First performance March 5, 1958, Berlin, Kammerspiele des Deutschen Theaters. Time: April 1778. Place. Sanssouci.

This exposure of the national legend is so biased and so charged with special pleading that in its turn it falsifies history. Hacks explains: "The subject is a man's pettiness. His pettiness is shown to originate in skepticism and his skepticism in a particular economic situation." The schoolbook anecdote about how Frederick the Great ordered a mill to be closed down because he was irritated by its noise, and subsequently decided in favor of the miller's rights and against his own comfort, had already attracted Brecht's interest for an interpretation drawing the opposite moral. Hacks interprets the king's concern for justice as a move in a political game of chess.

Frederick, the despot, goes through this farce in order to demonstrate that he is not a despot. Because he wants peace he orders his troops, as the climax of large-scale maneuvers, to invade Austria and conquer parts of Silesia. The clacking of a windmill annoys the sovereign, and some of his subordinates at once seize the opportunity to display their zeal. They ruin the livelihood of the unpopular crippled miller. The king wants to give the public a striking, effective proof of his respect for the law; he is prepared to recognize the miller's concession and to submit to the Codex Friedericianus which he himself introduced. But at an audience the little man of the people, trembling with fear, surrenders his rights. The king is cheated of his satisfaction. His minister de Catt has to apply army drill in rehearsing with the miller the exceptional scene of a man being freely permitted to express his opinion. The public at large is then treated to a performance of the scene in which the miller demands his rights before the king, while reiterating that he is ready to obey as a loyal subject. To universal applause the king submits to the law and at the same time makes use of it to call up the crippled miller's only servant for his army. As a result the mill cannot be worked and can be closed down.

The style develops from the shadow-play prologue. The king is a stylized poster figure of a self-satisfied poseur, and the celebrated officer corps are doddering old men who can only bark in chorus. This is the quintessence of didactic theatre.

DIE SCHLACHT BEI LOBOSITZ [The Battle of Lobositz]. Comedy in three acts. Prose. First edition in *Theaterstücke,* Berlin 1957. First performance December 1, 1956, Berlin, Deutsches Theater. Time: September–October 1756. Place: Saxony and Silesia.

This is a play about an anti-hero of the Seven Years War, and Hacks intends it as a lesson in positive sociology. "The play," he says, "constitutes part of man's efforts to abolish war. It claims to be more than a mere expression of displeasure. . . . The play presents war as a conspiracy of officers against the people. This point of view is of practical importance to the soldiers, for, if they think out its implications, it suggests the possibility of a conspiracy of the people against the officers."

First Lieutenant Markoni has by a trick pressed his Swiss servant Ulrich Braeker into the Lüderitz regiment of Prussia. However, the more brutal the methods by which the recruiting gangs proceed on behalf of their gracious king, the more often the unwilling recruits run away. Lieutenant Markoni has a brilliant idea: "How can an officer turn his men's natural hatred for him into hatred for the enemy? How is it to be done?" He substitutes condescending kindliness for inhuman drill. He wagers that Braeker and two other Swiss whom he has tricked will soon be so devoted and obedient to him that there will be no question of desertion. Nonetheless Braeker's two comrades prefer flight to glory in the forthcoming battle of Lobositz. Only Braeker sticks to his lieutenant with incomparable loyalty and is detailed to a suicide squad, for only when he is dead will he be, in the officers' eyes, a truly good soldier, immune to desertion. Whereupon Braeker, too, turns his back on the glorious flag, and with relief sets out for his Swiss homeland, while Markoni dies in the slaughter.

Hacks makes use of methods learned from Brecht, such as picture-book presentation with explanatory songs, a harsh, crude language, and striking, often impressive simplification.

DIE SORGEN UND DIE MACHT [The Cares of Office]. Play in five acts. Prose and verse. First edition in Fünf Stücke, Frankfurt/Main 1965. Time: October 1956 and January 1957. Place: the German Democratic Republic.

It is not certain whether Hacks sees the party standard as so oppressively absolute that its effect is, willy-nilly, satirical, or as so satirical that reeducation under it develops into absolute oppression. In this play, as so often in recent drama from the German Democratic Republic, we are shown how an insubordinate nonconformist is converted to party discipline. However, this time the reeducation is not so much ideological as private and personal. Even love has no footing unless it keeps step with the march of solidarity. At the same time Hacks shows the workers exposed to the temptations of power and thus to capitalist egotism. And the difficult road to socialist perfection eventually is lit up by the discovery— as categorical as a Kantian imperative—that power signifies cares, i.e. responsibility for the common weal. "The workers' power, we knew, must come before/ The workers' happiness. For that needs power./ The day

when power gives place to happiness/ Will only dawn for those who pay
their dues to power."
Even in the classless society prosperity is unequally distributed and gives
rise to a system of privileges. The workers in the briquette factory deliver
inferior fuel in vast quantities, for which the government heaps bonuses
and praise upon them. But because of their unusable briquettes, the glass
factory shows an increasing shortage in output and cannot meet its production quota. This affects the earnings of the girl worker Hede Stoll. For
love of her, Max Fidorra, a briquette worker, successfully insists on an im-
provement in the quality of the fuel. But production now takes longer,
wages drop, and the workers complain. The party is agitated about the
falling output figures and the factory management is afraid that the dissatisfied workers will go elsewhere. Zidewang, a former margarine dealer,
tries to satisfy the demands of his superiors by falsifying the records of
quality checks. By now Hede is doing well in the prospering glass factory.
Fidorra, on the other hand, is impoverished; he pushes through improve-
ments, despite the reluctance of his co-workers, so that in the future quality
and quantity will coincide. With his new self-assurance Fidorra can then
declare his intentions to Hede.
Hacks has managed to bring some detachment to this topical piece (which
includes also the party commentary on the Hungarian rising of 1956) by
the use of quotations. The parable of the mother (the government) and
her progeny (factories) is modeled on Brecht's topical reinterpretation of
the *Coriolanus* image of the belly and its rebellious limbs; the satirical
names are reminiscent of the political fairy-tale note in Aristophanes.
At the programmatic keypoints of political education the prose scenes
abruptly change over to blank verse.


## HAECKER, Hans-Joachim
(Germany, born 1910)


DER BRIEFTRÄGER KOMMT *[The Postman Arrives]*. Play in five scenes
and an epilogue. Prose. First edition Cologne 1962. First performance
March 31, 1962, Celle, Schloßtheater. Time: the present. Place: a furnished room and an unreal dream world.

In this play, distortions and a nightmare of vague fears are connected
only by the epilogue with reality and endowed with meaning. The unsuccessful author Rolf Winter has withdrawn from the world. Scraps of
memory, undigested fragments of experience, repressed desires, and the
oppressive claims of the unconscious create a strange world around him:

a postman arrives with a garbage disposal truck and with a pitchfork
buries Rolf Winter under a mountain of mail, but takes all the letters
away again because Winter cannot pay the postage due. The only letters
delivered to him contain greetings from Carolus, Xaver, and Meerschaum,
all three totally unknown to him. Carolus and Meerschaum are hurt that
Winter does not remember them, and drive him into the arms of his beloved. He succumbs to her despite police warnings. But obstacles get between the lovers. Winter cannot pay for his happiness either with money
or with strength or genius. He is beaten and mocked. Finally he pays with
his life and takes poison from his sweetheart. That is the only way out.
For his love is of such consuming exclusivity that he refuses anything that
is of this world: "This is the certainty that we shall never lose each other.
Life is a detour." The epilogue puts things back into their true perspective.
Winter has poisoned himself. Carolus, Meerschaum and the postman are
stripped of their fateful demonism and revert to their ordinary everyday
roles. They accompany the coffin to the grave. Suddenly Xaver rushes up—
he urgently needs Winter's deposition in a murder case. But Winter has
evaded the only genuine task of his life.


DREHT EUCH NICHT UM [Don't Turn About]. One-act play. Prose.
Written 1957–1961. First edition Cologne 1962. First performance April
21, 1961, Bochum, Schauspielhaus. Time: the present. Place: Rebecca's
and Miriam's living room in a German city.

A play about the impossibility of mastering the past. The author explains:
"What is common to my plays is that in them the world surrounding us
somehow begins to be transparent. . . . In these plays it is not merely a
question of tensions and counteraction within reality, but at the same time
always of reality itself. Thus they are an expression of astonishment at
existing and at the manner of our existence."
At first we are in the puppet world of a faded idyll—with two aged sisters,
fidgeting around tremulously and excitedly in their doll's room. Suddenly
our century's gloom erupts. The two old ladies are Jewish and have fled
from their appalling memories of death camps and gas chambers into a
fragile dream world; now Joseph Tibor, one of the blunt and obedient
henchmen of that time, speaks to them. His conscience will not let him
rest since he has discovered that the personnel manager of one of the
"economic miracle" business firms is the former commander of a death
camp—a man who counted out his victims with the help of the nursery
rhyme "Don't turn about, the knot's going round." To bring the criminal
to account, Tibor tries to persuade the sisters to come forward as witnesses.
They refuse, horrified, and withdraw into their solitude. In their fear

they realize that the ex-Nazi has followed Tibor to get rid of the dangerous witnesses. The horrors of the past have caught up with them. Without detriment to its realism, the psychological study turns into a nightmare.


## HALL, Willis
See WATERHOUSE, Keith


## HAMMERSTEIN II, Oscar, and LOGAN, Joshua
(both United States; Hammerstein, 1895–1960)

SOUTH PACIFIC. Musical play in two acts. Adaptation of short stories in *Tales of the South Pacific* by James Michener. Music by Richard Rodgers. First edition New York 1949. First performance April 7, 1949, New York, Majestic Theatre. Time: the Second World War. Place: the Pacific.

Its content, its form and, not least, its interpretation give *South Pacific* a special position among musicals. Its very theme—racial conflict and the stress of war—bring it close to opera. The hero, however, is not a radiant tenor lover, but a gray-haired widower worn by life, and the main part was indeed created not by any of the established Broadway stars, but by Ezio Pinza, who had for many years sung Don Giovanni at the Salzburg Festival. In spite of their popularity, his songs are never mere hits, but a means of psychological self-characterization. This up-graded libretto set the pace for the further development of the whole genre. Michener's original text was awarded the Pulitzer Prize, as was later the dramatic musical version.

During the Second World War, the American pilot Joseph Cable urges the planter Emile de Becque to help him carry out a suicide patrol. He wants to set up an anti-Japanese signal post on a neighboring Pacific island and needs de Becque's intimate knowledge of the district. De Becque, a widower and father of two Malay children, courts the nurse Nellie, but she does not want a ready-made colored family and refuses him. His disappointment drives him into jungle warfare. Cable is killed, de Becque is reported missing. Eventually he does return, exhausted, to find that Nellie's better nature has won the upper hand. She is looking after his orphaned children and waiting for him, the man she loves. The secondary plot, a love affair between Cable and the Polynesian girl Liat, underscores the plea for racial reconciliation. The musical themes of the Far East recur in Rodger's later work. *South Pacific* has won a number of prizes, its popularity enhanced by its widely played score.

## HANDKE, Peter
(Austria, born 1942)

PUBLIKUMSBESCHIMPFUNG *[An Insult to the Public]*. One-act play. Prose. First published in *manuskripte*, Graz, April 1966. First edition Frankfurt/Main 1966. First performance June 8, 1966, Frankfurt/Main, Theater am Turm ("Experimenta 66"). Time: the present. Place: an empty stage.

The origins of this study lie in distrust of the theater's suggestive power and of the way in which it can be manipulated, in misgivings about the deliberate purposiveness of the whole apparatus set in motion every evening, and in reservations regarding the uncontrollable seductive power of its ultimate effects.

Handke demolishes the theater insofar as it is the vehicle of a message and an escape into make-believe and rediscovers it anew in man's experience of himself and in the inexhaustible spontaneity of theatrical expression in word and gesture. The spectator enters the auditorium, hears the bell, the scurrying excitement behind the curtain, sees the lights go out, and, in other words, is intentionally put in the mood of expectation normal for each evening's audience. Thus prepared for gentle, noncommittal illusions, he is suddenly confronted with four ordinary young people on an empty stage. Instead of escaping into imagination, the public itself becomes the raw material of the action. The lights are on the spectator; he is directly addressed by the actors who become interviewers, and he is mercilessly referred back to himself, to the immediate present and his reactions to it.

In this, Handke was up against the philosophical problem of how to get hold of the *hic et nunc*. How can one make people consciously experience themselves without using analogies and conceptual abstractions, without foreshortening through a simultaneously assumed relation to the past or the future, without projection into another medium? This is reminiscent of the purism of producers of happenings, who clear the stage of all simulated significance, relying solely on the explosive spontaneity of the here and now. But Handke takes another path, one which does not exclude language and its mediating logic but objectivizes it, uses it as a record of actuality, as pure description. Somewhere between the forms of litany and brainwashing, pure objectiveness is reproduced. Significantly, this can happen only negatively. Actuality as such, without meaning and context, can be sighted only in the negation of its traditional denotation. The public ceases to be "the public" but becomes a number of different individuals reacting in different ways to impressions from the external world.

The stage is no longer "the stage" but a platform of boards which the speakers use to stand on. There is neither representation nor presentation. Things are simply what their qualities make them. So is the man in the audience—extinguished by anonymity, nothing but a sample of a collective whole, and yet at the same time individualized in the inventory of his physiological processes. Handke gives rhythm and articulation to this inventory by variations in viewpoint. He includes passages of critical argument about this "main actor, the public," as well as secondary analyses and glosses on the influence of sitting and standing on the spectator's apperception, or the final discharge of emotion in vituperation. This effort at complete identity of proceedings arises from a Heraclitean awareness of the unrepeatable uniqueness of every moment in time.

In a work which claims to be nothing but spontaneous reality, the problem of form becomes inescapable: even Handke's spontaneous reality can only be consciously shaped reality. The author uses two stylistic means, namely, factual description and emotive vituperation, in which, however, the emotional discharge of vituperating is again camouflaged as description, as dry statements of fact. In the descriptive passages the language is deliberately simplified. It is intended to record reality; for such purposes style would be an arbitrarily interposed medium amounting to falsification. This cliché language resembles a monotonous grammatical exercise. In a similar way an English phrase book gave Ionesco the idea of linguistic dismemberment in *The Bald Soprano*. But Ionesco deliberately used the clichés to construct a model of banality and meaninglessness. Handke does not want to build a model, but to lay hold of reality itself.

There are literary analogies for vituperation: Brecht at the first performance of *Dreams in the Night* confronted the public with billboards reading "Don't goggle so romantically!" But Handke differs from Brecht in that he uses his insults not as a means to *épater le bourgeois,* but as a form of theatrical *furioso,* as a relief from tension.

The producer is left to decide how the text is to be distributed among the four speakers; complete freedom of voice and gesture is permissible. Groups of sentences are repeated as leitmotivs, imperceptibly changed and then reintroduced in another context.

## HAVEL, Václav
(Czechoslovakia, born 1936)

ZAHRADNÍ SLAVNOST *[The Garden Party]*. Play in four acts. Prose. Written 1963. First published in *Divadlo* XIV, No. 7, Prague 1963. First performance September 26, 1963, Prague, Divadlo na zábradlí. Time: the present. Place: Prague.

Men have become helpless functions of an overriding phraseology. Young Pludek hopefully goes to a garden party, expecting to forward his career in the informal company of influential party bosses. The officials of the opposing offices for inauguration and liquidation populate the scene—their eyes radiating the brotherhood of party bonds, their hearts heavy with fear and misgivings, for every inaugurator is canceled in his very existence by an equally official liquidator. Merrily Pludek begins an acrobatic ascent through this tangle of dialectical purposes and counterpurposes and ends up as chief of a proposed central commission which is to set up a joint office of inauguration and liquidation. He introduces a new system of progressive inauguration-liquidation-inauguration; the system is extravagantly praised, although it is incomprehensible to all. Meanwhile his own parents no longer recognize the hero, for the dialectical cogwheels have made of him a verbal hash of clichés. The author is indebted to Ionesco not only for the attempt to express social criticism in clowning but also for his dramaturgy. The play with its conversational clichés, literal repetition of certain scenes to exemplify the mechanical process of life, and characters reduced to mere "balloons," all testify to the growing experimental spirit of the theater in Eastern Europe.

## HAY, Julius
(Hungary, born 1900)

ATTILAS NÄCHTE *[Attila's Nights]*. Tragedy in five acts. Prose. Written 1961. First edition in *Dramen*, Hamburg 1964. First performance July 22, 1966, Bregenz, Theater am Kornmarkt (Vienna Burgtheater ensemble at the Bregenz Festival). Time: A.D. 451–453. Place: Plain of Catalaunum, Attila's capital, and the outskirts of Rome.

Attila as god incarnate, who took over world dominion of Rome and aspired to give a new order to the people, is contrasted with the reality of his life in five crisis-filled nights. Between Attila's ambitious plans and his knowledge of their being condemned to failure, we see the conqueror aware of his responsibility and intent on unifying the world, the great benefactor of humanity tempted by a messianic sense of mission, the man alone with his doubts of god and his longing for redemption, with his helplessness and fear of death. On the eve of the battle of the Cataluanian fields Attila meets the Roman general Aetius, once the friend of his youth, now his enemy. They try in vain to save their peoples the senseless bloodbath of this battle, but the logic of the situation is stronger than the good will of individuals, and Attila loses his friend as one of the countless victims of the indecisive battle. He falls in love with the Gothic princess Mikolde and in defiance of every obstacle makes her his wife. She is a fervent Christian with but one choice open to her, either to convert the king or to kill him. But her rigid fanaticism is vanquished by Attila's humanity in the last redeeming act of his life. Death overtakes him, and the empire falls into chaos once more. Hay's major aim is that of identification. He writes in the foreword: "When the reader reads Attila, then it is Attila who is meant. . . . No doubt the characters are new dramatic creations, variously stylized in a tragic or comic sense, but there is no question of their being contemporary persons who have appropriated historical trappings for the sake of a sort of fool's freedom as in a fancy-dress ball." The subject matter has to be appreciated in the light of the problems, an operation which Hay deliberately withdraws from the stage and submits to the critical judgment of each individual. This slightly didactic and critical undertone, the careful, illusionist painting-in of the background, shows clearly how far the author's aims are from the light-hearted conception of history displayed by Giraudoux, Anouilh, or Dürrenmatt and how far, therefore, from the purposes of the contemporary theater.

DER BARBAR *[The Barbarian]*. Tragicomedy in five acts. Prose. Written 1955. First edition in *Dramen II,* Hamburg 1966. First performance January 30, 1965, Cologne, Städtische Bühnen. Time: 70–63 B.C. Place: Asia Minor and Rome.

"Every man lives and dies as material for world history." And this material in turn is used for theatrical aphorisms. Problems are dissolved in wisecracks, in a glossary of the twentieth century which conceals its bewilderment behind historical props. In the last century before Christ the world is already divided into two hostile power blocs. Mithridates Eupator, the great king of Pontus, rules over Asia with an almost divine absolutism. Rome, the master of the western world, has sent Pompeius the consul with a strong fleet to break the power of the East. In between swarm the eternal accessories of world politics: the little satellite rulers who are threatened and wooed by both sides and are prudently looking after their own interests; the drunken excitement of the masses skillfully stirred up by agents; the smart jobbers who under the flag of cultural exchanges go profitably back and forth between the opponents. As a strategist, scholar, and connoisseur, Mithridates has all his life been opposed to Rome and its conquests. All his thinking and planning is directed toward the West, to which he will always remain a barbarian despite his power and knowledge. His son Pharnaces feels that this longing is undermining their barbaric, native vigor and tries in vain to restore inner confidence to his father. At a banquet —a caricature of a political summit meeting, complete with the incomprehensible gibberish of some underdeveloped tribe—Mithridates tries to give reality to his dream and to shine as a man of the West, a poet and polymath. In the snobbish world of Rome he merely makes himself ridiculous and, furious with rage, betrays his secret plan for Asia's campaign against the West. The hubris of this plan, which is quickly played up as a sensation by the Romans, shocks the great king's army. It abandons its ill-starred ruler and at once Pharnaces makes a deal with Rome in order to safeguard his crown. Abandoned even by his mistress, Mithridates tries to kill himself with his own poison, the pride of his alchemical art. But it turns out to be harmless, and he has to send for the executioner—a joke of history which sends his mistress into fits of hysterical laughter. The passionate amateur is opposed by the hard-headed wielder of power and is defeated. "History is a duel between organization and unorganization."

GÁSPÁR VARRÓS RECHT *[Gáspár Varró and His Rights]*. Play in three acts. Prose. Written 1955. First edition in *Dramen II,* Hamburg 1966. First performance December 12, 1965, Wuppertal, Schauspielhaus. Time: beginning of 1953. Place: village and nearby district capital in the depths of the Hungarian plain.

This realistic tragicomedy of everyday life on a kolkhoz is directly inspired by contemporary problems and reaches out to the hopeless predicament of all mankind. The most moving part of the play is its frank and compassionate conclusion. The denouement, with a prefabricated recipe for truth, is not brought about by argument and accusation, or even by some political *deus ex machina* of the party, but by the search for truth envisaged as a continuous task and a lifelong challenge.

All his life old Gáspár Varró was an enthusiastic pig breeder, both during the time when their lordships owned the estate and now as a member of the "Unity" Agricultural Production Cooperative. In despair he sees his pigs dying off one after another because there is no fuel with which to prepare warm feed for them. The old man is accused of "gross negligence

in the administration of cooperative property." Secretly he steals barley
and straw from his foster brother, the free peasant Kova, in order to
alleviate the sufferings of his pigs, which have the misfortune to be born
"state property." Even Lujzi Pósa, the woman chairman of the cooperative,
sees no way out of this predicament brought about by state-planned economy. The only one who can help is Terka Oszkó, the district plenipotentiary, a pretty country girl who has managed to intrigue her way up the
ladder of the official hierarchy by means of training courses and influential
lovers. First she hushes up the unfortunate incident, for she only gives
help where a quick success can be ensured and exploited as propaganda.
Needing a scapegoat for the unsatisfactory situation which has resulted
from so much incompetence, Terka cold-bloodedly leaves Gáspár to be
tried: "Somebody has to pay for it! The state and the party are entitled
to demand action from us. . . . We need a political judgment, not a lot of
hot air about so-called justice." The swineherd is baffled by the dialectical
subleties of the charges he has to face before the tribunal, which has been
suitably instructed by Terka. "Does the court then really not understand
my rights? . . . Mr. Judge, I talk and talk, I say what is true. It's true as it
comes from my mouth . . . but when it reaches your ears it has become
something else." Lujzi commits suicide because she does not want to be
an accessory to injustice. A minor misunderstanding eventually shakes the
party secretary Tatar into ordering a full investigation into the deeper
causes of the pig mortality. The drama comes to an end with an anxious
question: Can truth be brought to light, regardless of private interests and
political expediency?

DAS PFERD *[The Horse]*. Comedy in three acts. Prose. Written 1960.
First edition in *Dramen,* Hamburg 1964. First performance August 21,
1964, Salzburg, Landestheater (Europa Studio). Time: first century A.D.
Place: Rome.

Camus sees in Caligula the rational man whose madness makes him reduce
a corrupt world *ad absurdum;* Hay treats the same material as an example
of the humiliation of man under tyranny. "Here no one dares to go about
looking satisfied because this might make him suspect. And no one dares
to look dissatisfied because this might make him all the more suspect. Men
are afraid to fear because nothing is more suspect than fear! And they are
terrified of being unafraid because the self-confident are most suspect of
all!" Young Selanus with his splendid dapple-gray horse has come to Rome
to seek his fortune. The shrewd consul Egnatius, whose statesmanlike wisdom has already put him on the execution list, succeeds in replenishing
the exhausted treasury when the stallion wins a surprise victory in the

chariot races. The delighted Caligula awards the rank of consul to the horse. This whim of the tyrant's sets off a centaur mania among the fear-ridden pedestrian bootlickers. Neighing and galloping become the latest fashion, along with hooves and horsetails. The new consul gets a human bride in the person of the banker's daughter Ameana, whom Selanus loves and suitably comforts. When Caligula dresses up as a horse and wants to play Jupiter and to enjoy forbidden fruit, he gets a painful, earthly thrash-ing. Jealous persons bring about the horse's death, and in a burst of magnanimity the emperor pardons the lovers, and they are allowed to depart to the provinces.


## HELLMAN, Lillian
(United States, born 1905)


TOYS IN THE ATTIC. Play in three acts. Prose. First edition New York 1960. First performance February 14, 1960, Boston. Time: the present Place: New Orleans.

A psychological play in the established Broadway style: lifelong neuroses are shown at the moment of their explosion and typified in social criticism. The sisters Anna and Carrie Berniers, two ageing spinsters worn out by their jobs, dream of their trip to Europe that never materializes, and dote on their younger brother Julian, a happy-go-lucky fellow who is always up to his neck in gambling debts. He is about to land a profitable blackmailing deal with the gangster boss Warkins, but out of jealousy his wife Lily betrays him. Warkins has Julian beaten up and robbed. Humiliated and penniless, Julian takes refuge with his sisters, who are happy to be allowed once more to take care of their "toy."


## HENSEN, Herwig (Florant Constant Albert Meilants)
(Belgium, born 1917)


DE ANDERE JEHANNE [The Other Joan]. Play in four acts. Prose. First performance January 3, 1959, Louvain, Municipal Theater. Time 1431–32. Place: France.

Hensen makes use of the tradition that for decades after Joan of Arc was burned at the stake, numerous pseudo-Joans kept putting forward their claims on the legend in order to summon up against the arrogance of national heroism all the unknown wives and mothers whose thankless everyday labors keep the world going. In other words, "to live for God is more difficult than to die for Him." The matter-of-fact fulfillment of duty, transitory as it is, is confronted with the secular claims of martyrdom. The wife of the English governor has taken pity on Joan, gotten her out of prison and hidden her in her own house, while a wax dummy is burnt at the stake. Both the rabid crowd and reasons of state are satisfied. Joan takes refuge in anonymity, marries Loys d'Argenne, brings up her children and hopes for a modest, ordinary happiness, but the myth of her past does not let her rest. Loys is tormented by self-reproach: has he, with his earthly love, cheated God of Joan's martyrdom? He seeks death in despair. Joan's brother is determined to force her back into the part of a national heroine; the authorities threaten her with the stake. Joan has become the plaything of her environment's varying purposes. Her family happiness and security are destroyed. Undeterred, her hopes fasten on her youngest, still unborn child: ". . . to stay here, to live is the more merciless fire." In interludes the "other Joan" of ordinary life and the historical martyr Joan confront each other before the curtain in dialectical argument and comment on the action. Hensen sceptically queries the pomposity of heroism in comparison with the courage of survival.

## HERBERT, Zbigniew
(Poland)

*[The Other Room]*. Three acts. Prose. Time: the present. Place: a room.

The clichés of language and behavior are used, as in Ionesco, to show up bourgeois everyday life. At the same time Herbert strives for psychological motivation of absurd situations. A married couple wish to acquire the "other room" occupied by an old woman. They aim at driving her out of her living space step by step by means of strategically contrived harassments. They insult her, intimidate her, try to provoke her by deliberate, malicious noises, and finally fake an official document ordering her eviction. At the same time they become more and more dominated by their apartment's fellow-occupier, whom they persecute with such hatred. They lie in wait for her, listen for the slightest sound from the next room, peep in through cracks and windows. The couple are completely possessed by this banal course of things. They hum songs, make plans for traveling, invent games. At last they discover that the old woman has died, quickly stifle their few pangs of conscience and gaily carry on as usual.

## HEY, Richard
(Germany, born 1926)

WEH DEM, DER NICHT LÜGT *[Woe to Him Who Does Not Lie!]*. Comedy in two acts. Prose. First edition Cologne 1962. First performance February 1, 1962, Hamburg, Deutsches Schauspielhaus. Time: the present. Place: Baron von Kappoffum's house and a film studio.

The subject is the conflict between the individual defending the integrity of his life against an oppressive farcical environment. Baron von Kappoffum, an aristocrat and retired imperial army officer, subsequently a comedian in a circus and a cactus fancier, is to be driven out of his house by a realty developer's building project. His military service during the war is to be made into a super-film. In the boiling witches' cauldron of the film studios, the Baron, with his anachronistic notions of honor, struggles to maintain his own authentic reality. For the film producer, "reality" means using artistic exaggeration to create an effect at any price. He alters and falsifies in an effort to transform the dead past into life and success. In the film, the aristocrat is played by Jens, a very up-to-date "killer." The scene where von Kappoffum is on his deathbed is used as a special tearjerker. The realty developer has the house blown up, and the explosion startles the cactus fan into new life. In the future, Jens will profit from his compromise with lies and thereby support the old baron. The cabaret style satire and the realistic, sentimental elaboration of a misunderstood man's woes reflect the mental contrast in form as well as in content.

## HILDESHEIMER, Wolfgang
(Germany, born 1916)

DIE EROBERUNG DER PRINZESSIN TURANDOT *[The Conquest of Princess Turandot]*. (First version entitled *Der Drachenthron [The Dragon Throne]*). Comedy in two acts. Prose. First edition in *Welt des Theaters*, Munich 1955; second version in *Modernes Deutsches Theater*, Vol. 1, Neuwied/Rhein 1961. First performance April 23, 1955, Düsseldorf, Schauspielhaus. Time: legendary past. Place: China.

From Gozzi to Schiller and Puccini the legend of the icy princess has passed through every stage of development ranging from the graceful playfulness of the commedia dell'arte to the psychological case history. Hildesheimer goes back to the comedy of types in making an existential model out of the old story. Power politics are the decisive element in this play about the real Turandot and the bogus Kalaf who have to take refuge in anonymity in order to keep their humanity. Turandot, the daughter of the old doddering emperor of China, orders all her suitors to be executed. Hitherto not one of them has been able to perform the allotted tasks or to defeat the clever girl in conversation. For Hü, the chancellor, the test is merely an instrument of his policy of conquest. China occupies the lands of the executed princes. Kalaf, the prince from distant Astrakhan, whose dialectical fencing wins the argument with the princess and also her heart, is exposed by the slave Pnina as a swindler who once promised marriage to her, too. Hü sends for the real prince of Astrakhan, a dull, coarse barbarian who misunderstands such high-level diplomacy and forthwith conquers the empire with his unbridled horde. Turandot wins the argument with this uncouth suitor. She bamboozles the strong man by convincing him that Pnina is the emperor's daughter and disappears with her pseudo-Kalaf into an inconspicuous, happy existence. The basic theme of the legend is how the inhuman command that turns men into robots, here exemplified by Turandot's suitors who must go through prescribed mechanical tests in order to win her, can be invalidated by love. This theme is further strengthened by the renunciation of throne and high office and by the triumph of the simple life. With stylized movement and pantomime, this piece of chinoiserie maintains an ironic detachment throughout.

LANDSCHAFT MIT FIGUREN [Landscape with Figures]. Play in two parts. Prose. First edition in Spiele, in denen es dunkel wird, Pfullingen 1958. First performance September 29, 1959, Berlin, Tribüne. Time: the present. Place: an artist's studio.

A kaleidoscope of nonsensical gags, existential symbols, and scenic analogies in a world of standardized functions are combined with the grotesquely distorted details of an arbitrary triangle story, which psychoanalysis digs up from the past in the shape of guilt complexes. The painter Adrian has to stand by helplessly as a strange glazier darkens his studio by putting in purple windowpanes. Smiling and happy the widow Sartorius sits for her portrait with her young lover Colin. The aged industrial boss from the Ruhr is painted as a member of the master race, booted and spurred astride a rocking horse. Adrian changes his props and background as necessary, thus evoking the wish dreams of each of his subjects. His wife Bettina enlivens the scene as a somnambulist in her nightgown. The widow and her lover quarrel over who is responsible for her husband's death. The creative process lasts for years, and in the meantime the models are locked up in cages. Finally Adrian completes his masterpiece, and, full of pride, displays his work—monochrome areas in pale purple. An old gentleman gives his expert opinion on the figures, has them act out their destiny, and buys them for his collection. This cryptic impersonation of a world judge remains a foreign body in a fashionable script which contains no trace of absurdity experienced or suffered.

DAS OPFER HELENA *[Helena the Victim]*. Comedy in two parts. Prose. Written 1955. First published in *Wirkendes Wort,* 1955. First performance October 7, 1959, Mainz, Zimmertheater. Adapted as a musical by H. D. Hüsch and G. Wimberger, 1968. Time and place: not specified.

The charming playfulness of this recent contribution to the theme of the Trojan War does not obscure the author's implacably bitter concern with politics as a game of chess; the abduction of beautiful Helena is merely one move in the game. The loving woman, who struggles to retain the purity of her feelings, is degraded into a pawn both by her husband Menelaus and her lover Paris, both of whom need her as a pretext for the long-planned war. These men who make such a moving show of their betrayals are in fact business strategists who, in their unscrupulous heroism, not only turn Helena into a helpless instrument but vitiate her intentions and eventually leave her at the mercy of the cheap pharisaism of the pious folk. The stage version in which Helena is the narrator and the action is seen only in flashbacks cannot disguise the original conception of the work as a play for radio.

PASTORALE ODER DIE ZEIT FÜR KAKAO *[Pastoral or Time for Cocoa]*. One-act play. Prose. Written 1958; revised version 1965. First edition in *Spiele, in denen es dunkel wird,* Pfullingen 1958. First performance November 14, 1958, Munich, Kammerspiele. Time: the present. Place: an idyllic landscape of forest and meadow.

A play of paradoxes inspired as much by idyll as by farce, by the macabre as well as by sentimentality. A vocal quartet meets in the meadow for its musical pastime. Glinke, president of a big firm and a stock manipulator, delights in his spiritual emotions, which are poured out in a stream of immortal phrases. Miss Fröbel lies in wait for a victim of her unsatisfied, loving heart. The two aged Asbach twins—Dietrich, from the mining industry, and Abel, the consul—are as happy as little boys at having escaped from their nurse. Dietrich (or possibly it is Abel) and Glinke succumb to the exertions of this jubilation. It is the servants who are the victors: Philip, the valet trained at evening classes, and Selma, the nurse who looks after the Ansbach twins with her baby carriage and flask of cocoa. There is much clowning, gags, and verbal wit, but the main dramatic effect is obtained by the recurring arbitrary reversal of conventional ideas, by the combination of opposing elements to form a nonsensical whole. There are many visual gags (such as testing the accuracy of a scale by holding up a mirror) and there are ridiculous images such as "The new president is very musical, he sings mezzo-soprano and at the same time accompanies himself on the flute, but only when no one is looking." This nightmare of the Absurd is turned into an abstruse but pleasant piece of hocus-pocus.

DIE UHREN *[The Clocks]*. One-act play. Prose. First edition in *Spiele, in denen es dunkel wird,* Pfullingen 1958. First performance April 18, 1959, Celle, Schloßtheater. Time: the present. Place: a room.

The spiritual erosion of modern man is shown in grotesque symbolism. Dominated as he is by institutions and machines, man loses contact with reality, to which he reacts but no longer experiences. Even the most elementary impulses are transferred to the competence of some authority, to the intermediary of some industrial product. A man and his wife wear out their lives in trite chatter. Suddenly the glazier comes to replace the windowpanes with black unbreakable glass—"untransparentlike prison walls"; the isolation, long a fact psychologically, is given visible expression. The workman helps the couple to share a few last ephemeral impressions from the outside world, which cause the husband and wife at once to play their part with feverish excitement—the only companionship they can still achieve is in make-believe, in a flight from themselves. An unctuously voluble salesman sells watches and clocks for every occasion. His arguments are unanswerable, and soon chronometers tick and whir away on the couple's wrists, on the walls, tables, and mantlepieces, all of them showing a different time. The machines have become an end in themselves. The glazier finishes his work and leaves with the injunction: "Let it dry. The putty must dry to make the glass eternal." The room is now a lightless coffin. Harried by the relentless ticktock of the clocks, the people stumble through the darkness.

DIE VERSPÄTUNG *[The Delay]*. Play in two parts. Prose. First edition Frankfurt/Main 1961. First performance September 14, 1961, Düsseldorf, Kammerspiele. Time: the present. Place: bar in a country inn.

A play on the various experiences of transience, failure, and decay, a "dry run" of hopelessness: ". . . what should we do? A fine, rich question, a bountiful question to which there are many delicious answers, a whole wood of answers. But the longer you push the question around, the lighter it gets in the wood of answers. And finally the point comes when you look about in vain for an answer. . . ."

At the inn of a decayed and deserted village a handful of people come together, all of them out of circulation in this isolated place—the burgomaster, the schoolmistress, the landlady. The professor from the city has been on an excursion, lost his way, and is now frantically trying to catch the last train. Maliciously the worthies tease the ignorant stranger who lives in a wish-dream of being a figure of worldwide renown. With his boastful stammering, he misses the train, the last opportunity of getting back into the world. The next day the situation is reversed. The professor, with masochistic cynicism, admits to his failure and puts the others in a panic by mercilessly exposing their crumbling existence. Fanatically he chases after the legendary bird Guricht, which he believes to be the origin of mankind. With a flood of oily eloquence, a traveling salesman plays off the characters one against the other. The professor collapses amidst his delusions. A gigantic coffin-maker, the silent figure of the play, alone dominates the scene. It is a hall of mirrors of anxiety, a play of torment without meaning or cause, which gets its fascination from the symbols of strangely fragile lives.

## HOCHHUTH, Rolf
(Germany, born 1931)

THE REPRESENTATIVE (also: *The Deputy*) *(Der Stellvertreter)*. Play in five acts. Verse. First edition Hamburg 1963. First performance March 20, 1963, Berlin, Freie Volksbühne. Translated by Richard and Clara Winston, New York, Grove Press, 1964, and by Robert D. MacDonald *(The Deputy)*, London, Methuen, 1963. Time: August 1942 to end of 1943. Place: Berlin, Rome, and Auschwitz.

This controversial play, written in a very free, iambically accented verse form, was the first of a series of attempts to use the technique of semi-documentary "stage reportage" to open up a discussion on events of the recent past, events ranging from the case of Oppenheimer to that of Vanzetti. The data are selected and arranged in accordance with certain points of view and thus made to serve as proof of some theory. The result is an argument which claims to be an empirical analysis and strict reproduction of fact and yet puts all the details taken from reality at the service of an unproved hypothesis. Could the Pope's open opposition have prevented the "final solution" of the Third Reich? Although it is inevitable, for the purposes of dramatization, to subject the historical sources to a definite idea and to align them to that idea, this casts doubt on the documentary value of the play. In a passionate accusal, Hochhuth takes issue with the detachment, the serene noncommitment, and the "higher considerations" which cannot be totally eliminated in any worldwide, tradition-bound and hierarchy-ridden institution, including the Church. Hochhuth's revolt is directed against an institution, but—with dramatic effect though historical dubiousness—he concentrates it upon one single person, the Pope. In this perspective Pius XII is bound to appear as a vain poseur: "He was no criminal for 'reasons of state,' he was a neutral quantity, overintent on his station, who later often passed the time of day with irrelevant games while the world in its agony . . . vainly waited for a word of spiritual leadership from him." The young Jesuit Father Riccardo Fontana witnesses the Jewish persecutions in Berlin. A report by SS Lt. Kurt Gerstein, a secret resistance fighter, on the annihilation camps in Poland rouses Riccardo from his impassive, unworldly contemplations, and with every means of entreaty and threat he tries to obtain assurance from the Papal Nuncio in Berlin and later from the cardinal in Rome that the Church should openly declare its opposition to Hitler's Germany and that the Pope should break off the Concordat. But all the higher dignitaries of the Church see its peace mission in coming to terms with the events "calmly, in a friendly way" and in avoiding everything that might make a matter of principle of the differences between the Curia and the Third Reich. The Jesuits succeed from time to time in saving single individuals from the murderous machine of the SS and Gestapo. However, Riccardo's desperate scheme to capture the Vatican transmitter and call the Catholics of Germany and the world to open resistance against the Nazi regime meets with nothing but embarrassed silence and horrified rejection. When the Pope in these days of persecution devotes himself to the financial transactions of the Curia, Riccardo decides, as a protest, to take the contemporary Jews' martyrdom upon himself, to wear the yellow star until "Your Holiness condemns, before all the world, the man who slaughters Europe's Jews like cattle." And thus the young priest in his revolt becomes the representative of "Christ's representative": ". . . and since the Pope, who after all is only human, can represent even God on earth, a poor priest may . . . perhaps . . . represent the Pope at the place where he should stand today." The ardent idealist voluntarily lets himself be deported to Auschwitz, but it is not granted to him to accompany his fellow sufferers into the gas chamber. Doctor Gerstein, a cynical sadist who means to challenge God with his inhuman experiments and to confirm a nihilistic world order, chooses Riccardo as his assistant. The doctor enjoys Riccardo's revulsion and keeps him as a "philosophizing pet." Gerstein tries to liberate the priest from the camp, but Riccardo wants to pass on this possible escape to a Jewish inmate. The doctor discovers the plot. Riccardo is shot, and his Jewish friends end up in the gas chamber.

SOLDIERS. AN OBITUARY FOR GENEVA. (Soldaten. Nekrolog auf Genf). Tragedy in three acts, prologue and epilogue. Free verse. First edition Hamburg 1967. First performance October 9, 1967, Berlin, Freie Volksbühne. Translated by Robert David MacDonald, London, André Deutsch, 1968. Time: Autumn 1964 and April–July 1943. Place: England.

Hochhuth takes up two themes. One is the demand for an international law of aerial warfare for the future protection of civilians. The other is the question of the unexplained death of the Polish leader in exile, General Sikorski. The lack of dramatic unity is not fully compensated by these two heterogeneous themes being made to intersect in the question of the necessary evil in politics, where to act means having the courage to do wrong, and only the survivors are in the right. It is not truth that decides, but utility.

Only one of the extras on the stage of history, Commander Dorland, can afford twinges of conscience and translate them into action. He had taken part in the senseless bombing of Dresden and twenty-one years later he writes a play about the discussions among Churchill, Sikorski, and Bishop Bell, which is to be produced in 1964 amid the ruins of Coventry Cathedral. This is the framework. Dorland protests against the present which has learned nothing and is still building up its air strategy. He wants to have a law on aerial warfare included in the Geneva Convention. He condemns his own son as a potential professional criminal, because he works on the staff of NATO as a planning assistant. Dorland, already doomed to death by cancer, is a nuisance to his contemporaries. The personal responsibility of a soldier has long since been diverted to superior orders, and ultimately Dorland's play is to be banned.

This play, which is then presented in dress rehearsal, shows Churchill in 1943 as Prime Minister. Larger than life size, already a myth, Churchill is portrayed as the pragmatist of an epoch. "Politics is what we don't speak about./ We have to keep quiet about much that was done in the war . . ./ Only the victor writes history." Accordingly he sacrifices London to the German bombs, in order to save the armaments industry. With similar coolness he plays off the allies one against the other. To his friend, General Sikorski, he has guaranteed the independence of Poland. But at the same time Churchill supports Soviet claims to Polish territory, in order to humor Stalin. Then the Katyn graves are discovered: they are those of Polish officers, victims of Stalinism. Sikorski wants justice and demands an international investigation. Stalin breaks with the Poles and recalls his ambassadors from London and Washington. Churchill fears a break-up of the alliance over the Polish question and a military understanding between Stalin and Hitler. Sikorski, whose unreasonable demands for justice threaten Churchill's policy, must be silenced; he dies in a plane crash over Gibraltar.

In all the voluminous memoirs of the Second World War there is such an obstinate silence about the affair that Hochhuth comes to the conclusion that the Secret Service was invisibly at work. Hochhuth most convincingly pursues the question: *"Cui bono?"* The struggle for humanity at the margin of world affairs is illustrated by the love episode between Lieutenant Helen, an officer of a women's service, and Captain Kocjan, a captain in the Polish underground army. Kocjan is the idealist who unreservedly sacrifices himself, and precisely because of his uncompromising attitude can never be more than a tool in the "dirty hands" of the pragmatists. Another advocate of humanity is Bishop Bell of Chichester. He wants to stop the bombing of defenseless populations, but is defeated by Churchill's ambition to get maximum results from the machinery of war, to which the bishop must resign himself. In all this Hochhuth is not sparing of the more grotesque aspects of Churchill acting himself and entranced with his own performance. He is shown enthroned in bed and displaying his prima-donna manners, or puffing and blowing as he steps out of his bath, or setting fire to a wastebasket with his inevitable cigar. At the same time Hochhuth endeavors to bring philosophical clarity into his historical material by portraying Churchill as not merely the savior of the free world but also the gravedigger of the Empire, because by his policy he is paving the way for a world which will be dominated by only two blocs, both outside Europe. The epilogue announces laconically that the production was banned.

Hochhuth's aim is intensification. The realistic scenes with Churchill are incorporated in three acts of a London *Kleines Welttheater*. The prologue, centered on the director Dorland, combines the parallel with *Everyman* with quick citations in the form of historical documentation. Even the characters' names are deliberate contributions to the style: the name of the author of the original *Everyman* is supposed to have been Peter Dorlandus. The framework includes the sort of resignation which accepts war as something unavoidable, and, as during a natural catastrophe, seeks to mitigate what cannot be abolished: "The unnaturally domesticated masses . . . are driven by an instinct to let themselves be sold down the river from time to time."

## HOCHWÄLDER, Fritz
(Austria, born 1911)

DONADIEU *[Donadieu]*. Play in three acts. Prose. Written 1953. First edition Hamburg 1953. First performance October 1, 1953, Vienna, Burgtheater. Time: June 1629. Place: a hall in Galargues Castle, southern France.

The theme of this play—renunciation of revenge on war criminals—is the same as that of C. F. Meyer's ballad "Die Füße im Feuer," and although Hochwälder's dramatization is clothed in historical garb, this detracts nothing from its relevance to our own time. True peace in justice is to be found only by the man who conquers himself and offers his anger to a higher power as a *don à Dieu,* a gift to God. "Say nothing of vengeance! To do right means to purify oneself of one's own evil."
For many years the Huguenot leader Donadieu has dreamed of the vengeance he would take on the monster who tortured his wife to death in the fireplace and caused the defenseless village to be exterminated. For that villain, Du Bosc, the fight for Catholic unity had merely been a pretext for his own sadism. Now fate brings him back to the scene of his atrocities. Together with Lavalette he is on his way as a courier of the king to bring the edict of toleration which will give the Huguenots the religious peace they have hoped for so long. But Du Bosc, butcher that he is, is betrayed by his own fear. After a hard struggle with his conscience, Donadieu forgoes his vengeance for the sake of hospitality and the forthcoming peace. He endures the treacherous provocation of the Royalist Du Bosc, who is brought to judgment by Lavalette, the impartial arbiter.
Conceived in the strict form of classical drama, this play is often held up as an example of perfect dramatic construction. With its unity of time, place, and action, its careful exposition by means of episodic figures, the rise and fall of the action, peripeteia and catastrophe looking toward catharsis, the construction of this play is a model of lucid yet unstrained motivation.

DONNERSTAG *[Thursday]*. A modern mystery play in three acts. Prose. First edition in *Dramen I,* Munich 1959. First performance July 29, 1959, Salzburg, Landestheater. Time: infinite present. Place: not specified.

A grandiose attempt at a comprehensive representation of modern man and the perils to which he is exposed in a world of technology and mass society. Although the play's spiritual polarities are intended to resemble those of *Jedermann* and *Faust,* its props and background are drawn from a grotesquely perfected and hypertrophied civilization. Maskeron, an engineer, is the tempter and Lucifer; he has become an infallible brain machine, and as technician and psychiatrist he personifies the hubris of progress, material things as the absolute. Wondrak, his assistant, is assigned the task of finding the man who is "significant of our time—that is, the man who is dead while alive." Such a man is found in the architect Pomfrit, who despairs of the façade of prosperity which he himself has erected. Pomfrit makes a pact with Wondrak, by which he is assured of an existence without suffering or soul. This firm guarantee of happiness without perturbation or without external change proves to be a technical delusion: the supermodern homestead as the *ne plus ultra* of prefabricated comfort, the conquest of outer space as the riskless occupation of every Tom, Dick, and Harry, and the provocative, animalistic sex of the call girl. In this temptation the architect is sustained by the warriors of light, the Dominican monk Thomas, and a childlike girl, the rag-picker Estrella. In the end, Pomfrit humbly finds his way back to faith.

Hochwälder has found inspiration from many periods in plays on the Last Judgment. As in the medieval dance of death the play is divided into stations and the characters are allegorical abstractions who introduce themselves as they appear, contrastingly strongly with Hochwälder's use of modern cinematographic and electronic effects.

DIE HERBERGE *[The Inn]*. Dramatic legend in three acts. Prose. Written 1955. First edition Zürich 1956. First performance March 30, 1957, Vienna, Burgtheater. Time: the present. Place: inn at a Volhynian village.

This play puts man on trial as he flounders between right and wrong. Justice and self-conquest do not appear with all the grandeur of an ethical imperative but in a fleeting moment's grace: "In the midst of wrongs dwells God's justice—like the stone in a fruit." The Slav soul, with its naive, sensuous, and lifelong struggle—in which it is tossed between the search for God, the convulsions of penitence, and the yearning for redemption—is used by Hochwälder for his abstract parable. What in other hands would be the construction of an all-too-conscious catharsis has here the detachment of a ballad set in the landscape of Tolstoy and Dostoevsky.

Smalejus, the magistrate, is investigating a theft in a gloomy, dilapidated inn. A chest full of gold pieces has disappeared. All concerned protest their innocence but gradually become involved in guilt and crime. The lumberman Minjotai has stolen the chest, so that despite his poverty he may marry the avaricious landlord's daughter. He admits the theft only when a beggar is about to be beaten into confessing it. The gold belonged to the usurer Berullis, who once cheated Minjotai's father of an equal amount. His servant Andusz is anxious to expiate a murder he committed. An instant of pure, relieved conscience unites all these people before they once more set off into life and new wrongs.

DER HIMBEERPFLÜCKER [The Raspberry Picker]. Comedy in three acts. Prose. Written 1964. First edition Munich 1965. First broadcast April 1965, Austrian television. First stage performance September 23, 1965, Zürich, Schauspielhaus. Time: the present. Place: The White Lamb Inn at Bad Brauning.

A political satire on the "unassimilated past." The ingredients of old-time farce, ranging from mistaken identity and the disloyal servant to inn-parlor intrigues and the village powwow, are used in a bitter lecture on contemporary affairs. At an inn at a spa two strangers turn up who are obviously dodging the authorities and who are anxious to get across the frontier as fast as possible. The rumor spreads swiftly that the "raspberry picker" has come back: a former concentration camp commandant who, being a nature lover, had killed his victims among the wild raspberries. The local worthies, all veterans with high party decorations, compete for the commandant's favor—after all, it is only self-defence to protect an old comrade from "the final extermination of the grass-roots elements" and at the same time to prevent one's own shady past from coming to light. Konrad Steisshäuptl, the jovial burgomaster and landlord, who in his days as a group leader invested several cases full of gold teeth from the death camps in his prospering business, rapidly makes his daughter Sieglinde available to the stranger. She is swept off her feet by the nordic superman. Dr. Schnopf, a specialist in euthanasia, Huett, the headmaster and erstwhile energetic executor of death sentences, the architect, Ybbsgruber, and Stadlmeier, the factory manager, endeavor to outdo each other in the raspberry picker's favor. Even the policeman Zierreis, whose duty it is to arrest the stranger, is forced by the comrades into their steely "blood and honor" association. Then Grappina, the newcomer's companion, reveals out of jealousy that the "raspberry picker" is only the housebreaker Alexander Kerz. Full of moral indignation and cheated of their mass murderer idol, the community are quick to discover in this scum of the earth the semitic subhuman, and, since the real raspberry picker is now proved to be dead, they can safely cultivate the façade of a good conscience.
In this play Hochwälder has renounced formal experiment and has successfully returned to his practised style—to polished dramatic craftsman-

ship, straightforward development, a clear message, and solid characters in realistic surroundings.


1003 [1003]. Play in three acts. Prose. Written 1963. First edition in *Dramen II,* Munich 1964. First performance January 9, 1964, Vienna, Theater in der Josefstadt. Time: the present, "from midnight to morning." Place: the living room-study of Ulrich Valmont, the writer.

A discordant play with echoes of the Don Juan story and Faust's pact with the devil, as well as touches of Pirandello and zealous moralizing. The writer Ulrich Valmont is working on a new play, "One Thousand and Three," and in the agonies of creation he struggles with his own ego which booms at him from a tape recording: "Drama is struggle, spiritual conflict with the self, the opponent, imperfect, culpable man!" And so Valmont imagines his "nonman" Hans Bloner as the modern Don Juan, an immensely rich man of the world, whose sources of wealth are as hidden as his scandals are public. The symbol of this soulless search for pleasure is the luxury car with the privileged number 1003—the record figure of the amorous successes of Mozart's Don Giovanni. Valmont is striving to create an incarnation of uninhibited modernity of his own so that he can then take issue with this most comprehensive negation and stand up to him as a kindred soul and counterpart, as "the opponent who sees through him, fights him, conquers him and ruthlessly rehumanizes him." When the writer is fuddled with whisky, there appears to him the cynically self-assured figure that has always eluded him in the attempt at creation, Hans Bloner. The man of the world offers the writer everything that the modern world has to give, from the skillfully launched best seller to the nudist party, demanding as a trifling return that curiosity, a virgin. Uncritically self-confident as he is, Valmont makes his pact with the tempter so as to try his own hand at the process of rehumanization. The writer becomes Bloner's bookkeeper, Solkofsky, and in an attempt to save the girl he blackmails his chief with the latter's shady deals. But the man of the world has no trouble in brushing aside the zealous moralist who has long been involved in his "exclusive parties." Valmont, who has to carry out Bloner's demands, creates in his imagination young Sonja von Stein and delivers her into the tempter's hands. At the same time he appeases his conscience with the idea that her pure innocence will purify and "save" the libertine. But the calculation behind this soothing reassurance does not work out. Unmoved, Bloner has enjoyed the innocent creature at the party. Valmont takes on the role of an elderly Austrian aristocrat, the commander of a knightly order and defender of the family honor, and calls his adversary to account. But Bloner is utterly unrepentant and thus invulnerable. Sonja is killed when car 1003 is in an accident. Valmont, now a criminal inspector, can prove that Bloner murdered his mistress who had become a nuisance, and yet he still has to yield to Bloner's deceitful dialectic. The following morning Valmont is startled out of his dream by the tape recording and must resign himself to his own powerlessness: "The non-man—projection of one's own baseness." Suddenly a cheerful type swaggers in, introduces himself as the writer's new neighbor, and invites him to come to a daring midnight party—in the dream car, number 1003. Valmont yields to this persuasion. A two-actor play, 1003 remains stuck in its crudely simplified symbolism.

THE PUBLIC PROSECUTOR (Der öffentliche Ankläger). Play in three acts. Prose. Written 1947. First edition Hamburg 1954. First performance November 10, 1948, Stuttgart, Staatstheater. Translated by Kitty Black, in Plays of the Year, Vol. 16, New York, Ungar, 1956, and London, French, 1958. Time: shortly before 1800. Place: office of the public prosecutor in Paris.

This is a study of the merciless functioning of a machinery of terror made up of cruelty and pedantry; the historical setting gives the play detachment without obscuring its disturbing contemporary relevance. "I have to carry out the law—wherever it may lead. . . . Everything is possible, once the grounds are given." Crime evades responsibility by making use of the law, of the dulling effect of routine, and of a hierarchy of authorities. For decades Fouquier-Tinville—the public prosecutor of the revolutionary tribunal, who was always dependably at the service of the powers that be—has sent to the scaffold first Royalists, then Girondins, Jacobins, Danton, and finally Robespierre. He has done it with the help of perjured witnesses and extorted confessions. Even the executioner Sanson, proud of his "decent and clean handiwork," revolts against the "mindless mass production" of this endless bloodbath. At last the flood of prosecutions subsides. The Republic feels secure and urgently wishes to overcome its own bloodthirsty past. To this end Fouquier-Tinville must fall and be sacrificed to the now tender conscience of the public. But only he himself, with his intimate knowledge of all the subterfuges of an unscrupulous jurisdiction, can clear up the case and guarantee at least the appearance of justice. Madame Tallien, "Notre Dame de Thermidor," carried to power by her legend, commands the prosecutor to arrange a nocturnal fake trial with a preestablished death sentence, in which the name of the accused is to be kept secret until the last moment. Fouquier-Tinville is delighted at this new evidence of his indispensability and pays no heed to any warning. Into his speech for the prosecution he puts the finest touches of rhetoric, only to find, to his utter consternation, that he is to be hanged by his own rope. No rest awaits those who are guilty of perpetrating this kind of "justice" which generates ever new distrust and suspicion. But they too will exculpate themselves with the same catchwords by which public prosecutors have always justified themselves—they will say that in a conflict of conscience and obedience the latter must prevail: "Accuse the time and the ideas which take possession of men, but leave the axe out of it! Bring to the bar those who prepare it! I was always merely the axe!"


# HOFMANN, Gert
(Germany, born 1932)


THE BURGOMASTER *(Der Bürgermeister)*. Play in two acts. Prose. Written 1962. First edition Frankfurt/Main 1963. First performance (in English) January 23, 1963, Bristol, Drama Studio of Bristol University. Time: the present. Place: Moll's best room.

The idea of Max Frisch's didactic play *The Firebugs,* in which Mr. Biedermann appeases his conscience while supporting the anarchists, is here carried through with disturbing logic to its conclusion, that is, the little man who takes the bit between his teeth so longs for initiative and power that he shoves his way into the job of the hangman. The municipal official Moll, a nonentity in his office, feels dissatisfied and insufficiently appreciated even by his wife Therese. Wilhelm Nachtigall, a disarmingly cheeky convict, comes and settles into the couple's home. He works for an underground movement, robs a jeweler, perpetrates bomb outrages, and murders. The criminal considers himself a "militant idealist" whose activity is ennobled by the "movement." The Molls soon become suspicious and gleefully use the public enemy to work off their own private discontents. They do indeed want to profit from the rule of violence and prudently give advice—always, of course, within the limits of the permissible—on additional acts of sabotage, pretending that they know nothing and wouldn't like to get involved in anything." Their welcome excuse for this lack of principles is tolerance: "It's easy to reject. It's more difficult to understand. It's not so much that I'm for these people. But I'm not against them either. They must have their reasons. I try to understand them. . . . One hasn't the right to reject something one doesn't understand." It is only when the revolutionaries are obviously in the majority and there is no risk that the dry-as-dust little bureaucrat rushes into bloodshed. Moll longs to be feared, sees himself as the future burgomaster, and plumes himself with the crimes of others. The professional murderer Nachtigall unexpectedly reveals him-

self as a man of tender sensibilities, a frustrated station master and amateur gardener. With the gesture of a Napoleon Moll takes his place, turns
his fellow citizens into terrified bootlickers, and, as the first step on the
road to power, sketches out a comprehensive program of executions.


## HOLME, Christopher
See SPARK, Muriel


## HUXLEY, Aldous
(England, 1894–1963)


THE GIOCONDA SMILE. Play in three acts from the short story of the
same name in Huxley's *Mortal Coils* (1922). First edition London and
New York, 1948. First performance June 3, 1948, London, New Theatre.
Time: summer in the early thirties. Place: living room in Henry Hutton's
house in the Thames valley, not far from Windsor.

A combination of detective story, conversation piece, and self-confession
leading toward an existentialist solution. The theme of *per aspera ad astra*
is developed on as many levels as life itself. Henry Hutton, a rich and
fastidious sensualist, leads a life of smiling noncommitment. He is tied to
an ailing wife, but his attachments are divided between Janet Spence, with
whom he shares a refined aestheticism and connoisseurship, and an indefinite number of secret amorous adventures. For Janet, a woman no
longer very young, Hutton becomes the focus of her unfulfilled life. She
unobtrusively poisons his wife, who is also her best friend. With her unfathomable "Gioconda smile," which so fascinates the art lover Hutton,
she now expects to win Hutton. Instead he chooses to marry his current
mistress Doris Mead, a pretty but empty-headed young girl. Janet hides
her hatred behind the mask of a devoted family friend and succeeds in
making the suspicion of murder fall upon Hutton, who is condemned to
death on the basis of circumstantial evidence. At the last moment the
family physician Dr. Libbard is able to prevent a judicial murder by trick-
ing the nearly insane Janet into a confession. While this almost overloaded
plot is coming to its climax, Hutton undergoes a spiritual transformation.
The incomprehensible death sentence suddenly gives his life meaning:
"That's why I'm here, I suppose . . . for resisting the spirit of God within
me; resisting it by means of lies, by means of lust, by means of insensitive-
ness towards other people, by means of every kind of selfishness." As they
take leave of each other, Hutton and Doris thus for the first time find

true companionship. The return to life, the unexpected charisma of self-conquest, puts everything in question once more, and in profound comprehension the absolute values are again set in the context of living, with its temptations and decisions: "Life has to be lived forwards; but it can only be understood backwards. I suppose that's why we always make the important discoveries too late."

# HUXLEY, Aldous, and WENDELL, Beth

THE GENIUS AND THE GODDESS. Play in three acts. After Huxley's novel of the same title (1955). Prose. First edition New York 1955. First performance December 10, 1957, New York, Henry Miller Theatre. Time: 1921 and the present. Place: the Maartens's living room in St. Louis and the Rivers's library in southern California.

A young student's progress to maturity is traced on two levels and is linked by the double role of the hero. The elderly physicist John Rivers tells his writer friend Matthew Barr the story of his early years as a young man and a young scientist. Having been taken into the house of the Nobel prize winner Professor Henry Maartens as an assistant, he worshipped the great authority on nuclear energy and platonically adored his wife Katy. Thus this awkward young man fresh from the provinces lived a few years between "the genius and the goddess." The genius proved to be an egocentric, capricious, and hypochondriac bundle of nerves. Without earning any thanks for it, Katy dutifully did what needed to be done, brought up the children Ruth and Timmy—and then one day just collapsed in a fit of despair. The startled young man has to watch his idol transform itself into a human being, and human, too, is the way out which these two overburdened, discouraged people find in their love. John is nagged by his conscience, while Katy placidly and gaily yields to her sentiments and at the same time remains a tender companion to her unworldly husband, who is twenty years her senior. Her teenage daughter Ruth, a budding lyrical poetess, jealously guesses the adulterous situation and steps between the lovers. John accepts a job in Syria; Katy and Ruth are killed in a car accident. Years later John finds peace in a harmonious marriage, whereas Henry Maartens, untouched by all these catastrophes, goes on brooding over his formulas and tables, to the end a slave of his mathematical genius. This is a cultivated society play, psychologically striking in its contrasts but always subdued in tone and removed from immediacy by the device of reminiscence.

## ILLYÉS, Gyula
(Hungary, born 1902)

*[The Queer Fellow]*. Two acts. Prose. First edition Budapest 1963. Time: about 1860. Place: Dresden, Vienna, Budapest.

This play is a historical picture book from the days of the Hungarian independence struggle against Hapsburg domination. Illyés endeavors to give a popular slant to the nineteenth-century independence movement, which was led by the nobility, and to present it as a precursor of the proletarian revolution.

In Dresden Count László Teleki, the leader of the Hungarian emigrés, meets his beloved, Baroness Orczy. He is arrested by the Saxon state police and sent to Vienna. The emperor Franz Joseph grants him his freedom in return for a promise not to engage in political activity in Hungary. In Budapest Teleki rapidly becomes an object of controversy between Austria, which wants to make a collaborator of him, and the national uprising. Signs of favor from Vienna make the count appear as a renegade in the eyes of the Hungarian patriots. To escape the conflict, he kills himself. Illyés does not shun melodramatic effects, in the hope of arousing patriotic feelings even at the present time.


## INGE, William
(United States, born 1913)

BUS STOP. Romance in three acts. Prose. First edition New York 1955. First performance March 2, 1955, New York, Music Box Theatre. Time: the present. Place: a restaurant.

A social study composed of vignettes juxtaposed to make up a flat, typed variant of the conflict between individual and society. Inability to communicate, overcompensation, trauma, and perversion are the key themes Inge has borrowed from psychoanalysis. A bus is marooned by a blizzard. The passengers take shelter in an isolated roadhouse, and in the course of waiting through the night each acts as the touchstone of another. Dr. Lyman, a college professor who has been sacked for getting involved with young girls and for habitual drinking, overcomes his weakness and spares the young waitress Elma, who innocently trusts him. The farmer Bo Decker wins the chanteuse Cherie with his hulking naivete, and the manageress Grace Hoyland has a brief amorous encounter with the bus driver Carl.

COME BACK, LITTLE SHEBA. Play in two acts. First edition New York 1950. First performance February 15, 1950, New York, Booth Theatre. Time: the present, late spring. Place: the Delaneys' house in a midwestern city.

Man's sufferings at his own hands and his sufferings caused by his environment, his inner loneliness and his escape into illusion are here the subjects not of a tragedy but of a behaviorist study sceptical in its diagnostics. The author remains true to his own dramatic purpose: to make visible something of the dynamics of human impulses and human behavior.

Instead of realizing his life's ambition to become a doctor, Doc Delaney runs aground in a commonplace marriage with Lola, becomes a chiropractor, and tries to forget his failure in drink. After a cure to break himself of the habit he emerges as a fanatic teetotaler who works for Alcoholics Anonymous. Lola, in her turn, tries to cover up the emptiness of her childless marriage with irrelevant chatter and the senseless search for her dog Sheba which ran away years ago. For sheer delight in exciting scenes she encourages the student Marie in an escapade with a husky, good-looking muscle man. Doc had been shyly and tenderly attached to the girl and, disillusioned, takes to the bottle again when Marie, with light-hearted unconcern, returns to her unsuspecting fiancé after her adventure. In the end, the married couple accept their hopeless reality. Both renounce their dreams and try, cautiously, to live for each other. Dreams and the unconscious, photographic fidelity in describing everyday life, and psychopathological case histories combine to make this play a realistic social study of the American lower middle-class.

PICNIC. Play in three acts. First edition New York 1953. First performance February 19, 1953, New York, Music Box Theatre. Time: the present. Place: a garden in a small Kansas town.

A domestic watercolor against the backdrop of an American small town with its gossip, eccentricities, and petty spite. A picnic—organized by a carefully scheming mother who intends to steer her eldest daughter, Madge Owens, into the safe harbor of a prosperous marriage—takes an altogether shocking course. The girl breaks the conventions of her middle-class family's comfortable morality and runs away with Hal Carter to share his bum's life. The waspish schoolteacher Rosemary Sydney acquires a husband, and the rest of the party relapse into their trifling daily round—a lifelong waiting for the fulfillment of a vague yearning: "I think we plan picnics just to give ourselves an excuse—to let something thrilling happen in our lives." Once more Inge beguiles a wide public with his concern for the homely, his gift of shrewd observation, and his ability to see the poetic in humdrum life.

### IONESCO, Eugène
(Rumania/France, born 1912)

AMÉDÉE OR HOW TO GET RID OF IT (Amédée ou comment s'en débarrasser). Comedy in three acts. Prose. Written 1953. First edition in Théâtre I, Paris 1954. First performance April 14, 1954, Paris, Théâtre de Babylone. Translated by Donald Watson in Plays, Vol. 2, London, Calder & Boyars, 1958. Time: the present. Place: a room in Amédée's apartment.

Men are incapable of giving their life a meaning, they let themselves down and others as well, they incur guilt out of weakness or fear of reality, and they suffer from life-long self-alienation through commonplace trivialities —Ionesco represents all this in an oppressively grotesque distortion of reality.

Amédée Buccinioni is an unsuccessful writer who has locked himself in his room for fifteen years in order to live entirely for his work, but has managed to write no more than two sentences. His wife Madeleine is seen as a frenzied telephone operator, ceaselessly connecting callers and giving information. Her hectic rush is as senseless as his fruitless waiting. In the meantime, mushrooms keep cropping up all over the apartment—an eerie menace which begins to get the better of the couple. Next door lies a corpse, which also displays a tendency to ceaseless growth. While the couple quarrel about who this victim of their murder might originally have been, the corpse itself keeps expanding and occupying more and more of their living space. They argue about missed opportunities and cheated hopes. In a brief flashback the promising beginning of their marriage is shown. Both are hopelessly locked within themselves. After prolonged discussion, the growing threat of the corpse's advancing feet leads them to a superficial agreement. They simply decide to throw the inconvenient dead man out of the window. Naturally enough, this creates a commotion among the "guardians" of public order. There is no end of trouble, and as a result Amédée literally "goes up in the air"—a gust of wind simply carries him away. The alarmed people are calmed by the police and return to their daily round. Profundity and nonsense are combined in a refreshing piece of clowning.

THE BALD SOPRANO (also: *The Bald Prima Donna*) (*La Cantatrice chauve*). An antiplay in eleven scenes. Prose. Written 1948. First edition in *Théâtre I*, Paris 1954. First performance May 11, 1950, Paris, Théâtre des Noctambules. Translated by Donald M. Allen in *Four Plays*, New York, Grove Press, 1958, and by Donald Watson *(The Bald Prima Donna)* in *Plays,* Vol. 1, London, Calder & Boyars ,1958. Time: the present. Place: a middle-class English home.

In contrast to the classical drama, whose concern it was to represent the so-called "eternal values" in a harmonious and beautiful form, Ionesco adopts the opposite approach: he reduces our daily behavior to cliché.

Two married couples, who in their every gesture and most secret thoughts are stereotyped "Made in England," meet for the inevitable ceremony of afternoon tea. The hosts, Mr. and Mrs. Smith, are adrift in their endless small talk about meals, illnesses, deaths. Words become increasingly detached from their meaning and become menacing cyphers with an independence of their own, as when the conversation turns to "Bobby Watson, the son of old Bobby Watson, the second uncle of Bobby Watson, who died." Mr. and Mrs. Martin's visit is the occasion for representing the disintegration of human companionship. The spouses meet in ice-bound isolation and seemingly unknown to each other and go through lengthy inquiries in order to prove that they belong together. A garrulous Fire Chief and a rhetorical maid complete this circus in which reality is destroyed.

The bald soprano of the title appears only in an irrelevant marginal remark—one of Ionesco's malicious traps for the incorrigible thinkers and interpreters among the audience. The consistent elimination of meaning eventually leads to the dissolution of all means of expression, which degenerate into gibberish, eventually into pure noise, cascades of vowels, unfettered rhythm, the free sweep of energy. Across the footlights comes the compelling impact of sheer mime, beyond logic or intelligibility. It ends in the mischievously profound joke of the interchangeability of all experience as the ultimate consequence of depersonalization: "All together shout at each other in a paroxysm of frenzy. The lights go out . . . Suddenly it stops. The stage slowly lights up again. The Martins are sitting exactly where the Smiths sat at the beginning of the play. The whole thing begins all over again, with the Martins saying the same sentences, while the curtain falls."

THE CHAIRS. *(Les Chaises).* One-act tragic farce. Prose. Written 1951.
First edition in *Théâtre I,* Paris 1954. First performance April 22, 1952,
Paris, Théâtre Nouveau Lancry. Translated by Donald M. Allen in *Four
Plays,* New York, Grove Press, 1958, and by Donald Watson in *Plays,*
Vol. 1, London, Calder & Boyars, 1958. Time: the present. Place: a semi-
circular room with ten doors.

Dreams, memories, longings, and illusions must help man through the
weariness of life. Ionesco explains: "The world sometimes seems to me
devoid of concepts, and reality seems unreal. This feeling of unreality, the
search for a substantial, forgotten, unnamed reality in which I believe
myself to be—this is what I wanted to express by my characters who are
adrift in unrelatedness and who own nothing except their fear, their remorse, their failure, the emptiness of their life. People propelled into a
Something devoid of sense cannot help appearing grotesque, and their
suffering is nothing but tragic mockery."
An aged married couple have surrounded themselves with a ceremonial
of anemic babble. He is her sweetie, a misunderstood genius whom she
admires. She is his Semiramis, trembling and kittenish. The atmosphere
of unreality around them is steadily intensified. They talk themselves into
the certainty that today, at long last, is the day when the old man will reveal his momentous legacy to an astonished world. The couple's feverish
fantasy summons up the invisible guests: "The Colonel . . . the Beauty . . .
the Photoengraver . . . the Lady." A spookish conversation begins among
the empty chairs, with the hosts intervening only occasionally with respectful agreement. Further "invisibles" now keep streaming in through
the doors, the room is soon crammed with chairs. As a climax the nonexistent emperor enters the room. At this stage the Orator appears; he is
to announce the great message. He is a real man of flesh and blood, a deaf-
mute who glides quietly among the empty chairs and hands out autographs. The couple jump out of the window and thus definitely enter the
world of permanent fantasy, for the intrusion of reality destroys illusion.
The Orator despairs of his senseless task, which he can never fulfill, and
departs helplessly. Silent and in vain the chairs are left waiting—a world
of empty chairs without meaning or purpose. In the end the open doors
admit the sounds of an impatiently waiting audience's coughs and
whispers. It is a sad farce about wrong contexts, about the ridiculousness
of the inappropriate, and the curse of futility. The freedom which lifts man
above the rest of creation, where all is predestined, has become the instrument by which he must come to grief.

EXIT THE KING *(Le Roi se meurt).* One-act play. Prose. First edition
Paris 1963. First performance December 15, 1962, Paris, Théâtre de

l'Alliance Française. Translated by Donald Watson in *Plays*, vol. 4, London, Calder & Boyars, 1963, and New York, Grove Press, 1967. Time: not specified. Place: a dilapidated throne room.

With voluptuous cruelty this "tragic Punch and Judy show" dwells on the process of transience, on the ritual of dying. King Berenger I is the ruler of a depopulated realm devastated by wars, earthquakes, and plagues. Even the cycle of the seasons and the vegetation are perverted in this non-country, and the non-king's death on his crumbling throne is merely the ultimate consequence of the general disintegration. Berenger must die because he no longer has any gift for resisting the universal decay. The law of death gains a hold over him because royal rights and powers have lost their meaning; the notion of another, outer force has become conceivable. His first wife, Marguerite, forces him coldly and ruthlessly to submit to the process of decay; his second wife, Marie, tries with the irrational obstinacy of a loving woman to reconquer the king's unique Promethean permanency of life. It is only by boundless faith in himself and his own powers that Berenger can withstand the impassive course of the centuries through which he has lived.

But Berenger no longer belong to himself, for he is gripped by overwhelming fear, by naked terror of death. He tries frantically to escape the ordained decline. Drunk with his enduring fame he retires into blatant egocentricity and vapid self-pity. For the first time in his life he feels spontaneous sympathy with a fellow human being, a plain servant girl, only to realize that this frail bridge to a human relationship is nothing but an attempt to buy time, to put off the day of death. There is no comfort either in the proud catalogue of his achievement, which Berenger the man draws up, or in his abrupt turn to destructive mania. Inexorably Marguerite and the king's personal physician, who is simultaneously also astrologer and executioner, drive Berenger into the euphoria of accepting his own death, until he consents to the ultimate renunciation of wanting nothing any more. One by one the things of the world around him are extinguished, until at last he himself fades away into the luminous mist. What had life been? "It was only a brief walk in a flowering avenue of trees, an unfulfilled promise, a smile that dies." A colorful self-deception while inevitable death lies in waiting. The author seems to have lost the one positive, saving grace that has so far marked his work—the courage to laugh. All the more compelling, therefore, is the bewilderment of the human being who feels contradicted and cheated in his own transience.

HUNGER AND THIRST *(La Soif et la faim)*. Play in three episodes. Prose. Written 1964. First edition Paris 1966. First performance December 30, 1964, Düsseldorf, Schauspielhaus. Translated by Donald Watson in

*Hunger and Thirst and Other Plays,* New York, Grove Press, 1969. Time: not specified. Place: changing interior settings.

Hunger and thirst in their banal and compelling daily recurrence are stronger than philosophy, ideals, and spiritual aims, which are man's irrelevant luxuries so long as he enjoys "provisional liberty" and can afford to play with his own self-satisfaction. All these are interchangeable and ineffectual compared with the needs of the body. Once more Ionesco finds a disconcertingly simple formula for man's inner conflict, for the natural limitations to his striving for liberty. In *Exit the King* the pompousness of self-assertion and world conquest came to grief on the ineluctable process of physical disintegration. In *Hunger and Thirst,* liberty is shown to be a variable function of man's animal nature. Banalities are necessary for life; and hence life's necessities are banal: "Everything will do to make ourselves a nest with, we cover ourselves up with our aspirations. We feed on our desires, we drink from the cup of hope. . . . Make a restful night out of the shadows of the past." The compulsion of eating and drinking fetters the wayward idealist to the anonymous community, where, a mere slave of his metabolism, he founders.

Three loosely connected "episodes," called the flight, the rendezvous, and the Black Mass in the good inn, show Jean—another version of Ionesco's character, Berenger—in his futile attempts at self-realization. At first, Jean and his wife Marie-Madeleine are in a damp moldy basement flat, which imperceptibly keeps sinking more and more deeply into the mud. Marie-Madeleine tries to create a home in this grim environment with her love. In serene modesty this woman can succeed anywhere in her destiny of creating "a house of habits," of enjoying the happiness of small things. Jean on the other hand is made restless by feverish expectations, by longing for what does not exist. Grotesque Aunt Adelaide, a will-o'-the-wisp of blurred illusions and missed opportunities, and a spectral female form in front of the fireplace remind Jean of past guilt and unfulfilled hopes. He pulls the "dog-rose of love" from his heart and sets out into the unknown.

In the second episode he is on the terrace of a museum, waiting in vain for his beloved who signifies freedom and salvation, the most comprehensive symbol of hopes fulfilled. He tries to describe her to the museum guards, but every statement, every realistic detail dissolves in an ecstatic trance. The two guards expose Jean's eternal dream life as failure in the face of reality, as a betrayal of his fellow man, and as boundless egocentricity. While Jean sets off once more through the darkness chasing a vain promise, the officials are content with their cosy ordinariness and look forward to a good meal.

In the third episode, Jean, worn out by his life-long, aimless quest, enters, for a brief rest, a walled-in institution, "a sort of monastery-barracks-prison." An anonymous brotherhood of cowled men, but without the Christian cross, do their best to look after him. Hunger and thirst bind Jean forever to this gray community, whose thirst for knowledge and hunger for power are aroused by the new arrival. In the most friendly manner, he is involved in a harmless conversation. The informal talk soon becomes menacing and becomes a test, the test turns into an interrogation, interrogation into a ruthless brainwashing. In honor of the guest and for his useful instruction, the brothers perform a "play of education and reeducation." The materialist Brechtoll—a transparent pseudonym—and the Christian Tripp sit in their respective cages. Both are old and starving, both suffer from "progressive malformations" because they have their own personal philosophy and thus offend the leveling community. Brother Tarabas performs a teasing game with the two piteous figures half demented by hunger, promising both of them the longed-for soup if they recant their convictions. In the end Brechtoll confesses faith in God, Tripp denies him—and both satisfy their hunger. Outside the walls Jean sees his wife Marie-Madeleine and their daughter Marthe who has meanwhile grown up. He is gratefully ready to make it his life's task to achieve a modest family happiness. But there is no way out of the walled-in space, the doors of his prison do not open any more. In return for the hospitality shown to him he is condemned to serve the hunger and thirst of others forever as a waiter. It is the dialectic of wishful dream and nightmare that give life to the action.

JACK OR THE SUBMISSION (also: *Jacques or Obedience*) (*Jacques ou La soumission*). One-act play, a naturalistic comedy. Prose. Written summer 1950. First edition in *Théâtre I*, Paris 1954. First performance October 13, 1955, Paris, Théâtre de la Huchette. Translated by Donald M. Allen in *Four Plays*, New York, Grove Press, 1958, and by Donald Watson (*Jacques or Obedience*) in *Plays*, Vol. 1, London, Calder & Boyars, 1958. Time: the present. Place: a neglected room.

The final scene of sentimentally transfigured happy-end bliss, where the oh-so-loving couple are united with the blessings of their family and in the proud contemplation of the heir, is Ionesco's ironic way of representing the conversion of an incorrigible nonconformist to the cosy idyll of hearth and home.
Three generations have gathered in indignation and despair around Jack, the family black sheep who is so depraved that he throws tradition to the winds and refuses the reliable, sound nourishment of bacon and fried potatoes. In the midst of all the hue and cry, the Robert clan arrives for

the ceremonial introduction of Roberta, who has been chosen as Jack's bride-to-be. Detailed personal inspection reveals the sterling quality of the product to be bartered. Only Jack refuses to be "exploited." He persists in his opposition to everything and declares that he wants a girl with three noses. Even this peculiarity of taste is met by Roberta II. Lovingly and obligingly she takes possession of him by accepting all of his reservations and nullifying them with her purring kittenish pliancy. The continuation of this idyll is shown in the one-act play *L'Avenir est dans les oeufs il faut de tout pour faire un monde (The Future Lies in the Egg, or It Takes All Kinds to Make a World)*. The purring idyll has been going on for three years, without the young couple doing anything to make their contribution to the population policy of the *grande nation* and safeguarding the continuance of the family. Again the family council, this voluble, menacingly grotesque majority, prevails and forces Jack into a breeding machine. A cackling Roberta produces mountains of eggs, under which the hard-tried husband collapses.

Ionesco underscores this satire by deliberate warped language, silly puns, stale jokes, grotesque alliteration, and monotonous internal rhymes, and by wisecracks out of context—all the clichés of family life are mirrored in linguistic craziness.


THE KILLER *(Tueur sans gages)*. Play in three acts. After the author's story "La Photo du colonel" (1955). Prose. First published in *Théâtre II*, Paris 1958. First performance April 14, 1958, Darmstadt, Landestheater. Translated by Donald Watson in *The Killer and Other Plays*, New York, Grove Press, 1960, and *Plays*, Vol. 3, London, Calder & Boyars, 1961. Time: the present. Place: not specified.

In self-protection, the individual tries to establish a convention with the murderer's totalitarian system. The individual relies on rational argument, enters into contracts and looks the other way—and thereby loses his defenses. The hand that executes murder is guided by a purpose, by a readiness to go to the utmost limits, and hence is stronger than a world that has become so absurd that it is not worthwhile to fight for. Berenger is shown around the promising city of the sun by the Architect, who is also commissar, civil servant, and psychiatrist. Technology has created a paradise on earth, but a mysterious mass murderer has made the idyll a place of horror shunned by all in panic. The monster is disguised as a harmless beggar; his habits are known, so are the scene of the crime and the murderer's own whereabouts. But there is no point in doing anything against him, because everybody, even the police on duty, are mesmerized by him. The rootless, unprincipled people of this world have nothing to oppose to the merciless principle of destruction. Only Berenger with his impulsive idealism still resists. When he finds a bag with the murderer's tools at his friend Edward's place, he vainly tries to get the anonymous apparatus of government to take action. Even the politicians, represented by La Mère Pipe—Mrs. Peep with her caretaker authority—have other things to do. By means of the Goose Party they proclaim the "mystification of the demystified," and launch the rabble-rousing slogan that mankind can be liberated from lunacy only by each single individual being turned lunatic: "Let us all march in goose-step!" A chaotic traffic jam eventually smothers Berenger's attempt to mobilize mankind against evil. He finally decides to go to the police chief himself and loses himself in a gray plain, divided by a wall as far as the eye can see. Suddenly Berenger is face to face with the murderer, a tattered, one-eyed man who stalks his victims with a grin. Berenger has two pistols, and is physically stronger than this infantile monster; but he wants to convert and understand the murderer. His opponent's blank grin, the cruel sureness of his knife, invalidate all the arguments of psychology, logic and charity. Berenger collapses, exhausted. Helplessly the victim awaits his destiny. Ionesco condenses his paradoxes into merciless diabolatry.

THE LESSON (La Leçon). One-act play. Prose. Written 1950. First edition in Théâtre I, Paris 1954. First performance February 20, 1951, Paris, Théâtre de Poche. Translated by Donald M. Allen in Four Plays, New York, Grove Press, 1958, and by Donald Watson in Plays, Vol. 1, London, Calder & Boyars, 1958. Time: the present. Place: the professor's study.

A parable of oppressive profundity. Life in its carefree growth, its unsuspecting spontaneity, its curiosity and ignorance is a challenge to the zealous classification of bloodless scientific pursuits. The activation of theory for its own sake inevitably implies the destruction of reality.
A girl student is introduced by the professor to the ABC's of all knowledge. The eccentric pedagogue entangles her in ever more labyrinthine hypotheses, a spectral confusion of ideas. The more devoid of substance and form the speaker's expositions become, the more frenzied grows his persuasiveness. The conversation turns into an interrogation, a ruthless brainwashing. The girl, at first so full of life, complains of pains and responds with growing apathy to the furious assault of empty phrases. The professor is drunk with his own power and speech to the point of raving madness. The sexual murder to which the girl eventually falls victim is merely the ultimate consequence of this man's obsession with his own talk, his own persuasiveness. Disapprovingly the maid removes the victim, the fortieth in the professor's successful teaching career. By a political slant

the murders acquire the complexion of a national necessity and thus of being normal cases not subject to penalty. Eager to learn, the next pupil enters the room. We are shown in this presentation our age's characteristic tendency to take means as ends, to treat functions as independent, and to submit to the dictatorship of clichés that instead of being an aid to understanding have developed into an isolating barrier between people.

THE NEW TENANT (Le Nouveau locataire). One-act play. Prose. First edition in Théâtre II, Paris 1958. First performance 1955, Finland. Translated by Donald Watson in Plays, Vol. 2, London, Calder & Boyars, 1958. Time: the present. Place: an empty room.

In an oppressively literal sense Ionesco "boards up" the world. An individual, crushed under the burden of tradition, buried under the junk of the past, deliberately chooses the peace and ultimate security of a casemate-like room. The "new tenant," a Charlie Chaplin figure of comic gravity complete with moustache, bowler hat, and patent leather shoes, takes possession of the bare room. The voluble caretaker vainly tries to establish her ascendancy over the new arrival. He needs neither her motherly sympathy nor her domestic services. In a screaming fit of anger she departs and leaves the field to two furniture movers, who nimbly and inexorably fill the room with junk. Soon the windows and doors are blocked up, the tenant's living space is more and more narrowly hemmed in by furniture, until he cowers helplessly in the dark and is smothered by his possessions. This piece of clowning is constructed like a ballet, with rhythmical intensification and symmetrical movement, and with the props as an essential ingredient of the play's dynamics. The language sometimes merely marks time, sometimes mounts to musical furioso.

RHINOCEROS (Les Rhinocéros). Play in three acts. Prose. First edition Paris 1959. First performance October 31, 1959, Düsseldorf, Schauspielhaus. Translated by Derek Prouse in Rhinoceros and Other Plays, New York, Grove Press, 1960, and by Donald Watson in Plays, Vol. 4, London, Calder & Boyars, 1958. Time: the present. Place: a provincial town in France.

Ionesco in this play says an energetic "No" to every kind of mass hysteria and fanatical cult of ideas. His innate sense of the theater, however, preserves him from an exclusive indictment of the absolute worship of ideologies, which would merely have resulted in yet another ideological play. Instead, he treats his polemic with the true comedian's light touch and sets it on the stage with an unerring stylistic sense that never wants to be more than play, a sculptured cascade falling back on itself and self-sufficient in this intoxicating activity.

Rhinoceroses suddenly turn up in the small provincial town, much to the alarm of its citizens. People are amazed, upset, indignant. But in their hysterical defense these honest people show themselves to be only too much like the equally honest beasts. All the citizens' hitherto latent rhinoceros qualities come irresistibly into the open: the trumpeting pugnacity, the heavy-footed selfishness, and the pachydermoid obstinacy in stampeding after any old catch phrase. Like an epidemic, rhinocerosism grips the people. The nobility, the clergy, the whole of officialdom join the new movement. The down-at-heels clerk Berenger is horror-struck at seeing his colleagues, his friend John, and eventually even his fiancée Daisy transformed into rhinoceroses. Whoever is not driven into the herd by his own rhinoceros nature, joins the mass movement from opportunism: "One has to be sensible. One must find a *modus vivendi*. One must try to come to terms with them. . . . We must try to understand their psychology, to learn their language." Others justify their adherence to the Rhinoceros party with the intention of fighting it from within. The result is always the same. Berenger alone is human to the end, hopelessly surrounded by the closed ranks of a rhinoceros world that will always be inhuman. He will never have access to this world, and in nagging self-doubt asks himself whether in this modern world of ours an individual has any right to exclude himself demonstratively and to disagree with the majority.

THE STROLLER IN THE AIR (also: *The Pedestrian in the Air*) (*Le Piéton de l'air*). One-act play. Prose. Written 1962. First edition in *Théâtre III*, Paris 1963. First performance December 15, 1962, Düsseldorf, Schauspielhaus. Translated by Donald Watson in *Plays*, Vol. 6, London, Calder & Boyars, 1965. Time: the present. Place: English countryside.

With a wealth of aphoristic images and figures Ionesco makes plain the ridiculousness of an outsider who dares transgress the limits of convention and gaze on the miracle of existence, its realities and unrealities, its beauty and terror.

The French writer Berenger and his family are spending their holidays in idyllic Gloucestershire. He despairs of the inadequacy of literature in capturing and rendering life. The glossy toy landscape complete with funicular and panoramic hills, the people decked out in their Sunday best and busily engaged in their polite, guaranteed genuine English small talk, and, not least, the naive devotion of his wife and daughter give Berenger a feeling of exuberant happiness. He is, as it were, borne upward by inner jubilation and thus realizes mankind's primordial dream: he can fly because he firmly and unreservedly believes that he can. While mankind are doing their best to forget how to walk, Berenger points out to them the delight of soaring in unbounded space. He becomes the "stroller in the air," and thereby also an outcast, suspect in the respectable world of pedestrians. People guess that it might be a new disease, they mock and at once try to set up rules for the incomprehensible. Berenger returns exhausted from his flight. He has seen the dark side of humanity—cruelty, murder, war, "bottomless caverns, bombs, mud, fire, and blood. Behind that there is nothing. Nothing but bottomless depths." Even the harmless passers-by are distorted into grotesque figures, seething with hate and attacking each other in a mania of destruction. Friendly Uncle John Bull mows everyone down with a machine-gun salvo. And then the apocalypse gives way once more to the cosy respectability of the beginning. No one seems to notice the timid wish uttered by Berenger's little daughter: "You must love people. If you love them, they are no longer strangers. If you're not afraid of them, they are no longer monsters. They, too, are afraid behind their armor. Love them, and there will be no hell any more."


VICTIMS OF DUTY (Victimes du devoir). One-act pseudodrama. Prose. First edition in Théâtre I, Paris 1954. First performance February 28, 1953, Paris, Théâtre du Quartier Latin. Translated by Donald Watson in Plays, Vol. 2, London, Calder & Boyars, 1958. Time: the present. Place: lower middle-class room.

Educational associations and vestiges of tradition, uproar and psychoanalysis, archaic symbolism of life and literary aphorisms are all mobilized for their theatrical value. All these elements become interesting and usable to Ionesco only when he can tear them from their context and distort them beyond recognition. Thus they acquire the explosive directness of clowning and make a violent impact that is both sensory and spiritual. Ionesco explains: "The artifices should not be concealed but displayed, unreservedly exposed and made plain. The grotesque and the caricature had to be radically reinforced. . . . The comic must be hard, exaggerated, without delicacy. And no dramatic comedies any more, but a return to the intolerable. Everything pushed to a paroxysm, to the point where the springs of tragedy flow."
A detective inquires of young Mr. and Mrs. Choubert whether a certain Mallot, who is supposed to have once lived here, spelled his name with a "t" or a "d" at the end. Choubert never knew the man, but to not seem disobliging he hesitantly advances some guesses. At this, the kindly official assumes an increasingly sharp tone. The informal conversation turns into

an interrogation, the interrogation into torture. Choubert has to search the utmost corners of his unconscious for Mallot. His wife Madeleine becomes a willing helper in this merciless brainwashing. Repressed feelings of guilt, wishes, loneliness, and disappointments flash across the path of the hunt which leads across oceans and continents. At last, Nicolas d'Eu, a frustrated poet, stops the torment. The detective insists on his duty and wants to continue the interrogation, but—a victim of duty—he is stabbed by Nicolas. Soon, however, Nicolas himself dutifully steps into the official's shoes, hands Choubert a large crust of bread, and commands: "Chew—swallow! . . . Chew—swallow!" The other victims of the system are not prepared to put up with this. In their turn, Madeleine and Choubert stuff bread into Nicolas' mouth: "While all of them command each other to chew and swallow the curtain falls."

Man has no defense against an anonymous system's words of command. The world consists only of people who, fed themselves, feed others, of victim-accomplices who act out their mechanized life in spineless guzzling.

## JAHNN, Hans Henny
(Germany, 1894–1959)

ARMUT, REICHTUM, MENSCH UND TIER *[Poverty, Wealth, Man and Beast]*. Play in four acts. Prose. First edition Munich 1948. First performance June 25, 1948, Hamburg, Deutsches Schauspielhaus and Wuppertal, Wuppertaler Bühnen. Time: the present: Place: Norway.

Jahnn sees the conflict of a man torn between two women as a symbol of elemental modes of experience. Love, in the form of the Dionysian myth of tearing and being torn, comes into the life of Manao embodied in two contrasting women. Anna's love is all possessiveness and desire for domination; against her there is Sofia, with her childlike devotion and spendthrift selflessness: "I can only be a small thing in your eyes. Something beside your house and herds. . . . I will try to overcome my failings, since we don't want to avoid each other any more."

In the solitude of the North, Manao Vinja has hitherto lived in communion with plants and animals, in close intimacy with nature's spirits, the troll Yngve and the watersprite Brönnemann, and as kith and kin to his mare Falada: "I love animals, horses above all. For me there is nothing strange about them except the mystery of their being created by an invisible power, like ourselves. . . . Certainly I could not be what I am if I did not find a pleasant music in their shape, their odor, their breath and their velvety hides." The nature spirits drive Manao to mankind: "How can your life be put on the true path if you do not understand your youth aright? If you give your love to solitude, which will dry you up? If you give your tenderness to some chance animal that does not want you? . . . You are doing everything wrong." Manao ought to marry and prove his worth as a man. He becomes engaged to the gentle maidservant Sofia Fuur. The proud peasant woman Anna Frönning thereupon considers that she has been cheated in her expectations and by force and cunning she gets the man for herself. She forges a letter in which Manao jilts his betrothed. Sofia is expecting a child by him and in despair flees to Gunvald, the hired man at the Frönning farm. Anna strangles the new born child and twists the evidence against Sofia. In the spring when Manao comes down to the valley from his pathless solitude, he finds that Sofia is in jail. He thinks she has betrayed him and, on the rebound, he marries Anna. The peasant woman has triumphantly achieved her purpose, but happiness is still denied her. With her suspicious jealousy she also has the horse killed, but in vain. Blackmailed by Gunvald, seduced by the farm laborer Ole, she sees that Manao rejects her and is reconciled with Sofia: "We have been small of spirit and wanting in experience. We have taken the gleam in our eyes as an event for all the world, and the signs of our fear as the footprints of a steely reality." Crushed and mortally ill, Sofia goes with Manao into the mountains, where he looks after the reindeer herds belonging to the troll Yngve. On her death bed she commits Manao to the stable girl Jytte, and Manao finds consolation with this elfish creature who has the same name as his dead mare. For the death of Sofia signifies nothing to one whose blood flows in the cycle of eternal renewal, of the coming to birth and passing away of all creation. So Sofia is replaced by Jytte. This is not to be measured in terms of human standards of affection, but as a child-like, naive nature symbolism which men develop like flowers and then fade away, each living on and working on in another. The scenes are separated by epical prose transitions. Supernatural manifestations, the participation of animals or crystals, magical occurrences in nature, all contribute to making the action a representative, visible section of the hidden forces of the cosmos.

THOMAS CHATTERTON [Thomas Chatterton]. Play in five acts. Prose. First edition Berlin 1955. First performance April 26, 1954, Hamburg, Deutsches Schauspielhaus. Time: 1767–1770. Place: Bristol and London.

The fate of the artist who suffers on account of himself and his vocation, and who with his suffering and his egotism incurs guilt toward his fellow-men as well, has more than once been used by Jahnn in creating the character of the alienated and irredeemably solitary individual. The person ruled only by his own inspiration must become a nuisance to the rest of the world. By taking refuge in imagination Chatterton is made free of many possibilities.

Young Chatterton, unhappy and lonely, endures an environment which includes the fussy incomprehension of his mother and of the seamstress Sarah, as well as the indifference of the lawyer Lambert, whose clerk he is. Then there appears to him Aburiel—it is not certain whether this is a real person or the personification of a dream—who reveals the redeeming world of poetry to him. To gain recognition as a poet, Chatterton takes refuge in a make-believe role from the remote past, in the life of Rowley the medieval monk. Thomas puts forward his own feelings and confessions as a discovery from the middle ages, as the records of this Rowley who never existed and whose potentialities Thomas magically fulfills. Jahnn intensifies the historical facts of Chatterton's life by dissolving history, the succession of generations, into an urgent simultaneity and enlarging it into archaic timelessness. Thomas confides his hopes and fears, his longings and restlessness to the fictitious "manuscript" of Rowley and takes his "medieval discovery" to the local historian Barrett. Very quickly Thomas is exposed as the author and a forger. Defiantly he goes to London and makes a meager living as a political hack writer. His friendship with William Smith and his love for Maria Rumsey disintegrate. The more fate humiliates him, the greater his pride becomes. "We are merely an attempt, not a success. Our pride—we were speaking of pride—is the only way to salvation. If we do not accept the humiliations, if we refuse to swallow the mortifications, if we renounce the little bit of hope that is sometimes held out to us, and ask for nothing more than what is our due—Heaven—then, with head held high, we shall know if even that is a disappointment." Thomas poisons himself with arsenic. Aburiel accuses the world of rejecting its elect, in order to preserve itself and its own standards. What Jahnn usually treats as a mythical destiny is in this play resolved psychologically with much detail.

## JAMIAQUE, Yves
(France, born 1918)

LES COCHONS D'INDE *[Guinea Pigs]*. Play in two acts. Prose. First published in *L'Avant-Scène*, No. 235, January 1961. First performance November 29, 1960, Paris, Théâtre du Vieux-Colombier. Time: the present. Place: provincial town in southern France.

Robust, naive, and ingenuous social criticism in the popular mood relies more on a thoughtful sense of humor than on radical pronouncements. Victor Matouffle is a mason and has built houses all his life for his fellow citizens. Now he and his family of seven are roofless, turned out into the street because the landlord needs room for breeding guinea pigs. Matouffle moves into the town's band pavilion, and his friends cannot be kept from demonstrating in front of the town hall with all the noisy exuberance of their southern French temperament. But the mayor mercilessly orders the "desecrated temple of the muses" to be cleared. The priest gives the family shelter in the sacristy. But now the Board for the Conservation of National Monuments intervenes, and insists on compliance with the rule that this artistic and historic building may be visited only during the official hours of opening. Eventually the ordinary people take a hand, and place the children, one by one, with separate families. In utter bewilderment Matouffle is left alone in the market place with his new and now useless washing machine, and broods over his fate: "The whole thing is no doubt a 'product of our time,' as they say. This funny time in which we live, and this odd world in which they've forgotten the windows. That's how it is: a building without windows. The likes of us will have to cut windows in this ill-built world, so that we can get a breath of fresh air from time to time."

## JÄRNER, Väinö Vilhelm
(Finland, born 1910)

EXEKUTIONEN [The Execution]. Play in two acts. Prose. First performance March 12, 1963, Helsinki, Svenska Teatern. Time: the present.
Place: a ruined site in a conquered country.

In a spiritual no-man's-land of the Beckett type, man overcomes the hopelessness of the endgame by his freedom to contradict. The menace of a
world that has become unreal and absurd is a challenge to the individual,
and the individual's resistance restores a meaningful reality to life which
is safeguarded forever by the individual's voluntary sacrifice and ruin.
Amid the rubble of a bombed site in a town, Ivo and Goggo are dismantling
a forgotten gun. They do not know whether they are prisoners or still
serving in the army. Vlov and Dlodi, two subordinates of the anonymous
government machinery, have arrested an unknown man, whom, after a
brutal interrogation, they intend to kill. This victim of theirs, Cliff, never
appears, but his execution assumes the significance of an execution of life
itself, and of an exposure of all the characters: the pleasure-loving tor-
turer Vlov, the tender dreamer Dlodi whom fear has turned into a henchman of inhumanity and who appeases his own conscience with the
self-deception that he is merely doing his duty, the obsequious opportunist
Goggo who is always on the side of the strong, and young Ivo, whom disgust with life and frustration suddenly lead him to defend Cliff's unknown
aims and who is taken away as the next victim of the ceaseless execution:
"And yet I shall have died for something . . . for my country . . . for a spot
of color on the map . . . for mankind . . . for a dream . . . for something that
does not exist at all. . . ."

TA FAST MALEN! [Catch the Moth!]. First performance May 21, 1964,
Helsinki, Kammarteatern. Time: the present. Place: living room in the
apartment of Elfi and Otto.

A macabre grotesque, in which absurd conclusions are deduced from real
premises. The customary triangular situation here has old people as its
protagonists, and thus appears as a moth-eaten museum piece beginning
to acquire a spectral life of its own. Elfi and Otto, a very aged couple, and

Bernhardine, the once so sparkling intruder and now a toothless bundle of misery crippled by gout, torment each other with their memories and with the obsession with which they try to revive the ardent amorous encounters of their youth. The two women rivals go on fighting for the man, and eventually with malicious delight they rob each other of their illusions: Bernhardine announces triumphantly that the couple's missing son has become a robber and murderer, and in turn is told that the Resurrection Chapel, the dream of her bigoted age, cannot after all be built because of an embezzlement. An old chest full of clothes, which throughout the play is repeatedly rummaged through in the search for moths, takes on the broader significance of heaps of memories.

## JEFFERS, Robinson
(United States, 1887–1962)

THE CRETAN WOMAN. One-act play. Verse. Based on the *Hyppolytos* of Euripides. First published in *Hungerfield and Other Poems,* New York, 1954. First performance 1951, New York, Provincetown Players. Time: antiquity. Place: in front of the house of Theseus at Troezen.

Turning now to psychology and now to myth, Jeffers uses a theme from antiquity to express his demand for a natural life. While he follows Euripides in having Aphrodite speak the prologue and epilogue, her encounter with Eros goes far beyond the vengeance of an offended goddess and she becomes a human being at the mercy of her inner chaos: "In future days men will become so powerful/ That they seem to control the heavens and the earth,/ They seem to understand the stars and all sciences—/ Let them beware. Something is lurking hidden./ There is always a knife in the flowers./ There is always a lion just beyond the firelight."
Phaedra, the young Cretan princess, is by the law of nature destined not for her gray-haired husband Theseus, but for Hyppolyto, her stepson of her own age, and in her passion for him loses all self-control: "She is like someone possessed by an angry god." He is an arrogant young man who lives only for the hunt and his pederastic inclinations, and when she confesses her love to him he rejects her. She is gripped by hatred of a man who evades the temptations of life, and tells Theseus, already forewarned by an oracle, that Hyppolytos has violated her. The prince is killed by his father's sword. Phaedra scornfully confesses her lie and commits suicide. Theseus recognizes himself as the true culprit, who sheltered behind the husband's legal claim on his wife and abandoned his nearest and dearest to their miseries and snares. Jeffers attempts to achieve a monumental

effect by means of verse and archaically simplified development of the action.

MEDEA. Two-act play. Verse. Freely adapted from the Medea of Euripides. First edition New York 1946. First performance October 20, 1947, New York, National Theatre. Time: antiquity. Place: before Medea's house in Corinth.

Jeffers with his "inhumanism," his profoundly skeptical view of civilization, turns the ancient myth into a confrontation between the vital spontaneity of primitive man defending his elementary right to live and the morbid, opportunistic, treacherous Western world.

Lust for power has made Jason abandon his wife Medea and marry Creusa, the daughter of the Corinthian king Creon. The woman from Colchis is to be banished because she is a reminder of an inconvenient past. Her alleged friend Aegeus, king of Athens, is ready to grant her asylum, but she realizes scornfully that he does so only to further his own cause. Jason boasts of the virtues of civilization to the victim of his treachery: "I carried you/ Out of the dirt and superstition of Asiatic Coolchis into the rational/ Sunlight of Greece, and the marble music of the Greek temples. . . ." To revenge herself upon the husband who betrayed her, Medea not only destroys Creon and Creusa, but kills her own children.

The theme of the tragedy is here reduced to the human scale. The chorus has given way to three helplessly babbling neighbors. Medea is an elementary human being who feels hopelessly trapped in the double-dealing, artificially dialectical world and looks for relief in destruction. For heightened effect the author relies solely on his dramatic technique—free verse in long lines and unity of place—which serves as a mere anti-illusionist framework.

THE TOWER BEYOND TRAGEDY. One-act play. Free verse. After Aeschylus and Jeffers' 1924 epic of the same title. First performance November 26, 1950, New York, ANTA Playhouse. Time: antiquity. Place: Mycenae.

The author's ideal of "inhumanism" takes shape in an archaically monumental reality, where even man's crimes are absorbed in the serenity of elementary events. Cassandra, taken by Agamemnon as booty from the Trojan war, is set against Clytemnestra. Even as a slave she is a visionary prophet and judge. To celebrate the victory, Clytemnestra causes her re-

turning husband Agamemnon to be killed by her lover Aegisthus. She tries
to deceive the people with her show of widow's grief. But the spirit of the
dead Agamemnon speaks through Cassandra and calls for vengeance.
Clytemnestra, by divesting herself of her robes, manages to placate the
crowd and to assure Aegisthus of his undisputed sovereignty. Eight years
later Electra and Orestes return from foreign lands to avenge their father.
Clytemnestra hypocritically seeks to conciliate Orestes, and only when she
masses her soldiers for attack does Orestes kill his mother in self-defense.
Deluded by approaching madness he sees his mother once more in Cassandra and kills her. He, who by matricide sacrificed the peace of his soul
for the sake of justice, roams restlessly through the world, while Electra
turns to her immediate concerns. Purposefully she has the blood washed
off the floor and takes command. As in his earlier epic, Jeffers uses in this
dramatized version long-line verse and the technique of interspersed commentary by the speaker.


## JELLICOE, Ann
(England, born 1927)


THE KNACK. Comedy in three acts. Prose. First edition London 1962.
First performance October 9, 1961, Cambridge, England, Arts Theatre.
Time: the present. Place: a room in London.

With beat-style gags and rhythms the **Don Juan** myth is made into a piece
of clowning. Social criticism becomes souped-up cabaret that is disarmingly lighthearted but hits the nail on the head. Erotic freebooting is
treated as a sport with its attempts at speed records.
Nancy, the country innocent who is looking for the Y.W.C.A. comes to the
hang-out of three young fellows. One of them is Tolen, the record holder
and hero of all the girls; he initiates Colin into the secrets of his triumphs
because Colin is unsure of himself and shy about making contacts. And
as all this takes place in the "scientific age," the crash course proceeds
through the statistics of behavioral research and questions of diet to a
guarantee of success. Thanks to the help of the practical Tom and the
lively imagination of the girl herself, who, when she revives after a faint,
believes she has been raped, nothing stands in the way of Colin's happiness.
Tolen is rebuffed and his belief in his irresistibleness is shattered. The
script of the play allows room for improvisation and for ad-libbing by the
actors. Only the cinema, with its movable viewpoint and multiple struc-
turing, was able to exploit the expressive range of the material to the full.

# KÄSTNER, Erich
(Germany, born 1899)


DIE SCHULE DER DIKTATOREN *[School for Dictators]*. Comedy in nine scenes. Prose. First edition Zürich 1949. First performance February 25, 1957, Munich, Kammerspiele. Time: the present. Place: an imaginary dictatorship.


With the sharply pointed humor of cabaret, Kästner demonstrates how the redoubtable leviathan of old-style government has been replaced by the interchangeable figure of the modern dictator, himself an anonymous function and the standard figurehead of a system. In a preliminary note, the author explains: "This book is a play, and its outline is twenty years old. At that time many, including the author, found themselves the poorer by all their hopes and the richer by an experience. They learned from the German example that man can be deformed beyond recognition, even though his photographic likeness is maintained. This book is a play and might be taken for a satire. It is not a satire, but shows man catching up with his caricature, without exaggeration. His caricature is his portrait. Can such a play have rewarding parts of the traditional kind? No. Can it have a subtle dialogue by which the characters are distinguished? No. Any development of character? No. Tragic conflicts? No. Such things are not applicable to degraded people dancing on their hindlegs. Greatness and guilt, suffering and purification, the hallmarks of noble drama, lie in the dust. This is to be regretted, but first it has to be noticed. . . ."

The bombastic Prime Minister, the Minister of War in his bath chair, and the estimable personal physician have set up a school for dictators, so as to have always at their disposal a willing figurehead of tyranny. The current President makes a mistake: right in the midst of a memorized speech he proclaims an amnesty. With inescapable solicitude he is therefore treated to an injection by the physician and gently sent to his death. He was the third of the doubles who, after the elimination of the original president, had been placed at the head of the goose-stepping nation to drum in slogans. Now a new candidate is selected from the school for dictators, where the professor keeps a pool of criminals, chosen for their resemblance to the president, and trains them to match the original in bearing, stride and speech. "Number 7," whose adaptability and intelligence mark him out as useful to the group as a factotum, but who is excluded from the highest office for reasons of security, overthrows the powers that be and tries to become the "tribune" of a just, moderate government. The people see nothing but a menace in their unaccustomed

freedom. A military junta seizes power and makes the "tribune" its instrument. In despair he jumps from the balcony, is given a state funeral and is
succeeded by a man who is his very spit and image—the new, old inerad-
icable system is confirmed.

## KERR, Jean
(United States, born 1923)

MARY, MARY. Comedy in three acts. Prose. First edition New York 1963.
First performance August 8, 1961, New York, Helen Hayes Theatre. Time:
the present, winter. Place: McKellaway's apartment in East Manhattan.

A popular hit that owes its success more to charm and wit than to characterization. Gently and insistently a recalcitrant ex-husband is trained
for matrimony. His tax lawyer proves to the young publisher Bob McKellaway that he simply cannot afford the alimony he pays his former wife
Mary. The expensive demands of his new fiancée, Tiffany Richards, and
Mary's flirtation with a film star and Bob's own jealousy all help to cure
him of his hasty decision to have nothing more to do with Mary and lead
him back contritely to home and hearth.

## KILTY, Jerome
(United States, born 1922)

DEAR LIAR. A comedy of letters in two acts. Adapted from the corre-
spondence of Bernard Shaw and Mrs. Patrick Campbell. First edition
London 1960. First performance October 5, 1959, Berlin, Renaissance-
Theater. Time: 1899–1939. Place: not specified.

A tribute to two masters in the art of producing themselves, bringing
George Bernard Shaw to life on the stage with all his lovable weaknesses
and maliciously intelligent sarcasm. Passion filtered through irony and
gentle malice melting into tender homage mark Shaw's correspondence
with the actress Stella Campbell, his life-long confidante. It was for her
that he wrote *Pygmalion*, but she was a lady of society and forty-nine by
that time, and it was a long while before she agreed to play the Cockney
flower girl. For years they quarreled about casting and interpretation. The
death of Shaw's mother and of Stella's son, who was killed in action, temporarily sadden the chatty tone. Then this conversation by letter con-

tinues loosely during the improvised rehearsals of *Pygmalion*. But the two artists were intoxicated with each other and each other's talents only during the first twenty years. The aging Stella, finding herself gradually impoverished, wanted to mend her finances by publishing the love letters, much to the vain dramatist's annoyance. But he got back at her by complacently incorporating a variant of their affair in *The Apple Cart*, which gave Stella her place in literature as the enchanting, capricious adulteress Orinthia. On both sides the troubles of old age eventually turned the impish malice of the early correspondence into spiteful acrimony. The bravura of these two stars who always lived for the public, provides today's interpreters with two splendid parts.

## KINGSLEY, Sidney
(United States, born 1906)

DARKNESS AT NOON. Play in three acts. Prose. Based on the novel of the same title by Arthur Koestler (1940). Written 1945. First edition New York 1951. First performance January 13, 1951, New York, Alvin Theatre. Time: March–April 1937. Place: cell in a Russian prison.

Koestler's autobiography, in which he draws from his Communist past, is presented with fade-in techniques and naturalistic harshness. Rubashov is waiting in prison for his show trial and for the predetermined death sentence. As a convinced bolshevik he had his share of all the dangers of the revolution, worked as an agitator and wrote ideological tracts. In Germany he was tortured by the SS for his convictions, and after his flight to Moscow was awarded decorations and celebrated as a national hero. A true fanatic, he sacrificed his friends and even his mistress Luba to Soviet justice. Whoever fails to meet the superhuman targets of the plan is condemned as a saboteur. Eventually the aggressive Gletkin causes Rubashov's downfall by just this accusation. The demoted official finds that many of his victims are now his fellow prisoners. He realizes with despair that the rigid dogma, which was supposed to liberate mankind from misery, has done nothing but increase misery in the world. After endless, agonizing interrogations Rubashov pleads guilty and, a broken man, waits for the relief of a bullet. The principle that all revolutions devour their own children serves to illuminate an aspect of recent history.

## KINOSHITA, Junji
(Japan, born 1914)

TWILIGHT CRANE *(Yûzuru)*. One-act Japanese fairy tale. Prose. First performance 1949, Osaka, Theatre of the "Budô-no-Kai." Translated by A. C. Scott in *Playbook. Five Plays for a New Theatre,* Norfolk, Connecticut, New Directions, 1956. Time: not specified. Place: Yohyô's hut in a snow-covered landscape.

This fairy tale of loyalty abused is rooted in ancient myths about animals and their power to become human. Greed and vanity destroy the unearthly dream. Out of love and gratitude, a crane has assumed the shape of the girl Tsû and as such has become the wife of the peasant Yohyô. This unexpected stroke of good fortune has made him complacent and lazy; he keeps nagging Tsû to weave more of the precious crane-feather fabric, which he hopes to sell for a high price. Under pressure from his greed, Tsû sacrifices the crane feathers and with them her life. Yohyô now possesses the precious fabric. Left alone, he sadly watches as a crane rises to heaven in crippled flight and disappears forever into infinity. Folklore and nature magic lyrically combine in a seamless unity.

## KIPPHARDT, Heinar
(Germany, born 1922)

IN THE MATTER OF J. ROBERT OPPENHEIMER *(In der Sache J. Robert Oppenheimer)*. A play freely adapted on the basis of documents in nine scenes. Prose. Written 1962–1963. First published in *Spectaculum VII*, Frankfurt/Main 1964. First televised January 23, 1964, Hessischer Rundfunk. First stage performance October 11, 1964, Berlin, Freie Volksbühne, and Munich, Kammerspiele. Translated by Ruth Speirs, London, Methuen, 1967. Time: April 12 to May 14, 1954. Place: Investigation Room 2022 in Building T3 of the Atomic Energy Commission, Washington, D.C.

This dramatic interpretation of documents of contemporary history drew a protest from Professor Oppenheimer, who asserted that the motives and the facts had been falsified. Nothing could better underline the play's own theme, which is that in our age everything factual is dubious and incapable of being verified. In the course of the wave of persecution that Senator McCarthy unleashed against everyone who was even slightly tinged with leftist sympathies, the distinguished physicist J. Robert Oppenheimer, the "father of the atom bomb" and professor at Princeton, is summoned before a Personnel Security Board. Photomontage, tape recordings, films, records of proceedings and the testimony of witnesses are used to present the antecedents of the case, namely: the insoluble conflict of the modern scientist who is divided between joy in discovery, obedience to the state, and pangs of conscience. The opposing viewpoints of the participants make plain the hopeless impotence of men faced with the demands of our time. Although Roger Robb, Counsel for the Atomic Energy Commission, cannot prove guilt by the facts adduced, he tries to make a case for "ideological treason" in order to punish even the slightest possible failure of duty. "I confess that it was Oppenheimer's case which made me realize the inadequacy of being strictly confined to facts in our modern security investigations. How rough and ready and unscientific is our basic approach if we do not go beyond the facts and take as the subject of our inquiries the thoughts, feelings, and motives that underlie the facts." The physicist's scruples, which restrained him from any further military atomic research after the bomb he had developed had been dropped on Hiroshima, are interpreted as high treason and indirect support of the Soviet Union. What he did and said in his youth is examined with the suspicion that has divided the present time into two hostile power blocs. Oppenheimer wanted to stop the manufacture of any more hydrogen bombs and advocated total disarmament.

Was he humanly justified in taking this line, or ought he to have left the question to the politicians and continued to do his duty as a physicist? Does he himself bear the responsibility for the exploitation of his discoveries, or can he take refuge in noncommitment by claiming that "discoveries are neither good nor bad, neither moral nor immoral, but merely matters of fact. They can be used or misused; both the internal combustion engine and atomic energy. In the end, however painful the intermediate stages, men have learned to use them." Is it possible and human to demand a sharp separation between the personal philosophy of a scientist and his objective work, which he has to do, without reservations, for the state which pays him? Is it right and proper to hail scientific work as implying no value judgment and then to exploit it for political purposes? And on the other hand, in the interest of its citizens' safety, ought not the state to do everything, even at the cost of some individual injustice, to exclude the slightest possibility of atomic treason? "Security measures are pragmatical. They are a question of what is to be made secure in what situation against whom. They lay no claim to absolute justice and impeccable ethics. They are practical." But what if the defense of freedom turns into such tyranny that everyone has in fact long ceased to be free? This jumble of confused, insoluble questions is illuminated by the predicament of one man. The Board reaches a decision by a narrow majority. Security clearance is withdrawn from Oppenheimer, that is to say, he is declared suspect. A few years later, on December 2, 1963, the man who was thus humiliated received from President Johnson the Enrico Fermi prize for services rendered to the atomic energy program. The conflict in these facts is the conflict of our time.

JOEL BRAND [Joel Brand]. The story of a deal in twenty-two scenes. Prose. First edition Frankfurt/Main 1965. First Performance October 5, 1965, Munich, Kammerspiele. Time: the spring of 1944. Place: Budapest, Istanbul, Cairo.

Initially a television documentary with extensive commentary and fade-in scenes, the stage version is an illusionistic drama much concerned with psychological nuances and the atmosphere of the time. In his use of historical data, Kipphardt concentrates on the conflict between the law and humanity perverted for a political game of chess.
The Nazi *Schutzstaffel* in Budapest wants to "mobilize the economic resources of world Jewry." In return for 10,000 new trucks, serviceable at the front, they are prepared to release a million Jews already sentenced to the Auschwitz gas chambers. For a fortnight Eichmann suspends deportations and sends Joel Brand as an undercover negotiator to the Jewish organizations and the Allies. Brand sees his mission as the imperative last opportunity of saving human lives. To his bitter consternation he discovers that mass murder is not to be eliminated from the world by business deals and agreements. For the sake of the condemned Brand is ready to push through the deal at any cost, even if he himself has to violate the law. With a faked passport he travels to Istanbul, along with the shady agent Bandi Grosz. He bribes the Turkish authorities, tries to persuade the Jewish representatives to use bluff, implores the British military to exceed their powers, to go behind the backs of their allies and submit to the *Schutzstaffel* blackmail. Brand, an idealist lost in Utopias and a political dilettante, pays no heed to the political and military consequences which would follow the deal with the Nazis. All that remains is bitter and senseless discussions between men who will never understand each other.

SHAKESPEARE DRINGEND GESUCHT [Shakespeare Wanted Urgently]. Satirical comedy in three acts. Prose. First edition Berlin 1954. First performance June 28, 1953, Berlin, Kammerspiele des Deutschen Theaters. Time: the present. Place: East Germany.

Kipphardt uses the 1953 "thaw" in cultural policy for a satirical settle-
ment of accounts with the culture bureaucrats. However, he does not forgo
the final apotheosis to the greater glory of the party. He combines topical
comment with crude, old-hat comedy and characters who are no more than
flat, superficial types.

Amadeus Färbel, the harassed drama consultant of an East German municipal theater, is a self-portrait in Kipphardt who at the time was drama
consultant of the German Theatre in East Berlin.

Amid all the resolutions and agitations, the didactic programs and practical applications which the theater has to implement in the service of
socialism, the drama consultant also has to provide good, actable plays. The
director Schnell, a servile party bootlicker with an inexhaustible supply
of phrases, always manages to trim his sails to the political weather whatever it may be: "We have to think dialectically: the press, the president—
one must have the courage to change oneself. Criticism and self-criticism."
Miss Glück, the secretary, is a fanatical cultural activist who checks the
output quotas with a stop watch. Färbel reacts with a sigh of protest
against her feelings of solidarity which gush forth in innumerable committees: "What we lack is a meeting of the Association for the Suppression
of Meetings Fanatics, so that now and then someone could have an opportunity of making an effort with his head instead of with his behind." Concoctions which enjoy high-level political protection have to be given prefer-
ential treatment. And proper respect must be paid to the lowbrow, but
influential leader of cultural mass activities, who until recently was a
splendid milk tester. Then Färbel discovers his "Shakespeare," a simple
locksmith called Raban who has written a play which depicts the world
plainly and realistically. Indignantly the director raises objections to the
play as being an "insulting criticism of our conditions, our achievements,
our heroes." It is surely the acme of high treason that this "unrealistic,
objective, cosmopolitan concoction" goes as far as to portray even a high
party functionary as an ordinary man and beer drinker. Then the party
intervenes as a friend and helper in the person of a woman official from
the Berlin Ministry of Culture. She has Schnell posted to a tractor station
as punishment and Färbel is made director. "With us a man is never alone
when he has a good case. The party is the conscience of the world of today.
The party is the brains of the world of tomorrow."

DIE STÜHLE DES HERRN SZMIL *[Mr. Szmil's Chairs]*. Satire in six scenes.
Based on the novel *Twelve Chairs* by Ilf and Petrov. Prose. Written 1958.
First published in *Junges Theater von heute,* Munich, n.d. First performance February 1, 1961, Wuppertal, Städtische Bühnen. Time: the present. Place: Soviet occupied zone of Germany.

A carefully calculated piece of topical social criticism, more interesting for
the abuses it often laboriously seeks to play up than for those it vociferously denounced. In style it is something between the hyperbole of Maya-
kovsky's social satires and traditional farce.

As a young rake, the nobleman von Szmilicz got through the whole of the
family fortune in his day; now an irreverent age has democratized him
into the registrar Szmil. He is delighted to learn of the death of an aunt,
from whom he has reason to expect an inheritance. The family jewels are
hidden in one of twelve chairs which had long since been torn from their
imposing drawing-room and profitably auctioned by the classless society.
A hoodlum, Kasch, takes charge of the hunt for the chair with its promise
of reward. In one role after another, as a sinister functionary, as an
imperialist counter-revolutionary, as a marriage imposter, swindler and
housebreaker, he intimidates the insecure petty bourgeois and incorrigible
property owners, who had looked forward to peaceful contemplation of
their vanished splendors from their feudal armchairs, rickety and moth-
eaten though they might be. These pusillanimous people are maliciously
caricatured. Breathless from the swift alternations of power in this century,
they are the eternal hangers-on forever worrying about their comforts and
quick to come to terms with whatever regime there may be. The disappointed academic, the senile general, a sentimental regional poetess, petty
shopkeepers are all exposed to acid ridicule, behind which is felt the presence of hidden tragedy. Average men and women, insignificant supernu-
meraries of the ordinary with their desire for peace and security have to
shed their principles in these times, for they haven't the stuff of martyrs
or heroes in them. All that is left at the end are twelve smashed-up armchairs and no valuables. It was all the aunt's wicked joke to hoax the
legacy-hunters. Kasch, the double-crossed double-crosser, turns the *Junker*
Szmil into a yapping cur—it is a cheap point to score as a concession to
the workers' paradise and to bring to its conclusion an otherwise daring
satire that hits out in all directions.


## KISHON, Ephraim
(Israel, born 1924)


THE LICENSE. Comedy in two acts. Prose. First performance May 17,
1961, Tel Aviv, Ohel Theatre. Time: the present. Place: a room at
Brozowsky's, in Israel.

The plumber Daniel Brozowsky has found the ideal husband for his
daughter Vicky in the person of young Robert, a professional employee
at the statistical office and his mother's darling at home. Before the mar-

riage with this authoritative young man, his mama wishes to inspect Daniel's marriage certificate. It cannot be found. The union between Daniel and his wife Ella goes back 25 years to the kibbutz, where love had not yet been overtaken by bureaucracy. The idea of just getting married over again founders on the objections of Ella, who would be only too happy to get freedom in exchange for her stodgy domestic tyrant. Eventually the document is found behind the engagement photograph. The marital crisis subsides, the wedding can take place. Vicky, in the meantime, has decided against the colorless office chatterbox and has got engaged to Bunky, who had been summoned from the kibbutz by Daniel to help clear up the facts relating to his marriage. Bunky is as disarmingly attractive as any national idol can be expected to be—unselfish, strong, a veteran, a football champion and even a nonsmoker. A marriage farce that combines social criticism, comic situations, and soulful genre scenes, its descent into clichés is more than compensated by Kishon's lively sense of the theater.

## KOHOUT, Pavel
(Czechoslovakia, born 1928)

CESTA KOLEM SVÊTA ZA 80 DNÍ [Around the World in Eighty Days]. Play in forty-five scenes. After the novel of the same title by Jules Verne. Prose. First performance January 27, 1962, Prague, S. K. Neumann Theatre. Time: the Spring of 1871. Place: interchangeable outline settings.

The action of the novel—a multivalent game of social satire—is used in double refraction with anachronistic alienation effects. To provide a framework, Jules Verne comments throughout on the adventures of his hero, represented by himself. The other partner in the conversation is a "youngish man" of today, who eventually turns out to be the astronaut Major Gagarin. The different levels of what the characters know provide an opportunity for maliciously clever skirmishing with the Punch-and-Judy puppets of a ludicrous bourgeoisie. There is hardly any party-political distortion on the bourgeois side; rather, these figures often serve as a pretext for pinpointing the excesses of the people's democracies. In fact, Kohout justifies his dramatization as "less risky than writing plays critical of contemporary conditions." The salient point for Kohout, as it was for Verne, is faith in technical progress as man's exclusive salvation; this is the fixed point that gives unity to the cabaret-style picture album. Around 1871 Jules Verne is writing his novel in Paris, and takes on the main part in it, that of the Englishman Phineas Fogg, who makes a bet at the Reform Club in London that he will make a trip around the world in eighty days, exactly in accordance with Cook's timetable. The astronaut Gagarin, the guest from the twentieth century, joins this intercontinental speed trial as the servant Passepartout. Detective Fix acts as a delaying element. He suspects Fogg of being a bank robber and tries by all possible means to delay him and arrest him. Briskly the world travelers' adventures flit across the stage: a widow in India is saved from suttee, obstacles such as typhoons, opium dens, Indian ambushes, and Mormon missionaries have to be overcome. It seems as though the handcuff-happy detective will cause Fogg to lose his bet, when the international dateline appears as a *deus ex machina* and makes an unexpected extra day available. Fogg is now sure of winning both his bet and a happy end with the agreeable widow.

An age to which a voyage round the earth in eighty minutes has become commonplace reenacts the daring of a feat of long ago—critical from its distance, sympathizing from its superior vantage point, a parody of itself, and yet with a tinge of nostalgia: "That was not mockery, that was the immortal smile of youth. And there will be others to smile about this youth, those that circle the earth in eighty seconds, and after those still others. And always it will be a compassionate smile, a smile of admiration."


TAKOVÁ LÁSKA *[Such Love]*. Play in two parts. Prose. First edition Prague 1957. First performance October 13, 1957, Prague, Realistic Theatre. Time: the present. Place: stylized variable settings.

A sensitive psychological study that crosses the bounds of reality into the law courts of the next world. The law student Lída Matys has committed suicide because of an unhappy love affair and now she has to face an imaginary trial. A "gentleman in a gown" shows the reasons for her suicide in an associative sequence of flashbacks. On the eve of her marriage with the designer Milan Stibor, Lída is gripped again by her passion for her girlhood's great love, the university lecturer Peter Petrus. Circumstances are against the lovers; Peter's wife fights for her marriage, the political boss demands the scientist's unreserved service for the state. Lída's girl friend insists that the lovers must separate for moral reasons. Lída realizes that Peter can never be pried loose from his past and his longed-for career, and jumps out of the train. The "gentleman in a gown" absolves her and imposes upon the others, who seemed to have nothing to do with her deed, the ineluctable awareness of their guilt.

## KOPIT, Arthur L.
(United States, born 1937)

CHAMBER MUSIC. One-act play. Prose. First edition New York 1965. Time: the present. Place: conference room.

The coexistence of two hostile power blocs juggling in mutual fear with aggressive wars and deterrent weapons is transposed into a lunatic asylum. The toolbox of politics has become a dangerous madness. Representatives of the women patients hold a grotesque summit meeting at the sixth annual assembly of the lawfully elected grievance (and tomorrow, perhaps, government) committee of Station 5, Women's Ward. Each of these women believes herself to be a historical personality. The company includes Gertrude Stein with her associative play on words; Joan of Arc, whose more-than-life-size crucifix becomes a sword of Damocles for all; Mozart's widow, feared by the whole circle because of her nerveracking, incessant record playing; a lady explorer on safari; a film star, and a pioneer aviatrix. A suffragette chairs the meeting. The women feel menaced by the other bloc, the men's ward. But they do not feel strong enough to wait for the men's attack, and decide they must forestall it. All the men are to be killed, that much is certain. But a moral alibi is wanted for the surprise attack. Since in such civilized times as today the only acceptable reason for murder is hunger, the ladies are prepared to start a new fashion of cannibalism and eat their victims. But this plan, too, has its drawbacks, since the ladies' appetite will no doubt not be sufficient to dispose of all of the victims, and the unconsumed dead might be held to have been killed for mere pleasure. The only help lies in an effective deterrent. The aviatrix is to be strangled and her corpse, decorated with the autographs of all the ladies, is to be sent to the men's ward as proof of the women's defensive power. Unlike Mrozek, who builds up his profound caricatures as closed worlds with their own immanent laws, Kopit does not forgo personal allusions and topical, polemic sniping.

OH DAD, POOR DAD, MAMMA'S HUNG YOU IN THE CLOSET AND I'M FEELING SO SAD. A pseudoclassical tragifarce in a bastard French tradition. Three scenes. Prose. First edition New York 1960. First performance January 7, 1960, Cambridge, Mass., Agassiz Theatre. Time: the present. Place: a lavish hotel room in Havana, Cuba.

An entertaining persiflage about the conventional portrayal of conventional perversions in conventional family life, such as dominated the stage some time ago when psychoanalysis was being exploited. Like the animalistic provocativeness of Jarry's *Ubu roi,* Kopit's play and its shock effects, too, have their origin in student theater. But the naive approach of the lively Punch-and-Judy show with its bloodcurdling deeds and impressive paunches has given way to a refined and voluptuous enjoyment of the manifestations of decadence.

Hounded by her passions, Madame Rosepettle travels aimlessly about the world. She has with her the stuffed corpse of her husband, a collection of growling carnivorous fish and plants, and her stuttering son Jonathan. Jonathan is seventeen, but dressed and treated like a boy of ten, who plays happily with his jingling coin collection and is guarded by the babysitter Rosalie. While Mama nearly causes her senile admirer Commodore Roseabove to suffer a heart attack thanks to her kittenish seductions, Rosalie purposefully tries to seduce her ward. Jonathan cannot measure out his passions and is so carried away that he smothers the girl to death, thereby displeasing his stuffed Papa so much that he pulls the misguided offspring by the legs. Madame Rosepettle disapproves of the confusion, and turns on her son: "This place is a madhouse. That's what it is. A madhouse . . . I ask you, Robinson. As a mother to a son I ask you. *'What is the meaning of this?'* "


THE DAY THE WHORES CAME OUT TO PLAY TENNIS. One act. Prose. First edition New York 1965. First performance March 15, 1965, New York, Players' Theatre. Time: the present, in May. Place: nursery of the Cherry Valley Country Club.

The collapse of the world order and the dissolution of social conventions under the pressure of an anonymous threat are satirized in a macabre farce: the world has become a nursery, mankind a fatuous and banal country club called Cherry Valley, where everyone every day indulges his complacency and malice. People spend their whole lives there, trying to acquire a little prestige from one golf hole to the next and to purchase with successive drinks an illusion of togetherness and sympathy. Suddenly an inconceivable occurrence upsets everything that has so painstakingly been built up for decades: eighteen women of doubtful calling step out of two Rolls Royces and, in a most embarrassing state of undress, proceed to play tennis on the courts reserved for club members. The Club committee convene in haste and crowd into the nursery, from where they suspiciously watch the doings of their unwelcome guests. Despite the early hour, they are all dressed in picturesque combinations of tuxedo and pajama. President Franklin Delano Kuvl unsuccessfully tries to summon the police. The wires have been cut by the "ladies," whose only response to all the remonstrances is of an evil-smelling fecal kind. Kuvl junior, twenty-five-year-old

Herbert Kuvl, blubbers on the rocking horse. Gayve, the aged secretary of the Club, seeks distraction from the tennis-playing disaster in trick objects like electric buzzers and exploding cigars. His son Rudolph, as chairman of the sports committee, ventures a last approach to the ladies and is beaten with tennis rackets. A bombardment of tennis balls causes the building to collapse, while the Club dignitaries helplessly sit in the nursery like children.

SING TO ME THROUGH THE OPEN WINDOWS. One-act play. Prose. First edition New York 1965. First performance March 15, 1965, New York, Players' Theatre. Time: not specified. Place: a room.

A play on the impossibility of clowning for one who is condemned in advance to be a clown and born into a "clownery." The jester seeks in vain by his grimaces to banish his own fear. The magician Ottoman lives in his dilapidated house furnished with a treasure chest, a throne, and a state bed; he is served by the butler, clown Loveless. They torment each other and are at each other's mercy in the imaginary circus game which they improvise. Every year Andrew, a little boy, turns up as a messenger of spring and life. He loves this dusty world and the two ridiculous old men with their circus tricks. Andrew returns to his own world where, though he may not act out his dreams, he does possess real existence. Ottoman dies alone and without anyone to see him, and with him dissolves his world, magic chest, fourposter and all. Only a little boy lost in daydreams wanders away —and it is left open whether the whole thing was not just a child's dream.

## KOPS, Bernard
(England, born 1926)

GOODBYE, WORLD. Play in three acts. Prose. First performance February 2, 1959, Guildford, Surrey, Guildford Theatre. Time: the present. Place: upper story in a block of flats in the London district of Paddington.

A sombre procession of down-and-outs in the cockney world. The juvenile delinquent John Martin escaped from prison when his mother committed suicide with gas. He now lives in a shabby boarding house run by the eccentric Miss Mead, and there gets caught between two women. He loves Susan and wants to free her from her lot as a prostitute, but in his turn he is pursued by the aging nymphomaniac Lola, who is eventually stabbed by her jealous husband Gaza, a blind clown. John gives himself up to the police. The only person who carries the torch of goodwill through this gloomy scene is the Irishman Paddy, a dissolute drunkard with the poetic soul of a child. Acute social criticism finds expression in dreamlike poetic language.

THE HAMLET OF STEPNEY GREEN. A sad comedy with some songs in three acts. Prose and verse. First published in *New English Dramatists,* 1, Harmondsworth, 1959. First performance May 19, 1958, Oxford, Playhouse. Time: the present. Place: the Levys' house and garden in Stepney Green, in London's East End.

A happy popular play, in which the most contrasting elements are molded together: social criticism of the Teddy Boys, petty bourgeois satire, Jewish folklore and religious customs, a parody of Hamlet and realistic descriptions of everyday life. Young David Levy, the son of a pickled-herring seller, dreams of being acclaimed some day by the masses as a popular crooner and in the meantime enjoys the melancholy of being misunderstood. When his father, Sam, feels that his end is coming, he spends his last hours in the garden, amid the noise of the children at play, surrounded by song and dance. His death raises David's delusions to fever pitch; he suspects the helpfulness shown to his mother Bessie by their neighbor Segal, and broods over the possibility of his father having been murdered by the couple. Sam has to take the trouble to come back from the other world as a ghost to disarm his vindictive offspring's Hamlet complex by recommending a harmless potion as reliable poison. David comes to his senses, gets engaged to his childhood playmate Hava and decides he can perfectly well sell herrings and croon at the same time. A loosely constructed, amiable pedagogic play about the transition from youth to adulthood.

## KORTNER, Fritz
(Germany, born 1892)

DIE ZWIESPRACHE *[The Dialogue].* Play in four acts. Prose. Written 1963. First edition Munich 1964. First performance April 11, 1964, Munich, Kammerspiele. Time: the present. Place: drawing room in Mehnert's villa.

This abundant drama takes up a bewildering profusion of problems, only to rest content in each case with making its polished point. The persecution of the Jews, atheism, Christianity, the conflict of the generations, the economic miracle, sophisticated stage refinements for the initiated, the pull of left- and right-wing extremism—such things are by no means all of the autobiographically conditioned ingredients which Kortner works in. He is frequently led to simplification and banality for the sake of his effective gags.

The lawyer Dr. Erich Mehnert and his wife Julia are celebrating their tenth wedding anniversary, when they get news that both their sons have been buried by an avalanche during a skiing holiday. During the anxious hours of uncertainty and fear, the couple settle their accounts with the whole of their life in a merciless and searching "dialogue." Mehnert is a free-thinker, a cool, calculating opportunist, who, behind the stiff façade of his money marriage, consoles himself with the chambermaid. Julia is a devout Catholic, whose first husband had been a leading SS murderer and who tried to appease her conscience by adultery with a Jewish professor. The two main characters are surrounded by lightly sketched secondary figures from the world of the economic miracle, including the Jewish Professor Ewald, the business tycoon Schostal and his adventurous wife, the song-hit composer Zietsch who is kept alive only by his alcoholic sarcasm, and the actor Leyrer who has long outlived the fiery stage hero of his youth. At the crossroads of all these destinies, the Mehnerts' marriage, for all the anniversary festivity, collapses in hatred and disillusionment. By the time the news comes that the boys are safe, the breach between the parents is irreparable.

Kortner's spiteful charm and penetratingly clever aggressiveness give the play some sort of stylistic unity—not the development of the action toward an end, but the multifarious playing with words of a passionate causeur and polemicist.


### KRASNA, Norman
(United States, born 1909)


SUNDAY IN NEW YORK. A new comedy in nine scenes. Prose. First edition New York 1962. First performance November 29, 1961, New York, Cort Theatre. Time: the present. Place: New York.

A humorous tale about the amorous troubles of a girl trying to rid herself decently of her decency. Young Eileen Taylor is a girl of good family, a hopelessly outmoded, inappropriate circumstance that she finds hard to cope with. Through her moral reserve she has lost her fiancé, Russell Wilson, to more accommodating women. Driven by tormenting complexes and desperate uncertainty, she takes refuge in the opposite extreme. She applies all the infallible means of the movies—a lesson well learned—in trying to seduce the newspaper reporter Mike Mitchell, a chance acquaintance; but it all ends in the same old failure. The reporter is put off by her innocence, whereas her ex-fiancé finally gives up every intention of marrying her in the face of her supposed guilt and the aura of her so painstakingly simulated disreputableness. However, in the meantime Mike has become so fascinated by Eileen's predilection for unnecessary complications, that nothing more stands in the way of a happy ending.

It is middle-class theater in the best Broadway tradition, where problems of living together are brought to their solution step by step in a psychological demonstration, without ever losing a sure sense of entertainment.


## KRISCHKE, Traugott
(Germany, born 1931)


KREUZE AM HORIZONT [Crosses on the Horizon]. Play in four acts. Prose. Acting edition Rowohlt, Hamburg 1960. First performance September 5, 1959, Hildesheim, Stadttheater. Time: "The war is not yet over." Place: "Somewhere in Europe."

The destiny of people born into a conflict of nations is shaped by the compulsion to hate and the courage to love. There is no specific time reference; the general moral predicament of this disruption is shown exclusively through the medium of the emotions of a young girl on the threshold of life. A village in the frontier area has been exterminated and its inhabitants shot as hostages. The sole survivors, in their hide-out, are seventeen-year-old Joana and her mute brother. Grimly the children now play at "putting to death," when suddenly Ivo appears, tattered and wounded. Joana hesitantly makes him welcome and experiences the miracle of first love. The young soldier has deserted from the enemy, because he could no longer bear the fratricidal war. And then Joana recognizes him: he was in charge of that fatal firing squad. She is expecting a child by Ivo, but nevertheless, after a violent inner struggle, shoots him and thus takes vengeance in obedience to her people's law. There is no issue and no answer to the dilemma of a world consisting merely of nameless recipients or orders: "You have the order. And because you've got the order, you'll do it. You're not responsible, for you have the order. And whoever gave the order, isn't responsible either, for he's got the law. And whoever made the law, isn't responsible either, for he's long dead. Murder is done—and no one is responsible for it."

## KRUCZKOWSKI, Leon
(Poland, 1900–1962)

PIERWSZY DZIEŃ WOLNOŚCI [The First Day of Freedom]. Play in three acts. Prose. Written 1958, new version 1961. First performance January 1960, Warsaw, Teatr Współczesny. Time: March 1945. Place: a small town in Germany.

Thanks to its power of expression in relation to contemporary problems, this became the play most often performed for several seasons running. Six Polish officers, prisoners of war, have spent years of their life behind barbed wire. Now, the murderous upheavals at the end of the war bring them their "first day of freedom." They see how the three teen-age daughters of a German doctor are assaulted by foreign laborers and take the girls into their brotherly protection. But the beautiful dream of humanity soon vanishes. Discord divides the Polish officers, wavering between vindictiveness and gallantry. Only Jan, who has fallen in love with bruised, abused Inge, and Michal let their better nature prevail: ". . . and we do, after all, need that hope, the hope that the world might change . . . and that it depends on us whether it does or not." A straggling German regiment renews the battle for the town, and at once people confront each other again as enemies with mutual suspicions. Inge flares out in wild defiance against Jan, whom she secretly loves: "I am sure you are a kind man. But it's the kind people, precisely, who make the world incomprehensible. Why do you prevent me hating people as they deserve?" To the general satisfaction, it is seen that the war has re-established national solidarity by a unifying hatred against the others. To defend her country Inge intervenes in the senseless battle with a stolen tommy gun, and, to save freedom, Jan shoots her.

## KUNDERA, Milan
(Czechoslovakia, born 1929)

MAJITELE KLÍČŮ [The Key Owners]. One-act play with four visions. Prose and verse. First edition Prague 1962. First performance April 17, 1962, Ostrava. Time: Second World War. Place: Kruta's apartment in Vsetin.

The destiny of a "supernumerary philosopher," who is forced to lose himself and his freedom. Instead of the customary glorification of the resistance, Kundera shows how in "dark times" the individual is condemned to the use of violence. Jirka, a student of architecture, has dissociated himself from the underground movement and has married the high-strung dancer Alena. At his in-laws, ex-major Kruta and his wife, he is forced into a stuffy lower middle-class life turning on the possession of the house key. The "key owner" is a symbol for all those who have complacently withdrawn into their private lives and come to terms with injustice in order to safeguard their own comfort. Věra, a girl comrade from Jirka's illegal days, turns up and needs shelter. To save her, he kills the caretaker Sedláček, a Gestapo snooper. Reluctantly Jirka leaves the family and goes underground. His wife and her parents have to pay for his "heroic deed" and are liquidated by the Germans. Jirka has no choice but to enter once more the rigid partisan movement, which, for the sake of general freedom, extinguishes him as an individual and forces him into violence. Memories of the past, Jirka's true kind of life, are blended in—his inner conflict, for instance, is made plain by a duel of words between the partisan leader and the Gestapo officer. Scenes of everyday family life are worked in, with the conversation polyphonically stylized.

## LAMPELL, Millard
(United States, born 1919)

THE WALL. Play in two acts. After the novel by John Hersey (1950). Prose. First edition New York 1960. First performance October 9, 1960, New York, Billy Rose Theatre. Time: 1939. Place: the ghetto in Warsaw.

The fatal story of the Warsaw ghetto told in contrasting types and a sensationally realistic description of the milieu. The author clearly wants to achieve his effects by transporting the audience into the actual environment and having them identify with the events, and thus to move and terrify them. The result is a naturalistic, emotional play.

The Jewish population of Poland has been abruptly torn from its habitual way of life and shut up in the Warsaw ghetto, under German guards as an "infested area." Conflicts break out among the people crowded into the far too narrow space—selfishness and panic, but also humanity and self-sacrifice. Pan Apt, the rich jeweller, spares neither obsequiousness nor money to purchase the good will of the rulers and with it the road to escape. His son Mordecai, a blasé amateur, is roused by the universal distress to face reality, hard work, and responsibility. The fanatic Katz and the Rabbi's daughter Rutka intend to preserve their human dignity in a futile, heroic revolt and to die fighting. Others counsel moderation and submission. Rutka's brother Stefan serves the Gestapo as a policeman. To buy his own life for a few more days, he brings about his father's deportation to the gas chambers. Dolek Berson, the complacent sensualist, succeeds in escaping, but later returns to the ghetto of his own free will and sacrifices himself for his neighbors. The uprooted aesthete finds himself and his vocation in death. The novel's abundance of action is transposed to the stage without any attempt at stylization.

## LAURENTS, Arthur
(United States, born 1920)

WEST SIDE STORY. Musical. Prose and songs. Music by Leonard Bernstein. First edition New York 1958. First performance September 26, 1957, New York, Winter Garden. Time: the present. Place: Manhattan.

The style of the musical gives way to a triumph of choreography as such, to sheer intoxication with movement. The "Romeo and Juliet" theme of the lovers condemned to enmity is transposed to the back streets of Manhattan, under the pressure of mass psychosis. Today's Romeo and Juliet cannot be expressions of their own most intimate sentiments, as they are in Shakespeare. They are predetermined parts of a community and their behavior is governed by social phenomena, in this case racial conflicts and street-gang fighting.

The racial conflict between the old-established slum dwellers and the Puerto Rican immigrants is taken into the streets by the violent feud between the teen-age gangs of the native Jets and the newcomer Sharks. Tony of the Jets and the Puerto Rican gang-leader's sister Maria fall in love. Their lyrical balcony scene takes place on a fire escape. Their wedding is an imaginary game set against the background of the bridal store where Maria works, which provides the props as well as window-display mannequins as silent witnesses. The lovers are repeatedly separated by the gang warfare and police raids. In full flight Tony stabs Maria's brother and himself falls victim to the vendetta of a Shark. Passions are translated into gesture and movement, into a collective frenzy of expression. The orgies of hatred, the brawls and knifings are stripped of their realism and concentrated in expressive dances. Dissonant jazz rhythms and languishing melodies help, by their contrast, to articulate the action.

## LAWLER, Ray
(Australia, born 1922)

SUMMER OF THE SEVENTEENTH DOLL. Three acts. Prose. First edition London 1957. First performance November 28, 1955, Melbourne, Union Theatre. Time: the present. Place: cottage in Carlton, a shabby suburb of Melbourne.

A social study of the life of the sugarcane plantations' laborers forms the background for a realistic psychological play about passion and illusion. For seven months of the year Roo and Barney do backbreaking work on the sun-scorched plantations, and during the layoff season join their girls Olive and Nancy in town. Every year they bring along a gorgeous doll as a present, which Olive proudly adds to her collection. What started as an adventure seventeen years ago has long become a profound human bond, without the persons concerned being quite aware of it. The "summer of the seventeenth doll" shatters the illusions of these primitive people, who, proud of their physical strength, cannot realize the fact that they are getting older. Foreman Roo had to give up his job to brawny young Dowd and shams an accident in order to conceal his failure. Barney is now a lady-killer only in boasts and overcompensates for his insecurity with aggressive behavior. Nancy has left him in order to get married. But he also disappoints Pearl, whom Olive has taken on for the lay-off season. Roo tries to face up to reality; he takes a job as an unskilled worker in town and wants to settle down and marry Olive. The girl hysterically defends her dream: she does not want a husband like any other, but the hero of the layoff season, the crew leader of the plantation, who no longer exists. Roo and Barney, both exhausted and disconsolate, team up and depart forever.

## LENZ, Siegfried
(Germany, born 1926)

ZEIT DER SCHULDLOSEN [Days of the Guiltless]. Play in two scenes. Prose. First published Cologne 1962. First broadcast as a radio play February 9, 1960, Norddeutscher Rundfunk, Hamburg. First stage performance September 19, 1961, Hamburg, Deutsches Schauspielhaus. Time: the present. Place: an imaginary country.

In "times of darkness" the world is divided between executioners and victims. To survive without guilt and to keep a clear conscience in so doing seems cheap self-deception: "We have no choice other than to accept existing guilt as our own; only then can it change us." The Governor wants to force the assassin Sason to betray his helpers and to this end causes nine arbitrarily chosen people to be locked up with Sason in his cell. They were picked up in the street and are to remain in jail until the "Sason case" is settled—by confession or death. The Governor "leaves it to the guiltless to do what he considers right! To kill." Egocentrically, these nine people look upon Sason as an enemy who robs them of their freedom. Hunger and thirst, business and family responsibilities beckon the prisoners back to life. No argument, no threat or mistreatment, not even the pressure of the majority induces Sason to speak. Only two of the nine, a young, idealistic student and the cynical and resigned consul, defend his convictions. They arrange that all should take turns at night in guarding him against being murdered. Nevertheless, under the cover of darkness and joint action, Sason is strangled in an unguarded moment. The Governor has made accomplices of the "guiltless" and readily gives back to them their freedom. Months later they are in prison once more. The rebels have overthrown the regime and demand Sason's murderer. In panic these ordinary people set on each other and try to fasten the murder on each other. Eventually the peasant, whose turn it had been at the time to guard Sason, takes the responsibility for the murder on himself. At this the consul shoots himself: "He died for his doubts. By his death he meant to prevent something he could not have borne." The student, today one of the new leading personalities of the government, sets the others free: "The deed is expiated, but the guilt will remain among us." This is a discussion piece, which simplifies ethical problems and projects them in a stage model.

## LEOKUM, Arkady
(Russia/United States, born 1915)

FRIENDS and ENEMIES. Two one-act plays. Prose. First performance September 16, 1965, New York, Theatre East. Time: the present. Place: apartment and restaurant.

When Strindberg involves his characters in an orgy of hatred, he always tries to give the motivation. Antecedents and psychopathological characteristics serve as a pretext for the *danse macabre* of the passions, psychology and probability as a peg on which to hang emotional eruptions and excitements striving for realization. Leokum merely sketches out the situation and the tensions between the characters, with the result that the psychological study turns into farce. Pleasure in tormenting and being tormented boils over into a psychological wrestling match, which Leokum formally divides into rounds. The theme is always the same: two people made inseparable by hate are at each other's mercy. The ambivalence of victim and executioner is made as plain as their mutual dependence. The individual as such is extinguished. He exists only in relation to another, who is both the condition and the aim of his own sadism.
*Friends* is about a lesson by a shabby tutor, who tries to teach reading to his only pupil, the overfed twelve-year-old son of a millionaire. The spoiled brat torments the old man in the most ingenious way. He delays and resists instruction in order to compromise the teacher in the eyes of his own parents at the examination and thus to deprive him of his living. He humiliates him with a banknote dropped as though unwittingly, causes delicacies to be delivered to the famished man and then to be taken back as a "regrettable error." He teases the teacher with a fictitious offer of a job as a private tutor and shatters the illusion of a happy marriage, the one dream that comforts the old man who has been crushed by life. This impertinent little mother's boy sets out to smother the old man's humanistic faith by means of a world of plastics, the indispensable, infinitely variable product of daddy's factories. The teacher in his turn lands an

occasional counterblow, when, for instance, he denounces the boy's dubious friendship with a sailor or leaves him prey to a sudden awareness of being forgotten by his indifferent, deadline-conscious parents. In the end the promising youngster mockingly pulls the rug from under the teacher's feet—he reads the lesson without a mistake and thus proves all the old man's efforts to have been useless.

*Enemies* is set in a small restaurant where Miller, retired before his time, is a daily customer. He enjoys the privilege of being served alone, an hour before opening time, which gives him an opportunity to make the waiter Gittelman the victim of all the malice and sense of power that he needs to console himself for his wasted life. He complains about the food, harasses the waiter, thinks up endless new ways of humiliating him, boasts about his own carefree and luxurious life. Then Miller learns that the patient, insignificant waiter, whom he so despises, has managed by skilful speculation to buy a house and become a partner in the restaurant. Miller's sadistic pleasures are over. He is, in reality, a poor invalid, dependent on his son's charity and always afraid of losing his precarious living. He begins to fawn upon the waiter in the hope of finding his way into big business with his help. Politely and aloofly, always the perfect waiter, Gittelman takes back everything he has said. Has it all been boasting? Is the practiced obsequiousness with which he reverts to the part of a downtrodden little employee his secret revenge? Neither Miller nor the audience knows. Henceforth Miller can no longer play his habitual dominating part, for he has lost the willing stooge he needs.

Leokum always gives us studies of everyday life in an alarmingly grotesque caricature, which sparks off emotional explosions.


## LEONOV, Leonid Maximovich
(U.S.S.R., born 1899)


ZOLOTAYA KARETA [The Golden Carriage]. Play in four acts. Prose. First published in *Oktyabr* No. 4, 1955. First edition Moscow 1957. First performance December 1955, Karaganda, Russian Dramatic Theatre. Time: immediately after the end of the Second World War. Place: a small Russian town in the former front area.

A textbook example of the aims of social realism: the "positive heroes" Marya and Timosha, a tractor driver, selflessly do their duty wherever the party has placed them. The intellectuals are, in the sense of the "personality cult," overbearing, decadent, selfish and estranged from the people.

The worst negative character is a manufacturer, who represents private capital, a deserter and enemy of the people. A family quarrel serves the author to develop a model of social pedagogics.

Twenty-six years ago the young teacher Kareyev had aspired to the hand of Marya, whose father, a high official, had contemptuously rejected him. Defiance and injured pride had driven the teacher out into the world, and he became a geologist. Now a famous professor and member of the academy, he returns with his son Juliy to the scene of his former humiliation. He now, in his turn, wants to humiliate the people of this small town. He wants to settle his accounts with the "golden carriage," the symbol of the outdated bourgeoisie, the vehicle of class consciousness, the power of money and social climbing. But his own middle-class ostentation shows him up only too clearly as a passenger of precisely such a vehicle. Marya is not happy in her marriage with a match manufacturer, but as chairman of the municipal soviet she enthusiastically and selflessly directs the reconstruction of the bombed town. She finds her life's happiness in love of her country and fulfilment of her duty. Her daughter Marka is courted by Juliy. Fate seems about to make up to the young generation for its former cruelty, and the golden carriage stands invitingly ready for the journey into a radiant, carefree future. But Marka chooses to remain faithful to her fiancé Timosha, who has come back blind from the war, and to live at his side as a loyal companion in his hard lot.

## LERNER, Alan Jay
(United States, born 1918)

MY FAIR LADY. Musical comedy in two acts. Prose and lyrics. Music by Frederick Loewe. First edition New York 1956. First performance March 15, 1956, New York, Mark Hellinger Theatre. Time: 1912. Place: London.

The theme of Cinderella suddenly rising into glittering society and finding her great good luck at the street corner has its place not only in the land of unlimited possibilities, but all over the world in the daydreams of millions of less than fully contented people. Shaw's mordant satire on the complacency of high society and the arrogance of science experimenting with human beings has here turned into a romantic and nostalgic elegy on good old England, where such sentimentality meets with irony but is also relished. To win his bet with Colonel Pickering, Professor Higgins, the phonetician, puts the flower girl Eliza with her outrageous cockney accent through a drill from which she emerges with the conversational tone and the graces of a duchess. At Ascot the girl successfully holds her own in society. At a ball she enchants all the guests and is taken indeed for an aristocrat. The professor has won his bet, but also Eliza's heart—an altogether unexpected circumstance which disturbs his studies a great deal. Stung by his lack of consideration and indifference, the girl resolutely prepares to put Professor Higgins through her own psychological treatment.

## LESSING, Doris
(England, born 1921)

EACH HIS OWN WILDERNESS. Play in two acts. Prose. Written 1956. First published in *New English Dramatists,* 1, Harmondsworth 1959. First performance March 23, 1958, London, Royal Court Theatre. Time: the present. Place: the hall of Myra Bolton's house in London.

Twenty-two-year-old Tony Bolton has completed his military service and returns to his mother Myra, who divides her life between socialist agitation against nuclear tests and a motley throng of changing lovers. At the moment it happens to be the turn of Sandy Boles, who is exactly the same age as Tony. Tony conceals his disappointed love for his mother, his sense of being unnecessary and misunderstood, behind a frenzy of aggressiveness. He would like to be off into the world, but is too attached to his familiar surroundings. Philip Durrant, one of Myra's past lovers, turns up with his fiancée Rosemary. The girl is another source of disappointment for Tony. In despair he takes refuge with Sandy's mother Milly, and here has his first encounter with love—which makes him still more disconsolate. His hysterical fits of hatred eventually drive away his mother, who is somewhat amused that she, of all people, should have given birth to this rebellious philistine. Like two frightened children Tony and Rosemary fall into each other's arms: "Leave us alone. . . . Leave us alone to live. Just leave us alone. . . ."
This flight into "inner emigration" is the doubtful solution of a misunderstood young generation, which revels in self-surrender and self-pity. This play, modeled closely after Osborne, is one great outcry of disgust with life.

PLAY WITH A TIGER. Play in three acts. Prose. First edition London 1962. First performance March 22, 1962, London, Comedy Theatre. Time: the present. Place: Anna Freeman's room.

Devotion to duty and public spirit are equated with inner self-destruction. Rootless intellectuals put so much effort into their emancipation, into standing apart as outsiders and self-styled "individuals," that they once more become typical and hence traditionally average. There are signs of a start at surmounting the purposeless anarchism of the "angry" generation by means of psychological differentiation that transcends ideological programs, and of healthy irony.

Anna Freeman, a widow and mother of a teen-ager, breaks off her engagement to Tom Lattimer, who is on the point of taking a job as business manager of a women's magazine and can offer her a secure future. She prefers to earn a bare living by occasional literary work and to retain her independence as a social outsider. Anna loves the American Dave Miller, a man "who is rootless on principle" and keeps running away from himself in a ceaseless round of changing jobs and love affairs. At present Janet Stevens is expecting his baby, but he feels bound to Anna and her freedom. They continuously abuse and deceive each other, yet are indissolubly at one in the intoxication of their self-deception, in the hot-headed rebellion against life's sheltered and successful favorites and in the lethargy of inner emptiness. Strictly according to the methods of Freud's analysis of dreams, they take turns in revealing their spiritual development, their disappointments and complexes. Anna has, ever since she was a child, suffered from her parents' ostensibly happy marriage, while Dave has a background of radical trade unionists and from an early age has rebelled against the smug upper middle-classes. Anna is fascinated by her "play with the tiger," the intractable wild animal that is Dave. But when she realizes that his loose bond with her is merely a pretext to relieve him of any responsibility, she is disillusioned and sends him packing. Dave takes the easy way out and marries Janet: the tiger is at last locked in the cage of convention.

Each of the two main characters is flanked, as though in a distorting mirror, by a corresponding figure which, as it were, anticipates the end of the road. In Anna's case it is her friend Mary Jackson, a nymphomaniac widow for whom sex has become the means of self-delusion, and in Dave's case it is his colleague Harry Payne, an aging journalist, a drunkard and hypocritical family man.

# LEVI, Paolo
(Italy, born 1919)

IL CASO PINEDUS *[The Pinedus Case]*. Play in two parts. Prose. First published in *Teatro-Scenario*, XIX, No. 2, February 1955. First performance November 20, 1954, Turin, Teatro Goletti. Time: the present. Place: an imaginary monarchy.

Kafka's hopeless entanglement in the machinery of judicial trial is transposed to a realistic description of an individual case.
The music critic Giovanni Pinedus refuses to pay a parking fee for his car in a controversial case. He has words with a policeman and is taken to the police station, where gradually the circumstantial evidence regarding an unsolved murder of a woman closes in on him more and more menacingly. An arrogant, complacently destructive review of his once drove the commissioner's niece, a moderately gifted singer, to suicide. He is haunted by this memory and his protestations of innocence become more and more hesitating. His fiancée leaves him, his paper exploits his case for a welcome polemic and election weapon against the government party. The judiciary need a culprit to cover up their failure. Worn down by interrogations, Pinedus signs the prepared confession and is condemned to death. His petition for pardon is rejected by the king for political reasons similar to those for which the opposition demands his acquittal. The Pinedus case has come to its fatal conclusion: "What one has done is of no consequence. . . . The only thing that matters is getting involved, having set in motion a mechanism that no one can stop. . . ."

INDIRIZZO SCONOSCIUTO *[Address Unknown]*. Play in two parts. Prose. First performance January 26, 1965, Neustrelitz, Germany, Friedrich-Wolf-Theater. Time: the present. Place: Rome.

A fanatic of justice who refuses to compromise is thereby driven to run amok. In his time, Michael Kohlhaas foundered on the feudal system; today, the individual is under pressure from anonymous influences, from the invisible hierarchy of "intervening authorities."
Police sergeant Aldo Bergami has arrested a couple of lovers in an unlit, parked car, for "offending against public decency." The man is Dr. Marti, director of a bank and brother of the Undersecretary of State, and most embarrassingly a married man. Police lieutenant Giacomo Sertorio is firmly warned from above that there must be no scandal. Bergami insists on his report. The lieutenant tries to intimidate his subordinate, to

threaten and persuade him, but Bergami will not comply. He doggedly persists in proclaiming everyone's equality before the law and takes the matter as far as the police chief General Briatico, who retires behind smiling incomprehension. In desperation Bergami, seeing himself disavowed by everybody, shoots the general. This scene, which introduces the play, is witnessed by a reporter, who subsequently presents the case in flashbacks with comments on it.

LEGITTIMA DIFESA [Self Defense]. Play in two parts. Prose. First published in Teatro-Scenario, XVI, No. 3, February 1952. First performance January 16, 1952, Rome, Teatro Eliseo. Time: the present. Place: Italy.

An extreme situation is analytically set out and generalized into a model case of freedom of will: every action, by deciding for one possible course, thereby negates all other aspects of any given situation. Spontaneous action in response to illusions, which is always self-consistent, and the reflecting mind which takes all possibilities into account, but must pay for its awareness with doubts and resignation, are irreconcilable existential manifestations.

The engineer Matteo, with his whole fortune in his pocket, is on the way to a nocturnal appointment with his mistress Grazia, with whom he plans to elope. She seems determined to leave her husband, the gangster Rocco. An unknown young man—Pietro, an accomplice of Rocco's—warns Matteo that Grazia has prepared a trap for him. Rocco is going to shoot him from an ambush and take his money. Matteo faces a desperate decision: if he heeds the warning and goes home, Rocco is bound to fall victim to his own machinations and after his death Matteo can win back Grazia. But his tranquil happiness will be clouded by the doubt of whether the loved woman would not have betrayed him today. Matteo chooses certainty and continues on his road to the guileless, loving Grazia of his illusion. Soon a shot is heard in the dark.

What actually happens is merely a point of reference for the multiple play of visions and makes visible the consequences that explain human destiny in terms of the polarity of spontaneous freedom and causal necessity.

# LEVITT, Saul
(United States, born 1911)

THE ANDERSONVILLE TRIAL. Play in two acts. Prose. First performance December 29, 1959, New York, Henry Miller Theatre. Time: August 1865. Place: the United States Court of Claims, Washington, D. C.

Levitt uses a historical court martial as an illustration of the conflict between moral responsibility and military obedience. The full significance of this question, by the author's own account, while latent at the time of the Andersonville trial, became clear to the world, and himself, only when the case was no longer one of a mere 14,000 dead in the remote American Civil War, but of six million victims of National Socialist concentration camps. In writing this play, he says, he felt himself to be part of the contemporary world's collective conscience.

After the end of the War of Secession Henry Wirz, the governor of Andersonville prison, has to face a court martial in the victorious United States. At Andersonville, 14,000 Union troops perished in inhuman conditions— of epidemics, hunger, shootings by sentries at the "deadline" and hunts with bloodhounds when trying to escape. The death sentence is a foregone conclusion before the trial ever starts, for political reasons and for the sake of the victors' moral prestige. Half paralyzed and apathetically the accused listens to the witnesses' testimony, which the Judge Advocate Chipman in his fanatic idealism wants to magnify into an indictment. But all the evidence shows is the compelling nature of the situation and the human weakness of Wirz, who was bound by his instructions. Against the advice of his defending counsel, a clever tactician who is in a position to invalidate a fictitious charge of murder fabricated by the chief witness for the prosecution, Wirz agrees to being cross-examined by the prosecutor. Chipman raises the problem of binding orders despite the warning of the presiding judge, General Lew Wallace: "If at the outbreak of war the government of the so-called Confederacy had stood on the moral principle of freedom for the black man and the government of the United States had stood for slavery, would a man have been bound on moral grounds to follow the dictates of conscience—even if it led him to the point of taking up arms against the government of the United States?" Chipman maintains that the dictates of conscience should have been overriding even to that point. The court, which consists of staff officers, is obliged to ignore the possibility of an officer refusing to obey orders for reasons of conscience; nor can it convict Wirz for having obeyed orders. His is sentenced to death for "conspiracy."

## LIBERÁKI, Margarita
(Born in Greece)

L'AUTRE ALEXANDRE *[The Other Alexander]*. Play in three acts. Prose. First edition Paris 1953 (in French translation). First performance October 12, 1957, Paris, Alliance Française. Time: a winter's night after the Second World War. Place: the surroundings of Athens.

Ever new aspects of the disintegration of society, the family and eventually the self are shown on simultaneous levels of action. Men are nothing real for each other any more, but merely an expression of longing or fear, hope or menace.

A mine owner has four legitimate children, Alexander, Aglaia, Grigori and Phokion, and also four illegitimate ones with the same names. This family dualism set off identity doubts in the individuals, a feeling of being lost. The dreamer Alexander has a vague longing for complementarity, for that "other Alexander" who alone could confer meaning on his own confusion but who cannot be found even with incessant search. The cold place-hunter Phokion is filled with hatred for his stepbrother Phokion, the pit foreman; he feels cheated of his uniqueness and is killed by his double. Grigori has been turned into a killer by the war, and can find rest only in an endless chain of real or imagined murders; he lets his stepbrother Grigori, an innkeeper, die in the flames.

The environment, too, is full of guilt and violence. Adultery disrupts the family, the children revolt against the domineering father and the miners against the boss; the existing order is undermined: "Everything slips every day, everything slips imperceptibily. . . . The loneliness is immeasurable, and the discord grows from day to day. . . . Flashbacks and dream scenes use stylized means, making reality seem unreal: "The style of the performance should be abrupt and impetuous—change of lighting, of setting, interpersonal relations, gestures, looks, screams. Fast pace. The play should exercise an almost physical effect on the audience. . . . Every person is a stranger to every other. For this reason dialogue sometimes turns into monologue. . . . Finale as in the circus. Each shows his number, lost in his own gestures and screams, and is deaf to those of the others."

## LIVINGS, Henry
(England, born 1930)

KELLY'S EYE. Play in two acts. Prose. First edition London 1964. First performance June 12, 1963, London, Royal Court Theatre. Time: August 1939. Place: beach and lodgings on the coast of Lancashire, England.

A man trained only for war and as an instrument of murder, takes his revenge for his degraded, defiled self by opting for evil in peacetime. Why should murder, only a few years ago a matter of praise and medals, now be prosecuted as a crime? Just as senselessly as Kelly killed the enemy in battle, he now murders his best friend and goes underground. The dead man accompanies the action and comments on it as an external observer. Kelly becomes a restless tramp forever in flight from himself. He meets Anna, a girl breaking out of her deadening, sheltered middle-class life, who sees in Kelly, for the first time in her life, the merciless compulsion for suffering. Sickened with life as he is, he opens for her the way to a daring decision and happiness. The two unequal individuals, both imprisoned in their own hopelessness, gradually begin to feel responsible for each other. For the sake of the other, each begins to fight for the meaning of life. The caricatures of bourgeois self-righteousness, Anna's father and a sensation-hunting reporter, destroy this precarious companionship. Kelly is driven to suicide, but his death now has a meaning, for it finally sets Anna free from convention and cheap conformity. The dead commentator concludes with a gentle reproach: "For Anna it has taken all this time to get to the beginning. And for these others, these proper men, what are we to make of their part in this story? Are these the only men we can set up against violence and cruelty? . . . Kelly was not the only one needed to learn to love his own, and therefore others', humanity."

## LOGAN, Joshua
See HAMMERSTEIN II, Oscar, and LOGAN, Joshua.

## LORD, James
See DURAS, Marguerite, and LORD, James.

## LUCKE, Hans
(Germany, born 1927)

KAUTION [The Surety]. Crime play in three acts. Acting edition Berlin, Henschel, 1955. First performance February 6, 1955, Dresden, Staatstheater. Time: 1953. Place: entrance hall of a country house on the west coast of the United States.

Even the standard crime play has been given a propaganda slant. The quest for the perpetrator of the crime is made the pretext for casting a light into the asphalt jungle of capitalism. The question of legality gets the laconic answer: "What for? We live in a free country!" Big business is shown up as the origin of the crime. "Everything turns on the law of the wolves. Devour, devour everything!" Its posterlike simplification made the play the hit of the East German theatre.

Vivian Deshields is found shot. Suspicion falls on her husband Steve, who has been seeking a divorce after her blatant adultery with Jeffry O'Brien. Vivian had asked for the return of her dowry, which had been deposited with the shipper Adamo as surety for Steve's job. Thus a social question is unobtrusively broached, namely, the suggestion that in the United States Steve's captain's certificate and his ability do not suffice for him to exercise his profession unless he can provide hard cash as surety. Hard pressed, Steve breaks out into threats against his wife who wants to get the money for him, and against the shipowner who refuses to let him have it. Finally the wicked capitalist Adamo is unmasked as the murderer who shot Vivian in order to keep the money in his firm. Subinspector McDowell wants to keep the innocent captain in custody in order to prevent a strike of the dockers and serve the "national interest." The story is developed by means of interrogation scenes and flashbacks.

## MAASS, Joachim
(Germany, born 1901)


DER ZWILLINGSBRUDER *[The Twin Brother]*. (also: *Das Leben nach dem Tode [Life after Death]*). Comedy in four acts. Prose. Acting edition Munich, Desch, 1958. First performance September 11, 1960, Vienna, Volkstheater. Time: the present. Place: living room at Schütte's, in a North German port.

A popular play with effectively typed characters, robust morals, humor, and just the right amount of sentimentality. Heinrich Schütte is a member of the lower middle class. His wife Lina persuades him to take advantage of an oversight in his deceased twin brother's death certificate and to take over, as it were, his twin's life. With his brother's name goes a customs official's pension and thus the prospect of a comfortable old age; but with it also goes his shady past, which now brutally invades Heinrich's parlor in the person of the smuggler Atje Peters. Heinrich is blackmailed into covering up for clandestine overseas deals in dynamite, until eventually dear uncle, a detective superintendent, sets everything right again with a great show of joviality and reproachful finger wagging.


## McCLELLAND, Allan
(England, born 1917)


BLOOMSDAY. Play in three acts. After the novel *Ulysses* by James Joyce. First performance January 28, 1958, Oxford, Playhouse. Time: Thursday, June 16, 1904. Place: Dublin.

The instructive thing with all dramatizations of Joyce is not so much the result, as the reason for failure. Here the entire novel is compressed into three acts, which give a sort of shorthand outline of the externals of the action. In thus putting the bare facts on the stage, the book's techniques of association, its language, and its depth are necessarily lost. One day, the 16th of June 1904, is lifted out of Dublin life. The poet Stephen Dedalus, the cynical medical student Buck Mulligan, and the insolent Oxford scholar Haines live in a martello tower. Stephen's conscience nags him because he refused a prayer to his dying mother, and he tries to quell it in drink and brothels. His friend Leopold Bloom, an advertising canvasser and resigned cuckold, vainly tries to rescue him for a life of cosy respectability. Bloom's wife Molly, a soprano with voluptuous physical charms, has the customary affair with her manager Boylan. Bloom takes refuge in inane philosophizing from his private indignity, the lack of understanding he meets, and humiliations he suffers because of being a Jew. This one day out of the life of Stephen Dedalus, personifying Joyce, has here become a "Bloomsday." The events are presented by a narrator and given concrete shape in Bloom, the main character, but come across somewhat coarsened in tone.


## McCULLERS, Carson (Smith)
(United States, 1917–1967)


THE MEMBER OF THE WEDDING. Play in three acts. Prose. Adapted 1950 from the author's novel (1946). First edition New York 1951. First performance January 5, 1950, New York, Empire Theatre. Time: August 1945. Place: back yard and kitchen of the Adams family in a small Southern town in the United States.

A landscape of pure innocence surrounds the psyche of an adolescent girl with her predicaments and troubles. Twelve-year-old Frankie has left the security of childhood, the untroubled fairy-tale world of toys, without as yet having found her entry into the world of the grown-ups. Reality is merely the raw material that the precocious girl constantly reshapes in wishes and fears, gushing exaggeration and contrariness. Her big brother's wedding, the club of the older teen-agers, and her own jealously guarded childhood friendships push Frankie into compulsive daydreams, which again and again come up against reality. True tragedy, like the death of her little playmate John Henry or the fate of the Negro Honey Camden Brown, whom the race hatred of the South drives to murder and suicide, fail to touch Frankie's egocentric puberty. Every day she improvises new roles for herself and acts them out until she loses her breath from sheer exhaustion. The highly differentiated language and a loving application of the art of understatement and suggestion turn this psychological study into poetry.


THE SQUARE ROOT OF WONDERFUL. Play in three acts. Prose. Written 1957. First edition Boston 1958. First performance October 30, 1957, New York, National Theatre. Time: the present, spring. Place: an apple farm near New York City.

Conflicts belonging to the well-known psychorealism of American litera-ture melt into soft melody. Human encounters, people's timid attempts to find a way to each other, and human yearnings and unfulfillments are pastel tones in a vast landscape of the soul.

Mollie Lovejoy finds in the architect John Tucker genuine affection, security and a limpid, firmly established happiness. But her troubled past keeps catching up with her. She is tied to the dissolute writer Phillip Lovejoy, whom she has already divorced twice; each time she was defeated by his demanding carnality and returned to him. Now her husband has been discharged from a sanatorium where his alcoholism had put him; he obstructs Mollie's timid attempt to build a new life: "I feel surrounded by a zone of loneliness. I try to reach out and touch, but I can only grab." Phillip is unable to face the challenge which his first literary success implies for his whole future, and his fears, self-hatred and weakness drive him ever more deeply into his dream life. Mollie perceives a duty precisely in the futility of such a common life: "Genius is, I suppose, something light and dark and lovable and failing, all at the same time." Phillip's complacent mother adds fuel to the frustrated writer's megalomania. His sister Loreena is a fading girl who mocks herself with biting sarcasm. None of these people are really evil, yet they keep driving each other more and more deeply into the "square root" of their failure: "The sin of hurting people's feelings. Of humiliating a person. That is the square root of sin. It's the same as murder. . . . The square root is there. You just have to figure it to be a higher power. War is the square root of humiliation raised to the millionth power. . . ." Mollie realizes that her bond with Phillip was self-deception and definitely chooses John, who will also be a loyal friend to her son Paris. Her entanglement has ultimately resolved itself into the "square root of wonderful," into a peaceful, unproblematic happiness. Phillip has a fatal accident, and his mother retires to the farm with the air of an eternal guardian of the Holy Grail.

## MacLEISH, Archibald
(United States, born 1892)

J.B. *A play in verse*. Eleven scenes and prologue. Verse. First edition Boston 1958. First performance April 22, 1958, New Haven, Conn., Yale University Theatre. Time: the present. Place: a circus tent.

Again and again men have tried to act out the roles of God and Satan and to deduce a theodicy. The meaning of suffering in this world is ultimately as much beyond comprehension as is Job's endurance by the strength of his faith. MacLeish relates his Job interpretation to the contemporary scene and makes the spontaneous facets of life emerge triumphant over everything. Initially he approaches the theme in a dialectical construction.

Zuss and Nickles, two unemployed actors who make a living by selling
balloons and popcorn, improvise the play *J.B.* in the empty circus tent.
Job is shown as the timeless victim, as degraded, stricken man himself. In
their struggle for interpretation, the two comedians hide their faces behind
masks. God's mask is blank and blind-eyed, Satan's a grin of anguish. The
actors tempt Job with misfortunes, illness, loneliness. Soon a "distant
voice" begins to take part in the play, and the masks realize with a shock
that they, too, are only pawns: Job "isn't in the play at all. He's where we
all are—in our suffering." Contentedly Job enjoys his prosperity in the
midst of his large family: God will "never change. A man can count on
Him." And then his children are taken from him by war, a car crash, a
sexual murder. Bombs destroy all his wealth. Illness and malice exile Job
from the world. Even his wife Sarah leaves him, disgusted with his humility
and meekness. Vainly Job broods over his guilt, the cause of his ruin. An
atheist, a psychoanalyst, and a priest offer slogans in place of comfort.
Only the certainty of a ceaseless new beginning leads him to himself. Bearing a branch of blossom, the symbol of new hope, Sarah returns: "You
wanted justice, didn't you? There isn't any. There's the world. . . ." The
spiritual heritage of Christianity and antiquity merge in a vague humanism. God becomes detached fate: "He does not love. He is." The rational
play within the play dissolves into an illusionist apotheosis, as the metaphysical model does in vitalist exuberance.


## MAGNIER, Claude
(France, born 1920)


BLAISE [*Blaise*]. Comedy in three acts. Prose. Written 1959. First published in *L'Avant-Scène* No. 219, 1960. First performance November 20,
1959, Paris, Théâtre des Nouveautés. Time: April 8 to 11. Place: apartment in Paris.

This is a riotous piece of vaudeville theatre, whose wealth of vulgar and
piquant language perhaps makes it stronger on the side of stage effect
than of good taste.
The fashion model Geneviève has two lovers, one young and penniless, the
painter Blaise d'Ambrieux, for whom she cares a great deal, and one elderly
and well-heeled, the business man Carlier, for whom she cares rather less.
She is trying to introduce the young lover into the older lover's house, to
the former's financial benefit. But Blaise's social climb into accomplished
immorality is thwarted by Marie, the picture of rustic innocence complete
with pigtails and saucer eyes, whose inept remarks make for much hilarity.

Through a maze of disguises, disrobings, mistaken identities, and ruses Marie eventually takes her Blaise away into less complicated conditions.

IT'S IN THE BAG *(Oscar)*. Play in three acts. Prose. First published in *L'Avant-Scène* No. 173, 1958. First performance March 20, 1958, Paris, Théâtre de l'Athénée. Adapted by Robin Maugham for production in London, May 25, 1960, Duke of York's Theatre. Time: the present. Place: drawing room in the Barniers' apartment in Paris.

Girls get mistaken one for another, luggage gets mixed up, people get madly drunk, and everybody gets into the most comic situations that all add up to a farce that is never at a loss for a striking effect.

The junior clerk Christian Martin is in love with a young lady who has given herself out as the daughter of his general manager Barnier. Having enriched himself by successful embezzlement and thus turned himself into an acceptable suitor, he requests and obtains the hand of Barnier's daughter—only to discover to his horror that the young lady is not only totally unknown to him, but stupid to boot and richer in inner than in outer charms.

The chauffeur Oscar not only obligingly lends his name to the title of the play, but acts as a catalyst in the confusing web of schemes and counter-schemes, which the author, with the experienced touch of an old hand in stage routine, finally disentangles and brings to a happy end.

## MALRAUX, André, and MAULNIER, Thierry
(both France; Malraux, born 1901; Maulnier, born 1909)

LA CONDITION HUMAINE *[Man's Fate]*. Play in twenty-five scenes. Adapted by Thierry Maulnier from Malraux's novel (1933). First published in *L'Avant-Scène* No. 107, Paris 1955. First performance December 6, 1954, Paris, Théâtre Hébertot. Time: the spring of 1927. Place: Shanghai.

Malraux's novel, which dates from the period when he still believed in communism, is based on his own experiences in China. He sees world revolution as the aim of humanitarian world salvation, and, painting on a broad canvas, makes his characters the active missionaries of his philosophy. Communist rebels fight side by side with the "Blues," Chiang Kai-shek's nationalists, in the civil war against the government dominated by France. The rebels are victorious. Chiang Kai-shek allows himself to be corrupted by foreign capitalism and rises to sole power by treacherously ordering the massacre of the "Reds." The torchbearers in this hate-clouded world are young Communists glowing with self-sacrifice and fraternity: the Chinese Tchen, who has to pay with his life for an assassination, the half-caste Kyo and the Russian Katow, both of whom die for their convictions. On the other side we are shown, as it were, psychological engravings of the rootless inhabitants of this decaying world: Baron de Clappique running away from reality into an unworldly aestheticism and Professor Gisors who tries to forget Europe in opium. In his heart, he never can break loose from his home country, yet he despises it because it keeps betraying its culture by an unscrupulous struggle for power.

Beyond the dated and, for Malraux, now long outdated revolutionary fire, and behind the nostalgic tribute to the contemplative East paid by a European trapped in his own restlessness, the work is a testimony to free humanity that can indeed be destroyed but never defeated.

## MANSFELD, Michael
(Germany, born 1922)

EINER VON UNS [One of Us]. Play in three acts. Prose. Written 1960. First performance September 23, 1960, Stuttgart, Staatstheater. Time: the present. Place: waiting room at a railroad station.

The problem of multiple identity, which Pirandello's virtuosity presented as an interplay of being and appearance, in this play is explored in depth and used to make plain an insoluble conflict of conscience. A shivering group of people are waiting at the station for a late homecomer from the war. To their consternation all these people realize that theirs is not a chance meeting, but that they have all come because of prisoner of war No. 6,426,410. The parents expect their son, the wife the father of her child, the foreigner the soldier whom she has loved, and the public prosecutor is waiting for the war criminal who was responsible for the execution of a deserter. The different points of view convey an altogether contradictory picture, which is now corrected by reference to the true picture shown in scenic flashbacks. All these people have wronged the man they are waiting for, and now try, through him, to come to terms with their own past. The mother, with her enthusiasm for war, brought up her son to be a hero; the girl seduced him and forced him to marry her; the foreigner misused his guileless love for her espionage activities; and the public prosecutor himself used the man to obey the inhuman orders for the execution of which he now wants to hold the homeowner responsible.

The loudspeaker announces that the prisoner of war has died during the journey.


## MANZARI, Nicola
(Italy, born 1909)

DIO SALVI LA SCOZIA [God Save Scotland]. Comedy in three acts. Prose. First published in Il Dramma, No. 270, March 1959. First performance January 16, 1959, Turin, Teatro Carignano. Time: the present. Place: sacristy in a small town in Scotland.

A popular play with a lot of humour and robust morals. The Reverend Mr. Cunningham, the new vicar, creates some salutary confusion among the upright members of his flock, and a lot of good among its black sheep. Instead of consorting with respectable spinsters and self-righteous colleagues of the cloth, he surrounds himself with flighty ladies of easy morals and with rough dock laborers, takes a hand himself on the loading ramp of the port and breaks the monopoly of the exploiting shipping companies. This forcible demonstration of active Christianity liberates people so far locked in indifference and prejudice. Cunningham happily goes off as a missionary to Africa. The familiar farcical situations of clerical comedy are here buttressed by well-aimed social criticism.


## MARCEAU, Félicien (Louis Carette)
(Belgium, born 1913)

THE EGG (L'OEuf). Play in two acts. Prose. Written 1956. First edition Paris 1957. First performance October 13, 1956, Paris, Théâtre de l'Atelier. Translated by Charles Frank, London, Faber, 1958; adapted by Robert Schlitt for New York production, January 8, 1962, Cort Theatre. Time: the present. Place: Paris.

Emile Magis, an employee in the lower ranks of the Civil Service, treats the public to a confession of his life. He has always been looking for the "system," the ultimate rules governing people's living together and getting along with each other. But he feels forever excluded from an incomprehensible environment, which seems self-contained like a round, smooth, impenetrable egg. The conventions of the others, the prearranged meaning of the whole thing elude Emile, confused by chance and startled by surprise as he is. The flashbacks of his life's changing situations never reveal the principles of the fool-proof "system." By means of a trick, Emile drives Gustave, who is in love with Georgette, into the arms of his own sister; the result is a perfectly ordinary marriage. He himself marries the daughter of his chief, keeps a mistress and enjoys a game of cards; but he is disgruntled and feels he is victimized by small fortuities, for life still owes him the discovery of the great, decisive rules of the game. Now the petty bourgeois takes a hand at playing fate: in self-tormenting triumph he facilitates his wife's adultery with Dugommier, and eventually shoots his wife and manages to "frame" Dugommier by means of a calculated chain of circumstantial evidence. Now at last Emile is satisfied, for he has learned how to handle life's system whereby one can "get away with murder." Social criticism is expressed with playful levity and a delight in formal experiment.

LA PREUVE PAR QUATRE [Two and Two Make Four]. Two parts. First edition in Théâtre, Paris 1964. First performance February 3, 1964, Paris, Théâtre de la Michodière. Time: the present. Place: Paris.

This is a sparkling and frivolous sophisticated piece which, with the help of alienation effects, cabaret gags, and flashbacks, trebles the customary triangular situation and thus makes fun of the total approach of psychoanalysis.

The industrial manager Arthur Darras leads such a hectic life that he has become a bundle of nerves. He outlines to his friend, the writer Champlon, a new psychotherapy he has invented and which he hopes will prove the perfect recipe for living. Arthur will henceforth split up all his emotions, anxieties, instincts, and longings into partial aspects and isolate them. Having thus concentrated the ingredients of his psyche on one single point, he hopes to master and dominate them more easily. The vague anxieties which so far oppressed him are concentrated in the person of a redhead, who now becomes the butt of all his revulsion, with the result that Arthur's vital activities are disintoxicated and cleared of all feelings of hatred and fear. With love he deals equally consistently; he chooses three different female temperaments for his three emotional approaches: for physical passion, the curvaceous beauty Lulu; for platonic flirtation and tender dalliance, the romantic student Jacqueline; and for the familiar domestic security his wife Caroline. The smart manager now happily enjoys his well-structured psychological life, which no longer leaves room for emotional instability or imbalance.

All this is upset, however, by the unanimous protest of the women, who see themselves degraded into objects without a will of their own. They are not content with the segment of Arthur's personality which he entrusts to them for "psychodiagnostic" treatment, and long for the man as a whole with all his contradictions. Thus Arthur eventually loses all three of them for happier, if psychoanalytically less advanced, rivals. But he knows how to repair this breakdown in his system. He simply changes the functions around: he desires Jacqueline and writes soulful poems to Lulu in the moonlight. With this reorganization of his psychological mechanism Arthur has achieved his masterpiece and can now sit back in self-satisfaction.


## MARCEL, Gabriel
(France, born 1889)


THE FLORESTAN DIMENSION *(La dimension Florestan)*. Satirical comedy in three acts. Prose. First edition Paris 1958. First transmission October 17, 1953, Radiodiffusion Nationale. Staged in English December 13, 1961 in Boston, a Poets' Workshop production. Time: the present. Place: a small town in south Germany.

A profound play about the tragic ambiguity of reality which forever changes as it is registered in the individual's experience and can never be grasped as an absolute certainty. Marcel does not disdain a dialectical use of the weapons of comedy in his—sometimes rather transparent—attacks on his opponents and their worldly existentialism.

Professor Hans Walter Dolch, thanks to his great philosophical work *Die Wacht am Sein (The Watch on Being)*, has not only acquired a world reputation as a prophetic thinker, but is also the leading spirit in the Florestan Research Group. The latter's purpose is to propagate the literary legacy—profundity clothed in sibylline unintelligibility—of the poet Florestan, whose real name was Gustave Affenreiter. Professor Dolch, who wants to exalt himself in this solemn exegesis, has a lot of trouble with his ecstatic collaborators. The philologist Schattengräber is trying to bring to light the unembellished facts of the dead idol's life and indulges his thirst for knowledge without any concern for mystical veneration. As a precious memorial to Florestan, the Countess, who was his mistress, publishes the "Letters to Altair," which she herself has written. A far more genuine legacy of his, namely her daughter Verena, has to disappear for the sake of the myth. Another victim of the legend is Frieda Herzog, who, too, was once Florestan's mistress and now turns up again—most inconveniently, for by mistake Florestan had already lamented her death in moving elegies. "I decide that nothing has happened. . . . I decide what is the truth"— thus Professor Dolch, *ex cathedra*. And thus the whole thing procures the philosopher a most exclusive amusement about the naughtiness of philosophy. The disintegration of identity leads to theatrical somersaults: "Each of us know the Florestan she deserved."


ROME N'EST PLUS DANS ROME [Rome Is No Longer in Rome]. Play in five acts. Prose. First published in Les OEuvres libres, No. 63, Paris, August 1951. First performance April 18, 1951, Paris, Théâtre Hébertot. Time: the winter of 1951. Place: Paris and Brazil.

A man's discovery of himself is combined with political problems such as patriotism and national honor. In the hands of a German writer this sort of thing might come dangerously close to the "blood and soil" myth and the glorification of racial ideals, but the specifically French approach to life turns it into a dialectical struggle over the ultimate questions of human existence.

Like many others, Pascal Laumière, a professor of literature of national-catholic leanings threatened with deportation by anonymous letters from the Communists, is driven into a panic by the Korean crisis. Although he has so far condemned emigration as ignoble flight, a discussion with the fanatic Marxist Robert Velars convinces him that in these confused times France can be saved only by preserving the spirit of the "grande nation" abroad. His wife Renée has managed to obtain an invitation for him to a chair of literature at a new university in Brazil. He takes up his new task with enthusiasm and is cruelly disappointed. He has lost Renée to the Brazilian Carlos Martins, who, as a "gentleman's" gesture of gratitude, helped him to his new position. He is expected to adapt himself completely to the Latin-American way of life and his lectures are criticized. When Pascal takes refuge in his love for his sister-in-law Esther, he incurs the censure of the rigidly orthodox church. He confesses his error in a radio talk. If men of good will betray and abandon their country, they betray themselves, become the plaything of events and lose their vocation. Overwhelmed by this insight, Pascal collapses and dies.

Corneille was wrong in saying, in one of his tragedies, that "Rome is no longer in Rome, it is where I am." It is a play with a message, but its attraction lies less in the dubious message itself, according to which an individual is fully valid only in the country of his birth, than in the grace of its lucid style.

# MAULNIER, Thierry (Jacques Talagrand)
(France, born 1909)

LA CONDITION HUMAINE. See MALRAUX, ANDRÉ, AND MAULNIER, THIERRY

LE SEXE ET LE NÉANT *[Sex and Nothingness]*. Comedy in three acts. Prose. First published in *L'Avant-Scène* No. 221, June 1960. First performance March 5, 1960, Paris, Théâtre de l'Athénée. Time: the present. Place: Paris.

A satire on the formation of legends and the bestseller racket in modern literature. Annibal Leborgne is a failure as a writer and a man. His nihilistic books attract no readers, and he is humiliated by his domineering wife Augusta and has to pay in hard cash for the self-deception of a brief happiness with Denise. Suddenly he is roused into action by the romantic admiration of a girl student and runs away. Augusta has her missing husband declared dead and releases to the popular press the heartrending story of his misunderstood genius. Annibal's lascivious concoctions are published in large editions, his brave abnegation is celebrated as a significant manifestation of the times. Augusta rakes in prizes and royalties. Annibal returns from anonymity to take his share of the unexpected golden shower. But businesslike as she is, Augusta forces him back into his nonexistence, whence he is allowed carefully to smuggle a new, mature work into the officially posthumous writings. Its much higher level condemns the book as a flop. Maulnier's personal literary difficulties, with their effective polemics, overshadow the problem of a man deprived of his identity.

# MAURIAC, François
(France, born 1885)

LE FEU SUR LA TERRE, OU LE PAYS SANS CHEMIN *[Fire on Earth, or Land without a Path]*. Play in four acts. Prose. First edition Paris 1951. First performance October 12, 1950, Lyons, Théâtre des Célestins. Time: the present. Place: the country property of the du Prat de La Sesque family in France.

The family du Prat de La Sesque is living on its inherited property in poverty but with aristocratic arrogance. All of them are bullied by the eldest daughter Laure, an aging spinster, whose frustration finds an outlet in a consuming passion for her younger brother Maurice. Maurice is reading law in Paris and every penny of the scant family fortune has been spent on him in the expectation of his marriage to a rich local heiress. Suddenly he returns home with his wife Andrée and their little son Eric. He has married secretly and instead of preparing for his law degree has become a painter. Laure feels cheated and robbed. She wants to annul the marriage and instead have Maurice marry Caroline, the beautiful heiress whom she herself has chosen for him. Maurice very nearly succumbs to the compulsion of her iron will, but the marriage sacrament leads him back to Andrée's side. Yet Laure's hard and demanding passion remains a disturbing element in the life of all her family.

In a world without faith man's inner fire turns into destructive passion. The individual's longing for the bonds of love and security is bound to lead him into error and guilt so long as it is directed to the things of this earth. The bewilderment of Mauriac's characters has its origin in the world's lack of order and faith.


LES MAL-AIMÉS *[The Unloved]*. Play in three acts. Prose. First edition Paris 1945. First performance March 1, 1945, Paris, Théâtre-Français. Time: the present. Place: country house of M. de Virelade, France.

The uncertainty of all earthly bonds is demonstrated through two "difficult personalities" who lack Hofmannsthal's sensibility. They do not have enough egotism to effect what would make them happy, but fail out of weakness and indecision. The intrigues of their environment are a mere pretext for their own impotence, and the rapture of self-sacrifice is justified in terms of a religious decision. Elisabeth de Virelade, a girl past the first blush of youth, and the young doctor Alain have decided to seal their childhood friendship with marriage. But the squire of Virelade finds it convenient to keep his eldest daughter to run his house and read to him. Elisabeth's sister Marianne, twelve years her junior, blackmails Alain with a flirtation some years back and theatens suicide, until her spiteful egocentricity succeeds in forcing him to marry her. The lovers renounce their love, but a year later vainly try to elope together and eventually are resigned to their situation. Mauriac paints his psychological nuances so subtly that the symbolism of his religious plays often passes unnoticed.

## MEICHSNER, Dieter
(Germany, born 1928)

BESUCH AUS DER ZONE *[A Visit from the Other Side]*. Play in three acts. Prose. Originally written as a radio play. Acting edition Hamburg, Rowohlt, 1958. First performance January 25, 1958, Saarbrücken, Stadttheater. Time: the present, before the erection of the Berlin wall. Place: West Germany.

A play on the division of Germany, based on well-drawn types and compelling conflicts. The smug pity which participants of the German economic miracle dole out to the poor relations on the other side, and the latter's envy of their better-off brethren threaten to turn the political frontier into a final separation between people.
Walther Reichert hopes that his West German business associate Brötscher will find new outlets for the sale of the plastics he produces at his factory at Gonar, in East Germany. But Reichert's partner Kleinschmidt has settled down in the West together with some key specialist, and developed an improved product. Brötscher is now in a position to do without his Eastern associate, whose patents are the basis of the economic boom. What a victory for the free world! But instead Brötscher offers Reichert a profitable chance of finding a place in the economic miracle. Reichert declines and returns to the East, taking his family with him. He means to stay with his old workers, notwithstanding the nuisance of interference by party officials, output targets, and the threat of expropriation. By means of unassuming, painstaking goodness at the level of individual relationships he wants to give reality to Germany as such, which has long sunk into official oblivion on both sides of the frontier.

## MEIER, Herbert
(Switzerland, born 1928)

DIE BARKE VON GAWDOS *[The Bark of Gavdos]*. A Romanian tale in three acts. Prose. Written 1950. First edition Zürich 1954. First performance June 17, 1954, Zürich, Schauspielhaus. Time: the present. Place: Romania.

Meier believes in man's goodness and in the meaning of this message. This gives him courage for the redeeming catharsis, for the idealistic *per aspera ad astra*—which, however, he removes from reality and sets in an unworldly dream of wish fulfillment: "We come from an island called Gavdos. There we killed our brothers. And they expelled us. . . . And then we sailed across the Black Sea in an old bark. . . . Your curses, your hatred screamed like black gulls around the mast. In their shadow you were reborn. In this bark a yellow dragon slid out of you: Iorgu Koruga, who devoured love."

Outlawed and tormented by feelings of guilt, the tinker Koruga roams the world. Sitis, his demonic antagonist, drives him further and further: "I am your hatred, your scream. I have fastened my teeth in the back of your neck, I bestride you." Istra and Ion, a young couple, remain guiltless in their pure love, because they drown with the leaking boat during the trip to Gavdos, the island of peace. For "Gavdos, that's unknown here. It seems one has to drown to get there." The action has the simplified outlines of a woodcut and is presented in stylized mythological form with the help of rhythmical prose and gloomy images full of oriental nature magic.

JONAS UND DER NERZ (also: *Die weißen Stühle*) *[Jonas and the Mink Coat*, also: *The White Chairs]*. Play in twelve scenes. Prose. Written 1957–1958. First edition in *Theater im S. Fischer Verlag*, Vol. 1, Frankfurt/Main 1962. First performance March 24, 1959, Bern, Stadttheater. Time: the present. Place: stylized settings.

The conflict of the generations and the task of coming to terms with the past are distilled into an ambiguous symbol of menace: "Look around you, they all have power over us, those old people who are hardened, petrified, and are enthroned on their chairs, unthreatened themselves because they threaten us by their very existence. They are unafraid because they sow their grass seed over the death camps and their business prospers again. They smile when someone says love, and they corrode us, they corrode the faith that it's worth while. . . ."

Jonas Anders is preparing for his wedding with Anja, when the past suddenly intrudes between the lovers. Jonas' father had been driven to suicide when his wife eloped with the speculator Golker. Bankrupted and devalued by life, these specters of Jonas' youth reappear. His mother has become the "lady in lilac" who wanders from place to place in a motheaten mink and guiltily tries to find her son. Golker is the "man in the top hat" who was so avid for profit that he let children starve, and who now sponges his way around the world with nebulous inventions. Irreconcilable and hard-hearted, Jonas does not tell his mother who he is. History seems about to repeat itself in his friend Edgar, who courts Anja. Jonas' mother has poisoned herself. Jonas has failed, and his failure stirs him into a willingness to incur guilt in the future. He embarks with Anja on the adventure of life.

This somewhat slender tale is embroidered with masks, dances, and changing stylizations. Often the content seems to be determined only by the form of expression. The author explains: "The mask, it seems to me, combines with the tale, the organized material, and with the décor to form the 'world' of the drama. . . . And this world determines the model, not the other way around, both are variable because historically conditioned, and hence their unity and content also change. . . . And dramatic language seems to me authentic when it echoes the mimed, choreographic element."

## MEISTER, Ernst
(Germany, born 1911)

EIN HAUS FÜR MEINE KINDER *[A House for My Children]*. Play in three acts. Prose. Acting edition Berlin, Kiepenheuer, 1964. First performance March 20, 1966, Wiesbaden, Staatstheater, Studio. Time: the present. Place: living room in a house near Paris.

A conversation piece intensified into grotesque profundity. People live only by their lost longings and dreams. Madame Bautain has set herself one aim in life, and that is to have her daughter Beatrix and her son-in-law Henry live happily in an idyllic suburban house. She has secretly saved the money for building the house, lovingly chosen the site and, with the architect, designed every detail. At the same time she carefully restrained her motherly solicitude, so as not to stand in the way of the young couple's independent development. In the end Madame Bautain is forced to realize that the young people have quite different aspirations. With their temperament and tastes they could never feel at home in the mother's dream house. The old lady's wistful plans are distorted by grotesquely caricatured busybodies and are exploited to serve the most diverse interests. For Meister, the lyrical poet, the action is merely a pretext for playing in a melancholy and graceful fashion with characters, with the soul's melodies, with encounters and occurrences.

## MELL, Max
(Austria, born 1882)

JEANNE D'ARC *[Joan of Arc]*. One-act drama. Prose. First edition Wiesbaden 1957. First performance July 19, 1956, Bregenz, Landestheater (Vienna Burgtheater Ensemble at the Bregenz Festival). Time: 1431: cell in Rouen Castle.

In Mell's interpretation, a blend of psychological exploration and religious emotionalism, St. Joan is seen as the enduring force of good in the world: "That is her truth. And I am not sure that it is hers alone. That it is not one which should be the truth of us all." At the center, Mell places not the supernatural miracle, but the human being struggling through doubts and temptations to find faith and, once found, to stand up for it.
M. de Ligny, the uncouth country gentleman, has delivered Jeanne into the hands of the English and now bargains for his pieces of silver. The trial is conducted by Bishop Cauchon, a disinterested fanatic for order. In fear of death and in hopes of a happy marriage Jeanne follows the advice of the lawyer Peter Manuel and signs the recantation which saves her. But the acquittal is the worse punishment, for Jeanne is to be imprisoned for life, eating the bread of adversity and the water of affliction. The voices of the saints arouse the girl to a sense of her mission, and she goes to the stake as though to salvation. The sceptical rationalist Manuel and de Ligny's kindly wife are moved by Jeanne's faith in God to start a new life in faith: "It is a cruel soil on which we are born. The one consolation is that even this cruel soil cannot prevent saints growing on it."

## MERZ, Carl, and QUALTINGER, Helmut
(both Austria; Merz, born 1905, Qualtinger, born 1928)

DER HERR KARL *[Mr. Karl]*. One-act monologue. Prose. Adapted from a sketch for the authors' cabaret. First edition Munich 1962. First broadcast November 1961, Austrian television. First stage performance November 26, 1961, Vienna, Kleines Theater im Konzerthaus. Time: the present. Place: cellar of a delicatessen store.

For Wedekind's "Marquis von Keith" life is a constant zigzag; in the perspective of Mr. Karl this comes out as follows: ". . . at least twenty times I've built my life over again in the course of my life . . . And what's left of it?" Karl is a bundle of human failings. His selfish intent to feather his nest in all possible circumstances is carried out in such a matter-of-fact way, in the total absence of even the possibility of any pang of conscience, that it begins to seem almost like an animal's innocence. His physical super-vitality is after the good life, leaving no room for any kind of intellectual or spiritual reservations. Such an attitude finds its place somewhere between Brecht's "Baal," the incorporation of a mythical zest for life, and the shabbiness of an egocentric. With advancing age, Karl has become a shop assistant in a delicatessen store, and, surrounded by yards of salami and stacks of bottled wine, he looks back on the vicissitudes of his life. As a "nonpolitical man" Karl has managed to look after his financial interests by milking all political parties, whether of a socialist, Christian-democratic or nationalist brand. His very philosophy is determined by the mutability of a chameleon: "I mean, I'm Catholic all right. Not very much. But still. Such as most of us are." Somehow he is always on the spot wherever there is an accident or some political demonstration, and enjoys himself greatly on these occasions. Nor is he averse to a bit of fun with the girls. Eventually he marries an elderly widow and lazes about in her restaurant. As the treasurer of a savings club he is an unscrupulous as he is a few years later as an NSV official.* Skillfully he dodges military service, makes profitable deals after the war with the occupation powers and, to the extent that he can still sell his prowess, is kept by professional ladies. However timeless and universal the sordid attitude of such a Mr. Karl may be, the character himself is so deeply rooted in the recent history of Austria that the play could hardly fail to call forth indignant protests from all those who saw in it an attack on the "nation's most sacred patrimony." Originally written as an attraction for the two authors' Vienna cabaret, the play has found its place in the history of the drama as a political documentary.

## MESTERHÁZY, Lajos
(Hungary, born 1916)

PESTI EMBEREK [People of Budapest]. Play in two parts. Prose. First edition Budapest 1961. First performance October 24, 1958, Budapest, Vigszinház. Time: 1941–1957. Place: Budapest.

An individual's life is shaped by the collective destiny of the people and in turn helps to create the latter, so that it is at once derived and productive. The idea of evolution takes a moralizing turn. "In this play," says the author, "I have not written a dramatic story, but have tried to drama-

* An official of the National Socialist Public Welfare agency.

tize our life. What I had to say I elaborated not so much in depth as in breadth. I follow the life of a few characteristic types of our age and society, in an attempt to induce the audience to think about their own life and about the outstanding questions of their life." The author aims to make an inventory of Hungary's contemporary history—the fascist Arrow-Cross movement under Szalassy during the Second World War, the guerilla warfare, the establishment of the Communist People's Republic, the Stalinist purges under Rakosi, finally the Petöfi circle whose reform proposals sparked off the 1956 revolt. Without glossing over the errors and excesses of the Marxist system, Mesterhazy tries to justify his Communist convictions in his own eyes and those of his contemporaries: "I have brooded over it night and day, have eaten out my heart. . . . There were things that were not right, of course. Abuses, errors. . . . But I looked at the whole, and it won. It won again and again. . . ."

Chance brings Monika and Sandor together at a crossing after sixteen years and reawakens the unfulfilled love of their youth. Monika is a widowed teacher, her face marked by resignation; Sandor a high government official in the foreign service. Images of the past are recalled: the garden party at the boarding school, when all Sandor's friends danced attendance on Monika and later keep crossing her path. Bela is the idealist rebel, who in 1956 calls the people to revolt without having tested his aims against reality. Gyula is an opportunist, who did as well under the fascists as he does as a vociferous party official. Tamas, the pianist, perished in the persecution of the Jews. Laszlo, though himself a victim of Stalinist tyranny, has preserved his faith in the Marxist salvation. He opposes Bela and the October revolution of 1956, and becomes the author's mouthpiece in addressing his contemporaries: ". . . our path is not an easy one, and it does not lead straight to our aim. But we must believe in it . . . for whoever does nothing but work is tired unto death at the end and his strength fails him. But whoever has conviction, builds the Communist future, and his life has a meaning." Laszlo is killed in the upheavals of the revolution. Monika and Sandor, who are finally joined together, will be the torchbearers of his faith in the future: "When once we pass away peacefully, after a life of suffering and exertions, full of harmless little joys and unbroken confidence, when we are reunited with the earth from which we have sprung, then we shall bequeath to history a script which, despite a few crooked strokes, is as streamlined and pure as that of no other generation before us." The action is given the appearance of Marxist-slanted reportage by means of film montage and fade-in techniques and a commentary by a newspaper seller.

# MÉSZOLY, Miklös
(Hungary, born 1921)

AZ ABLAKMOSÓ *[The Window Cleaner]*. One-act burlesque tragedy. Prose. First performance March 15, 1963, Miskolc, National Theatre. Time: not specified. Place: an apartment.

A parable of modern man and his unrelatedness is set in a carefully unrealistic no-man's-land. The menacing antithesis between self-obsessed negation of the rest of the world and self-surrender in completely standardized mass is resolved by the ever new miracle of motherhood: "faith in the invincibility of continuity." Mészöly comments in his foreword: "The play is set in no specific time or place, it could happen wherever private life is out of harmony with external power. The intention is to enter a clarifying protest against the inhuman and disastrous possibility of such a disharmony or indeed against the memory or repetition of it. . . . It was my intention to mobilize the alarming 'more' so as to succeed better in protesting against the real 'less' that threatens us."
Martin has given up his profession as an actor, which meant perpetual lying and deception. With his wife Annie he withdraws from the rest of the world, in the hope of finding his true self in the doll's house of his marriage. The idyll is disturbed by a window cleaner, who proceeds to make the glass walls of isolation once more transparent for everybody. He is a disguised official of the regime and, with the help of a change of sex, proves that Martin's dream of private happiness is nothing but self-deception. The caretaker and his wife Fanny are called in. In his uncertainty, Martin takes refuge in a love affair with Fanny, while Annie consoles herself with the window cleaner. The caretaker, a fanatic for order, hangs himself to escape this anarchy. Eventually Martin and Annie are reunited and decide that henceforth they will jointly strive for a compromise between the self and the outside world. It is a discordant attempt to find a new form for a play on contemporary problems by demonstrating a theme on the stage and directly involving the audience in the argument.

## MICHELSEN, Hans Günter
(Germany, born 1920)

DREI AKTE *[Three Acts]*. Play in three acts. Prose. First edition Frankfurt/
Main 1965. First performance March 26, 1965, Ulm, Ulmer Theater.
Time: the present. Place: cellar, forest clearing, hallway.

Michelsen is concerned not with an action, but with the emptiness behind
mechanical actions, with the shock "which perhaps everyone suffers when
he comes to think that he's thinking of nothing. . . . Until the end one
thinks, and one doesn't know how, whether one is afraid of it or not, and
who one is. Or was. In one's heart is this growing terror of one's own ignorance." In his play *Lappschiess* Michelsen decomposes reality by showing
how any one occurrence is experienced in different ways by the different
individuals it concerns, dissolves reality into fluid associations and waves
of consciousness. In *Three Acts* he proceeds in the opposite direction. No
occurrence, no external fact is subjectivized or shown in multiple refractions in the interplay of different sensibilities; instead, Michelsen objectivizes what goes on inside man's soul. The shock of self-alienation radiates
outward and alters reality. The collapse of bourgeois existence is depersonalized to the utmost degree and repeated in a chain reaction from one
act to the next, always with reference to a different character.
Right in the middle of his sixtieth birthday celebrations Niegsch rushes
away, away from his fussy, voluble, well-meaning wife, away from his
estranged daughter Anne, away from his correct, uneventful official's life—
away into the cellar. He is filled with despair about wasted opportunities,
with fear of the power of day-to-day conventions in his family and job,
which turn him into a mere function in a mechanical round of events.
He is determined to break out of such a pseudoexistence. Anne finds him
in the cellar, but however much he tries to explain his predicament, she
goes on chattering uncomprehendingly about their beautiful, carefree togetherness. Disconsolately, Niegsch goes away for ever. Anne is calmed by
her fiancé, the neighbors' son Bernd.
Bernd's parents, the Schrohls, have lost their way in the mountains during
a holiday tour. As night falls in the no-man's-land of this situation, Mrs.
Schrohl suddenly feels how the thoughtless, everyday conventions are
shattered within herself, that there is no point in getting cross about the
breakfast coffee or worrying about having enough money to keep up their
accustomed style of life after retirement. She can well understand Niegsch
and his refusal to go on living on those terms. She is beset by doubts about
the meaning of her life consisting of an empty round of work, success,
enjoyment, and contentment. Does one have to be the way one is? Mr.

Schrohl has no use for such hysterics. Husband and wife face each other as strangers, an unbridgeable gulf between them.

Anne in her turn has been transformed by her father's destiny. Without regard to any taboos or bourgeois decency, she claims Bernd's love at once and without reservations. Helplessly, the well brought-up young man takes refuge in the familiar phrases which rise to his lips so smoothly and thoughtlessly. He talks of their common future, makes plans, while Anne loses heart in her loneliness and despair. Michelsen creates a deliberate interchangeability of situations and language. Commonplaces, the trite chatter habitual to all, hide the collapse of the individual and terminate in helpless silence.

HELM [Helm]. One-act play. Prose. First edition Frankfurt/Main 1965. First performance September 17, 1965, Frankfurt/Main, Städtische Bühnen. Time: the present. Place: clearing in a wood.

This is the first play in which Michelsen chooses a situation comprehensible in concrete terms. The classical pattern of cause and effect in crime and punishment, of a higher nemesis remaining invisible yet encompassing everything in irresistible destruction, is only apparently transposed into modern times. The theme of the unassimilated past which catches up unawares with its hirelings is only a pretext for showing man face to face with catastrophe—man in his false self-assurance, his unfreedom, his trite squabbles, selfishness, and hypocrisy.

The innkeeper Helm has invited his wartime superior officers on a spree and subsequently has left them stranded in an unfamiliar clearing in the woods. Helm had been Colonel Kenkmann's mess sergeant. For reasons of personal ambition the division commander had convicted Helm of "demoralizing the armed forces" and posted him to a riffraff battalion, from which Helm returned a permanent invalid. Today's "rough but hearty" gathering had been a veritable orgy of vociferous patriotism, sentimentalities, and steely reminiscences, and everyone had laughed at Helm's capital idea. Meanwhile he was intending to put to good use on his instructors his training as a perfect machine for murder and his skill. Helm cannot be found. At first amused, then cross and finally panic-stricken, one after another of the men sets off for home. Every now and then a shot is heard. Those that still remain suddenly realize what is happening: perched high in a tree, Helm is presenting the bill for his wasted life, bullet after bullet. The former officers begin to hurl accusations against each other and enjoy the murder of each successive comrade as a quiet triumph of self-affirmation. Until the very last the colonel is convinced that he alone is innocent and as such immune from Helm's justice. A German folksong

returns as a leitmotif, in a permutation by which Helm becomes murderous destiny hobbling through the woods.

As in Weiss's *Nacht mit Gästen*, horror finds expression in oversimplified
naïvete in the destructive mania of children's games, and the voluptuous
cruelty of fairy tales.

STIENZ *[Stienz]*. One-act play. Prose. Written 1955. First edition Frank-
furt/Main 1963. First performance March 16, 1963, Frankfurt/Main,
Städtische Bühnen. Time: the present. Place: the major's room.

This is the tragedy of self-discipline for its own sake, of insisting that everything must be just so and not otherwise, without taking into account
changed circumstances, but instead taking refuge in the self-sufficiency of
stubborn carrying-on. "To capitulate now is as bad as desertion, or worse."
The longing for something unalterable to hold on to, drives men into
mortal rigidity. The major talks big and broods over his memoirs which
he will never write; around him the dilapidated house is slowly crumbling.
His daughter Mechthild wastes her life in domestic chores without getting
any thanks for it, and dreams of a lieutenant whom she once loved and
who has disappeared. This could be the point of departure for one of
those gloomy ballads about lost reality, and failure, and flight into illusion, such as O'Neill has more than once composed. But Michelsen pierces
the pychological reality of an individual destiny and creates a grotesque
nightmare.

In the basement Stienz guards the entrance. He is a former sergeant-major
grown dull and animal-like from the mechanical stamping up-and-down
of sentry duty. For years the occupants of the house have not been able
to go out; they are provided with necessities by means of a basket let down
on a string. Lieutenant Paul, who has returned to life, is permitted to provide the wherewithal of the family by this means, but nonetheless remains
a contemptible base-wallah in the eyes of the major, for whom the entire
world is divided into those who give and those who receive orders. The
major sees everyone, including himself, as functions of an existence that
has long been obsolete. He clings to his past which assures him the illusion
of a strategy of life, the pseudotask of a command. He needs the ceaseless
parade step and the stereotyped "Yessir!" of his sergeant-major, no less
than the meaningless personal peril of the crumbling house. "And one
cannot simply begin all over again somewhere without knowing what truly
happened, and to what end we were called. The past lives on! . . . I have
given myself my word of honor to sit it out." With a crash half the house
falls in. Mechthild tries in vain to find a way through the ruins out into
the open. Even the major now admits that they will have to use the door
which Stienz guards and thus break the rule which he himself has estab-

lished. Threateningly the sentry bars the way and is shot down in self-defense by his commanding officer. But this petrified world allows of no escape. Mechthild stiffens into the posture of a sentry, stamps mechanically up and down and utters only one growling sound: "Yessir!"

## MIHURA, Miguel
(Spain, born 1916)

MELOCOTÓN IN ALMIBAR [Peaches in Syrup]. Comedy in two acts and a prologue. Prose. First edition Madrid 1962. First performance November 20, 1958, Madrid, Teatro Infanta Isabel. Time: 1957. Place: a drawing room in Madrid.

The familiar theme of the defeat of criminal cunning by disarming innocence is transposed to the sophisticated theater. After a successful burglary, four gangsters with their haul of jewelry take up lodgings with Dona Pilar, all under false names. The chief of the gang, Cosme Suarez, falls ill with pneumonia and is nursed by Sister Maria. The little nun is inquisitive, voluble, and provokingly trustful. She looks in the arm chair for loose coins to give to the poor, and finds a pistol as well as gloves reeking of chloroform. She inspects the bathroom and exposes Federico and Nuria, who pretend to be married but use different toothbrushes. The gangsters take Maria's guilelessness for a crafty police trap, take flight and leave the booty behind in a flower pot. With disarming impudence Sister Maria now wheedles the precious jewel-plant out of the landlady: "There's so much misery in the world. And when the poor can put a flower pot on one of their shabby window sills, they are as happy as though they'd been given a treasure. . . . God will reward you!"

## MILLER, Arthur
(United States, born 1915)

AFTER THE FALL. Play in two acts. Prose. Written 1963. First edition New York 1964. First performance January 23, 1964, New York, ANTA–Washington Square Theatre. Time: the present. Place: ". . . in the mind, thought, and memory of Quentin."

Ibsen once declared that in his plays he was passing judgment on himself; to this same task, Arthur Miller brings to bear all the psychoanalytically sharpened tools of his intellect: "I think that for many years I looked at

life like a law case, a series of proofs. . . . And all that remained was the
endless argument with oneself—this pointless litigation of existence before
an empty bench. Which, of course, is another way of saying—despair. . . .
It's that I no longer see some final saving grace! Socialism once, then love;
some final hope is gone that always saved before the end!" There is no
need here to go into the question of the extent to which this stage autobiography is to be understood as a justification and excuse for Miller's own
life or simply as a pursuit of self-knowledge, in which Marilyn Monroe's
tragic destiny is used to sharpen the effects. What gives this play, in spite
of all reservations, a claim to be taken seriously as an attempt at creative self-realization is that the complacent pose of self-reassurance—"whoever goes to save another person with the lie of limitless love throws a
shadow on the face of God"—is wiped out by an awareness of one's own
involvement.

The lawyer Quentin is alone on the empty stage, surrounded by a number
of platforms on which the changing figures of his reminiscences appear—
lit up suddenly, delivering their cues, intermingling in response to erratic
associations and disappearing again. The different scenes are superimposed
upon each other, displace and interrupt each other, are suddenly taken
up again and continued, and are repeated to provide a leitmotif. Situations seem to cast doubt on themselves by their own contradictions or
are indirectly illuminated by contrasts. After two unsuccessful marriages
Quentin is about to make a third attempt with the Austrian girl Holga.
The gruesome ruins of a concentration camp make him feel guilty for
being one of the carefree survivors. The great common guilt of our century causes him to pass under review all the wrongs that have piled up for
many years in his own private life. His friend Lou is accused of being a
communist—it is the time of the McCarthy persecutions—and asks Quentin for his help. Quentin undertakes Lou's defense only reluctantly and is
secretly relieved when the latter settles the case by suicide. The marriage
of Quentin's parents breaks up with the loss of their fortune; because
Quentin's professional aspirations demand that he should go to college,
his brother Dan has to be content with staying home and doing business
in a small way. Quentin's marriage with Louise is destroyed by selfishness
and wearing triviality. Nothing but a chain of misunderstandings underlies his subsequent marriage with Maggie, who is as beautiful as she is
commonplace and makes a meteoric rise from anonymous telephone operator to celebrated vaudeville and television star. The girl misinterprets
Quentin's initial shyness of a sex symbol as personal respect, paid to
her—much to her astonishment—for the first time in her life. Once married to Maggie, Quentin masks his instincts, which alone bind him to her,
behind moral phrases, and obstinately tries to improve her so as not to
have to despise her. She in turn finds her carefree exuberance hemmed in

by the tormenting fear that he, the intellectual, has to be ashamed of her. She is nothing for him but "a joke that brings in money." The limelight of publicity, the exhausting show business, financial troubles and, not least, the two partners' mutual uncertainty which generates distrust and animosity, make this marriage a hell. Quentin leaves his second wife, even though he knows that she is being driven to suicide by the loneliness to which he thereby exposes her. And now uneasiness and resignation cloud Quentin's new happiness with Holga. But hope is eternal, however senseless it may appear to Quentin after his life-long disillusions, and in some inexplicable way gives him the courage for a new beginning: ". . . after the Fall, after many, many deaths. Is the knowing all? . . . I think one must finally take one's life in one's arms."

ALL MY SONS. Play in three acts. Prose. First edition New York 1947. First performance January 29, 1947, New York, Coronet Theatre. Time: "August of our era." Place: backyard of the Keller home on the outskirts of an American town.

This is a play of analytical social criticism, which derives from Ibsen both its construction and its theme. The prosperous and popular manufacturer Joe Keller, one of those respected, reliable "pillars of society," is overtaken and destroyed by his troubled past. To make more profits, he supplied the Army Air Force during the war with cracked airplane parts and thus become responsible for the loss of many pilots who did not survive. During the trial he manages to fasten the crime on his business partner and thereafter suns himself in the glory of the present, so firmly under his control and so comfortably secure. But then he learns that his son Larry, who was killed in action and thereby enabled Keller to assume the heroic pose of a heart-broken father, was driven by shame and despair about the corrupt war profiteer to seek his own death. Keller loses also his surviving son, Chris, who leaves his home forever. Utterly crushed, Keller, whose criminal greed was merely a result of his misguided love for his sons, takes his own life.

THE CRUCIBLE. Play in two acts. Prose. Written 1952. First edition New York 1953. First performance January 22, 1953, New York, Martin Beck Theatre. Time: the spring of 1692. Place: Salem, Massachusetts.

The nightmare of mass psychosis and destructive mania, which are only changing names for the ever unchanging primitive bloodlust that keeps flaring up on religious, political or racial pretexts, is put before our eyes in a historical case. The satisfaction men can derive from the wildest accusations, the intoxication of denouncing others, and the greediness of insignificant hangers-on who pay lip service to justice while keeping their eye on lucrative business—all this is frighteningly timeless. Betty, the daughter, and Abigail, the niece of the clergyman Parris, are caught in the woods at the licentious games of adolescents. So not to be punished by their prudish elders, the girls take refuge in pathological fantasies; they pretend they are possessed by the devil, innocent victims of witches and fiends, including some of Salem's most respected inhabitants. Abigail is driven to the most hair-raising accusations by her hatred and spite generated by sexual unfulfillment. Because the farmer Proctor has paid no attention to the teen-ager's wanton seductiveness, he and his wife Elizabeth are picked out as the first victims. The puritanical and self-righteous clergymen Parris and Hale revel in passing judgments of biblical harshness. A witch-hunt of mutual accusations grips the little town. Each feels all the more just and virtuous as he heaps charges on his neighbor. But even this catastrophe acquires meaning through sacrifice and steadfastness. The innocent men and women condemned to death meet their end with composure. Abigail has found no peace in her deeds of destruction and is still relentlessly driven by her lust for life.

Miller uses the same theme as does Feuchtwanger in *The Devil in Boston* and raises it to symbolic level, in spite of its topical relevance to McCarthy's anti-Communist campaign.

DEATH OF A SALESMAN. *Certain private conversations in two acts and a requiem.* Prose. First edition New York 1949. First performance February 10, 1949, New York, Morosco Theatre. Time: 1948. Place: Loman's house and yard in New York and various places he visits in New York and Boston.

A commonplace destiny is made into poetry. Even in his own family life a man becomes an outcast as a result of the attrition of his professional life, his boastful lies to himself, and his hectic defensive reactions against his uncongenial surroundings.

Willy Loman is a salesman grown too old for his job. His sales figures decline, he is worn and tired. Yet the money for his family has to be earned as before. His sons Biff and Happy have both failed in their professions and look for compensation in brief adventures. When the firm for which Loman has been working for decades fires him as useless, he represses the awareness of his own failure by means of forced gaiety and feverish planning of new schemes. Missed opportunities and unfulfilled dreams and aspirations appear in flashbacks. In vain Willy's wife Linda tries in her loyal, worried, and unassuming way to smooth out the emerging conflicts in the family, which are leading to mutual reproaches and nagging. Rejected by his sons as well, Loman ends his life in a faked accident. A sizable insurance payment remains as the last credit item of a wasted life, which never became true and valid except in moments of unreality: "Willy was a salesman. And for a salesman, there is no rock bottom to the life. . . . He's a man way out there in the blue, riding on a smile and a shoeshine. And when they start not smiling back—that's an earthquake. . . . A salesman's got to dream, boy. It comes with the territory."

INCIDENT AT VICHY. One-act play. Prose. Written 1964. First edition New York 1965. First performance December 3, 1964, New York, Lincoln Center Theatre. Time: 1942. Place: Vichy, France.

This is a vignette of the office routine of one of the innumerable raiding squads that pick up Jews in the streets and pack them off to Auschwitz in cattle wagons. But Miller does not stop at an accusation which divides humanity into executioners and victims. He probes into the causes of the incomprehensible mania of destruction that has gripped all concerned. Among the persecuted, too, indifference, selfishness, and irresponsible euphoria create the alibi of a "good conscience," which seeks a logical justification for the doom of others in order to deduce a guarantee of one's own safety.

A handful of passers-by, whose noses are longer than suits the Aryan racial image, are arrested at Vichy, the seat of the government installed by the Germans; after many hours of detention, they are still waiting to be interrogated. For each individual among them the encounter with the bureaucratic machinery of murder becomes a test of himself. The actor Monceau incorrigibly sticks to the logic with which he disproves the danger: "But an atrocity like this is . . . beyond any belief." The painter Lebeau seeks a way out in senseless provocation: ". .. you get tired of believing in the truth. You get tired of seeing things clearly." An old Jew withdraws into silent submission, and a boy defends his small duties to the very last. But even those who realize their doom, take their courage from some fiction: the electrician Bayard, a fighter for the Marxist world order, sees in Hitler a monster of capitalism; for Prince von Berg, a lonely aesthete from Vienna, Hitler is the leader of the proletarian mass movement which dispossessed him. The psychiatrist Leduc loses himself in selfish hopes, which eventually bog down in dull despair: ". . . all this suffering is so pointless—it can never be a lesson, it can never have a meaning. And that is why it will be repeated again and again forever." Indecision causes them to miss the chance of breaking out by force, and the German major in self-contempt fulfills his military duty, which in effect turns him into the stooge of an SS professor. Only two of the group escape the gas chamber. The pass to freedom is granted to the business-man Marchand because he is economically indispensable, and to the melancholy degenerate from Vienna because of his political insignificance. Prince von Berg, however, cedes his pass to Leduc and sacrifices himself in helping the other to escape. Voluntary self-sacrifice is the only way in which Berg can redeem the inner reproach of being safe and, therefore, unconcerned in these dark times. Just then a new lot of doomed men arrives—the automatic mechanism of destruction keeps going.

With the means of the realistic theater—unity of time and place, psychologically analyzed characters and environment—the author at the same time gives us a valid symbol of man exposed to an extreme situation and called on to prove himself in it.

A MEMORY OF TWO MONDAYS. Play in one act. Prose. First edition New York 1955. First performance October 20, 1955, New York, Coronet Theatre. Time: Monday morning "in a bygone year." Place: shipping room of a large automobile warehouse in Manhattan, New York.

Miller's pessimistic psychorealism is in this play shown as social criticism. Two Mondays in an automobile spare-parts warehouse are each the occasion for an inspection by the dreaded supervisor Eagle and thus for decisions on the workers' future. In each we are shown glimpses of the wage slaves' inner life. Dreams and aspirations decay into torpid self-deception for lack of the strength to turn them into reality. Drink, the dullness of daily routine, and the pursuit of cheap eroticism turn the men into robots. Alone among all of them, young Bert manages to go to college with his savings and to build up a better life for himself. It almost seems wrong to him that he should have escaped this place of damnation. He feels that as long as he lives he will still be there in spirit and that everyone who stays on deserves to have a statue put up to him in the park. An empirical study of an environment with the poetic quality of a requiem for human submission.

THE PRICE. Play in two acts. Prose. First edition New York 1968. First performance February 7, 1968, New York, Morosco Theatre. Time: the present. Place: attic in Manhattan.

The x-ray analysis of the past that Miller produced in *After the Fall* with such reckless experimenting with formal means is continued in this play with the most conservative theatrical methods of illusion and psychological subtlety. Two basic attitudes toward life are propounded in terms of the old theme of two hostile brothers. In this play Miller excludes so much that the subject effortlessly observes the unities of time, place, and action. In a manner akin to Ibsen's his analytical probe penetrates buried, repressed strata of the soul. But Miller does not morally censure; he leaves everything in suspense, shows no way out. "It's that everything was always temporary with us. It's like we never were anything, we were always about-to be. . . . I look at my life and the whole thing is incomprehensible to me."

After many years Victor comes back to the scene of his childhood, to the "old lumber" in the attic, the relics of past patrician splendor. It is all to be sold. And it is all saturated with memories—his mother's harp, the foil with which Victor won his first fencing victories. Now he is a police sergeant on the eve of retirement with his thoughts on a secure old age, whereas his wife Esther is still dreaming of some extraordinary future. During the slump of the twenties his father had lost his fortune. To help him, Victor gave up his studies and became an inconspicuous, ordinary official. The consciousness of having done his duty and sacrificed himself had given meaning and justification to his life. And he had never forgiven his brother Walter for living his own life, finishing his studies and taking no responsibility for their father. Walter, a successful surgeon, feels guilty. To justify himself, he demonstrates to Victor that his sacrifice was purposeless and that their father did not need him. He offers his brother a well-paid position, but Victor refuses it. He cannot give up his lifelong self-deception because it was justified and validated by the sacrifice of himself. In life Walter is proved right, the egoist who remained true to himself. He is the active one of the two brothers, he has the courage to do injustice. The chaffering between the brothers about guilt and responsibility is counterpointed by the haggling over the furniture with the veteran dealer Solomon, in whom Miller successfully creates an archetypal figure of oriental cunning.

A VIEW FROM THE BRIDGE. Play in two acts. Prose. First edition New York 1955, second version New York 1957. First performance September 29, 1955, New York, Coronet Theatre. Made into an opera by R. Rossellini, 1962. Time: the present. Place: Eddie Carbone's apartment.

The gripping interplay of social grievances and private jealousy are displayed. The longshoreman Eddie Carbone, a Sicilian immigrant, has two of his cousins staying with him, who have come from Sicily to get their share of the unlimited fleshpots of America but have no residence permit and are being hidden by Carbone from the police. The tensions in the small apartment become intolerable when the happy-go-lucky Rodolfo, the younger of the two newcomers, falls in love with Eddie's niece Catherine. Eddie is passionately devoted to the girl and in his jealousy betrays his more successful rival to the police. Rodolfo's wedding with Catherine is off, but Eddie's passion needs another victim. In self-defense Marco, Rodolfo's brother, has to disarm the raging Eddie and kills him with his own knife. This penny dreadful is redeemed by the desolate background of the waterfront quarters, the wistful balladlike lyricism and the comments of the lawyer Alfieri that frame the action.

## MISHIMA, Yukio (Hiraoka Kimitake)
(Japan, born 1925)

THE DAMASK DRUM (Aya Nô Tsuzumi). One-act Nô Play. Prose. First performance 1955, Tokyo. Translated by Donald Keene in Five Modern Nô Plays, New York, Knopf, and London, Secker & Warburg, 1957. Time: the present. Place: street at third-floor level—a lawyer's office on the left, a fashion salon on the right; Japan.

A contemporary projection of Japan's ancient poetic myths of love and death. The palace gardener of the legend has become a care-worn office attendant, the heartless princess is a client of the fashion dressmaker. The aged office attendant Iwakichi has written no fewer than thirty love letters to the capricious society lady Hanako Tsukioka, whom he has seen from time to time in the fashion salon opposite. His glowing tributes to the "laurel princess of the moon" were never even shown to the spoiled customer; they raise a laugh with the gentlemen and eventually are used to clean combs. At last Hanako is told, as a curiosity, of the old man's passion and is talked into a cruel joke. She sends Iwakichi a damask drum, together with a promise that at the sound of the instrument she will be his. The old man vainly tries to coax a sound out of the textile drum, and in despair jumps out of the window. But his love is so strong that from the other world it produces a resounding drum-roll. Mockingly Hanako pretends to hear nothing, and drives the ghost back into his loneliness. The psychological motivation in no way detracts from the fairy-tale atmosphere, from the magic of the miracle.

# MOBERG, Vilhelm
(Sweden, born 1898)

DOMAREN *[The Judge]*. A tragicomedy in six scenes. Prose. First edition Stockholm 1957. First performance December 28, 1957, Stockholm, Intima Teatern. Time: the present. Place: the imaginary kingdom of Idyllia.

A satirical settling of accounts with a social order is ruled not by justice but by the articles and paragraphs of the law. The young writer Krister Langton returns home after traveling for several years in Italy. He is faced with bankruptcy, because Judge Cunning, a highly respectable man who looked after his interests in his absence, has, covered by powers of attorney, quite legally robbed him of all his property. Langton appeals to the law and to the press; neither can help. Anyone, whether he is a lawyer or a newspaper editor, who takes up the cause of the man to whom this wrong has been done, stands in danger of being put in prison or in a lunatic asylum as a rebel against the established order. Voluptuously the judge relishes the omnipotence of the legal machinery which has reality in its grip. Realistic social criticism is combined with the grotesque intensification of nightmare.

# MOERS, Hermann
(Germany, born 1930)

DER KLEINE HERR NAGEL *[Little Mr. Nagel]*. One-act play. Prose. Acting edition Cologne, Kiepenheuer & Witsch, 1965. First performance October 24, 1964, Frankfurt/Main, Kleines Theater am Zoo. Time: the present. Place: living room at Gülden's.

Moers's characters are the functional skeletons of men and their behavior a typed demonstration of the social crisis. The "haves," well established in their own lack of principles, are confronted by the new generation, the adolescents fighting without compromise for their revolutionary ideals. Between the two, "little Mr. Nagel" kicks against the personal injustice done to him and thereby gets into conflict with the young world reformers.

After six years in jail Nagel, formerly the owner of a printing works and a perfectly harmless citizen like any other, forces his way into the ostentatious luxury apartment of Gülden, the newspaper publisher. The dictator of opinion had once set a trap for Nagel with an alleged order for ambiguous leaflets, and thereupon got rid of him by a political denunciation. Nagel disappeared in jail, Gülden took over the printing works, and his wife pocketed the personal fortune of the vanished printer. Now, all the answer that Nagel can get out of the Güldens is smug mockery, until he pulls out his pistol in exasperation and sets the panic-stricken couple to attack each other. At this moment Ute, the Güldens' daughter, intervenes. For this young fanatical champion of justice Nagel is an idol, the pioneer and martyr of his revolutionary convictions. Chastened, she realizes that the decent little man was merely the accidental victim of scheming greed. Both Nagel and Ute founder on the unrealizable claims of their utopias of justice, while the Güldens, both feet firmly placed in life's baseness, are left in possession of the field and rebuild the hearty façade of respectability.

Even though the subject is never taken further than the clichés of social criticism, certain details are instructive as symptomatic of modern dramaturgy. In scenic interludes, metaphors are repeatedly taken literally and illustrated by means of spontaneous improvisations. The bestial instincts of the Güldens are sometimes whipped up into a lion tamer's turn, and Nagel's humiliations degenerate into a game voluptuously enjoyed. In this way Moers uses certain devices of alogical play, relying for its stresses on pure mime as a means for the psychological interpretation of his tale.

KOLL [Koll]. One-act play. Prose. Written 1962. First edition Cologne 1962. First performance September 26, 1962, Berlin, Tribüne. Time: the present. Place: food store.

As viewed in the perspective of a small grocer's store, the totalitarian regime's accession to power appears as a farce. This changes nothing in the tactics of using false legal phraseology and of crushing identity by brutal violence.

Self-satisfied and without a worry in life, the retailer Vogel is sitting in his shop after closing time and going over his accounts. Then Koll turns up with an empty chest. Full of curiosity, Vogel lets him in, procures him a crowbar, hands him his overalls, and trustfully shows him round the shop. Koll describes his enthusiasm for groceries. From it he deduces his right to take over the store, and forces Vogel to sign a deed of sale and to go through a back-slapping act of transfer in the show window, for the benefit of passers-by. Just when Koll is about to liquidate his "predecessor" in the cellar, Vogel manages to attract a few people by his cries for help, and together they put the opponent to flight. The story and its purported "deeper significance," probability, and abstraction get in each other's way.

ZUR ZEIT DER DISTELBLÜTE *[When the Thistles Bloom]*. One-act play. Prose. First edition Cologne 1962. First performance September 26, 1958, Bochum, Schauspielhaus, and Saarbrücken, Stadttheater. Time: the present. Place: prison yard.

The theme of Sartre's *Huis clos* is developed in *Zur Zeit der Distelblüte* into a model, and prison life made absolute in the form of life imprisonment. Life has lost its soul and become a mechanical drill, but is reborn in a flowering thistle. The purposeless natural process is set against the prison regulations and makes man's imagination flower. In a game, oblivious of all else, he wins freedom and himself. Five prisoners, reduced to mere numbers and deprived of any will of their own, obey the warden's orders and exhaust themselves in meaningless and monotonous activities. No. 3 and No. 5 indulge in unfeasible plans of escape. No. 4 is an opportunist; he comes to terms with the situation, and, having been promoted meal distributor thanks to his bribes, he now longs for a further promotion to world meal distributor. The thistle flower which pushes up through a crack in the wall and renews the prisoners' dreams of freedom, is crushed. The prisoners' hypnotic game of negating and transforming reality has come to an end. Scornfully they take from the warden's hands the keys which inevitably lead only into their own cell. Moers puts the means of the experimental theater and mimic improvisation at the service of the idealistic theater's catharsis, man's faith in a *per aspera and astra*.

## MONTANELLI, Indro
(Italy, born 1909)

I SOGNI MUOIONO ALL'ALBA *[Dreams Die at Dawn]*. Play in two acts. Prose. First edition Milan 1960. First performance November 3, 1960, Milan, Teatro Sant'Erasmo (Ensemble of the Teatro delle Novità). Time: November 3–4, 1956. Place: a room in the Duna Hotel, Budapest.

Contemporary events are documented through a series of individual destinies. Five Italian newspapermen are in Budapest at the time of the failure of the Hungarian uprising, which is crushed by Russian tanks. The star columnist Andrea is deeply upset by the bloodshed of the civil war. His colleague Gianni takes it in stride and busily chases after sensational news, which is good for his career. Alberto and Sergio are Communists and have to adjust their ideals to the bloodstained reality. But "dreams die at dawn": the tender romance between Sergio and the young freedom fighter Anna goes down under a hail of bullets in the street fighting along with a whole people's hopes of freedom and happiness.

## MONTHERLANT, Henry de
(France, born 1896)

THE CARDINAL OF SPAIN *(Le Cardinal d'Espagne)*. Play in three acts. Prose. First edition Paris 1960. First performance December 18, 1960, Paris, Comédie Française. Translated by Jonathan Griffin for production at the Yvonne Arnaud Theatre in Guildford, England, 1968. Time: November 1517. Place: Madrid.

A historical incident serves to demonstrate the counterplay of action and inaction, of political commitment and passive renunciation both leading men into guilt. In Montherlant's own words, this is "the drama of a man who knows that his political achievement is destined to disappear, the drama of ingratitude and disillusionment. Ximenez ultimately dies of hurt sensibility."

Cardinal Francisco Ximenez de Cisneros is Regent and absolute ruler of the Spanish Empire for the sixteen-year-old King Charles, who resides in Flanders. He is so obsessed with his life's work that, at eighty-two, he has become a cruel, malevolent old man, proud never to have yielded to any request all his life and full of icy arrogance. After decades of a life of prayer and mortification of the flesh, during which he gained the reputation of being a saint, he was entrusted by the queen mother, Joanna the Mad, with the highest office of state. Coming from an unworldly life of meditation, the Cardinal for the first time experiences the intoxicating consciousness of the power of authority and the triumph of active achievement. He seems to be drawing new vitality from the smoldering hatred of the court and the universal impatient expectation of his death. The counterpart of this ceaselessly active statesman who sacrifices everything to his purposes, is Joanna, a quarrelsome, blubbering madwoman who maltreats her court, has fits of bestial frenzy, yet then can utter ultimate wisdom in a dreamlike trance. Fear of a life which inevitably implies guilt for a monarch has driven her to take refuge in her hallucinations. "I do nothing, or if I do anything it is with such torments . . . and beyond anything I do is another torment, that there is nothing to do any more, and that is the void." This total abnegation outrages the Cardinal, who does not want to lose the principal figure in his political game of chess. He is angered by this unlived life, which derives its innocence from weakness and omission. Joanna has only pitiful derision for the politician's tireless scheming. She cannot even accept the convenient formula "ad maiorem gloriam Dei," which for centuries has served to cover up so much injustice. God, for her, is the "great nothing." The discussion shakes the Regent's self-assurance. The "voice of truth from the mouth of madness" reawakens his longing for monastic self-obliteration, for ascetic renunciation. He dreams of being fortified by Joanna's blessing. At the same time he is fascinated by the idea of shocking and horrifying the world by bringing the queen to the stake for blasphemy. "I do not want what I love, and I want what I do not love." His abrupt dismissal by the King, whose displeasure he has aroused, brings to an end the Cardinal's life.

Montherlant is concerned not so much with the destiny of an individual, as with the confrontation of existential positions in human relationships. This symbolic presentation nevertheless results in gripping theater and is renewed proof of Motherlant's characteristic gift of creating an exciting tension between sensibility and abstraction.

CELLES QU'ON PREND DANS SES BRAS [Women One Takes in One's Arms]. Play in three acts. Prose. Written 1949. First edition Paris 1950. First performance October 20, 1950, Paris, Théâtre de la Madeleine. Time: the summer of 1949. Place: Ravier's study in Paris.

Three entirely different personalities are confronted in a world without faith. They warm to ideals, and yet when it comes to the point cannot escape their self-centered natures. These cynical self-tormentors are condemned to failure in their own eyes. In all their hopelessness, there remains only the grace that ennobles: the grace of resignation and self-mockery, the sadness of unspent kindness, of conscious self-delusion and the precariousness of all feelings. The art dealer Ravier, an epicure with a surfeit of all the good things of life, woos eighteen-year-old Christine Villancy with all his immense wealth. The unspoiled girl rejects him. Her girl-guide years have left her with a passion for fierce independence and proud virginity. The unaccustomed refusal shakes the vain connoisseur, so that he begins to look on Christine not as a desired woman, but as an understanding human being: "For an instant you opened a door into another world for me. . . . I mean the world of integrity, pride and courage. . . . The intruder in this impeded love affair is Mademoiselle Andriot, an embittered and clever old spinster. She mothers Ravier, who is the sole compensation for her unlived life. Ruthlessly she prods for the truth in this psychological conflict, and that is enough to drive the lovers more and more deeply into prejudice and self-doubt. Financial need puts Christine at Revier's mercy. He goes into raptures at anticipating the generosity with which he will forgo the girl's compulsory "gift of gratitude." But his generosity melts away in desire when the moment arrives. He passionately draws the girl to himself: "There are women one takes in one's arms, and there are others. Nothing can be baser, more common, than the way in which I now take you. But almost everything that is born on earth is born unclean. It comes from the gutter. . . . From now on I shall worship you. I shall awaken in you a delight in love by which I shall kill you, and in which you will die with a blessing for me." The methods of drawing-room comedy are combined with dialectical logic to capture the ambivalence of life with all its unpredictability and predicaments.

CIVIL WAR *(La Guerre civile)*. Play in three acts. Prose. First edition Paris 1965. First performance January 27, 1965, Paris, Théâtre de l'OEuvre. Translated by Jonathan Griffin in *Theatre of War,* Harmondsworth, Penguin, 1967. Time: July 15–17, 48 B.C. Place: Caesar's and Pompey's camps south of Dyrrhachium.

Montherlant takes up a historical vantage point for delivering his disillusioned and sarcastic judgment on the contemporary world's political situation. The Roman Empire is torn by civil war. Two opposing power blocs bestride the civilized world in the name of liberty: "a liberty that will multiply fear, a liberty no one will dare to use. . . . There! Our life will be wasted, and our death will be wasted: it is total disaster." Pompey, the worn, irresolute representative of the Republic, and Julius Caesar, the upstart determined to gain sole power, face each other for the decisive battle—both of them vain poseurs, flirting with their ailments, slaves of their own public image, and having bought their successes with their self-respect: "I don't need people who see clearly, I need people who'll back me. . . . I need enthusiasts—that is, people who don't see clearly." Pompey, an innovator out of sheer indecision, allowed Caesar to come to power by purchasing the latter's repeated assurances of peace by more and more concessions. Around him gather a number of turncoats like the tribune Laetorius and Captain Fannius, who see their financial speculations threatened by Caesar. Others, like Brutus and Cicero, are waverers. Cato, the only disinterested doubter, is an upright man and as such a ridiculous anachronism is resented as a nuisance by both parties. His stirring speech before the battle of Dyrrhachium gains Pompey victory over Caesar, yet Pompey sends him into exile, because he cannot measure up to Cato's uncompromising democratic views. After the victory Pompey's followers busily draw up a blacklist, with the intention of enriching themselves at the expense of their political opponents. Pompey feels his defeat to be imminent and takes refuge in the victor's pride. The chorus gives an unconcerned account of the ruin of all those who are now triumphant. The historical lesson is generalized by means of polished antitheses, in which Montherlant's aristocratic approach seems ready to embrace deGaullism: "Does this minister to his ambitions? Who cares? Does he want the dictatorship? Who cares? Let people stop boring us with platitudes and hoary warnings against dictatorship. A dictatorship is worth what the man is worth. And in fact Caesar's enterprises have always coincided with the good of the people."


THE LAND WHERE THE KING IS A CHILD *(La Ville dont le prince est un enfant)*. Play in three acts. Prose. Written 1951. First edition Paris 1951. First performance December 1967, Paris, Théâtre Michel. Translated by Henry Reed and produced by the British Broadcasting Corporation, 1958. Time: the present. Place: a Catholic boarding school in Paris.

For more than sixteen years Montherlant refused to authorize professional performances of this controversial, austerely poetical work. In this so-called "pure landscape" of the soul, the bewilderment of the heart beset by longings and frustrations, the struggle for love and understanding, dedication and renunciation, come dangerously close to making the play a study of homosexuality. Abbé de Pradts, the master in charge of the "intermediate division" in a boarding school for boys, jealously watches over his favorite pupil, fourteen-year-old Serge Souplier, a gifted but lazy and recalcitrant rascal. He shapes the boy entirely after his own spirit and regards him as his sole achievement. Not only has the Abbé refused a brilliant preferment in Rome in order to stay near the boy, but he also secretly does his homework for him, to cover up his protégé's inadequate scholastic performance, and in general misuses his authority to give preference to his favorite. At the same time the priest tries to hide his affection for the boy as something illicit. To his annoyance he notices that Serge has found a sincere friend, whom he idolizes, in André Sevrais, a pupil two years older who is preparing for the university, a first-rate scholar and dreamy introvert. The Abbé gets other boys to spy and inform on the two friends, confuses them by insinuations and destroys their mutual confidence by making their friendship "official." Yet all these precautions fail to set the Abbé's mind at rest. He still feels betrayed, excluded, and superfluous. Eventually he provokes a scandal, contrives to have Sevrais's matriculation declared invalid and, although his performance has so far been the pride of the whole school, to have him expelled at once. Thanks to his authority as a priest, he convinces Sevrais that this injustice is a necessary sacrifice and extorts from him his word of honor never to see Souplier again in all his life. With relief the master now once more knows himself to be the sole influence in Souplier's life. He wants to take the boy for three weeks to an isolated country house, in order to intensify his education. The principal of the school, Abbé Pradeau de la Halle, warns the master not to "poison things." De Pradts regards himself as an instrument of providence in making others suffer, for what leads man to himself is always life's injustices, humiliations, and bitterness. When the principal expels Souplier in his turn, the master objects desperately and is prepared to renounce his priesthood rather than lose the boy. The principal reminds de Pradts of the purifying power of suffering, which the latter has so far always deliberately imposed only on others. Utterly crushed, de Pradts accepts the sacrifice of renunciation. His superior comforts him with kind words of counsel: "There is another love, M. de Pradts, another love even toward men. If it achieves a certain degree of absoluteness, thanks to its intensity, its permanence, and self-forgetfulness, it comes so close to love of God that one is tempted to say God has made His creatures only to lead us back to Himself."

MALATESTA *(Malatesta)*. Play in four acts. Prose. Written 1943–1944. First edition Lausanne 1946. First performance December 19, 1950, Paris, Théâtre Marigny. Translated by Jonathan Griffin in *The Master of Santiago and Four Other Plays,* New York, Knopf, and London, Routledge, 1951. Time: 1468. Place: Rimini and Rome.

This play is a perfect example of man's zest for living, whether for good or evil, and the tragedy of an individual who goes too far. Very fittingly, this dithyrambic play is set in the Italian Renaissance, when people took their enjoyments with ferocious relish. The central theme is the ambivalence of human existence: every moral judgment evaporates in the face of contradictory historical valuations. Malatesta is a shining hero and a common brawler, the Pope is the kindhearted father of Christendom no less than he is a cruelly scheming princeling and a self-satisfied bigot. Men are at the mercy of their own unpredictability and hence torn by inner conflicts, which are reflected in an era of decline, a time of disjointment.

After a dissolute life, the *condottiere* Sigismondo Pandolfo has become absolute ruler of Rimini. He revels in his own cruelty as much as in his subjects' hatred. Especially do the scholars and scribes, including Porcellio Pandone and Basinio Parmense, resent the usurper's brutal violence and cannot forgive him his exuberant vitality. They are kept like domestic pets at his court, for the purpose of writing his monumental biography which is to proclaim his fame to posterity. At the moment, he is engaged in hostilities with Pope Paul II, and when the Pope makes ready to take Rimini by force, Malatesta in his primitive unconcern plans to settle the conflict quite simply by murdering the Holy Father. But the Pope's cunning is superior to the adventurer's brute force. The Pope puts Malatesta in the wrong, extracts a confession of remorse from him and then, with a generous gesture of Christian forgiveness, appoints him "pontifical *condottiere.*" Unsuspecting, Malatesta is caught in the trap and is pleased at the reconciliation; he is in effect stripped of all his power and left with nothing but the command of the ridiculous Vatican guard. When the truth dawns on him, he cannot accept it with anything like the equanimity of the historian Platina, who knows perfectly well that the Pope's disfavor will soon cost him his life, but calmly goes on concentrating on his studies. Thanks to the diplomatic skill of his wife Isotta, who loyally stands by him in spite of his own numerous infidelities, Malatesta is allowed three months' leave from the Vatican. Back at Rimini, he at once turns with furious energy to plans of revenge. Instead, he is poisoned—by the sycophantic Porcellio, who hopes by this deed to compensate for his lifelong humiliation and self-contempt. With all the hatred of the oppressed he tears up the famous biography in front of the dying Malatesta's eyes, thus destroying the latter's hope of immortality.

THE MASTER OF SANTIAGO (Le Maître de Santiago). Play in three acts. Prose. Written 1945. First edition Paris 1947. First performance January 26, 1948, Paris, Théâtre Hébertot. Translated by Jonathan Griffin in The Master of Santiago and Four Other Plays, New York, Knopf, and London, Routledge, 1951. Time: January 1519. Place: Avila, Old Castile.

Unbending to the point of selfishness, perfectionist to the point of denying reality—this is how Montherlant presents his hero, an aristocratic, hard man answering only to himself. In the religious field, as elsewhere, he seeks to exalt ascetic rigor, self-surrender and voluntary obedience to the strictest law. This is how Montherlant interprets his Master of Santiago: "What is his love of God except love of his own idea of himself? . . . He thanks God for disencumbering him of people. His God is destruction rather than love."

Don Alvaro Dabo has retired to his crumbling castle. He is Master of the once powerful Knightly Order of Santiago, whose only activity now is a monthly meeting for a common meal. Spain, which Alvaro faithfully served in its war of liberation from the Moors, has itself become an oppressor in newly discovered America. When Don Bernal de la Encina wants to win him for a lucrative expedition overseas, Alvaro indignantly refuses to have anything to do with it. For a moment it looks as though a cunning scheme of the courtiers would lead him to change his mind, for the spoil brought home from the proposed campaign is supposed to provide a generous dowry for his daughter Mariana and thus to ensure a happy marriage for her. But Mariana renounces her love for Don Bernal's son and exposes the fraud. Honest to the point of self-sacrifice and arrogant in the strength of their faith, father and daughter withdraw from the temptations of this world behind the walls of a convent: "Let Spain perish, let the universe perish! If I gain my salvation and you yours, every-thing is saved and everything done."

PORT ROYAL *(Port Royal).* Play in one act. Prose. First edition Paris 1954. First performance December 8, 1954, Paris, Théâtre Français. Translated by Jonathan Griffin in *Port Royal and Other Plays,* New York, Hill & Wang, 1962. Time: August 1664. Place: visitors' room in the convent of Port Royal, Paris, Faubourg Saint-Jacques.

This religious play is about the conflict between conscience and obedience. Because the Jansenists believed God's grace alone to be decisive for the salvation of the soul, they were in conflict with the Pope. Pope Alexander VII condemned their proposition, which detracted from the importance of men's striving for the good, and demanded a formal oath of renunciation from all members of the church. The nuns of Port Royal, under the leader-ship of the coadjutrix Mother Cathérine-Agnès de Saint-Paul and of the subprioress Sister Angélique de Saint-Jean, refuses obedience to this order, which the Archbishop of Paris brings to them. The two champions of resistance are relatives of Professor Arnauld of the Sorbonne, himself a leading Jansenist theologian. Sister Flavie, a woman consumed by ambi-tion, who is assigned to be the "tierce" watching over the conversations of her fellow-nuns, reveals to the Archbishop the names of the heads of the resistance, who are thereupon dispersed, with the help of the police, among other strictly orthodox convents. The twelve white-gowned Sisters of Port Royal, martyrs of their faith, are replaced by twelve black-gowned Visita-tion Nuns, fanatical followers of the Pope. This makes a profound im-pression on young Sister Françoise, who has so far lightheartedly and in-differently kept out of the dispute. Full of enthusiasm she rebels against the compulsion and will henceforth be uneasy in her conscience. This is the tragedy of pure hearts which, because they are uncompromising, con-tinually call into question the established order and condemn authority to the offense of being obliged to destroy this rebellious idealism.

# MORAVIA, Alberto (A. Pincherle)
(Italy, born 1907)

THE FANCY DRESS PARTY (La mascherata). Tragicomedy in three acts and a prologue. After the 1941 novel of the same title. Prose. First edition in Teatro, Milan 1958. First performance April 14, 1954, Milan, Piccolo Teatro (Compagnia Stabile). Translated by Angus Davidson, New York, Farrar, Strauss & Young, 1952. Time: the present. Place: an imaginary country ruled by a dictator.

Moravia sets his social satire not, realistically, in today's society, but in a striking, imaginary stage world. The medium thus acquires an independent existence of its own and the luxurious costume drama becomes naively identical with the play's theatrical effects.
General Tereso Arango, the dreaded dictator, attends a fancy dress ball in order to woo Marquesa Fausta Sanchez. The beautiful courtesan sells her favors for lucrative army contracts and plays off her admirers against each other, whether they are kitchen boys or counts. An intricate web of intrigues is woven around the fancy dress ball, replete with jealousy and frivolous play, conspiracies and treason. The aristocratic admirer dresses up as a servant. Fausta falls victim to a pretended attempt on her life organized by the secret police to demonstrate its own indispensability. Sheer theatrical effect is so overdone that the satire is buried by the melodrama.

# MORTIMER, John
(England, born 1923)

THE DOCK BRIEF. Comedy in two scenes. Prose. First edition London 1958. First stage performance (after radio and television productions) April 9, 1958, London, Lyric Theatre, Hammersmith. Time: the present. Place: a prison cell.

Mortimer looks for the paradox in everyday life. By means of the grotesque, he exposes daydreams and disillusionment without detriment to realistic relevance. The "humorous man" of the traditional English comedy of manners is modernized.
Fowle has murdered his wife because he could think of no other way of escaping her infuriating cheerfulness. The unsuccessful lawyer Morgenhall has been detailed for his defense, and the senile incompetent is anxious on this occasion to make the speech of his life, as he has always dreamed

of doing. In preparing his brief, he confuses the facts by quite inappropriate legal tricks, like surprise witnesses and contesting the alibi and the medically certified cause of death, and revels in the intoxication of his imaginary strategy for the trial. But in court he is a complete failure and allows Fowle to be condemned to death without making any counter-arguments. His delusion that he is a misunderstood genius is at last dispelled: "I had lived through that moment so many times. It happened every day in my mind, daydreaming on buses, or in the doctor's surgery. When it came, I was tired of it. The exhaustion came over me. I wanted it to be all over. . . . Being too tired to make my daydream public. . . . I was tired out by the long wait, and when the opportunity came—all I could think of was sleep. . . . So I failed." Fowle wants to cheer the dejected lawyer and feigns admiration for his clever conduct of the case: his intimidating silence during the interrogation, his calculated indifference, his stupefying tactics of creating confusion by ignorance. Fowle is reprieved for the reason that he manifestly had an "old crock" as a defense counsel. Much relieved, Morgenhall sees this as a rehabilitation of his own daydreams and goes on looking forward to a great career.

LUNCH HOUR. One-act comedy. Prose. First edition London 1960. First performance February 14, 1960, Stuttgart, Staatstheater (Kammertheater). Time: the present. Place: a hotel room in London.

The truth behind convention is brought to light by the improvisation of a play within the play and by the white lies of everyday life. While Pirandello shows the gap between truth and reality in tragic relativity, Mortimer takes a moralizing view of it. During the lunch hour "the man" and his employee meet in a seedy station hotel, where they hope to give fulfillment to their love which so far has not been able to flower in the hectic business atmosphere. For the sake of the garulous manageress, they have to pretend that they are married and spontaneously improvise conjugal domesticity. In the course of this, the man's selfishness and unkindness become so obvious that the girl is startled out of her illusions and leaves him.

TWO STARS FOR COMFORT. Play in two acts. Prose. First edition London 1962. First performance April 4, 1962, London, Garrick Theatre. Time: the present. Place: a bar in Sam Turner's riverside hotel.

A tragicomical everyday romance revolves around a failing master in the art of living, who wants to please everyone and with his indiscriminate complaisance disappoints his girl friend's trust: "You can't just give people what they want because it's easy to see their grateful faces." The retired lawyer Sam Turner thoroughly enjoys his cheerful existence as a hotel keeper in the provinces. Every summer a few young couples stay with him for the regatta and fill the house with their noisy gaiety. Sam is a splendid host, always ready to join in the fun and never averse to a little flirtation. This time he befriends the student Ann Martin and bestows his love on her, the ugly wallflower. His wife feels that this is the end and sues for divorce. The old barman Drake, whom Sam in his kindness has been training for victory in the "Golden Sculls," is defeated on Regatta Day. The hotel's creditors are getting insistent. Sam has formed a deep attachment for Ann and hopes to begin a new life with her. But in his anxiousness to oblige everyone he is himself so helpless that he cannot protect the girl from the mockery of the others. Ann leaves him, and for the first time in his life Sam grasps the naked truth about himself.

## MORUCCHIO, Umberto
(Italy, born 1893)

METALLURGICHE TISCORNIA [Tiscornia Armory]. Comedy in three acts. Prose. First published in Teatro-Scenario XVIII, No. 6, August 1954. First performance November 3, 1953, Savona, Teatro Reposi. Time: the present. Place: an industrial town in northern Italy.

This is a social satire which cunningly plays the ideals of the class struggle against the reality of business life. A malevolent destiny has presented Maffeo Tiscornia with the unhappy lot of being a modern factory owner. If he wants to dismiss a drunken, incompetent workman, he is told by the trade union that the man is a "national hero" of the resistance who cannot be dismissed. If he is pressed to meet an important delivery date, the workers, all enthusiastic Communists, invariably happen to go on strike just then in sympathy with some political incident or other in darkest Africa. Exhausted, Tiscornia gives up the management; he turns over the armaments works to the staff, along with the related responsibilities. Henceforth he plans to contribute only as an adviser, a simple employee among all the new owners. In a rush of pacifist enthusiasm the workers at once convert the factory to the production of agricultural machinery. A lucrative armaments order from America soon puts an end to these ethical good intentions. But the about-face fails to produce the expected golden blessing. Shocked by the Communist joint ownership, the Wall Street strategists cancel the order. Within a year aimless management and mutual suspicions ruin the business. The proud owners at the work bench react to the trading loss by cutting down wages and implore Tiscornia to take back his dubious gift. In the end he generously yields to their entreaties.

## MOSEL, Tad
(United States, born 1922)

ALL THE WAY HOME. Play in three acts. Based on the autobiographical novel *A Death in the Family* by James Agee. Prose. First edition New York 1961. First performance November 30, 1960, New York, Belasco Theatre. Time: May 1915. Place: in and around Knoxville, Tennessee.

This play shows man between love and death, temptation and loneliness in a psychologically subtle representation of middle-class family life. Mosel's psychorealism, his mosaic of banalities, proves to be deliberate dramatic design and his understatement a gesture of respect for elementary reality: "People fall away from us, and in time, others grow away from us. That is simply what living is, isn't it?"
Even in his marriage with Mary, Jay Follet has preserved his liberty to disappear suddenly and to have a good time in unknown inns along the open road. This world of dreams and chance encounters is closed to Mary. The life of the family bubbles along, without disturbance, without problems, seemingly safe for eternity. The family goes to call on great-grandmother and each emotionally takes leave of the centenarian. Jay is trying to give his son Rufus a liberal education and is looking forward to the expected new baby. There are small excitements and small joys, many conversations with relatives, some crossness with Jay's brother Ralph, a drunkard. Ralph calls Jay to their father's bedside, self-importantly pretending that the old man is seriously ill; Jay is killed in a car accident on his way. Her misfortune drives Mary into a religious crisis and gives little Rufus an opportunity to boast to his playmates that "My daddy's dead!" Life goes on, after its own fashion. But for Mosel what is triumphant is life itself in all its gaiety—a far cry from the optimistic pedagogics of the usual American psychotherapeutic play.

## MROŻEK, Sławomir
(Poland, born 1930)

THE MARTYRDOM OF PETER O'HEY (*Meczenstwo Piotra O'Heya*). Play in three parts. Prose. Written 1959. First performance 1959, Cracow, Teatr Groteska. Translated by Nicholas Bethell in *Six Plays*, New York, Grove Press, 1967. Time: the present. Place: O'Hey's apartment.

A grotesque caricature of modern man's existence. O'Hey is literally torn to pieces by the ruthless institutions of modern civilization, by bureaucracy, science, the arts, politics, and the welfare system. He is ruined by what was originally meant for his protection. At the same time the author builds up a bitter symbol of the spread of power; the humble citizen goes along hesitantly with things so as to be left in peace, but precisely this reluctant acquiescence leads to his ultimate downfall. Peter O'Hey, an honest, ordinary citizen and *pater familias*, placidly endures his wife's babbling and reads his paper as usual. An official comes to announce that a tiger is hiding in O'Hey's bathroom. O'Hey would be only too glad to shrug off this obvious nonsense, but nonsense given validity by the authorities becomes an ordinance to be obeyed. His protests are silenced when even his youngest son is infected by the psychosis and declares that he has seen the animal. O'Hey admits its existence in the hope of thus finally settling this tiger story. This first step gives rise to increasingly strict demands on the part of the authorities and O'Hey's life becomes more and more restricted. A tax collector appears, and after him a scientific expert, a circus manager with his following, an old Siberian "leatherstocking," an Indian Maharaja; for all of them the tiger is a pretext for settling in with O'Hey. To the sound of horns, hunters roam through the apartment with their hounds. As the animal never appears, everybody grows more and more irritated with O'Hey. At the instigation of the Indian, who has been given a free hand by the authorities for political reasons, O'Hey eventually has to sit in the bathtub as a living bait. When even this expedient fails, he is shot by the trigger-happy hunters.

OUT AT SEA *(Na pełnym Morzu)*. One-act play. Prose. First performance 1961, Cracow, Teatr Stary. Translated by Nicholas Bethell in *Six Plays,* New York, Grove Press, 1967; under the title *At Sea,* translated by Maia Rodman, produced April 23, 1962, New York, Mermaid Theatre. Time: the present. Place: a raft at sea.

In this grotesque drama the author provides a haunting symbol for the abuse of power and the dubious attempts at justifying the abuse. On the high seas a raft drifts, carrying three elegantly dressed survivors of a shipwreck, the Fat One, the Small One, and the Medium One. The last can of veal and peas has gone, and as tactfully as possible the three gentlemen now hint to each other that one of them will have to be slaughtered. Clearly the Small One, being the least able to defend himself, will be the first to be eaten. Led by the Fat One, they begin the minuet of excuses by which mankind eternally tries to gloss over the right of the stronger, the abuse of power. Each pleads his point of view in emotional election speeches and vainly tries to falsify the vote. The Fat One hits upon a sentimental approach as an effective means of pressure: he declares himself and the Medium One to be poor orphans, whose unmerited misfortune can be mitigated only by turning the Small One into sausages. A mailman, puffing and blowing, swims up to the raft with a telegram attesting that the Small One has just been orphaned. Now the Fat One marshals "historic justice": given that he is a lumberman's son, he has a clear right to take a knife to the Small One who comes from a white-collar family. Again reality disproves his argument: a chauffeur emerges from the sea and obsequiously reveals the Fat One to be a count. Eventually the Fat One gets his way with massive brutality. The Small One, in his turn, discovers the pride of those about to die: if "ordinary freedom" has long vanished under the compulsion of dictatorship, man still has the "true freedom" to yield and to howl with the wolves. He determines to die not as a passive victim, but as a hero. In his helplessness he intoxicates himself with a handful of slogans which the Fat One generously offers him, and goes to the slaughter as a "glorious example of selflessness," as a "voluntary sacrifice for the community." At once something like envy comes over the Fat One: he senses a dedicated happiness which even the most luscious dish of human meat cannot confer upon the cannibal.

THE POLICE (Policja). Play in three acts. Prose. Written 1958. First performance June 27, 1958, Warsaw, Teatr Dramatyczny. Translated by Nicholas Bethell in Six Plays, New York, Grove Press, 1967; under the title The Policemen, adapted by Leonidas D-Ossetynski, produced November 21, 1961, New York, Phoenix Theatre. Time: the present. Place: an imaginary dictatorship.

This satire on the absolute police state fits all institutions, not only those of the Eastern bloc, that transgress their subordinate function of keeping order and degenerate into an end in itself. The state's only prisoner suddenly retracts his political opposition and after ten years of imprisonment turns into the Regent's most zealous adherent. As a loyal citizen he has to be released. Since, as everybody vociferously proclaims, there are none but completely happy citizens under this peace-loving, just system, no punishable political or criminal acts are to be expected in the future. The police apparatus, hitherto the most powerful institution in the state, is out of work and hence unnecessary. The police sergeant in disguise roams through the streets as an *agent provocateur,* but can find no victim. Instead, he is beaten up by the angered populace all faithfully following the official line. Gone are the good old days when he first met his wife: "It is a long time ago. He denounced me, I denounced him, and so we met. . . ." Under orders from the Commissioner of Police, the sergeant himself must insult the state by assassinating someone. He is arrested and provides the police regime with an alibi. The former prisoner, now a happy convert to loyalty to the government, has in the meantime risen to become the General's Adjutant and expert for subversive activities. A round of mutual arrests sets in: the Commissioner of Police is arrested because he over-hastily released the Adjutant, and the Adjutant because he did not prevent the assassination. In the end even the Regent is detained, because he recklessly exposed himself to such a danger: "The police has its hands full." The distinguishing feature of Mrożek's style are the quick climax, the explosive cabaret form, and the division into separate numbers; clearly, the author has not departed from his one-act techniques in this, his first full-length play.

STRIPTEASE *[Striptease]*. One-act play. Prose. Written 1961. First published in *Dialog*, 1961. First performance 1961, Warsaw, Teatr Współczesny. Time: the present. Place: an empty room.

While in his one-act play *Out at Sea* Mrożek with mordant mockery exalted the collapse of the individual in the face of violence as "true freedom," in *Striptease*, he takes up the same problem in terms of the contrast between "inner and outer freedom."
Two gentlemen are most ungently thrown onto the empty stage. After the first shock, they excitedly try to make out what this inexplicable occurrence may mean. They were busily pursuing their customary occupations, undeterred by the fog—when suddenly they were collared, maltreated, and propelled into this bare room. The first gentleman is an amateur philosopher and chooses "inner freedom." He prefers to remain a prisoner of this situation, rather than to take any action and by action become a "prisoner of his own making." For every action, once done, destroys the liberty to choose another alternative. His companion in misfortune wears himself out in futile attempts to get out of this dilemma. A giant hand appears and, bit by bit, strips the two men of all their clothing, chains them together, and blindfolds them. While the two still argue whether the mounting catastrophe has been provoked by the inactivity of the one or the vain attempts to escape of the other, they are both dragged offstage by the hand. Thus Heidegger's formulations about men being thrown into the world and being under a hand there are taken literally and distilled into a dramatic nightmare.

TANGO *(Tango)*. Play in three acts. Prose. First performance May 1965, Warsaw, Teatr Współczesny. Translated by Nicholas Bethell and Tom Stoppard, London, Cape, 1968. Time: the present. Place: a room.

As always, Mrożek exaggerates social phenomena and, by taking their logic literally, reduces it *ad absurdum*. In *Tango* the conflict of the generations is simultaneously trebled and broadened into a conflict of ideologies. Youth can affirm itself only in rebelling against tradition. But since we have by now had three successive generations of avant-gardists and eternal iconoclasts drunk with hollow proclamations, the competition for originality at all costs becomes more and more fierce.

The parents, the doggedly experimental artist Stomil and his frivolous wife Eleonore, have dispensed with all spiritual and moral standards. Proudly they live with absolute freedom in an anarchical way of life: "rebellion, that is progress in its potential phase." The tango, which they once introduced as a revolutionary novelty, was the emblem of universal licentiousness. Grandma Eugenia and Uncle Eugene have, like everyone else, accepted the "compulsion of immortality." In token of their emancipation, these two good folk, bourgeois respectability personified, play cards with a suspiciously unkempt individual called Edek, Eleonore's lover.

Arthur, the son, reaches the conclusion that, since "nothing is no longer possible, just because everything is possible," he must first create a world order so that he can derive from it his right to revolt against it. He wants to create "significance" and to introduce order into the jumble of incidentals. Thus he demands a return to rules and social conventions. As a protest against free love, he proposes to marry his cousin Ala, strictly according to old-fashioned custom. His parents are forced to perform a formal ceremony, complete with tails and a long dress with a train, hand-kissing and grandmotherly blessing, tears of maternal emotion, and a solemn photograph as a keepsake. Arthur has to admit that these clichés amount to no new reality. Eventually he discovers in dictatorships the long-sought-for system that represents "rebellion in the form of order." Murder, so he realizes in a flash of genius, is the infallible means of turning the utopia of slogans into fearful reality. Edek, who has already been helping Arthur as a butler in renewing the conventions, eagerly puts himself at his disposal for more bloodthirsty tasks. And then Arthur finds out that Ala is unfaithful to him. She felt debased as the guinea pig of an ideology and found consolation with Edek. Jealous, Arthur wants to shoot his rival, but is killed by Edek. The latter now takes over Arthur's system in his own way and terrorizes the family. The new tyranny accedes to power with an elaborate tango. Overdone sophistry alternates with theatrical excitement.

# MÜLLER, Heiner, and MÜLLER, Inge
(both Germany; Heiner, born 1929; Inge, born 1925)

DIE KORREKTUR [The Correction]. Play in five scenes with prologue and epilogue. Prose and verse. First edition Berlin 1959. First performance on the professional stage May 15, 1958, East Berlin, Maxim Gorki Theatre. Time: 1956. Place: an industrial combine in East Germany.

Abuses and defects in industry provide the theme of this object lesson for workers of all kinds. The prologue recalls the reconstruction situation in Heiner Müller's play *Der Lohndrücker* [The Sweatshop]: "You saw how it was in 1949:/ the beer thin, tobacco scarce,/ produce more was the order of the day./ But he first was bitten by the dogs." Then comes a fade-in to a further stage in the process of socialist reconstruction, seven years later. The individual sweatshop has become a collective, the work-brigade a combine. "We show how one brigade out of a thousand/ (and not the best) learned by trial and error. . . . We are the others, unknown by name,/ but indispensable for the good result . . . Unknown doers of great deeds." The question is always to win outsiders for the overriding aims of the party. "We can afford to build socialism even with people not interested in socialism. That's as far as we've got. We can't dispense with them. We can't yet go as far as that. And when we can, it won't be necessary any more, because then they will be interested in socialism."
Bremer, the activist, takes over the leadership of a run-down brigade. Any shortage of the output target is made good by means of false entries in the records. Faulty planning results in unproductive waiting periods and loss of earnings. Discord between the workers and the engineers holds up the work flow. "The major," a former officer of the thousand-year Reich downgraded to bricklayer in the workers' state, introduces Bremer to the swindle of "output juggling": "What we don't produce on the site, we produce on paper." The new brigade leader refuses to go along and is removed. Foundations are laid with badly mixed concrete and they settle. Bremer is responsible and is to be penalized. Thereupon a young workman admits that the collective is to blame. The major with his inflammatory speeches is expelled, and they see the need for working together: "We snatch the new world/ out of the old one that's dying,/ on every building site between the Hwang-Ho and the Elbe,/ with ax and steam shovel, with spade and crane,/ cursing and stumbling, but never stopping,/ left, left in the march of five-year plans." The prologue and the epilogue in verse, quotations from letters, and discussions are combined in a montage with acted scenes.

## NASH, N. Richard
(United States, born 1916)

THE RAINMAKER. Comedy in three acts. Prose. First edition 1954. First performance October 29, 1954, New York, Cort Theatre. Time: "a summer day in a time of drought." Place: the living room of the Curry ranch and the sheriff's office in a western state of the United States.

This play of thirsty fields and thirstier souls in a sun-parched landscape is borne along by poetry and solid realism. What triumphs is not the escape into the rainmaker's fantasies, but the sober matter-of-factness of everyday life. A long heat wave has dried up the Currys' ranch. The adventurer Bill Starbuck offers to charm up some rain in return for a hundred dollars. In their plight the family enter into his nonsense with some amusement. While Bill gets his hocus-pocus going, he exercises a genuine charm on Lizzie, the sadly fading daughter of the house. The rainmaker tells her: "You don't believe in nothin'—not even in yourself. You don't even believe you're a woman. And if you don't, you're not." For him, Lizzie is the fairy-tale Melisande, whom he tenderly leads to believe that she is beautiful and desirable. For the first time in her life Lizzie finds herself courted. But she decides against Bill and for the rough heartiness of deputy sheriff File. To his utter amazement Bill witnesses a sudden downpour and for once in his life he can go on his way with honestly earned money.

## NEMETH, László
(Hungary, born 1901)

GALILEI [Galilei]. Historical drama in four acts. Prose. Written 1953. First published in Történeti Drámak, Vol. 1, Budapest 1956. First performance October 20, 1956, Budapest, National Theatre. Time: 17th century. Place: Rome.

From Brecht to Broszkiewicz, East European playwrights have taken the dilemma of Copernicus and Galilei as a metaphor for a world in which truth is not allowed to coincide with reality. The individual's freedom comes into conflict with the prefashioned institutional model, disinterested scholarship with political purpose. There is no solution to the dilemma of surrender through submission and compromise with the lie, or paying for one's convictions with death.

Galilei is called to account by the Holy Office in Rome. He has confirmed Copernicus' discovery that the earth revolves around the sun and has elaborated it in a formal theory. The scholar is surrounded by violence and incomprehension, is spied upon and eventually tortured to the point of denying his knowledge. Galilei has thus saved his life, but must pay for it with doubts and self-contempt: "The spirit of science is like the fears of men, unfortunately, indivisible. It is difficult to prune it like a shrub at one place and to let it grow at another." The counterpart of the ruined scholar torn by self-reproaches is Cardinal Barberini, the brother of Pope Urban VIII, a practical politician who takes reality as he finds it and accepts it in order to transform it: "I do not examine the Holy Father's decisions with a view to discovering whether I can agree with them; rather I try to find out how—in full compliance with Christian and brotherly obedience—I can manage to carry them out with least damage."


AZ UTAZÁS [The Journey]. Comedy in four acts. Prose. Written 1962. First published in Mai témák, Budapest 1963. First performance May 11, 1962, Budapest, National Theatre. Time: the present. Place: the small town of Küngösd in Hungary.

An admirably frank exposition of men's conflicts of conscience under a totalitarian regime. This play is significant of the "thaw" in Hungary a few years ago and of the new tendency to self-criticism and open discussion. The secondary school teacher Jószef Karádi was dismissed years ago for political reasons and downgraded to a petty official. By chance he took part in a delegation which made a trip to Russia. After his return the inhabitants of the small town are most anxious to hear what he has to report. But his descriptions are at once rewritten by the newspaper into Communist paeans, while his friends, secret opponents of the regime, find his objective attitude much too close to the party line and begin to suspect him. The conflict seems to be spreading to his own family, to his daughter Margit and son-in-law István. The party secretary Forgács tries by low journalistic tricks to exploit the situation of the homecomer for political purposes. And all around is the busy tribe of opportunities, whose vociferous communism is rewarded by the party with lucrative posts, but who at the same time would be reluctant to do without a despised and politically persecuted figure like Karádi as a sop to their good conscience.

## NEVEUX, Georges
(France, born 1900)

LA VOLEUSE DE LONDRES *[The Thief of London]*. Play in two acts. Prose. First edition Paris 1961. First performance April 9, 1960, Amsterdam, Stadsschouwburg. Time: the end of the eighteenth century to the beginning of the nineteenth century. Place: London.

This is a frivolous comedy about scoundrels and a purposeful attack on the middle-class moral code. Teddy is a cashier of such touching honesty and correctness that he is quite unsuited to a different sort of "professional" life. His wife Pamela has to provide for them being a pickpocket and confidence trickster. She has, as a "rich widow," successfully caught the apparently equally well-to-do M. Beltram in her net, and plans to fleece him thoroughly. But then he, too, turns out to be a marriage imposter. The mutual disappointment of the swindled swindlers kindles true love between them, without detriment to their professional morals. Pamela develops into a peerless prima donna of her nimble-fingered trade. She amasses a fortune and prudently invests it in America. The abandoned Teddy is no good even as a thief; with his incorrigible honesty the best he can do is to be an informer. Out of jealousy he denounces the two swindlers to the police. The gallows looms menacingly close when the police chief, one of Pamela's dubious acquaintances, remembers his duty as a *deus ex machina* and sends the pair off into the country of unlimited possibilities. There is nothing to stop them now from stepping over the border into bourgeois respectability. This is sophisticated theater spiced with lyrics, elements of the ballet, and many an impertinently charming borrowing from world literature. In range it is between Gay's *Beggar's Opera* and Anhouilh's *Thieves' Carnival*.

## NICOLAJ, Aldo
(Italy, born 1920)

LA CIPOLLA *[The Onion]*. Comedy in two parts. Prose. First published in *Il Dramma*, No. 342, March 1965. First performance April 30, 1962, Vienna, Kleines Theater der Josefstadt in Konzerthaus. Time: the present. Place: Piero's study, Italy.

The claims of the standardized welfare society cause the individual to disintegrate into a confusion of contradictory aspects. He must live his life not as a personality, but as the impersonator of varying roles. Like an

onion the theatrical producer Piero peels himself off in layers when, determined to commit suicide, he looks back upon his life. The past is shown
in flashbacks. All his life Piero was exploited by his environment. As an
individual, he was allowed to represent only whatever corresponded to
the others' selfish demands on him. Because he loved Bianca, he helped
her to a career on the stage, provided her with all the luxuries of life and
helped even her impudent braggart of a brother, Mimmo. It turns out
that dear brother was in fact Bianca's lover, who is quite prepared, for
suitable compensation, of course, to allow the aging patron his customary
tender hours. Disconsolately, Piero looks for comfort with his family. His
wife Giulia has no other use for him than his paying the bills of her life
of luxury. His son Nando, a student of psychology full of scientific conceit,
proves his father's failure statistically. Piero's daughter Lisa has nothing
in her head except sport and flirtations. Piero is on the point of shooting
himself, when he learns that Mimmo has left Bianca for Giulia. Overjoyed Piero, the temporary makeshift, returns to his Bianca and gives up
the idea of a melodramatic death. Like Félicien Marceau, Nicolaj uses
metaphysical and alienation effects for effective theater.


IL MONDO D'ACQUA [The World of Water]. Play in two acts. Prose.
First published in Il Dramma, No. 306, March 1962. First performance
May 28, 1963, Vienna, Volkstheater. Time: the present. Place: a town in
Italy.

With a light hand and infectious exuberance the author mixes the most
contrasting elements—from the impulsive realism of Italian family life
through a satirical parody of office affairs to the poetically surrealist ending of a fairy tale—to make effective theater out of the defeat of a dreamer
who refuses to be forced into the straitjacket of a mechanized, disillusioned world ruled by bustling utilitarianism. "I wanted to get away, far
away, from everything that is ugly and bad in this world. I wanted to be
free, free. . . . But now, now my life is just the same, and how can I change
it? I'm left only with dreams. . . ." Young Celestino Viola has dreamed
of the "world of water" ever since he was a child—the free, windswept life
of a fisherman on the sea. But his ordinary, practical family pushes him
into the secure job of a minor employee and, purposefully inconsiderate,
takes as its own due the time-payment comforts of the Joneses—complete
with television, refrigerator, and washing machine. The ubiquitous solicitude for his well-being with which all of them are allegedly concerned
allows of no contradiction and condemns Celestino to helpless compliance.
He gladdens the lonely evenings of Mattea, his woman colleague at the
office, and lets himself be talked into marrying the calculating Amelia, who

is already pregnant. He cannot realize even the modest dream of making his life a little more tolerable by fishing on Sunday. His environment firmly insists that it is his duty to be happy. Eventually Celestino has had enough. He transforms himself, perhaps, into a goggle-eyed goldfish, the pride of the aquarium—in one moment he is gone, and, for the first time able to follow the vital laws of the "world of water." The disconsolate family, deprived of the useful goldfish with his possible salary rise and pension rights, is left with only an abandoned umbrella.

## OBALDIA, René de
(France, born 1918)

JENUSIA *(Genousie)*. Comedy in two acts. Prose. First edition Paris 1960. First performance September 26, 1960, Paris, Théâtre Récamier. Translated by Donald Watson, in *Jenusia and Seven Impromptus for Leisure*, London, Calder & Boyars, 1965. Time: the present. Place: drawing room in a castle.

The well-tried devices of society theater—romantic castles, drawing-room conversation, a triangular situation around a beautiful stranger from the musical comedylike country of Jenusia—are applied in the style of the grotesque Theater of the Absurd, and ultimately given a neat psychological motivation. It remains uncertain whether this is meant to be a literary experiment or a parody of the "endgames" of modern playwrights. The interplay of identities is externalized and presented as a crude joke involving changes of costume.

Madame de Tubéreuse annually gives an extravagant party at her castle. This time everybody's attention centers on the dramatist Philippe Hassingor and his young wife Irene, who comes from remote Jenusia and hardly speaks a word of French (or any other language that the others know) and hence becomes negligible for human contacts. Her incomprehensible gibberish makes all the others feel understood and right without contradiction. Irene and the young lyric poet Christian Garcia are gripped by a sudden mutual passion. Officiously the hostess arranges a duel with the betrayed husband, in which the latter is shot by Christian. The guests quickly put on fancy-dress and make a game of it. Madame de Tubéreuse dresses up as a nurse, Professor Vivier as a Napoleonic general, the organist Jonathan as a monk. Love has endowed Irene with the gift of intelligible speech, and at once the lovers quarrel and are chastened. Hassingor revives and is glad to return to his wife. Christian finds himself disowned by the party, stripped of his identity and menaced by the conceptual chaos of mutilated phrases; he runs amok. A fade-in takes us back to the drawing room small talk of the beginning. Madame de Tubéreuse suggests playing theater this time, and improvising a sort of "pocket western" in which Hassingor is to be shot. In happy anticipation the parts are distributed and Christian once more feels carried away by the course of events.

WIND IN THE BRANCHES OF SASSAFRAS *(Du vent dans les branches de sassafras)*. Play in two acts. Prose and rhymed verse. First edition Paris 1966. First performance: first version February 17, 1965, Brussels, Théâtre de Poche; second version November 29, 1965, Paris Théâtre Gramont. Translated by Donald Watson, London, Calder & Boyars, 1967. Time: early nineteenth century. Place: living room at the Rockefellers' in Kentucky.

The mass consumption of products of the tear-jerker industry and well-tried cinematic clichés are combined, sometimes forcibly, in a quodlibet. The mass public's latent expectations are transposed into penetratingly voluptuous and titillating situations with which everyone can identify: the joys and sufferings of love, the conflict of the generations, complexes and the supercomplex of avoiding complexes, self-sacrifice and heroic renunciation all serve as a pretext for outré cabaret.

John Emery Rockefeller, the patriarch with a powerful command of vituperative language, repulses an attack by the Comanche Indians with the help of his clan made up of the most contrasting types. He is also helped by the warm-hearted harlot Miriam, with the nickname "Bull's Eye," who in noble self-sacrifice paralyzes the art-appreciative savages with a strip-tease act, apparently meets an "elegiac death" and eventually has a respectable conjugal idyll with the drunken quack and medicinal mass murderer, who had fled the district. All the others are allowed to assume the part of saviors. For the benefit of her family, Rockefeller's daughter Pamela is prepared to give herself to the devilish Indian, Lynx Eye, and is saved from this fate worse than death by the shining hero Carlos. Even Rockefeller's son Tom, the scoundrel, is seen to have become a criminal only to thwart the much more scoundrelly Calder gang. In this parody of tragedy and tear-jerker, arias and rhymed epic are combined and made effective by the rhythms of forced choreography and calculated tableau effects.

## O'CASEY, Sean
(Ireland, 1880–1964)

THE BISHOP'S BONFIRE. A sad play with the tune of a polka in three acts. Prose. First edition London 1955. First performance February 28, 1955, Dublin, Gaiety Theatre. Time: the present, an evening in autumn. Place: the village of Ballyoonagh in the Irish Republic.

Councillor Reiligan and the Very Reverend Timothy Canon Burren rule their parish with the merciless whip of puritanism. To welcome the bishop on his visit to his home town, they arrange for a "great bonfire" of "bad books and evil pictures on top of it"—books that do not shun the obscene word "love" and sinful roses, too, all for the purification of the soul. By this Pharisaism Reiligan's two daughters Keelin and Foorawn are cheated of their love. Keelin renounces Daniel's cheerful poverty, and Foorawn is drawn to the convent, but is killed by her disappointed lover Manus. Father Boheroe, the rough but well-meaning village priest, vainly tries to save joy and humanity in this world of self-righteous pride.

Unconcerned with such things as dramatic style and construction, O'Casey just turns the pages of his zestful Irish picture book: the humor of tramps and servants, social theory, satire on the clergy, the melodrama of love with a tragic ending, Irish folklore, and Gaelic fairy tales all make their own artless effects regardless of literary form and structure. He also shows a grimly humorous defense of the liberty and happiness of ordinary life, which are so often sacrificed to slogans and bigotry.


## ODETS, Clifford
(United States, 1906–1963)


THE COUNTRY GIRL. Eight scenes. Prose. First edition New York 1951. First performance November 10, 1950, New York, Lyceum Theatre. Time: the present. Place: a theater in New York.

The problems of marriage and the claims of the theatrical profession are sharply drawn and contrasted in a context of social criticism by this psychological study of theater life. The actor Frank Elgin has quickly ruined his successful career by dipsomania. After ten years of involuntary absence from the stage, he is suddenly offered a big part by the director Bernie Dodd. Bernie is determined to give Frank the chance of a comeback. His sympathy is gained by Frank's complaints about his wife Georgie, a wearingly hysterical country girl, whose excesses, he says, have caused all his misfortunes. Bernie drives away Georgie, this evil spirit in Frank's life. But the actor takes to the bottle again and endangers the whole production. Bernie realizes that Georgie in fact sacrifices herself in selfless loyalty and has been slandered by her psychopathic husband. Bernie and Georgie become fond of each other, but renounce their chance of happiness—Frank has now achieved his first success and needs the simple country girl more than ever if he is to keep that evening's promise. The play is a stunt, which dresses up its tendency to melodramatic effects as psychological astuteness.

## O'NEILL, Eugene
(United States, 1888–1953)

HUGHIE. One-act play. Prose. Written 1941. First edition New Haven 1959. First performance September 21, 1958, Stockholm, Kungliga Dramatiska Teatern. Time: the present, at night. Place: lobby of a small hotel in New York.

When the seedy *bon vivant* Erie Smith returns to his lodgings in a shabby hotel after a few nights of hard drinking, he finds a new night clerk. Being afraid of the loneliness of his miserable room, he looses a hectic flow of speech. He was a friend of Hughie, the former night clerk, who had been at the hotel for many years before he died. To that ordinary little man, Erie had been able to talk big to his heart's content, despite his failure in life. In those few minutes of nightly conversation at the reception desk, Erie believed himself to be a shrewd Broadway tycoon admired and feared by all. The new clerk retires behind a screen of indifferent courtesy, while he lets his imagination pursue the meaning of the dark city's noises. Erie is just about to give up and stop his vociferous boasting, when the clerk reveals a shy interest in gambling. Now Erie gets going again in full spate; he plays dice with the clerk, thoroughly cheats him, and gets carried away by this manipulated stroke of luck, which obviously presages a brilliant future.

Once more we find a man locked in the illusionary world of his dreams and longings. O'Neill's basic theme has found its most concise expression in this sharply outlined monologue.

THE ICEMAN COMETH. Play in four acts. Prose. Written 1939. First edition New York 1946. First performance October 9, 1946, New York, Martin Beck Theatre. Time: the summer of 1912. Place: bar and back room at Harry Hope's waterfront saloon, New York.

Like Ibsen, O'Neill battles against the falsehoods of life. He accepts the cheap illusions, the opiates of the lower-middle class, because they alone bring consolation and reassurance into a time that has lost all gods and standards: "They manage to get drunk, by hook or by crook, and keep their pipe dreams, and that's all they ask of life. I've never known more contented men."

Every year Hickey celebrates his birthday with rounds of drinks at Harry Hope's Bar, which has become home to a handful of down-and-outers. An ignominiously degraded police lieutenant, an intellectual has-been, several cashiered officers, and a jobless circus man dream themselves into an illusionary world of unattainable hopes, talk big of their plans, and lose themselves more and more in drink and hallucinations. This time Hickey makes "Iceman Death" a guest in the usual company. He forces each of his pals to try to make his pipe dream real. All of them fail him, like Harry, who believes he has it in him to be a successful politician and must now admit that he can't cope even with the traffic in the street. Hickey is satisfied, for all he wanted was to make his friends face reality and to destroy their crippling illusions. A fanatic for truth, he is convinced that proper self-appraisal is bound to confer true happiness on these dipsomaniacs. But they are disenchanted, fed up with life, and hopeless. They learn that Hickey has shot his wife. He freed himself by a deed of violence from the life-long remorse and sense of guilt which accumulated in him by his wife's unswerving and loving forgiveness. Relieved, he now waits for the sentence. Only Larry Slade, a one-time syndicalist-anarchist disappointed by his ideals, and young Don Parritt, who betrayed his mother to the police for money, gain freedom—in death. All the others relapse into drink and illusions. The author paints on a broad canvas with social compassion and subtle psychological shades.

LONG DAY'S JOURNEY INTO NIGHT. Play in four acts. Prose. Written 1940. First edition New Haven 1956. First performance February 10, 1956, Stockholm, Kungliga Dramatiska Teatern. Time: a day in August 1912. Place: living room in James Tyrone's summer home.

With bitter irony O'Neill uses his own family history to paint a gloomy psychological picture. All the characters are trapped in some neurosis. James Tyrone is a successful, complacent actor speeding from one guest performance to the next. He cannot forget the poverty of his youth and tyrannizes his family with his pathological avarice, which, experienced performer that he is, he masks with high-sounding phrases and winning gestures. His ingrained meanness has already been responsible for the death of one of his sons, and the consciousness of this guilt has driven Tyrone's wife Mary into morphine addiction. The drug helps her to close her eyes to the fact that her husband's avarice is pulling down the whole family. The elder son James takes to drink, the younger son Edmund, a poet—O'Neill's self-portrait—suffers from consumption, which the family treat as a minor cold to save the expense of a doctor. The hopelessness of their situation drives these people into cruel anger; they taunt and bludgeon one another but can never break loose from each other. Each is "a stranger who never feels at home, who does not really want and is not really wanted, who can never belong, who must always be a little in love with death."

A MOON FOR THE MISBEGOTTEN. Play in four acts. Prose. Written 1941–1942. First edition New York 1952. First performance February 20, 1947, Columbus, Ohio. Time: early September 1923. Place: the home of tenant farmer Phil Hogan, in Connecticut.

O'Neill's sensitive psychological insight and his realistic appreciation of detail in *A Moon for the Misbegotten* soar into poetry, into the dream of a purer self. Josie Hogan, a fading virgin, and Jim Tyrone, a dissipated estate owner, come together in the conversation of a lonely, moonlit night: "We've agreed there is only tonight—and it's to be different from any past night—for both of us. . . . Everything is far away and doesn't matter—except the moon and its dreams, and I'm part of the dreams—and you are, too." But in the grip of their environment and their own lethargy as they are, they lack the strength to make the dream real. They will continue to wear the life-long masks behind which they hide. Josie, still innocent and full of longings, next morning will once more be the rough, merry slattern who drives her drunken father Phil to work, if necessary by blows, and who boasts cynically of her numerous lovers. Tyrone goes back to the bottle and the brothels, where he has been seeking self-forgetfulness since his mother's death: "It was as if I wanted revenge—because I'd been left alone —because I knew I was lost, without any hope left—that all I could do would be to drink myself to death." Phil tries to turn these two hapless people's mutual affection to his own advantage: Josie is to manoeuver the drunken Tyrone into a compromising situation and with the help of pre-pared witnesses force him to marry her. The Irish peasant cunning of her father, who by this trap hopes to trick Tyrone into renewing the tenancy, casts doubts on the girl's pure hopes and confirms her in her renunciation. Josie is left with nothing but mockery for all that life failed to give her: "I thought there was still hope. I didn't know he'd died already—that it was a damned soul coming to me in the moonlight, to confess and be for-given and find peace for a night. . . ."

MORE STATELY MANSIONS. Play in three acts. Prose. Written February 1935–1941. First edition New Haven 1964. First performance November 9, 1962, Stockholm, Kungliga Dramatiska Teatern. Time: October 1832 to the summer of 1841. Place: Massachusetts.

This play was meant to be the fourth of O'Neill's planned cycle *A Tale of Possessors Self-dispossessed* and is the continuation of *A Touch of the Poet*. It reflects the deepening gloom in the poet's mind, the *tedium vitae* and desolation of a man fatally sick. In this world without principles, the pur-suit of possessions and dominion has spread even to the realm of the soul.

Human relationships, the bonds between mother and son, the companionship of husband and wife, are subject to calculation, to the cold profit motive of business: "Love should be a deal forever incomplete, never finally settled, with each party continually raising the bids, but neither one concluding a final role." This apparent cynicism is to expose the moral self-deception of an age where in their family life people indulge themselves in the illusion of a disinterested better self to justify their brutal and unscrupulous fight for existence. In this inflation of ideals it is cynically admitted that "life means selling yourself." Happiness can consist only of possession, power, and enjoyment. Good is what exists and can prevail over the weak. But even this ultimate consequence of materialism cannot solve man's conflict, self-assertion in the world cannot completely bury man's longing for paradise lost: "He lives split into opposites and divided against himself! All in the name of Freedom! As if at the end of every dream of liberty one did not find the slave, oneself, to whom oneself, the Master, is enslaved!"

Simon Harford grew up under the care of his capricious mother Deborah, in a remote, dreamlike Arcadia of poetry and fairy tales. Recoiling from her husband, who lived only for his business, Deborah retired into her strange garden. Sitting in her summerhouse, she dreamed herself into a distant, shadowy rococo life, in which she saw herself as a courtesan and schemer at the court of Versailles. Under his mother's influence Simon feels himself to be a poet. He wants to write a book on the evils of wealth, that in the spirit of Rousseau will describe the utopia of a humanity without possessions. He marries Sara Melody, a practical girl devoid of imagination. Remembering only too well the poverty of her childhood, her new wealth is a source of security and happiness for her. Her influence turns Simon into a cold businessman exactly like his father. He takes over the firm, develops it, and makes his way in the world insatiably and without scruples. What began as a trading concern he expands by acquiring a shipping company, a railway line, a bank. Harford cotton grown on Harford plantations and processed in Harford textile mills, is sold in Harford stores. Harford slave ships bring labor from Africa. With insatiable aggressiveness Simon plans to establish a monopoly by which buyers, too, would become his firm possession, his consumer slaves.

Deborah cannot get over the fact that Sara has taken her son from her and made him into a caricature of himself. She wants to reconquer Simon. She pretends that she is reconciled to her daughter-in-law and appears to be the modest, utterly content grandmother. Sara is so intent on having her place in Deborah's aristocratic way of life that she consents to this idyllic arrangement, where the display of friendship hides distrust and the struggle for the sole domination over Simon. The businessman sees himself degraded into an object of the women's secret contest and responds with psychological horse trading. He turns his wife into a whore. Night after night he pays for her love with a cheque, makes over to her a share in the business: "And strip yourself naked and accept yourself as you are in the greedy mind and flesh. Then you can go on . . . successfully . . . with a clear vision . . . without false scruple . . . on to demand and take what you want . . . as I have done!" He forces his mother back into her rococo garden and entangles her more and more deeply in the delusion of her false part. Yet Simon longs for the selfless dreams of his youth: "I have never forgotten the anguished sense of being suddenly betrayed, of being wounded and deserted and left alone in a life in which there was no security or faith or love but only danger and suspicion and devouring greed!" Simon tries to force his way into the summerhouse, behind the doors of which madness lurks. Deborah sacrifices herself for her son and finally fades away in her fantasies. Simon remains at the mercy of his purposeful wife, who henceforth will also have to act as his mother.

A TOUCH OF THE POET. Play in four acts. Prose. Written 1936. First edition New Haven 1957. First performance April 1957, Stockholm, Kungliga Dramatiska Teatern. Time: July 27, 1828. Place: the dining room of Melody's Tavern, in a village near Boston.

O'Neill had planned eleven plays for the great cycle which, under the title *A Tale of Possessors Self-dispossessed,* was to trace the fortunes over 150 years of the rise and fall of a New England family. He actually completed only four of these plays. He destroyed two of them, *Greed of the Meek* and *Give Me Death,* on February 21, 1943; the two others, *A Touch of the Poet* and *More Stately Mansions,* were found among his manuscripts after his death.

The theme of dreams versus reality, the false pathos of illusion and the happiness of selfless devotion to duty, is presented in this play not in the exclusive terms of a postulate but diffused in a subtle representation of human characters. Cornelius Melody, one-time landowner and major in the British Army, was forced by an affair of honor to emigrate to the United States; he now runs a neglected tavern with his wife Nora. He lives in memories of his cavalry career, declaims Byron, and supports a band of boon companions, willing toadies who applaud his military feats. He keeps an expensive riding horse and plays the gentleman, while Nora, whose rustic simplicity he despises, and their daughter Sara struggle to keep the debt-ridden, unsuccessful business going. Sara hates her father's self-satisfied pose as much as the humble devotion of her mother, who endures Melody's airs because she loves him. Sara's own first love is a rich, spoiled young man called Simon Harford, who in a romantic mood has taken up quarters at the tavern. At first, she is attracted to him by the prospect of a carefree life, but later she feels the certainty of unreserved happiness by his side. The Harfords' lawyer Nicholas Gadsby, who is supposed to settle the affair by means of an appropriate payment, only succeeds in making the eccentric gentleman-innkeeper challenge Harford to a duel and shock Simon's capricious mother Deborah with his clumsy attentions. He starts a fracas in front of the Harfords' mansion and is clubbed by the servants. This shock shatters Melody's façade. He accepts the truth about himself and turns into an innkeeper with a broad Irish brogue and hearty vulgarity. He shoots his mare and finally buries the dream figure of the Major. With rough tenderness he turns to his wife: "I'll be a real husband to you, and help you run this shebeen, instead of being a sponge." Released at last from the "hell" of his pretensions, he is content to settle for his proper station.

## ORTON, Joe
(England, 1939–1967)

ENTERTAINING MR. SLOANE. Comedy in three acts. Prose. First edition London 1964. First performance May 6, 1964, London, New Arts Theatre. Time: the present. Place: Kath's lounge in a house in London.

Unfettered instincts, perversion and brutality are exaggerated beyond the point of tolerance at which they can still be understood and experienced as problems. Instead, we get a rebound into strident comedy kept going by a display of the abnormal, by a blasphemous and unsavory dialogue, by the peculiar situation. The cynical challenge which, in the hands of Genet and Albee, still had its dissonant justification on the stage, is degraded to a macabre popular entertainment, which, however, has the fascination of remarkably sure characterization.

Kath, a frustrated, aging spinster, has made the conquest of the homeless Mr. Sloane, twenty-one years her junior. He readily accepts her seductive invitation to let himself be spoiled as her lodger and in return he will cater to the needs of her heart. But Kath's brother Ed, a big shot in business, intervenes. He, the perfumed friend of athletic young men, simply cannot put up with such immorality. He remembers only too well how his sex-starved sister years ago had ruined a "little matie" of his and taught him "nasty" things. He offers Sloane, the universal favorite, a job as chauffeur with very special duties by day and by night. The cunning lad is only too pleased to pursue his career in this lucrative fashion. But there is yet another member of the family. Senile Dadda Kemp, a blubbering,

half-blind wreck of a man pushed around rudely by everyone, recognizes
Sloane as the murderer of his former employer, a photographer and specialist in "certain interesting features," who had been killed by a boy
streetwalker. Sloane's reaction to these insinuations is to kill the old man.
Brother and sister are shocked—not, of course, because they cared for their
father at all, but because they feel Mr. Sloane really need not have been
so direct. This sort of thing is apt to create a nuisance. But is that a reason
why the charming guest has to be given up to the police? Surely, he is much
too desirable for them. They come to an agreement; they will pretend that
the incident was an accident, and thus will have a permanent hold on
Sloane. Henceforth he will be at the service of both in turn.


LOOT. Play in two acts. Prose. First edition London 1967. First performance February 1965, Brighton, England. Time: the present. Place: a room
in McLeavy's house.

Orton shifts his provocative cynicism from sex to religion and the cult of
the dead, the last strongholds of human piety. Derision is used for shock
effects. All taboos are fair game and are material freely available for every
kind of triviality, gag, and comic situation. Mrs. McLeavy lies in her coffin,
embalmed and with sky-blue glass eyes, while her intestines, eyes, and
other perishable ingredients are stored away in a little casket. Engrossed
in his rose-growing hobby, the widower fails to notice the purposeful proposals of nurse Fay, who has already expedited seven husbands into the
hereafter by fanciful accidents and has thus become a sevenfold heir. Her
love is magnetically drawn from McLeavy to the undertaker Dennis, just
as she learns of the latter's successful bank robbery. With the help of Hal,
McLeavy's son, Dennis has hidden the loot in a wardrobe at McLeavy's
house. Inspector Truscott, disguised as an employee of the Water Board,
is already on the track of the hoodlums.
A merry game of hide-and-seek sets in: first the money is in the coffin, the
mother's body naked in the wardrobe, then the money is in the casket, the
glass eye rolling on the floor. Swathed and tied up in bandages like a
tailor's dummy, the corpse is passed from hand to hand. The police disregard the confessions of the culprits and beat the innocent into confessions of crimes not committed. Truscott forgets about the bank robbers
and also about Fay, who has Mrs. McLeavy's murder to her credit as well,
takes his share of the loot and arrests the provocatively innocent McLeavy
for murder. In order to save him the trial and the proof of his innocence,
the policeman agrees to arrange a fall from the prison window—an accidental death. Conscious of his duty, he takes charge of the loot. This grotesque thriller makes play with the paradoxes, misunderstandings, and
clichés of a distorted reality.

# OSBORNE, John
(England, born 1929)

THE ENTERTAINER. Play in thirteen numbers. Prose and verse. First edition London 1957. First performance April 10, 1957, London, Royal Court Theatre. Time: the present. Place: a large coastal resort in England; a music-hall stage with the Rices' flat as an inset.

Osborne's challenge to convention is focused and objectivized in sociological terms. The hollow, outdated world, which was the setting of Jimmy's conflicts in *Look Back in Anger,* has become a variety caricature of itself, empty but kept going only by its own routine.

Jimmy, who gambles his life in his despair of it, is replaced by Archie, a "dead beat" professional comedian. The permanent instantaneous revolt of the "angry young man" is petrified in a bravura part. This is the result of a transition from programmatic self-representation to an objective understanding of the world: "Why, we have problems that nobody's ever heard of, we're characters out of something that nobody believes in. We're something that people make jokes about because we're so remote from the rest of ordinary everyday, human experience." The English music-hall tradition has had to give way to rock 'n' roll and the "New'd Look," and as a result the Rices, a family of comedians, are uprooted, have lost their livelihood and their life's work. The "entertainer," whose witty, improvised comments used to accompany the audience through the program and whose satirical songs used to link the separate numbers, has sunk, in Archie Rice, to a weary teller of gags. Desperately he offers his wares, which raise no laughs: "I 'ave a go, don't I? I do . . . I 'ave a go."

He is a plain failure, radiating a forced mood of generosity and irresistibility, playing the part of child prodigy notwithstanding his gray hair, merely to evade his responsibilities. He cannot make a success of life and comes to terms with his weakness by laughing at himself ironically. Archie enjoys his humiliations as much as any opportunity for boastful scenes. His wife Phoebe is now old and resigned, and quite insignificant. Once she was proud to have won the idolized star, now she drowns her disillusionment in the most ordinary pleasures. Their daughter Jean, in the alert distrust of youth, has broken off her engagement and wears herself out in a stubborn attempt to teach art to "Youth Club kids." Her two brothers are sharp contrasts: Frank refused to be called up and went to jail for it, while Mick, as a "sensible boy," does his civic and military duty and loses his life in the Suez crisis. Archie's father Billy dreams of his past successes on the stage and cultivates his grotesquely anachronistic British pride of colonial vintage. Archie hopes to save his "washed-up, tatty show" by taking his father into it as a draw, and as a result of all these excitements brings about the old man's death. For years the entertainer has as a matter of course been accepting financial assistance from his brother William, a successful lawyer. This was convenient enough, but when his brother offers to pay for his emigration to Canada, so that he can start a new life with his family as a hotel keeper, Archie declines and cynically prefers to go to prison for his tax debts: "Here we are, we're alone in the universe, there's no God, it just seems that it all began by something as simple as sunlight striking on a piece of rock. And here we are. We've only got ourselves. Somehow, we've just got to make a go of it." As an anti-illusionist device the action is set on a music-hall stage and develops in a sequence of "numbers," repeatedly interrupted by Archie's, the Entertainer, gags. He addresses his jokes directly to the audience and sings topical songs about "the salt of our dear old country." It is a remarkable attempt to exploit the music-hall technique for the purposes of social satire.

INADMISSIBLE EVIDENCE. Play in two acts. Prose. First edition London 1965. First performance September 9, 1964, London, Royal Court Theatre. Time: the present. Place: a solicitor's office in London.

A modern man's spiritual agony takes its course in the no-man's land between dream and reality. Life is a stock of clichés now falling to pieces. Even man's rebellion against the ruling order, his addiction to drink, adultery, and shady business are incidental and ordinary. He needs more and more excesses to escape the awareness of his own nonentity: "I am almost forty years old, and I know I have never made a decision that I didn't either regret or suspect was just plain commonplace or shifty or scamped and indulgent or mildly stupid or undistinguished."

His inferiority and guilt complexes propel the solicitor Bill Maitland into a waking dream in which he is in the dock before his own employees. His managing clerk Hudson is the apathetic judge and young Jones is going to lead for the prosecution. Bill is a man incapable of either accepting or reciprocating affection and is equally incapable of making decisions; he is lethargically subsisting with the help of his pills. He tries to give himself the illusion of self-assurance by spicing his legal advice with bravado and obscene jokes. This repels his clients, whose divorce affairs and sexual offenses he vicariously relishes—of course, only to understand fully the facts of the case. The actual conduct of business is left to the employees. They give notice when Bill calls in false witnesses and in consequence is to be called to account by the Law Society. He gives vent to his anxiety in endless monologues on the telephone; it is uncertain whether there actually is anyone at the other end of the line. Bill refuses to take part in his daughter Jane's birthday party—he even forgets whether she is seventeen or eighteen. He also offends his wife Anna just to have the weekend free to go away with his mistress Liz. Bill's secretary Shirley is pregnant by him and gives up her job to marry another man. As a consolation, Bill seduces the telephonist Joy in the office after hours while his mistress is expecting him and his wife keeps ringing up. But even sex does not save Bill from himself; "But what sort of object is that? Is it an enjoyment, a duty, an obligation, a necessity, or just the effort of fighting, of fighting off the end, whatever is to come to you." Not knowing what he wants, he eventually drives away even Liz, who really loves him. The long weekend for which he has fought so hard he will now have to spend alone with his frustration. People and situations lose their identity and dissolve into the hallucinations of utter rootlessness.

LOOK BACK IN ANGER. Play in three acts. Prose. First edition London 1957. First performance May 8, 1956, London, Royal Court Theatre. Time: the present. Place: the Porters' one-room flat in a large Midland town.

A neurasthenic family crisis is amplified into a diagnosis of the "angry young men," the generation lost between the ruins of the war and the hectic economic miracle of reconstruction. Without purpose and standards, rootlessly adrift in an inflation of ideals, young Jimmy Porter wears himself out in aimless provocations, so as to shock his environment out of its noncommittal reservations. He no longer wants a part in a world devoid of convictions and passion, and because of this becomes an actor in it, a poseur dominated by his whims of the moment. Having been unsuccessful in his studies, Jimmy now makes a living selling candy. He is at odds with himself and the world and tries to shock and humiliate his wife Alison, whose aristocratic background he resents and for which he tries to compensate with vulgarity. He boasts about his premarital adventures and asserts himself with ear-splitting music and parties with his friend Cliff. Even in his moments of spontaneous affection this young man, who can never be himself, plays a part. In such moments he calls Alison his "beautiful, great-eyed squirrel," and he is her "jolly super bear . . . a really marvelous bear." It is an escape into the naturalness and sincerity which reality denies them. Alison is expecting a baby, but does not tell her unpredictable husband; instead, on the advice of her friend Helena Charles, after a hysterical scene she returns to her parents. In his injured vanity, Jimmy makes Helena his mistress and soon afterwards the butt of his customary irritability. Alison loses the baby and returns to her husband. Hesitantly the couple grope for a new beginning. It is not by accident that the action is divided into scenes, solo numbers, and monologues, for the fascination of a bravura part has to replace the lost certainty of a comprehensible world view.


LUTHER. Play in three acts. Prose. First edition London 1961. First performance June 26, 1961, Nottingham, Theatre Royal. Time: between 1506 and 1530. Place: Germany and Italy.

This chronicle play shows the great reformer as an "angry young man" at war with himself and tradition. He is tormented by self-doubt and filled with a passion for perfection. The battle of the spirit is complete with all the abusive polemics and filthy vulgarities of that rough-hewn age. Luther's constipation is as important as his religious zeal; the latrine is juxtaposed with the tabernacle in full equality of rights.

Martin Luther, in 1506, is received into the Order of Eremites of St. Augustine at Erfurt much to the displeasure of his father Hans, who sees himself cheated of his ambitious plans for his son. Even as a novice he stands apart from the others. The monks' unctuous confession about broken plates and a forgotten scapular is interrupted by a fit of madness that expresses the frenzied anguish of his inner doubts. Luther is tormented by his awareness of incessantly renewed sin: "It's this, just this. All I can feel, all I can feel is God's hatred." Luther believes himself to be acting in the spirit of the Church in preaching against the oily tirades of John Tetzel, the seller of indulgences, and against his duke's futile mania for relics.

On October 31, 1517 he summarizes his protests in Ninety-five Theses and nails them to the church door of All Saints, the castle church at Wittenberg. Armed with an "impossible standard of perfection," he opposes the world, the church, and the secular authorities: "For you must be made to know that there's no security, there's no security at all, either in indulgences, holy busywork, or anywhere in this world." The Papal Legate Cajetan vainly pleads with Luther to retract his theses and thus to reestablish the unity of Christendom. Luther delivers the Christians unto themselves and their own responsibility; he deprives them of comfort and security, of blind faith in indulgences, and of the infallibility of the clergy. What remains is solitude—such as the reformer himself was to experience all his life. "If we're lucky we can be persuaded in our own mind, and the most we can hope for is to die each one for himself." Luther's struggle for the purity of the word and its message gets entangled in politics. In the Peasants' Revolt, he had to take sides against the oppressed whom he himself had inspired with the love of freedom. He knows that the peasants are fighting for justice, but he betrays them for reasons of state. In all circumstances Luther is in conflict with his conscience—even in his marriage with Katherine von Bora, in conversation with his prior Staupitz, and in watching over his little son's sleep. He had "to learn a hard lesson, which is that a human being is a helpless little animal; he's not created by his father, but by God. It's hard to accept you're anyone's son, and you're not the father of yourself."

The facets of history are set against a stylized background—the time and place of the events are announced from the stage, and the action is foreshortened and without depth.

A PATRIOT FOR ME. Play in three acts. Prose. First edition London 1966. First performance June 30, 1965, Royal Court Theatre. Time: 1890–1913. Place: Austro-Hungarian Empire.

Osborne uses the famous espionage case of Colonel Redl for participating, from the stage, in the discussion concerning the reform of criminal law in England and for pleading that homosexuality should not be punishable. He is not above exploiting his theme to the full; it is obvious that he is out for a *succés de scandale* with such devices as a prolonged transvestite ball, melodramatic effects, and much unsavory detail.

Perseverance and indefatigable hard work have enabled the gifted Alfred Redl, in spite of his humble origins, to advance in the army over men who have the advantage of an aristocratic name or influential protection. The insignificant lieutenant from a provincial garrison in Galicia becomes the inscrutable staff colonel in the Imperial counterespionage services. The Russian secret service under Colonel Oblensky has long been following the unusual rise of the bourgeois outsider. They assign one of their agents, Countess Sophia Delyanoff, to a brief exploratory romance with him, which, however, founders on Redl's peculiar tastes. He makes expensive presents to his young boy friends and, overwhelmed by debts and threatened in his position by blackmail, he eventually becomes the Russians' willing tool. For large sums, he sells them the Austrian army's strategic plans. Eventually his treason is discovered and he is forced to settle the scandal by shooting himself. In the Chamber of Deputies the case provides a pretext for an anti-Semitic campaign, taking advantage of Redl's having had a Jewish mother.

Unlike Christopher Fry, who, in his comedy *The Dark Is Light Enough,* successfully transplanted the old Austrian atmosphere and talk into an English setting, Osborne sticks to his main purpose, which has nothing to do with literature. His language is as obvious as that of a poster.

## OSBORNE, John, and CREIGHTON, Anthony
(Creighton, England, born 1920)

EPITAPH FOR GEORGE DILLON. Play in three acts. Prose. First edition London 1958. First performance February 11, 1958, London, Royal Court Theatre. Time: the present. Place: sitting room and hall in the home of the Elliot family, just outside London.

Outsiders and society are in this play only apparent contrasts, they impose on each other and effect a compromise. The artist becomes an exciting stimulant for the conformist, and by this is necessarily driven into a pose. "I play 'scornful parts'—anyone a bit loudmouthed, around my height, preferably rough and dirty, with a furnace roaring in his belly. The rougher and dirtier the better."

George Dillon, whose lack of success as a writer has condemned him to an office existence, is taken into Mrs. Elliot's family. He is to replace her son Raymond, who was killed in the war, and in exchange he gains enough economic security to indulge in the illusions of his modest talent. Too weak to give inner form to his aspirations, yet too sensitive to be content with a commonplace destiny, George Dillon acts out his part: he accepts the pent-up motherly feelings of the aging Mrs. Elliot, but at the same time despises the lower-middle-class narrowness which affords him a carefree life. He seduces Mrs. Elliot's daughter Josie, who, when she expects a baby, finds out that he is already married. Eventually George Dillon puts his ideals into effect by betraying them and becoming a well-paid manufacturer of cheap trash for the stage. The philistines are happy that their darling after all does not disappoint them, and applaud him even when he recites a cynical epitaph on his true, lost self. Osborne's basic theme, the contradiction of youth, merges smoothly into psychological realism with a touch of social criticism.

## PAGNOL, Marcel
(France, born 1895)

JUDAS [*Judas*]. Play in five acts. Prose. Written 1955. First edition Paris 1956. First performance October 6, 1955, Paris, Théâtre de Paris. Time: the Passover feast, A.D. 32. Place: Jerusalem and surroundings.

A psychological interpretation of the Judas tragedy in the setting of a realistic, broadly conceived environment. Judas is the most pious and the most devoted among the apostles. Neither his father, the vintner Simon, nor his betrothed Rebecca approves of his unconditional devotion to Jesus. When Judas hears his master predict the betrayal, he takes it as a mission, the more so since his arrest by the Roman centurion Marcius and the offer of the thirty pieces of silver seem to be signs of providence. Judas is convinced that Jesus is merely waiting for the moment of his arrest to reveal himself in all his glory. After the deed, the traitor is plunged into torments of doubt: was the master just a man without power, who must now innocently die, or was he the Messiah, whose hour had not yet come? What drives Judas to suicide is the burning desire for certainty at last. Marcius, the cold-blooded executioner, is converted by Christ's death on the cross. It is not Jesus, but Judas who is seen as the most pitiable victim, necessary for salvation, of the Gospel story.

## PATRICK, John (J. Patrick Goggan)
(United States, born 1905)

THE HASTY HEART. Play in three acts. Prose. First edition New York 1945. First performance January 3, 1945, New York, Hudson Theatre. Time: the Second World War. Place: a British military hospital in Southeast Asia.

A typical war play which makes good use of the popular theater's best qualities of humor, thoughtfulness, and sentimentality. The Scot Lachie, who is destined to die of a kidney wound in a few weeks' time, arrives from the front at the hospital and, not knowing his own fatal condition, has to adapt himself to the community spirit of the convalescent ward, where all the others meet him with comprehension and friendship. But Lachie is a hard, reserved character, who all his life has obstinately repressed the "hasty heart" of human sympathy. His misanthropic sullenness melts away when the others present him, on his birthday, with a kilt that he has long coveted. At this point he learns about his hopeless condition from the Colonel. In hatred and disillusionment he turns away from his new friends, whose friendliness may be nothing but a show dictated by pity. Ultimately Lachie comes to terms with his destiny and gratefully accepts the security of the group for the short time that he may still enjoy it.


THE TEAHOUSE OF THE AUGUST MOON. Play in three acts. Adapted from the novel by Vern Snyder. First edition New York 1954. First performance October 15, 1953, Martin Beck Theatre. Time: after the end of the Second World War. Place: Okinawa.

A political satire on the Americans' democratic missionary zeal and their complacent faith in reason and innovation. Their effort to press all things into the standard pattern of democracy is bound to come to grief on the East Asians' equanimity. Having turned out the Japanese, the Americans now proceed to reeducate the natives of the island of Okinawa and turn them into model democrats.

According to Plan B every village is to have its municipal government, its Ladies' League for Democratic Action, and a school, naturally in the shape of the famous Pentagon. Lectures and discussions are to be organized. Captain Fisby, from Psychological Warfare, utterly fails with this committee-room strategy in Tobiki village. In no time he finds himself the master of the attractive geisha Lotus Blossom and cannot escape the conclusion that the only effective contribution to understanding among nations is to distill brandy. In strict adherence to democracy he yields to the wishes of the majority; the women demand lipsticks and perfume as the achievements of civilization, while the men vote for a modern teahouse instead of the school. Colonel Purdy at General Headquarters is outraged at this irreverent humanitarian perversion of his reeducation scheme and orders the teahouse to be destroyed at once. But in the meantime the press has discovered Tobiki as a model of American "get-up-and go," a congressional committee is on the way from Washington, and the colonel gets his general's stars. Fisby is in some doubt as to who has really taught and educated whom: the self-confident victors with their slogans of freedom and democracy, or the islanders with their genius for taking their fate with grace and dignity. Sakini, the interpreter, guides the audience through the action with sly comments and at the same time is one of the main figures in this ironic and impish tale.

# PFEIFFER, Hans
(Germany, born 1925)

LATERNENFEST *[Lantern Festival]*. Play in three acts. Prose. First edition Berlin 1958. First performance September 1, 1957, Dresden, Staatsschauspiel. Time: July 1946. Place: Nagasaki.

The song of songs of humanity and love triumphs over the thirst for revenge and the mania for destruction. Amid the suffering, incurable victims of the Nagasaki atom bomb, the Japanese girl Yuki Yamamoto and the American medical student James Kennedy come together. The fathers of the loving couple are deadly enemies, with their ideals made up of honor, steel, racial delusion, and heroic death. Akira Yamamoto, now blinded by radioactivity, took part in the attack on Pearl Harbor and dropped the first bomb, which killed James Kennedy's oldest brother. James's father, Major Kennedy, once a jovial manufacturer of candy, spurred by thirst for revenge for his son's death and national pride, had released the atom bomb on Nagasaki. Now he is a member of the American commission studying the effects of the bomb. In order to put an end to their children's love affair the two enemies, with their officers' pride, become allies. The Japanese officer's attempt to kill James misfires, but he stabs the major and his own daughter and commits hara-kiri. The lovers suppress the memory of their dead fathers' vengeful spirit and confidently set forth into a new life. The new day dawns on the Lantern Festival, the Japanese equivalent of All Soul's Night, celebrated with lamps and paper boats.

# PINGET, Robert
(Switzerland, born 1919)

CLOPE *(Ici ou ailleurs)*. Play in three acts. Prose. First edition Paris 1961. First performance December 5, 1963, Zürich, Schauspielhaus. Translated by Barbara Bray, in *Plays*, Vol. 1, New York, Hill & Wang, and London, Calder & Boyars, 1966. Time: the present. Place: a railway station.

Man is indissolubly chained to the mercy of self-deception in illusions, dreams, wishes and memory. This farce demonstrates that certainty, in which men so often look for security, can consist only of the unalterable fact of death. As a protest against the love of travel, this gift of self to the future, Clope has built himself a brushwood hut in the station hall and proclaims an absolute standstill. A French grammar, the last legacy of the "good old times of disasters," becomes the ritual of his existence. The only thing that vouchsafes certainty is the skeleton of the language. Clope mistrusts its content and disintegrates it into a linguistic system in which cases, numbers, and functions all have their immutable position. Opposite his hut, Mme. Flan, the purveyor of exciting faraway places, has her newsstand. She is also a fortune-teller and her cards forever dazzle the housewives with new hopes and transfigure with inexhaustible possibilities the humdrum life of those who never board the train. Pierrot, who in despair broke out of the treadmill of his office routine, is converted by Clope to the nihilistic dogma of the grammar, and ultimately escapes into the wide world. The spell of the unknown, the ever new adventure that is called life, and the promise of the "elsewhere" have defeated Clope's nihilism: "One can't do without traveling when one is alone and unhappy and, to boot, suffocates in poverty." Extreme existential experiences are transformed into gentle clowning.

DEAD LETTER (Lettre morte). Play in two acts. After the author's novel Le Fiston (1959). Prose. Written 1959. First edition Paris 1959. First performance March 29, 1960, Paris, Théâtre Récamier. Translated by Barbara Bray, in Plays, Vol. 1, New York, Hill & Wang, and London, Calder & Boyars, 1966. Time: the present. Place: bar and post office in a French provincial town.

Life has become a passive waiting without sense and purpose, trickling away into emptiness. For this hopeless and sad state Pinget has found a gripping parable expressed in realistic terms. Levert's son has been absent and not heard of for years. All the old father's thoughts and longings, all his self-reproaches and feelings of guilt center on the son's return. Levert doggedly clings to every crumb of hope that his sad environment sends his way. In self-tormented fascination he watches, in the bar, as the comedians Lili and Fred perform scenes from a cynical travesty of "The Prodigal Son." Next morning the old man calls again, as every day, at the post office, hoping for a sign of life from his missing son. All that is left to him is the bulky packet of his own letters, marked "addressee unknown."

# PINTER, Harold
(England, born 1930)

THE BIRTHDAY PARTY. Play in three acts. Prose. First edition London 1960. First performance April 28, 1958, Cambridge, England, Arts Theatre. Time: the present. Place: living room in Meg's boarding house.

The extinction of the individual by the executives of an anonymous system in this play has the intensity of a nightmare. Personal tragedy becomes an official act, personality the malleable product of brainwashing, death an exchange of functions. Stan is the only visitor in Meg and Petey's run-down seaside boarding house. He boasts of his long-past successes as a pianist and in panic tries to hide from reality; but reality catches up with him. Two officials, Goldberg and McCann, envoys of an unnamed organization, arrive. The two arrange a wickedly grotesque birthday party for Stan, smash his spectacles, abduct his mistress Lulu, and put him through a brainwashing from which he emerges a completely broken man: "You're what's left! . . . What makes you think you exist! You're dead . . . You can't live, you can't think, you can't love. You're dead. You're a plague gone bad. There's no juice in you. You're nothing but an odor!" Next morning he is taken away in a car. The officials have fulfilled their assignment. Platitudes, the monotony of trite repetition, and standard situations develop their weird independence in this dismantlement of the soul.

THE CARETAKER. Play in three acts. Prose. First edition London 1960. First performance April 27, 1960, London, Arts Theatre. Time: the present. Place: a room.

Pinter chooses a closed space—notwithstanding his realism, his "rooms" presuppose no outside world—to query the validity of human companionship and of social conventions. The psychological study of three contrasting characters makes a sudden leap into farce: the differences between the real and the unreal are blurred, things need not necessarily be either true or false, they can be both at the same time, so the author explains, and the more intense an experience is, the less articulate is its expression.
The old tramp Davies, disheveled and without a roof over his head, comes to live with the brothers Aston and Mick. Alternating between calculating obsequiousness and malevolent self-assertion, he plays off the two landlords against each other. Aston, a gentle eccentric, was thrown into a lunatic asylum by a heartless world and there subjected to electro-shock treatment. As a result he has lost all contact with people, collects junk, and

keeps himself busy "doing up" things. Aston provides Davies with clothes and arranges a caretaker's job for him. The burden of gratitude irritates the tramp, he kicks against the traces and threatens to have Aston sent back to the lunatic asylum. He also tries to persuade Mick to get rid of his "nutty" brother and to run the house as a profitable business. But Davies finally goes too far. The brothers see through his intrigue and throw him out.


THE COLLECTION. One-act play. Prose. First edition London 1963. First presented by Associated Rediffusion Ltd. May 11, 1961; first stage performance June 18, 1962, London, Aldwych Theatre. Time: the present. Place: Harry's house in Chelsea and James's flat in Belgravia, London.

This is a bitter farce playing ambiguously with paradoxes. On the different sets juxtaposed simultaneously on the stage, the author explores two human relationships that have long declined into indifference. James learns from his wife Stella that she has been unfaithful to him with Bill, a chance acquaintance in a hotel. The husband calls on the young fashion designer and finally extracts the liberating confession from him as well. But then Harry intervenes indignantly. He is an older man who patronizes Bill, and he so energetically denies the amorous slip that Bill and Stella eventually admit that he is right and in their turn deny the occurrence. It turns out that the two suspects have made up the whole thing, letting their imagination dwell voluptuously on how it would be if. . . .
Strictly according to the rules of gentlemanly behavior the most embarrassing subjects are discussed in dry and polite conversation, with visits and return visits, drinks and stereotyped phrases. And all this demonstrates that adultery is so embarrassing for modern society that to all intents and purposes it very nearly never happens at all. With this, however, the absurd jest becomes oppressive. In this party-going circle—all the protagonists belong to the world of high fashion—eroticism has become a parlor game, to which limits are ultimately set by reality, so that desire is satisfied only by sexual phantasmagoria and the impotence of semantic excesses.


THE DUMB WAITER. One-act play. Prose. First edition London 1960. First performance January 21, 1960, London, Hampstead Theatre Club. Time: the present, an autumn evening. Place: a basement room in Birmingham, England.

In the first place this play shows us the situation of contemporary man in the distorting mirror of a stage play juggling with paradoxes: two people locked in a world that consists only of the mechanical reception of orders and an invisible authority. The meaningless performance of duty for its own sake ceaselessly produces murderers and victims. But at the same time so much realistic detail is incorporated in the play, so much consistent motivation within a sharply drawn environment, that the outer framework of the psychological study is never forcibly broken.

Two men, Ben and Gus, wait and doze in a bare room. For years an anonymous organization has been sending them to some town or other, where they must wait in an empty room for a nameless victim and kill him: a straightforward job and good pay. The monotony of their wait is filled with the clichés of everyday actions: small talk about the news and football, the annoyed search for a cigarette, complaints about the lavatory that does not function. Gus, the younger and more sensitive of the two, is puzzled at the meaning of their activity, sympathizes with the victims and objects to being a mere function without a will of his own, a perfect machine for murder without any power of decision. Ben has long been dulled into just carrying on. A "dumb waiter" rattles up and down in the wall behind a serving hatch. Slips of paper bring orders for dishes which the two men in the room cannot possibly provide. They take refuge in mechanically rehearsing their instructions. Ben gets the expected order that always announces the victim. Automatically he points his gun at the man who enters—it is Gus, a tottering wreck expecting his death.

THE LOVER. One-act play. Prose. First edition London 1963. First presented by Associated Rediffusion Ltd. March 28, 1963; first stage performance September 18, 1963, London, New Arts Theatre Club. Time: the present. Place: a detached house near Windsor.

Inability to communicate and self-disgust drive a married couple into a lascivious double life. Pinter once explained that in his own view the problem was not so much one of inability but of unwillingness to communicate; rather than do this terrible thing, to establish an understanding with anyone else, people prefer to avoid talking to each other about the real basis of their relationship.

The married couple Richard and Sarah never tire of thinking up and acting out for each other new situations of seduction and resistance, desire and sudden chastening. For the purposes of this macabre little game, every day Richard slinks like a lover into his own home, where Sarah is expecting him in the guise of a mistress called Dolores or of a slut called Mary. The lovers keep inventing ever new variants. Thus Mary is importuned by a stranger in the park and is saved by the park keeper whom she subsequently tries to seduce in his hut. In the end the couple try to give up their game and get at the truth. But in the sphere of reality the last shred of companionship has long vanished, and they have no choice but to return to the exciting game and to the fascination of being different.

THE HOMECOMING. Play in two acts. Prose. First edition London 1965. First performance June 3, 1965, London, Aldwych Theatre. Time: the present, summer. Place: room in Max's house in North London.

Pinter turns the spotlight of naturalism on an environment of deepening depravity and at the same time clothes the action in a travesty of myth. The homecoming of a nymphomaniac, who commercializes her sex and keeps her lovers alive by her earnings as a call girl, harks back to archaic mother cults. The Universal Mother of Knossos, giver of life and fertility, and Circe's magic power of transforming men into beasts provide material for symbols of the modern predicament. The primitive need for images in prehistoric cultures has its counterpart in the objectivization and materialization even of the things of the spirit. Feelings have become objects, love a material asset.

Teddy has managed to become a professor of philosophy in America and returns with his young wife Ruth for a few days to his father's home, a neglected household of four bachelors. Teddy's father Max, filthy and grumbling, looks after the chores; of his sons, Lenny is a pimp and Joey an unsuccessful prizefighter. Uncle Sam, the simple moralist pushed around by the others, is a chauffeur and earns a living for all of them. Teddy, the intellectual, prides himself on his abstract, detached view of the world. He looks upon all this eating and being eaten with indulgent pity, which does not prevent him from ravenously gobbling up a cheese-roll meant for Lenny. An equally spontaneous ravenous hunger drives the unwed brothers to lay claim to Ruth's body. Ruth was a prostitute before Teddy retrieved her for middle-class respectability, and she thoroughly enjoys this promiscuity. She readily accepts Lenny's suggestion that she should again take up her amorous profession and thus keep the whole family. This is all the more necessary as Sam, hitherto the breadwinner, drops dead after revealing the secret which he has guarded all his life, namely, that Max, in his time, unwittingly shared his wife with his admired friend McGregor. The barter of women returns in archetypal variation. The realistic jumble of spleen, uneasiness and irritability assumes supernatural aspects in the grotesque glorification of sex.

# POUND, Ezra Loomis
(United States, born 1885)

WOMEN OF TRACHIS. One-act play. Adapted from the *Trachiniae* by Sophocles. Free verse. First edition London 1956. First broadcast British Broadcasting Corporation April 25, 1954. First stage performance May 9, 1959, Berlin, Schillertheater. Time: mythical. Place: not specified.

Pound translated the ancient tragedy into modern language not in order to reinterpret the myth, but to show how incomprehensible, senseless, and surpassingly horrible it is when human life is abruptly extinguished by unreason and blind passion: "And put some cement in your face,/ reinforced concrete, make a cheerful finish/ even if you don't want to . . . [the gods] see the things being done,/ calamities looked at,/ sons to honor their fathers,/ and of what is to come, nothing is seen. Gods!/" With his negation of any theodicy and his acceptance of a humanism purely of this world Pound comes close to the French existentialists.

Daysair is awaiting her husband Heracles, who so often leaves her in order to perform his heroic deeds in the great world. Now he has destroyed the realm of King Eurytos and brings the women captives home as slaves. Daysair welcomes the captive Iole with sympathy, but learns that Heracles passionately woos the girl. To possess her is the sole aim of all his conquests. The queen tries to win her husband back by a love spell which a centaur once gave her. With the best of intentions she spreads the poison on his tunic, and Heracles succumbs to the belated vengeance of the beastman. Daysair commits suicide. The dying Heracles weds his son Hyllos to Iole and accepts his fate: "Come at it that way, my boy, what/ splendor, it all coheres."

Pound uses current language, not disdaining even the help of colorful idiomatic expressions, but removes it from reality and lifts it into poetry by his free verse. The chorus acts not as a counterpart, but as a commentary, a lyrical echo of the events.

## PRIESTLEY, John Boynton
(England, born 1894)

AN INSPECTOR CALLS. Play in three acts. Prose. First edition New York 1945. First performance Moscow, summer 1945; first London performance October 1946, New Theatre. Time: 1912. Place: dining room in the Birlings' house in Brumley, an industrial city in the North Midlands.

The coldness and indifference of our socialized welfare world are critically demonstrated by an everyday case from so-called good society. The industrialist Arthur Birling and his closest family are celebrating his daughter Sheila's engagement to Gerald Croft, the son of a competitor. The happy occasion is suddenly interrupted by a police inspector with the news of a young woman's suicide. He wants some information, and in the course of his interrogation the complacent family's reputation crumbles, piece by piece—for each one of them has in one way or another failed the wretched girl who has now thrown away her useless life. Every one of them is guilty. Sheila, a spoiled customer of the shop the girl had worked in, had capriciously complained about her, which led to her losing her job. Both Sheila's brother Eric and her fiancé Gerald have taken advantage of the girl in brief adventures. Birling dismissed her because she was defending a just claim. Mrs. Birling, finally, added the last straw: as a hypocritical member of a Brumley Women's Charity Organization, she had only two weeks before sacrificed the girl to her own ideas of morality and caused her to be refused the help she asked. Outraged, the family try to decline responsibility for all this, when it suddenly turns out that there is no such person as police inspector Goole and that nothing is known of any suicide either. With much relief they are just about to enjoy their newly found good conscience and pretend that nothing has happened, when a telephone call announces that a police inspector is on the way to ask some questions in connection with a young girl's suicide. The gap between factual social criticism and the personification of fate by the nonexistent inspector is bridged by masterly stagecraft.

THE RACK. Play in three acts. Written 1958. First performance October 27, 1959, Bremen, Städtische Bühnen. Time: the present. Place: living room in the Marleys' bungalow in the West Indies.

A disturbing demonstration of how the cold war destroys all human values. The defensive ideological fronts undermine confidence and companionship and drive the individual into distrust and anxiety.

Alan and Joyce Marley rejoice in the prospect of their early return to England. Alan, a scientist, has been carrying out a research project in the West Indies, and has at long last succeeded in finding the formulas for the production of artificial proteins, thereby solving the food problem for the whole of mankind. His colleagues, the lethargic drunkard Lee Dexter and his wife Clare, seem to share the Marleys' happiness ungrudgingly. But suddenly the Marleys are assaulted by Lee and the failed student Hiltz, whom Alan once had to dismiss for incompetence. Both are emissaries of "the party" and intent on getting hold of the strategically invaluable formulas for their totalitarian regime. Lee, a cynical and brutal agent who has dissembled only for the sake of his secret mission, puts the scientist through a ruthless brainwashing. But Alan's power of resistance is not broken even when his wife's unfaithfulness is proved to him. Clare Dexter and Brennan intervene as liaison agents of an American counterorganization, and arrest the Eastern spies. The Marleys relax in the belief that the nightmare is now over. But in effect the vivisection of Alan's soul proceeds more forcefully than ever, because he is suspect in the West as a former "party" member. The scientist buys his release from torture by handing over a false formula to Brennan. Trapped in a chaos of suspicions, distrust, cruelty and deception as they are, the couple attempt, with much trouble, to come together again.


THE SCANDALOUS AFFAIR OF MR. KETTLE AND MRS. MOON. Comedy in three acts. Prose. Written 1955. First edition London 1960. First performance September 1, 1955, London, Duchess Theatre. Time: the present. Place: Kettle's living room in the small town of Brickmill, England.

Mr. Kettle, branch manager of a bank and a respectable citizen of Brickmill, suffers from the usual Monday morning blues and, instead of just indulging in a bit of bad temper, he decides to do something serious about it for once. In one fell swoop he gets rid of all the trappings of his former life—the boring job, the stiff collar, the endless round of daily duties and his wearyingly correct behavior. Henceforth he will belong to himself only and "go on a lark" whenever he pleases. In utter consternation Brickmill's staid dignitaries—Alderman Hardacre, Police Superintendent Street, and also the bank manager Clinton—watch Kettle absorbed in children's games, making a lot of noise and generally having a wonderful time. In this obviously serious case of revolt even the psychiatrist, the last resort of our age, is helpless and the alarmed Brickmillians have no option but to let their *enfant terrible* proceed into his light-hearted, playful, and carefree future. Kettle, this new Adam, has in the meantime found a playmate in Mrs. Delia Moon, who happily leaves all her preoccupations with progressive committees behind and escapes into boisterous merriment.


## PUGET, Claude André, and BOST, Pierre
(both France; Puget, born 1905, Bost, born 1901)


UN NOMMÉ JUDAS. [A Man Named Judas]. Play in three acts. Prose. First edition Paris 1954. First performance April 2, 1954, Paris, Comédie-Caumartin. Time: A.D. 32. Place: Jerusalem.

This is not meant to be either a passion play or a biblical period piece; it deals in modern terms with a deluded idealist's inner conflicts. Thus the characters include neither Jesus nor any of the clearly established, well-known disciples. Judas is represented as a world reformer, who has already served a two-year prison sentence for his determined championship of his ideals. While the other disciples are devoted to Jesus in their open-hearted faith, Judas is an intellectual who has been led by rational concepts to the doctrine of redemption, in which he sees the possibility of saving the world. But the uncompromising nature of Christ's message of salvation is bound to appear as sterile romanticism to the practical politician that Judas is. When he hears from his mistress Lea, a former prostitute, about Christ's tribulations on the Mount of Olives, the whole world collapses around Judas and his speculations. He is convinced that the Messiah has betrayed his mission for the sake of his humanity. By his own betrayal Judas now wants to force Jesus to reveal his divine right: "The God that he is must be put with his back against the wall. So much with his back against the wall that he cannot retreat any more, that he has no other possibility except to display the God that is within him." When, instead of the expected glory, ordeals and the crucifixion are meted out to the master, Judas kills himself.

## QUALTINGER, Helmut

See MERZ, Carl, and QUALTINGER, Helmut.


## QUOIREZ, Françoise

See SAGAN, Françoise

## RADOK, Marie, and RADOK, Alfred
(Czechoslovakia, born 1914)

ŠPAŇELSKÁ ZAPALKA *[The Safety Match]*. Comedy in three acts. Based on themes from stories by Chekhov. Acting edition Prague, Dilia, 1961. First performance December 20, 1961, Prague, Komorní Theatre. Time: around 1890. Place: a Russian garrison town.

This play is a graceful arrangement of themes from Chekhov outlined with Gogol's satirical sharpness. The characters of this Russian provincial society are so clear-cut and unmistakable, so traditionally typed, that there is no need of any plot. What action there is, is introduced casually, blown up and exploded—just a piece of voluble, subtly discriminating self-deception.

Kusmich, the chief of police, is giving a dinner party, an epicurean celebration complete with *Weltschmerz*, romantic outpourings, boredom, elaborate courtesies, and the cynical pose of narcissism. Suddenly the worthy company are confronted with reality. It seems that the estate owner Klausov has been murdered. But the ceremonious game of vanities goes on. The magistrate, his clumsy assistant, the snappy doctor, the not very bright commissar all act out their roles, investigate and suspect. Fascination with the unlimited possibilities of the complicated Russian soul leads everyone to advance the most unlikely conjectures. After all, they've all read their Dostoevsky and they all believe in the latest triumph of science, psychology: "You know . . . in the end people always confess their crime. Always . . . At least, they do with us in Russia." At last, the supposedly murdered man is found, as alive as could be, in the bedroom of the police chief's wife. The safety match, one of the lady's luxuries, brings the affair of the heart to light and restores calm to the agitated little town.

Radok, an experienced hand at anything to do with the theater and founder of the Prague "Laterna magica," presents all this as pure stage entertainment with an unerring sense of effects, ludicrous types, and grotesque scenes. Themes and characters originally heavy with acid social criticism and devastating caricature, are softened in imitation and adaptation and by the distance of time. What remains is a collection of lovable eccentrics, harmless leftovers from the fund of Russian literature. "The world has room for all of us. All we have to do is to realize it."

# RATTIGAN, Terence
(England, born 1911)


THE DEEP BLUE SEA. Play in three acts. Prose. First edition London 1952. First performance March 6, 1952, London, Duchess Theatre. Time: a day in September 1948. Place: the sitting room of a furnished flat in north-west London.

One out of the innumerable obscure human destinies in this play is treated with psychological subtlety. Hester Collyer tries to end her wretched life by turning on the gas. Death appears to her as the "deep blue sea," the sea of security in which she lets herself sink. She left her husband William in order to live with Freddie, a former fighter pilot, but she had nothing but disappointments from that. Freddie is uprooted and has never found his way back from the part of a much decorated war hero to ordinary civilian life. The additional responsibility for Hester worries him, and more and more he takes refuge in drink. William vainly tries to win back his wife. It is left to Mr. Miller, a doctor who was once jailed and removed from the medical register, to shake Hester out of her lethargy and give her strength and courage for a new beginning .


SEPARATE TABLES. Two plays. Prose. Written 1954. First edition London 1955. First performance September 22, 1954, London, St. James's Theatre. Time: the present. Place: a small, slightly seedy private hotel at Bournemouth, England.

Two separate playlets "Table by the Window" and "Table Number Seven" are linked by a common setting and environment. In both the protagonists are outsiders, rootless and lonely people whom a self-righteous society has driven into the isolation of "separate tables." They timidly explore the possibilities of renewed self-affirmation. The private hotel has become home to a number of failures sheltering from reality behind a protective wall of illusions.
John Malcolm was once a successful politician; then an unhappy marriage drove him to drink and a scandal ended his career. Now he is reduced to "a penny-a-line" and has to thank only Miss Cooper, the owner of the hotel, and her tender concern for his last refuge, the "table at the window." This evening he is joined at this table by Anne Shankland, his divorced wife—a domineering egotist whom he still loves. Miss Cooper, in her turn, loves Malcolm enough to renounce him and carefully leads the couple together. A year and a half later it is again Miss Cooper who gives the destiny of

aging Major Pollock a happy turn. The guest at "Table Number Seven" suffers from pathological inhibitions and knows nothing of love except what he deceives himself with in dark cinema auditoriums. He meets the faded spinster Sybil, who has escaped from her mother's domineering ways into a hysterical neurosis. These two human beings who have so far been locked out of life are attracted to each other, but Sybil's dragon of a mother, Mrs. Railton Bell, has in the meantime discovered the Major's questionable past and is determined to have him hounded out of the hotel. But Miss Cooper refuses, and the two psychopaths find in their unexpected companionship the courage to start living their own life.

THE SLEEPING PRINCE. An occasional fairy tale in two acts. Prose. First edition London 1954. First performance November 5, 1953, London, Phoenix Theatre. Time: 1911. Place: Royal suite in the Legation of Carpathia, Belgrave Square, London.

This play is an excursion of competent boulevard theater into the realm of dreamy fairy-tale dalliance. Grand Duke Charles, Prince Regent of Carpathia, has come to London to represent his miniature country at the 1911 Coronation. He seeks a little light diversion for the evening by inviting a young American chorus girl to his room. But Mary Morgan, the chosen young lady, deals roughly wth the Regent's exalted whims, makes short shrift of his aristocratic eccentricities, and soon makes him see that he is nothing but a bogey. After this chilling episode the Regent not unnaturally wishes to break off this would-be adventure the next morning. But one of the Grand Duchess' ladies-in-waiting has fallen ill, and, to save the day, Mary has to take her place in accompanying the Duchess to the Coronation. Subsequently Charles's sixteen-year-old son, the king, insists on taking the dancer to the ball. Thus the Regent cannot get rid of his unpleasant memories, for the resolute little American keeps crossing his path and with her natural, warm humanity ultimately awakens his proud Highness to life and love. Overjoyed, the Grand Duke now wants to keep her forever. But Mary knows only too well how fleeting is the moment. She is content with a princely farewell present and returns to her theater, sensibly realizing that while it may be a little sad to awaken from a beautiful dream, the dream is no less beautiful for that.

# REINECKER, Herbert
(Germany, born 1914)

NACHTZUG [Night Train]. Play in two parts. Prose. Acting edition Munich, Desch, n.d. First performance March 20, 1963, Vienna, Theater in der Josefstadt. Time: the present. Place: compartments in a train.

A contemporary play in which a handful of people are abruptly faced with the necessity of making a decision without being prepared for it. The plea not to disappoint a refugee's trust becomes an ineluctable test for each individual's worth or failure in his own eyes. A night train is rushing through the Soviet zone toward the Federal Republic. In two compartments the sleepy travelers are dozing and chatting. Suddenly a young East German jumps on the train and looks for a hiding place so as to escape to freedom. Naturally, the federal beneficiaries of the "economic miracle" have every sympathy for him, but it is only after prolonged resistance that a few of them are prepared to commit the offense of "aiding and abetting flight from the republic" and to endanger their own freedom. These few cannot prevail against the massive egoism of the others, and the refugee jumps from the moving train in despair. A simple everyday occurrence is magnified to the scale of an existential charisma and presented in the sharply drawn outlines of a sensational story.

# RICE, Elmer (E. Reizenstein)
(United States, 1892–1967)

DREAM GIRL. Comedy in two acts. Prose. First edition New York 1946. First performance December 14, 1945, New York, Coronet Theatre. Time: the present. Place: changing settings suggested by props.

Applied psychotherapeutics and playful irony combine to bring an alienated outsider back from illusion to reality. Georgina Allerton runs a small bookshop with a friend, has written a gushing novel that nobody wants to read, and loves the man who is married to her sister. So there is nothing left for the poor thing except to indulge in self-pity for her heart-rending unhappiness and to revel in dreams: she sees herself courted and envied, now an applauded star and now a romantic adventuress. Suddenly wish-fulfillment is at hand—Jim is divorced and wants to take Georgina with him into the world. But she shrinks from the claims of her actualized illusion. The enterprising newspaper man Clark Redfield does win Georgina for himself, but she still has inner reservations about exchanging her dream world for the reality of marriage: "Do I have to give up dreaming altogether? Couldn't I just sort of taper off?" Finally she understands that one can dream and not make dreams your master!


# RICHARDSON, Jack
(United States, born 1935)


GALLOWS HUMOR. Play in two parts with a prologue. Prose. First edition New York 1961. First performance April 16, 1961, New York, Gramercy Arts Theatre. Time: the present. Place: a prison cell and a suburban kitchen.

Men vainly strive for freedom and self-realization; they are standardized and predetermined in their environment, their tasks, even their reactions and feelings. Richardson assigns his actors two different parts and two different situations equally without issue. The prologue is spoken by death personified. He is perplexed at finding himself in an age when the living and the dead, the executioners and the victims have become indistinguishable: "Indeed, in the last years, I seem both to have expanded and blurred my activities without knowing it. The grave's dimensions suddenly have grown to include those who have not yet achieved the once necessary technicality of ceasing to breathe. It appears I now infiltrate those still bouncing to music, still kissing their wives, still wiggling their forefingers in the air to emphasize those final truths by which they think their lives are lived. But are they, after all, living?"
Walter, a lawyer, has killed his wife in an effort to buttress his shaken sense of justice by the inexorable logic of capital punishment. During the night preceding his execution, the prostitute Lucy, who, according to the latest policies of humane prison management, is to spend Walter's last night with him, pries him loose from his rigid principles and converts him to her female charms. In the second part, the spotlight shifts from the convict to the executioner. The executioner Phillip is as satiated with his profession as with his wife, who betrays him with the warden. He tries to break out of his narrow confines and to live the sort of life he has long dreamed of. But convention is stronger and forces him back into the old yoke.

# ROBLÈS, Emmanuel
(France, born 1914)

MONTSERRAT *(Montserrat)*. Play in two acts. Prose. First edition Paris 1949. First performance April 23, 1948, Paris, Théâtre Montparnasse, and Algiers, Théâtre du Colisée. Adapted by Lillian Hellmann, New York, Dramatists' Play Service, 1950. Time: July 1812. Place: guardroom of the general's palace at Valencia, Venezuela.

The individual's struggle against an inhuman soldiery, the conflict between personal guilt and service to an idea, the predicament of having to decide among many contradictory "truths"—all the conflicts of man having to prove himself in a community—are projected in a historical model case.

The Spanish colonial army is wreaking havoc and destruction on the inhabitants of Venezuela, who are fighting for their freedom under their leader Simon Bolivar. Lieutenant Montserrat takes sides with the exploited people and helps Bolivar to elude a trap. Captain Izquierdo, Montserrat's commanding officer, decides to force Montserrat to reveal Bolivar's hiding place, and to this end rounds up six Valencians as hostages, to be shot unless Montserrat betrays the secret. Montserrat is faced with an insoluble dilemma: Shall he save the six hostages, who implore and threaten him, and thus sacrifice Bolivar and the country's freedom? He eventually chooses the uncertain chance that the ailing leader may yet escape his pursuers and carry on the revolt; he sacrifices the hostages who curse him and until the very end think only of their own skins. "What must be saved at any price is hope—the sole and at the same time the last hope."

Under the influence of Camus, Montserrat is an "homme révolté," who protests with his own destruction against senseless inhumanity. The existentialist message is presented with an oppressive theatrical realism, which is not devoid of excessively crude effects.

### ROSE, Reginald, and BUDJUHN, Horst
(Rose, United States, born 1921; Budjuhn, Germany, born 1910)

TWELVE ANGRY MEN *(Die zwölf Geschworenen)*. Play in three acts. Prose. German stage adaptation by Budjuhn of Rose's television play first published in *Six Television Plays,* New York 1956. First edition of Budjuhn's stage version, Cologne 1962. First performance of German stage version October 14, 1958, Munich, Kammerspiele. Time: the present. Place: a jury room in the United States.

A social study of the jury system broadened to deal with the conflict between personal responsibility and collective power claims, between freedom of opinion and the prejudices of the anonymous mass. It may be difficult enough to get at the truth, it may even be impossible; but this is no justification for taking the easy way out and accepting a half-truth. A crushing mass of circumstantial evidence suggests that a nineteen-year-old boy has stabbed his father to death. The jurymen must hand down a unanimous verdict. Persuaded by the arguments of the public prosecutor, they are prepared to pronounce the defendant guilty at once, when juryman No. 8, against the protests of the others, goes over the whole case once more. He is an intellectual concerned with truth, not with a vengeful judgment, and he succeeds in casting doubt on all the evidence. The testimony of the witnesses is not unambiguous, the facts can be interpreted in the defendant's favor. In the verbal swordplay the self-assurance of the jury is slowly eroded. Only No. 3 remains unconvinced; obsessed with a mania for destruction, he wants the judgment to be the electric chair. He himself, a violent family tyrant, once tormented his own son to the point of picking up a knife in self-defense. But No. 3 painfully struggles through to freedom from his own hatred, and the jury pronounces a unanimous verdict of not guilty.

The play is a masterpiece of stagecraft. Human destinies and problems with which everyone can identify are presented with unity of time and space, in a sharply drawn environment, and in the clear language of factual, concise dialogue.

# ROSEWICZ, Tadeusz
(Poland, born 1921)

THE CARD INDEX *(Kartoteka)*. One-act play. Prose. First performance March 25, 1960, Warsaw, Teatr Dramatyczny. Translated by Adam Czerniawski, in *The Card Index and Other Plays,* Playscript 6, London, Calder & Boyars, 1967. Time: the present. Place: a room.

Rosewicz transposes the collage technique of surrealist painting onto the stage, with mimic reactions, visual gags, psychological reflexes, conscious and unconscious elements linked by nonlogical associations in clowning. Without any motivation or significance, characters and situations are reduced to the instant's spontaneous impression and are registered by the public as by a sensitive film. In the meaningless recital of a dictionary, that litany of the heterogeneous, words gain a spectral life of their own, language degenerates into noise, and sense into provocative nonsense.
The hero, a man in his prime who is administrative manager of a musical comedy theater, is lying in bed and daydreaming. Memories and expectations, the past and the future, intertwine in a dreamlike sequence of pictures. The hero at seventeen is scolded by his parents for his habit of stealthily pilfering sugar. Olga, his abandoned mistress, makes a scene. She fades out to make room for war reminiscences, in which the hero appears as a Partisan. A voluble reporter, a teacher seen as an insistent inquisitor, the secretary with the appointments book are all reflections of standard situations in an ordinary life. The chorus of old men and a burlesque skit on Greek tragedy furnish a trite commentary. Suddenly there is a pause, the stage remains lit, the curtain up: "Maybe the play is merely interrupted . . . for an hour, for a year."

THE LAOCOÖN GROUP *(Grupa Laokoona)*. Play in four scenes. Prose. First published in *Dialog, Miesiecnik Póswiecony Dramaturgii Wspólczesnej teatralnej, filmowej, radiowej,* No. 8, August 1961. First performance March 14, 1962, Warsaw, Teatr Dramatyczny. Translated by Adam Czerniawski, in *The Card Index and Other Plays,* Playscript 6, London, Calder & Boyars, 1967. Time: the present. Place: a compartment in a train, a living room, a museum.

This is a bitter satire on platitudes and ready-made phrases, this time in the setting of aestheticism. Led by Papa, who has just returned from a trip to the beauties of eternal Rome, the whole family hold forth in emotional tones in praise of beauty and harmony, noble simplicity, and silent greatness—and in so doing consistently overlook the fact that the teen-age son is losing all interest in life and that his whole inner life is buried under this mountain of affected talk. Mother is undecided whether she is to go in for abstract painting or instead to express her personality by adapting Shakespeare's plays. Ecstatically she tells her friend: "It's true I've always got to go into the kitchen, but all the same I listen, always listen. . . . Marvellous how they literally take the word out of each other's mouth. They can sit like that for hours, two of them or three. . . . Today Jan was telling us of the Laocoön Group. I must confess quite honestly that it is only under the impact of his description that I really came to understand the essence of this matter. In our atomic age people are so unstable, so lacking any center of gravity, that they hardly have a sense of beauty. I can feel in an almost plastic way how Jan transfers beauty to the boy, with the valiant help of grandfather, even though he may nod from time to time." When grandfather suddenly loses his "faith in beauty," this spectral, hollow world threatens to collapse. An idea of the cabaret type, perhaps spun out too far.


THE WITNESSES *(Swiadkowle albo nasza mala stabilizacja)*. Play in three parts. Prose and free verse. First performance December 8, 1962, Głiwice, Students' Theatre "Step." Translated by Adam Czerniawski, in *The Card Index and Other Plays,* Playscript 6, London, Calder & Boyars, 1967. Time: the present. Place: room and café terrace.

Three aggressive short scenes bear witness to people's disgust with a paradise of washing machines and institutions. The key word for the stagnation of a mechanized world frozen in utilitarianism is "stabilization": "Stupidity is reduced to normal proportions . . . love and hate are less demanding . . . I am afraid, you know, I am afraid I might lose it . . . lose just this nothing . . . our little stabilization. Is it perhaps only a dream?"
A married couple has long drifted apart. The monotonous round of days, the clichés of their eternally repeated, threadbare gestures and thoughts relegate them into hopeless loneliness. With equal indifference they both note how a kitten—isn't it sweet—is first cuddled and then tormented to death by children. The occurrence no longer makes any spontaneous ethical or existential impact upon people, who instead respond with purely aesthetic reflections, the automatic reflex of an anonymous convention of taste. Two café guests, the "second" and the "third" man, are additional witnesses. Conversation turns into a monologue of misunderstood individuals, the monologue into a sequence of stuttered, disconnected words. A vague menace turns up in varying shapes, inapprehensible except by way of surmise, yet inexorably coming closer. No one can make

up his mind to run away and give up the position acquired by a whole lifetime of compromise and self-degradation. The source of disturbance in the welfare paradise proves to be a revolting, stinking piece of carrion— the dead can create uneasiness in more than one sense. The rousing problem of existence pales once more into an aesthetic discomfort. Turning up their noses a little, people put up with the stench, make it part of their "stabilization" and rely on the institutions. Only the street cleaners are perhaps in a position to do something some time about this pollution. A series of variations is made up of episodic action and associative language: "Our language is as inadequate as a stepladder with broken rungs."

# ROUSSIN, André
(France, born 1911)

UNE FEMME QUI DIT LA VÉRITÉ and LES GLORIEUSES *[A Woman Who Speaks the Truth* and *Saints in Glory]*. Two comedies. Two acts, prose, and three acts, verse. First edition Paris 1961. First performance September 15, 1960, Paris, Théâtre de la Madeleine. Time: the present. Place: drawing room of a Paris apartment.

Ever since Molière the French have delighted in examples of the smug, pedagogic style; one of this species is put through its paces in vaudeville theater. The two pieces were loosely joined together under the title "School of Marriage" on the German stage, but what they have in common is theme and star performance rather than any message they may convey.
*Une Femme qui dit la vérité* is a piece of dialogue virtuosity, *Les Glorieuses* a farce in bombastic alexandrines. In *Une Femme,* husband Marcel and lover Jean grieve together over the farewell letter of charming Nicole, who has fled from the lie of their triangular life. The two involuntary widowers comfort each other with a sarcastic discussion of their psychological state. Suddenly it turns out that the letter was written years ago. The lady will come back quite unconcerned. The lie of the past has long become an acceptable truth, and the two men are content to possess Nicole's love, if not her faithfulness.
In *Les Glorieuses,* the unsuccessful comedy writer Gilbert Carruche gives the ladies of his circle a lesson from a school for wives. In his latest comedy he paints a portrait of his own family. His wife Yvonne is a silly society woman who ecstatically fastens onto whatever celebrity happens to be fashionable; his mother-in-law is one of those widows who, in the hope of fame and royalties, exploit the memory of their late poet husband and

make a ritual of worshipping the "immortal master." The comedy is a hit. Gilbert, thus suddenly become famous himself, finds to his horror that Yvonne's exasperating admiration is now lavished upon him. The hard-tried author decides he must now write a sure-fire flop, perhaps some piece in alexandrines, for instance something like *Les Glorieuses* . . .

THE LITTLE HUT *(La Petite Hutte)*. Comedy in three acts. Prose. First edition Monaco 1948. First performance October 28, 1947, Brussels, Théâtre des Galéries. Translated by Nancy Mitford, London, Hamish Hamilton, 1951; New York, Dramatists' Play Service 1953. Time: the present. Place: a desert island.

This is an attack on our private taboos and social white lies worked into a brilliant feat in the best French boulevard tradition. Capricious Susan, her husband Philip, and her lover Henry, the sole survivors of a ship-wreck, are stranded on a lonely island. To make sure that Henry can continue to enjoy his secret pleasures, the liaison has to be made "official." The obliging lady gets hopelessly entangled in the strategy of her seductions, for any tender attention to one partner always means a slight to the other, who then has to be pacified by an extra portion of charm, which amounts to another gross disadvantage to the first. Similarly, the gentlemen's well-meant attempts at discretion are unintentionally embarrassing and disturb the peace. The situation becomes unbearable. Is destiny really going to be so cruel as to deprive the severely tried members of high society of their last spice of life? Philip, a banker, knows how to organize things and finds a way out. The husband and the lover agree that Susan is to change partners once a week. Philip is visibly rejuvenated by the knowledge that he has a rival in his wife's favors; after this rude awakening from the cosy round of conjugal days, he playfully courts Susan and thereby provokes the wrath of Henry, who sees himself cheated of his role as a glorious lady-killer. When one of the islanders turns up and threatens the marriage idyll, Susan is only too willing to "sacrifice" herself and to follow the native into his little hut, sure that he is an exciting jungle prince. But once more the little female becomes a victim of her romantic soul, for the Negro prince turns out to be a simple ship's cook. A ship takes these artists of life and love on board and carries them back home. Henry plans to persuade his friend Philip that he, Henry, has now finally broken with Susan, so that henceforth he can again enjoy the charms of secrecy without fear of disturbance.

## ROZOV, Viktor Sergeyevich
(Russia, born 1913)

IN SEARCH OF HAPPINESS *(V poiskach radosti)*. Comedy in two acts. Prose. First performance 1957, Moscow, Central Children's Theatre. Translated by Nina Froud, London, Evans, 1961. Time: the present. Place: Savina's room in a Moscow suburb.

Without shedding the moralizing, didactic intent, Rozov shows the "positive hero" in the differentiated terms of his contradictory human nature. Russian everyday life with its good and its bad moments, the life of humble folk in all its impulsiveness are described in living detail, yet always seen *sub specie aeternitatis* of solidarity: "Why should I be thinking only of my own happiness, of myself alone? . . . One should always think of the people who are worse off than one's self. It's our business, after all, to see to it that everybody's life gets better and happier. Is it worth while living at all, otherwise?"
Crowded together in a tiny space Savina lives with her four children in an old suburban apartment, smoothes out quarrels and sees to it that eventually the fulfillment of one's duty to the community and personal satisfaction become one and the same thing for each other. Fyodor, the eldest son, has been so absorbed by his scientific career and by his wife's selfish zest for life that he has lost all family sense and readiness to help. Fyodor's wife inconsiderately stores in the tiny apartment all the furniture she manages to acquire, until the second son, Olyeg, the enthusiastic scribbler of verses, smashes up the precious junk in a fit of rage. Fyodor and his wife leave his mother's apartment. In the meantime, the daughter Tanya chooses an honest farm laborer in preference to an arrogant scientist, and the youngest son Kolya loyally stands by his Marina, whose mother has just been arrested for dealing on the black market.

VECHNO ZHIVYE *[Those Who Live Forever]*. Play in three acts. Prose. Written 1955. First edition Moscow 1956. First performance February 1956, Leningrad, Komisarzhevskaya Theatre. Time: before and after the Second World War. Place: Soviet Union.

A picture of the times is colorfully painted on a broad canvas, showing how the war erupts into an average family group and becomes a test for each member of it. Realistic and detailed description of everyday life successfully prevails over the simplified, pedagogic intent.
Young Boris volunteers for the front, leaving behind his promising scien-

tific career and his fiancée Veronica. He is reported missing. His father, a doctor, and the rest of the family are evacuated from Moscow. Total strangers selflessly help each other. Even those who are otherwise indifferent and carefree are spurred into meeting their responsibilities in these "dark times." The only asocial element in the family circle is an artist, cousin Mark, the pianist. He not only manages to evade military service, but also successfully courts the discouraged and fickle Veronica. But he soon tires of his marriage with her and falls under the spell of a demi-mondaine, a *femme fatale* who attracts all the evil bourgeois forces that have not entirely vanished as yet even in the Soviet Union. An honest factory girl is deflected from her work and demoralized as a chambermaid. A corrupted crowd of drug addicts, culture bosses, and women clerks pursue their black market deals at the expense of the starving population and enliven this shady side of life, which is drawn in voluptuous detail. After the war Veronica, too, has learned that she must accept her responsibilities. She finds a loyal companion in the young soldier Vladimir, whose life Boris saved during the battle and in so doing was killed. Vladimir will also carry on his dead friend's scientific work. "The people bequeath the work of their hands and their mind. . . ." The migration of the cranes, which was nothing but a thoughtlessly repeated nursery rhyme for Veronica all her life, is now for the first time a reality that she experiences in the countryside, happy and looking forward to the future.

## SACHS, Nelly
(Germany, born 1891)

ELI *[Eli]*. A mystery play on the sufferings of Israel. Seventeen scenes. Free verse. Written 1943–1944. First edition Malmö 1951. First broadcast 1959 by the Swedish radio as an opera with music by Moses Pergament. First stage performance March 14, 1962, Dortmund, Städtische Bühnen. First performance as an opera, with music by Walter Steffens, March 5, 1967, Dortmund, Städtische Bühnen. Time: "after the martyrdom" of the Second World War. Place: Poland and Germany.

In the darkly glowing ardor of Hasidic mystical reality, the world of the dead, men, plants, and stones are all fused in a cosmos of sound, a lament in vivid incantatory language for the sufferings of Israel. The author explains: "I was at all times intent in transposing the unspeakable onto a transcendental plane, so as to make it bearable and to convey in this night of nights a glimmer of the sacred darkness in which the quiver and the arrow are hidden."

German soldiers have destroyed a Jewish village in Poland and massacred virtually all the inhabitants. The few survivors gather together and grieve, lamenting especially young Eli, the pious shepherd boy, who in the midst of the bloodbath tried to call down God's help with the sound of his flute and was killed by a German soldier. The bootmaker Michael has the Ba'al-Shem* eye and is one of the thirty-six righteous men for whose sake, according to Hasidic belief, the world is saved, "one who follows the course of the waters and hears the earth turning, . . . one who wears the shoes of Israel's wandering. . . ." Visible to Michael alone, the murderer's face magically appears on Eli's shroud, and an inner voice commands Michael to set forth and call the murderer to account. Michael struggles through an eerie no-man's-land where the stones talk and the skeleton fingers of the executioners ceaselessly do their deadly work. The lonely wanderer vicariously suffers the torments of his people and dies innumerable deaths. He finds the murderer as a prosperous tenant farmer in Germany, who justifies himself in terms of his military duty and had misinterpreted Eli's flute as a signal of attack. His unrepenting wickedness claims another innocent victim, for his own child dies of a fever. The crushing reproach of the whole of creation causes the murderer to disintegrate, limb by limb. Michael, too, disappears from the earth. His mission is fulfilled, and he enters into the glory of God.

The play is an oratorio with monumental imagery, and the biblically

---

* According to Hasidic belief, a wise man who does wonders by use of the name of God.

exalted language of the psalms combines with the expressive ardor of
Hasidic ecstasy to make an impact of compelling unity.


## SAGAN, Françoise (Françoise Quoirez)
(France, born 1935)


CASTLE IN SWEDEN (Château en Suède). Comedy in four acts. Prose.
Written 1959. First edition Paris 1960. First performance March 11, 1960,
Paris, Théâtre de l'Atelier. Translated by Lucienne Hill, produced in
London May 23, 1962. Time: the present. Place: drawing room in a
Swedish castle.

A melancholy farce in which profundity and banality, cultivated drawing-
room conversation and macabre brooding, psychology, and cliché are
whipped up into an entertaining soufflé. The landowner Hugo let it be
known that his wife Ophelia was dead, while in fact he had locked her up
as mad in his remote castle, so as to be free to marry the seductive Eleonore.
The latter enjoys the security of this marriage, but at the same time has an
erotic attachment to her brother Sebastian, a cynical poseur. She amuses
herself by starting a flirtation with any guest who happens to be overtaken
by the winter and snowbound in the isolated castle. This time it is a distant
cousin, Frederic, a self-satisfied lady's man. In an artful crescendo the husband, the brother, and the sister drive the seducer into a panic, until
Frederic flees from the dark hints of murder and perishes in the icy
countryside. All the other male guests had also met with a similarly violent
death. The family congratulate each other on this new success, and Eleonore begins to dream of the next arrival.
Although this fancy-dress jest (a cranky aunt insists that they all wear
rococo costumes) places this comedy close to Anouilh and his elegant am-
biguities, the black humor has more in common with Strindberg than the
mere setting of crushing hopelessness. Spleen and disgust with life are the
origin of these charming vices, behind which we glimpse the horror of an
existential dance of death: "Time always stands between us and what we
want."

LA ROBE MAUVE DE VALENTINE *[Valentine's Mauve Dress]*. Play in two
acts. Prose. Written 1962. First edition Paris 1963. First performance
January 16, 1963, Paris, Théâtre des Ambassadeurs-Henry Bernstein.
Time: the present. Place: Paris.

Puppets of modern society flit about with entertaining frivolity among
banalities, piquant dialogue, and moments of thoughtfulness: "You know,
in effect that's all we have to defend. Worn-out words that sound high-
falutin, and behind which tremble profound, and sometimes bloody truths."
A nymphomaniac, who takes pleasure for granted with natural unconcern,
is the central figure in today's general pursuit of pleasure. Marie is fighting
doggedly for her late husband's inheritance, with the help of a lawyer who
does not stop short of a marriage proposal. She and her son live at present
in a shabby hotel, where they are unexpectedly joined by her touchingly
helpless, younger cousin Valentine. Valentine's husband, the film magnate
Jean-Lou, has politely but firmly sent her away with a generous check for
travel so that he can devote himself undisturbed to his latest mistress.
Valentine has lost the money in gambling, and with natural naivete
takes refuge with her poor relations. "There are people whose life could be
summarized in a few such desperately vague words. In your case, they
would be: charm, tulips, balconies, absent-mindedness, laziness." Valentine
proceeds to divert herself with romantic flirtations, picture transfers, her
mauve dress, and blue tulips.
Marie's son Serge, an insignificant advertising artist who imagines himself
a budding Van Gogh, is so carried away by his aunt Valentine's persecuted
innocence that he consoles her with all his youthful passion, even though
it means being unfaithful to his mistress. Marie wins her case, and Valentine's love affair can now be carried on in puce silk, in the best style of
women's magazine fiction. Suddenly the idyll is disturbed by the appearance
of her husband Jean-Lou. It turns out that in fact it is Valentine who over
and over again goes off with her husband's money to enjoy successive
adventures, large and small. Jean-Lou loves her enough not to be afraid
even of ridicule, and always waits for her return quietly and without reproach. Now she would like to stay with Serge, but he with his strict
principles wants to have nothing further to do with her. The capricious
lady floats off to Italy with her husband as—a no doubt temporary—escort.

## SALACROU, Armand
(France, born 1899)

L'ARCHIPEL LEÑOIR OU IL NE FAUT PAS TOUCHER AUX CHOSES IMMOBILES [*The Lenoir Archipelago, or One Must Not Touch Immobile Things*]. Comedy in two parts. Prose. First edition Paris 1948. First performance November 8, 1947, Paris, Théâtre Montparnasse. Time: the night of July 3, 1935. Place: drawing room at the Lenoir family's castle, Calvados, France.

In the best boulevard tradition, this comedy maneuvers successfully in the archipelago of stage effects using the macabre, the grotesque, and the crime story. The powerful Lenoir clan consists of an archipelago, a confusion of island existences. At their head is the seventy-three-year-old liqueur manufacturer Paul-Albert Lenoir, and all of them are kept afloat by more spiritual and lucrative liquids than is usually the case with archipelagos. Carried away by the fire of his products, grandfather Lenoir has taken one liberty too many with his secretary. There is a threat of scandal, the reputation of the firm is in danger, and the aristocratic in-laws, acquired by hard dowry cash, are shocked. With much feeling it is explained to the old man what a convenient moment this would be for a respectable death, and how satisfactory for all concerned. But Grandpa remains obstinate even when his son-in-law Adophe presses him to accept the most useful present of a gun. The two men are left alone and suddenly, to everybody's relief, a shot is heard. Next morning the most bewildering speculations are rife: What happened? Is Grandpa dead? Or did he shoot Adolphe in justified self-defense? But all is well, as soon becomes clear with the help of the butler who is well versed in family intrigues. Conflicts are puffed away in witty remarks which may not be the most credible, but are certainty the most entertaining way of getting the better of them.

LES NUITS DE LA COLÈRE [*Nights of Anger*]. Play in two parts. Prose. First edition Paris 1947. First performance December 12, 1946, Paris, Théâtre Marigny. Time: April 1944. Place: the Bazires' dining room at Chartres.

This is a drama of the French resistance, and it typifies the contrasting attitudes and options of the French under the Vichy regime. The chemical engineer Jean Cordeau reacts to the defeat of France and the terror of the German occupation as to a personal challenge and joins the Maquis. He is injured when blowing up a train and takes refuge with his old friend

Bernard Bazire. Bernard is a respectable man with a family to look after; he always obeys the governing power and tries to keep out of trouble by not drawing attention to himself. Out of fear he betrays Jean, and in his turn the neighbor Pisançon, an opportunist collaborator, "does his duty." Jean dies under the tortures of the Gestapo, and the informers from bullets of the resistance fighters. As corpses they still argue fiercely about justice and guilt. The episode of the final bloodbath serves to anticipate and frame the action, into which the antecedents are worked in brief scenes.

## SALOMON, Horst
(Germany, born 1929)

KATZENGOLD *[Cat Gold]*. Play in five acts and a prologue. Free verse. First performance June 11, 1964, Gera, Bühnen der Stadt. Time: the present. Place: a mine in East Germany.

This is a didactic utility play written collectively for the Agitprop movement. Salomon, a miner, brings together the colliers from the Wismut mines and the party officials for a discussion at which proposals for amendments are brought forward. He also consults with theater people and state dramaturgists. This method of manufacturing a play by the teamwork of various specialists, as though it were some piece of sound craftsmanship turned on a lathe, may seem incomprehensible to Western aesthetes, but it corresponds to the Marxist conception of the social application of art.

Everyday conflicts in a coal mine are illustrated by sharply contrasted types. There is the arrogance of the "educated" members of the pit management and their jealousy of the colliers who intervene with constructive proposals in business planning. Suspicion and misunderstandings divide the party officials and the technicians. Piontek, the instructor, is downgraded as a result of false accusations, in order to make possible the promotion to foreman of the ambitious and unscrupulous Gäbler. Justice is made to prevail thanks to a rising of the apprentices, a bunch of "golden-hearted toughs," and to a pit accident in which Piontek's humanity shows its worth. "Cat gold," the valueless mica whose glimmer shows the trapped miners the way to safety, is the symbol for the unassuming, anonymous "positive hero" who proves his worth in a crisis.

## SARKADI, Irme
(Hungary, 1921–1961)

OSZLOPOS SIMEON *[Simeon the Stylite]*. Three acts. Prose. First edition Budapest 1962. Time: the present. Place: the studio of the painter Kis.

This farce is directed against the outsiders who do not meet the demands of social reality. The revolt of the individual against the rules of everyday life and the compromises of society are historically exemplified by the Syrian saint, Simeon the Stylite (died A.D. 459), who elected to live on the top of a column in order to avoid contact with the earth. The painter János Kis carries to the extreme his challenge to society. Drinking and philosophizing, he pursues his bohemian existence. His girl friend Maria, who was hoping for middle-class security, leaves him. Because he is a failure as a drawing master, he is expelled from his teaching job. He seduces a young married woman and soon deceives her, whereupon she stabs him. Individualism is seen from the Marxist point of view; it is branded as nihilistic destruction and antisocial wrong and is equated with the Christian asceticism of the stylite.

## SAROYAN, William
(United States, born 1908)

THE CAVE DWELLERS. Play in two acts. Prose. First edition New York 1958. First performance December 7, 1956, Darmstadt, Germany. Time: the present. Place: an abandoned theater on the lower East Side, New York.

A dreamy fairy tale about the world, that transient scene, is represented by an abandoned stage. The political and social conflicts of his time are only raw materials for Saroyan, who lets his imagination play with the self-abandon of a child: "Nobody *belongs* here, but here we are . . . because we *don't* belong here. It's not our place. It's a cave. What are we doing in a cave? We're angels. What are we doing in bodies?" An empty, dilapidated theatre in the slums is the last refuge of a handful of down-and-outers: the "King" and the "Queen," an aging couple of actors, go on dreaming their parts; the "Duke" is a prizefighter who twenty years before had lost a title match and now cannot overcome his fears; a roofless family of bear-keepers arrive with their baby and their bear. Only the "Girl" stands with both feet in reality, and she proceeds to pound some sense into this hopeless group. The "King" goes out to beg and steal for the starving infant; the "Duke" yearns for the girl's love but renounces her when he guesses her affection for the milkman's boy. A wrecking crew arrives and starts to pull down the protective cave. But the people in it are ready to step out into a reality which is transformed for them. The past's sins of commission and omission, conjured up on the many levels of a dream, here lose their psychoanalytical function and are ennobled in the poetry of little things.

LILY DAFON. Play in three acts. Prose. First performance February 27, 1960, Vienna, Burgtheater. Time: the present. Place: Paris. [This play has been performed only abroad.]

Saroyan's graceful tribute to Paris and its feminine charms. After a lifetime of work, care, and responsibility, an "American in Paris" learns to be light-hearted and gay, to accept everything as an enchanting gift and to let it go without regrets. This bitter-sweet romance about the incompatibility of age and youth is clothed in language of old-fashioned, lovingly ornate indirectness.

A horse and a gift of flowers lead to the encounter between the rich Texas farmer Hannaberry, who is breaking away from his fixed, sensible existence, and little Lily Dafon. In Paris the American chases after the unfulfilled dreams of his childhood. He forgets his domineering wife and the approach of old age. Lily tries to teach the blunt Texan elegant conversation and introduces him to her droll family with all its gradations of generations up to great-grandmother. He fascinates her by his simple humanity. But then his grown-up sons arrive from the United States and make him realize how much he is needed at home. Tenderly he leaves his love for Lily in the world of dreams and buys her a country place where she is to live a happy, philoprogenitive life with her fiancé, as befits her youth.

Saroyan surrounds this unequal pair with a quaint crowd of secondary figures in a world of gay nonsense. Lily's fiancé refashions trees because he thinks they will fit better into his reality with new colors; the broker Leloup plays *deus ex machina* and becomes the asthmatic victim of his appetite; and mother, grandmother, and great-grandmother give joy as charmingly faded portraits of the girl. Talking dogs and birds provide mordant comments. Men's feelings suddenly break out into song. Scenes and situations are juxtaposed by film-cutting techniques, and the story thereby given a poetic light.

### SARTRE, Jean-Paul
(France, born 1905)

THE CHIPS ARE DOWN *(Les Jeux sont faits)*. Script for a film by Jean Delannoy. First edition Paris 1947. Translated by Louise Varese, New York, Crown, 1948 and London, Rider, 1951. Time: the present. Place: an imaginary dictatorship.

Man's loneliness is overcome by love. Love restores their freedom to those "in camera"—this time in the inevitability of the world of the dead. And this freedom gives men a chance to choose for the community, for responsibility, and for a futile, yet necessary self-sacrifice. As the leader of a resistance group, the worker Pierre Dumaine has prepared a revolt against the dictator, but on the eve of the appointed day falls victim to an act of revenge and is shot in the street. Eve Charlier is poisoned in the midst of her frivolous life of luxury by her husband, a high police official of the regime. The two young people, who have thus been forcibly removed from life, get into a macabre and droll world inhabited by the dead who move invisibly among the living, observe everything, mockingly comment on everything, and are quite human in their indulgence of their curiosity and little vanities. But they have been relieved forever of the unceasing hurry which drives the living. The miracle of a great love blossoms between Eve and Pierre, and the old lady in the registry of the dead must, though disapprovingly, apply the law which permits any couple that were destined for each other but were prevented by life's vicissitudes from meeting on earth, to return to the world of the living for one day. If, in this span of time, the lovers preserve their mutual confidence in spite of all obstacles, a new life is granted to them.

Pierre and Eve return to the world of the living. Pierre tries unsuccessfully to get his friends to call off the revolt, which he now knows to be betrayed and therefore senseless; the fact of his knowing Eve marks him out as a class enemy and traitor. Eve, in her turn, is regarded as ridiculous when she turns up among her snobbish acquaintances with the rough diamond Pierre. Both of them offend the world by their love and therefore fail in their desire to help the community. Eve cannot save her sister Lucette from the wicked designs of her own husband, who poisoned her. The environment proves stronger than the lovers' love. They doggedly pursue their senseless tasks and thereby lose each other and the chance of a new beginning. Sadly and hopelessly they return to the realm of the invisible. There they at once meet another young couple ready to try their luck. Once more the test is to be applied. Elements of the Orpheus myth are modernized in the setting of a social problem.

THE CONDEMNED OF ALTONA (also: *Loser Wins; Altona*) *(Les Séquestrés d'Altona)*. A play. First edition Paris 1960. First performance September 23, 1959, Paris. Théâtre de la Renaissance. Translated by Sylvia and George Leeson, New York, Random House, 1963; London, Hamish Hamilton, 1960 *(Loser Wins);* Harmondsworth, Penguin, 1962 *(Altona)*. Adapted by Justin O'Brien for American premiere February 3, 1966, New York, Repertory Theater, Lincoln Center. Time: the present. Place: the family mansion of the Gerlachs, near Hamburg, Germany.

In the midst of a blood-stained age that has calmly returned to its ordinary routine, one man is driven by his conscience to accept guilt and penance. This brings him into conflict with the rest of the world, in whose busy prosperity there is no room for justice.

Throughout his life the German industrialist and shipyard owner Gerlach never regarded his country's successive governments as anything other than business partners to be used for buttressing his own power. His son Franz during the second world war committed what in his own eyes was a crime. As a mere boy, an eighteen-year-old lieutenant, he wanted to save a rabbi from the Gestapo but desisted under the persuasion of his father's "political reasonableness." Obeying orders, he caused Russian prisoners to be tortured to better protect his own men against partisan attacks. Now his conscience will not let him rest and for the last thirteen years he has imprisoned himself in his room. Only his sister Leni has access to him and loves him with passionate exclusivity. Franz is obsessed with his mission of defending humanity before the thirtieth century's judges, who are reduced to the state of mere crabs, and to explain to them humanity's inhuman attitude. He is convinced that Germany, in the name of justice, survived the last war only as a burnt-out crater condemned to sterility. "The razed cities, the broken machines, the dismantled industrial plant, the rapidly mounting unemployment and tuberculosis, the steep plunge of the demographic curve—none of this I failed to notice." In his burning need to atone, Franz makes tape recordings of his speeches for the defense and, half crazy, immures himself amid conches, justificatory delusions and penitential writhings, and subordinates his whole life to his obsession.

This rejection of reality comes to determine the life of the whole family, who in their turn isolate themselves to preserve the appearance of unblemished family honor. As far as the outside world is concerned, Franz is covered by an Argentinian death certificate. Eventually the father succeeds in making Johanna, the wife of his younger, altogether ordinary son Werner, call on Franz. The young woman, who, in the soulless despotism of this aristocracy of money, for the first time finds a task to be done, might lead the maniac back to reality, but Leni is driven by evil jealousy to step between the lovers. Franz goes to his death with his father, who has an incurable cancer of the throat that is stripping him of his power. Their death is carefully disguised as an accident, so that nothing will cloud the family's reputation.

Sartre's endeavor to translate his philosophy into detailed stage action occasionally leads him into artificial expedients. The inhumanity and dogmatism of the Third Reich are represented as the direct outcome of life-denying, ascetic Protestantism. Leni's incestuous obsession stands for the racial pride and family conceit that Sartre observes as a characteristic of the German nation: "I was born a Gerlach, that means mad with pride, and I can go to bed only with a Gerlach. Incest is my law, my destiny." Flashbacks and symbolic gestures are used in an attempt to find a new way of transposing contemporary events into universal terms.

DIRTY HANDS (also: *Crime Passionel; Red Gloves*) *(Les Mains sales)*. Play in seven scenes. Prose. First edition Paris 1948. First performance April 2, 1948, Paris, Théâtre Antoine. Translated by Lionel Abel, in *Three Plays*, New York, Knopf, 1949, and by Kitty Black *(Crime Passionel)*, in *Three Plays*, London, Hamish Hamilton, 1949. Adapted by Daniel Taradash *(Red Gloves)* for New York production December 4, 1948, Mansfield Theatre. Time: 1943–1945. Place: Illyria, an imaginary country somewhere in Europe, between the German and the Russian fronts.

The insoluble conflict between Antigone and Creon, between the idealist who defends the purity of his moral ideal even unto death and the practical politician, who does not mind "dirty hands" and, if need be, achieves worthy ends by base and unscrupulous means.

The young intellectual Hugo has been driven by his ardent love for humanity and his passion for self-sacrifice to join the Communist party, where his bourgeois origins always make him an outsider. He volunteers for the mission of assassinating the current party leader Hoederer, who advocates a coalition with the bourgeois and royalist camp; he, therefore, has become unacceptable to the fanatical bolsheviks. Hugo falls under the spell of Hoederer's compelling humanity, which causes him to compromise and to forget about his principles whenever the moment's needs or a spontaneous demand challenge his human feelings. Hugo is shaken in his loyalty to the party. It takes a sudden fit of jealousy, provoked by Hugo's coquettish wife Jessica, to send on its way the fatal bullet which kills Hoederer and forces Hugo again to toe the line. Released from prison two years later, Hugo learns that, in the changed political circumstances, Hoederer is now worshipped as a martyr by the party. Hugo, who believed that he was the executioner of a just sentence, has become a common murderer. Embittered, he refuses to change his mind once more, and allows himself to be shot by comrades with a less sensitive conscience. Flashbacks are used in building up this exciting discussion drama, which is marked by the self-doubts of the early postwar years.

KEAN, OR DISORDER AND GENIUS *(Kean ou désordre et génie)*. Play in five acts. Based on a play by Alexandre Dumas, père (1836). Prose. First edition Paris 1953. First performance November 16, 1953, Paris, Théâtre Sarah Bernhardt. Translated by Kitty Black, London, Hamish Hamilton, 1954; adapted by Peter Stone for New York production, November 2, 1961, Broadway Theatre. Time: 1824. Place: London.

What Sartre lifts out of the brilliant costume play by the romantic playwright Dumas is the noted actor's inner conflict. Kean is so feverishly intent on his efforts at characterization, at feeling himself into the most extreme parts and mastering them, that he ends up by losing his private self: "I shall go on imitating the natural until it becomes my second nature." He loses his grip on reality; his affection for Elena, the wife of the Danish Ambassador, and for the simple girl Anna Danby becomes a mere flood of self-intoxication. Eventually the eternal player is turned into a plaything of royal whims, when the Prince of Wales, who bestows his favors upon Elena, has Kean exiled to America. All the well-tried devices of theatrical make-believe, from the play within a play to secret doors and a riot of props, are mobilized for an evening's brilliant entertainment in which everything is subordinated to virtuosity.

LUCIFER AND THE LORD (also: *The Devil and the Good Lord*) *(Le Diable et le bon dieu)*. Play in three acts. Prose. First edition Paris 1951. First performance June 7, 1951, Paris, Théâtre Antoine. Translated by Kitty Black, London, Hamish Hamilton, 1953; also, under the title *The Devil and the Good Lord*, New York, Knopf, 1960. Time: 1524–1526. Place: Germany.

Almost simultaneously Sartre and Cocteau came forward with plays from the reformation era, in which they tried to apply intellectual analysis to the solution of the given conflict between good and evil, freedom and necessity. Sartre justifies the historical background of his philosophical play in existentialist terms: "I believe that the thesis of the reformation, according to which everyone is a prophet, is much more illuminating than the thesis of the French Revolution, according to which all men are born equal. This thesis of the absolute and religious value that every man has for all others, made me prefer the reformation and especially the peasant prophets of that time to all other historical situations and personalities. . . . Today's problems concerning human liberty and man as such should make us reexamine our relationship to God from the same point of view as during the reformation. The problem of political evil cannot be put in different terms today if we believe in transcendence."

Three entirely different kinds of people are engaged in a struggle for their moral and religious existence: Goetz, a man of action, Heinrich, a man of the church, and Nasty, an enthusiast. Commander Goetz and his soldiery are besieging the rebellious town of Worms, at the instance of the archbishop. Goetz is a libertine, a violent man who suffers from the futility of existence and counters it with the cynical challenge of absolute evil. He gains possession of Worms by treason on the part of the poor men's priest Heinrich. Heinrich has betrayed the people and their trust in him, in order to serve the authorities and save the clergy from the rebels. He believes this evil deed to have made him pleasing in the sight of God and providence. Goetz, who has so far turned to evil only out of Promethean revolt, is persuaded by Heinrich that in this grim world genuine resistance can lie only in enforcing the good. He changes fronts, becomes the "captain of the good" and with undiminished frenzy tries to reshape the world. He gives away all his property, turns the oppressed peasants into landowners and preaches nonviolence. His actions earn him the suspicion of the lowly folk and the enmity of the nobility, who are afraid of losing their privileges.

Chastened, Goetz realizes that his ardent pursuit of the absolute good has caused more hatred and upheaval, more suffering and death of innocent victims than the wildest excesses of his former evildoing. Even the stigmatization which Goetz blasphemously performs upon himself so as to bring suffering and redemption into his own, free human life, cannot wipe evil off the face of the earth. There is only one man who seems to be happy in the confusion of that age, and that is the sectarian preacher Nasty, for his fanatic obsession has made him proof against inner doubt. For Goetz, Sartre's existentialism is the only consolation: good and evil merge indistinguishably into each other. Man is not a datum, he discovers his true self only in freedom and responsible action: "I shall be alone with the empty sky above me, because only thus can I be with all. . . . In this world and in this age good and evil are intermingled; I must resign myself to being evil, in order to become good." Goetz takes sides with the exploited peasants, even though he is convinced that the fight can lead to nothing. Sartre explains this moral attitude as follows: "Goetz, a monster in evil and a saint in goodness, understands the good as something absolute, because he wants to maintain a certain relationship with God. When he descends to men, he renounces every demand for the absolute—because he has become modest and no longer relates himself to God, and he does so in the conviction that the good is impossible in a society founded on injustice. If the whole of society is evil, all one can do is to take part in the fight, even if the fight is hopeless, as it was in the peasants' war against the nobility."

NEKRASSOV *(Nekrassov)*. Play in eight scenes. Prose. First edition Paris 1956. First performance June 8, 1955, Paris, Théâtre Antoine. Translated by Sylvia and George Leeson, London, Hamish Hamilton 1956. Time: the present. Place: Paris.

*Nekrassov* is Sartre's answer, from his own leftist point of view, to the anti-communist hysteria of McCarthyism. More than one satirical device is overelaborated into the terms of an all too obvious political pamphlet, and while this is historically understandable, it has not helped the play.

The newspaperman Sibilot, who urgently needs a scoop, introduces the notorious swindler Georges de Valéra as Nekrassov, a former Soviet Minister of the Interior "seeking freedom." Nekrassov readily obliges the public in love with its own fears with a wealth of bloodcurdling details about Russian conditions: "Life is like a panic in a burning theater. Everyone looks for the exit, no one finds it, they hit out at each other, and whoever falls is unlucky, he gets trampled on at once." The sensation-mongering press and the unscrupulous politicians, who, though they are quite aware that the whole thing is a hoax, see in it a golden opportunity for another boom in the armaments industry, eventually become too much for de Valéra's conscience. He elopes with Sibilot's daughter, a faithful fellow traveler. The wicked capitalist press at once launches the story that Nekrassov, who all this time has been spending a holiday in the Crimea without an inkling of the whole affair, has been kidnapped by the Russians and forcibly repatriated. No denial by the desperate de Valéra can prevail against the conspiracy of the wicked warmongers.

THE RESPECTFUL PROSTITUTE (also: *The Respectable Prostitute*) *(La Putain respectueuse)*. Play in two scenes. Prose. First edition Paris 1946. First performance November 8, 1946, Paris, Théâtre Antoine. Translated by Lionel Abel, in *Three Plays,* New York, Knopf, 1949, and by Kitty Black, in *Three Plays,* London, Hamish Hamilton, 1949. Adapted by Eva Wolas for New York production, March 16, 1948, Cort Theatre. Time: the present. Place: a furnished room somewhere in the Southern United States.

This is a protest against racialism in the context of the broader problem of the "guided decision," of individual opinion shaped by "official" phraseology in today's mass society.

During a train journey the prostitute Lizzie has been molested by a young rascal of very good family. In the subsequent fight a Negro is shot; he happened to be there but had nothing to do with it all. His pal is now to be lynched by the hate-inflamed whites to provide a culprit for the whole occurrence. The Negro flees to Lizzie, who at the time is enjoying the favors of Senator Clarke's son Fred. The Negro asks Lizzie to tell the truth, which alone an save him from his persecutors. Fred, who is a cousin of the true culprit, and his self-righteous papa offer Lizzie money for a perjury and convince her with fine phrases that it is a national duty to sacrifice one or other of the useless black beasts of labor for the "rash" action of a highly placed white. Reluctantly the girl agrees, betrays the Negro and henceforth can count on both father and son from the respectable senatorial family among her lecherous "regulars." Lizzie's heart is with the Negro—they are both degraded, abused instruments in the hands of the rich. None of the oppressed has the courage to rebel. It is a play with a message, and it tells its message in the crude black-and-white outlines of a poster, in an effort to denounce an evil and rouse a protest.

THE VICTORS (also: *Men without Shadows*) (*Morts sans sépulture*). Play in three acts. Prose. First edition Lausanne 1946. First performance November 8, 1946, Paris, Théâtre Antoine. Translated by Lionel Abel, in *Three Plays*, New York, Knopf, 1949, and by Kitty Black *(Men without Shadows)*, in *Three Plays*, London, Hamish Hamilton, 1949. Time: 1945. Place: French village school.

The crude brutality of a war episode is stripped of its material aspects and shown as a means of moral purification which, in accordance with Sarte's philosophy, implies knowledge. Five members of the French resistance have fallen into the hands of their Fascist compatriots and are being tortured. They are to reveal their leader's hideout. They do not know where he is, they are tortured for nothing, and by the futility of their suffering lose hope. Then their comrade Jean, taken to be a harmless passerby, is locked up with them; he has every expectation of being released very soon by his unsuspecting captors. For the others, physical torture now becomes a terrible spiritual test. The temptations of conscience are more agonizing than the pain of their maltreated bodies. One of them jumps out of the window. Jean feels expelled from the circle of his friends, for the compulsion to go on living is guilt in the face of those who have to die. Even Lucie, who used to love him, loses her feelings in the tension of self-abnegation. Her brother, a teen-aged boy named François, does not have the strength to withstand torture. His collapse might endanger Jean's release, and in order to prevent that, the others strangle him in tacit agreement—a sacramental death, true to the principle that the individual (François) must sacrifice himself for the group, and the group in its turn for the individual (Jean). Jean returns to freedom in a hopeless and oppressed state, planning a ruse by which his comrades are to be liberated as well. But one of the guards breaks his word, with the result that the prisoners lose their lives.

Although this play is often mistakenly regarded as a contribution to the literature of the Maquis, it is, like all Sartre's other works, to be understood in terms of the basic situation of existentialism: in the cruelty of these absurd times, the individual can find genuine freedom only in commitment even to the point of death, only in the voluntary acceptance of responsibility.

## SASTRE, Alfonso
(Spain, born 1924)

LA CORNADA *[Death in the Arena]*. Play in two acts with prologue and epilogue. First edition Madrid 1961. First performance January 14, 1960, Madrid, Teatro Lara. Time: the present. Place: Madrid.

Man as an object, his degradation into a mere function, is studied by Sastre in terms of Spain's national institution, the bullfight. The destiny of the bullfighter José Alba, who dies in the arena, is shown in flashbacks. Alba has become a victim of his own fear. He had always been pulled this way and that by the ambition of the dictatorial impresario Marco, who harried him from fight to fight, and by the love of his wife Gabriela, who longed for tranquil, peaceful happiness. Desperately he tries to kill himself, but, although wounded, he is driven by the merciless Marco to fight. The bull wins and Marco looks for another victim of his trade in death.

## SAUNDERS, James
(England, born 1925)

NEXT TIME I'LL SING TO YOU. Play in two acts. Prose. Written 1962. First edition London 1963. First performance June 18, 1962, Ealing, London, Questor's Theatre. Time: not specified. Place: bare stage.

Several levels and perspectives keep overlapping and annulling each other throughout the play. In the here and now of an evening in the theater, four actors, Rudge, Dust, Meff, and Lizzie, have gathered round an old experienced player to improvise the story of a hermit, who died at eighty-four in 1942, in an attempt to discover the meaning of such a strange life. The performers hide under trite jokes and personal small talk the helplessness with which they face their unfamiliar task. They doggedly try to avoid even the slightest action and decision. Nevertheless: "How can you do what you're doing when you don't know what you're *supposed* to be doing!" Even though they do their best not to acknowledge their situation, its challenge shapes their attitude. On this second level, the scene broadens out into the world as such where each has to master the eternal task of living. Rudge is the sponsor of this search for truth. He sets up rules, marks boundaries, and yet must admit that the play is gaining its own independence. Dust is the opponent who, with his cynical restlessness and self-tormenting mockery keeps questioning everything over and over again. Lizzie and Meff are full of love and life, happy dolts from the eternal realm of clowning. These archetypal temperaments provide the fixed starting points for the improvisation of scenes from the hermit's life, such as they might have come to pass. The actor who plays the hermit is discouraged by the fluctuating play of contrasting possibilities which overwhelm him: "It's a difficult enough part as it is, in fact it isn't a part at all, it's just a . . . hole in the play which I have to sit in while all of you shovel earth in on me. The earth being your own ideas of what kind of character I am. . . ."

And here we are at yet another, deeper level—the dissolution of everything that can be said in words into fluid ambiguity: "Do you want your identity in terms physical, psychological, biological, biochemical, sociological, statistical or mystical? Answer." Personality disintegrates, space and time and development vanish in the face of the spontaneous shapeless instant which encompasses all possibilities: "How are we to know . . . that God did not create the Universe once and for all only a moment ago, together with all the evidence necessary to prove that it had existed for three hundred billion years? How are we to know that we were not created suddenly with our memories and our wrinkles and our pretensions to maturity,

*now*—or now, or now, or now." The actor who plays the hermit takes
refuge in his part from the isolation and hopeless alienation of this world
and dies the old man's death in protest against the relativity of all that
exists. Looking at his dead body, the four comedians, perhaps thanks to
the same protest, gain an awareness of their own flesh-and-blood existence,
which just because of its conflicting nature is flexible and limitless.

The author has mobilized all the devices of the unfettered mime theater,
from clowning to montage, from debauched stupidity to sad meditation.
The whole thing is presented as an improvisation, the characters scoff and
jeer, declaim purple phrases, and read a vacuous text now forward, now
backward. It is the laughter of fear, such as overcomes children left alone
in the dark, high spirits forced to the point of incipient horror: "There lies
behind everything . . . a certain quality which we may call grief. It's always
there, just under the surface, just behind the façade, sometimes very
nearly exposed, so that you can dimly see the shape of it. It bides its time,
this quality. And if you do catch a glimpse of it, you may pretend not to
notice or you may turn suddenly away and romp with your children on
the grass, laughing for no reason."

A SCENT OF FLOWERS. Play in three acts. Prose. First edition London
and New York, 1965. First performance September 30, 1964, London,
Duke of York's Theatre. Time: the present. Place: a room, a church,
and a graveyard.

A requiem on the transitoriness of one man's fate—and of man's, nameless
and anywhere—so gay and playful in its tragedy, so ironically detached in
the face of death and so full of restrained lyricism in its dry humor, so
profound and severely architectural in its seemingly improvised structure
that the critics at the first performance hailed it as a new Mozartian style
in literature. Events are seen on two interconnected levels.

The student Zoe has committed suicide because of unhappy love, the coffin
is carried into the church, the Mass for the Dead is celebrated, and in the
graveyard the funeral proceeds. At the same time Zoe is brought to life in
scraps of memory from her childhood, youth, and downfall. These visions
from the past appear in a loose chain of associations, take shape around
some particular figure, and recede again. One after the other the vestiges
of the past drop from Zoe like burnt-out slag. In an inexorable process of
extinction she withdraws from the world, to the descant of the burial
ceremony in the background. The two levels of death and the life that
preceded it are connected by the loneliness that anticipates death: "This is
what loneliness really is—to have no way, no way of stopping your
thoughts. . . . This is terrible; frightening; you begin to feel as though

you're possessed. . . ." The whirling memories are, both in form and in substance, the counterpart of physical decay.

Since her childhood Zoe never found security and confidence with her stepmother Agnes, whose cold intellect offered psychological understanding rather than love. David, Zoe's father, was weak and indifferent. Only her stepbrother Godfrey was a real companion, and she loved him. As a student, the object of her passion had been a married university lecturer. In the insoluble dilemma between the claims of happiness and of her Catholic faith she chooses suicide. The scenes gradually become a mere monologue divided among different voices, until even memory fades and Mr. Scrivens, the undertaker and, in act two, the priest celebrating the Mass for the Dead, politely but firmly show the girl to her grave. Her last words are: "Just a little silence, a light rain falling from a colorless sky, and a slight scent of flowers."

A SLIGHT ACCIDENT. One-act play. Prose. First performance October 24, 1961, Nottingham, England, Playhouse Theatre. Time: the present. Place: Penelope's drawing room.

The "profoundly tragic event" with its claims on the emotions and pathos becomes the theme of a farce which combines the devices of the Theater of the Absurd with the typical, dry humor of the English. Right in the midst of a decent, uncomplicated, well-balanced ordinary marriage, Penelope shoots her husband Harry, carefully wraps the body in the fur of a polar bear and now wants to talk over the "slight accident" with her best friend, Camilla. But the conversation is nothing but a spectrally grotesque string of platitudes. Camilla's husband praises his way of life, which long since has become quite mechanical as a protection against the unforeseen. Harmless interjections by the guests eventually worm the confession of murder out of Penelope. She felt she had become like an automated being in the course of events, and by this autonomous deed wanted to prove herself as an individual. Camilla finds this proposition so fascinating that she in turn shoots her spouse. But the two ladies, so intent on their titanic self-assertion, finally have to admit that they always remain prisoners of reality.

WHO WAS HILARY MACONOCHIE? One-act play. Prose. Written 1962. First performance June 9, 1963, Ealing, London, Questors Theatre. Time: October 19, 1962. Place: a drawing room in the English style.

The glorification of the Empire, the wistful nostalgia for everything that has made England great, is reflected with biting sarcasm in the distorting mirror of the Theater of the Absurd and reduced to empty phrases and stereotypes. In form, the profound farce is a literary parody: the gushing, flowery prose of diary confessions, the argumentative style of certain scholars who hide every statement in a semantic maze of reservations "on the one hand, on the other hand," the maid's chatter which provides neatly classified footnotes to all that happens.

Two officious widows meet for the inevitable game of cards, combined with a playful striptease. In the mechanical flow of associations from the sphere of national history and domestic chores, we get uncertain and ambiguous glimpses of what has happened earlier. One woman got rid of her husband in 1932 by means of an exploding hotwater bottle to be free to devote herself to her weird and demoniac lover, Mr. Hilary, who happened to be the other woman's first husband. The betrayed wife wanted to take her own life with the help of another hotwater bottle, but by accident killed her desired husband instead. Now the two women, both Hilaryless, many years after these events boast over their teacups about the erotic prowess of their respective spouses. The maid, who indiscriminately had to look after the husband's and lover's needs in this respect, too, and records her own experiences in footnotes, becomes the judge in this macabre contest. Exhausted by their dispute, the two women eventually make the embarrassing facts disappear by covering them up with a few handy doubts: perhaps neither of them was ever married at all?

## SAUVAJON, Marc-Gilbert
(France, born 1909)

DEAR CHARLES (*Les Enfants d'Edouard*). Comedy in three acts. Adapted by Sauvajon from the original English *Dear Charles* by R. Bottomley and F. Jackson. First edition Paris 1949. Readapted into English by Alan Melville, in *Plays of the Year*, Vol. 8, London and New York, Elek, 1953. Time: the present. Place: Paris.

A skillful family farce made up of the interplay of frivolity and respectability. The successful journalist Denise Darvel is in an awkward spot. Her two elder children, Walter and Martine, are about to marry into the family of the late sardine canner Douchemin, whose widow is a lady of notoriously high morals. Denise is thus forced to confess to her three children that behind the pious memory of their deceased "father" Charles, she has been hiding no fewer than three gentlemen, all very much alive and each the father of one of her offspring. All three—Sir Michael Anstruther, the Polish pianist Jan Letzaresco, and the gallant Dominique Lecler—are only too anxious at present to marry her. When Madame Douchemin herself weepingly reveals her own dreadful secret, the portrait of "dear Charles" is restored to its place of honor to watch over his family as before.


## SAVORY, Gerald
(England, born 1909)


A LIKELY TALE. Comedy in three acts. Prose. First edition London 1957. First performance March 22, 1956, London, Globe Theatre. Time: the present. Place: the Petershams' living room in Wimbledon, London.

An effective selection of ultra-English eccentricities whirled around in well-tried slapstick situations with mistaken identities: the result is a riotous entertainment not unduly concerned with probability and originality.

The aged Petersham brother and sisters, Lola, Mirabelle and Oswald, go through the daily ceremony of afternoon tea with as much style as through the evening of their life and cultivate their autumnal reminiscences and gentle malice. Suddenly reality bursts in. Their hundred-year old papa is dying, which as such would not create much disturbance. But before the end the mischievous head of the family lets it be known that his fortune is used up, and what is left of it is to be bequeathed to the maid Ursula Budgeon, who is the only efficient member of this degenerate household. This is shocking enough, but matters get worse with the sudden appearance of Jonah, Oswald's ne'er-do-well son. He skips from scene to scene with flattery and blackmail, attacks on alternating fronts but for all his greed is eventually foiled by the jeweller Gregory Lupton who, with a fine show of renunciation and honesty, earns Ursula and the happy end.


A MONTH OF SUNDAYS. Comedy in three acts. Prose. First edition London 1957. First performance May 28, 1957, London, Cambridge Theatre. Time: the present. Place: an old farmhouse in a remote part of Cornwall.

The customary family comedy is leavened with amiable idiosyncrasies of an Anglo-Saxon cast, such as the back-to-the-land enthusiasm, the do-it-yourself mania and the cult of the pioneer spirit of bygone days.

The bankrupt publisher Oliver Sylvester has retired with his wife Mary and their three daughters to an inherited farm in the depths of Cornwall.

With enthusiasm he has taken to the "natural life" and forces his women-folk to do without the comforts of civilization and to live only on what, unskillfully, is sown and harvested. His Bible is the highly moralizing diary of his grandfather, who went to America as a farmer. It takes the young agriculturalist Tim Riley and his practical sense to put a damper on these fads. He and the eldest daughter Sarah take over the farm, while Oliver with the rest of his family leaves the life on the land which is so obviously not for him and returns to his desk in London. The traditional English comedy of manners, playing off the humor of its characters one against the other, is effectively applied to contemporary eccentricities.


## SCHÉHADÉ, Georges
(France/Lebanon, born 1910)


L'EMIGRÉ DE BRISBANE [The Emigrant from Brisbane]. Play in nine scenes. Prose. Written 1961. First performance January 12, 1965, Munich, Residenz-Theater. Time: about 1925. Place: the small village of Belvento in Sicily.

Schéhadé softens into feathery poetry even the hard, calcined world of Sicilian peasant honor. The play is a cruelly simple fairy tale about wealth that cannot die with its owner, but becomes a fatal legacy and a test of the survivors: "Whoever has money does not die, he merely alters his way of life. And history goes on! So long as people are not buried together with their fortune, there can be no justice and no culture."
Returning from a lifetime in Australia, an emigrant hires a coachman to drive him to his native village in Sicily. He dies during the night at the fountain, alone and unknown. In his pocket there is a fortune, destined for his illegitimate son. The villagers proceed to an "agonizing reappraisal" in their consciences. Nobody can remember the dead stranger. There are only three women—Rosa Picaluga, Laura Scaramella and Maria Barbi, all of them respectable wives and mothers now—who might conceivably have smuggled this unknown son into their marriage. Distrust, self-doubt, avarice and jealousy break out among the couples. Picaluga, known as "the just," overcomes his doubts and trusts his wife's faithfulness. Scaramella is not so sure, beats his wife but eventually silences his suspicions for the sake of domestic comfort. Barbi is convinced that his Maria is blameless, but the thought of all that money gives him no rest. He is obsessed by the plan of selling his wife's honor to make one of his sons the stranger's heir. Maria indignantly refuses this shameful bargain and is stabbed by the

miser. The village celebrates the murderer as the avenger of his honor, who has punished his wife's unfaithfulness and is duly rewarded by the emigrant's money. Like a national hero Barbi goes to the police. At this moment the coachman comes along again with another emigrant who crossly remonstrates that he has been taken to the wrong village. The coachman admits with a sly grin that he always takes all new arrivals to the pretty village of Belvento, because of the view and because it's nearer for his poor old horse. Yesterday's stranger, too, had asked to be taken to another village, but nevertheless had been quiet and content.

This smiling final twist lifts the conflict of destiny into pensive playfulness. There are things stronger and more durable than the confusions of human life: the quiet market place in the evening breeze, the "silver spider" of night, the melancholy song of a child, the inexhaustible, flowering telling of tales.

MONSIEUR BOB'LE [Mr. Bob'le]. Play in three acts. Prose. First edition Paris 1951. First performance January 30, 1951, Paris, Théâtre de la Huchette. Time: the present. Place: Paola Scala and a port hospital.

A colorful, spontaneous tale of the happiness of an active life, of the trans- figuring power of the pure heart and the restless wanderings of man in search of himself. "Out of a sense of duty and humor and from love of prayer" Monsieur Bob'le has been administering the small town of Paola Scala and has become everybody's fatherly friend. Now he leaves in order to take up the job of director on a distant island. His man-servant Arnold sweeps up the odd words lying around on the floor and packs twenty-three pairs of slippers, so that his master can also tread softly and cautiously when he is abroad. The "Trémandour," the gray copybook in which Bob'le has noted his wisdom, is left behind as his testament. Henceforth it is the metropolitan Nicolas who administers the little town, which lives en- tirely on its memories of Bob'le. Young Michel dreams of him so much that he never notices that Corée loves him. At last, José Marco, a native of the island and educated by Bob'le, brings news that Bob'le has dis- covered some mineral deposits, is teaching the natives how to mine them, and for the rest meditates on the beach. Finally Monsieur Bob'le sails for home and dies miserably in a hospital in port. But his testament works on. Before he dies, the captain of the ship on which he was traveling comes to claim him on behalf of the passengers and crew, all of whom have been transformed by his gentle understanding. The hospital attendant Alexandre will be driven by a strange restlessness all his life to look for Paola Scala and the "Trémandour." It is a play of fairylike figures and images.

LA SOIRÉE DES PROVERBES [An Evening of Proverbs]. Play in three
acts. Prose. Written 1953. First edition Paris 1954. First performance
January 30, 1954, Paris, Théâtre Petit Marigny. Time: the present. Place:
an inn and a country house.

In dreamlike sounds and images, in lyrical symbols, Schéhadé explores the
melancholy of oncoming age, the sadness of transience. From the most diverse directions and backgrounds a group of people are converging on the
nocturnal meeting place of the "Four Diamonds." A mysterious "evening
of proverbs" is being held, at which they hope to find their former selves
again and all the purity and innocence of their youth, long lost in the
dirty struggle for existence: "In the evening of life . . . when the fiends
approach . . . man's body is full of maggots. . . . His thoughts trickle into
the ground. . . . And on the rock of unhappy snow . . . grazes the red-eyed
sheep . . ."
At this place, a generation ago, a handful of enthusiastic young people had
congregated around the sage Evangelil. Ardent and pure, they were going
to remain true to their aspirations for ever: "But that night . . . was the
night of hopes—it was dream, confession, and truth! They all sat around
this table! . . . All of one mind, like one single tree!" But life turned the
music-loving dreamer Sola into a suspicious usurer, the young sailor Topo-
loff with his roving yearnings into a disgruntled old "fish corporal," and
the beautiful, romantic Martha into a malevolent old spinster. Their ideals
have shrivelled in the course of the years into ludicrous eccentricities and
the inspired exuberance has blown away in bombastic phrases and hollow
extravagance. On this evening of proverbs, which arrogantly sets itself
apart from life and wants to force reality into rigid formulas, they "uncork
the bottle of legends, rummage in the age-worn chest of truth and the
crystal cupboard of lies, and pluck the oats of reason from the feed-trough
of philosophical ideas." And then the young poet Argengeorge steps into
this group of specters from the past with all the passionate sympathy of
his unspent heart. Spitefully they lock out his inspired youth and entrench
themselves complacently behind their old age: "Innocence cannot replace
age. . . . If God exists, it is because he is old! . . . Because he has lived
through many things and is so very, very old that he bends down to us!"
Argengeorge meets the gloomy hunter Alexis, whom disappointed love has
robbed of his reason. Alexis, too, was once full of hopes, but life has made
nightmares of his dreams. The poet realizes that he, too, will surely have
to betray himself over and over again in lifelong compromises and will
end as a caricature of his ideals. He sacrifices his life and gets Alexis to
shoot him. He has slipped out of reality's grip and entered into truth. The
empty phrases of the evening of proverbs are invalidated forever. A chorus
softly intones a dirge.

VASCO *(Histoire de Vasco).* Play in six tableaux. Prose. Written 1956. First edition Paris 1956. First performance October 15, 1956, Zürich, Schauspielhaus (Compagnie Renaud-Barrault). Translated by Robert Baldick in *Theatre of War,* Harmondsworth, Penguin, 1967. Time: about 1850, during a war. Place: South America, Germany, or Italy.

Quite mistakenly this play, when first performed in France, was taken as a didactic piece of pacifism and shocked the public. Schéhadé in fact does not accuse or pronounce any value judgment; without ulterior motive, he gives us a fairy tale about the ugly and the beautiful things of life. He explains: "The story of Vasco is a play about the impracticability of senti- ments . . . a book of pictures, a reverie which I dreamed as I sat in my chair, smoking slowly, through an autumn, a winter and a summer. Every time, before beginning to write, I took my son's toy soldiers out of their box and looked at them, taking pleasure in their bright colors and their innocence. . . . My son's little soldiers killed Vasco. . . . And I came to ask myself whether there are not certain things so accursed that the curse per- meates even their lovable external appearance . . . I am talking, of course, of my son's little lead soldiers."

Vasco, the little village barber, obstinately refuses to go to war, in spite of the hostility and contempt of the others and his own economic ruin. The gentle no of this timid little man is more than the stereotyped "heroes" can take. What neither pressure from above nor the whipped-up noisy patriotism of the neighbors were able to achieve is eventually brought about by a ruse.

Lieutenant September brings Vasco the message that he is urgently needed for a secret military mission. In his innocence the barber believes that he is to beautify a few high-ranking ladies and eagerly sets out with his comb and scissors. The Mirador sends Vasco off to carry a secret order through the enemy lines. Given that the enemy already know of the project, they are to be deceived by the illogical appearance of a perfect antihero. Vasco thinks he is carrying a letter about trout-fishing and, armed only with a parasol, starts on his way. His childlike innocence is his best protection. He is undeterred by a grotesque patrol dressed up as women, by the hail of bullets, and by the enemy camouflaged as trees. Taken prisoner, he very nearly saves himself by the hair-raisingly confused answers he produces during the interrogation. But then the wine goes to his head. He works himself up into the part of a hero who insists on a hero's death. He is shot, and the soldier who interrogated him so successfully is promoted to sergeant major. Vasco's grandiloquent inventions help the Mirador to a victory, which is to be celebrated by a parade. Only Marguerite, the daughter of the strange dogcatcher Caesar, has secretly loved Vasco and now sees herself cheated of her happiness. This sad fable of innocence that is not of this world and therefore is destroyed is presented with so much playful grace and magic that even death is encompassed in a consoling wisdom.

LES VIOLETTES *[The Violets]*. Comedy in eleven scenes with lyrics. Prose. Written 1959. First edition Paris 1960. First performance September 21, 1960, Bochum, Germany, Schauspielhaus. Time: the present. Place: Madame Borromée's boardinghouse.

Schéadé's contribution to the protest against the mania for technical experiments, against irresponsible nuclear tests and the public's unconcerned acceptance of projects whose implications cannot be foreseen is not a purposive didactic piece with a massive deterrent message, but a profound grotesque in which accusations dissolve in gentle dreams.

Not only are the clocks out of order since the nuclear physicist Professor Kufman has taken lodgings in Madame Borromée's boardinghouse, but her niece Pierette pursues no fewer than three men with her boundless ardor: the athlete Colombo, the philistine Adam, and the bookkeeper Zanzi. But since she is a respectable girl, she duly gets engaged to each one of them. Zanzi has read so many novels about pirates that he has contracted a fatal seasickness. The girl loses her two other fiancés to the professor, whose technical games fascinate the young men more than Pierette's eyes. Kufman's raw material for nuclear fission is neither uranium nor cobalt, but scented violets such as grow by the thousands in the surrounding fields. When the henhouse is to be blown up in a first experiment with the new weapon, Baron Fernagut, a world reformer so far condemned to inactivity, sees his chance. With the help of the servant Aristoteles he issues a rousing call of protest in defense of the cackling, innocent creatures. However, the professor's counterslogans about the nobility's spiritual duty to further the sciences and progress soon turn Fernagut into an enthusiastic nuclear champion. Eventually Kufman has pangs of conscience about his work of destruction and elopes with Pierette into more peaceful regions. Fernagut is so obsessed with his zeal and sense of duty that he blows up the whole world. The loose sequence of scenes with interspersed songs sets a new, charming tone for the theatrical treatment of contemporary problems.

LE VOYAGE *[The Voyage]*. Play in eight scenes. Prose. First edition Paris 1961. First performance February 17, 1961, Paris, Théâtre de France. Time: around 1850. Place: Bristol, England, and an imaginary South Sea.

Play and dream rebel against reality and try to transform it and to light up its dark side. Young Christopher dreams of the sea and faraway countries while he briskly and obligingly serves the customers in Mr. Strawberry's button shop. He would like to write the "history of the wind." His sober and prosaic boss gruffly scolds him for such extravagant ideas. For him the wind is a wild and unpredictable ruffian, but always a friend of England, the best country in the world, which Christopher so recklessly wants to leave. Quartermaster Alexandre Wittiker, who seems to be in a strange hurry, offers Christopher his naval uniform for an evening. He proudly puts it on and is so filled with the dignity it confers on him that he insists on playing Quartermaster Alexandre even when the role involves him in being brought to trial by three hard-bitten old salts. They are investigating the death of Midshipman Hogan, whom Alexandre has allegedly killed in self-defense. In a flashback the Quartermaster is seen committing a treacherous murder in a fit of jealousy. Christopher watches this cruel episode in the "El Gringo" tavern with the utmost bewilderment, and when it is over he asks to be heard and tries to justify the occurrence in terms of his idealized notions of the seaman's profession. The same events are reproduced by the harmless personalities of Christopher's button-shop world. The filthy southern tavern is now a place of out-and-out English respectability, and Christopher, in the innocence of his mind, can convincingly prove that it was all an accident. Admiral Punt acquits him. He suspects the truth and warns Christopher against such dangerous games with the South Sea, pistols, ships, uniforms, and parrots.

Next morning Christopher is made the offer of which he has dreamed for years: a voyage round the world. Courageously he sticks to the button trade and England's traditions. Strawberry at once rewards this meritorious attitude with a raise in pay. The sly Reverend Lamb puts one of his hilarious cock-and-bull stories to good use in giving a helping hand to the timid love affair between Christopher and the girl apprentice Georgia. Christopher's dream voyage lands him safely in the port of wedlock.


### SCHISGAL, Murray
(United States, born 1926)


LUV. Comedy in two acts. Prose. First edition New York 1965. First performance April 24, 1963, London, New Arts Theatre. Time: the present. Place: a bridge in New York.

Love and marriage, illusion and anxiety, the need to communicate and frustration, all these manifestations of our overindulged contemporary psyche and at the same time hackneyed clichés are taken literally: love is merely a progressive development due to physical attraction, complementary professional interests, and social adjustment.

Harry Berlin is about to jump from the bridge. He is fed up with life. Since the time when, as he was pursuing his ideals, an impudent mongrel lifted his leg on him he has been overwhelmed with his disgust of life. It so happens that his school friend Milt Manville passes by. They have not seen each other for fifteen years. Milt has become a stockbroker and refuse collector and is comfortably off. He holds forth to Harry about love, life's magic potion. His trouble is that he is tied to his wife Ellen and thus risks losing his girl friend Linda, and he proposes that Harry should take on the inconvenient spouse. The would-be suicide suffers from attacks which block his nervous system. Sometimes he is dumb or paralyzed, sometimes deaf or blind. When Milt in his turn wants to jump into the water, Harry accepts the bargain. Ellen, a perambulating collection of quotations, is hastily polished up by her husband with mascara, rouge, and a Persian lamb coat, as is fitting for a special offer worth its price. Ellen has neatly recorded her husband's unfulfilled marital duties in a diagram. Now it is her turn to want to jump from the bridge. Harry has to hold the neglected wife back by feigning a love he does not feel. They find common ground in a contest over whose childhood was worse. They come to blows, destroy each other's valuables, and torment each other just to satisfy their curiosity about whether their love will stand up to such trials. Enthusiastically they get Milt to approve their new bond.

A few months later Ellen and Milt meet on the bridge. He has been jilted by his mistress, and she has so thoroughly exercised her mind on Harry, whose nickname is Dostoevsky, that her diagram looks even sadder than before. The couple want to get together again and to this end try to help Harry to the suicide he missed. But Harry now wants to stay alive, and Milt falls twice into the water in his helpful attempts to expedite his friend into the other world. Complaining about the inadequate expression of their love, Ellen returns to Milt. In despair Harry jumps from the bridge, drifts back to the shore and is pursued by a dog. The style of this lighthearted piece of clowning owes everything to the repetition and analogy of theatrical gags. A trite and endlessly repeated love song keeps the whole thing moving.

THE TIGER. One-act play. Prose. First edition New York 1963. First performance February 4, 1963, New York, Orpheum Theatre. Time: the present. Place: a shabby basement.

A bitter farce, which with unsparing objectivity shows its own accusation against self-deception to be nothing but self-deception itself. Ben wants to take his revenge on the world for the insignificant, ordinary postman's life to which he is condemned and dreams himself into the part of a bloodthirsty "tiger." He assaults Gloria, a good little housewife, carries her off to his shabby lodgings and tries to challenge his century by a sexual murder. But the menacing situation by and by turns into a ridiculous and moving exchange of monologues between two bewildered human beings. In spite of his love for learning, Ben failed his exams. As a result he consoles himself with the part of an unappreciated, asocial hero. In her turn Gloria, who is disappointed in her ordinary marriage, discovers within herself long-buried ideals and cautiously responds to the outsider. They get all worked up over their spiritual alliance which is to fight the world of conventions. Excited by their scheme and by self-pity, the two world reformers go to bed with each other. A quick casual love affair soon gets the better of all their eccentric ideals. They settle back into the much-maligned world with new hopes and new lies. Reality is sharpened into paradox without detriment to psychological consistency.


THE TYPISTS. One-act play. Prose. First edition New York 1963. First performance February 4, 1963, New York, Orpheum Theatre. Time: the present. Place: an office.

A life swallowed up by the desolate and mechanical round of daily work shrinks to the monotony of a single, gray office day. The social criticism is not expressed in argument, but is implicit in the situation stereotyped to the point of absurdity.
Paul Cunningham introduces himself in the office as a newcomer and is given his first briefing by Sylvia Payton, the secretary: he is to copy pages and pages of addresses from the telephone directory for the purposes of a promotion campaign. In the course of this one working day, which stands for all of them, forty years go by. In the evening the two typists are old and worn. Paul is a worried family man who unsuccessfully spends his free time trying to study law; Sylvia is an aging spinster sacrificing herself for her family without getting any thanks for it. They confess their love for each other, but all their life they lack the courage to make this love real. They take refuge in small illusions and insurrections, little outbursts of hate against the invisible boss, they deceive each other with sham importance or give way to self-pity. The one thing they never do is to recognize and accept reality as the cause of their plight.

## SCHNEIDER, Reinhold
(Germany, 1903–1958)

DER GROSSE VERZICHT *[The Great Renunciation]*. Play in five acts. Prose. First edition Wiesbaden 1950. First performance July 18, 1958, Bregenz Festival. Time: thirteenth century. Place: Italy, Germany, France.

Across nations and generations, this play of *vanitas vanitatum* shows the futility of power and dominion in this world. The compulsion to do wrong and the conflict of evil on earth are overcome in the humility of the "great renunciation": "What, then, am I to do? I am sorry for the fishermen when they catch no fish, and for the fish when they are caught. There is no way out of guilt." Right is not with the man of action, but with the man of prayer. This insight dawns in suffering on those who all their life never come to rest between pride and the longing for redemption.

The election of a Pope is thwarted time and again by suspicions and disputes between opposing power groups. Led by cardinals Gaetani and Rosso, the Roman Curia is ranged against the party of Charles of Anjou, king of Naples, and of the ambitious patrician cardinals of the Colonna family. By common agreement the choice finally falls on the unworldly, innocently pious hermit Petrus of Murrhone, whom everyone hopes to be able to exploit as the instrument of his own power politics. Under the name of Celestine V he accedes to the throne of St. Peter, and his humility is to restore peace to the strife-torn world of Christendom. Against Gaetani's wishes he unsuspectingly accepts King Charles's invitation to Naples. The king has merely simulated penitence, and the Pope is taken prisoner when he refuses to bless the king's fleet, which is about to sail against Sicily and to support the king's plans of conquest in Germany. Celestine could avenge himself by hurling the Papal anathema against the king, but forgoes doing so and thereupon is forced by Gaetani to abdicate. This ambitious cardinal now succeeds him as Boniface VIII, and uses his new power to deprive his rivals of the cardinal's hat and to persecute them. The Colonna brothers flee to Paris and form an alliance with King Philippe of France. They try to get hold of Celestine and to use him as a legitimate weapon against the new Pope. Boniface in his turn sends out his agents to kidnap Celestine, but when they find him, he is dead.

Celestine's seeds of peace bear fruit only much later. Louis, King Charles's only son, comes to realize the inhuman conduct of his father in exterminating the issue of Conradin, rightful ruler of Naples, and in revulsion abandons the throne for the priesthood. King Charles renounces his unscrupulous lust for power and chooses a crown of straw. As master of all divine and secular power, Boniface declares the rulers of France and Germany unlawful so as to gain world dominion for himself. The rulers thus menaced by the Pope proceed to make him prisoner. He dies of grief for his frustrated plans and, at the end, is converted to Celestine's gentle humility. A colorful chronicle unfolds in nineteen scenes involving no less than fifty-five personages, but the plethora of events nearly drowns the intended parable.


## SENDER, Ramón José
(Spain, born 1902)


THE PHOTOGRAPH. One-act play. After Sender's story in Spanish. Prose. Published in English 1953. Time: the present. Place: a photographer's studio.

A psychological study in the form of a farce which shows that in the disintegration of identity and the blurred ambiguity of emotions the machine with its incorruptible functionality is the sole yardstick and fixed point of life.

A photographer is vainly trying to take a photograph of his wife for their twentieth wedding anniversary. Reality is never equal to the supersensitive reactions of the camera or to the artistic ambitions of its owner. Sometimes the woman's sentiments are wrong, sometimes her attitude is not correct, or her appearance is too ordinary. A family friend is an element of discord between husband and wife. During a walk with her he fell into the river and was drowned. Did she kill him? Or was it suicide? The wife surprises her husband, who knows he cannot beget children, with the confession that she is pregnant. The man's suspicions and the many variants of the woman's protestations obscure the true connections. At this stage the camera demands its due. The elaborate mechanism cries out for application. They set the camera for automatic release, arrange themselves in a sentimental pose and, for the sake of the prospective photograph, enjoy an ever so blissful happiness.

## SHAFFER, Peter
(England, born 1926)

FIVE FINGER EXERCISE. Play in two acts. Prose. Written 1958. First edition London 1958. First performance July 16, 1958, London, Comedy Theatre. Time: the present. Place: the Harringtons' weekend cottage in Suffolk.

The individual unable to bear himself and therefore unbearable also to others is shown in the broad setting of his whole family. All the characters try to live their lives after their own fashion and thereby are a nuisance to the others, with the result that each is pushed further into his own isolation and the conflicts are sharpened. All say and do things they do not really mean. Everyone strives for self-realization, for the meaning of life, always at the expense of the others. Action becomes mere uncontrollable reaction to the hostile environment. In this frantic defense each character becomes distorted to the point of no longer being able to identify himself with the resulting caricature. The problem of living together turns into a helpless struggle: "Feelings don't unite us, don't you see? They keep us apart. And words are no good because they're unreal. We live away in our skins from minute to minute, feeling everything quite differently, and any one minute's just as true about us as any other. . . . Oh, it goes on and on. No meeting . . . never. . . . Why can't we be important to each other?"

Walter Langer, a German, was driven away by the unrepentant fascism of his parents' home and has escaped to liberal England, where he takes a job as tutor with the Harringtons, a tormented and problem-ridden family. Harrington is amiable but somewhat rough, a man who has worked himself up from humble beginnings as a carpenter to being a furniture manufacturer. He grudges his family no luxury, but becomes an outcast in this carefree household. His wife Louise fancies herself in the part of a sophisticated Frenchwoman suffering under a plebeian husband, adores the arts, and feels herself to be "misunderstood." Clive, the nineteen-year-old boy, is torn between his parents' conflicting educational ideas and hides his loneliness behind cynical rebellion and drinking. Only fourteen-year-old Pamela is protected from these smoldering family troubles by her teen-age petulance. "What's it matter? You start a family, work and plan. Suddenly you turn round . . . there's nothing there. Probably never was. What's a family anyway? . . . There's no reason why they should like you." Each one of these self-imprisoned individuals now expects confirmation from Walter. Clive wants him exclusively for himself and is led by jealousy to suspect Walter and Louise. Louise in turn is deeply humiliated as a woman when she discovers that the young German appreciates in her merely her motherliness and suspects him of a questionable attachment for Pamela. Eventually they drive Walter away so as not to be forced to readapt themselves to the example of a well-balanced, disciplined personality. The idealist, who has tried so hard to help those for whom he feels responsible, thus sees his efforts condemned to failure and makes a suicide attempt but is rescued in time. The family resign themselves to their hopeless disharmony: "The courage . . . for all of us. Oh, God—give it!"

THE PRIVATE EAR. One-act play. Prose. Written 1961. First edition London 1962. First performance May 10, 1962, London, Globe Theatre. Time: the present. Place: Bob's bed-sitting room in Belsize Park, London.

Bob, a withdrawn and imaginative office clerk, has so far lived entirely for his love of classical music; his friends regard him as not a bad fellow at all and realize that his feelings are genuine and profound, but on the whole less a help than a hindrance to him. He is now making his first, timid attempt to entertain a girl in his room. To help him over his embarrassment, he has invited not only Doreen herself, but also his extrovert and experienced friend Ted. The girl falls for Ted's carefree merriment, and Bob, richer by the disappointment, has to resign himself to the fact that he will never have access to the others' lighthearted world.

THE PUBLIC EYE. One-act play. Prose. Written 1961. First edition London 1962. First performance May 10, 1962, London, Globe Theatre. Time: the present. Place: Charles Sidley's office.

The legend of Orpheus and Eurydice, the eternal symbols of the constancy and perils of lovers, is turned into a psychoanalytical investigation of a conjugal crisis. Under the guidance of the solicitor and tax consultant Charles Sidley, his young wife Belinda has grown in her marriage into a sensitive, consciously living woman. But with his own psychological inhibitions, his pedantry, the narrowness of his whole nature, he cannot satisfy the profound character he has awakened in her. Belinda henceforth lives in vague, dreamy expectations. Charles feels that she is slipping away from him and engages the private detective Julian to check up on her. For the first time Belinda is aware of the real interest of a man who persistently follows her, and she gives her heart to this faithful stranger. Julian, the "public eye," forces the self-righteous husband to follow Belinda for one month wherever she goes, selfless and devoted like Orpheus at the beginning of time, until their love transcends the caverns of death where indifference and strangeness lurk. While Charles is thus being re-educated in love, Julian will substitute for him in the office. The age-old triangular situation of the boulevard play takes a novel turn on the borderland between psychology and surrealism.


THE ROYAL HUNT OF THE SUN. A play concerning the conquest of Peru in two acts. Prose. First edition London 1964. First performance July 7, 1964, Chichester Festival. Time: June 1529–August 1533. Place: Spain, Panama, the Upper Province of the Inca Empire (stylized bare set with an upper level).

Shaffer condenses the history of the conquistadors into the pathology of the conqueror as such. The myth of the leader serves as a narcotic to a world doubting itself and its destiny. Seeking salvation from the despairing awareness of his transitoriness, man escapes into a destructive mania and acts himself out in senseless cruelty and greed.

Pizarro, a man despised for his illegitimate birth and his poverty, yearns for a new world in which nothing is as yet preestablished and apportioned. He is intoxicated with America's rich opportunities. Here he can realize his lifelong dream of power without having to subordinate his own will to law and privilege. With a handful of adventurers, all driven by their lust for gold or power, Pizarro sails into the great unknown. He is accompanied by the Dominican Valverde, imperious in the strength of the true faith, and by the haughty courtier Estete, the Spanish King's Overseer, who are to make sure that the lion's share of the still unknown booty goes to the Church and State. The Spaniards invade Peru and their greed is put to shame by the sun god's empire. Under the Inca Atahuallpa, who is worshipped as a god, all men are equal and content. Like plants they grow under the sun of their ruler and fade away again in humility and patience. No one has any privileges and all feel secure in the omnipotence of their sun-emperor. The Christians now bring them the "right to hunger," the driving force of desires, the unfulfilled wishes, the spur of avarice. The only weapon the white men have in the immensity of the continent and against its native aborigines is the arrogance of their bearing, the pride of their race, the Pharisaism of their only true religion.

Pizarro comes as a god and is trustfully welcomed by Atahuallpa as his brother. The Inca is lured into an ambush and his retinue killed. Pizarro promises him his own freedom in exchange for the fabulous gold treasure of the empire. The ransom is paid and in utter despair the conqueror comes to realize that he must break his word and kill Atahuallpa if he is not to endanger his life's aim—the sole possession of a new world. Deeply stirred Pizarro accepts the gentle religion of the Incas and is confessed by Atahuallpa, who in his turn is forcibly converted to Christianity and killed. Pizarro hopes for the resurrection of the immortal sun-god, but finds himself cheated, too, in the Inca religion which he has chosen— banished with his guilt and no comfort for his conscience.

The play is given a formal structure by the double role of Martin Ruiz, who, as a young page, accompanies his master throughout the action and, as an aged survivor, speaks the comments which lead into the flashbacks. Skillful use is made of the polyphonic sonorities of the Inca language, now in chorus chants, now in staccato individual voices. Nothing could better describe the stage effects of this play with its "rites, mimes, masks, and magics," than Shaffer's own words: "It is a director's piece, a pantomimist's piece, a musician's piece, a designer's piece, and of course an actor's piece, almost as much as it is an author's."


## SIMON, Neil
(United States, born 1927)


BAREFOOT IN THE PARK. A new comedy in three acts. Prose. First edition New York 1964. First performance October 23, 1963, New York, Biltmore Theatre. Time: the present. Place: an apartment on East 48th Street, New York.

The well-tried boulevard mixture of humor and sentimentality, frivolity and thoughtfulness, and sheer foolery are underpinned, however, with serious psychological motivations, all resting on the carefully calculated dosage of punch lines and scenes. The occasion for all this forced gaiety are the inexpert steps that the young couple Corie and Paul Bratter are trying to take along the much-obstructed road to conjugal bliss. They have a top-floor walk-up apartment in which nothing ever functions; a mother-in-law, who persistently wants to share their intimacy; and a neighbor who develops astonishing talents as a bluebeard and cat burglar. Corie is an extravagant girl and is soon bored with Paul, a supercorrect, stuffed-shirt lawyer. A party where they get tipsy enough to wash away their complexes, a good row, and a scandalous scene of being "barefoot in the park" eventually clear the way to the rose-colored happy ending.

## SIMONOV, Konstantin
(Russia, born 1915)

CHETVĚRTY *[The Fourth]*. One-act play. Prose. First published in *Teatr* No. 7, 1961. First edition Moscow 1962. First performance October 23, 1961, Leningrad, Gorki Theatre. Time: the present. Place: changing, dreamlike settings.

Simonov puts on the stage the "positive" hero, who, after lifelong errors, discouragements, struggles against his own selfishness and inner cowardice, finds his way to self-criticism and self-conquest in the service of socialism. The author explains: "With all his sins, and weaknesses, and shortcomings, I have made him the hero of the play, because in the end, after a long inner struggle, he finds the strength to say no. And thereby he justifies his existence on earth and also in my play, for if he had not roused himself to that no, I should never have written a play about him."
An American newspaperman finds out that the United States is going to test a new antiradar device in secret flights over the Soviet Union. And this means a grave risk of war for the whole world. Is he to publish the news of this secret mission and thus, at the cost of his own existence, prevent it being carried out? The past adds its voice to the inner conflict through the deaths of others for which he was responsible. He fought with the popular front in the Spanish Civil War, but when he later had to explain his pro-Communist attitude to an investigating commission, he cleared himself under duress by betraying his friend. He left his wife, whom he loved and who was that same friend's sister, in order to further his career by another marriage, and opportunities eventually landed him on the extreme right. Confronted with his sins of commission and omission, he finds the inner strength to take his stand against the government and to avert the danger of war. The antecedents are presented in analytical flashbacks and thus become an integral part of the action.

## SIMPSON, Norman Frederick
(England, born 1919)

ONE WAY PENDULUM. A farce in a new dimension in two acts. Prose. First edition London 1960. First performance December 22, 1959, London, Royal Court Theatre. Time: the present. Place: The Groomkirbys' house in London.

Two of the sacred cows of English family life—do-it-yourself and the hobby—are shown in hilarious exaggeration, which creates an amiable variant to the Theater of the Absurd. We look into the depths of an absurd world, which in fact merely reflects the slightly crazy situations of the customary household routine and thus becomes an inexhaustible source of nonsense.

Arthur Groomkirby is in charge of parking meters and is so entranced with his job that he takes it to absurd lengths. He becomes his own best customer, conscientiously drops his sixpence into the slot as required and then patiently stands by the parking meter until time is up. At home he relaxes from this exhausting activity, and, to the horror of his wife, clears out the living room in order to build a replica of a court at the Old Bailey. His current hobby is "institutions." His son Kirby likes to dress in solemn black and, for the sake of overriding logic, has to justify his mourning clothes by dispatching forty-three persons into a better world. He rehearses the "Hallelujah" chorus from Handel's *Messiah* with five-hundred "Speak your weight" automatic weighing machines, in which enthusiastic pursuit he is sorely troubled by the musical idiocy of the bass weighing machine. Sylvia, his teen-aged sister, has so thoroughly studied her Darwin that her dearest wish is to have knee-length apes' arms and an appropriate new set of glands. Aunt Mildred is bitten by the travel bug; having exhausted the possibilities of wheelbarrows, roller skates, rickshaws and a camel, she now swears by a wheelchair as a means of locomotion and has herself pushed around in it, notwithstanding her excellent health; she is sure she has just arrived in the Outer Hebrides. To clear some space in the overcrowded larder, the family rely on the services of Myra Gantry, an enormously fat professional eater who performs miracles of voracious labor in consuming every bit of food in sight.

Robert Barnes, a family friend, provides comments to guide the public through this logical maze and eventually, as a detective sergeant, exposes Kirby's serial murders. Arthur's do-it-yourself courtroom is accorded the honor of a real trial, in which Kirby is acquitted because the judges do not want by premature haste to dim the brilliant prospect of the numerous future crimes and trials to be expected of this talented homicide. The black humor of the Theater of the Absurd is introduced into drawing room comedy by the backdoor of eccentricity.


# SNYDER, William
(United States, born 1900)

THE DAYS AND NIGHTS OF BEEBEE FENSTERMAKER. Play in three acts. Prose. Written 1962. Time: the present. Place: New York and Arizona.

Ordinary people suffer from being ordinary; they cannot resign themselves to being just beasts of burden or anonymous wheels in the economic machinery and thus live in life-long frustration. Beebee's tragedy is that she feels within herself a possibility of creative self-realization but has neither the strength nor the substance to fight for it against a world of incomprehension. Beebee Fenstermaker has been brought up in a respectable provincial home and has been to college. She now expectantly comes to New York and wants to make a life for herself in the big city. A girl of many half-talents, she tries to write a novel, tries to paint, and eventually works as a nameless typist in an export office. But she cannot escape the dream of artistic flights. A feeling of inner emptiness drives her from one job to another; four years later she is back in a routine job in export. In love, too, Beebee remains a hopeless dabbler, who again and again comes to grief on the exclusivity of her emotions. The amateur philosopher Ed Busby soon takes flight from the exaggerated construction which Beebee puts on their affair. A motley band of successors follows, ending with Bob Smith, a naive country lad. Hesitantly Beebee allows herself to be infected with his practical sense of reality, renounces her illusions, and finally puts her secretarial competence to good use.
Painting on a broad canvas, the author shows us how a maturing woman suffers at her own hands and those of her environment. He thereby puts on the stage the kind of sociological insights which so far were the prerogative of the realistic psychological novel.

## SPARK, Muriel
(England, born 1921)

DOCTORS OF PHILOSOPHY. Play in three acts. Prose. First edition London 1963. First performance October 2, 1962, London, New Arts Theatre Club. Time: the present. Place: living room and terrace in Charlie Delfont's house overlooking the Regent's Canal.

The *femmes savantes* of our age are psychoanalytically and most entertainingly dissected in this play. Professor Delfont's household has disintegrated into an assembly of militant experts in the most diverse academic disciplines. Mama's subject is Assyriology, cousin Leonora's ancient languages, and daughter Daphne's is philosophy. The motive power behind all the women's disputes and their occasionally very robust behavior is their common longing for a child. Wish fulfillment and escapism, repression and overcompensation are the ingredients of this ironic, sparkling, and profound drawing-room comedy.

## SPARK, Muriel, and HOLME, Christopher
(Holme, England, born 1907)

THE BALLAD OF PECKHAM RYE. Stage version of Muriel Spark's novel (1960). Two acts. Prose and verse. First performance August 17, 1965, Salzburg, Landestheater (Europa Studio). Time: the present. Place: the London suburb of Peckham.

Lesage holds up a malicious mirror to the morals of his contemporaries with his *Diable boiteux*. Muriel Spark, too, shows us a deformed figure of a devil who comes to disrupt a standardized, secure bourgeois world. The author, a Catholic convert, writes a sort of morality play around the black angel Dougal Douglas, who provokes evil in modern industrial society. He wears the manifold masks of the pursuit of success and willingly caters to the consumer demand of his environment. The devil Dougal and his material worldliness have their counterpart in Nelly Mahone as the personification of possible religion; she is a religious fanatic who flits across the scene with her monotonous singsong. She is a perversion of the good, just as Dougal is a perversion of metaphysical evil. Both make play with the world's bad conscience, and they form an alliance which demonstrates the ambivalence of ethical values.

Dougal takes his name from his ancestor Archibald Douglas, the black knight of the Hundred Years' War. Half myth and half caricature, he possesses all the qualities and properties of our cinema superidols. In Peckham, an industrial district of London, he poses as an expert in industrial relations, tosses around words like "human research" and "vision," and goes from promotion to promotion in two companies at the same time without giving up his occupation as ghost writer of an aging musical-comedy star's memoirs. This knight of fortune has his own James Bond "speciality," a backhand clutch at the throat, to deal with his opponents. He is supreme in the role of Don Juan for innumerable office girls, but he is also a psychopath given to fits of weeping and to flirting with his own self-pity. He plays off against each other both his employers and his numerous girl friends. He uses Nelly, his religious counterpart, as an informer, and provokes the enmity of Trevor Lomas, whose standing as a local hero he utterly destroys. Dougal sows distrust between the secretary Merle Coverdale and her chief, whose mistress she has been for many years and who now kills her with a corkscrew. Unperturbed Dougal descends into his local hell. The scene he haunts is Peckham and Peckham Rye, a large common, but actually what he does is turned to evil only by the environment.

Numerous songs and musical transitions link the separate scenes, which come and go like film shots on a screen. Music, dance and pantomime, devices borrowed from the orgiastic choreography of *West Side Story* complete with a Jamaica Band and knife duels, and from director Joan Littlewood's scenic agitation, the "stations" technique of expressionism, and a somewhat forced attempt at topical cabaret merge in a kaleidoscopic picture of a hectic fair, in which the novel's abundant action is distributed among 43 actors and 22 scenes.

## SPEWACK, Bella, and SPEWACK, Samuel
(both United States, both born 1899)

KISS ME KATE. Musical comedy in two acts. Music and lyrics by Cole Porter. First edition New York 1953. First performance December 30, 1948, New York, New Century Theatre. Time: the present. Place: a theater in Baltimore.

A self-portrait of Broadway and its producer system is set in Baltimore. Shakespeare's comedy *The Taming of the Shrew* figures as the play within the play in fragments and thematic variations based on the everyday life of a group of actors.

Fred Graham is partnered on the stage by his divorced wife Lilli Vanessi.

He acts Shakespeare's Petruchio, who by dint of boorishness, provocation, and mockery succeeds in breaking his Kate's obstinacy and whims. The lovers' skirmishes, with their challenge and defiance, are continued in the dressing rooms, until finally Lilli, too, gives in to her Fred. Another quarreling couple converted to love are the soubrette Lois Lane and the incorrigible gambler Bill Cahoun. A variety show of literary satire ("Brush Up Your Shakespeare"), a parody of sentimental waltzing bliss nevertheless accepted by the public as true emotion, and jazz rhythms are as complementary in their contrasts as are Shakespeare's English with modern Americanisms and the technical jargon of the stage door.

## SQUARZINA, Luigi
(Italy, born 1922)

ROMAGNOLA [Romagnola]. Kermess in three parts. Prose. Written 1952–1957. First published in Sipario, No. 156, April 1959. First performance February 6, 1959, Rome, Teatro Valle. Time: June 28 to April 11, 1945. Place: Northern Italy.

A ballad of the passage of years in Romagna, presented with the help of well over fifty characters in thirty-two scenes. A handful of individuals is thrown off balance by the events and destroyed. Young Cecilia Borghi, betrothed to a professor, distributes Fascist literature among the farmers. She falls in love with the peasant Michele Foschini, but at the same time does not disdain the advances of Count Gardenghi, an aging estate owner. She uses the rich nobleman's influence to promote the interests of her lover. She represents Michele as a painter, although his talents are quite inadequate, and tries to prevent his being called up for the army. He in turn feels that this means degrading him to a toy and volunteers for the front. Later he deserts, in despair over the failure of his love, and joins the Communist partisans. When Michele renews contact with Cecilia, the Count, who is a close collaborator of the Germans, is about to denounce him but is killed by Cecilia. At this point she learns that Michele has married in the meantime. She still loves him, but in her disappointment betrays him to the Fascists whose tortures he does not survive. Cecilia falls into the hands of the partisans and is shot.
At first sight Romagnola is pure sensationalism, superficial, and passionate southern theatricality. But the crude effects are merely the framework for a densely packed picture of an epoch with all its contradictory detail. The author conveys the simmering crisis atmosphere of a time of political upheaval, when every spiritual conflict is bound to be also a social and po-

litical conflict, and men live their lives not as individuals, but only with reference to some overriding authority.

## STEINBECK, John Ernst
(United States, born 1902)

BURNING BRIGHT. Play in three acts. Prose. After the author's novel. First edition New York 1950. First performance September 27, 1950, New Haven, Shubert Theatre. Time: the present. Place: circus, farm, and port in the United States.

An extreme case of psychological distress in an abstraction which makes it an allegory of the sacredness of the human race. The sacred flame of life prevails over the moral code as a matter of unquestioned, self-evident fact. Beyond good or evil, everything that lives is sacred.
Joe Saul's marriage with Mordeen is childless and he is getting old. He is still hoping for a child, but the growing disappointment threatens to destroy the happiness of the marriage. Knowing that Joe is sterile, Mordeen out of her great love for him gives herself to the muscle-man Victor and conceives a child. Joe is happy to see the meaning of his life fulfilled, until Victor, cheated of his paternity, reveals the truth. After an inner struggle Joe accepts the child he has wanted so much, in the realization that the continuity of the human race is more important than personal blood ties. He thus becomes worthy of Mordeen's sacrifice. The action develops in four scenes—representing unease, maturity, despair and fulfilment—and against the contrasting backgrounds of a circus, a farm, and a port. The play is a psychological study which avoids dithyrambic excesses in praise of life and instead propounds new values with realistic argument.

## STEVENS, Leslie Clark
(United States, 1895–1965)

THE MARRIAGE-GO-ROUND. Comedy in two parts. Prose. First performance October 29, 1958, New York, Plymouth Theatre. Time: the present. Place: an American college.

The traditional triangle is transplanted into an academic setting and amplified into a satire on the educational system. Paul Delville and his wife Content both teach at the same institute; he is Professor of Cultural Anthropology and she is Dean of Women. From their respective lecture desks they publicly propound theoretical problems, strictly classified according to the male and the female point of view. But in their own marriage they get into a situation that defies all scientific axioms. Katrin Sveg, the daughter of a professional colleague, comes from Sweden to stay with them as a guest for the summer, and for the sake of a scientific eugenic experiment wishes to have a child by Paul. The professor seems not altogether disinclined to grant the fair charmer her wish—out of sheer professional interest, naturally. His learned spouse thereupon falls back on the proven physics of conjugal warfare, that is, artificially fanned jealousy and a spectacular flight home to mother. Chastened, Paul is preserved for the domestic hearth and, to boot, can use his adventure for a new lecture on monogamy. A stunt, but a highly entertaining one.


## STOPPARD, Tom
(England, born 1937)


ROSENCRANTZ AND GUILDENSTERN ARE DEAD. Play in three acts. Prose and verse. First edition London 1967. First performance August 24, 1966, Edinburgh, Cranston Street Hall (Oxford Theatre Group); first professional performance April 11, 1967, London, Old Vic Theatre (National Theatre Company). Time: the Elizabethan period. Place: without any visible character.

Stoppard, the late-comer, no longer shares Shakespeare's confidence in the unalterable fact, nor believes in the purifying power of the bloodbath and the distinction between guilt and atonement, doer and victim. He focuses on the Hamlet tragedy from the angle of the two stooges Rosencrantz and Guildenstern, who, unsuspecting and unconcerned, meet their death amid the twists of the plot. They are just two average people, in effect anonymous, for they are continually being mistaken for each other until they no longer know who is who and become more and more irrevocably alienated. Thus minor figures of the baroque theater become the symbol of modern man who finds himself at the mercy of events he cannot understand, still less influence. He is a function and is expendable. His reactions are calculated in advance and predetermined. Thus *Waiting for Godot* seems to be transposed into the hectic bustle of a living world. Rosencrantz and Guildenstern, breathless with duties and distractions, yet await a destiny, a call, the liberating moment of self-realization that might justify their existence. "All your life you live so close to truth, it becomes a permanent blur in the corner of your eye, and when something nudges it into outline it is like being ambushed by something grotesque."

They have been summoned with the utmost urgency to the Danish court, and then they are kept waiting. They think up bets and games. Desperately they seek a world that would act as a foil to their reality and make it comprehensible. But all they encounter is the troop of players, who make everything seem a repeatable pretence. What Rosencrantz and Guildenstern have hitherto supposed to be their unmistakeable identity turns out to be merely parts which the players easily adopt. In identical costumes and with identical gestures they double for the courtiers and make them superfluous. Scenes from Shakespeare's *Hamlet* mark the progress of the action. The quotations are used as mere punctuation and enable the author to reduce external events to their reflection as experienced by the two minor figures, for example, the play within the play, the murder of Polonius, the journey to England. Secretly Hamlet turns the king's order for assassination against the two bearers of the message, Rosencrantz and Guildenstern. Finally Fortinbras, gazing at the tableau of the heroic dead, learns of the quite unheroic death of the two stooges. And to the two English ambassadors who deliver the message, not understanding what has happened, and not concerned, there suddenly comes a message, an urgent command. Irresistibly these two are also caught in the undertow of some unknown event. It is by such digression that Stoppard makes plain the interchangeability of the situation and its characters. He makes purely ornamental use of baroque rhetoric with its ingeniously spun hairsplitting arguments, so that sophistry becomes a revelry of language, a forensic session in the face of nothingness. The characters try to circumscribe the here and now, to fix it and make it evident by means of paradoxical paraphrases, alienated montage of quotations such as the pseudo-Biblical "Give us this day our daily round," and logic carried to absurdity.

## STRINDBERG, Axel
(Sweden, born 1910)

MOLONNE *[Molonne]*. Play in three acts. Prose. First performance March 18, 1959, Stockholm, Kungliga Dramatiska Teatern. Time: the present. Place: a drawing room.

This scenic phantasmagoria explores the borderland of the unconscious: "A man and his potentialities are always two, two opposing currents in the world's soul. One man is what happens, the other, what might happen." Strindberg draws on psychoanalysis—the whole toolbox of suggestion, trauma, hysteria and hypnosis—as much as on fantastic motives from the realm of spiritualism and nature magic, such as exotic conjuration of the dead, fetishism, and ecstasy expressed in dance.

Dark, opposing forces compete for the soul of the young pianist Virginia, who lives in her mother's house as though in a trance, surrounded by exotic plants and the sultry atmosphere of a conservatory. A doctor, who years ago committed a ritual murder in the West Indies, binds the girl to himself with the nature magic of the natives. Virginia's former fiancé, a geologist, makes vain efforts to draw her into a sober, healthy life. Increasingly she falls under the power of Molonne, her imaginary double, who speaks and acts through Virginia. Fascinated by this strange existence within her, Virginia yields to it and shoots the doctor. After that she finally does become Molonne herself, an impersonal mask. The "dybbuk" which possesses men and has to be exorcised, a recurring theme of Hasidic literature, is here divested of its metaphysical implications and is treated as a clinical case, making effective theater.

## SUASSUNA, Ariano
(Brazil, born 1920)

THE ROGUES' TRIAL (Auto da Compadecida). A popular play from North Brazil in two acts. Prose. First performance September 11, 1956, Recife, Teatro Santa Isabel. Translated by Dillwyn F. Ratcliff, Berkeley, University of California Press, 1963. Time and place: not specified.

Conceived on the world scale, this play with compelling simplicity encompasses on a few bare boards heaven and earth, life and afterlife, laughter and weeping. Ever since the shows of medieval fairs, the moralities and clowning acts, since the gay *Interludes* of Cervantes, the exuberant mimic drive of the popular theater has pulsated in the episodic tangle of plays which make no distinction between blasphemy and piety as expressions of an explosive zest for life. The author himself appears as a buffooning commentator, a shrill fairground barker; he explains his intentions as follows: "The author who wrote this play in order to pillory the worldly attitude of his Church, reserved to himself the part of a clown. He meant to show thereby that he knew better than anybody that his own soul is nothing but a beggar's bag of foolishness and deceit. He had no right to treat this theme. But he dared to do so all the same, because he believed that these people who suffer are an uncorrupted people, and deserve our trust."

The central figure is the baker's boy Joao Grilo, a sly rogue, impudent and childlike, malicious and pious, rough and cunning, familiar with every sharp practice and of unbeatable gumption—the scum of the earth, born into eternal servitude and always prompt to go to war with his sly tricks against those with a full belly and a self-confident soul. Here is a new, delightful permutation of the picaresque tradition that has survived irrepressibly since antiquity. The baker's wife is set on giving a Christian burial to her adored pet dog. Grilo quickly placates the vociferously outraged clergy by alluding to the "dog's testament," which makes generous provision for the shepherds of the flock. Thanks to hard cash, the dog's corpse is interred to the accompaniment of incense and litany. A rich officer who remembers God only when he happens to be in some trouble or other is helped by Grilo's schemes to an involuntary, but salutary thrashing. The fearful robber Severin quite unaware helps the merry Brazilian folk to their own ascension ending in the Last Judgment. Christ, in the person of a Negro, must sorrowfully leave to the devil the whole pack of rogues, who on earth never paid heed to his commandments. But the hero of the play, the master rogue of them all, turns to Mary, Our Lady of Mercy, and her intercession wins the grace of another chance for human weakness. The avaricious upper classes, clergy, and citizenry alike tumble into purgatory. Grilo is allowed to return to earth, so that laughter should not die out there.

Nothing would be more mistaken than to see in this longing for leveling justice an anticlerical, class-conscious political message. The clergy are ridiculed just because men preserve the faith and certitude of the church in their hearts, untainted by doubt; and the rich are harshly caricatured, just because basically people accept the hierarchy of the world's values.

## SUPERVIELLE, Jules
(France, 1884–1960)

THE COLONEL'S CHILDREN (Le Voleur d'enfants). Comedy in three acts and an epilogue. After the author's novel (1926). Prose. First edition Paris 1949. First performance October 16, 1948, Paris, Théâtre de l'OEuvre. Translated by Alan Pryce-Jones, London, Secker & Warburg, 1950. Time: the present. Place: Bigua's apartment in Paris.

Tragicomedy of a would-be father is captured in a compellingly human everyday fairy tale. Colonel Philemon Bigua, who has exchanged his native South America for hectic Paris, longs so passionately for a son that he does the craziest things in his innocent and at the same time wise way. He busily sews baby clothes on a sewing machine, lays in a supply of talcum powder, and makes a nuisance of himself with the doctors, who cannot help his wife to have a child. He keeps getting into trouble with the police for befriending strange children. Eventually chance and an overburdened

father present him with sixteen-year-old Marcelle, who with some perplexity finds herself moved from her privations into a life of luxury.

Bigua has his educational principles, which he applies by making the
servants carry on their backs blackboards with good advice. The girl's
resistance and obstinacy soon change into love, when she begins to realize
how touchingly helpless her foster father really is, and he himself has more
than paternal feelings for her. Tormented by self-reproaches, he jumps
into the Seine with the sole result that he catches cold. Feeling rejected,
Marcelle goes off with the good-for-nothing rascal Justin. A year later
Bigua rediscovers her, with a new baby, both abandoned by Justin. Here
at last is what he wanted, and full of radiant joy he forthwith takes possession of his "almost" legitimate grandson. It is all good comic theater combined with psychological subtlety.

## TARDIEU, Jean
(France, born 1903)

FAUST ET YORICK [Faust and Yorick]. A parable in one act. Prose. First edition in Théâtre de Chambre, I, Paris, 1955. First performance November 1952, Paris. Time: not specified. Place: a study.

The problem of life unlived is concentrated in an oppressive farce. In a sketch of seven pages Faust traverses his whole life from the young scholar to the old man dying of senility. His point of reference for all the unsolved existential questions is the skull, the Hamlet prop: "The skull is the main issue."
Faust is looking for evolution to that "higher stage," of which, to be sure, nothing at all is known, but which was the *idée fixe* that led him to all his observations and analyses. Vainly the nurse reminds this obsessed scientist of his wedding day; subsequently, his young wife cannot get him interested in their first baby. Indefatigably he measures skulls, compares them, catalogues them—while around him his children grow up, make unhappy marriages, become embittered and lonely. How unimportant, after all, are these family troubles in comparison with the task of determining the maximum possible volume of the human skull. Faust ages visibly. The hypothesis of the "higher stage" has gained acceptance throughout the world, although even the possibility of its existence has not as yet been proved. Only when the scientist himself has collapsed and died does the eager group of young scholars find the long-sought-for proof in his own skull. This sad and macabre piece of clowning about pseudoscience, the symbol of any rigid purposefulness in the service of a slogan, banishes the naive spontaneity of life into the no-man's-land of abstraction.

THE LOVERS IN THE METRO (Les Amants du métro). Ballet comedy without dance and without music in two scenes. Prose. Written 1951. First edition in Théâtre II: Poèmes à jouer, Paris 1960. First performance April 22, 1952, Paris, Théâtre Lancry. Translated by George Wellwarth for New York production, January 30, 1962, Van Dam Theatre. Time: the present. Place: platform and carriage of the Paris subway.

Language and action become nothing but ciphers for emotions, which are conveyed to the audience not by statements but in terms of music and choreography. The elementary impetus of love in the midst of a soulless, puppetlike and noncommunicating environment is the theme of this outburst of gestures and words: "The whole thing should make the impres-

sion of a kind of ballet, with reality transposed into rhythm." Platitudes
and the exuberance of love alternate in changing, stylized facets.

He and She, "the lovers in the metro," happily waltz onto the station platform: "I want to be you. You are I. For you, around you. Through you,
toward you, across you. One to exist for the other. One single being."
They are crowded into a packed carriage and their kinetic impulse has to
be sacrificed to the means of mass transport. Indifferent passengers in the
masks of anonymity get between them—"they are impersonal, blank-faced,
with a fixed gaze, as though they were all shop-window dummies." Persistently, now courteously, now rough or pushing, He works his way past
the passengers. As He passes each one, the Newspaper Reader, the Offended
Flirt, the Plumber, the Would-be Movie Star, the Individual about to melt
into the crowd, He has to adjust to the appropriate platitude, the last
vestige of a dismantled personality. He reaches her just as She, too, turns
into an equally standardized automaton. His love saves her, She becomes
human again and the couple hurriedly escape the mechanized nightmare.


## THOMAS, Dylan Marlais
(England, 1914–1953)


THE DOCTOR AND THE DEVILS. Screenplay from the story by Donald
Taylor. Prose. First edition London 1953. First performance Septem-
ber 26, 1959, Wuppertal, Städtische Bühnen. Time: 1827–1829. Place:
Edinburgh.

The historical facts behind the involvement of the Scottish surgeon Dr.
Robert Knox in a trial for murder in 1829, used by James Bridie in *The
Anatomist,* was employed by Dylan Thomas for his film script. The scientist in a narrow-minded world cannot pursue his research otherwise than
through an alliance with crime: "To think, then, is to enter into a perilous
country, colder of welcome than the polar wastes . . . where the hand of
the unthinker is always raised against you, where the wild animals, who
go by such names as Envy, Hypocrisy, and Tradition, are notoriously
carnivorous. . . ."

His genius, his unerring dedication to his purpose, and not least his success have made the anatomist Dr. Thomas Rock an outcast in Edinburgh.
Society cold-shoulders him because he dared take Elizabeth, a simple girl
of the people, not for his mistress, but for his wife. He is in conflict with
the law for secretly buying from shady characters called "Resurrectionists"
the corpses he needs for his anatomical experiments. This practice gives
the two drunkards Broom and Fallon the lucrative idea of killing un-

known guests who call at their tavern and selling the goods fresh to Rock. The case is discovered and Fallon executed. Rock's connection with the case is carefully hushed up by the influential medical profession. Eventually Rock, hunted by the mob, estranged from his family, and shunned by the students, remains alone with his voracious and insatiable desire for knowledge.


UNDER MILK WOOD. Play in two acts. Prose. Originally a radio play. First edition London 1954. First performance October 24, 1953, New York. Time: the present, spring. Place: Llareggub, South Wales, Great Britain.

As in Thornton Wilder's *Our Town*, the day-to-day life of a small town provides the theme, the background, and the title. But while the American lovingly traces a family idyll, looks at the hereafter in cosy middle-class terms, and conveys the poetry of little things, the Welshman mobilizes the whole town with its teeming multitudes—the stage version has a cast of no less than thirty-eight. This multiplicity and ubiquity make small-town life into something disturbingly unreal. Thomas also discloses the nocturnal side of his characters, their dreams and frustrations, their longings and fears. Blind Captain Cat is the guide through this invisible world and "voices" accompany the day through its course: "It is night moving through the streets . . . dewfall, starfall, the sleep of birds in Milk Wood. . . . Behind the eyes of the sleepers, one can hear their dreams. . . ."
In a string of associations we are shown people's early morning dreams, their occupations during the day until nightfall once more. The first to rise is the Reverend Eli Jenkins, the collector of bardic songs; the butcher's daughter, a demure schoolteacher, dreams of the bartender; twice-widowed Mrs. Ogmore-Pritchard fusses in her dust-defying bedroom. Zestful Polly can hardly count her children any more, let alone remember their fathers, and yet, despite the contempt of the "wedding-ringed" Mothers' Union, rejoices over each new life she carries; the Owens' marriage proceeds happily amid drink and mutual blows. The little world of "under Milk Wood" has as much room for down-and-outers like Lord Cut-Glass and Nogood Boyo as for innocent children's games. Nightfall once more brings to the fore the spectral world of nature's magic and murmuring sprites: "The thin night thickens. A breeze from the creased water sighs the streets close under Milk waking Wood . . . whose every tree-foot's cloven in the black glad sight of the hunters of lovers, that is a God-built garden. . . ." It is a prose poem divided among many parts and by virtue of the language and style becomes truly lyrical.

## TRAUTWEIN, Martin
(See TUCHOLSKY, Kurt, and TRAUTWEIN, Martin.

## TROYAT, Henri (Lev Tarassov)
(France, born 1911)

SÉBASTIEN [Sebastian]. Comedy in three acts. Prose. Written 1949. First edition Paris 1949. First performance March 1, 1949, Paris, Théâtre des Bouffes Parisiennes. Time: the present. Place: the painter Arbisseau's drawing room.

The self-righteous pseudorespectability of the philistine is confronted with genuine hooliganism, and their interaction results in an entertaining mixture. Since the painter Ernest Arbisseau became a well-paid specialist for pictures of saints, his lachrymose wife Hortense and his not-so-young daughter Mathilde have to make a show of religious fervor—for business reasons. This, as it were, compensates for Jacques, the family's incorrigible black sheep, who is just working off a prison sentence for theft. Madame Vial, a lady as rich as she is bigoted, has commissioned a painting of St. Sebastian.

By accident the painter finds a model who—the very spit and image of the ideal—is even called Sebastian. He is taken into the painter's house and soon grows enthusiastically into his saintly role. But when Jacques comes home, he discovers to his surprise that Sebastian is the leader of the gang of burglars. Ernest's conscience has no chance against the lucrative commissions for a whole series of Sebastian paintings. Sebastian himself turns his eyes piously to heaven and points out to his accomplices that Madame Vial has admirable jewels—a most welcome temptation, which he will resist with the pose of the saint. But when the clumsy Jacques now prepares to "go it alone," his virtuous papa is terrified of a new arrest and consequent scandal. He therefore implores Sebastian to take charge of the burglary. With Sebastian's professional experience and his—almost—saintly way of life the blessings of heaven surely cannot fail to materialize. Generously Sebastian fulfills the hard-tried father's request and steals the jewels. Looking at his own portrait as a martyr, Sebastian prefers to take away the painting and Mathilde, whom he loves, and leaves the jewels behind, untouched. Profoundly stirred, Madame Vial thrills at this incomprehensible "miracle of St. Sebastian."

# TUCHOLSKY, Kurt, and TRAUTWEIN, Martin
(both Germany; Tucholsky, 1890–1935)

SCHLOSS GRIPSHOLM *[Gripsholm Castle]*. From the novel by Kurt Tucholsky. Five chapters with a prologue. Prose. Acting edition Hamburg, Rowohlt, 1963. First performance October 30, 1963, Mainz, Städtisches Theater. Time: yesterday and perhaps also today. Place: on the road and Gripsholm Castle.

By adding to the basis provided by his novel *Schloß Gripsholm* passages from *Lottchen beichtet einem Geliebten* and *Rheinsberg,* Tucholsky, with his easygoing narrative art, breaks up the stage version into even more facets. Yet there is no fragmentation of style in this play of innumerable refractions.

In a light, gossipy manner a narrator follows the holiday trip of Peter and Lydia, the "princess" of his heart, to Sweden and the idyllic Gripsholm Castle on Lake Mälar. For several animated scenes the lovers bring into the play their friends Karlchen and Billie who with their uninhibited pleasure in a good story introduce into the action a whole crowd of characters. Some are already known, others invented, with the result that an endless prospect opens up. It is an inexhaustible play of aphorisms in the form of verbal wit or stage gags, a profusion of thoughtful trifles, frivolities, gentle and not so gentle mischief. Lydia and Peter spend some carefree summer weeks, rescue a child from its harsh governess—the regulation wicked fairy in this idyll—and unselfconsciously fool about with silliness and wisdom. "We lay in the meadows and dandled our souls."

The lovable controversialist side of Tucholsky comes out; and serenely like Shakespeare's wise fools, he contemplates this world—and beyond: "We fled to each other from the solitude of the world. There was a gram of malice in it, a little spoonful of irony, nothing languishing, very much will power, very much experience and very much innocence . . . and there with scepticism, understanding, incapacity, and plenty of strength, we concocted an attitude for ourselves . . . which often makes us keep silent while others buzz wildly about."

## TURNER, David
(England)

SEMI-DETACHED. Satirical comedy in three acts. First edition London 1962. First performance June 8, 1962, Coventry, Belgrade Theatre. Time: the present. Place: the home of Fred Midway in the London suburb of Dowlihull.

Fred Midway, a ruthless insurance man, has made a profitable business enterprise of his family. The working capital consists of sex and legacy expectations. At present the family is in trouble. The daughter Eileen has fallen in love with a married man, an engineer whose skill is indispensable to Fred for his model railway. The younger daughter Avril wants a divorce from her husband Nigel Hadfield, because the wealthy uncle has altered his will. With the help of a baby which was really fathered by young Tom Midway but is foisted on the startled uncle, Fred smooths out this particular difficulty and, to make doubly sure of the inheritance, maneuvers Eileen into the uncle's arms.

A trenchant satire on the art of making life pleasant at any price. The whole play is an experiment with new potentialities in boulevard comedy —a ceaseless crescendo of complications and a second stylistic level of comments addressed directly to the audience.

## USTINOV, Peter Alexander
(England, born 1921)

THE LIFE IN MY HANDS. Play in two acts. Prose. First performance 1965, Nottingham. Time: the present. Place: stylized variable settings.

With the polemical impact of a billboard poster, Ustinov puts on the stage a highly effective intervention in the discussion concerning criminal law reform, circumstantial evidence, and the abolition of the death penalty. The reporter Arthur Long is shocked out of his usual routine hunt for news by the "Martovsky case." Martovsky has been sentenced to death for the rape of a halfwit, who died, perhaps as a result of it. The public's outcry at this crime induces the courts to disregard the extenuating circumstances—the victim suffered from a weak heart and was a nymphomaniac, and neither the actual cause of her death nor the fact of rape is conclusively proved. Long's paper clamors for "justice," not to save Martovsky, but to exploit him as dynamite in a press campaign. In fighting for the convict's life, Long acquires an unexpected ally in John, the Minister's son. John demonstrates to his self-righteous father that Martovsky was the victim of unfortunate circumstances. He himself and his father, the Minister, owe the appearance of respectability only to a lucky chance which concealed their own crimes. But for the sake of his reputation as a legal authority, the Minister lets Martovsky be executed and thereby drives his son into such disgust with life that he commits suicide. The jubilant press can now represent Martovsky to the public as a martyr. Deeply stirred, the Minister pardons the next prisoner awaiting execution, but once again is made the butt of the newspaper's attacks, which now bewail the unpublished crime. Long finally has enough of this double-edged manipulation of public opinion and sacrifices his job to his conscience. The scenes blend into each other by the use of film fade-out techniques and are interrupted and highlighted by Long's comments without detriment to the topical relevance.

THE LOVE OF FOUR COLONELS. Play in three acts. Prose. First edition London 1951. First performance May 23, 1951, London, Wyndham's Theatre. Time: 1948. Place: the village of Herzogenburg in the Harz mountains.

A plethora of assorted devices—the farce of a futile summit conference, a psychoanalytical fairy tale and the always serviceable play within a play—are mobilized for this entertainment which, for all its gentle social criticism, ultimately remains noncommital: "We can't do right without doing wrong, and we can't do wrong without doing right. Every act is the renunciation of another. We must do one thing or the other, and when we do one thing, the other is undone." All the characters are telescoped into debating points.

Four colonels represent their respective Allied Military Administration in a German village, where they have been fighting their paper battles for two and a half years. The question of taking possession of a nearby castle occasions a jumble of protocols, votes, amendments, protests, and adjournments. The trouble is that the castle is cut off by impenetrable undergrowth which mysteriously keeps closing up again every night. To their utter amazement these desk strategists are told that behind this barrier the Sleeping Beauty waits to be awakened by Prince Charming from her long sleep. Two strange personifications of good and evil come to the rescue of the perplexed victors. The "wicked fairy" turns up in the person of a tramp. Since time immemorial the wicked fairy has created discord among men, as the serpent in paradise and through other temptations. The "good fairy," the warning angel, is the attractive Auxiliary Territorial Service girl, Private Donovan. Together, they take the four colonels to the castle and show them the sleeping princess on an elaborate early nineteenth century stage. For each one of them the princess represents his secret ideal of beauty and love, to which they now have to measure up. In four successive scenes set among changing epochs, situations, and characters, the Frenchman, the Englishman, the American, and the Russian encounter the princess as the woman of their respective dreams, "the elusive bird which flutters in [their] heart," and try to win her. The Frenchman Aimé Frappot is defeated by the innocence of the princess, since he, a man of principles, wishes to be merely the lover of a married woman in the gallant rococo style. The Englishman Desmond de S. Rinder-Sparrow approaches his love in the person of an Illyrian nun in coarse Shakespearean times and is put to flight by the ghost of her mother. The American Wesley Breitenspiegel is a methodist preacher among gangsters, as strong in his faith as with his fists, and is deflected from his love by his woman psychiatrist. Finally, the Russian Ikonenko, fails from sheer passiveness in a Chekhovian idyll replete with melancholy and solemn trifles.

The wives of the four unsuccessful wooers now·turn up and exchange their psychoanalytically based experiences. Aimé and Wesley resign and stay in the castle to share the princess's magic sleep. Desmond and Ikonenko feel that the world must not be deprived of them and return to power politics.

PHOTO FINISH. An adventure in biography in three acts. Prose. First edition London 1962. First performance April 25, 1962, London, Saville Theatre. Time: the present. Place: in the study of Kinsale House in London.

Time sequence and unity of person are ingeniously abandoned so that the balance sheet of a man's life can be drawn up through a jigsaw of situations and causalities divided by decades. The disintegration of personal identity, which Evreinoff in his *Theatre of the Soul* treated as a tragic mystification, is in *Photo Finish* an entertaining bluff, a balancing act with latent possibilities: "Changing course . . . selling fractions of our soul every now and then for the sake of peace and quiet, but counting the change jealously all the same at every transaction for the sake of honor. . . ."

Tied to his wheelchair as he is at eighty, the writer Sam Kinsale is completely at the mercy of his tyrannical wife Stella. Suddenly his past literally comes up to meet him in the persons of himself at different ages—at twenty, at forty, and at sixty. Sam Twenty is just getting enaged to Stella, to the horror of his older selves who have to pay throughout their life for his youthful enthusiasm. Sam Forty is an unkempt idealist, rather proud of being misunderstood and determined to leave Stella for the sake of true love. But then she is pregnant and so forces Sam back into the broken marriage. Sam Sixty a complacent poseur, serves the broad public with his literary manufactures and rakes in his plentiful royalties. Occasional love affairs make his life with Stella tolerable. None can help either himself or any of the others. In Sam's sorrow about the literary opportunities he missed, we suddenly seem to hear the voice of Ustinov the routine entertainer himself: "It's not writing that's the trouble, . . . it's thought, and it's protecting thought against elegance, wit, style. How I hate it. . . . Style's a way of lying. Style's an ornament which hides the architecture." Undeterred, Sam Eighty makes ready for the "photo finish" and continues to write his memoirs—a slave of his brilliant talent to the end.

ROMANOFF AND JULIET. Comedy in three acts. Prose. First edition London 1957. First performance April 2, 1956, Manchester, Opera House. Time: the present. Place: the smallest country in Europe.

The certainly far from harmless ingredients of contemporary politics appear in this political satire as riotously unproblematical confections. Romeo has turned into the Russian naval officer Igor Romanoff, who must win his Juliet in the cold war between the big powers. As the son of a Soviet ambassador he is at first horrified about this revolting ideological aberration of his sentiments, which attract him to the daughter of the

American ambassador. His love becomes a protest against national prejudices and "reasons of state." The Ruler of this musical-comedy country, which has as many political parties as it has citizens and exploits its political vicissitudes merely as a tourist attraction, is an avuncular dictator who by a ruse gets the young couple safely wedded.

The two papas are at first outraged at this national treason, but then drop their respective ideologies with a sigh of relief and remain as immigrants in the little country, whose soldiers pass the time of day with word games and where all conflicts are resolved in the third act at the latest. With obvious gusto Ustinov aims many a passing dart at current affairs and thus turns the play into a political cabaret. There is the gentle but very definite pressure of East and West on the neutral state for a defense treaty, the grotesquely exaggerated stool-pigeon system in Soviet families, and the two-faced espionage services of the neutrals—all elements which fit somewhat uneasily into the glib smoothness of an evening's light entertainment, but thanks to the author's brilliant stagecraft are not felt to be out of place.

# VALÉRY, Paul
(France, 1871–1945)

MON FAUST [My Faust]. Two plays: Lust, la Demoiselle de Cristal [Lust, the Young Lady of Glass], comedy in three acts (the fourth and last act is missing), prose; and Le Solitaire ou Les Malédictions de l'univers [The Recluse or The Maledictions of the Universe], dramatic fantasy in one act and an interlude, prose and verse. Written 1940. First edition Paris 1946. First performance January 10, 1947, Brussels, Théâtre du Parc. Time: not specified. Place: Faust's library and garden; a glacier.

Faust, the Promethean challenger of chaos looking for meaning and activity throughout the universe, has become a skeptic indulging in mental acrobatics and is lost in the absolute void of disillusionment. Valéry's Faust is a "man without qualities" in Musil's sense, for whom every fixed stand in reality implies an inadmissible limitation of potentialities and of the free play of aspects and associations. His life is a mere "disorder of attempts." Genius "is all very simple. It's just a matter of sensibility to chance." Logically, Faust's attempt to dictate his autobiography to his secretary Miss Lust is bound to fail. It is all meant to be playful and fragmentary, as indeed is evident in the very design of the work, which consists of fragments of two entirely separate plays.

Faust goes through three situations of conflict in his encounters with Miss Lust, with the Recluse, and with the fairies. These symbolize man's confrontation with the confused area of the emotions, with abstraction for its own sake and with the dreams of fantasy. The interplay of emotions subjects man to the external world. If man allows the constructions of his mind to turn him away completely from the world of the senses, he ends by negating existence. The domination of the unfettered imagination, finally, is fated to spend itself in beautiful make-believe. Faust stands the ordeal of these three encounters, he remains true to himself and to his device: "to master the mind by the mind."

Faust is dictating his memoirs to Miss Lust, his secretary, and is hard put to think up yet further fantastic embellishments by which to outdo the innumerable variants of his fate extant in literature and music. Mephistopheles sees himself invalidated by mankind's obsession with progress. In a world of moral ambivalence, of events taking their indifferent course beyond good and evil, the devil has become a standardized concept. Faust is now the active partner who renews the pact in order to rescue Mephistopheles from the "inertia of his eternity" and to return to the world with him. In so doing, Faust escapes the seduction of Lust, whose femininity disturbs his pose as a dispassionate genius. He warns the disciple to beware of love. This young man, rejected by Lust and discouraged by the futility of all the achievements of the human mind buried in the library, falls into the hands of the devil. "On the roof of the world," in the solitude of the glacier, Faust encounters the Recluse, who has to face the fact that his scornful rebellion has long become a commonplace routine in this mass age. He hurls Faust down from the rock into a world of fairies, creatures of the fleeting imagination. They want to give Faust back his youth and to entangle him in boundless possibilities. Faust turns them down. He wants to know no more, to do no more: "However great the powers here to me unfurled/ They cannot give me any pleasure in the world." By denying himself to the external world with his No, he also annuls the power of the supernatural.

## VAN DRUTEN, John
(England/United States, 1901–1957)

BELL, BOOK AND CANDLE. Comedy in three acts. Prose. Written 1948–1949. First edition New York 1951. First performance November 14, 1950, New York, Ethel Barrymore Theatre. Time: the present. Place: Gillian Holroyd's apartment in New York.

In the strictly standardized world of the American way of life a coven of witches are exercising their jolly art. Thanks to her spellbinding talents, Gillian Holroyd captivates the heart of the writer Shepherd Henderson at first sight and thereupon readily gives up black magic in order henceforth to rely on the magic of love alone. Weird Aunt Queenie and brother Nicky stick to the cauldron and suitably bewitch the witch-hunter Sidney Redlitch. An unusual and happy variation of the society comedy's customary progress toward its happy ending.

## VAN ITALLIE, Jean-Claude
(American, born in Belgium, 1936)

AMERICA HURRAH. Three one-act plays: *Interview; TV; Motel.* Prose. First edition New York 1967. First performance November 7, 1966, New York, Pocket Theatre. Time: the present. Place: America.

A critical audit of the affluent society and its façades, the palliatory phrases which barely conceal the underlying mania for destruction. These improvisations were written for the Open Theatre and make creative use of the group's style, its acrobatics, lightning character changes and miming.

In three one-act plays behavior patterns of the American way of life are exaggerated to a grotesque level. In the first, four applicants go to an employment agency for an interview. In the second, three employees are monitoring television programs. In the third, the voice of a woman motel-keeper, on stage as a grotesque, life-size doll, is heard ceaselessly extolling the virtues of the standardized hotel room as a man and a woman, also grotesque dolls, enter and within a few minutes casually destroy everything in the room, including finally the motel-keeper herself. These basic situations are filled out with caricature stills: the hysterics of a pedestrian swamped by the street crowds; a gym class of small Americans developing their charm and self-confidence; behavior patterns on the subway and while awaiting a telephone connection. Shock elements from everyday life are introduced; for example, the girl who has just witnessed an accident seems a spoilsport at the immediately following party. Or a peaceable citizen is seized with panic as he sits watching television. In between comes the ballyhoo of a state governor's election campaign in which the public is stuffed with indiscriminate promises. The gossip of the employees in the television testing room mingles with reports from the war in Vietnam and touching family scenes from the White House. Finally the people in front of the screen, with their phrases and standardized gestures, become indistinguishable from the characters on the screen. Van Itallie makes use of rondo form and masks in the choreographic stylization of his waxworks.

## VAUTHIER, Jean
(France, born 1910)

CAPITAINE BADA [Captain Bada]. Play in three acts. Prose. Written 1950. First edition Paris 1952. First performance January 12, 1952, Paris, Théâtre de Poche. Time: the present. Place: Bada's room.

Man's freedom, his chance of self-realization in daring and decision, are now, in Vauthier's view, confined to the game, to the free, self-oblivious, spontaneous exploration of all contradictory possibilities. He explains: "The work aims at a sort of dramatic poetry not to be looked for in the individual's reactions to events, but on the contrary in the 'secretion' of the event through the spiritual state of the individuals. It is a duel lived on the few square feet of the stage. The action turns in a circle and dictates rhythmical figures, which are now stopped short and now set in motion again by the 'breaks' in intentions, speeches, and tone color (spiteful, violent, plaintive). The gestures are sometimes quite commonplace, but nevertheless have a tendency to choreographic stylization or even true ballet."

Bada, "a strange young man making an almost exotic impression," has to make the hard choice between an ascetic, lonely path of spiritual purification at the end of which beckons the poet's laurel, and a small, comfortable, average happiness at Alice's side. The frustrated genius finally succumbs to the woman. The wedding is performed in a ritual dance with the pursuing male pressing more and more closely in on the fleeing female. The excesses of the sex go as far as a suicide attempt on Alice's part, after which she happily and naturally accepts her lot. Twenty-seven years later Captain Bada again lives wholly for the claims of the spirit; he has not stepped outside the neglected room for twelve years, works on a nebulous manscript, and is a tyrannical husband looked after by Alice with ceremonial solemnity. He indulges in grotesque fits of temper in self-pity and relishes the crown of misunderstood genius. His secret diaries preserve a vestige of his inalienable self; they are the "radiant hope" which justifies the gloom of his existence. Just when Bada, in a fit of ecstatic reforming zeal, wants to start an entirely new life, he falls off a cupboard and breaks his neck. A government official takes him away through the window in a silver gondola.

In the epilogue Alice celebrates the memory of a man in perpetual struggle with himself. Polarities such as man and woman, mind and emotion, creative power and malleable material, fighting and yielding, are personified in the loving opponents Bada and Alice, and the currents are discharged in a magnetic field of vibrant spiritual forces. The spontaneously accidental aspects of this ceaseless flux of associations are controlled by the rigor and choreographic stylization of expression.

LE PERSONNAGE COMBATTANT *[The Struggling Individual]*. Play for one person and a waiter, in forty-two sequences. Prose. Written 1952. First edition Paris 1955. First performance February 1, 1956, Paris, Théâtre Marigny. Time: the present. Place: a hotel room.

In struggling for his past, man has to settle his accounts with the seemingly so secure present. Or, in Vauthier's own words: "It is my wish that choice and suggestion should be one, that they should take place spontaneously and simultaneously on the stage and in the audience rather than in an interior decorator's workshop; what is not possible in the style of an overprecious prose priding itself on its attempt at magic performed for its own sake should not be possible on the stage either. And all that for the sole purpose of respecting and buttressing the meaning of this play, which is that we should surrender enough of ourselves to reality so that, by way of compensation, we are rewarded with so complete and close a presence that we perceive even whispered remarks. . . . The audience must bear with the actor who assaults them!" This one-character play mounts to a fortissimo in the spiritual tension between two texts: the draft of a short story written long ago by the well-known author Raymond Ducusso and the empty phrases of his present existence.

As a successful author Duccusso returns to the scene of his first, hesitant attempt. The shabby room in a provincial hotel, the view of the railway station, the noise of the trains clattering past—all that is to reawaken inspiration. He passes amused judgment on the naive and awkward language of the manuscript, which he begins to rewrite. He reads out whole pages of it. In this spooky dialogue with his superannuated self he gradually sheds the vain arrogance and self-assurance of the successful writer. He discovers in the manuscript an unexpected seriousness and a truthfulness that expose as a lie his subsequent emergence as a fashionable author and the whole proud success story of his life. With alarming suddenness he sees his present invalidated, and once more he becomes the struggling, vulnerable man of his beginnings. Desperately he tries to revive the creative tensions of that time, and to this end forcibly turns the room into what it was then, tearing down the wallpaper and smashing the knickknacks. A strangely menacing waiter and the noises from the next room— to the left a couple of rag-pickers end their lives by murder and suicide, to the right an old professor is having a good time with a prostitute—intervene in the violent spiritual struggle of his nocturnal brooding, until he is nearly demented. The futility of his efforts, his sense of being abandoned and rejected by his own past, and his profound solitariness drive him to despair. A sacrifice appears the only possible way to salvation. He throws his money and his luggage out of the windows, destroys the typewriter, that immanent temptation to insincerity, and—now down to bedrock—is able to pray for the "tiny chance" of a new beginning. He has finally paid his ransom and broken free from fraud and in exchange is given once more the poet's freedom to change the world. An attempt is made to convince him that this is nothing but yet another self-deception, for the hotel was built only a few years ago and his youthful experience is only a fiction; he is arrested under suspicion of murder, beaten up by the waiter, and dragged from the stage like cattle to the slaughterhouse. But even the most profound humiliation cannot rob him of the exalted certainty of his vocation.

In substance and in form this is a musical score: the rhythmic tension between pause and action, crescendo and decrescendo, between the true man and the poseur enslaved by his own rhetoric—the movement and language, dance and pantomime, the counterpoint of the offstage noises—the fuguelike construction. The result is ecstatic theater of extreme formal rigidity.

LES PRODIGES [The Prodigies]. Play in two parts. Prose. First edition Paris 1958. First performance January 10, 1959, Kassel, Staatstheater. Time: the present. Place: a large lounge.

This is Theater of the Absurd, conveying no message accessible to the mind, but mere affective reactions, mere sensory delusions. The substance of reality is decomposed into an interplay of changing points of view and possibilities, its form into a loose musical sequence. Man can gain access to this alienated reality only by becoming a "man without qualities" in Musil's sense, that is, if he never fixes his point of view, never becomes a rounded personality intelligible in terms of causally determined patterns of behavior, but instead retains the freedom of spontaneity—in the absurd. "The fade-out of one effect, the fade-in of the next, the false miracles, the utopias, allusions, mirages, hallucinations, and delusions all reveal one clear intent, which is to point to the miracles closest at hand that are present everywhere: to harmonize the love of the uncreated with the love of creation."

Three characters confront each other in will-o'the-wisp chaos. The man, Marc, feels himself to be a misunderstood genius and bewails the missed opportunities of self-realization. He is in the power of the girl Gilly, eternal femininity that needs no self-realization because it "is" and always has been. Gilly revels in extreme emotional outbursts, is unpredictable and seductive, and driven by a dangerous love-hate. In the background there is a nurse, a grotesque monster, who is eventually burned in the kitchen stove. Her sadness is silent like an animal's, she is the satyr in this play of love, a mere prop like Gilly's stuffed dog, an object to speed the pace of the action.

The couple indulge in the excitements of what is not present, grieve over missed opportunities, and dream of future ones. The decisive point is the absence of psychological consistency: "Nothing in nature has the right not to be used!" This puts at Vauthier's disposal the full range of all means of expression, the seething chaos of a world before the first day of creation. The lovers, who cannot get together in the disruption of life, are not content with the habitual "as-if," with the cheap deception of superficial companionship, but accept isolation, accept being outcast, accept the immanent break in the world and turn it into a philosophy. The temperature curve of their outbursts alternating between abandon and indifference, exuberance and depression, sadism and masochism, excitement and soberness fluctuates so wildly that the individuals become the plaything of this counterpoint of their nerves. It is left to the chance of "affective harmony" whether any human encounter, any spiritual bond is at all possible.

The estrangement and helpless abandonment of these characters is reflected in alienation effects at various levels. In regard to content, there is first of all the device of making the subconscious evident; thus Gilly in one scene simultaneously renders two different experiences. The refractions of memory, the facets of experience are so inextricably intermixed that neither can be recognized any more. In form, Vauthier uses similar devices. The worn language, washed out by everyday usage, is made by alogical means to yield new effects—advertising slogans, lyrical bombast, babble, anecdotes, sheer noise are abruptly juxtaposed. Even the actor's expressional means, standardized by a long tradition are decomposed into nonsensical, disconnected impact energies: "This is the beginning of the most erratic, tiring and exaggerated sequence of improvisations which can possibly be demanded of a young woman's larynx. Different poses, the body contorted. . . ." All this results in a glittering apotheosis of sensuous theater without any message. But we should not overlook the cathartic function of this unfettered game; everything susceptible of expression and disfigured by the patina of a thoughtlessly accepted tradition, by outdated scales of value, misunderstandings and conventions, is tested by Vauthier in the crucible of elementary creation itself. It is decomposed into minute units of communication, stripped down to its physical origins, and ultimately thrown like an elemental sound, pure and all-encompassing, into a world emptied of meaning.

This is how Vauthier's own interpretation is to be understood: "This whole expenditure of energy, the innumerable hours, this passion clinging to the provisional but intensive for all that—the ultimate aim of it all, without my knowing it, is simplicity. . . ."


## VERCORS (Jean Bruller)
(France, born 1902)

ZOO OU L'ASSASSIN PHILANTHROPE [Zoo or The Philanthropic Murderer]. A juridical, zoological, and moral comedy in three acts. Prose. First edition Paris 1964. First performance July 6, 1963, Carcassone. Time: the present. Place: Criminal Court, Old Bailey, London.

A dialectical comedy is developed within the framework of a trial. The ancient question of man's nature is posed anew. Pirandello's probing dialectic and his device of disintegrating identity are handled with the comedian's levity and permutated step by step. Individuals cannot be precisely defined in terms either of appearance or origin, language or interpretation. Everywhere the transitions are fluid, the accents interchangeable. The chance constellation of circumstances and the moment's point of view determine what particular concept of truth is to be valid.

A research expedition encounters in the depths of Australia the *Paranthropos erectus* ("tropi"), a species of quadruped walking erect on two legs, which is a link, so far believed to be extinct, in the biological chain of evolution between apes and men. The newspaper reporter Douglas Templemore crosses a tropi and a human by artificial insemination, kills the strange hybrid, and faces trial. The jury has the insoluble task of deciding whether the tropi is to be regarded as human and Douglas therefore condemned as a murderer, or whether this archaic form of life is to be classed as an animal and Douglas therefore acquitted. A contradictory confusion of experts' opinions and hypotheses proves only one thing, namely, that the stage of human evolution depends always only on the single individual. "The philanthropic murderer . . . thus demonstrates to the world that to be human is not a state to be borne, but a dignity to be fought for. . . . There is no humanity in the human being, unless it is created." Douglas is acquitted and has achieved his purpose of shaking the thoughtless self-assurance of the others.

A whole series of maliciously clever problems is grouped around the main theme. Justice Draper is at once busily canvassed by a number of people who—God forbid—do not want to deflect justice, but merely want to give him good advice. The uncertainty of scientists, who fanatically look for a jawbone thousands of years old but who are all perplexity and bewilderment when for once their sterile search for knowledge is confronted with reality, has its counterpart in the ambivalence of the witnesses' testimony which allows both prosecution and defense to pick out whatever happens to suit either. The conflict is not—as it usually is—developed out of the plot, but out of the discrepancies of reality: "The circumstances have led you, doctor, to issue a death certificate for a creature to which you would never have given a birth certificate." "Much fun is made, too, of officials who hold an office and a correspondingly determined view, but no opinion. For in this trial one piece of circumstantial evidence cancels another. The author's Gallic relish for playing with ideas and his light comic touch make a standard out of shifting subjective colors and turn them into an impressive case study.

## VERNEUIL, Louis (Louis Colin du Bocage)
(France, 1893–1952)

AFFAIRS OF STATE. Comedy in three acts. Prose. First performance September 25, 1950, New York, Royale Theatre. Time: the present. Place: George Henderson's home in a suburb of Washington, D.C.

This play, written in English, follows Scribe's popular tradition of the witty "diplomat" comedy around a noble father figure juggling with polished intrigues in a spirit of elegant and ironic detachment. It is now transposed into the modern democratic setting, without detriment to the original nonchalance and aristocratic flair.

When the elderly American statesman Philip Russell retires, it looks as if, along with his position, he will also lose his wife Constance who is twenty-five years his junior. She wants a divorce so that she can marry the up-and-coming young politician George Henderson, who is trying to get elected to the Senate with Philip's help. With indulgent mockery Philip asks for a short period of grace, which he uses to mount a brilliant intrigue by which to reconquer his wife. Within a few days George finds his career jeopardized by an unknown opponent. Full of sympathy, his paternal friend Philip advises a quick marriage, which is bound to go down well with the virtuous American public. Philip has already arranged for someone as a partner in this marriage of convenience, to wit, his niece Irene, who agrees to accept a salary for acting the part of George's loving wife. Things move to their foregone conclusion: the young couple fall in love. When Philip generously offers to set his wife free, he finds—to his well-played surprise—a chastened, conscious-stricken young woman only too relieved to return to security at his side. With grace and wit Verneuil creates a new variant of the traditional drawing-room comedy's obligatory triangular situation.

## VIAN, Boris
(France, 1920–1959)

THE EMPIRE BUILDERS (Les Bâtisseurs d'empire ou le Schmürz). Play in three parts. Prose. First published in Cahiers du Collège de Pataphysique, No. 6, 1959. First edition Paris 1960. First performance December 22, 1959, Paris, Théâtre Récamier. Translated by Simon Watson Taylor. Produced in London, July 31, 1962, New Arts Theatre Club. Time: the present. Place: different rooms in the same house.

The Schmürz is a silent, bandaged, rag-encrusted figure. He wears one arm in a sling, with the other he leans on a stick. He limps, bleeds, and is revolting to look it. He is a symbol of conscience, always silenced and betrayed by men, those thoughtless builders of life's empires.

An inexplicable noise alarms and terrifies a family. The parents, their daughter Zenobia and the maid, who answers to the charming name of Mug, all flee upward from story to story to just under the roof. Although the father carefully bars all entries, the inexorable advance of the terrible "outside" hems them in more and more. Everywhere the family come up against an indefinable, repulsive something that they call "the Schmürz." This bundle of misery is an outlet for all their moods and tensions, they treat it to kicks and blows and grind it to death. Every banality, every thoughtlessly repeated platitude is a new torment for this personification of conscience.

By some obscure fate, the household keeps diminishing; Mug escapes from the oppressive restriction, Zenobia moves to the neighbors (in ruthless logic her return is barred when the door slams behind her), mother has an accident on the stairs and dies before she reaches the attic, father's last refuge. Until the end, when father, too, is destroyed by the catastrophe, he remains a poseur enamored of his own phrases. Exalted by self-justification, he even tries to make his peace with the Schmürz until he falls to his death with a scream. "The Noise invades the room and darkness descends. And perhaps the door opens and perhaps schmürzes enter, vague outlines in the dark . . ."

THE GENERALS' TEA PARTY (Le Goûter des généraux). Play in three acts. Prose. Written 1951. First published by the Collège de Pataphysique in Dossier 18–19, 1962. First performance November 4, 1964, Braunschweig, Staatstheater. Translated by Simon Watson Taylor in Theatre of War, Hardmondsworth, Penguin, 1967. Time: some indefinite time in the future. Place: France.

A vicious farcical attack on church and state is dressed up as scintillating stage entertainment. These venerable institutions are so distorted as to appear as menacing puppets, ridiculous and insidious bogeys furnishing each other a butt for their wicked jokes. General James Audubon Wilson de la Pétardière-Frenouillou is a henpecked gentleman, as he has been all his life, and still stands in awe of his Mama. But for once this formidable lady's watchfulness has slackened for a moment, and immediately he has escaped from the nursery and, together with Prime Minister Léon Plantin, has dreamed up a war.

War is a national blessing, for the wave of destruction is to sweep away the overproduction of men and goods which is causing serious trouble for the French economy. The Archbishop is equally pleased at the prospect of being able to try out new effects of unctuous exhibitionism when interceding for victory. Audubon's colleagues on the General Staff launch their preparations with all the zeal of naughty schoolboys and a grandiloquent proclamation is to promote the national enterprise. On second thoughts, Audubon discovers to his dismay that in all the general enthusiasm nobody has remembered to decide who is to be the necessary enemy. Just the job for the diplomats! Hastily the ambassadors of the various major powers are summoned. But to their immense regret, the representatives of the United States, Russia, and Communist China have to forgo this unique opportunity of a war with the *grande nation*.

The fire of the gentlemen's military ardor, which held out such splendid hopes, is dimmed by political considerations and geographical distance. Is nothing to come, then, of the lovely war, and is France's economic prosperity to be sacrificed to the petty interests and reservations of peaceful foreign countries? The top brass are quite up to this discouraging situation. They decide to wage a senseless, but all the more lengthy war against Algeria. Two years later the fiery heroes sit, disgruntled, in their underground command post and pass the time of day with silly games. Deadened by yawning boredom as they are, their nerves can finally be titillated only by a party game of suicide. One after another dispatches himself to the hereafter. Only one of them is left at the end, and he will take care of carrying on the war—for the economy must prosper. . . .

## VIDAL, Gore
(United States, born 1925)

THE BEST MAN. Play in three acts. Prose. First edition Boston 1960. First performance March 31, 1960, New York, Morosco Theatre. Time: perhaps July 1960. Place: a hotel suite in Philadelphia during an American political party convention.

A political play with an ethical message: in the political jungle a man must at some stage choose between being honest or successful. There is a violent struggle at the convention as to who is to get the party's nomination as presidential candidate. The two men who have the best chances are the former Secretary of State William Russell, a moderate, sensitive idealist, and Joe Cantwell, the typical ruthless careerist. Cantwell tries to get rid of his rival by having him declared mentally unstable, on the basis of faked medical certificates. Russell is in possession of material about a moral scandal in which Cantwell was involved and by means of which he could demolish the political freebooter, but as an intellectual, Russell shrinks from fighting with such dirty weapons. Art Hockstader, a former President, has every sympathy for this moral rectitude, but nevertheless decides to back Cantwell, because he feels that if America is to assert itself in the world it needs a ruthless, strong man of action at the helm. At this Russell throws away his chances, withdraws from the race and releases his supporters in favor of a third candidate, who so far was not in the running but who now wins the majority. The old problem of "dirty hands," Kreon's problem, is reinterpreted in this documentary of American politics.

## WALSER, Martin
(Germany, born 1927)

DER SCHWARZE SCHWAN *(The Black Swan)*. Play in two acts. Prose. First edition Frankfurt/Main 1964. First performance October 14, 1964, Stuttgart, Staatstheater. Time: the present. Place: a clinic for nervous diseases.

Martin Walser says *Der schwarze Schwan* could equally well have been a book of memories. It is the theme of the inflammatory process of recollection, of the German past still not overcome. He realized that the "fear and misery of the Third Reich" cannot be directly transplanted onto the stage, for inevitably the theater turns into play what is inconceivably appalling, prettifies it in presentation, reduces it in scale by selection, and falsifies it in aiming at effect and intensification. The play shows the revolt of conscience. The crimes of the concentration camps appear only in indirect refractions, in repressed elements of the subconscious, recollections of children's games and carefully glossed-over euphemisms. The mainspring of all the characters is their relationship to the past.

The former concentration camp doctor Professor Leibniz has gone underground with the pseudonym Liberé and is now director of an isolated clinic for nervous diseases. To account for what he did in the war years he has invented the story of a harmless, idyllic earlier life in India and has taught that story to his unsuspecting daughter, whom he has transformed from a hearty German Hedi into an inoffensive Irm. "I have tamed what has been, turned it into a little rodent." Liberé has imposed upon himself a private penance. Every day he makes a larger number of wire brushes than was laid down as the norm for camp prisoners, eats out of a tin bowl and sleeps on a plank. He adopts Tinchen, a mentally retarded thirty-year-old woman who, as though she were still a child in the League of German Girls, goes on collecting for the Winter Help and paying tribute to her Führer at the summer solstice. For her the past has become a pseudo-present to which she clings fanatically.

Dr. von Trutz, the assistant doctor who is engaged to Irm, seems to have found the most effective recipe for dealing with the inconvient past. He belittles past and present alike and reduces both to his own shallow banality. "In Minsk I ran out of eau de Cologne . . ." is all he remembers of the war. Professor Goothein, like Liberé a valiant former champion of the millennial misery, has come to terms with the past thanks to his adaptability. He was known as the "Black Swan," the notorious gas-chamber specialist at the Rosenwang concentration camp; having sat out his four years in prison, he is now sunning himself in his new and well-deserved

respectability. But the festering ulcer of conscience which everyone disregards suddenly breaks out in Goothein's son Rudi. Born in 1940, he
learned only the macabre details of the extermination camps which he
and Hedi introduced into their childhood games. Then, in the midst of
the booming economic miracle he comes upon a forgotten instruction
signed by his father. The blood-stained document impels the young man
into complete identification with the "Black Swan," the official mass
murderer. Quickly Goothein calls in his psychiatrist friend to treat this
distressing divagation, this "ethical hypertrophy" which gives rise to such
an inexplicably sensitive conscience. Rudi is struck with Hamlet's madness; he feels an exile in a world steeped in guilt and shame, and, in his
feverish frenzy, sets out to provoke the respectable gentlemen by staging
a play entitled "The Domestication of the Erinyes by Dr. F." But the
worthy gentlemen with butchers' hands choose not to understand. Irm
owns up to being the former Hedi, but her sound vital instincts make her
prefer a carefree marriage with Trutz, however ordinary he may be, rather
than make a common stand with Rudi against this shameful world and
die in the attempt. She is convinced that in our age self-sacrifice is nothing
but a ridiculous eccentricity. Rudi capitulates and shoots himself.
Liberé gives himself up and faces trial, either as a gesture of genuine expiation or perhaps in order to acquire a legitimate place in the sun of the
economic miracle. One thing only is certain, namely, that his punishment
will be welcome to the pharisees of the present with their full bellies. "The
fact is that they have no notion of what guilt is, but instead a costume and
an expression which they have learned by heart. And that is the punishment, the borrowed gravity with which they treat you. In public, before
people who do well for themselves. The gallows is what they would like
best. But in any case they want to appear spotless. That's the purpose I am
to serve."

THE DETOUR *(Der Abstecher)*. Play in three scenes. Prose. First published in *Theater heute,* No. 12, December 1961. First performance November 28, 1961, Munich, Werkraumtheater der Kammerspiele. Translated by R. Grunberger in *Plays,* Vol. 1, London, Calder & Boyars, 1963.
Time: the present, at night. Place: Ulm, Germany.

A vicious farce on the German middle classes, whose happiness so comfortably spreads itself between latent sadism and honest-to-goodness respectability. The company director Hubert makes a little nocturnal detour
to Ulm during a business trip. He sends his driver Berthold off with money
for a gay evening and calls on his former mistress Frieda, whom he sent
packing four years ago. In the interim she has married Eric, a locomotive en-

gineer. The husband happens to be absent, Frieda is as appetizing as ever, and Hubert looks forward to a tender evening. It is some shock to his amorousness when Frieda darkly tells him that she has poisoned her husband with potassium cyanide. Hubert is upset. He is a decent chap, after all, and even though he is not averse to occasional discreet adultery, he would never go so far as to express his feelings with murder. However, so as not to deprive himself of the pleasures to come, he makes an effort at human understanding—true to his sympathetic, true-blue German heart. Eric turns up unexpectedly and apologizes for Frieda's macabre hoax. In embarrassment because of his bad conscience, Hubert denies having any affection for Frieda, whereupon the indignant couple sentence him to death by electrocution.

During the voluptuous preparations for the execution, Hubert tries to save himself by pretending to Frieda that he loves her passionately and imploring her pardon. Thereupon the jealous husband condemns him to death all the more emphatically. Then Hubert holds forth on his high, beer-garden ideals, his unscrupulous business methods, his secret escapades, and his open display of golden-hearted family affection. Eric is moved and overwhelmed. Each discovers himself in the other's banality. Two ordinary souls have found each other and celebrate their friendship with a bottle of wine. Frieda is quite forgotten. She scornfully gives the two gentlemen who are so satisfied with themselves a piece of her mind and goes away. The methods of the Theater of the Absurd are used to expose the falseness of human relationships.

THE RABBIT RACE (Eiche und Angora). A German chronicle in eleven scenes. Prose. Written 1962. First published in Theater heute, No. 11, November 1962. First edition Frankfurt/Main 1963. First performance September 23, 1962, Berlin, Schiller-Theater. Translated by Robert Duncan in Plays, Vol. 1, London, Calder & Boyars, 1963. Time: April 1945 to 1960. Place: the "Eichkopf," the hill above the German town of Bretzgenburg.

At the concentration camp, Alois Grübel, a former Communist, was both physically and spiritually sterilized of his "subhumanity" and made into a submissive nominal member of the ruling party. He acquires a new outlook on life: "So if only everyone would always just go along at once, there wouldn't be these cruel nuisances. Instead we would have a development. . . . But what happens? There's always this stubborn resistance to what is bound to come. And then people are surprised if someone gets killed. If they behave like that, people naturally do get killed. History has to go on." His contemporaries, the splendid representatives of German civic virtue, with brutal and unconcealed opportunism adapt this outlook to suit the changing times.

The dashing Storm Trooper Potz, who is April 1945 meant to save the Reich with the help of the Home Guard, and the District Leader Gorbach shortly afterward become underground resistance fighters and convinced opponents of war. The establishment of the Bundeswehr necessitates a new tack for these expert turncoats. In an attempt to reensure themselves in respect of the East, they then go through yet another change. But simple-minded Alois does not so easily rid himself of the catchwords drummed in during the Nazi period. The pliant patriots take a dim view of his back-sliding. While his wife Anna, in despair at the destruction of her mar-riage, takes to drink, Alois applies the eugenic teaching of his period in the concentration camp to the large-scale breeding of Angora rabbits. But this hobby is forbidden by the ex-Nazis just as much as his cherished desire to shine in the choral society thanks to his beautiful castrato tenor voice. Finally this bothersome reminder of the past is locked in a lunatic asylum along with the Jew Woizele who persists in searching for his liquidated family. At last Alois is happy. A man of the twentieth century, the security of the cage and of prison walls has become indispensable to him. A didactic play on that past which has been only too overwhelming—aggressive, bitter, uncompromising. The form, too, with its easy-going use of cabaret methods, suggests new potentialities for the play on contemporary themes.


ÜBERLEBENSGROSS HERR KROTT *[Mr. Krott, Larger Than Life].* Requiem for an immortal in thirteen scenes. Prose. Written 1963. First edition Frankfurt/Main 1964. First performance November 30, 1963, Stuttgart, Staatstheater. Time: the present. Place: Hotel Excelsior in the mountains.

This is a ballad of the omnipotence of money in the alarming personifica-tion of Mr. Krott. This "dance around the golden toad" compellingly high-lights the questions of domination and subjection, possession and responsibility, complicity and lethargy. Krott, the symbol of big business, is tired of his domination over the world. Larger than life, older than time, immortal, he squats, with the staying-power of a toad, on the terrace of the mountain hotel and wearily acts out his part. He knows that he has long outlived himself, but there is nothing that could take his place in the order of values. The disgruntled poseur is surrounded by a train of fol-lowers spellbound by the magic of money: his wife Elfchen and Malfalda, his sister-in-law and mistress, go into raptures about their own silliness; the waiter Ludwig Grübel and his wife Rosa, whose son Hansi is being prepared for the lofty career of a virtuoso, but also ends up as a waiter, look after Krott's physical comfort. They cater to his soul by performing a sad family scene for him in the guise of his daughter Erni and her fiancé Frederik. But Ludwig's principal duty is to care for the collection of dead victims, which keeps growing thanks to Krott's powers of destruction: Selzhammer, the director, commits suicide because he cannot obtain an interview with Krott; Sepp, the mountaineer, comes to grief on the Wall of Death in order to provide the ladies with a little mild entertainment; meaning to shoot birds, Krott accidentally kills a washerwoman.

When the trade union official Strick forces his way into Krott's presence, the latter hopes for release by assassination. But Strick succumbs to the temptation of wealth, forgoes the avenging shot and disappears into the unnumbered army of sycophants. To his sorrow, Krott endures—an account that is no longer profitable but that no one has the courage to close. Krott is a Brechtian figure, reminiscent of "Baal," to which he owes the monumental dimension and the balladlike language, and of "Puntila," which contributed the epic construction in a sequence of scenes as well as the basic design. He stands for the canker of capitalism taken in the absolute, whose danger consists in contaminating everything, smothering every protest, corrupting every opponent. What we meet here is not a plutonic fairy-tale king, as in Aristophanes, but all-encompassing tyranny, final and irresistible, because it does not acquire its power by illegitimate means but is power itself and all resistance melts before it.

## WALTER, Otto F.
(Switzerland, born 1928)

ELIO ODER EINE FRÖHLICHE GESELLSCHAFT [Elio, or A Merry Party]. Play in three acts with prologue and epilogue. Prose. Written February 1963. First edition Munich 1965. First performance February 27, 1965, Zürich, Schauspielhaus. Time: the present. Place: the Schaubs' living room in a small town.

This is a profound requiem on reality, irresistibly changing, and man's forever unchanged yearnings which in the form of an *idée fixe* dominate his life. It is on the conflict between the day and the dream, on the misleading nature of all human statements and sentiments, which, in relation to the outside, immediately become false and uncontrollable and are filled with other contents and determined by other refractions. Only death vouchsafes the security that lies in the unalterable: "You and I have overtaken time. Everything is here, not once more—for everything is now, is here; I believe you have overtaken these years. Or rather: invalidated them. . . . Now everything can be new—from some origin new and good, and everything solved by an angel whom perhaps we do not know as yet."

The chemist Albert Schaub and his wife Ella have no problems in their comfortable middle-class marriage, when suddenly an escaped convict seeks refuge in their apartment. He is wounded and hunted by the police. He gives his name as Friedrich, but Ella, fascinated as in a dream, welcomes him as Elio, the hero of her teen-age longings and the personification of everything that life has failed to give her. When she married Albert she gave him this imagined name and saw in him a champion of the protest against reality, an idealistic rebel; later she had to watch this erstwhile Elio make his pedantic compromise with life. Now the intruder becomes the prop of her lifelong yearning. Ella's unfulfilled and unspent tenderness and her romantic longing for danger weave a web of lies and fairy tales to defend this newly-won property of hers. In her husband she sees nothing more than a function and an unwanted tie. Albert defends himself and tries to get rid of Friedrich/Elio. Through a maze of gossip with the housekeeper, disputes and trite squabbles we see how indifference and sins of omission have ruined this marriage. Albert has a child by another woman. Ella, in her middle-class comfort, has forgotten about her promise to Elio that every seven years they should somewhere begin a new life. When she realizes that even today's Elio, the car thief in flight, might well in the course of the years turn into someone as smug as Albert, that her longing can never win against the course of reality, she shoots him.

The "merry party" of bridge players, which is repeatedly referred to as a leitmotif and background to this phantasmagoria of an unfulfilled life, can now finally continue. Ironically the author uses triangular situations and crime, the most conventional props of the theater, as raw material for this interplay of identities.

## WATERHOUSE, Keith, and HALL, Willis
(both England; Hall, born 1929)

BILLY LIAR. Play in three acts. Adapted from the novel by Keith Waterhouse. Prose. First edition London 1960. First performance September 13, 1960, London, Cambridge Theatre. Time: the present, on a Saturday. Place: living room and garden at Goeffrey Fisher's home in the North Country.

This is a loving character portrait of a daydreamer and teller of tall stories possessed of inexhaustible imagination and energy, both of which, however, dry up at once if they are to serve some useful and profitable purpose in everyday life and work.

Billy Fisher defends his chaotic and carefree child's world with every possible means. He does not want to grow up lest he lose himself, but he fails to notice that in his constant buffoonery he is not really himself at all, but is submerged in a flood of shapeless potential selves. Billy is troubled by himself and his nineteen years as much as by his lower middle-class environment. He is a day-dreamer who passionately enjoys his invented experiences, recklessly swindles all the level-headed commonplace people around him and plays them off against each other. In his emotional insecurity he has become engaged to three girls at the same time and has tried his hand, unsuccessfully, at several jobs. At present he is an undertaker's clerk and creates a lot of mischief in this serious business. Unexpectedly he is given an opportunity to start a new life in London as a writer, an old dream of his around which he has woven grandiose fantasies for years. But in the end Billy shrinks from reality and retires into self-pity for being eternally misunderstood.

## WEINGARTEN, Romain
(France, born 1926)

L'ÉTÉ *[Summer]*. Dramatic tale in six days and six nights. Verse and prose. First published in *L'Avant-Scène* No. 377, April 1, 1967. First performance May 29, 1965, Darmstadt, Landestheater. Time: not specified. Place: a garden.

A play of shadows and reflections is captured impressionistically in a summer garden. The romance of lovers meeting is, like the plants, gentle and sad. There is none of the violence of passion on display, none of the indiscretion that is implied in every "contrived" representation of emotions. Longings, fulfillment and disappointment are made known only by their reflections in the life of children and animals.
In the dark, a woman's voice conjures up the memory of her love: "I stand where I saw you for the first time, and if I look about me carefully, I understand the meaning of the lines in that hand that never ceases to implore. The begging summer all around . . . and that moment that lives on in me, incomprehensible today as it was then. I do not want to torment you, dearest, only to cherish the desire that united us in the radiance of that same day, that same light." Invisibly—betrayed only by the windows lighting up and darkening—the lovers meet in the isolated boardinghouse run by the teen-age girl Lorette and her stuttering, simpleton brother Simon. The counterparts are two tomcats—Half-Cherry and His Garlic Highness—impersonated by two nimble gentlemen in lounge suits. "The

cats, rather disgruntled aesthetes during the day, become mysterious wizards during the night. As though they were the secret priests of some cult, they prepare all the places for events to come and already known to them." The animals are vain, combative and obstinate, graceful clowns and at the same time eerily paradoxical in their ubiquity—nature's creatures in the depths of a "midsummer night's dream." "Things happen. We know them already. We knew them already. The footprint before the step. Caught!" The housefly Manon, His Garlic Highness's ladylove and a critical reader of Sartre, causes many a jealous skirmish with her flighty nature. Then again the cats get all worked up by the idea of power and greed, which would make them swallow up the whole earth and eventually devour each other.

Everything all these creatures do is sparked off by the couple of lovers, whom they watch with fascination. The lovers' ring, which in the course of the play is lost, found, hidden, tricked away and lost again, sets the rhythm, as it were, for this dance of nebulous associations. The woman no longer loves the man and leaves him to go with another. Thus everything loses its meaning for the inhabitants of the garden. A grief other than his own makes Simon into a sensitive person. Pretending to be Pierre and Lila, he and his sister reenact the affair—meeting, love, parting. The imaginary Lila, too, betrays Simon, and all that remains is Lorette's sisterly comfort. Once more they escape into the self-oblivion of illusion, so that the game called life should go on: "You don't understand a thing. Nor do I. It cannot be explained. Even if one repeats the words like a parrot, one knows nothing of the wherefore. Why are we here and not elsewhere, together or not together, happy or unhappy?"

## WEISENBORN, Günther
(Germany, born 1902)

BALLADE VOM EULENSPIEGEL, VOM FEDERLE UND VON DER DICKEN POMPANNE [The Ballad of Eulenspiegel, Federle and Fat Pompanne]. Represented on the stage with a prologue and choruses in forty-three scenes. After the old Merry Pranks. Prose and verse. First edition Hamburg 1949. First performance March 17, 1949, Hamburg, Deutsches Schauspielhaus. Time: the late Middle Ages. Place: a platform stage, no specified place.

The eternal play of executioner and victim, of oppression and rebellion, is presented on bare boards in the manner of the wandering players. The characters, which have their origin in the medieval Peasants' War and were later simplified to the sharply contrasting types of the Punch-and-Judy show, are timeless and as flat as a woodcut. They represent the attitudes which constantly recur in times of despotism.

Eulenspiegel, the wag, is the only individual to fight, cunningly and courageously, against the Lord High Steward and his lawless mercenaries, but refuses to merge himself in the anonymous collectivity of the peasants' uprising. The Lord High Steward appears as the Dickwanst-Wüterich [Bigbelly Tyrant] of the old folk theater. His mistress Federle makes a deal with injustice for the sake of her comfort: "Life is too terrible to be good . . . I'm afraid of the whip, so I stay with those who do the whipping." Only her love for Eulenspiegel makes her develop into a human being. The coarse camp follower Pompanne makes a fortune in times of war and famine. The dumb peasants Kasperlein and Dummschussel are led by the nose, as always, and have to pay for the noisy heroics of the others. Eulenspiegel has to stab Federle to save her from the Lord High Steward. He kills the tyrant and everything leads up to the concluding moral: "You have heard how things have come about/ When the little man got mad./ Let's press on and not be sad,/ Since the darkness will not last, no doubt."

Brecht's alienation theory is coarsened into naive crudity. Lyrics are introduced as commentary and breaks in the action; the decoration on the bare stage is entrusted to the dialogue and the "moral of the story" is emphatically proclaimed—all means are used to take the ideologically "committed theater" back to the spontaneously improvised folk play.

FÜNFZEHN SCHNÜRE GELD [Fifteen Purses of Money]. Play in eight scenes. After the Chinese of Chu Su-chen. Prose. First edition Munich 1956. First performance August 30, 1958, Hamburg, Thalia-Theater. Time: not specified. Place: China.

The subject matter of this play can be traced back in the national literature of China to legends of the twelfth century. After it was put down in writing by Chu Su-chen about 1650, it continued to be reshaped during the following centuries and at one time was enlarged to a total of twenty-nine acts. Weisenborn has distilled the mythic material in a striking parable by the use of stage techniques inspired in part by the restraint and stylization of the East Asian theater and in part by Brecht's epical didactic treatment.

The happy-go-lucky, bibulous butcher Yu Hu-lu has let his shop run down. His sister gives him fifteen purses of money to save him from complete bankruptcy. But the rescued toper gets no chance to enjoy his golden blessing, for that same night he is stabbed and robbed by Lou, the bum, known as "the rat." The dead man's niece Su Shu-chuan, who had been driven out of the house the evening before as a result of an unfortunate joke, falls under suspicion of having committed the murder. Hsiung Yu-lan, a young trader who was Su's chance companion on a journey, is arrested as her supposed lover and accomplice. Puffed up with his own self-importance, the judge Kuo Yu-chih declares himself satisfied with the suspicion which is cunningly strengthened by Lou, and delivers the death sentence. The prefect Kuang Chung is to supervise the execution. Kuang suspects a miscarriage of justice. But is he to act contrary to the emperor's commands, defer the execution on his own initiative and cast doubt on the administration of justice? Just because of his uneasy conscience is he to get into conflict with the all-powerful hierarchy of authorities? However, "to save a single life is better than building a pagoda." Kuang overcomes his misgivings about his own fate; he stakes his life and his position, wakes the dreaded governor from his sleep and pledges his head to his outraged superior so that he may seek out the truth. The governor is enraged at this obstinacy, for he cannot rely on such insubordinate judges. Yet "is it not equally important that the people should be able to rely on its judges?" By a trick Kuang extracts a confession from "the rat." Su and Hsiung, who have shyly made friends in their misfortune, are free to set out toward an unburdened and happy future. And Kuang is left musing, with gentle scepticism: "Will it not always be so, that to fight for the truth is a bitter and ungrateful task?"

DIE ILLEGALEN [The Illegals]. Drama of the German Resistance Movement in three acts. Prose and verse. First edition Berlin 1947. First performance March 21, 1946, Berlin, Hebbel-Theater. Time: the Second World War. Place: a town in Germany.

A realistic picture book of the activities of the German resistance movement: "We illegals are a silent community in the country. We dress like everyone else, we have the same habits as everyone else, but we live between treason and the grave. . . . The world loves victims, but the world forgets them. The future is forgetful."
Walter, son of the innkeeper Weihnacht, operates a clandestine radio transmitter. Lill, the waitress, makes use of his love for her to get him to join an illegal resistance group. Walter sacrifices himself; he is found in possession of incriminating material and shot while attempting to escape. The episode is presented in too broad an outline to be of much interest today as a political record, though it can stir our human sympathy. As counterparts to the young people's spirit of rebellion there is the mother who, with her fears, wants to remain unpolitical even in "dark times."

There is the little girl whose spontaneous filial love unwittingly betrays her father, who has gone underground, and thus delivers him into the hangman's hands. There is also the neighbor Sargnägelchen whose own suffering has made him indifferent to any political cause. These individuals with their human failings are stronger than the ideological summons to solidarity. "How vulnerable is man and how forlorn/ when the monster attacks him, it is stronger,/ with dagger, with murder, with gas, with the scaffold . . . and experience teaches too that man/ . . . is uncommonly feared by the monster,/ for there is nothing stronger on earth/ than groups organized and determined/ to go their way, come life or death."

## WEISS, Peter
(Germany, born 1916)

THE INVESTIGATION *(Die Ermittlung)*. Oratorio in eleven cantos. Free verse. Music by Luigi Nono. First printed in *Theater 1965,* special annual issue of the review *Theater heute.* First edition Frankfurt/Main 1965. First performance October 19, 1965 at sixteen theaters: Altenburg, Landestheater; West Berlin, Freie Volksbühne; East Berlin, Deutsche Akademie der Künste; Cottbus, Theater der Stadt; Dresden, Staatstheater; Erfurt, Städtische Bühnen; Essen, Städtische Bühnen; Gera, Bühnen der Stadt; Halle, Landestheater; Cologne, Städtische Bühnen; Leipzig, Städtisches Theater; London, Aldwych Theatre; Munich, Werkraumtheater der Kammerspiele; Neustrelitz, Friedrich-Wolf-Theater; Potsdam, Hans-Otto-Theater; Rostock, Volkstheater. Translated by Alexander Gross, London, Calder & Boyars, 1966. Time: the present. Place: a law court.

What Weiss is after in his stage documentary on the Frankfurt Auschwitz trials of 1963–1964 is not merely a requiem, but at the same time a criticism of the modern world. "I want," he says, "to stigmatize capitalism which goes as far as to have dealings with gas chambers . . . I have not added any sauce of my own, but have of course consciously brought out certain trends." Weiss originally had the idea of a vast poem, of the range of Dante's *Inferno,* and in the final version has maintained the division into cantos. He describes them as a "big collage" which contains "nothing but facts as they emerged in the court proceedings. Personal experiences and confrontations had to yield to anonymity." The eighteen accused in the trial keep their names, but are symbols rather than individuals. The testimony of the four hundred and nine witnesses at the Frankfurt proceedings are concentrated in nine anonymous witnesses who now and then change their roles. Witnesses one and two exculpate the accused, while the remainder speak for the innumerable victims. The actual defending counsel, who murdered twenty-four, are represented by one right-wing extremist and his rhetorical tirades. He raises objections against witnesses who "are inspired by hatred," against "exaggerations and calumnies directed by a certain circle" and waxes enthusiastic about the nation "which during the time under discussion was fighting a bitter battle at great sacrifice." The accused often smirk with pleasure at this belated publicity.

In the eleven cantos Weiss has given shape and form to the documentation of the inhuman reality and made it comprehensible. Through this structure Weiss forces his contemporaries to an intellectual showdown. The reality which was revealed at the Frankfurt trial had instinctively been met with abhorrence; that is, with a defensive reaction, with psychological self-defense. Weiss stands back and lifts the nightmare from the realm of the emotions into that of reason. First he outlines the scenes in the "Canto of the Ramp," "Canto of the Camp," and "Canto of the Swing." Then he contrasts the fate of the prisoners—in the "Canto of the Possibility of Survival" and the "Canto of the end of Lili Tofler," who refuses to be an informer and is shot—with that of their tormentors, in the "Canto of Sub-Group Leader Stark," who, aged twenty, is boning up on "Goethe's humanism" for his matriculation examination and in the meantime shoots a mother and her children. Individual murder techniques ("Canto of the Black Wall") are cumulated in the special operations ("Canto of Phenol," "Canto of the Cell Block") and finally terminate in the mass annihilation of the gas chambers ("Canto of Zyklon B") and in the inescapable final phase of physical extinction ("Canto of the Furnaces").

The evidence of the witnesses illustrates the separate procedures of the death machinery. On the ramp the doctors sort out the "usable material" from among the new arrivals, and a number is tattooed on each one. A Red Cross ambulance, which the prisoners interpret as a sign of humanity, carries the poison gas. The sadism of a Kaduk and a Bednarik, the swing torture invented by Boger, the medical experiments, are made plain. The black wall is the scene of mass shootings. The medical orderly Klehr wields the hose. In the standing cells the prisoners are condemned to slow wasting away, and the dying tear each other to pieces and trample each other down as they struggle to reach the air hole. Those sentenced to the camps, prisoners and executioners alike, are stripped of all sentiments of humanity. The greatest threat is not physical extinction, but the denaturation of the spirit.

The accused have lapses of memory or plead higher orders. Industrial profiteers, who at the time increased their output tenfold thanks to "unlimited consumption of manpower" and are now honored members of their trade associations, are circumspectly uninformative on the witness stand. A "Society for Justice and Freedom" put pressure on the witnesses by means of anonymous letters and also tries bribery. The accused Mulka, in his self-assurance, has the last word: "Today, when our nation has once more worked its way up to a leading position, we should concern ourselves about other things than reproaches which must be considered as long superannuated." It is not so much in the bestiality of individuals that the system reveals itself, as in its terminology. The language makes it possible to manipulate the moral sense of the individual, the phraseology perverts his sense of justice, obscures the promptings of conscience, because it makes use of the same logical abstractions. It does not oppose the moral order with anarchy, but it infiltrates it with a scale of pseudovalues and catchwords. The official language makes the ultimate horror commonplace and manageable. That kind of phraseology ineluctably links executioner and victim, makes them interchangeable, mere faceless material of the system.

The many performances of this play were all readings rather than theatrical productions. The aim was to communicate factually, to bring home the enormity of it all rather than to achieve an equivalent of the horror in theatrical terms aiming at the subjective nuances of emotional effect.

NACHT MIT GÄSTEN [Night with Guests]. Murder story in one scene. Verse. First published in Akzente 4, 1963. First performance October 14, 1963, Berlin, Werkstatt des Schillertheaters. Time: not specified. Place: a house.

A gripping experiment in a style made up of elements drawn from the uncouth violence of Grand Guignol, from Artaud's Theatre of Cruelty, and the physical demonism of the Japanese kabuki theater. A murderous robber has crept into the house and threatens a family. The parents and children lavish the most bewitching kindliness on their questionable "guest" in order to do him in at some unguarded moment. Cunningly they stimulate the intruder's desire for a treasure chest which is supposed to lie at the bottom of a lake. The husband is sent out into the night to make sure of the gold. Meanwhile the wife and the children urge their guest to assume the father's role, and he cannot resist the inviting double bed. The "warner" announces the appearance of robbers in the neighborhood. The father, who is dragging along the chest, is taken by the warner to be a housebreaker and is killed. The wife tries to go to her husband's assistance and is killed by the guest. Then a bitter struggle breaks out between the warner and the guest for possession of the treasure chest and it costs each of them his life. Full of curiosity the children open the coveted chest and find it contains nothing but beets. The bloodbath had been caused by fodder from the cattle shed. The meaningless cruelty of life makes sense only in the dangerously innocent world of children's nursery rhymes, and the inextricable deception of all human relationships is explained only in a silly grimace.

THE PERSECUTION AND ASSASSINATION OF MARAT AS PERFORMED BY THE INMATES OF THE ASYLUM OF CHARENTON UNDER THE DIRECTION OF THE MARQUIS DE SADE *(Die Verfolgung und Ermordung Jean Paul Marats, dargestellt durch die Schauspielgruppe des Hospizes zu Charanton unter Anleitung des Herrn de Sade).* Drama in two parts. Various verse forms. First edition Frankfurt/Main 1964. First performance April 29, 1964, Berlin, Schillertheater. Translated by Geoffrey Skelton and Adrian Mitchell, New York, Athenaeum, and London, Calder & Boyars, 1965. Time: July 13, 1808. Place: Charenton asylum in France.

This is dialectical pseudofireworks masking behind its brilliance the absence of any true dramatic intention—an aesthetic farce befitting a time of stagnating affluence. Weiss has created a fascinating symbol, rich in meaning, for an age paralyzed by success and self-sufficiency. He chooses the year 1808, a time of prosperity and world conquest, of self-righteousness and strong nationalism in France. The people of France, ecstatic under the sun of their successful dictator, are reduced to the scale of inmates of a lunatic asylum. This uniform community, anonymous and forcibly united by an all-powerful institution, is representative of the whole people. Like the world at large, this community busies itself with burying the past and reenacting the horrors of the revolution in play, so as to enjoy with all the more complacency the security protected by iron bars.

The Marquis de Sade, a luxury patient who even here has managed to preserve some sort of fool's freedom for himself, acts as the *maître de plaisir* and organizes a performance of Marat's murder by Charlotte Corday. In the crude outlines of a billboard poster, Sade and Marat represent two irreconcilable modes of experience beyond any hope of constructive compromise. Marat is a revolutionary for love of mankind, who uses tyranny in order to help the exploited proletariat and who must ultimately learn to his despair that power always implies injustice to the weak. The counterpart to this ideologist of action is Sade, the perverse introvert, who knows only one fitting form of protest, and that is self-destruction from disgust with life. Sade is the unscrupulous individualist petrified in a pose of self-fascination and deluded by his idolatry of his own body, which reacts in ever-changing ways to his probing intellect. He stands alone, while Marat's enthusiastic ideals of world reform are represented in a number of different mutations—the ex-monk Jacques Roux propounds an anarchistic brand of communism, and even Charlotte, who stabs the demagogue in the bath where he seeks relief for his skin disease, is very close to her victim with her vague national enthusiasm.

The style of the work, with its multiple refractions, is expressed by a series of puppetlike demonstration types, who often step out of the action, comment upon it and link the separate episodes together. They include the mischievous dolt of a Herald, who introduces the personages in clumsy rhymed verse. The nameless small folk have four spokesmen, the grotesque popular singers Cucurucu, Kokol, Poloch and Rossignol, who deploy the grievances of the eternally exploited in sharp-tongued ballads. Coulmier, the director of the asylum, personifies authority, which may indeed be amused by what goes on but immediately stops any attack that goes beyond the neutrality of an amateur performance. He radiates the newly won respectability of 1808, which is right because it is successful and has made its utilitarian arrangements with the survivors of the blood-stained past. Militarism is once more a profitable national virtue, toy guillotines are a popular Christmas present and the reign of terror, which has been over for a whole eternity of fifteen years, is an object of aesthetic coquetry. The final chorus of madmen is a cynical tribute to the achievements of the new standards of the time.

Weiss combines a deliberately coarse simplicity with glittering virtuosity, popular song hits with subtle and intellectual discussions about world philosophy, melodrama, thriller, circus and pantomime. But for all this profusion, there is no development, no conflict which is logically solved. The play within a play is a device for arguing about irreconcilable positions, and the arguments themselves are a pretext for the play—a fascinating round of self-delusion in ceaseless experimentation, in the triumph of theatrical means over the play's message, and hence a distorting mirror which as a symptom has its justification.

## WENDELL, Beth

See HUXLEY, Aldous, and WENDELL, Beth.

## WESKER, Arnold
(England, born 1932)

CHICKEN SOUP WITH BARLEY. Play in three acts. Prose. First edition Harmondsworth, England, 1959. First performance July 7, 1958, Coventry, Belgrade Theatre. Time: October 1936 to December 1956. Place: London.

In this first play of *The Wesker Trilogy* social conflicts and family psychology are traced over the course of thirty years in a Jewish family named Kahn. The repercussions of economic and social events are shown in the lives of otherwise anonymous "humble people," in their hopes and aims, their disappointments and worries. Characteristically for our century, they are all politically committed.
In 1936 there is a Communist demonstration in London's East End against a Fascist meeting. Sarah Kahn champions her revolutionary ideals with so much enthusiasm that everyone is carried away. Only her husband Harry hides with his mother at the decisive moment. Snapshots from the years 1946, 1947, 1955 and 1956 show how political enthusiasm gradually wanes under the pressure of the cares of life. The contempt which makes Harry with his indecision and timidity an outcast in his own militantly class-conscious family also causes him to fail in his job. Most often he is out of work, dreams himself into false importance and ultimately wastes away in self-pity after a stroke. His daughter Ada marries Dave Simmonds, who has fought for his ideals in the Spanish Civil War. But now the young couple turn their back on politics and are determined to build themselves a little happiness of their own. Harry's son Ronnie tries his hand as a writer and, chastened, withdraws from Communism when the Hungarian revolt is drowned in blood. Only Sarah, the irritable mother, holds fast to the slogans which by now have become part of herself.

CHIPS WITH EVERYTHING. Play in two acts. Prose. First published in *New English Dramatists,* London 1959. First performance April 27, 1962, London, Royal Court Theatre. Time: the present. Place: a Royal Air Force camp in England.

A psychological study of the problem of the outsider in a community with an all-male setting, parade-ground slang, the vestiges of personalities deformed by the military machine, and a surfeit of disarmingly obvious mediocrity: "I will die of good, well-meaning, and intelligent people who have never made a decision in their life." Nine National Service recruits—

nine different characters moulded by different backgrounds—are getting their basic training under crusty Corporal Hill. The student Pip Thompson is led by his opposition to a carefree life of luxury and to his father, who, as a general and banker, made his way into the privileged classes, to mix with the humble people, where hopes and aspirations fade away in the daily odor of French fried potato chips. But his unpredictable sensibilities are offended by the distrust and rough heartiness of the proletarian boys as much as by the arrogant camaraderie of the officers. He comes to doubt himself when the Pilot Officer scornfully proves to him that all that drives him into the ranks of the "lower classes" is ostentation and lust for power. Conscript "Smiler" Washington, whom everyone teases for his constant grin, makes an unsuccessful attempt to run away, and the otherwise so discordant and indifferent group spontaneously rises to his defense. Their courageous humanity threatens to bring them all before a court martial, but Pip saves the situation by sacrificing his freedom and accepting his superiors' compromise that he should become an officer. Wesker narrows social conflict down to the predetermined pattern of an exceptional environment.

I'M TALKING ABOUT JERUSALEM. Play in three acts. Prose. First edition London 1960. First performance April 4, 1960, Coventry, Belgrade Theatre. Time: September 1946 to 1959. Place: farmhouse in Norfolk, England.

In this third play of *The Wesker Trilogy* the young generation of Kahns fails in its attempt to break out of the pattern of industrial society and to make Rousseau's "simple life" a contemporary reality. Their delight in exercising a craft under the open sky is bound to founder on the competition of machines. In 1946, Dave Simmonds and his wife Ada move to a primitive house in Norfolk. Tired of the sociological and political theories by which the world is to be improved, he wants to construct a simple, independent existence for himself. The couple endure the skepticism of the Kahn relatives as well as the cynical pessimism of Dave's war pal Libby Dobson, who has got nowhere with his own plans for social renewal. Dave cannot make a living either by his job on Colonel Dewhurst's estate or as an independent carpenter. He just does not get any orders, and his apprentice Sammy is attracted by the more efficient factory. Disillusioned and exhausted Dave and his family return in 1959 to London's tenements, his "Jerusalem" unattained. The initial social criticism and enthusiasm for reform in the trilogy are supplanted by resignation to the inevitability of the mass age.

THE KITCHEN. A play in two parts with an interlude. Prose. Written 1958. First edition London 1960. First performance September 13, 1959, London, Royal Court Theatre. Time: the present. Place: a large kitchen in the Tivoli restaurant.

Man's subjection to the world of institutions and machines whose mechanism regulates his life is realistically set in a large kitchen and gradually pushed to farcical exaggeration. The author explains: "All kitchens, especially during service, go insane. There is the rush, there are the petty quarrels, grumbles, false prides, and snobbery. Kitchen staff instinctively hate dining-room staff, and all of them hate the customer. He is the personal enemy. The world might have been a stage for Shakespeare but to me it is a kitchen, where people come and go and cannot stay long enough to understand each other, and friendships, loves and enmities are forgotten as quickly as they are made."

The kitchen, shiny with aluminium, rigid in its functional utility, constantly filled with the roar of gas ovens, is the prison in which fourteen cooks have to live out their daily lives under the menacing, gentle, and watchful eye of the proprietor Marango and under the pressure of ceaseless orders by impatient waitresses. The cooks' products, ranging from poultry and roasts to cold buffet and dessert, matter more than their names and individuality. Small, ordinary destinies are glimpsed through all this hectic rush: a cuckolded husband, an ineffectual dreamer, the coarse sensualist, the resigned dullard. The supervisors shun responsibility, the strong take it easy at the cost of the weak. An accident is caused by the selfishness and indifference of the others. Rows keep breaking out, whether they have to do with the "foreign" Cypriot staff or with political tensions in connection with the new young Irishman. Even the dreams of these captives are nightmares.

The main character is Peter, a German, who is overcome by his love for the married waitress Monique and takes refuge in boisterous merriment. Their affair has been going on for three years, but Monique will never be prepared to give up the material security of her marriage and she condemns Peter's unborn child to destruction. After her final betrayal Peter runs amok, smashes the gas supply pipe and paralyzes the kitchen. Thus abruptly released from the spell of this witch's cauldron, they all stand around perplexed in the sudden stillness. But soon they'll be back at their old places in front of the ovens. In gentle triumph Marango watches over his victims: "What is there a man can't get used to? Nothing! You just forget where you are and you say it's a job . . . I don't know know what more to give a man. He works, he eats, I give him money. This is life, isn't it?"

ROOTS. Play in three acts. Prose. First edition Harmondsworth, England, 1959. First performance May 25, 1959, Coventry, Belgrade Theatre. Time: the present. Place: a village in Norfolk, England.

In this play, the second of *The Wesker Trilogy*, Wesker leaves the Kahns and the metropolitan proletariat escaping from their gray everyday life into the wish fulfillment of political ideologies, and turns his attention to village workers. In the country, there are no slogans creating any sense of solidarity; people are isolated, exposed without defense to their lifelong worries about how to make a living, to the clichés of the entertainment industry, and to the exhausting course of their own mediocrity.

Beatie Bryant, a waitress in London, is spending a few days' holiday in her native village. She is engaged to be married to Ronnie Kahn, the hectic intellectual, and has faithfully copied the outsider's extravagant style of life. The simple country girl paints abstract pictures and tries with some violence to "reeducate" her family. Mother must be weaned from cursing and from her favorite popular hits, sister Jenny must give up the recreation of gossiping, and brother-in-law Jimmy Beales must be pulled out of his easygoing sloppiness. For Ronnie is shortly to be introduced to the family. The neurotic young writer excuses himself by letter and breaks off the engagement. In her rage at being jilted, Beatie accuses the lower middle-class world from which she comes of being responsible for her misfortune and makes a determined attempt to break out of the prefabricated mold of mass society: "There are millions of us, all over the country and no one, not one of us is asking questions, we're all taking the easiest way out. . . . We don't fight for anything, we're so mentally lazy we might as well be dead. Blast, we are dead! . . . it's our own bloody fault!"

## WHITING, John
(England, 1917–1963)

THE DEVILS. Play in three acts. After Aldous Huxley's novel *The Devils of Loudun*. Prose. First edition London 1961. First performance February 20, 1961, London, Royal Shakespeare Theatre. Time: about 1634. Place: Loudun, France.

In this play the predicament of the individual is shown in twilight at the turn of an age, when the institutions of state and church are still jealously defending the medieval dogmas which shelter the individual in anonymous security. Individualism is the work of the devil: "For all vanities are an assertion of self, and the assertion of self in Man is the ascendancy of the Devil."

The priest Urbain Grandier is a man of the new age, who accepts himself as an individual with all his doubts and feelings. He has the courage and experimental spirit to seek out the meaning of life on his own, and takes refuge in the aesthetic enjoyment of this world: "Words are playthings in our situation. Expect music from them, but not sense." This worldly and vain vicar of Saint-Pierre-du-Marché at Loudun seduces Philippe, the daughter of the public prosecutor, and opposes Richelieu's edict to pull down the city walls. A man who over and over again succumbs to temptation, he desperately means to challenge God by his licentiousness and to find peace in self-annihilation. He pours out his spiritual struggles in conversation with a sewerman. Suddenly mass hysteria erupts among the nuns of St. Ursula's Convent. The crippled prioress declares that she is possessed by the devil in Grandier's shape. Supported by ill-meaning citizens, father Barre, the inquisitor, and the politician de Laubardemont exploit the nuns' fantastic accusations in order to get rid of the inconvenient priest. Torture and the stake show Grandier his way to God: "They do not understand the glory of mortality, the purpose of man: loneliness and death." Film techniques are used for smooth transitions among the numerous scenes and characters.

THE GATES OF SUMMER. Comedy in three acts. Prose. First performance September 11, 1956, Oxford, New Theatre. Time: early summer of 1913. Place: a country house near Athens.

This engaging piece of quixotism is devoted to one of those eternal stock heroes who sets out to conquer freedom for a whole country and in the end is relieved if he can make one single woman happy. After ten years the playboy John Hogarth meets his former sweetheart Sophie again in Athens. Both have so far lived without commitment and responsibility and have followed only their spontaneous inclinations; but both, too, have tried to trick life into meaningfulness by means of an irrevocable decision. Sophie has taken refuge in marriage with the aging archaeologist Selwyn Faramond and exiled her capricious temperament amid inaccessible sun-baked excavations. John lavishes his fortune and enthusiasm on some obscure revolution in the Balkans. Sophie is dictating her memoirs and in the passages dealing with their past relationship, John encounters his own legend, which he resolves to fulfill—like Byron—by a hero's death for Greek freedom. At this stage he meets Caroline, Selwyn's daughter by his first marriage. What begins as a flirtation eventually turns into love, though not without a grotesquely futile death potion in the Tristan tradition. In this new, unquestioned assumption of mutual responsibility John at last discovers the absolute truth that he has been chasing all his life to the point of self-sacrifice.

Whiting raises this conflict of a man between two women from the boulevard theater level to that of an existential decision.

MARCHING SONG. Play in three acts. Prose. First edition London 1954. First performance February 8, 1954, Cardiff, Prince of Wales Theatre. Time: the present. Place: the ultramodern house of Catherine de Troyes set on the heights above a capital city in Europe.

No man striving for self-realization in action can escape guilt; whether he succeeds or fails in his life's struggle, he is ultimately at fault and the bill has to be paid by others.

General Rupert Forster has to atone in prison for a lost war. His mistress Catherine de Troyes waits for him in her house, her room which is "a shell caught within a web of glass and steel." She holds court among a group of sorry failures intoxicated with the lost opportunities of wasted lives; there is the aging film director Harry Lancaster, who never again achieved anything as good as his first work and now seeks forgetfulness in drink; there is Father Anselm, a dissolute priest; and there is Dr. Matthew Sangosse, a physician without patients. Unexpectedly Forster is set free. The world needs a scapegoat, and so a big trial is to be held at which the vanquished general is to be accused of cowardice in the face of the enemy and the public thus reassured in its complacency. The aged chancellor John Cadmus has turned his country from a despised heap of rubble into a valued business partner by lies and self-betrayal; he does not want to stir up the shady past and tries to persuade Forster to commit suicide. Catherine knows that her love is buried under the years of separation, but nevertheless tries to win Forster back to life. Harry's girl-friend Dido, an insignificant, zestful little thing, is to serve her purpose. All his life Forster was trapped in "a prison of pride and ambition," and found his conscience only in his last military action, when he had to shoot down a whole children's colony. This action paralyzed his strategy and brought on the collapse, but at the same time Forster, the infallible, automatic fighting robot turned into a defeated, broken, but feeling human being. Forster tries in vain to explain the blessings of this transformation to the young captain Bruno Hurst, one of the eternal stock types of hero. All he can see in it is the betrayal of a sacred duty, abuse of a patriotic mission. In the face of a world of rigid self-obsession Forster resigns himself and chooses suicide. Cadmus had anticipated this outcome and announced it to the world beforehand; this purposeful and practical man allows him-

self only one brief moment of emotion in response to Forster's lonely decision. Then he hurries off to Parliament, where he will put an evil construction on Forster's death and falsify reality for the sake of the national
good.

All the characters are strangely understated and observed with a certain
diagnostic detachment, which accentuates the character of the play: "Each
one of us has the line of communication stretching out. With some of us
it is weak and with some of us it is strong according to our courage. The
line goes back to other people, places, and ideas. From you and Catherine
back into the past: from myself and the girl out to the immediate happening. But we all call it by the same name, don't we, Cadmus? Love. And as
long as that line remains open we have to live."

A PENNY FOR A SONG. Comedy in two acts. Prose. First performance
March 1, 1951, London, Haymarket Theatre. Time: morning of a day
in the summer of 1804. Place: the garden before Sir Timothy Bellboy's
house in Dorset, England.

The insubstantial picture-book world of this play owes as much to Shakespeare's wise fools as to Schéhadé's crotchety eccentrics and Paul Willems's
cranks: "Rather than reveal our human imperfections we will turn ourselves, even for the beloved, into a fair-booth. . . . We cry our wares hoping
the naked baby cowering at the back of the booth will not be noticed. . . .
Everyone attempts to be other than they are."

The country gentleman Sir Timothy Bellboy has made it his life's task to
save England from the impending invasion by Napoleon's army. He has
recruited a private army from among the villagers, but much to his regret
has had to hand it over to the professional officer Selincourt. Now he plans
to disguise himself as Napoleon and to appear in the enemy ranks at the
critical moment, so as to confuse them by senseless orders. His younger
brother Lamprett is equally absorbed in fire-fighting on the grand scale,
while Lamprett's wife Hester lovingly refurbishes a brass breastplate to
wear with the new Amazon Corps which is to help save the country. A
mock maneuver by the Home Guard sparks all these eccentricities into
hilarious conflict: for "this would be hell if we acted always by reason and
cold fact. . . . You must learn to accept things—attitudes—especially if
you're going to be in love. . . . For love itself is only a delicious pose to gain
for ourselves the comfort we all so deeply need." Eventually the protagonists discover a mutual love of cricket and all is well. In the midst of this
uproar a tender romance blossoms briefly between young Dorcas Bellboy
and the blind soldier Edward, who is being led by a small boy on his quest
to seek out the king and ask him to stop the war; the dream of love is only

touched on, for Edward soon goes his way on his endless errand: "Because our destination is unimportant. . . . We journey forward only to discover the reason for our traveling."

SAINT'S DAY. Play in three acts. Prose. Written 1947–1949. First edition London 1957. First performance September 5, 1951, London, Arts Theatre. Time: the present, January 25. Place: a room in Paul Southman's house.

An abyss of anxiety and chaos is suddenly revealed behind an idyllic and dreamy lifelong marriage. The lament of *vanitas vanitatum* mounts to a doomsday mood of baroque and shimmering ecstasy: "I only know that I am possessed by a loneliness hard to bear—a loneliness which I should imagine attends forsaken lovers. . . . They are wise, for that is the purpose of any memory—of any experience—to give foundation to the state of death. Understand that whatever we do in this house—in this damned house—will provide some of the material for our existence in death and you understand my fear." The "saint's day" is the eighty-third birthday of the poet Paul Southman, whose bitter satires turned the public against him well over twenty years ago and who has since been overlooked in persistent silence. Thus the literary rebel has become the morose tyrant of his home in a dilapidated country house and satisfies his need for hatred by feuding with the neighboring farmers. An equally decisive No to the world and its pursuit of success has brought to the same wilderness the young painter Charles Heberden, the husband of Paul's granddaughter Stella and one-time celebrated boy prodigy. These odd artists have lost their creative power as well as their public and for years have stagnated in tormenting, barren discontent. Only Stella has preserved her energetic sense of reality in this crumbling environment. When the writer Robert Procathren turns up to fetch Paul to London for a formal birthday dinner, she pleads with him to help her for the sake of her unborn child and to regain the family its due place in society. Politely and with indifference he promises to do what she asks. In the same way he reluctantly accepts a pistol which Paul presses upon him for joint defense against the impending attack by the villagers. Suddenly the pistol goes off in Robert's hand and Stella is killed. The unwitting murder abruptly puts an end to his overbearing manner.

All his past life consisted of elegant detachment in an ivory tower, but now he is seized with a fanatic destruction mania which he turns against the reality that all unawares has covered him with guilt and disonor. He joins three marauding deserters and they set fire to the village. He does nothing to prevent his companions hanging Paul and Charles. On this

saint's day all these people's hopes have turned to evil. Stella was fighting
for the life of her future child and died. Paul was dreaming of an exalted
return to the world of literature and ends up dangling on the very tree he
had planned to cut down himself. Charles was hoping to mature by his
self-renunciation and all he ever became was a frustrated eccentric. Robert
is overwhelmed by life's reality as though by a plague: "I thought the
power invested was for good. I believed we were here to do well by each
other. It isn't so. We are here—all of us—to die. Nothing more than that.
We live for that alone. . . . Knowing it is not a question of finding but of
losing the pieties, the allegiances, the loves."


## WILDER, Thornton
(United States, born 1897)


A LIFE IN THE SUN. Drama in three acts and a satyr play. Prose. First
performance August 24, 1955, Edinburgh. Time: mythical antiquity.
Place: courtyard at King Admetos's palace.

Into Euripides's fable of voluntary, sacrificial death for love of a husband,
Wilder has put modern, "exposed" people exiled from the self-evident
world of myth into a search for meaning and justification in life. Wilder
does not limit himself, as other versions of the story do, to the instant of
heroic decision; he includes antecedents and an epilogue, and thus gives
us a drama of development and lifelong self-realization. Nevertheless his
interpretation does not lead to the existentialists' humanism, but is inspired by the transcendent idea of Christian redemption—the God who
has become man and leaves in man the mark of grace.
At an early age Alcestis has dedicated herself as a priestess to Apollo. She
is doubtful about her love for King Admetos and beseeches heaven for a
sign. The king releases the girl who is so at odds with herself and by this
renunciation wins her love. The seer Tiresias, weakened by age, makes the
obscure announcement that one of four filthy, barbaric shepherds is
Apollo, serving the king for a year. Alcestis tries to recognize the god among
the wild lads. In each of them there is some unmistakable sign of Apollo's
realm of light, but in every case it is obscured by laziness, corruption, and
repulsive vulgarity. God's reality is a promise possible to all men. After
twelve years of marriage Admetos is about to die of a wound inflicted on
him by one of the shepherds. Alcestis leaves her children and family and
gives her life for her husband. The boisterous and kindly Heracles brings
her back from the underworld. Another twelve years pass and Alcestis is a

miserable slave of King Agis, who has conquered Thessaly and killed Admetos. The plague depopulates the town. Alcestis is accused of having caused this misfortune by her impious flight from the realm of the dead. Agis loses his daughter by the plague and, heartbroken, relinquishes the throne he has usurped. Gently Alcestis leads him to self-knowledge through suffering. She hands the reins of government to her son Epimenes when he returns, and, relieved, starts on her way back to the underworld.

In the cabaret-style satyr play Apollo, as a kitchen hand, gets the three Fates drunk and tricks the funny old spinsters into giving him the life of his friend Admetos. They impose the condition of a voluntary death sacrifice and the god has a premonition of the suffering to come. The old theme is treated symbolically as a matter of human conscience. It is loosened and articulated by the dialectical commentary of the disputation between Apollo and Death, by the boisterous Heracles scene and by the witty, lively satyr play.

THE MATCHMAKER. Play in four acts. Prose. Based on a comedy by Johann Nestroy, *Einen Jux will er sich machen* (Vienna, 1842), which was in turn based on an English original, *A Day Well Spent* (London, 1935) by John Oxenford. The original version of the play was first published in New York, 1930, under the title *The Merchant of Yonkers,* and first performed on December 12, 1938, Boston, Colonial Theatre. First edition of the new, revised version in *Three Plays,* New York 1957; first performance August 23, 1954, Edinburgh, Royal Lyceum Theatre. Musical version *Hello, Dolly!* book by Michael Stewart, music and lyrics by Jerry Herman, first performance New York 1964. Time: the early 1880's. Place: Yonkers and New York.

Nestroy's farce *Einen Jux will er sich machen* is pointed up by elements borrowed from Molière's *L'Avare* and transposed into a comfortable New York middle-class setting. Horace Vandergelder, a storekeeper in the small town of Yonkers, is about to marry from motives of avarice: "Marriage is a bribe to make a housekeeper think she's a householder." While he goes to nearby New York to call on his intended, his clerk Cornelius Hackl and the apprentice Barnaby in their turn are out for an adventure in the big city, whither Vandergelder's prim and well-bred niece Ermengarde has also gone, followed by her painter sweetheart. While Nestroy leaves his famous "special circumstances" to take care of the complications of the plot, Wilder introduces a *femme d'intrigue* to tangle the threads. Mrs. Levi as the matchmaker with a heart manages the maze of mistaken identities with a twinkle in her eye and a strategic skill which eventually lands the duped suitor in her own net. Nestroy's cut and thrust is broadened out into a realistic middle-class comedy, in which the couplets are replaced by moralizing comments addressed to the audience.


## WILLEMS, Paul
(Belgium, born 1912)


IL PLEUT DANS MA MAISON [It's Raining into My House]. Play in three acts. Prose. First edition Brussels 1963. First performance April 1, 1958, Vienna, Theater in der Josefstadt. Time: the present. Place: a room.

Willems attempts to capture life's essence in its reflection in wishful images, in the spell of dreams, the transfiguration of the fairy tale. Reality and man's longings are merged in a seamless unity. Nature takes a hand and relieves men of gravity, which evaporates into a "reflex": "Ah! Reflexes! The key to everything! . . . I have in mind the reflection that comes and goes, and returns, that disappears and grows, that dries up and gushes out, shines and dies away—and we, we who are alive, need it as much as we need warmth."

Madeleine, a secretary, has unexpectedly inherited an old, neglected country house somewhere in the depths of the provinces. There is an enormous tree there that was once introduced as a pretty house-plant and has now grown all over the building and through the roof. The sun and rain come in unhindered. The house is inhabited by the caretaker Germaine, the old fisherman Bulle, the girl Toune and the poacher Thomas. With immense care Bulle fishes the delicate reflections of willows and song-birds in the blue sky out of the pond and makes his bed with them. Sun-rays are strung diagonally across the room and hung with silver cobwebs and the natural sounds of the forest. It may happen that someone unawares topples over into the hereafter, but is transported back to earth by the friendly spirit George, who once shot himself for unrequited love. Madeleine, unromantic and businesslike as she is, wants to make money out of this impractical dream paradise by running it as a hotel for eccentric millionaires and eventually selling it. This plan is foiled by a dose of poison and a helpful spook from the other world. Madeleine and her fiancé Hermann Galion are converted to the idyll. The gentle forest magic will henceforth be home for them, too.

OFF ET LA LUNE *[Off and the Moon]*. Play in three acts. Prose. First performance February 1, 1955, Brussels, Théâtre National. Time: the present. Place: a room at Milie's in a small town in Belgium.

Willems does without the heavyweight device of an existential parable in this illustration of how humanity is threatened in a technological world tuned to utilitarian applications. With his Flemish gift of gab he solves the conflict in a faintly surrealist fairy tale, in which he combines humor, idyllic romanticism and moonlit sentimentality.

Louise, newly married, feels herself cheated of her teen-age dreams. Her husband Pierre, a truck driver and dogged money earner, is away for weeks on long-distance trips and for reasons of economy will not let her have a child. Louise is to spend her time more profitably in learning bookkeeping. Then Eric enters her life. For reasons of propriety she refuses his love. Off, a stray dog with human speech, carries messages between them with naive loyalty. He feels threatened by the cold moon, says his prayers to St. Barry every evening and—the most human creature on the whole earth—comforts the sorrowful. Louise remains with Pierre and her shrew of a mother Milie. She is going to have a baby, but can hardly endure her clumsy husband. The lovers part and bury their dream of happiness which foundered on their own timidity. Off is alone again on the street. In his awkward way he offers another equally abandoned creature, Milie's unhappy admirer Raymond, his dogdream of a free life: "They're all prisoners. But we, old gentleman, we now live the true life, a man and a dog in the woods and the fields . . . and maybe—who knows—maybe one day we'll go to sea!"

WARNA OU LE POIDS DE LA NEIGE *[Warna or The Weight of Snow]*. Play in four acts. Prose. First performance April 25, 1963, Brussels, Rideau de Bruxelles. Time: an indefinite past. Place: Warna's country house in Flanders.

Can personal happiness in these "dark times" of universal distress and oppression be nothing but self-deception and flight into illusions? For this conflict, which occupied Brecht, too, Willems has found a poetic parable. Love becomes egoism, the "trap of convenience"; happiness that is concerned only with continuation becomes a petrified ritual.

War and pestilence have devastated Flanders. In her castle, Warna has been celebrating the "great love" of her life for twenty-five years, and turning one brief instant of passion many years back into a lifelong, voluptuous ceremony. The man she loved, Chevalier Rodrigue, has long consoled himself with young Marie. He kills the girl's friend Malo and elopes with her into the wide world. Warna waits and wraps herself more and more closely in her illusions about the snow feast of her love. Disappointed by life and abandoned by Marie, Rodrigue returns. Full of bitterness he rejects Warna, wants to kill her as a revenge for the reality he has missed, and is shot by the tavern lad Gérard. In that moment of menacing hatred, of mortal danger, Warna for the first time experiences her love as real. Then she relapses into her dream, writes more letters to her sweetheart, wears herself out in aimless waiting.

With his style designed to express the unreal, a style of gentle, mildly surrealist flourishes, Willems had hitherto concentrated on poetic comedies of the soul. He was bound to fail in an attempt at high tragedy in a historical setting.

## WILLIAMS, Tennessee (Thomas Lanier Williams)
(United States, born 1914)

CAMINO REAL. Play in sixteen "blocks" and a prologue. Prose. First edition Norfolk, Connecticut, 1953. First performance March 19, 1953, New York, National Theatre. Time and place: not specified.

*Camino real* may be translated either as "royal way" or as "way to reality." The play's mysterious action is as glittering and ambiguous as its title. Cultural associations, symbols, and literary quotations flit through this unreal city wilting in the tropical heat at the edge of a desert.

The Lady of the Camellias Marguerite Gautier is being wooed by Casanova, now down-at-heel and senile. Lord Byron frets over his unattainable ideals. This hell of unlived potentialities is dominated, like everything else, by money. Everyone has his exchange rate and accordingly is assigned his place either in the luxury hotel run by the hard-hearted Gutmann or in the miserable corrugated-iron shacks of the natives. All desperately await an airplane to take them away from this place of exile, but at the decisive moment no one has the strength to get himself a place on it.

This spectral world of puppets who have lost their functions is stirred up by the arrival of two intruders: the wandering knight Don Quixote, who protects himself against reality by his dreams, and the young American sailor Kilroy, who has to prove himself in this inhuman world. He finds love and disappointment with the gypsy Esmeralda, he is persecuted, beaten, and robbed. Only a clown can he preserve his humanity in this degenerate world. Kilroy has a heart of pure gold, "as big as the head of a baby," which always makes him emerge intact from ill will and persecution. Quixote, abandoned by Sancho Panza, takes the incorrigibly trustful lad with him as his new companion and sets out into the unknown. Both of them know that their faith in this world's goodness and beauty can be betrayed and humiliated, but never destroyed: "The violets in the mountains have broken the rocks"—a symbol of meekness persistently and unwearyingly pushing its way through to the light. In a world full of perils and fear, temptation and persecution, hunger and loneliness, humanity's continuance depends on the individual's inviolate courage.

CAT ON A HOT TIN ROOF. Play in three acts. Prose. First edition Norfolk, Connecticut, 1955. First performance March 24, 1955, New York, Morosco Theatre. Time: the present. Place: bed-sitting room of Big Daddy's plantation home.

The family empire of a wealthy plantation owner seems safe for eternity until its members' waywardness causes the collapse of the old order. Williams explains: "The bird that I hope to catch in the net of this play is not the solution of one man's psychological problem. I'm trying to catch the true quality of experience in a group of people, that cloudy, flickering, evanescent—fiercely charged!—interplay of live human beings in the thundercloud of a common crisis."

Big Daddy, the rich owner of a cotton plantation, is dying of cancer, but the fact is hidden from him by the forced gaiety of his family. Each of his relatives has an eye on the fortune. The elder son, Gooper, a lawyer, and his philoprogenitive wife, Mae, flood the house with their noisy brood of "no-neck monsters" and fear a rival in Brick, the younger son, temporarily crippled after an accident and fast becoming an alcoholic. Brick's wife Margaret is driven to distraction by the frustrations of an unfulfilled marriage; tormented by her instincts and writhing like "a cat on a hot tin roof," she exacerbates the tensions with her hysteria and hatred. She has driven Brick's football pal Skipper to his death with her jealous accusation that he was harboring an unnatural affection for Brick. Brick punishes her with icy contempt, but in his heart he is uncertain whether his attitude stems from hatred of the slanderer or to the lingering suspicion that she may have been right. In his desperate search for the truth he tells his father of his hopeless condition. When Margaret feigns pregnancy in order to dampen the Gooper tribe's triumphant banality, Brick resumes his conjugal duties for the sake of his father's life's work. The exposure of the crumbling pillars of society is too intense to be real, and neuroses and traumata acquire the morbid glow of rare hot blossoms.

THE MILK TRAIN DOESN'T STOP HERE ANY MORE. Play in two acts. Written 1962. First edition New York 1964. First performance first version July 1962, Spoleto Festival, Italy; second version, December 6, 1962, New York, Shubert Theatre. Time: the present. Place: Mrs. Goforth's luxury villa on Italy's "Costiera Divina."

Williams combines such reliable ingredients as lust for life and the approach of death, mythical analogies, the psychoanalytical dissection of life in a luxury hothouse, sex kept going with drugs, and the abuse of poetic youth. In form, this play goes beyond the usual psychological realism in that Williams, as it were, displays the mechanism of these effects: two assistants in changing parts set the scene and break the illusion with their comments. To the same end, the sounds of a heart beating through a loudspeaker in a highly dramatic scene, and in thus beating time act as a diversion device. Symbols are used in such posterlike simplification that instead of setting the mood they merely serve as abstract punctuation.

High on the rocks of Capri the millionairess Sissy Goforth is spending the end of her eventful life—above her the southern sun, that "old, hungry lion," and the flag with her own emblem—protected by her bodyguard Rudy and a pack of bloodhounds, and feared by her secretary Blackie, to whom the "dying monster" dictates her memoirs during exhausting nights. Mrs. Goforth has prostituted her way up from the slums through the Ziegfeld Follies and six marriages with dying lechers to her present industrial millions. Now she is dying herself, and kept going only by injections, alcohol, and one of those casual lovers whom she keeps like domestic pets. When Christopher Flanders turns up, an unsuccessful poet and amateur constructor of mobiles, he is expectantly housed in the pink Villa Cupido. The tattered, half-starved beatnik has the reputation of being an angel of death, whose unexpected visit has already provided many an old, love-hungry lady with a romantically transfigured end. Confident of her powers of survival, Mrs. Goforth takes up this challenge of destiny and—now sulking, now spiteful—begins her usual game. Even the question of the meaning of life becomes a dalliance from desire to its satisfaction. For all her obsessed vitality, Mrs. Goforth is abruptly overtaken by death. The servants take possession of the ownerless property, the flag is hauled down. The situation marks a starting point and at the same time an end. The intensity which Williams in other plays achieves through plots as full of tension as thrillers is here the result of a static situation, but for all that no less effective.

THE NIGHT OF THE IGUANA. Play in three acts. Prose. First edition New York 1962. First performance December 28, 1961, New York, Royal

Theatre. Time: the summer of 1940. Place: a hotel at Puerto Barrio in Mexico.

Once more Williams conjures up a tropical hothouse atmosphere in a nightmare vision of man in his environment, people driven by their instincts in the midst of luxuriant vegetation, alcoholism in the damp sultriness of the rainy season—existence incomprehensibly lost and always renewed. Williams said of this play that its theme was life beyond despair, life in spite of itself.

Maxine is letting the hotel she inherited from her husband deteriorate and seeks comfort for her loneliness in the arms of her native employees. Suddenly a party of American schoolteachers arrives, together with Shannon, the tour guide. The ladies are outraged, for Shannon, a clergyman "locked out of his church" because of a moral scandal, has seduced a seventeen-year-old girl. Now he loses his present job as well and without protest accepts the refuge offered to him in the plainest possible terms by the sex-starved Maxine. Shaking with nervous collapse as he is, she has him tied fast with ropes. Shannon is trapped like the iguana, the tropical lizard that is captured and bound, until Maxine gets hungry and indicates that it is time for the slaughter. Two other strange guests arrive for the night: the ninety-seven-year-old poet "Nonno" Coffin, half blind and almost incoherent, yet continuously laboring to improve his songs, and his granddaughter Hannah, an aging spinster full of motherly comprehension. She makes portrait sketches and sells them, and with the help of random charity preserves the old man's illusion of persisting fame. Talking to Shannon during a wakeful night, she gives him a glimpse of another possible kind of human existence. He rouses himself abruptly from the neurotic egocentricity and feverish exaltation of a wasted life and for a fleeting moment wins the beautiful clarity of a decision of his own: he cuts the iguana loose. Then he goes to obey Maxine's calling of her erotic pet to his duty, "for something that works for us in our lives—even if it isn't on the highest kind of level."

ORPHEUS DESCENDING (also: *The Fugitive Kind*). Play in three acts. Prose. First edition Norfolk, Connecticut, 1957. First performance March 21, 1957, New York, Martin Beck Theatre. Time: the present. Place: a small-town store in the Southern United States.

The classical myth of faithful love is turned into two people's flight from their isolation into emotion: "What on earth can you do on this earth but catch at whatever comes near you, with both your hands, until your fingers are broken?"

Death has lost its fateful dimension and has become the destructive tool
of a hypocritical, malicious small-town clique. Years ago, "Lady" Torrance
lost her father in a riot directed against him as an Italian immigrant and
friend of Negroes. She is tied in childless marriage to the storekeeper Jabe
Torrance, a shriveled, spiteful old man dying of cancer. Suddenly the
wandering guitarist Val Xavier turns up, a young man of irrepressible
gaiety who has spent his life so far in search of the miraculous birds that
stay all their life on their wings high in the sky, and "never light on this
earth but one time when they die." This latter-day descendant of Orpheus
wears a remarkable snakeskin jacket, his lyre is a guitar covered with autographs of jazz musicians. "Lady" takes the man on as a shop assistant and
as a lover. But this, the first happiness and security of her life, is soon
disturbed by hypocritical, scandalmongering gossips and by the husband's
suspicions. Jabe was responsible for his father-in-law's death and now,
sneeringly triumphant, shoots his wife. Skillfully he frames Val, who is
lynched by the townspeople. The world which consists of only two kinds
of people, "the ones who are bought and the buyers," has successfully rid
itself of an outsider.


PERIOD OF ADJUSTMENT. A serious comedy in three acts. Prose. First
edition Norfolk, Connecticut, 1960. First performance November 10,
1960, New York, Helen Hayes Theatre. Time: the present, Christmas
Eve. Place: Ralph Bates' home in a suburb of a mid-southern city,
United States.

In this psychiatric dissecting room all human relationships are disturbed,
all connections perverted, every natural reaction pathologically distorted.
People are wrecked in a psychological chaos of trauma, inhibitions, complexes, and neuroses.
Abandoned by his wife Dorothea, Ralph Bates sits brooding alone on
Christmas Eve. Suddenly he receives the unexpected visit of his old war
buddy George Haverstick, and his bride Isabel, who are on their honey-
moon in a funeral limousine they picked up cheaply. George suffers from
a nervous tremor; he has given Isabel a shock on their wedding night and
now wanders off miserably into the night, leaving his wife with Ralph.
The two are total strangers and, to ease the embarrassing situation, analyze
each other. The young woman has had to give up her profession as a nurse
because she cannot stand the sight of blood. Ralph has married Dorothea
only for her father's millions; she was an aging, unattractive girl constantly under psychiatric treatment for "psychological frigidity," whom he
cured of her complexes. For this service his father-in-law pays with a respectable sinecure job, wealth, and status. But now Ralph has renounced

this golden cage, in which he was a mere chattel. This has cost him his wife and his livelihood. The Wall Street millionaire ruthlessly empties the house of all its contents. George returns and the friends plan a joint future for the three of them. They want to breed Texas longhorns for use in television Westerns. Unexpectedly Dorothea turns up, makes up with Ralph and is ready for a new beginning. Her decision gives Isabel the courage to get through her own difficult "period of adjustment."

THE ROSE TATTOO. Play in three acts. Prose. First edition Norfolk, Connecticut, 1951. First performance February 3, 1951, New York, Martin Beck Theatre. Time: the present. Place: Serafina's house and front yard in a village on the Gulf Coast between New Orleans and Mobile.

Williams is one more concerned with describing instincts, but this leads him not into a psychopathological study but into a ballad of unruly exuberance spending itself in extremes. Williams takes the noisy, carefree world of Sicilian immigrants as the setting for this unrestrained outpouring of joy and sorrow, desire and hate.
Serafina delle Rose, the widow of Rosario, truck driver and smuggler, makes a cult of her dead husband with her impulsive emotions; the urn containing his ashes becomes the center of the household, while Serafina herself goes to pieces, neglects her daughter Rosa and her dressmaking business, and passionately recalls the oath of eternal love that she once exchanged with Rosario and that he confirmed by tattooing a rose on her breast. Three years after his death the dressmaker learns from the malevolent mockery of an old spinster that Rosario had also made Estelle Hohengarten happy with the rose tattoo. Rage at this humiliation restores Serafina to life, and she takes young Alvaro, the stranger, into her house. Her daughter Rosa, who at her mother's command has so far reluctantly had to be content with the timid admiration of the sailor Jack, now shows that she has her full share of the family's passionate nature and runs off to join her boy friend at the hotel.
Somewhat unusual for Tennessee Williams, this play epitomizes the victory of healthy nature and Dionysiac naturalness over the absurd and artificial. Southern folklore contributes a plain, hard, poetic note.

A STREETCAR NAMED DESIRE. Play in eleven scenes. Prose. First edition Norfolk, Connecticut, 1947. First performance December 3, 1947, New York, Barrymore Theatre. Time: the present, spring, summer, and early fall. Place: New Orleans.

Ibsen's theme of self-deception is varied by means of a psychoanalytical dissection of the soul. In this play Williams has succeeded where some of his other plays failed, namely, in creating an entirely natural combination of brutal presentation of environment and psychopathic study, while giving these elements poetic intensity as existential symbols of man overcome by his disturbing instincts. The love-hate between the spiritually shattered intellectual woman frittering herself away in dreams and the man freely following his animal instincts may be seen as representative of the conflict between the degenerate European civilization narcissistically nursing its reminiscences and the unbroken primitive strength of the New World, without attributing to the matter more than a fleeting association; or it may be interpreted as the disenchantment of a contemporary writer who no longer believes in the soul's visionary longing and its power to transform reality and sees no other refuge for it in our institutional world than behind the bars of an insane asylum. But whatever view we take, the fact remains that Williams has rarely been so profound and so restrained in his overtones.

Blanche Dubois, a young teacher from the country, hopes to find shelter with her sister Stella and the latter's husband Stanley Kowalski. Blanche has ruined her life with drink and indiscriminate adventures with her seventeen-year-old pupils. A streetcar with the symbolic name of "Desire" has taken her to the Kowalskis' lower middle-class home. Out of her missed opportunities she builds up a dream world which gives her the enjoyments of a drug; she plays the successful lady and in hysterical self-assertion provokes life's secure and settled favorites, of whom her rough, vulgar but shrewd brother-in-law Kowalski is one. He lays claim to Stella's portion of the inheritance, exposes Blanche's past and drives away from her his friend Harold Mitchell, a timid admirer who had already decided to propose to her. Finally Kowalski himself takes Blanche and later arranges for her to be removed to an insane asylum. Naturalism and a will-o'-the-wisp life of dreams merge in a suggestively impressionistic landscape of the soul.

SUDDENLY LAST SUMMER. One-act play. Prose. Written 1958. First edition Norfolk, Connecticut, 1958. First performance January 7, 1958, New York, York Theatre. Time: the present. Place: garden room in a mansion at New Orleans.

The therapeutic intention which accompanies the psychoanalytical approach in nearly all of Tennessee Williams's plays is enlarged into a clinical demonstration from a psychiatrist's practice. All human bonds are shrivelled up in overriding self-obsession: "Yes, we all use each other and that's what we think of as love, and not being able to use each other is what's—hate. . . ."

In a fantastic jungle-garden of carnivorous plants, old Mrs. Venable imperiously guards the memory of her son, the poet Sebastian, who "suddenly last summer" perished in strange circumstances in a southern port. Only young Catherine Holly was a witness to these events and she suggests that they were attended by such horrors that Mrs. Venable brings all her influence and wealth to bear in her attempt to prevent a scandal and to silence the girl. Since the occurrence Catherine has been a prisoner in luxury mental institutions. Her family is bought by Mrs. Venable, this "ecstatic nun" worshipping her son's memory, and the psychiatrist Dr. Cukrowitz is to be induced by a generous research grant to obliterate the memory of the inconvenient witness by an operation.

Sebastian was a youth who had never grown up, and he had perverse inclinations; under his mother's jealous domination, he used to travel far and wide in an attempt to make an idealistic work of art of his life: "My son . . . and I constructed our days, each day, we would—carve out each day of our lives like a piece of sculpture." In his search for God the aesthete probed the world's cruelties in self-tormenting fascination. Every year he wrote one poem, the fruit of a morbid, licentious summer. Last summer it was Catherine who, at first unwittingly, had to take over the mother's role in procuring subjects for the poet's homoerotic desires. In a tropical port Sebastian—the decadent personification of the Dionysiac myth of the poet-god torn to pieces—falls victim to the bloodlust of an excited gang of street urchins. A truth drug wrests from Catherine the description of this nightmare. Aghast, the listeners at once take refuge in doubts, for, "truth . . . they say it's at the bottom of a bottomless well."

SUMMER AND SMOKE. Play in two parts. Prose. First edition Norfolk, Connecticut, 1948. First performance October 6, 1948, New York, Music Box Theatre. Time: the turn of the century through 1916. Place: Glorious Hill, Mississippi.

A social study after Ibsen's model: environment and upbringing interfere with two people's love that began hopefully as a carefree childhood friendship. The clergyman's daughter Alma Winemiller meets John, her childhood friend, now a budding young doctor, at the same fountain with the stone angel where fifteen years ago the two children used to meet every day for play. He sees in her an affected, standoffish prig, and she has nothing but puritanically righteous contempt for his drunken and licentious behavior with Rosa, the Mexican girl. By an ingenious plot Alma breaks up this affair, but in so doing causes the death of John's father. The young doctor gets engaged to be married to Nellie, Alma's music pupil, and Alma, in abject misery, strikes up a conversation with a stranger at the fountain and goes off with him for the evening. Williams' psychological realism in this play is not yet pushed to elementary levels as it was to be in his later ones.

SWEET BIRD OF YOUTH. Play in three acts. Prose. Written 1958. First edition Norfolk, Connecticut, 1959. First performance March 10, 1959, New York, Martin Beck Theatre. Time: the present, Easter Sunday. Place: The Royal Palms Hotel on the Gulf Coast, and Boss Finley's house in St. Cloud.

Youth is here the fleeting bird of transience borne away by time, away out of reach. The inevitable loss can be made good only by spiritual development and human maturity. These are not granted to Williams' instinctive, zestful characters. For them time is an enemy to be outwitted: "The age of some people can only be calculated by the level of—level of rot—in them." The aging film star Alexandra del Lago is doggedly fighting for a comeback. She is rich enough to be able to afford a substitute for her vanishing youth in the shape of drugs and the spice of a young lover, "the only dependable distraction." Chance Wayne happens to be the gigolo on duty, and he drowns his disgust with his occupation in drink and in a life of "wild dreams." A feeling of guilt and the hope of a new beginning drive Chance back to Heavenly Finley, whom he had seduced and infected. Boss Finley, the father, a powerful local politician, is afraid that Chance's return will create a scandal just in the middle of a rousing election campaign for the purity of the white race. He is determined to have the young man castrated and thus threatens the only force of self-assertion that exists for Chance in the "beanstalk country, the ogre's country at the top of the beanstalk, the country of the flesh-hungry, bloodthirsty ogre." Chance does not really want to save himself, for he sees in Heavenly the proof of his youth and his lost self. For the first time something like selflessness and love stirs in this cauldron of egocentricity. Chance resigns himself. Alexandra meanwhile goes on chasing success and leaves Chance to be lynched.

# WILLIAMS, William Carlos
(United States, 1883–1963)

THE CURE. Play in three acts. Prose. Written 1952–1960. First edition Norfolk, Connecticut, 1961. Time: May–June 1952. Place: the Mitchell's living room in an old farmhouse at the outskirts of a village in upstate New York, not far from the Genesee Valley salt mines.

Thoroughgoing psychoanalysis, naturalistic social drama, and an attempt at sex symbolism are not always successful in stylistic combination. The shock of a motorcycle accident hurls the young gangster Prospero into the perfectly ordinary and placid marriage of George and Connie Mitchell. With equal violence the young woman is thrown off balance by the intruder. The awareness that someone needs her brings out long-forgotten aspects of her nature; she turns into a motherly nurse, an understanding companion, almost a mistress. But her fear of her own feelings drives her back into her conventional marriage, and Prospero goes off into a cheap but uncomplicated affair with a casual sweetheart.

A DREAM OF LOVE. Play in three acts. Prose. First edition Norfolk, Connecticut, 1948. First performance July 1949, New York, Hudson Guild Playhouse. Time: a few years before the Second World War. Place: a suburb near New York.

In the borderland between social study and mystery, an ordinary case of adultery illustrates happiness imperiled and fulfilled, the precariousness and harmony of love, self-realization and sacrifice. The dissecting instruments of psychoanalysis are used as a medium of lyrical expression.
Myra Thurber unsuspectingly believes in her conjugal happiness, when her adored husband Daniel, a doctor and poet, suddenly dies—in a hotel room and in the arms of another woman. Myra sees her whole life of love degraded into a lie, and doggedly tries to learn the background of that night in the hotel from her rival Dotty. Myra has an obscure feeling that this incident must be the key to the incomprehensible deception. In a dream, her dead husband reveals to her the longings of his nature that were always in tormenting conflict with reality: "A man must protect his price, his integrity as a man, as best he is able. . . . He must create a woman of some sort out of his imagination to prove himself. Oh it doesn't have to be a woman, but she's the generic type. It's a woman—even if it's a mathematical formula for relativity. . . . A woman out of his imagination to match the best. All right, a poem. I mean a woman, bringing her up to the

light, building her up and not merely of stone or colors or silly words—unless he's supremely able—but in the flesh, warm, agreeable, made of pure consents." His unfulfilled creative urge necessarily became the origin of ever renewed unfaithfulness. Myra accepts the imperfection of her marriage as a task and proving ground, and is reconciled with her destiny. The transition from an extraordinarily subtle spiritual mood to a very direct therapeutic purpose is not completely successful.

## WITTLINGER, Karl
(Germany, born 1922)

DO YOU KNOW THE MILKY WAY? *(Kennen Sie die Milchstraße?).* Comedy in two acts with a prologue and an epilogue. Prose. First edition Zürich 1961. First performance November 26, 1956, Cologne, Studio der Bühnen der Stadt Köln. Produced, in English, in New York, October 16, 1961, Billy Rose Theatre. Time: the present. Place: a sanatorium.

Loss of identity and escape into illusion are shown in a clinical case from the psychiatrist's practice. In the experimental form of a seemingly improvised play, a realistic tale underlies the menacing grotesque.
Believing himself to originate from an unknown star in the Milky Way, a patient in the lunatic asylum gives the psychiatrist a play in which he describes his previous existence. The patient and the psychiatrist thereupon improvise, in alternating parts, the play *Do You Know the Milky Way?* On returning from the war, the patient found himself nonexistent as a person —his wife had married again, his property had gone to new owners, his name had been officially annulled by a declaration of death. Outside society as he was, he had to earn his living by hiring himself out at country fairs in such turns as "Bill, the man who doesn't know death," the star attraction in the "Flying Saucers." In the hope of reaching a remote star from which no one could ban him, he kept accelerating and eventually crashed. Carried away by the game, the psychiatrist sets out with the patient for the Milky Way, the place of freedom.

SEELENWANDERUNG *[Transmigration of Souls].* A parable. Prose and verse. Originally a television play. First televised October 2, 1962, Westdeutscher Rundfunk, Cologne. First edition television version in *Jahrbuch VI des Westdeutschen Rundfunks,* Cologne 1964. First performance stage version December 21, 1963, Frankfurt/Main, Städtische Bühnen. Time: the present. Place: Germany.

A critical fairy tale from the world of the German economic miracle. Two unemployed workers, Axel and Bum, make their discouraged way through life. Suddenly Bum, under the helpful influence of drink, comes to the brilliant conclusion that it is only his good-natured soul which has so far kept him away from the fleshpots of a big-time operator. He packs up the burdensome hindrance in an old cardboard box and with Axel's help pawns it for five marks. Much to the astonishment of his friend, the now soulless Bum no longer needs a boon companion. The five marks become the investment capital of a wholesale trade in scrap metal. Bum marries into a factory owner's family, becomes a politician, a trade delegate, a millionaire. When he eventually dies of the inevitable heart attack, his fellow citizens erect a statue to him. But without a soul Bum is denied entry into the world of the hereafter. In despair he begs Axel, whom in his lifetime he has repudiated and against whom he even brought lawsuits, to give him back the soul once so despised. Axel promises, and in return Bum makes him a present of the bronze statue, which represents considerable scrap value. But this gift from the other world, which Axel demolishes in good faith, brings him into conflict with the law. The reward for his deed of friendship is several months in prison. However, Axel has enough soul to be glad of it. The original television version showed the whole action within the framework of the trial whereas the stage version treats the theme more loosely, in cabaret fashion.

ZUM FRÜHSTÜCK ZWEI MÄNNER [Two Men for Breakfast]. Comedy in thirteen scenes. Prose. Written 1962. Acting edition Berlin, Bloch Erben 1963. First performance September 8, 1963, Mannheim, National Theater. Time: the present, a Sunday in summer. Place: Lilith's living room.

A choreographed dialogue testifying to the author's pleasure in his theatrical craftsmanship. Lilith is the name of the delicate creature, a fashion model and would-be actress, who consumes "two men for breakfast" as a matutinal appetizer. One of them is Sandy Brown, an unworldly scholar who out of sheer timidity became a chemist of genius and invented a formula for disintegrating matter. Lilith's dessert goes by the name of Markus Donald and is a rich manufacturer. The breakfast gourmet displays her passion for the theater in capriciously teasing the gentlemen, but eventually she loses both her admirers and has to settle for the obligatory check.

ZWEI RECHTS, ZWEI LINKS *[Two Right, Two Left]*. Comedy in three acts. Prose. Acting edition Berlin, Bloch Erben, n.d. First performance March 10, 1960, Zürich, Schauspielhaus. Time: the present. Place: Bettina's apartment.

A featherweight farce that is also a parody of itself, insofar as it takes its dramatic scaffolding literally: two rooms, two couples—old and young, two levels—reality and make-believe, present and past—these are the premises for this play as for many another. But here no problems are raised, no conflicts are developed out of profound characters; the dramatic structure remains at the stage of a draft. The characters in turn are mere outlines; as in a light-hearted experiment they are confronted and have to improvise "living." Seventy-year-old Bettina and eighty-one-year-old Till can look back on a common career on the stage. The successes that in the past failed to materialize are now transfigured into jealously guarded memories. Day after day the two old people celebrate their "as if," an indistinguishable jungle of experience and invention, longings and desires, which takes shape in ever new variations. Suddenly life intrudes into this fragile make-believe world. The university assistant lecturer Wolf Pranke becomes Bettina's lodger, but finds his room occupied by the woman student Sabine, to whom the scatter-brained old lady has also promised a lodging. The tricky situation gets altogether out of Bettina's control with the sudden appearance of Till's younger brother Tom, for whom she had nurtured tender feelings fifty years ago. The years have done nothing to temper this Don Juan's impetuosity. At once he purposefully takes possession of Bettina's heart and her room as well. The young couple in the adjoining room have in the meantime, after a sour-sweet exchange of words, decided on a "natural way out," that is, have got engaged to each other. The same solution is obviously indicated for the ludicrous old folks, when it turns out that Tom's entry was merely a new part assumed by Till in order to confess to Bettina his love which he had suppressed all his life. The play owes its success to its theatrical effectiveness and to the attraction of star parts for well-loved actors, and to the fact that it does not strain after significance.

## WOUK, Herman
(United States, born 1915)

THE CAINE MUTINY COURT-MARTIAL. Play in two acts. After the author's novel *The Caine Mutiny* (1951). First edition New York 1954. First performance October 12, 1953, Santa Barbara, California, Granada Theatre. Time: February 1945. Place: General Court-Martial Room of the Twelfth Naval District, San Francisco, and banquet room in the Hotel Fairmont, San Francisco.

What really faces the court is the ambivalence of reality—the manipulation of facts whose testimony can be altered at will by combination and interpretation. Lieutenant Stephen Maryk is to be court-martialed for mutiny. As executive officer of the destroyer U.S.S. *Caine* he relieved the insane Lieutenant Commander Queeg from his duty as commanding officer in order to save the ship in a typhoon. His defense counsel, Lt. Barney Greenwald, is in the airforce and has to suffer, like Maryk, from narrow-minded, pedantic commanders, and in exposing Queeg he means to expose the whole system, its drill and intolerance. The situation looks hopeless for Maryk. Not only do Queeg's many years of excellent conduct speak for him, but the psychiatrists can find no signs of insanity. Greenwald fights his duel with alternating tactics of intimidation and attribution. He interprets the experts' opinions as confirming abnormal symptoms, analyzes Queeg's petty chicanery in psychopathological terms and in his cross-examination of the captain exploits the latter's guilty conscience to drive him into panic and persecution mania. Queeg's nervous breakdown in front of the court makes the closing argument of the defense useless and Maryk is acquitted.

The officers celebrate the occasion with champagne, and far gone in his cups Greenwald now makes his big speech for the defense—the defense of Queeg whom he sacrificed. It is the "stuffy, stupid" regulars, and they alone, who saved the country from the enemy, and with it the Jew Greenwald. Greenwald also settles his accounts with the novelist Keefer, whose curiosity for a psychological experiment had driven his friend Maryk, in the first place, into the part of a lonely, heroic rebel.

## WÜNSCHE, Konrad
(Germany, born 1928)

LES ADIEUX ODER DIE SCHLACHT BEI STÖTTERITZ *[Les Adieux or The Battle of Stötteritz]*. Play in two acts. Prose. Written 1964. Acting edition Frankfurt/Main, Suhrkamp, 1964. First performance November 12, 1964, Darmstadt, Theater im Schloß. Time: 1813. Place: cellar at Stötteritz; Leipzig drawing room.

Arrabal in his *Guernica* places those who suffer the visitation of war in an unequivocal inferno; Wünsche expands the same theme to ambivalence on many levels. The banal in the midst of collapse, the remains of a now meaningless idyll preserved from happy bourgeois days—this is what determines the image. There is no longer any question of the guilt of a responsible opponent, but only the dallying frivolity of dilettante generals. In place of accusation we get the placid comment: "What's the point, dear God, of your Last Judgment? We have long since killed each other." The battle of Leipzig is shown in two aspects. First we see the little, peripheral victims who have to pay for the heroism of those who make history.

At Stötteritz village Max and his half-crazy, dumb aunt, have sought shelter from the war in the cellar of his ruined house. Despite the horrors of war Marie, the young piano teacher, lingers on in her world of études and lessons. She waxes sentimental over Beethoven's sonata "Les Adieux" and falls victim to a gang of soldiers. One of the brutes, a mortally wounded young ensign, takes refuge in the cellar. Right to the end the characters remain marionettes whose string are pulled by the universal fury of destruction. Although near his last, Max tries to shoot the dying ensign, who wants to get back to the battle, and is finally strangled by the aunt.

The satyr play in the second part contains the beginning and the antecedents of the first part. The Tsar and the king of Saxony, opponents in the forthcoming battle, are allies in an amorous skirmish with the accessible wife of the burgomaster of Leipzig. With martial bravado the Russian lets his rival have the plan of battle, which is finally acquired by the burgomaster's wife as a trophy of her gallant adventure. Playfully she sends her nephew, the favorite among her lovers, into the battle. He is the self-same ensign who came to an inglorious end in the first part. The thematic aims of the two studies are more interesting than their stylistic realization.

JERUSALEM, JERUSALEM [Jerusalem, Jerusalem]. Play in three acts. Free verse. First edition Frankfurt/Main 1966. First performance September 22, 1966, Wiesbaden, Hessisches Staatstheater. Time: the Middle Ages. Place: Jerusalem.

Wünsche uses material from Torquato Tasso's *Gerusalemme liberata* (the conquest of the city by Godfrey of Bouillon and the romance of Rinaldo and Armida) in order to expose the fanatical claim to dominance of an idea in the absolute. The conversation mania of the crusaders under Godfrey of Bouillon stands for the intellectual terrorism of all ideologies: "He wanted to be the savior/ Of a world that did not need salvation./ Not spared by scruples/ He drove himself to a unique sanctity/ Yet secretly suspected/ That the world was full of saviors like himself,/ To the very day before the last." Here salvation is equated with destruction, conversion with terrorism and self-assertion. Jerusalem, the goal of this gory proselytism, is the symbol of "life untroubled," an idyll of peace, hospitality, and gladness. Because "faith must cause suffering," such simple humanity is an abomination to the crusaders: "Whoever works for the mission/ Calls Jerusalem Hell,/ . . . They are appalled to find the marks of Satan here./ They denounce our festive table as consumption,/ And the clothes and the houses we make/ Are obscure monsters to them. . . . The abundance of life/ Is Hell to their noble minds. . . ."

Deprivations and setbacks cause the crusading army to disintegrate. Godfrey tries to rekindle the waning martial ardor by means of propaganda tricks. For him God has become a political prop to be manipulated, and prayer a blasphemous exhibition. But neither his mortifications and penance nor the great show of the Ecce Homo travesty will stimulate the warriors. The spirit of conquest is reawakened by the interests of the traders, the ambition of the everlasting campaigners, the greed of the whores. Then Rinaldo, the examplary hero and darling of the public, turns into an anti-Parsifal. He presses on to Jerusalem and there is converted not to glory but to satiety. It is not the mystical sacrifice that triumphs but the exuberance of life. The love of the courtesan Armida and the pleasures of her richly spread table make him forget the catchwords of soldierly duty and national mission. But nothing can appease the conversion mania of the besiegers.

Wünsche makes use of a device from Bruckner's *Elisabeth von England* to expose the dubious nature of power politics. He makes the opponents call simultaneously on the same god in the same words to grant victory to their own side, the only just one, the only one that serves peace. Victory goes to the justice that is affirmed by the destruction of all who think otherwise. Godfrey conquers Jerusalem and in so doing becomes a cripple. He wishes to be crowned and seize power as "Defender of the Holy Sepulchre."

His rival Avist stabs him and tries to blot out Jerusalem forever by building a new city. He is killed by the people who want to avoid that sort of strenuous pioneer work. Father Cesarius vainly tries to gather round him the men of good will among both friend and foe in order to do what is simply a matter of pure humanity, without any ideology or special pleading. But he too is left in the lurch by the people once more on the search for a myth that will liberate them from freedom and responsibility. Wünsche makes use of a loose sequence of scenes and achieves points by his flat and impulsively direct theatricality. He imparts rhythm to the action by lyrics, litany, takeoffs, blasphemous ceremonies, orgiastic ballets, chases, broad tableaux, and the counterpoint of the chorus and the protagonists.

ÜBER DEN GARTENZAUN *[Across the Garden Fence]*. One-act play. Prose. Written 1962. First edition Frankfurt/Main 1962. First performance November 21, 1962, Darmstadt, Landestheater. Time: not specified. Place: garden in the evening light.

Feelings and longings are stylized, appear as though masked, and slide into parody. To express vulnerability and timidity, the language plays preciously with dalliance by the garden bower—it is poetic drama toying with its own complexes.

At the garden fence Clara takes farewell of her cousin Robert and of her hopes for a happiness to which she has only just awakened. At thirty the girl is guarded by an Argus-eyed mama and strictly shielded from any reality that goes beyond playing with dolls and growing flowers. Robert is dispatched by his officious uncle Baron von Berg to South America, the classical situation in the lavender-scented memories of many a girl who has been left behind. The elegiac, languishing gesture is all that is left to Clara by way of a small, becoming consolation. Then Count von N. sends his servant with a tender invitation. The girl goes into ecstasies of heavenly expectations, which are persistently ruined by her mother and her uncle. With a sudden explosion Clara rebels against this world of deceptive sweetness. Then she resigns herself and with mama continues her aimless journey through life.

It is a sardonic play of associations fluctuating between humor and melancholy, full of sounds and images. "Like raindrops falling at night they say: plop, plop, plop, plop, plop. Where has the first plop gone? It's trickled away. The second plop? Trickled away. The third? Trickled away. They still tremble a little. Lots of notes, but not a melody."

DER UNBELEHRBARE *[The Unteachable]*. Play in five scenes. Prose. Written 1963. First edition Frankfurt/Main 1964. First performance November 30, 1963, Darmstadt, Landestheater. Time: the present. Place: drawing room at Professor Thalwitzer's Schneeberg.

The Hamlet theme has been steeped in the "light of a poisonous melancholy" and sharpened into trenchant mockery. The story of the parricide and the frustrated avenger is transposed to the twentieth century, which means that there is no tragic resolution, no election of good or evil, no struggle for certitude. A melange of petty bourgeois malice and banality constitutes both cause and purpose of the action.

Paul, the young epigone of Hamlet's restless spirit, is shown with merciless objectivity as anything but a highminded hero who goes to his death for the sake of purity and goodness; instead, he appears as a narrow-minded, unimaginative prig inhibited by complexes, who behaves decently only because he is infantile and weak. Professor Thalwitzer is poisoned by his wife Lydia just when he is having one of his customary escapades with the maid Trude. Two years later he haunts the house, greatly amused because his son Paul is just expected home after five years spent in absorbing culture in Italy. Before he went off with his tutor, Dr. Meyer, to satisfy his hunger for the humanities, Paul, then still at secondary school, had had a brief affair with Fritze Zwicker, a manufacturer's wife. In the meantime the lady has become a respectable widow and, in her carefully studied makeup, is waiting to carry Paul off to the registrar's office. Because the lady knows about the murder, Lydia has had to agree to this "barter of human flesh" and to lavish attentions on "her best friend," the affected widow of the wax flower manufacturer. Paul is accompanied to his home by Dr. Meyer. He keeps fidgeting with the nervousness of an overtaxed model pupil who does not quite know his lesson. Meyer is a mephistophelian culture maniac who tyrannizes everyone under cover of his obsequious phrases. His alarming inventions, such as a camera which can photograph itself and "the photographing of the photographing," or a conversation machine which will once and for all settle all interpersonal contacts, invade the cosy, well-padded Thalwitzer home.

Trude enlightens Paul about his father's death. But he timidly ducks and rattles off the school texts he has learned by heart. The maid, who is equipped with that tiresome sense of right and wrong which persons of inadequate education and insufficient *savoir vivre* often exhibit, proceeds to make some poisoned coffee for the murderess. Whereupon Thalwitzer, disguised as Santa Claus, appears and straightens out this out-of-step son of his. Paul, the "unteachable," meant to be something better than his parents. He tries to behave with more decency than his highly respectable adulterer of a father, and not to be a murderer like his precious mother.

Anyone so obviously out of touch with the age must clearly be eliminated, so that the others can recover the satisfactions of wealth and unconcern. Thalwitzer presses on his son the poisoned coffee and angrily dispatches him into the blessed hereafter. A bitter farce that keeps the action going mainly by the driving force of the language and uses macabre, cabaret-type cracks.


VOR DER KLAGEMAUER [At the Wailing Wall]. One-act play. Prose. First edition Frankfurt/Main 1962. First performance November 21, 1962, Darmstadt, Landestheater. Time: not specified. Place: the ruins of a city wall.

The play takes its title from a poem by Nelly Sachs: "We stones/ When someone lifts us/ He lifts primeval ages. . . . When someone touches us/ He touches a wailing wall." An inconclusive dialogue that circles round itself and takes up different aspects of remote layers of consciousness and modes of being.
A handful of people have fled from the burning town to the shelter of the ruined wall. Clemens Svozky and his sister Rosa have murdered their father, the colonel, for the sake of his jewels. Clemens is injured and collapses in delirium. Karel Kaizl, the beater, has plundered the colonel's abandoned mansion and brings the booty to Rosa, whom he has long looked upon with desire. In mounting fear the girl runs away and leaves her brother to die. All the refugees hope for safety in the nearby little town of Pritzlau. But they keep putting off their escape into the unknown. Finally the entire population rush away in a wild panic, murder the governor who opposes them, and by their lack of discipline seal the destruction of all. Karel robs the butcher Wondraschek and strips even Clemens of his last belongings. But there has long since been no resting place where the fruits of evil deeds can be consumed. Rosa has joined with the soldiery and scornfully denies her former self. She alone in this inferno has managed to break through to the security of anonymity. For "We wanted to go abroad, but the dust of our house cloaks us, this cloud that goes with us." The play is a nocturne that toys with the ruins of a blackened reality without being able to discover a new unity behind the disintegration of reality.

## ZAVATTINI, Cesare
(Italy, born 1902)

COME NASCE UN SOGGETTO CINEMATOGRAFICO [*How a Film Script Is Born*]. Monologue in two acts. First edition Milan 1959. First performance July 15, 1959, Venice, Teatro la Fenice (ensemble Piccolo Teatro della Città di Milano). Time: the present. Place: Italy.

A creative individual's striving for self-realization is sharpened in content to satirical criticism and in form to a dialectical juggling with reality and appearance. The creative author's plane of action keeps being disturbed by the intrusion of the characters created by his imagination. His spiritual purpose assumes shape only in ceaseless adaptation to reality, which means an endless process of deformation. The patron, the public, the author himself with the limited potentialities of his ability—all these are resistances against which the persuasive force of the work should prevail. But contradiction is paralyzed by compromise, the work of art is ultimately the product of numerous interests.

Antonio, who has gained affluence and fame on credit, is working on a film script. He is followed by the critical and watchful eyes of the censor Chiaretti and the producer Saloni, and whenever the disciple of Pegasus in his labors diverges by an inch from the well-tried clichés they at once give notice of moral or economic misgivings. Antonio is out to capture life in its harshness and beauty—in the love of two working-class youngsters and the temptation of a jobless worker to sell his eyesight to the factory owner. However, the two institutions—money and criticism—destroy the truth of the action. Antonio returns to his former miserable quarters.

But in the lower-middle-class gossip and ostentation he finds as little response to unconditional, unvarnished reality as in the cinema, where he hopes for the public's comprehension. The community of which the author dreams consists merely of an indiscriminate assembly of isolated egotists. In despair Antonio shoots himself. But the soulful phrases which the censor and the producer lavish on the white hope of poetry pass away all too soon and make him jump out of his grave with indignation. Resignedly Antonio sits down at the typewriter—just as he did at the beginning of the play—and writes the script which satisfies everybody. The play as a whole is a loose improvisation, a "monologue" made up of internal reservations and external resistances, self-justification and a glossary to literature in the making.

## ZAWIEYSKI, Jerzy
(Poland, born 1903)

MAZ DOSKONALY *[The Blameless Man]*. Drama in five scenes and two interludes. Prose. First performance March 30, 1945, Cracow, Teatr Stary. Time: the biblical past. Place: the Land of Uz.

In our century Job, the man who had more than his due of suffering and wrongs, has become a key figure in literature. A victim of despotism, a tragic clown of his faith, a man suffering innocently, but also the bearer of a message of consolation, Job has been variously interpreted by such writers as Kokoschka, Roth, Lauckner, Welti, Barlach, and MacLeish. Zawieyski goes back to the religious content of the fable. Wholly dedicated to prayer and burnt offerings, Job lives on the sacred hill of Uz. His wife Ruth looks after the everyday chores, sees to it that their possessions increase and provides the earthly conditions for Job's unworldly piety. God tries his servant, takes from him his children and his wealth. The "Stranger" tempts Job and incites him to deny God. It is only in his doubts and in his deprivation that Job finds his true self and now freely chooses his faith. The land bears fruit again and new life stirs in Ruth's womb.

## ZUCKMAYER, Carl
(Germany, born 1896)

THE DEVIL'S GENERAL *(Des Teufels General)*. Play in three acts. Prose. Written 1942–1945; revised version 1966. First edition Stockholm 1946. First performance December 14, 1946, Zürich, Schauspielhaus. Translated by I. and W. Gilbert in *Masters of the Modern Drama,* H. M. Block and R. G. Shedd, eds., New York, Random House, 1962, and adapted by Robert Gore-Browne and Christopher Hassall for London production, Savoy Theatre, 1953, and British Broadcasting Company, 1960. Time: 1941. Place: Berlin.

Immediately after the war, this contemporary play stimulated much fruitful and liberating discussion. Today, it seems remarkable more for the striking and sensitive reproduction of the background of Nazi leadership than for its moral issues, effective as they are on the stage. The conflict between fulfillment of duty and humanity is simplified to the outlines of a poster.

The German Air Force General Harras is an opponent of the Third Reich, which he despises but whose decorations he only too willingly accepts in the course of his brilliant military career. Heart and soul a soldier, he glories in the knowledge that he is indispensable, indulges in the indiscreet talk of an *enfant terrible,* and to placate his conscience saves a handful of Jews. Sabotage in the aircraft works under his command gives the SS an opportunity to exert some pressure on him through Dr. Schmidt-Lausitz of the Propaganda Ministry. The General discovers that his friend Chief Engineer Oderbruch is a member of the underground movement and as such doing his bit to end the war by means of sabotage. Conscience-stricken, the General realizes how his selfish noncommitment has made him the "Devil's General." He covers up for his friend and voluntarily crashes to his death in an aircraft he knows to be defective. The government settles the case with a state funeral for the national hero. Some similarities to General Udet's fate were exploited to produce this effective hit, but it is just this melodramatic slant, relying more on emotions than on argument yet claiming documentary truth, which casts doubt on the conclusions of this masterpiece of stagecraft.

DER GESANG IM FEUEROFEN *[The Song In the Fiery Furnace].* Play in three acts. Prose. Written 1950. First edition Frankfurt/Main 1950. First performance January 30, 1951, Göttingen, Deutsches Theater. Time: December 1943 and the spring of 1945. Place: Haut-Chaumond, a village in the Savoy Alps.

A real occurrence provides Zuckmayer with the theme for a symbolically intensified period piece from the days of the French resistance in a play which is half requiem and half a dramatic psychological study. Louis Creveaux is tried by a court of two angels as a collaborator and traitor. His accusers include the quick and the dead, friend and foe, but their self-assured accusations crumble under the impact of the guilt in which each of them has his part.

Creveaux had been an outcast in the village ever since he was a child. He was despised for being the son of a vagrant woman, suspect because of his knowledge and the technical experiments to which he was addicted, and rejected in his unhappy love for the innkeeper's beautiful daughter Sylvaine Castonnier. And so he became a traitor to his country. He lured a Jewish refugee family into an ambush and betrayed a meeting of resistance fighters at Chaplain Leroy's château. German troops surrounded the building and burnt it down.

Zuckmayer is careful to avoid any one-sided accusation. The symbolic figures of Father Wind, Mother Frost, and Brother Mist intervene in the play. By the dramaturgical device of having Frenchmen and Germans, friend and foe, played by the same actors in similar gradations ranging from idealism to fanatical murder, the author raises the inhuman events to the scale of the whole world's failure.

DAS KALTE LICHT [The Cold Light]. Play in three acts. Prose. First edition Berlin 1955. First performance September 3, 1955, Hamburg, Deutsches Schauspielhaus. Time: 1939–1950. Place: England, North America, and the Atlantic.

Elements from the fate of the atomic spy Klaus Fuchs are worked into a contemporary chronicle with effective contrasts. Zuckmayer explains in his afterword: "The subject of the play is not atomic fission, but the crisis of confidence. Or, more generally, the crisis of thought and faith in our age. The fact of 'ideological' or even 'idealist' treason exemplifies a personal conflict of conscience such as can be matched only in periods of religious wars." There is some disharmony between the theme and the plot—on the one hand the high-flung, insoluble dilemma between creative self-realization, a worthwhile end in itself, and political ideology which at once misuses every creative impulse as an instrument of power, and on the other hand the penny-dreadful story of police terror and a jealous woman's betrayal.

Kristof Wolters, a student of physics and former member of the German Communist Party, emigrates to England, where he joins a nuclear research team. He meets his former fellow student Hjördis Lundborg, now the wife of his chief Ketterick. Given that atomic weapons are used as a means of blackmail among nations, Wolters passes important research results to the Russians through the contact man Buschmann in an attempt to reestablish political equilibrium in the world. Hjördis betrays him from jealousy, and to his relief the scientist sees a chance of expiation in his pangs of conscience. Hjördis's husband meets with a fatal accident and, now in love with Wolters, she is ready to wait for him. The problem of the responsibility and neutrality of scientific research is shown in the chance setting of an individual's destiny and remains unsolved.

DAS LEBEN DES HORACE A. W. TABOR [The Life of Horace A. W. Tabor]. A play from the days of the last robber barons in five acts. Prose. Written 1964. First edition Frankfurt/Main 1964. First performance November 18, 1964, Zürich, Schauspielhaus. Time: the time of great improvisations, April 1879–April 1899. Place: the world of great good luck and enormous losses, Colorado and Washington.

On a broad canvas, Zuckmayer composes the ballad of the American pioneers. Man is continually challenged by the unlimited possibilities and the chances of a country still without government rules. Violent speculation, the fever of economic transactions and of the stock exchange crash mirror the struggle for life itself. A new, unreal dimension is added to the striving for self-realization between the personal challenge of reality and the extinction of the individual who is reduced to a function of gigantic processes. Zuckmayer explains: "For men like Tabor such things as happiness, power, wealth and greatness were fundamentally still of magic origin. Tabor believes in his belated good fortune, full of fear and awe, full of doubt and hope, full of arrogance and humility, as he might believe in a gift of the gods, but also fully prepared to fight for it or suffer for it. He is a man to whom fortune remains true even in misfortune, because he loves it."

Horace A. W. Tabor lives in one of the dilapidated gold-rush settlements of Colorado. There he is postmaster, grocer, and saloon keeper, the center of a rough social life, and the selfless helper of all who need help. Suddenly he has an opportunity of exchanging a jugful of whisky for a two-thirds stake in a rich silver mine, which a half-starved cobbler has discovered in the mountains. His avid determination to exploit this stroke of luck to the utmost robs him of his peace of mind and contentment. His fabulous riches tempt him into a great many projects, and in carrying them out he becomes a bully and boss. As the most powerful of the bonanza barons and silver kings, Tabor rebuilds the town and presents it with an opera house. He becomes a general, a governor and eventually a senator, while the emaciated miners band together and are trampled down by the cavalry. Moreover, "Lady" Augusta with her resolute simplicity is no longer good enough as a wife for the upstart. He divorces her and marries the night-club star Baby Doe, his mistress for many years. Intrigues, enmity, and a general stock-exchange crash topple the façade of Tabor's enterprises.

As a poor prospector he sets out for the mountains once more to try his luck again. At peace with the two women of his life he dies in the miserable blockhouse which he had built in his youth. His good luck, that eternal temptation and restlessness, has given way to a gentle acceptance of the inevitable. Careful study of the sources for the historically authenticated characters is subordinated to a wide-screen panorama with lively and realistic characters and colors.


DIE UHR SCHLÄGT EINS [The Clock Strikes One]. Contemporary historical drama in nine scenes. Prose. First edition Frankfurt/Main 1961. First performance October 14, 1961, Vienna, Burgtheater. Time: 1953–1954. Place: West Germany and Indochina.

An indiscriminate jumble of every conceivable contemporary social problem and social conflict is presented in gross oversimplification: the conflict of the generations, euthanasia, outstanding accounts with the past still remaining to be settled, juvenile drug addiction, disillusioned idealists turning to crime in their rebellion, scientists as opportunist turncoats, tragic destinies in the Foreign Legion, and mystical death-bed transfiguration—all these are used as material for a dozen news features, some of them sensational, some sentimental.

Intent on making sure of their German economic-miracle prosperity, the manufacturer Holtermann and his wife have left their children to themselves and thus have lost the latter's confidence and love. Their daughter Isabel escapes into a loveless but reasonable marriage with a university lecturer called Flühvogel, who has been quick to leave his SS past behind and to develop into a model democrat. Their son Gerhard is addicted to marijuana, joins a group of gangsters, has to flee the country, and disappears in the Foreign Legion, only to be killed in the course of hand-to-hand fighting in Indochina.


## ZWEIG, Arnold
(Germany, born 1887)


BONAPARTE IN JAFFA (also: *Napoleon in Jaffa*) *[Bonaparte at Jaffa]*. Historical drama in five acts. Prose. Written 1934–1938. First edition in *Soldatenspiele,* Berlin 1956. First performance March 19, 1955, Berlin, Volksbühne am Luxemburgplatz. Time: the spring of 1799. Place: Jaffa, Palestine.

A historical case of mass murder provides the occasion for a confrontation between humanity and political necessity. During his Egyptian campaign, Napoleon sees his strategy jeopardized by three thousand Turkish prisoners of war, who unexpectedly fell into his hands at the conquest of Jaffa. He has barely enough food for his own armies, there are no guards and no means of transport. To free his hands for an immediate assault on Akko fortress, he orders—with the agreement of his generals—the defenseless prisoners to be killed. Even Grosjean, who was born in the gutter and is a champion of the revolution, regards this course as a necessary sacrifice to progress, a "relay for humanity." He hates Napoleon and yet serves him, because he sees in him the only weapon against the reactionaries. Only one person resists: the physician Dr. Desgenettes, who risks his life in caring for plague victims to the point of experimenting on himself, but he has to capitulate to the reasonableness of the counterarguments. A discussion play in which the characters are reduced to mere vehicles for the message.

# Index of Play Titles

*The page on which the description of the play begins is listed. Titles are listed in their original language only if they have never appeared in English.*